THE VICTORIA HISTORY
OF THE
COUNTIES OF ENGLAND

———

A HISTORY OF
WILTSHIRE

VOLUME IX

THE VICTORIA HISTORY
OF THE
COUNTIES OF ENGLAND

EDITED BY R. B. PUGH

THE UNIVERSITY OF LONDON
INSTITUTE OF
HISTORICAL RESEARCH

Oxford University Press, Ely House, 37 Dover Street, London, W.1

GLASGOW   NEW YORK   TORONTO   MELBOURNE   WELLINGTON
CAPE TOWN   SALISBURY   IBADAN   NAIROBI   DAR ES SALAAM   LUSAKA   ADDIS ABABA
BOMBAY   CALCUTTA   MADRAS   KARACHI   LAHORE   DACCA
KUALA LUMPUR   SINGAPORE   HONG KONG   TOKYO

© UNIVERSITY OF LONDON 1970

SBN 19 722736 8

PRINTED IN GREAT BRITAIN

INSCRIBED TO THE

MEMORY OF HER LATE MAJESTY

QUEEN VICTORIA

WHO GRACIOUSLY GAVE THE TITLE TO

AND ACCEPTED THE DEDICATION

OF THIS HISTORY

The Chalk Escarpment, Looking East Towards Clyffe Pypard

A HISTORY OF

WILTSHIRE

EDITED BY ELIZABETH CRITTALL

VOLUME IX

PUBLISHED FOR

THE INSTITUTE OF HISTORICAL RESEARCH

BY

OXFORD UNIVERSITY PRESS

1970

Distributed by Oxford University Press until 1 January 1974
thereafter by Dawsons of Pall Mall

CONTENTS OF VOLUME NINE

LIST OF ILLUSTRATIONS

Thanks are rendered to the following for permission to reproduce material in their possession and for the loan of prints and photographs: Swindon Public Library, the Royal Commission on Historical Monuments (England), the National Portrait Gallery, the Courtauld Institute of Art, University of London, Mr. Leonard Lines, the Victoria and Albert Museum, the Wiltshire Record Office, Wiltshire Newspapers (Westminster Press Ltd.), British Railways (Western Region), Brasenose College, Oxford, and the Warwickshire Record Office.

LIST OF ILLUSTRATIONS

LIST OF MAPS AND PLANS

All the maps and the Swindon street plan were drawn by K. J. Wass of the Department of Geography, University College, London, from drafts prepared by Elizabeth Crittall, Janet H. Stevenson, and K. H. Rogers. They are based upon the Ordnance Survey with the sanction of the Controller of H.M. Stationery Office, Crown Copyright reserved. Parish boundaries on the hundred map and maps of *c.* 1773 are taken from the tithe maps of *c.* 1840. Thanks are due to Mr. R. E. Sandell, Miss Winifred M. Evans, and Mr. K. H. Rogers for help with the preparation of the hundred map.

EDITORIAL NOTE

THE present volume, the ninth in the Wiltshire series to be published, has been prepared like the previous ones under the superintendence of the Wiltshire Victoria County History Committee. That committee, whose origin and constitution are described in the Editorial Note to the *Victoria History of Wiltshire*, Volume VII, has been good enough to continue, and indeed to enlarge, its generous grant. Consequently it was possible in 1968 to appoint a second assistant editor in addition to the editor and assistant editor already employed. The University has thus been able to continue publication and takes pleasure in renewing the expression of its gratitude to the participating authorities in Wiltshire for their friendly co-operation.

It is unfortunately necessary to record three losses by death that the committee has sustained since the last Wiltshire volume was published. In 1968 Alderman S. V. Christie-Miller, C.B.E., chairman of the committee since 1961, died. In 1967 Mr. R. V. Lennard, and in 1968, Professor T. S. Ashton, F.B.A., died: both had been members of the committee since 1949 and had played important parts in guiding its early steps. Sir Henry Langton, D.S.O., D.F.C., was elected chairman to succeed Alderman Christie-Miller. In December 1965 Mr. Colin Shrimpton resigned from the assistant editorship, and was replaced in July 1966 by Miss Janet H. Stevenson. The post of a second assistant editor was filled in September 1968 by Mr. D. A. Crowley.

Thanks are rendered to many persons who have helped in the compilation of the volume by granting access to documents in their care or ownership, by examining drafts, or by offering advice. Many are named in the footnotes or in the preamble to the List of Illustrations. Particular mention must here be made of the Swindon Borough Librarian and members of the staff of the Reference Library; officers of several departments of Swindon Corporation, especially the Town Clerk's Department, the Education Department, and the Borough Architect's Department; the extra-mural class working under the direction of Mr. H. Ross in Swindon during 1964 and 1965; the Wiltshire County Archivist; and the Hon. Librarian of the Wiltshire Archaeological and Natural History Society.

LIST OF CLASSES OF DOCUMENTS
IN THE PUBLIC RECORD OFFICE
USED IN THIS VOLUME
WITH THEIR CLASS NUMBERS

Chancery

		Proceedings
C	1	Early
C	2	Series I
C	3	Series II
C	54	Close Rolls
C	60	Fine Rolls
C	66	Patent Rolls
C	78	Decree Rolls
		Inquisitions post mortem
C	136	Series I, Ric. II
C	137	Hen. IV
C	138	Hen. V
C	139	Hen. VI
C	140	Edw. IV
C	142	Series II
C	143	Inquisitions ad quod damnum

Court of Common Pleas

	Feet of Fines
C.P. 25(1)	Series I
C.P. 25(2)	Series II
C.P. 40	Plea Rolls
C.P. 43	Recovery Rolls

Exchequer, Treasury of the Receipt

E 40	Ancient Deeds, Series A

Exchequer, King's Remembrancer

E 126	Entry Books of Decrees and Orders, Series IV
E 134	Depositions taken by Commission
E 142	Ancient Extents
E 150	Inquisitions post mortem, Series II
E 178	Special Commissions of Inquiry
E 179	Subsidy Rolls etc.
E 199	Sheriffs' Accounts
E 210	Ancient Deeds, Series D

Exchequer, Augmentation Office

E 310	Certificates of Colleges and Chantries
E 315	Miscellaneous Books
E 317	Parliamentary Surveys

E 318	Particulars of Grants for Crown Lands
	Ancient Deeds
E 326	Series B
E 329	Series BS

Ministry of Education

Ed. 47	Awards

Home Office

H.O. 67	Acreage Returns
	Various, Census
H.O. 107	Population Returns
H.O. 129	Ecclesiastical Returns

Justices Itinerant

J.I. 1	Assize Rolls, Eyre Rolls, etc.
J.I. 3	Goal Delivery Rolls

Exchequer, Office of the Auditors of Land Revenue

L.R. 2	Miscellaneous Books
L.R. 14	Ancient Deeds, Series E

Ministry of Health

M.H. 12	Poor Law Union Papers

General Register Office

R.G. 9	Census Returns, 1861

Court of Requests

Req. 2	Proceedings

Special Collections

S.C. 2	Court Rolls
S.C. 6	Ministers' Accounts
S.C. 8	Ancient Petitions
	Rentals and Surveys
S.C. 11	Rolls
S.C. 12	Portfolios

Court of Star Chamber

Sta. Cha.	Proceedings, Jas. I

Court of Wards and Liveries

Wards 2	Deeds and Evidences

NOTE ON ABBREVIATIONS

Among the abbreviations and short titles used the following may require elucidation:

B.N.C. Oxford	Brasenose College, Oxford
Brit. Trans. Hist. R.O.	British Transport History Record Office
Char. Com.	Charity Commissioners
G.R.O.	General Register Office
Goddard MSS.	Papers and manuscripts concerning the Goddard family in Swindon Pub. Libr.
Hants R.O.	Hampshire Record Office
Hist. MSS. Com.	Historical Manuscripts Commission
P.C.C.	Prerogative Court of Canterbury
Sar. Dioc. R.O.	Salisbury Diocesan Record Office
Sar. Dioc. Regy.	Salisbury Diocesan Registry
S.R.O.	Somerset Record Office
Warws. R.O.	Warwickshire Record Office
W.A.S.	Wiltshire Archaeological and Natural History Society
W.A.S. Libr., Devizes	Library of the W.A.S. in the Museum, Devizes
W.A.S. Rec. Brch.	Records Branch of W.A.S.
Wilts. Cuttings	Volumes of Wiltshire newspaper cuttings in W.A.S. Libr., Devizes
Wilts. Pamphlets	Collection of pamphlets in Swindon Pub. Libr.
Wilts. Tracts	Collection of pamphlets in W.A.S. Libr., Devizes
W.R.O.	Wiltshire Record Office
Winch. Coll. Mun.	Winchester College Muniments
Andrews and Dury, Map (W.A.S. Rec. Brch.)	Crittall, Elizabeth (ed.) *Andrews' and Dury's Map of Wiltshire 1773* (W.A.S. Rec. Brch. viii)
Cal. Feet of F. Wilts. 1195–1272, ed. Fry	Fry, E. A. (ed.) *Calendar of Feet of Fines Wilts.* 1195–1272 (W.A.S. Devizes, 1930)
Chalfield and Malmesbury Garrison Accts. (W.A.S. Rec. Brch.)	Pafford, J. H. P. (ed.) *Accounts of the Parliamentary Garrisons of Great Chalfield and Malmesbury* (W.A.S. Rec. Brch. ii)
Crown Pleas Wilts. Eyre, 1249 (W.A.S. Rec. Brch.)	Meekings, C. A. F. (ed.) *Crown Pleas of the Wiltshire Eyre, 1249* (W.A.S. Rec. Brch. xvi)
Dugdale, *Mon.*	Dugdale, W. *Monasticon Anglicanum* (edn. 1817–30)
Early Stuart Tradesmen (W.A.S. Rec. Brch.)	Williams, N. J. (ed.) *Tradesmen in Early Stuart Wiltshire* (W.A.S. Rec. Brch. xv)
Endowed Char. Wilts. (1908)	*Endowed Charities of Wilts.* H.C. 271–3 (1908), lxxxi
Feet of F. Wilts. 1272–1327 (W.A.S. Rec. Brch.)	Pugh, R. B. (ed.) *Abstracts of Feet of Fines Wilts. for Reigns of Edw. I and Edw. II* (W.A.S. Rec. Brch. i)
First Pembroke Survey, ed. Straton	Straton, C. R. (ed.) *Survey of Lands of William, First Earl of Pembroke* (Roxburghe Club, 1909)
Hoare, *Mod. Wilts.*	Hoare, Sir Richard Colt, *Modern Wiltshire* (1822–37)
Jefferies, *Swindon*	Jefferies, Richard, *Jefferies' Land, a History of Swindon and its Environs*, ed. Grace Toplis (London, etc. 1896)
Morris, Swindon	Morris, William, *Swindon Fifty Years Ago* (Swindon, 1885)
Nightingale, *Wilts. Plate*	Nightingale, J.E. *The Church Plate of Wiltshire* (Salisbury, 1891)
P.N. Wilts. (E.P.N.S.)	*The Place-Names of Wiltshire* (English Place-Name Society, xvi)

NOTE ON ABBREVIATIONS

Pevsner, *Wilts.*	Pevsner, N. *The Buildings of England: Wiltshire* (1963)
Phillipps, *Wilts. Inst.*	Phillipps, Sir Thomas (ed.) *Institutiones Clericorum in Comitatu Wiltoniae* (priv. print. 1825)
Q. Sess. and Ass. 1736 (W.A.S. Rec. Brch.)	Fowle, J. P. M. (ed.) *Wiltshire Quarter Sessions and Assizes, 1736* (W.A.S. Rec. Brch. xi)
R.C.H.M. (Eng.)	Royal Commission on Historical Monuments (England)
Reg. Ghent (Cant. and York Soc.)	Flower, C. T. and Dawes, M. C. B. (ed.) *Registrum Simonis de Gandavo* (Canterbury and York Society, xl–xli)
Reg. Martival (Cant. and York Soc.)	Edwards, K. (ed.) *Registers of Roger Martival, Bishop of Salisbury, 1315–30* (Canterbury and York Society, lv)
Reg. St. Osmund (Rolls Ser.)	Jones, W. H. Rich- (ed.) *Vetus Registrum Sarisberiense alias dictum Registrum S. Osmundi Episcopi* (Rolls Series, lxxviii)
St. Mark's 1845–1945	*St. Mark's Swindon 1845–1945, A Record written by Priests and People* (Swindon, 1945)
Sar. Chart. and Doc. (Rolls Ser.)	Jones, W. H. Rich- (ed.) and Dunn Macray, W. (ed.) *Charters and Documents illustrating the History of Salisbury* (Rolls Series, xcvii)
Sess. Mins. (W.A.S. Rec. Brch.)	Johnson, H. C. (ed.) *Minutes of Proceedings in Sessions, 1563, 1574–92* (W.A.S. Rec. Brch. iv)
Swindon Studies	Grinsell, L. V. and others, *Studies in the History of Swindon* (Swindon Borough Council, 1950)
Taxation Lists (W.A.S. Rec. Brch.)	Ramsay, G. D. (ed.) *Two Sixteenth-Century Taxation Lists, 1545 and 1576* (W.A.S. Rec. Brch. x)
Walters, *Wilts. Bells*	Walters, H. B. *The Church Bells of Wiltshire* (Devizes, 1927)
W.A.M.	*Wiltshire Archaeological and Natural History Magazine*
Wilts. Inq. p.m. 1242–1326 (Index Libr.)	Fry, E. A. (ed.) *Abstracts of Wilts. Inq. p.m. 1242–1326* (Index Library xxxvii)
Wilts. Inq. p.m. 1327–77 (Index Libr.)	Stokes, Ethel (ed.) *Abstracts of Wilts. Inq. p.m. 1327–77* (Index Library xlviii)
Wilts. Inq. p.m. 1625–49 (Index Libr.)	Fry, G. S. and Fry, E. A. (ed.) *Abstracts of Wilts. Inq. p.m. 1625–49* (Index Library xxiii)
W.N. & Q.	*Wiltshire Notes and Queries.*
Wilts. Q. Sess. Rec. ed. Cunnington	Cunnington, B. H. (ed.) *Extracts from the Quarter Sessions Great Rolls of the 17th Century* (Devizes, 1932)

THE HUNDRED OF KINGSBRIDGE

THE AREA covered by the modern hundred of Kingsbridge lies towards the north of the county. Much of it is heavy clay-land, flat and low-lying. But in the south it climbs the chalk escarpment of the Marlborough Downs and here reaches heights of over 700 ft. The greensand belt, which runs beneath the chalk escarpment, has provided the site for several of the settlements within the hundred. Some of these settlements are still village centres, but some have declined in size and in the 20th century are represented only by large farmsteads. A fairly narrow ridge of corallian limestone runs right across the hundred from east to west and on its crest heights approaching 500 ft. are reached. Roughly in the centre of the hundred another elevation rises from the clay, formed by the exposures of Purbeck and Portland Beds on Swindon Hill.

Much of the land of the hundred is, therefore, good grassland and is dairy-farming country. In the 18th century it was renowned for its cheeses. There was also sheep-farming on a considerable scale in those parishes touching upon the chalk uplands. In the 1960s it was still mainly dairy country, although modern machinery and fertilizers made it possible greatly to increase the amount of arable. All along the limestone ridge numerous small quarries have been worked in the past to produce stone for roads and local building. Stone for a wider market was dug from quarries on Swindon Hill. It was not a region deeply involved in Wiltshire's cloth industry, although there is evidence of some of the trades connected with that industry. Since 1845, however, when the railway works of the G.W.R. came to Swindon, Wiltshire's only large industrial town has been included within the bounds of the hundred.

The modern hundred is formed from the ancient hundreds of Kingsbridge, Blackgrove, and Thornhill. The three, which were always royal hundreds, had probably been grouped together for administrative convenience by 1236 but, as will be shown below, they continued to retain their separate identities within the group until the 16th century. It will, therefore, be necessary to consider briefly the composition of the three before they finally became completely merged. Between 1084 and the time of the final merger a few important changes occurred as well as a number of minor variations. The evidence for the minor variations comes, however, from the lists compiled for purposes of taxation, and small places were clearly grouped in different ways by different collectors or on some occasions altogether ignored as separate units. Such variations, therefore, are probably of little significance. But an attempt will be made to trace the more important changes.

As is discussed in another volume of the *History*,[1] there are difficulties about determining exactly which places constituted the three hundreds in 1084. Thornhill at that date seems to have been made up of estates in Wanborough, Chiseldon, Liddington, Draycot Foliat, and possibly, it has been suggested, Aldbourne.[2] Wanborough, Chiseldon, Liddington, and Draycot Foliat continued to lie in Thornhill, but Aldbourne, if it was part of Thornhill in 1084, had been transferred to Selkley hundred at least by 1274.[3] Little Hinton (Hyneton) was reckoned to belong to Thornhill in 1254 and 1274,[4] although in 1254 its suit had been withdrawn from the hundred court for the

[1] *V.C.H. Wilts.* ii, pp. 197–8 (Kingsbridge), 206–7 (Thornhill), 215–17 (Blackgrove).
[2] Ibid. p. 207.
[3] *Rot. Hund.* (Rec. Com.), ii (1), 269.
[4] Ibid. 233, 275.

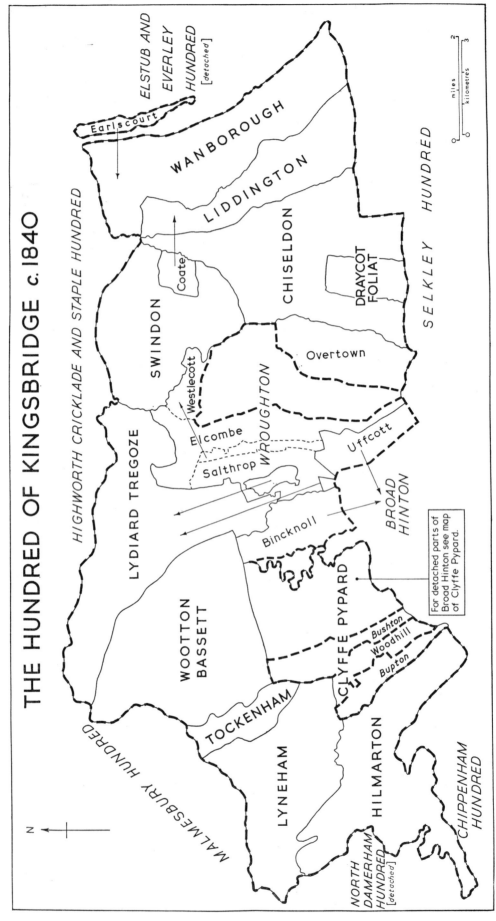

THE HUNDRED OF KINGSBRIDGE c.1840

ELSTUB AND EVERLEY HUNDRED [detached]

Earlscourt

WANBOROUGH

LIDDINGTON

HIGHWORTH CRICKLADE AND STAPLE HUNDRED

Coate

SWINDON

CHISELDON

DRAYCOT FOLIAT

SELKLEY HUNDRED

Westlecott

Overtown

WROUGHTON

Elcombe

Uffcott

Salthrop

BROAD HINTON

LYDIARD TREGOZE

Bincknoll

For detached parts of Broad Hinton see map of Clyffe Pypard.

WOOTTON BASSETT

CLYFFE PYPARD

Bushton

Woodhill

Bupton

TOCKENHAM

MALMESBURY HUNDRED

LYNEHAM

HILMARTON

NORTH DAMERHAM HUNDRED [detached]

CHIPPENHAM HUNDRED

N

miles
kilometres

Sources for parish boundaries: W.R.O. tithe maps; *for tithing boundaries:* W.R.O. map of Lord Bolingbroke's estate, 1766, Elcombe tithe and inclosure maps, Wroughton church rate bk., 1845, map in sale catalogue of Meux estate, 1906; map of Goddard lands in Clyffe Pypard, 1742, *penes* Mr. P. W. Wilson, Clyffe Pypard.

past 44 years by the Bishop of Winchester (see below). In the *Nomina Villarum* of 1316 Little Hinton is given under both Thornhill and Elstub hundreds,[5] but thereafter it was probably reckoned to be part of Elstub, which by 1249 belonged to the Prior of St. Swithun's, Winchester, as did the manor of Little Hinton.[6]

The hundred of Kingsbridge in 1084 contained lands in Lyneham, Clyffe Pypard, Hilmarton, Highway, and possibly Broad Hinton.[7] Of these, only Lyneham continued to lie wholly within the hundred. Bupton, in Clyffe Pypard, which was probably part of the Bishop of Salisbury's manor of Bishop's Cannings by 1086,[8] was probably also reckoned to be part of the bishop's hundred of Cannings by that date. It was certainly placed in that hundred by the tax assessors of 1428 and it subsequently became part of the hundred of Potterne and Cannings.[9] Another estate in Clyffe Pypard, Bushton, was also at some time detached from the hundred of Kingsbridge. In 1377 Bushton was allotted by the tax assessors to Thornhill hundred,[10] but it was a manor belonging to St. Swithun's Priory, Winchester, and like the priory's other Wiltshire estates, it was eventually transferred to the prior's hundred of Elstub. Exactly when this occurred is not known, but it was considered to be part of that hundred by 1545.[11] Beversbrook, in Hilmarton, was probably a detached part of the hundred of Calne in 1084 and certainly was by 1334.[12] Highway was lost entirely to Kingsbridge hundred probably by 1219 when, as has been explained elsewhere, it was transferred to Cannings hundred.[13] If, as suggested above, land in Broad Hinton lay in Kingsbridge hundred in 1084, this may have comprised the tithings of Bincknoll and Uffcott, but, if so, both tithings were subsequently transferred to Blackgrove hundred (see below). Tockenham, on the other hand, seems to have been added to Kingsbridge hundred from Blackgrove by 1254 (see below). Thus Kingsbridge hundred finally consisted of the parishes of Lyneham, Clyffe Pypard (except Bupton and Bushton), Hilmarton (except Beversbrook), and Tockenham.

The changes in the composition of Blackgrove hundred are even more complicated to trace. In 1084 the hundred seems to have corresponded to Swindon, Wroughton, Lydiard Tregoze, Wootton Bassett, and Tockenham.[14] Tockenham had probably been transferred to Kingsbridge by 1254.[15] The whole of Wroughton seems to have been still regarded as part of Blackgrove in 1274, although the Prior of St. Swithun's was claiming extensive liberties for his manor of Lower Wroughton (see below), and Lower Wroughton was probably soon afterwards transferred to the prior's hundred of Elstub.[16] But four substantial tithings in Wroughton continued to be regarded as part of Blackgrove hundred. These were Overtown, Elcombe, Salthrop, and Westlecott, all of which were closely connected with other manors in parishes within the hundred.[17] By 1274 Bincknoll, a tithing in Broad Hinton, was attached to Blackgrove hundred, although Broad Hinton itself was in Selkley hundred.[18] Another tithing in Broad Hinton, Uffcott, was part of Blackgrove by 1334.[19] These two tithings in Broad Hinton with the four in Wroughton and the parishes of Swindon, Lydiard Tregoze, and Wootton Bassett then made up the hundred of Blackgrove. Thus when about the 16th century the three hundreds were finally merged under the title of Kingsbridge,[20] that hundred comprised the parishes of Wanborough, Chiseldon,

[5] *Feud. Aids*, v. 207.
[6] *V.C.H. Wilts.* v. 50, 52; *Feud. Aids*, v. 207.
[7] *V.C.H. Wilts.* ii, p. 198.   [8] See p. 30.
[9] *V.C.H. Wilts.* vii. 177, where Bupton is said incorrectly to lie in Highway.
[10] Ibid. iv. 311.
[11] *Taxation Lists* (W.A.S. Rec. Brch.), 3.
[12] *V.C.H. Wilts.* ii, p. 182; ibid. iv. 298.
[13] Ibid. vii. 175.   [14] Ibid. ii, p. 217.

[15] *Rot. Hund.* (Rec. Com.), ii (1), 233.
[16] Ibid. 243.
[17] These connexions have not been worked out fully and are reserved until the history of Wroughton is written.
[18] *Rot. Hund.* (Rec. Com.), ii (1), 243.
[19] *V.C.H. Wilts.* iv. 297.
[20] No distinction was made between the three in 1545 or 1558: *Taxation Lists* (W.A.S. Rec. Brch.), 20-22 and E 179/198/276.

Liddington, Draycot Foliat (all formerly in Thornhill), Lyneham, Clyffe Pypard (except Bupton and Bushton), Hilmarton (except Beversbrook), Tockenham (all formerly in Kingsbridge), Swindon, Lydiard Tregoze, and Wootton Bassett (all formerly in Blackgrove), and the tithings of Elcombe, Salthrop, Westlecott, Overtown (all in Wroughton parish), Uffcott, and Bincknoll (both in Broad Hinton parish). By 1624 the four tithings in Wroughton parish, together with the tithing of Uffcott in Broad Hinton, were known collectively as the five tithings,[21] a title which they retained in the 19th century.[22]

In the 13th century numerous estates and persons in the three ancient hundreds had either withdrawn their suit from the hundred or claimed specified liberties within it. In the hundred of Blackgrove in 1255 William de Valence had withdrawn the suit due from High Swindon and Gilbert Basset that from Nethercott (Swindon). The Bishop of London, the Prior of St. Swithun's, Winchester, and Sir John Lovel claimed return of writs.[23] In 1275, in the same hundred, the Prior of Bradenstoke had withdrawn his suit for two holdings in Chaddington (Lydiard Tregoze); John Tregoze for a holding in Lydiard, the Prior of Wilton for a holding in Quidhampton (Wroughton); the Abbot of Stanley for a holding in Costow (Wroughton), and an unnamed person for a holding in Mannington (Lydiard Tregoze). The Prior of St. Swithun's, Sir John Lovel, the Earl Marshal, and William de Valence claimed gallows and the assize of bread and ale. The prior also claimed return of writs and to hold fully *de namio vetito*.[24] These claims by the prior presumably presage the transfer of his estate at Lower Wroughton to his hundred of Elstub (see above).

In the hundred of Kingsbridge in 1255 the township of Tockenham had withdrawn its suit as had the men of Geoffrey de Wancy at Clevancy.[25] In 1265 the Prior of Bradenstoke was granted exemption from suit at the hundred court for those lands which he held in demesne at Tockenham and elsewhere.[26] In the hundred of Thornhill in 1255 the men of the Bishop of Winchester had withdrawn for the past 44 years the suit due from Little Hinton, which may already have been transferred by the Prior of Winchester to his hundred of Elstub (see above). In the same year the Bishop of Bath was said to have withdrawn the suit due from Badbury (Chiseldon) for the past 35 years. Stephen Longespée, the Prior of St. Swithun's, the Abbot of Glastonbury, and Sampson Foliot all claimed return of writs.[27] In 1275 in the same hundred the following claimed gallows and assize of bread and ale: the Prior of Winchester in Little Hinton, the heirs of Stephen Longespée in Wanborough, Sampson Foliot in Draycot, and the Prioress of Marcigny in Broome (Swindon). The Abbot of Glastonbury claimed return of writs as well as gallows and assize of bread and ale.[28]

As in the other royal hundreds, these claims and numerous withdrawals of suit led to the grouping of the three hundreds, partly no doubt to ensure sufficient business in the hundred court. Kingsbridge, Blackgrove, and Thornhill had probably been so amalgamated under one bailiff, appointed by the sheriff, by 1236.[29] Thereafter, as far as record survives, the sheriff held his tourn for the three hundreds together.[30] In 1275 the men of Thornhill hundred complained that this practice of holding one court for the three hundreds together was inconvenient to them.[31] The three were valued separately in 1255 when Kingsbridge and Blackgrove were reckoned to be worth 40s.

[21] *Chalfield and Malmesbury Garrison Accts.* (W.A.S. Rec. Brch.), 92–93.
[22] W.R.O. Land Tax Assessments.
[23] *Rot. Hund.* (Rec. Com.), ii (1), 235.
[24] Ibid. 243.
[25] Ibid. 233.
[26] *Close R.* 1264–8, 148.
[27] *Rot. Hund.* (Rec. Com.), ii (1), 233.
[28] Ibid. 275.
[29] *V.C.H. Wilts.* v. 3.
[30] Record of tourns survives for 1439, 1502, and 1511: *W.A.M.* xiii. 105–18; S.C. 2/208/29; W.R.O. 192/26.
[31] *Rot. Hund.* (Rec. Com.), ii (1), 275.

each, and Thornhill 42s.[32] In 1275 Blackgrove was worth £5 and the sheriff rendered £3 7s. 11d. as tithingpenny for Thornhill.[33] At tourns held at Martinmas and Hockday 1291 the sheriff accounted for 65s. 3d. on both occasions as tithingpenny, apparently for the three hundreds together under the title of Kingsbridge.[34] At the tourn of 1439 £3 3s. 5d. was paid as tithingpenny.[35] At the first tourn of 1502 tithingpenny totalled £2 9s. 0d. and at the second tourn of the same year the sum was £3 14s. 5d.[36] At the Easter tourn of 1511 all profits of the court were reckoned to be £4 17s. 4d. while at the Michaelmas tourn they were £2 15s. 5d.[37] By 1651 the tourn was held once a year only, at Michaelmas, but the three weekly courts were said to be held in the usual place and according to custom. Lawday silver, or tithingpenny, payable at the tourn, then only annual, amounted to £8 15s. 8d., and this with all other profits of the court, brought the value of the hundred to £13 15s. 8d.[38]

In 1439 18 tithings appeared at the tourn. These were: Clyffe Pypard, and Broad Town; Hilmarton, Clevancy, Corton, and Witcomb; Liddington, and Medbourne; Lydiard Tregoze; Tockenham; Wanborough; Bincknoll (in Broad Hinton); Eastrop, Westrop, and Hodson (all in Chiseldon); Salthrop, Over Wroughton, and Westlecott (all in Wroughton).[39] Although Wanborough sent its tithingman to the tourn, he claimed exemption from making presentments or paying tithingpenny, and asserted his tithing's right to the assize of bread and ale. Swindon, Wootton Bassett, Lyneham, and Badbury (in Chiseldon), owed no suit, as a result, no doubt, of the claims and withdrawals made in the 13th century by William de Valence, the Earl Marshal, the Prior of Bradenstoke, and the Bishop of Bath respectively (see above). The 18 tithings appearing in 1439, with the addition of Uffcott (in Broad Hinton), owed suit at the tourns of 1502 and 1511.[40] Presentments on all occasions for which record survives were almost exclusively concerned with the repair of roadways, the removal of nuisances, and the exaction of illegal tolls by millers.

The meeting-place of Blackgrove hundred in the days when it met separately was almost certainly near Blagrove Farm in Wroughton.[41] The meeting-place of Thornhill hundred is unknown. It was presumably at some time in the tithing of Thornhill in Clyffe Pypard. But from 1084 Thornhill was always, so far as is known, reckoned to be, like Clyffe Pypard, part of Kingsbridge hundred.[42] According to tradition, the meeting-place of Kingsbridge hundred was in Clyffe Pypard, ½ mile north-west of Woodhill Park.[43]

The hundred bailiff was apparently sworn into his office publicly so as to make him known throughout the three hundreds. In 1275 some freemen of Thornhill hundred tried to excuse themselves for failing to attend an inquest at Salisbury, some 25 miles away, on the grounds that they had been summoned by someone who had not been so sworn into office, and was thus unknown to them. They were, none the less, heavily fined by the sheriff for their failure to attend.[44] In 1347 the bailiff of the combined hundreds had been imprisoned in the Marshalsea of the household for oppressions perpetrated in the course of his duties and upon his release was again accused of similar oppressions.[45] In the 1570s the hundred had two constables.[46]

[32] Ibid. 233, 235.
[33] Ibid. 243, 275. No record of the court held for Kingsbridge in 1275 survives.
[34] E 199/47/4.
[35] W.A.M. xiii. 105–8.
[36] S.C. 2/208/29.
[37] W.R.O. 192/26.
[38] E 317/Wilts. 11.
[39] W.A.M. xiii. 105–8.
[40] S.C. 2/208/29; W.R.O. 192/26.

[41] P.N. Wilts. (E.P.N.S.), 274.
[42] Ibid. 281. Thornhill in Clyffe Pypard was part of Kingsbridge hund. in 1084 (V.C.H. Wilts. ii, p. 198) and was returned under that hund. in 1334 and 1377 (ibid. iv. 300, 309).
[43] W.N. & Q. i. 413–15.
[44] Rot. Hund. (Rec. Com.), ii (1), 275; H.M.Cam, Hundred and Hundred R., 147.
[45] Cal. Pat. 1345–8, 308.
[46] Sess. Mins. (W.A.S. Rec. Brch.), 31.

CHISELDON

THE PARISH of Chiseldon[1] adjoins the borough of Swindon in the north and the distance from the centre of Swindon to Chiseldon village is about 5 miles. It is a long, narrow parish typical of those in this region which stretch northwards from the chalk escarpment of the Marlborough Downs. From north to south the distance is some 5 miles. Across the northern tip it is less than ¼ mile wide, but at its widest point, in the south, it is about 3 miles broad.[2] In 1891 the area was 4,884 a.[3] Three years later the entire ancient parish of Draycot Foliat (705 a.) was transferred to Chiseldon.[4] In 1928 a small area at Coate in the north of the parish, including part of Coate Water (see below), was transferred to Swindon and a few years later 5 a. in the same region were similarly transferred.[5] After these changes the area was 5,561 a.[6]

The geology of the parish is varied and that of the northern part, where there are small zones of Pectinatus Sands and Portland Beds, has been described elsewhere.[7] Chiseldon extends from the low-lying clays in the north across belts of Gault and Upper Greensand to the Upper Chalk of the Marlborough Downs in the south.[8] At their lowest point the clay lands do not rise above 350 ft.[9] To the south of the clays there is a gently rising belt of Gault which stretches right across the parish and on which is situated Burderop Wood, a densely planted area of woodland.[10] Beyond the Gault is the ridge of Upper Greensand, also well-wooded, on which are situated the three main areas of settlement in the parish, namely, the village of Chiseldon and the hamlets of Hodson and Badbury.[11] On the ridge the ground is distinctly hilly and at several points, notably to the south-east of Hodson and to the west of the parish church, deep tree-lined coombs have been gouged out of the chalk. The greensand ridge is succeeded to the south by the Lower Chalk Terrace at the foot of the Marlborough Downs. Here is an expanse of flat treeless land lying mostly at 500 ft. But beyond the chalk terrace the ground rises steeply to the Upper Chalk of the downs and at Burderop Down in the south-west corner of the parish it reaches to over 800 ft.[12] The parish has, therefore, a great variety of soils ranging from the heavy clays in the north, best suited for dairy farming, to the more-easily drained land of the Lower Chalk Terrace in the south which in 1967 was partly arable and partly pasture. On the Upper Greensand there was in 1967 a large nursery garden growing tomatoes.[13] Bricks are made on the Gault Clay south of Badbury Wick.[14]

A tributary of the River Cole rises north of Chiseldon village and flows northwards out of the parish by way of Coate Water. North of the reservoir this tributary, anciently known as the 'Dorcan', forms the northern and extreme north-western boundaries of the parish.[15] The River Ray, since diverted by the construction of Coate Water, formerly rose in Burderop Wood.[16]

The parish is crossed by a number of ancient tracks of which some still served as roads in 1967. The Ridge Way enters directly south of Chiseldon village and crosses the parish in a south-westerly direction. Most of the eastern boundary of the parish is formed by the 'Eldene Hegheway' which runs west of Liddington Castle northwards towards Snodshill. Part of the Roman road between Cirencester and Mildenhall, known for some of its course as 'Brokene Street', is now part of the main road between Swindon and Marlborough and runs right through the parish from north to south.[17] It probably only became the main road after 1819 when it was turnpiked. Until then the main road southwards ran due south from Burderop up the steep slope of Burderop Down and thence south-eastwards to Marlborough via Ogbourne St. Andrew. This road was turnpiked in 1761–2.[18] In 1967, as a minor road, it formed the western boundary of the parish. A track, called Gipsy Lane in 1845, forms part of the southern boundary.[19] The road running south of Burderop Park eastwards towards Chiseldon village was turnpiked in 1813–14[20] and two former toll-houses still stood on it in 1967. At the time of the turnpiking the course of the road through the village was diverted a little and extended eastwards to join the high road between Swindon and Marlborough.[21] Where it left the village the road became known as New Road. One or two small lanes in the village itself were disrupted when the railway line was constructed through Chiseldon in 1881.[22] Butts Road, leading towards Badbury, was known as Butt Way in 1781.[23] The hamlet of Badbury lies on the secondary road running from Liddington westwards towards Chiseldon. In 1773 the nucleus of the hamlet seems to have clustered between this road and a lane which ran to the north of it[24] but in 1967 the lane was only a rough track.

The railway line between Swindon and Andover was opened in 1881 and cut right through the centre of the village where there was a station.[25] A halt for Chiseldon Camp (see below) was opened in 1930.[26] The railway was closed in 1961 and in 1967 the

---

[1] Grateful thanks are due to Miss J. M. Calley for her help during the preparation of this article.
[2] The following maps have been used. O.S. Maps 6", Wilts. XV, XVI, XXII, XXIII (1st edn.); 1", sheet 157 (1958 edn.); 1/25,000, SU 17, 18 (1953 edn.).
[3] Census 1891.
[4] Ibid.; V.C.H. Wilts. iv. 344.
[5] V.C.H. Wilts. iv. 344; Census, 1931. [6] Census, 1951.
[7] For an acct. of the geology of the area, see W. J. Arkell, 'A Geological Map of Swindon', W.A.M. lii. 195.
[8] Ibid.
[9] O.S. Maps 1/25,000, SU 17, 18 (1953 edn.); Geolog. Survey of Britain 1857, sheet 34.
[10] Geolog. Survey of Britain 1857, sheet 34.
[11] Ibid.
[12] Ibid.; O.S. Maps 1/25,000, SU 17, 18 (1953 edn.).
[13] Plough Hill Nurseries.

[14] See p. 17.
[15] O.S. Maps 1/25,000, SU 17, 18 (1953 edn.).
[16] Andrews and Dury, Map (W.A.S. Rec. Brch.), pls. 14, 15; O.S. Map 1", sheet 157 (1958 edn.).
[17] O.S. Maps 1/25,000, SU 17, 18 (1953 edn.).
[18] V.C.H. Wilts. iv. 263; Andrews and Dury, Map (W.A.S. Rec. Brch.), pl. 15.
[19] W.R.O. Tithe Award Map.
[20] V.C.H. Wilts. iv. 263.
[21] Andrews and Dury, Map (W.A.S. Rec. Brch.), pl. 15; V.C.H. Wilts. iv. 257, 263.
[22] Andrews and Dury, Map (W.A.S. Rec. Brch.), pl. 15, and see below.
[23] Burderop MSS. Estate map, 1781.
[24] Andrews and Dury, Map (W.A.S. Rec. Brch.), pl. 15.
[25] V.C.H. Wilts. iv. 289, and see p. 115.
[26] Ibid. 291.

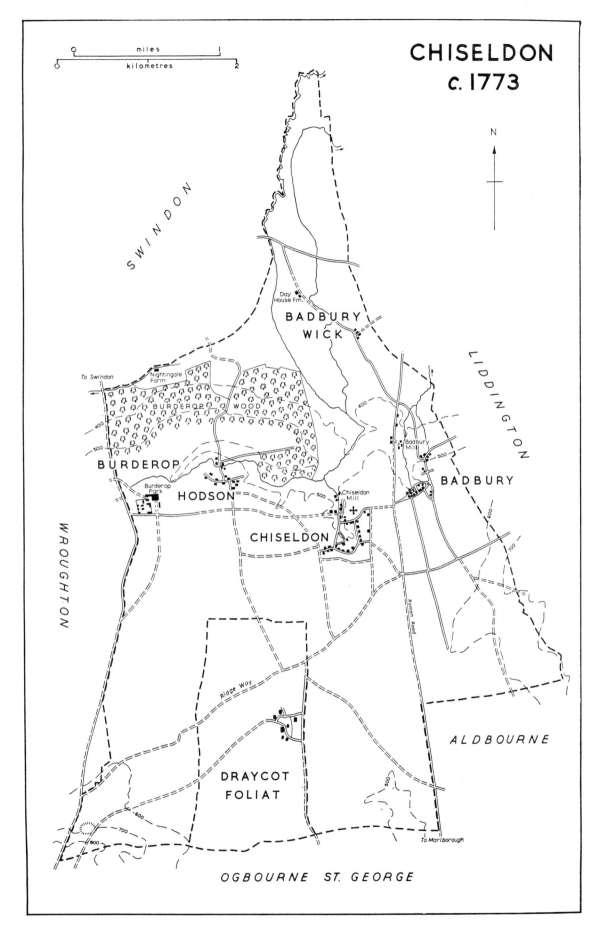

CHISELDON
c. 1773

line through Chiseldon had been pulled up and the station was derelict.[27]

The prehistoric archaeology of Chiseldon provides evidence of continuous habitation since Neolithic times. A stone circle of this period, first found by Richard Jefferies to the east of Day House Farm, was made up ot 9 recumbent stones.[28] The parish has 3 bowl barrows[29] and a disc barrow on Burderop Down[30] was found to contain Iron Age sherds.[31] Sherds of this date were also found in 1951[32] in a quadrilateral 'kite' excavated in Burderop Park.[33] The most numerous remains in Chiseldon are those of Romano-British origin, and include traces of huts[34] and fragments of a hypocaust.[35] The Roman highway from Corinium (Cirencester) to Cunetio (Mildenhall) passes the length of the parish[36] and an extensive field system of similar date stretches from the downs at Badbury and Burderop southwards to Smeathe's Ridge.[37] On Burderop Down an earthwork, which formerly inclosed a plantation and was probably of 18th-century date, was placed over an earlier field system.[38]

By the late 13th century Chiseldon manor was made up of three parts, Eastrop, Westrop, and Hodson.[39] The first two must be variants of East and West Chiseldon, two of the four or five tithings into which the parish was divided for certain purposes until the 19th century.[40] There was also at the end of the 13th century a place known as 'Cumbe', presumably lying in or near one of the deep coombs which are a feature of the parish.[41] Land belonging to the Cardeville family was known at the beginning of the 14th century as 'Cardeville-swick' and may have been situated near the Burderop estate with which it was merged in the mid 14th century.[42]

The modern parish contains a number of settlements. The three largest are the village of Chiseldon, the hamlet of Hodson, and the hamlet of Badbury. All three are ancient settlements. Chiseldon and Badbury certainly are the subjects of 10th-century charters. A charter of 901 concerning land at Chiseldon, also includes a reference to Hodson under the form 'Horeston'.[43] Descriptions of these three places are given below. Two miles north of Chiseldon village are a few houses belonging to the tithing of Coate, by far the greater part of which forms a detached portion of the parish of Liddington.[44] In 1822 the great reservoir for the Wilts. and Berks. Canal, known as Coate Water, was built along the boundary between Swindon and Chiseldon, so that until the boundary change of 1928 (see above) half the water lay in each parish.[45] Coate Farm, to the

north of the reservoir, the birth place of Richard Jefferies, was also taken into Swindon in 1928.[46] North of Coate the narrow northern tip of the parish is occupied by the two farms of Upper and Lower Snodshill.

Badbury Wick, which lies about a mile north-west of Badbury, may once have been a larger settlement. A few cottages are shown here on a map of 1773.[47] But in 1967 there was only Badbury Wick Farm with its farm buildings and the brick works just to the south of the farm. A region in the west of the parish may have been known as Burderop from early times. In the form 'Burithorp' it occurs as a tithing in 1249.[48] The Abbot of Hyde's manor of Burderop emerges by that name in the mid 14th century.[49] In 1967 Burderop Park still retained some of the features of a great estate but part of the land was built over during the Second World War (see below).

In 1086 six burgesses in Cricklade were attached to the manor of Chiseldon and another Cricklade burgess contributed 5d. to the manor of Badbury.[50] When assessed for taxation in 1334 Chiseldon was rated at 126s. 8d. and with Liddington had the second highest assessment in the small hundred of Thornhill.[51] On this occasion Badbury was assessed separately at 86s.[52] In 1377 there were 145 poll-tax payers in Chiseldon and 78 in Badbury.[53] There were 3 contributors in Chiseldon to the Benevolence of 1545 and 4 in Badbury.[54] In 1576 there were 14 taxpayers in Chiseldon, Badbury, and Hodson together.[55] In 1801 there were 904 people in the whole parish.[56] The population then rose gradually until 1841 when it was 1,176.[57] Of this total Chiseldon village accounted for 547, Badbury 395, and Hodson 234.[58] In 1851 the population of the parish had fallen to 1,137 but had risen slightly by 1861 when it was 1,246.[59] For the rest of the 19th century there was little significant change, since the addition of Draycot Foliat to the parish in 1884 only added 56 people.[60] In 1911 the population was 1,197 but in 1921, after the military camp had been established in the south of the parish (see below), it rose to 1,688.[61] Thenceforth the population rose as more and more people working in Swindon made their homes in Chiseldon. In 1961 it was 2,598.[62]

The old centre of Chiseldon was to the west of High Street, where an open space known as The Square lay at the head of the steep coomb which runs north-westwards from the village. The Square was obliterated when the railway was constructed along the coomb and through the village. The Elm Tree Inn, which overlooked The Square, has been rebuilt.[63] The village streets, all south of the church,

---

[27] See p. 115 and see pl. facing p. 14.
[28] V.C.H. Wilts. i (1), 56–57.
[29] Ibid. 165.
[30] Ibid. 217.
[31] Ibid. 56–57.
[32] Ibid. 56.
[33] Ibid. 264.
[34] Ibid. 56–57; W.A.M. xlvi. 101.
[35] V.C.H. Wilts. i (1), 56–57.
[36] Ibid.
[37] Ibid. 274.
[38] Ibid. 264.
[39] B.M. Harl. MS. 1761, f. 111v.
[40] W.R.O. Tithe Award, 1845.
[41] B.M. Harl. MS. 1761, f. 117.
[42] See p. 10.
[43] G. B. Grundy, Saxon Land Charters of Wilts. 200–10.
[44] See p. 66.
[45] W.A.M. l. 491.

[46] See p. 116.
[47] Andrews and Dury, Map (W.A.S. Rec. Brch.), pl. 15.
[48] Crown Pleas Wilts. Eyre, 1249 (W.A.S. Rec. Brch.), 216.
[49] See p. 10.
[50] V.C.H. Wilts. ii, pp. 127, 124.
[51] Ibid. iv. 302.
[52] Ibid.
[53] Ibid. 311.
[54] Taxation Lists (W.A.S. Rec. Brch.), 21.
[55] Ibid. 105.
[56] V.C.H. Wilts. iv. 344.
[57] Ibid.
[58] Ibid.
[59] Ibid.
[60] Ibid.
[61] Ibid. 326, 344.
[62] Census 1961.
[63] A. Williams, Villages of the White Horse, 93–94.

contain a number of old buildings, most of which have walls of local chalk stone and thatched roofs. On the north side of Turnball are several ranges of cottages dating from the 17th and 18th centuries. The former toll-house at the junction of Turnball and New Road was probably built *c.* 1814 and consists of a three-sided brick addition to one of these ranges. Cottages in Slipper Lane have walls faced with stone and brick but may originally have been of timber-framed construction. Nearby the thatched outbuildings of Dykes Farm include a long **L**-shaped barn. In Mays Lane the Cottage, formerly Chiseldon Cottage, appears to be a stone house of the early 19th century but carries date stones of 1583, 1615, and 1841. Further south a reconditioned house at right angles to the road has a dated chimney of 1623. In Church Street, facing the churchyard, is a thatched range of buildings some of which were originally timber-framed and possibly of medieval origin. A tablet of 1699 may record the date at which one of them was faced with stone. Glebe Cottage, at the east end of the range, was converted from derelict buildings *c.* 1954.[64] Parsonage Farm, immediately west of the church, has a ground floor of stone, probably of the 17th century, and an upper story of 19th-century brick. Two larger houses in the village have some claim to architectural distinction. The former Southfields House, re-named Chiseldon Manor in the 20th century, is a late-18th-century brick building with a symmetrical front and two low flanking wings. Chiseldon House, an elegant stucco-faced villa of *c.* 1825, has an arcaded verandah and a cast-iron balcony with Greek key-pattern ornament.

The first houses to be built in the village for people travelling daily by rail to Swindon are situated in New Road and Butts Road. They are semi-detached or terraced brick houses, uniformly urban in style, carrying date tablets of 1904–8. Much housing development took place in Chiseldon between the two World Wars. Houses were built in the north of the parish along either side of Butts Road and northwards to Plough Hill along the western side of the road from Swindon to Marlborough. Houses were also built at this date along the east side of Station Road and along the road between Burderop and Chiseldon. After the Second World War considerable development took place to the north of the railway line on either side of the allotment gardens. In 1955 land behind the Y.M.C.A. hall was developed and in 1959 a council estate, which contained a number of old persons' bungalows, was built on the site of the allotment gardens to the north-east of Station Road. In 1964 houses were built on the former Recreation Ground in the west corner of the village and also on ground along New Road to the east of Chiseldon House.[65]

In 1968 the hamlet of Hodson remained almost unaffected by modern building. It consists largely of chalk-stone cottages with thatched roofs, forming several picturesque groups on either side of a steep and thickly-wooded road. Hodson House is a larger building with a roof partly of stone slates. The oldest house is Hodson farm-house which consists of a medieval cruck-framed range and a taller cross-wing probably added in the 16th century. The remnants of two smoke-blackened cruck trusses survive in the older range which was formerly an open hall. To the east of the road to Burderop Wood is a cottage which shows traces of timber-framing. Nearly opposite a chalk-stone cottage with a thatched roof has a date stone of 1714 with initials 'I.H.M.'; this was the house of the principal character in *The Gamekeeper at Home* by Richard Jefferies (see below).

At Badbury a few new houses and bungalows were being built in 1968. There was formerly a group of old cottages at Badbury Bottom, a steep coomb lying west of the hamlet.[66] Several have been demolished, but survivors include an altered house with a thatched roof, chalk-stone walls, brick dressings to the windows, and a dated brick chimney of 1689. The stone is said to have been quarried in the side of the coomb. A smaller cottage has walls of Sarsen stone. Several springs rise at Badbury Bottom and further down the coomb lie the site of Badbury mill and the ruins of the mill house.

From 1811 to 1831 race-meetings were held at Burderop Down under the auspices of Thomas Calley of Burderop Park, one of the stewards of the course.[67] During the First World War a hutted army camp was built in the south of the parish east of the ancient parish of Draycot Foliat. It covered a considerable area of ground, extending about $\frac{1}{2}$ mile from east to west and from north to south. After the war it was used for a time as a vocational training centre and during the Second World War accommodated both British and American troops. It was occupied by the army until about 1963 but by 1967 the married quarters alone were used.[68] The camp had its own chapel, dedicated to St. Michael and St. George, but this had been closed by 1967.[69] Shortly before 1939 land from the Calley estate was acquired by the Royal Air Force as an addition to Wroughton R.A.F. Aerodrome and Hospital. During the Second World War an American Base Hospital was built in Burderop Park.[70] The hospital was vacated by the Americans about 1965 and was taken over by the South-West Regional Hospital Board.

In 1619 William Calley (*c.* 1565–1641) purchased Burderop Park with the proceeds of a successful business transaction with the Spanish court.[71] His friends and correspondents included Endymion Porter and Sir Francis Cottington, English Ambassador in Spain.[72] He was knighted in 1629 and in 1632 was appointed, together with his son, Receiver General of the Crown Rents of Oxfordshire and Berkshire in recognition of his services.[73] Richard Jefferies (1848–87), the poet-naturalist, was born at Coate Farm[74] which was situated in Chiseldon until 1928 (see above). His boyhood was spent wandering

[64] *Church Guide*, Holy Cross, Chiseldon, 9.
[65] Ex inf. Area Planning Officer, 36 Milton Road, Swindon.
[66] For a description of Badbury Bottom in the early 20th century see A. Williams, *Villages of the White Horse*, 111–14.
[67] *V.C.H. Wilts.* iv. 381.
[68] Ex inf. Major R. M. Scott, H.Q. Salisbury Plain Sub-District.

[69] Ex inf. the Revd. J. F. Collins; *Swindon Evening Advertiser*, 24 Sept. 1965.
[70] Chiseldon W.I. Scrapbks. (Microfilm in Co. Libr., Trowbridge)
[71] *W.A.M.* xxxi. 174.
[72] Gervas Huxley, *Endymion Porter*, 27–28.
[73] *W.A.M.* xxxi. 173.
[74] *D.N.B.* and see p. 67.

in the countryside around Chiseldon and it was then that the foundations of his knowledge of the countryside and of natural lore were laid. *The Gamekeeper at Home*, written in 1877, commemorates his friendship with Benjamin Haylock, a gamekeeper on the Burderop estate.[75] An account of the conditions of farm and countrylife on the Burderop estate was given in 1880 in *Roundabout a Great Estate*.[76]

MANORS AND OTHER ESTATES. Land at Chiseldon was devised to the Old Minster at Winchester by King Alfred who stated in his will that this and other lands were to be given to the church there in accordance with the wishes of his father.[77] About 900 the monks of the Old Minster appear to have surrendered this land[78] to Edward the Elder who granted the estate about 901 to his newly-founded abbey of St. Peter at Winchester, otherwise known as the New Minster.[79] It is uncertain whether the grant of Edward the Elder was made up of 40 or 50 hides, but at the time of the Domesday Survey the land held by the monks of the New Minster at Chiseldon was estimated at 40 hides.[80] In 1109 the New Minster moved to Hyde Mead and thereafter was known as Hyde Abbey.[81] It was noted in 1388 that from time immemorial the Abbot of Hyde and his predecessors had held as their own portion the manor of *CHISELDON*.[82] The estate continued to be held by Hyde and its abbots until 1538 when the house was dissolved.[83]

In 1540 the king granted the manor with its appurtenances in Chiseldon, Hodson, and Badbury to Sir John Bridges of Blunsdon,[84] later Lord Chandos, who died seised of it in 1558.[85] Lord Chandos was succeeded by his son Edmund, upon whose death in 1572[86] the estate passed to his son Giles, who was seised of the manor, known as that of Chiseldon and Hodson, jointly with Frances his wife.[87] Giles, Lord Chandos (d. 1593) and his wife conveyed the manor together with lands, tenements, and rents in Chiseldon, Hodson, and Burderop to Thomas (II) Stephens in 1579.[88] Before his death in 1596 Thomas (II) settled the manor and rectory upon his second wife Dorothy for life. After Dorothy's death the manor passed to Nicholas Stephens, the eldest son of Thomas (II), although it seems that his brother Thomas (III) disputed the succession unsuccessfully.[89] Nicholas Stephens died in 1611 and was succeeded by his son Thomas (IV) Stephens (d. *c.* 1631),[90] who in 1619 conveyed the manor to trustees. In the same year they reconveyed it to William Calley the elder, citizen and draper of London.[91] On the death of William Calley in 1641, the manor

passed to his son William (II) Calley, who in 1660 was succeeded by his son, yet another William.[92] William (III) Calley died without issue in 1670, whereupon the manor passed to his brother Oliver.[93] Oliver Calley died in 1684 and on his death the estate was inherited by his second son, Oliver (II) Calley, who died in 1715 and was succeeded by his son William.[94] William Calley died in 1768 and his heir was his son, Thomas Browne Calley, who died in 1791, and was succeeded by his son, another Thomas.[95] This Thomas died in 1836 and was succeeded by his son John James Calley, upon whose death in 1854 the direct male line of the Calley family failed.[96] J. J. Calley was succeeded by his cousin Henry, son of his father's younger brother.[97] Henry Calley died in 1881 and the estate passed to his son Thomas Charles Pleydell Calley, who died in 1932.[98] In this year the manor of Chiseldon passed to his only child Miss Joan Marion Calley,[99] who owned the estate in 1967.

The Cardeville family held a small estate in Chiseldon as early as the 13th century. At some date before 1236 Thomas de Cardeville conveyed to John de Cardeville a hide and 4 a. of land in Chiseldon,[1] and in 1236 John regranted Thomas half of the lands as a life estate with reversion to John and his heirs.[2] In 1305 Agnes de Cardeville, daughter and heir of a Thomas de Cardeville, granted land in 'Cardevilleswick' and in all places within the parish of Chiseldon to Hyde Abbey.[3] At this date Agnes also conveyed to the abbey all her land and tenements in Burderop and Hodson together with the reversion of 1 virgate, 2 a. of meadow, 2 a. of woodland, 12d. rent, and also the reversion of a messuage then leased to her sister Alice.[4] In 1306 the king pardoned the abbey for acquiring land in Chiseldon from Agnes de Cardeville.[5] Agnes was said to hold no other lands than those which she had conveyed to Hyde.[6] It was noted in 1355–6 that the Abbot of Hyde had acquired a carucate at 'Cardevilleswick' and also a messuage, 2 virgates, 26 a. of land, 2 a. of meadow, 4 a. of woodland, and 3s. rent, all parcel of an estate by then called the manor of *BURDEROP*.[7] The abbey of Hyde was again pardoned by the king in 1361 for acquiring the lands of Agnes de Cardeville.[8] In 1482–3 Agnes, wife of Thomas Dobyns, died seised of certain unspecified lands and tenements in Burderop and Hodson.[9] No more is known of the manor or estate of Burderop in the Middle Ages, but in all probability it remained with Hyde Abbey and was surrendered with the manor of Chiseldon in 1538.[10]

In 1540 Burderop manor and a grange called 'Monkebaron' were granted with Chiseldon to Sir

[75] *W.A.M.* xlvi. 535–6; *D.N.B.*
[76] *W.A.M.* xlix. 499.
[77] *V.C.H. Wilts.* ii, pp. 86–87.   [78] Ibid.
[79] Ibid. p. 94.   [80] Ibid.
[81] *V.C.H. Hants* ii. 116.
[82] *Cal. Inq. Misc.* v, p. 56.   [83] *V.C.H. Hants* ii. 120.
[84] *L. & P. Hen. VIII*, xv, p. 295.
[85] C 142/114/71.
[86] C 142/163/59.   [87] Ibid.
[88] C 142/309/193; C.P. 25(2)/240/21 Eliz. I East.
[89] Req. 2/153/37.
[90] C 142/325/203; *W.A.M.* xxx. 127.
[91] *W.A.M.* xxx. 127; ibid. xxxi. 175–6; C.P. 25(2)/371/7 Jas. I Trin., and see p. 9.
[92] 'J. Tharlett', 'The Society's MSS. Chiseldon and Draycot', *W.A.M.* xxxi, pp. 173 sqq.; Burke, *Land. Gent.* (1952), s. v. Calley.

[93] *W.A.M.* xxxi, pp. 173 sqq.
[94] Ibid.
[95] Ibid.
[96] Ibid.
[97] Burke, *Land. Gent.* (1952), s. v. Calley.
[98] Ibid.
[99] Ibid.
[1] *Cal. Feet of F. Wilts.* 1195–1272, ed. Fry, 24.
[2] Ibid.
[3] B.M. Harl. MS. 1761, f. 108v.
[4] Ibid. f. 109.
[5] *Cal. Pat.* 1301–7, 458.
[6] *Wilts. Inq. p.m.* 1242–1326 (Index Libr.), 323.
[7] B.M. Harl. MS. 1761, f. 111.
[8] Ibid. f. 110.
[9] C 140/83/23.
[10] See above.

John Bridges (see above).[11] On his death his lands passed to Sir Edmund Bridges, Lord Chandos[12] who in 1561 received a licence to alienate the capital messuage of Burderop Farm, together with Monke-baron grange and the tithes of both, to Thomas (II) Stephens of Burderop.[13] In 1561–2 the conveyance took place when messuages and lands in Burderop were transferred to Thomas (II) Stephens,[14] who died seised of Burderop Farm in 1596.[15] Before his death he had settled Burderop upon his first wife Elizabeth (d. 1574) as her jointure, with the intention that after his death his third son John should stand seised of the estate for the payment of legacies.[16] After this period the property was to remain to his eldest son Nicholas in tail male.[17] On the death of Thomas (II) Stephens trouble arose over the term of 6 years assigned to John.[18] In 1596 Nicholas and John Stephens agreed that Nicholas should have peaceful possession of the manor house of Burderop, together with demesne and parkland for the 6-year term, but the following year dissention arose and Nicholas accused his brother of wasting the park and reviving an old lease granted to Thomas Stephens (see below) in order to circumvent the 6-year term.[19] The dispute must have been resolved satisfactorily, since in 1611 Nicholas Stephens died seised of the manor and farm of Burderop,[20] and was succeeded by his son Thomas (IV) Stephens.[21] The estate thereafter followed the descent of the main manor and passed into the Calley family with whom it remained.

Burderop Park stands within extensive grounds in the north-west corner of the parish. The square three-storied stone house appears from the outside an entirely Georgian structure.[22] Internally the existence of an earlier house is revealed by two rooms with panelling and enriched plaster ceilings of the late 16th or early 17th century. Their position, one at the south-west and the other at the north-east corner of the present house, suggests that the original building may have consisted of two or more ranges disposed round a courtyard. It is possible that the main entrance was on the west side where a surviving Tudor doorway may have led through the west range to the courtyard. The original north-east room has an enriched plaster frieze above its oak panelling. The ceiling design includes the initials 'T.S.' and 'E.S.', possibly belonging to Thomas (II) Stephens (d. 1596) and his first wife Elizabeth (d. 1574). The initials 'W.C.' and figure '36' may have been added by William Calley (d. 1641) in 1636. An upper room on the north front has, above the fireplace, the painted arms of William (III) Calley, dated 1663. The north side of the house appears to have been remodelled at this date and at the same time was extended by a long wing projecting westwards. The main conversion probably took place before the middle of the 18th century and may have been carried out in more than one stage, the façades showing certain variations in detail. When it was complete the old building, except for the west wing, had been enclosed in a new square structure of formal classical design. To this a third story, of brick faced with stone, was added. A fine early-18th-century staircase occupies what is thought to have been the site of the courtyard. The most imposing of the façades are those facing south and east, the former being of five bays and having a central doorway with a segmental pediment. In front of it a forecourt is flanked by outbuildings which were evidently re-modelled to match the house. A straight avenue leading southwards to the road has now disappeared.[23]

Burderop Farm lies immediately west of the fore-court, part of the farm-house being incorporated in one of its flanking buildings. The house has a projecting two-storied porch on its long south front and appears to be basically a 17th-century stone structure, much altered in the 18th and 19th centuries.

In 955 King Eadred was said to have granted Badbury in Chiseldon, then assessed at 25 hides, to St. Dunstan, Abbot of Glastonbury.[24] But it is probable that the grant, although authentic, was made to another, possibly secular person and that the name of Dunstan was a later interpolation.[25] The manor of *BADBURY* was certainly held by Glastonbury at the time of the Domesday Survey, when it was reckoned at 20 hides.[26] In 1168 Alexander III confirmed the manor to Henry of Blois, Bishop of Winchester and administrator of Glastonbury.[27] Bishop Savaric united the see of Bath with the abbacy of Glastonbury in 1200 and, in the subsequent apportionment of lands, Badbury was allotted to the Bishop of Bath in 1203.[28] In 1219 an agreement regarding the temporalities of Glastonbury and Bath was reached and Bishop Jocelin restored the manor to Glastonbury Abbey.[29] The agreement was repeated in 1266 between Walter, Bishop of Bath and Wells, and Abbot Robert of Glastonbury.[30] Finally in 1280 Abbot John and the convent of Glastonbury were regranted Badbury in chief.[31] The manor continued to be held by Glastonbury until the house was dissolved in 1539.[32]

In 1543 Sir William Essex of Lambourn (Berks.), and his son Thomas, received a grant of the manor of Badbury.[33] Sir William Essex died c. 1548[34] and was succeeded by his son Thomas (d. 1575),[35] who in 1571 conveyed Badbury to Thomas Browne, a London merchant.[36] By 1576 the property had passed to Thomas Kibblewhite, who died seised of the capital messuage and site of Badbury manor in 1579.[37] It appears that Badbury passed at an unknown date to Thomas's grandson John Redferne, elder son of his daughter Elizabeth, who had married

[11] L. & P. Hen. VIII, xv, p. 295.
[12] See p. 10.
[13] Cal. Pat. 1560–3, 373.
[14] W.N. & Q. iv. 505.
[15] C 142/247/101.
[16] Req. 2/153/37.
[17] C 142/247/101.
[18] Req. 2/120/13.
[19] Ibid.
[20] C 142/325/203.
[21] W.A.M. xxx.142.
[22] See pl. facing p. 14.
[23] Andrews and Dury, Map (W.A.S. Rec. Brch.), pl. 15.
[24] V.C.H. Wilts. ii, p. 96.

[25] Glaston. Cartulary (Som. Rec. Soc. lxiv), iii, p. ccxxvi.
[26] V.C.H. Wilts. ii, p. 124.
[27] Glaston. Cartulary (Som. Rec. Soc. lix), i. 129.
[28] Ibid. 77.
[29] Ibid. 88.
[30] Hist. MSS. Com. Wells, i. 311.
[31] Cal. Chart. R. 1257–1300, 226.
[32] V.C.H. Som. ii. 98.
[33] L. & P. Hen. VIII, xviii (1), p. 543.
[34] P.C.C. 18 Populwell.
[35] C 142/173/3.
[36] C 66/1197 m. 3.
[37] P.C.C. 24 Fenner, Will of Arthur Redferne; C 142/188/8.

Arthur Redferne.[38] John died in *c.* 1609–10 and was succeeded by Thomas Redferne, his younger brother, who in *c.* 1621 conveyed certain lands within the manor to William Norden.[39] In 1623 the residue of the manor was conveyed to Ferdinando Hughes.[40] Hughes had no land in Badbury at the time of his death in 1640,[41] and it is possible that he conveyed his part of the manor to William Norden, who died in 1638 seised of the manor and farm of Badbury.[42] William Norden was succeeded by his son Richard, who died seised of the estate in 1640.[43] The manor then passed to his younger brother John (d. *c.* 1670–1),[44] who subsequently sold it, together with other lands, to William Mellish of London.[45] William Mellish was first named as lord of the manor in 1682 and after his death in *c.* 1691[46] his widow Dorothy and her nephews[47] Robert and Edward were seised of the manor, the capital messuage called Place House, Badbury Farm, and Dairy Farm.[48] Dorothy Mellish died in *c.* 1702 and her moiety was inherited by Robert and Edward. Edward Mellish died intestate in 1707 seised of his moiety and was succeeded by his son Edward (II).[49] Robert likewise died intestate in 1710 and his moiety passed to his elder brother Charles, who settled lands including the moiety of Badbury manor on his wife Elizabeth upon trust for sale after his death.[50] Charles Mellish died in 1713.[51] In 1717–18, the remaining tenants-in-common, Edward (II), Bridget, and Elizabeth Mellish made arrangements for the sale of the manor to James Stone of London,[52] who had acquired it by 1718.[53] The manor hereafter descended in the Stone family until the 20th century.[54] On the death of James Stone in 1743[55] the manor passed to his son John, who was succeeded on his death in 1774 by his son John (II) Stone.[56] This John Stone died in 1792[57] and the estate passed to his son John (III) Stone (d. 1858).[58] John (III) was succeeded by his daughter Catherine, who married William Warry in 1860[59] and died a year later.[60] The estate presumably passed to her son William Ellis Warry-Stone, who died in 1944.[61] Before his death W. E. Warry-Stone devised a life interest in Badbury to a cousin Mr. R. G. W. Stone,[62] and left the estate absolute to another remote cousin Miss Jane Rosemary Alethe Stone,[63] both descendants of his great-uncle Robert Stone (d. 1853).[64] Miss Jane Stone married Mr. D. Buchan in 1948.[65] By 1967 the manor was represented by West and Folly Farms, which had, at some date previously,

been purchased by the Whatley family firm of Chiseldon Grain Driers.[66]

The house known in 1968 as The Manor, and earlier as Badbury House, stands on high ground between the hamlet and the deep coomb to the west of it. It incorporates a stone building of three bays with a date tablet of 1597.[67] The only visible features of this period are heavy ceiling beams with carved stops of several different patterns. Much alteration, including the addition of a staircase wing to the east, appears to have taken place in the 18th and early 19th centuries. A depression in the ground to the north-west of the present house is thought locally to mark the site of an earlier one.[68] It is also possible that terraced ground on the edge of the coomb had some connexion with the medieval capital messuage.

It is possible to trace a number of small estates within Chiseldon. In 1242–3 Oliver of Earlscourt held ¼ knight's fee of Sampson Foliot, who held of Earl Richard as of the honor of Wallingford.[69] The land had passed to the Wroughton family by 1393 when the escheator was ordered to release 10 virgates in Chiseldon, Hodson, and Draycot lately held by William Wroughton, to Wroughton's widow Isabel.[70] It remained in the Wroughton family and descended for the next hundred years in the same way as the manor of Woodhill (Clyffe Pypard).[71] The estate, which in 1428 was said once to have been held by Oliver of Earlscourt, is last mentioned in 1496 when John Wroughton died seised of 12 virgates in Chiseldon and Hodson then held of Hyde Abbey.[72]

The Walrond family had a small estate at Chiseldon in the 14th century, held before 1318 by William Walrond and his wife Joan.[73] By 1400 William had been succeeded by his son John.[74] In 1438 Ingram Walrond and his wife Elizabeth, probably members of the same family, conveyed 2 carucates in Chiseldon to John Byrd and Isabel his wife.[75]

A number of small estates held by the Hodson family at Hodson in the 13th and 14th centuries eventually passed to Hyde Abbey. In 1223 Stephen of Hodson conveyed ½ hide there to Walter, Abbot of Hyde.[76] Other land in Hodson apparently passed to Stephen's daughter Emma, wife of Henry de Gal of Woodhill (in Clyffe Pypard). In 1270 Henry and Emma conveyed a virgate in Hodson to Joan de Bocland, who reconveyed it to the abbey between 1270 and 1281.[77] In the later 13th century Roger of Hodson conveyed 10½ a., parcel of Chiseldon manor,

[38] P.C.C. 108 Wingfield, Will of John Redferne.
[39] Ibid.; C 2/Jas. I/F 8/58.
[40] C 2/Jas. I/F 8/58; C.P. 25(2)/372/20 Jas. I Mich.
[41] *Wilts. Inq. p.m.* 1625–49 (Index Libr.), 323.
[42] Ibid. 321.   [43] Ibid. 319.
[44] *Wilts. Visitation Pedigrees* (Harl. Soc. cv, cvi), p. 146; W.R.O. 117, View of frankpledge of Badbury manor, 1640–1932.
[45] W.R.O. 374/41.
[46] W.R.O. 117, View of frankpledge, 1640–1932.
[47] W.R.O. 374/41.
[48] C 78/1382 Entry I.
[49] Ibid.
[50] Ibid.
[51] Ibid.
[52] Ibid.
[53] B.M. Add. Ch. 53501.
[54] W.R.O. 117, View of frankpledge, 1640–1932. There is a modern genealogy of Stone inserted in this document.
[55] Ibid.
[56] Ibid.
[57] Ibid.
[58] Ibid.

[59] Ibid. Genealogy of Stone.
[60] Ibid.
[61] Ibid. View of frankpledge, 1640–1932.
[62] Ibid. Genealogy of Stone.
[63] Ibid.
[64] Ibid.
[65] Ibid.
[66] Ex inf. Mr. N. Whatley, Badbury, to whom thanks are due.
[67] One of the initials which accompanies the date is 'M', perhaps recording a tenancy by a member of the Morse family.
[68] Ex inf. Mrs. N. Whatley.
[69] *Bk. of Fees*, ii. 727. For the honor of Wallingford, see *V.C.H. Berks.* iii, pp. 523 sqq.
[70] *Cal. Close*, 1392–6, 161.
[71] See p. 32.
[72] *Feud. Aids*, v. 278; *Cal. Inq. p.m. Hen. VII*, i, p. 505.
[73] C.P. 25(1)/253/36/34.
[74] *Cat. Anct. D.* vi, C 4607.
[75] C.P. 25(1)/257/63/1.
[76] *Cal. Feet of F. Wilts.* 1195–1272, ed. Fry, 12.
[77] Ibid. 60; B.M. Harl. MS. 1761, f. 101v.

to William Than, who granted it to Abbot Roger of Hyde (1282–92).[78] Some time during the 14th century another member of the family Robert, son of William of Hodson, granted 1 virgate, 12 a., and pasture for 2 oxen in Chiseldon to Hugh of Ogbourne. Hugh later granted the land, saving the rights of Robert, to Abbot Walter of Hyde (1319–1362).[79] Robert also conveyed a virgate which Philip the miller held of him in Hodson to the abbey.[80]

In Badbury, as in Chiseldon, there were a number of small estates. In 1189 Geoffrey Foliot held 4 hides there by knight service of Glastonbury Abbey.[81] The land held by the Foliot family at Badbury passed to Roger Foliot, who held land there during the abbacy of Michael of Amesbury (1235–52).[82] In 1242–3 Geoffrey (II) Foliot held ½ knight's fee in Badbury.[83] Before 1241 Geoffrey (II) Foliot conveyed 34 a. of land to the Abbot of Glastonbury, who in return granted him certain pasture rights in 1241.[84] It was Geoffrey (II) Foliot who in c. 1265 relinquished his entire holding in Badbury to Glastonbury Abbey.[85] It seems that the estate remained intact into the 15th century, since in 1428 William Wereman held of Glastonbury those lands which had once been held by Geoffrey Foliot by service of ½ knight's fee.[86]

A number of small estates in Badbury were acquired by Glastonbury Abbey in the 13th century. In 1214 Stephen the clerk conveyed to Jocelin, Bishop of Bath and Glastonbury, ⅓ hide there which had previously been held by Richard Sampson his brother.[87] Alice le Champion, sister of Stephen and Richard, in 1227 quitclaimed the land to Stephen the chamberlain, an obedientiary of Glastonbury Abbey to whom the estate had evidently been allotted.[88] In c. 1235 Simon, son of William of 'Berwick', confirmed ⅓ hide in Badbury to Everard, son of John the miller.[89] The land passed to Everard's widow Gillian, who in c. 1269 conveyed her entire holding to her son John.[90] In 1269 John conveyed the lands he had received from his mother to Glastonbury Abbey. John had also at some date received lands from Henry de Montfort, which he now also granted to Glastonbury.[91] In c. 1296 William Steven of Broome (in Swindon) conveyed a virgate at Badbury, an estate which he had previously acquired from Robert atte Grene to the abbey.[92]

In the later Middle Ages an estate called 'Strangbows' in Badbury was held immediately of Glastonbury Abbey. In 1424 John Mychell of 'Stratton' and his wife Alice conveyed land in Badbury and Badbury Wick to Robert Shottesbrook and Edith his wife.[93] This small estate was first called 'Strangbows' in 1428 when Robert Shottesbrook held it of

Glastonbury for ¼ knight's fee.[94] By 1470 it was held by Richard Estbury of Chute, who granted a messuage and land, which he said he had by feoffment of Robert Shottesbrook, to William Yorke the elder, a London merchant, William Mille of Ramsbury, chaplain, and John Ewen of Draycot Foliat.[95] Land known as 'Strangbows' was part of Badbury manor in 1718.[96]

The estate of Badbury Wick is not mentioned by name until the 17th century,[97] but it is possible to identify it with land held in Badbury by Thomas Morse, described as of Badbury Wick, who died seised in 1581 of 183 a. there.[98] He was succeeded by his son Richard, also of Badbury Wick.[99] Richard died seised of the same lands in 1616 and his heir was his son William, who may possibly be identified with the William Morse who conveyed tithes in Badbury and Badbury Wick in c. 1651.[1] It is probable that Richard Morse the elder who in 1664–5 conveyed a messuage and land in and around Badbury to Richard Morse the younger, Jane his wife, and others, was the son of this William.[2] At some date before 1689 Jane Morse, widow, and William and Richard her sons, conveyed the capital messuage of Badbury Wick, commonly known as 'Badham Weekhouse', as well as pasturelands in Badbury Wick amounting to 27 a., and called Newlands, and Upper and Lower Cowleaze, to John Haskins.[3] It eventually passed to William Codrington (d. 1842) of Wroughton and he was succeeded by his younger brother Oliver Calley Codrington (d.s.p. 1855),[4] who in 1845 owned Badbury Wick House and c. 28 a. land.[5] Subsequently the estate passed to a member of the Crowdy family, since in 1885 the farm known as Badbury Wick and about 44 a. were said to have been lately in the possession of Francis Crowdy.[6] Mr. John Sutton owned the farm in 1967.[7]

The Morse family was apparently well-established in Badbury in the 16th century for between 1518 and 1536 the demesne of the manor was being farmed by John Morse.[8] Between 1518 and 1520 William Morse, a free tenant of Badbury manor, had a holding called 'Blaks'.[9] This is elsewhere described as a 2-virgate estate held by military service, which Thomas Morse his father had bought from William Dayley.[10] In 1564 a William Morse, possibly either the William mentioned above or his son, conveyed a messuage and 2 yardlands known as 'Blakys' to Richard Morse of Badbury, who was said to have been already leasing it.[11] It was this Richard, presumably, who died seised in 1578 of 12 a. and other lands which were lately part of Badbury manor.[12] His heir was his son William, a boy of seven.[13] William, at his death in c. 1581, held 4 a.

[78] B.M. Harl. MS. 1761, f. 103.
[79] Ibid. ff. 99, 100.   [80] Ibid. f. 100v.
[81] *Inq. Glaston. Abbey Manors*, ed. J. E. Jackson, (Roxburghe Club), p. 1.
[82] *Rentalia et Customaria Monast. Glaston.* (Som. Rec. Soc. v), 3.
[83] *Bk. of Fees*, ii. 732.
[84] C.P. 25(1)/251/12/5.
[85] *Glaston. Cartulary* (Som. Rec. Soc. lxiv), iii, p. ccxxviii.
[86] *Feud. Aids*, v. 278.
[87] *Cur. Reg. R.* vii. 238.
[88] C.P. 25(1)/250/7/85.
[89] *Glaston. Cartulary* (Som. Rec. Soc. lxiv), iii. 676.
[90] Ibid. 677.
[91] Ibid. p. ccxxvii.
[92] Ibid. pp. ccxxvi, ccxxvii, 679; *Glaston. Feodary* (Som. Rec. Soc. xxvi), 10–11.
[93] *Cat. Anct. D.* i, C 109.

[94] *Feud. Aids*, v. 278.   [95] *Cat. Anct. D.* i, C 1387.
[96] B.M. Add. Ch. 53501.
[97] C 78/1391 Entry 1.
[98] C 142/197/83; P.C.C. 6 Tirwhite.
[99] C 142/197/83; P.C.C. 99 Rudd.
[1] C 142/355/58; C.P. 25(2)/608/1651 Mich.
[2] C.P. 25(2)/744/15 & 16 Chas. II Hil.
[3] C 78/1391 Entry 1.
[4] All inf. from W.R.O. Land Tax retns. for Kingsbridge hundred.
[5] W.R.O. Tithe Award.
[6] W.A.S. Libr., Devizes, Sale Cat. 1885.
[7] Ex inf. Mr. N. Whatley, Badbury.
[8] B.M. Harl. MS. 3961, f. 99v; S.C. 6/Hen. VIII/3953.
[9] B.M. Harl. MS. 3961, f. 99.
[10] Ibid. f. 99v.
[11] C.P. 40/1226 Carte rot. 8.
[12] C 142/187/103.   [13] Ibid.

in North Mead, 6 a. in Badbury, 12 a. of pastureland at Snodshill (in Badbury), and 3 a. in the Foremead, all formerly part of Badbury manor.[14] In addition William was seised of a messuage and 28 a. which he had held of Thomas and John Kibblewhite as of their manor of Badbury.[15] William's heir was his brother John Morse[16] who died seised of the same lands in 1611.[17] John's heir was his son Richard, then a minor,[18] but no more is known of the estate.

In 1618 Joan Harding held a life estate in a messuage and 2 virgates of land in Badbury and granted the reversion to her son Nicholas.[19] It appears that Nicholas predeceased his mother in 1636,[20] but before his death he had acquired other lands in Badbury. These amounted to some 88 a. which he had acquired in 1626 from a James Looker, son of William Looker.[21] This land probably represents the messuage and 3 virgates of which Nicholas Harding died seised, together with the reversion conveyed by his mother. Nicholas's heir was his son Robert, a boy of six,[22] and in 1636 his widow Edith was granted the wardship and custody of Robert and of certain lands in Badbury.[23] In 1668–9 Robert Harding (d. 1687) and Elizabeth his wife were holding what appears to be the same estate.[24] By 1690 his son Nicholas Harding and Nicholas's wife Anne had conveyed this estate to Peter Sayer.[25] In 1723 Peter Sayer, Dorothy his wife, and their son Peter, sold the estate to Isabel Calley, widow.[26]

Other branches of the Harding family seem to have held land in Badbury. In 1630 Robert Harding died seised of an estate there and was succeeded by his son Robert (II).[27] Robert (II) was seised of his father's lands and also of the reversion of 34 a. called 'Greenhill', late parcel of Badbury manor and purchased from Thomas Redferne. Robert the younger died in 1631 and his heir was his son Thomas.[28] No more is known of the estate until 1698 when Thomas Harding, possibly the son or grandson of Robert the younger, and Dorothy his wife, conveyed some land to Thomas Cresby.[29] The land was held by John Cresby in 1780 and by 1830 it had passed to Mary Anne Cresby, who in 1845 held some 13 a. north of Badbury village.[30]

Land in Badbury was held by the Collet family. In 1602 William Collet died seised of tenements there and was succeeded by his son Henry.[31] What is probably part of the same holding was conveyed in 1687 by another Henry, possibly a descendant of William Collet or his son, to Thomas Hardyman.[32] It is likely that the Collet family still held some land in Badbury after this date, since in 1700 Richard Collet and his wife Elizabeth conveyed Westrop's

House and some land to John Allen of Upham (in Aldbourne).[33] Two years later other lands in Badbury were also conveyed by Richard and Elizabeth Collet to John Allen.[34]

ECONOMIC HISTORY. In 1086 estates at Chiseldon and Badbury were surveyed separately. In the time of King Edward Chiseldon was assessed for geld at 40 hides. Here, in 1086, there was land for 22 ploughs. Of this land 17 hides were in demesne and had 5 ploughs. There were 40 a. of meadow and pasture ½ league long and 4 furlongs broad, while there was woodland 3 furlongs in length and 2 furlongs in breadth. On the demesne there were 6 serfs. Elsewhere on the estate there were 45 villeins and 13 bordars with 10 ploughs. The estate had increased in value from £18 T.R.E. to £24 in 1086.[35]

A survey of the manor of Chiseldon, most probably of either late-13th-century or early-14th-century date, showed the estate to comprise 5 distinct areas, Eastrop, Westrop, Hodson, Burderop, and the Coomb ('Cumbe').[36] On the estate as a whole there were 20 free tenants,[37] while in Eastrop there were 10 customary holdings of ½ hide[38] and 3 of 1 virgate.[39] There do not appear to have been any holders of half-hides in Westrop but here there were 23 virgaters of whom 3 held 1½ virgate each.[40] Westrop also had 3 holdings of ½ virgate.[41] Twenty cottars' holdings[42] and 5 cotsetlings are also mentioned,[43] but it is not clear whether these were the total number on the whole estate, or in Westrop alone. No customary tenants are mentioned at Hodson. There were 17 other tenants in Coomb, who held no more than a few acres each for money rents.[44] The total rents of the manor were worth £20 8s. 7d. at this time.[45] The rents of the free tenants amounted to £7 1s. 8½d.[46] Each holder of ½ hide owed a rent of 5s.[47] and the virgaters in Eastrop and Westrop, as well as the cottars, all owed average rents of 2s. 6d.[48]

The same survey specifies certain labour services. Duties owed by those tenants who held ½ hide in Eastrop included, besides sheep-washing and shearing, the carrying of wool and cheese to Hyde Abbey. In addition, these tenants were expected to hoop barrels and to provide 2 men for 3 days' work when the lord's meadow was mowed, for which they received certain privileges, including 2 rams, 2 wethers, and 2 cheeses, which were had in common by all the mowers as recompense for every 2 meadows mowed. Those who held ½ hide also owed haymaking services and each was liable to have to provide a man and a horse for hay-carrying and

[14] C 142/200/14.
[15] Ibid.; see p. 11.
[16] C 142/200/14.
[17] C 142/324/129.
[18] Ibid.
[19] Wilts. Inq. p.m. 1625–49 (Index Libr.), 184.
[20] Ibid.
[21] C 142/411/155; W.R.O. 212B/Ch. 1 H, Alienation, Looker to Harding and Richmond, 1626.
[22] Wilts. Inq. p.m. 1625–49 (Index Libr.), 184.
[23] W.R.O. 212B/Ch. 2, Grant of wardship, 1635–6.
[24] Ibid. Ch. 4, Final concord, Harding to Foster and Collins, 1668–9.
[25] C.P. 25(2)/887/1 Wm. & M. Trin.
[26] W.R.O. 212B/Ch. 17, Deed, Sayer to Calley, 1723–4.
[27] Wilts. Inq. p.m. 1625–49 (Index Libr.), 90.
[28] Ibid. 109.
[29] C.P. 25(2)/889/9 Wm. III East.

[30] W.R.O. Land Tax retns. for Kingsbridge hundred; ibid. Tithe Award.
[31] C 142/281/14.
[32] C.P. 25(2)/803/2 Jas. II Mich.
[33] W.R.O. 212B/Ch. 10, Deed, Collet to Allen, 1700.
[34] C.P. 25(2)/889/13 Wm. III Trin.
[35] V.C.H. Wilts. ii, p. 127.
[36] B.M. Harl. MS. 1761, ff. 114–17. For location of 'Cumbe', see above p. 8.
[37] Ibid. f. 114.
[38] Ibid. ff. 114v–115.
[39] Ibid. f. 115v.
[40] Ibid.
[41] Ibid.
[42] Ibid. f. 116v.
[43] Ibid. f. 117.
[44] Ibid.
[45] Ibid.
[46] Ibid. f. 114.
[47] Ibid. f. 115.
[48] Ibid. ff. 115v–116v.

Burderop Park

Station in 1963, shortly before demolition

CHISELDON

Chiseldon: Washpool Cottage to the West of the Church

Liddington Castle: Iron-Age Hill Fort

4 men to stack hay for 4 days. Ploughing, harrowing, wattling, walling, and fencing services could also be exacted.[49] Virgaters in Eastrop were liable for exactly half the services expected of those who held half a hide,[50] and those of Westrop might expect to render similar services.[51] Cottars on the manor at this time could choose to pay rent instead of doing 3 days' boonwork.[52]

In the late 13th or early 14th centuries Chiseldon manor had 2 open fields, namely, East and West Fields.[53] Common pasture lay in the Marsh, on the Down, on East Haddon, West Haddon, and at Coomb. Those who held half a hide in Eastrop were entitled to 6 a. on the Down, 3 a. in the Marsh, 2½ a. of meadow land elsewhere and an extra ¼ a. in an unspecified place.[54] Virgaters in Eastrop had 7 a. in one field and 7 a. in the other, as well as half the amount of land held on the Down and in the Marsh that was allotted to the half-hiders.[55] The tenants of Westrop and Hodson were allowed similar amounts in the open fields, while those of Hodson were allowed an additional ⅛ a. in the second field.[56] East Haddon and West Haddon were apparently pasture lands and the tenants of Hodson were said to hold a marsh in the cultivated part of East Haddon, which they claimed to be their common pasture.[57] The cottars of Chiseldon were allowed 5 a. in both the East and West Fields.[58] The tenants of Burderop held a croft called 'Chalvecrofte'.[59] There were several small inclosures, presumably of pasture, on the manor at the time of the survey and at least 5 free tenants had a small inclosure amongst their lands.[60]

Chiseldon lay in the cheese-producing region of Wiltshire. In 1282–3 from May to Michaelmas 165 cheeses were made, of which 52 were sent to Hyde Abbey.[61] The manor also supported a fairly large flock of sheep. Some time between 1203 and 1218 there were 200 ewes and 110 hoggets on the manor.[62] A demesne flock was still kept at Chiseldon in 1282–1283, when there were 209 ewes, 6 rams, 94 wethers, and 116 lambs as well as 84 hoggets, which were disposed of. The wool-fells produced in this year totalled 320 gross, of which 32 went in tithe, 4 were sold, and the remaining 284 went to Hyde Abbey.[63] A considerable herd of cattle was kept at Chiseldon during the 13th century. Between 1208 and 1213 the manor supported 48 oxen and 2 cows,[64] while in 1282–3 there were 56 oxen, 10 cows, 1 bull, 6 calves, and 22 bullocks of varying ages, of which 12 remained at the end of the year.[65]

Between 1203 and 1218 the manor was reckoned to be worth £31 3s.,[66] while in 1468–9 it was valued at about £28.[67] In 1540 the manor of Chiseldon with Burderop (see below) was let for a farm of £27 6s. 8d.[68] Assessed rents were reckoned at £5 7s. 11½d., rents of customary tenants at £12 15s. 10d., and perquisites of the court at 6s. 8d.[69]

The woodland mentioned in Domesday is probably to be identified with Burderop Wood. This covered 60 a. in 1540 and was valued at £20.[70] The woodland, in which oaks were numerous, included at this date Norrey Coppice (25 a.), Sunmarsh (18 a.), and Holme (7 a.). Three years earlier Thomas Stephens acquired a lease of the woods, excepting the 'great' trees, for 62 years at a yearly rent of 6s. 8d.[71]

By the early 14th century Hyde Abbey's manor of Chiseldon included lands which may be identified with the later manor of Burderop.[72] Chiseldon and Burderop then seem to have passed together,[73] and after 1619, when Sir William Calley purchased the two manors,[74] the lands were known jointly as the Burderop estate. The land once belonging to the church was probably also acquired by Hyde Abbey at an early date.[75] It was probably this estate, then forming part of the Burderop estate and known as Parsonage Farm, which was estimated at c. 439 a. in 1781.[76]

By the 18th century East Chiseldon, West Chiseldon, and Hodson all had their own sets of open fields, which covered a total acreage of 1,230 a. in 1779.[77] The fields in East Chiseldon were known as North and South Fields.[78] The progress of the inclosure of this arable has not been traced. In 1779 inclosures of arable, meadow, pasture, and woodland totalled 460 a. and under a private Act of that year rights of common were extinguished.[79] An award was made the following year, and besides allotments received in lieu of tithe, Thomas Calley as lord received five parcels of land, totalling some 114 a. and lying chiefly in the North Field of East Chiseldon and in the East and West Fields of Hodson.[80]

The Stephens family, who later acquired the freehold (see above), leased the Burderop estate in the 16th century. In 1537 Thomas Stephens, already described as of Burderop, together with his sons Thomas and Nicholas, leased the site of the manor there and a grange called 'Monkebaron' from Hyde Abbey.[81] In 1789 Elizabeth Haverfield, late Elizabeth Calley, widow, leased Burderop Farm to John Canning and his son Richard for 12 years.[82] In 1825 Thomas Brown, a member of a well-known Wiltshire farming family, and a pioneer of steam-ploughing, had a lease of the farm, then reckoned at 770 a. of which 310 a. were downland and 460 a. arable.[83] This farm was reckoned at 984 a. in a terrier of the Burderop estate compiled in 1845, and

[49] Ibid. f. 114v.
[50] Ibid. f. 115v.
[51] Ibid.
[52] Ibid. f. 116v.
[53] Ibid. f. 115v.
[54] Ibid. f. 114v.
[55] Ibid. f. 115v.
[56] Ibid. f. 114v.
[57] Ibid. f. 115.
[58] Ibid. f. 116v.
[59] Ibid. f. 117.
[60] Ibid. f. 114.
[61] Winch. Coll. Mun. Hyde Abbey 12192/66.
[62] *Interdict Doc.* (P.R.S. N.S. xxxiv), 27.
[63] Winch. Coll. Mun. Hyde Abbey 12192/66.
[64] *Interdict Doc.* (P.R.S. N.S. xxxiv), 27.
[65] Winch. Coll. Mun. Hyde Abbey 12192/66.
[66] *Interdict Doc.* (P.R.S. N.S. xxxiv), 27.
[67] Winch. Coll. Mun. Hyde Abbey 12189/64.

[68] E 318/168.
[69] Ibid.
[70] Ibid.
[71] Ibid.
[72] See p. 10.
[73] See pp. 10, 11.
[74] Ibid.
[75] See p. 20.
[76] Burderop MSS. Estate Map, 1781.
[77] Chiseldon Incl. Act, 19 Geo. III, c. 95 (priv. act).
[78] Ibid.
[79] Ibid.
[80] W.R.O. Chiseldon Inclosure Award, 1780, and see p. 20.
[81] Req. 2/120/13.
[82] W.R.O. 212B/Ch. 26, Lease, Eliz. Haverfield to John and Ric. Canning, 1789.
[83] Ibid. 374/447, Lease, Thos. Calley to Thos. Brown, 1825; *V.C.H. Wilts.* iv. 86–87.

other properties at this date were listed as Chiseldon Farm (584 a.), Lower Farm (96 a.), Hodson Farm (19 a.), and Lambert's (76 a.),[84] which had been bought in 1840.[85] In 1919 Charles W. Whatley began to farm c. 1,000 a. at Burderop as tenant of Gen. T. C. P. Calley. He was still tenant in 1941.[86]

The manor of Badbury was assessed at 20 hides T.R.E. and in 1086 there was land for 10 ploughs. There were 13½ hides in demesne and here there were 3 ploughs, while on the remaining 6½ hides there were likewise 3 ploughs. There were 100 a. meadow land in 1086 and pasture land 1 league long and 3 furlongs broad. There were 4 serfs on the demesne, while on the remaining land there were 11 villeins and 10 bordars. T.R.E. Badbury had been worth £8 but by 1086 it was worth £10.[87] The total of 25 tenants in 1086 had increased to 38 by 1189, which included 16 virgaters, 11 cotsetlers, and a crofter.[88] Some time between 1235 and 1252 there were 39 tenants on the manor, including the same number of virgaters, cotsetlers, and crofters as in 1189.[89] There were 20 tenants during the period 1518 to 1520, a number which included 3 free tenants, 16 customary tenants, and a cottager. Most of the customary tenants held one virgate.[90]

In 1189, when Abbot Henry of Sully surveyed the manors of Glastonbury Abbey, holders of half-hides and single virgates were all liable for general hay-making services, while cotsetlers had to mow at the lord's command. Services were owed daily from Midsummer to Michaelmas, but for 3 days only during the remainder of the year.[91] Badbury services were more explicitly defined in Abbot Michael of Glastonbury's custumal of c. 1235–52. Virgaters owed fallowing and ploughing services from Midsummer and from Michaelmas respectively. Virgaters also owed ploughing, harrowing, and mowing duties. Haymaking was rewarded by 1 'richel' and after mowing duties had been performed, the virgaters were paid 12d. and were allowed to choose, by sight and not by touch, a sheep from the lord's fold. Virgaters also owed multifarious general agricultural duties, such as carrying, grinding, and reaping. Fold-repair, shearing, and sheep-washing services might also be demanded, and virgaters were expected to render the lord 5 sheep at Easter. Cotsetlers at Badbury could be required to do 3 days' work each week for the lord from Michaelmas to Midsummer, and were also liable for the same general duties as the virgaters. The reeve, hayward, and shepherd were all allowed certain privileges. The reeve's perquisites included an acre of land and a piece of meadow above 'Nettleford', those of the hayward, a piece of meadow, while the shepherd was allowed to graze 15 sheep with the lord's flock,

and to use the demesne plough at specified times during the ploughing season.[92]

A series of manorial accounts extending from the late 13th to the early 16th century survives among the records of Glastonbury Abbey.[93] From these rolls it appears that early in the 14th century the paid farm servants at Badbury included an oxherd, a shepherd, a dairyman, and 2 carters. Paid labour was also employed at this time for weeding and harvest work.[94] In 1299–1300 a payment of 27s. 6½d. was made from the manor to the larder at Glastonbury, and was apparently an annual charge.[95] The accounts reveal a considerable amount of interchange in both stock and grain between Badbury and other manors in the neighbourhood belonging to Glastonbury Abbey.

Part of one of the abbey's demesne flocks was maintained at Badbury. The survey of Abbot Henry of Sully shows a flock of over 100 sheep on the manor in 1189.[96] There were also apparently fairly large tenant flocks and during the period 1235–52 a total of 22 customary tenants were bound to render 5 ewes each to Glastonbury at Easter.[97] In 1312–13 the demesne flock was pastured on Gavelhill and sheep came to Badbury from Ashbury (Berks.) and Winterbourne Monkton, both Glastonbury Abbey manors.[98] In the mid 14th century of the 5 flocks maintained by the abbey on the North Wiltshire downs, one was pastured on the downs around these three manors.[99] There continued to be much interchange of stock: at Badbury in 1333 there were 118 wethers, which were sent to Ashbury, and 267 hoggets, of which 100 were sent to Ashbury and 80 to Winterbourne Monkton.[1] In the same year 337 sheep fleeces and 61 lamb fleeces were rendered in tithe, while 40 sheep-fells and 45 lamb-fells were sold. Six sheepskins and 16 lambs' skins were also sold.[2] In 1333 there were 3 ploughs and 3 horses on the manor, which maintained a herd of breeding, as well as working, cattle.[3] The breeding herd in 1333–4 was made up of 16 cows, of which 8 were sold and 3 sent to South Damerham (then in Wilts.), another Glastonbury manor.[4]

In 1333 95 qr. of wheat, 37 qr. of oats, and 46 qr. of barley were produced at Badbury and the following year 63 a. of wheat, 20 a. of oats, 38 a. of barley, and 6 a. of beans were sown.[5] A certain amount of grain was consumed on the manor, some was sold, and as in the case of livestock, there were also considerable exchanges of grain between Badbury, Ashbury, and Winterbourne.[6] As far as is known, no grain was ever sent to the granary at Glastonbury and it seems possible that the larder rent mentioned above was to some extent in place of this.

At the time of the compilation of Abbot Beere's

[84] W.R.O. 374/179, Terrier of the Burderop estate, c. 1845.
[85] Ibid. 374/25, Chiseldon Poor Rate, 1839.
[86] W.A.M. xlix. 371.
[87] V.C.H. Wilts. ii, p. 124.
[88] Inq. Glaston. Abbey Manors, ed. J. E. Jackson (Roxburghe Club), 120.
[89] Rent. et Custom. Monast. Glaston. (Som. Rec. Soc. v), 57–61.
[90] B.M. Harl. MS. 3961, ff. 109v–114v.
[91] Inq. Glaston. Abbey Manors, ed. J. E. Jackson (Roxburghe Club), 120.
[92] Rent. et Custom. Monast. Glaston. (Som. Rec. Soc. v), 57–61.
[93] These are included among some 70 rolls of bailiff's accts. for the Glastonbury estates at Longleat House. Those for the later Middle Ages have been worked on by

I. J. E. Keil, 'The Estates of Glastonbury Abbey in the Later Middle Ages' (Bristol Univ. Ph.D. thesis, 1964).
[94] Longleat MS. 11271.
[95] Ibid. 11272; Rent. et Custom. Monast. Glaston. (Som. Rec. Soc. v), 60.
[96] V.C.H. Wilts. iv. 21.
[97] Rent. et Custom. Monast. Glaston. (Som. Rec. Soc. v), 58–59.
[98] Longleat MSS. 10655, 10656.
[99] I. J. E. Keil, 'Glaston. Abbey Estates', 129 (see n. 93 above).
[1] Ibid.   [2] Ibid. 80.
[3] Ibid. 117.
[4] Ibid. 113.
[5] Ibid. 90.
[6] Ibid. 89, 98, and accts. among Longleat MSS.

terrier of 1518–20 virgaters and half-virgaters on the manor were still said to owe general agricultural duties such as mowing and haymaking.[7] The land held by Glastonbury Abbey within the parish at this date included Badbury, Badbury Wick, and an area to the north known at this date as Snodshill.[8] The terrier records two open fields at Badbury, known as East and West Fields.[9] There were apparently 6 common meadows at this date, named Northmede, Stertmarsh, Nywelond, Formede, Cotsetylmede, and Losmere,[10] while in 1534–6 a further four, of which three, from etymological evidence, were probably inclosures, were called Reveharme, Haywardsharme, Cowmede, and Goseharme.[11] The low-lying clays at Snodshill were preeminently suitable as pasture land and in 1518–20 this area contained *c.* 45 a. of pasture which were held in common.[12] Two of the free tenants on the manor were allowed to pasture 15 plough beasts and 12 other animals with those of the lord at this date, while the virgaters were allowed to pasture 7 similar animals, and the half-virgaters to have 4 beasts and their pigs on the pasture with the lord's beasts[13]. All tenants held pasture at Snodshill according to the size of their holdings.[14] There were apparently small inclosures of arable land within the manor at this time.[15] The East and West Fields were inclosed in 1748 and rights of common extinguished.[16] The main allotment made under the inclosure award of 1749 was one of 426 a. made to John Stone, as lord of the manor, in the East and West Fields which lay south of Badbury village.[17]

From 1534–6 John Morse farmed the demesne of the manor. At this date it comprised 201 a. of pasture in Gavelhill, Northcliff, Closelacke, and Shappeclose, 22 a. of arable land and pasture in 'Burycrofte' (an unidentified parcel of land), 2½ a. in the common meadows, and 198 a. of arable in the open fields.[18]

In 1718 James Stone, who that year acquired the manor of Badbury, had an estate which included 50 a. of pasture land called Waxhill, 70 a. known as the Plain, and 50 a. called Gainehill.[19] In 1839 John Stone, great-grandson of James, farmed 227 a. at Day House, which was mainly a pasture farm.[20]

The manor of Badbury was broken up at an early date into a number of smaller estates. In 1845 there were seven farms at Badbury and Snodshill, all of which lay entirely under pasture. The estate, then owned by Baynton Stone, which represented the remainder of Badbury manor, was farmed in two parcels of 82 a. and 62 a. John Stone farmed 208 a. at Day House, while John Brown owned Greenhill, then estimated at 38 a., but formerly

parcel of the manor, and reckoned at 50 a. in 1718. There were three farms at Snodshill in 1845: one of 95 a. and another of 52 a. were owned by William Morse Crowdy, while one of 52 a. was owned by Jonathan Belcher. All were worked by tenant farmers.[21] In 1967 five of the six farms in Badbury and Snodshill were entirely under pasture. These were Badbury Farm, Day House, Badbury Wick Farm, Lower Snodshill, and Upper Snodshill. The former manor, then known as West and Folly Farms, was owned by the Whatley family firm of Chiseldon Grain Driers and was devoted to mixed farming.[22]

The Burderop estate survived intact into the 20th century. In 1967 the estate comprised Parsonage Farm, with 400 a. which supported a herd of 70–80 cows,[23] Nightingale, Burderop, and Hodson Farms, besides Draycot Farm[24] with 577 a. acquired in 1867.[25] All were given over to mixed farming except Nightingale Farm which was completely under grass at this date and supported beef and other cattle. A herd of pedigree Jersey cows was kept at Burderop Park in 1967.[26]

A brickworks was operating on the Gault Clay in the parish as early as 1736 and was probably connected with the Burderop estate.[27] This may have been situated north of Burderop Wood.[28] A brickyard at Badbury Wick, probably quite distinct from the earlier one, was being worked in 1857,[29] and had been acquired by the Swindon firm of Edward Hill by 1903.[30] This firm still owned the brickyard in 1931.[31] In 1947 Hill's brickpit at Badbury Wick displayed a section 10–12 ft. deep.[32] The brickyard was still worked by a Swindon firm in 1967 and employed mainly foreign workers,[33] who were accommodated in cottages beside the brickyard. A foundry which stood in Chiseldon high street opposite the railway station in 1887,[34] provided a little work for the parish in the later 19th and early 20th centuries. Owned in 1901 by W. E. N. Browne of Chiseldon House, it comprised workshops which included a moulding shed, a blacksmith's shop with two forges, and a fitting shop.[35] In 1913 the foundry, owned by a Swindon firm, employed 34 men and was largely engaged in repair work, although a few farm waggons and carriages were made.[36] Formerly it was said to have made steam-traction and ploughing sets.[37] In 1967 it was used as a grain-drying plant for Parsonage Farm.[38] At this date most of the inhabitants of Chiseldon travelled to Swindon to work, although some were still employed on the farms within the parish.

MILLS. At the time of Domesday Survey there was a mill at Chiseldon which paid 40*d*.[39] A mill there

---

[7] B.M. Harl. MS. 3961, f. 114.
[8] Ibid. ff. 99–114v.   [9] Ibid. f. 100.
[10] Ibid. ff. 109v–114v.
[11] S.C. 6/Hen. VIII/3953; Ekwall, *Dict. Place Names,* 214.
[12] B.M. Harl. MS. 3961, f. 99.
[13] Ibid.
[14] Ibid. ff. 109v–114v.
[15] Ibid.
[16] Badbury Incl. Act, 22 Geo. II, c. 7 (priv. act).
[17] W.R.O. Badbury Inclosure Award, 1749.
[18] S.C. 6/Hen. VIII/3953, and see p. 13.
[19] B.M. Add. Ch. 53501.
[20] Ibid.
[21] W.R.O. Tithe Award, 1845.
[22] Ex inf. Mr. N. Whatley, Badbury; see p. 12.
[23] Chiseldon W.I. Scrapbks. (Microfilm in County Libr., Trowbridge).

[24] Ex. inf. Miss J. M. Calley.
[25] See p. 46.
[26] Ex inf. Miss J. M. Calley.
[27] Burderop MSS. Clay Work Bk., 1736–41.
[28] *W.A.M.* lii. Geological map of Swindon facing p. 195.
[29] Ibid. 206.
[30] *Kelly's Dir. Wilts.* (1903).
[31] Ibid. (1931).
[32] *W.A.M.* lii. 206.
[33] Ex inf. the Revd. J. F. Collins, Chiseldon.
[34] O.S. Map 6", Wilts. XV, XVI, XXII, XXIII (1st edn.).
[35] Wilts. Cuttings, vii. 329.
[36] A. Williams, *Villages of the White Horse,* 98–103.
[37] Ibid.
[38] Chiseldon W.I. Scrapbks. (Microfilm in County Libr., Trowbridge).
[39] *V.C.H. Wilts.* ii, p. 127.

was mentioned in 1305 when Philip atte Mulle conveyed it, together with a virgate of land, to Richard of Chiseldon.[40] A mill, perhaps the same, is mentioned in 1341[41] and at some date in the 14th century Nicholas the miller, a free tenant of Chiseldon manor, held a mill and ½ hide of land there.[42] In 1370 William Stodlegh and Joan his wife, who held a messuage and 2 carucates of land in Chiseldon, granted the reversion of this small estate to William Wroughton and his heirs.[43] In 1391 Margery, the wife of Thomas Calston, gave up her life interest in lands which included a mill and 2 virgates in Chiseldon and Hodson granted her by William and Joan Stodlegh, in favour of William Wroughton and Isabel his wife, and in the following year Joan Stodlegh, now the wife of John Burcy, finally granted the mill, with a messuage and 2 virgates of land, to the Wroughtons.[44] No more is heard of a mill at Chiseldon until 1690 when William Taylor and his wife Anne granted a watermill, together with a messuage and 2 a. of meadow land in Chiseldon, to William Hill.[45] In 1773 the mill at Chiseldon lay directly north of the main village and was fed by a tributary of the River Cole.[46] The mill is not marked on maps of the 19th century.

By 1887[47] a windmill stood to the west of the cemetery at the corner of Butts Road on ground known as Windmill Piece. In 1901 Windmill Piece (9 a.) was sold on the instructions of W. E. N. Browne to an unknown purchaser.[48] This mill was still standing in 1967 but had no sails and had been converted into a dwelling house.

The earliest mention of a mill at Badbury occurs in 1086, at which date it was paying 40d.[49] It may have been this mill which fell into ruin at some date during King Stephen's reign, and in 1189 the loss to the lord of the manor was reckoned at 15s.[50] Badbury mill had been rebuilt by c. 1235–52, when John the miller, a free tenant of the manor, held a mill there as well as 3½ a. of land and small amounts of meadow.[51] No further mention is found of a mill until 1767 when it was held by Robert Berry and known as Berry's mill.[52] In 1773 Badbury mill, presumably that held a few years earlier by Robert Berry, lay to the north of the hamlet beside the Roman road and was fed by a tributary of the River Cole.[53] Robert Walker occupied the mill at Badbury in 1825, the last reference found to it.[54]

LOCAL GOVERNMENT. Rough drafts of the proceedings of the court-leet and view of frankpledge for the manor of Chiseldon exist for the years 1695–

1732 and 1738–84.[55] There are also court books for 1738–61, 1801–53, and 1854–81.[56] By 1738 the court met once a year only to appoint tithingmen for East Chiseldon, West Chiseldon, and Hodson and to deal with the usual small matters of agricultural concern.[57] Frequent presentments about the provision of stocks in Chiseldon were made in the 18th century, as in 1743, 1746, and 1753.[58] Encroachments upon the waste and the erection of a pound were often presented also. In 1839 the question of a public footpath from Hodson to Swindon was brought before the court.[59] The court continued to meet once a year during the 19th century and tithingmen for the same three tithings were appointed. A hayward and a constable were also appointed during this century.[60] In 1803 fines for non-attendance were imposed upon jurors but by 1853 the court had become a mere formality. It sat in the later 19th century at the 'Patriots Arms',[61] and for the last time in 1881.[62]

In the later 13th century Glastonbury's franchises in Badbury included view of frankpledge, return of writs, and the right to hold assizes of bread and ale. All these rights were exercised in the court-leet.[63] A court-leet and a hallmoot court were held at Badbury twice a year by the steward of the Abbot of Glastonbury for the tenants of that manor. Records of these courts survive from the mid 13th century until 1533.[64] After the beginning of the 14th century the two courts were held together and little distinction seems to have been made between the types of business dealt with by each. The court-leet then dealt with Glastonbury's franchisal jurisdiction, such as offences against the assize of ale, as well as exaction of excessive tolls by millers and many complaints of nuisances and breaches of manorial custom, which could equally well come before the hallmoot court. The court-leet also heard complaints about straying animals and defective buildings. A court book for view of frankpledge for Badbury manor survives for the period 1640–1932. The entries are similar to those contained in the court books of Chiseldon manor. Law-day quit-rents at Badbury are first recorded in 1742 but had probably been customary before this date, and continued to be paid in 1932.[65]

Churchwardens' accounts exist for the period 1778–1837 while the vestry minute book, begun c. 1834, was still used in 1967.[66] The accounts of the surveyors of highways for the tithing of Badbury run from 1766–1836. From 1824 the surveyors were nominated yearly at the Plough Inn by the local inhabitants.[67]

[40] *Feet of F. Wilts. 1272–1327* (W.A.S. Rec. Brch.), 52.
[41] *Inq. Non.* (Rec. Com.), 162.
[42] B.M. Harl. MS. 1761, f. 114.
[43] C.P. 25(1)/255/51/26.
[44] C.P. 25(1)/256/56/21; C.P. 25(1)/255/51/26; C.P. 25(1)/256/56/25.
[45] C.P. 25(2)/887/1 Wm. & M. East.
[46] *Andrews and Dury, Map* (W.A.S. Rec. Brch.), pl. 15.
[47] O.S. Map 6", Wilts. XV, XVI, XXII, XXIII (1st edn.).
[48] Wilts. Cuttings, vii. 329; W.A.S. Libr., Devizes, Sale Cat. 1901.
[49] *V.C.H. Wilts.* ii, p. 124.
[50] *Inq. Glaston. Abbey Manors*, ed. J. E. Jackson (Roxburghe Club), 121.
[51] *Rent. et Custom. Monast. Glaston.* (Som. Rec. Soc. v), 60.
[52] W.R.O. 117, View of frankpledge of Badbury manor, 1640–1932.
[53] *Andrews and Dury, Map* (W.A.S. Rec. Brch.), pl. 15.
[54] W.R.O. 569/2, Surveyors of Highways Accts. 1766–1836.
[55] Burderop MSS. Drafts of proceedings.
[56] Ibid. Ct. bks.
[57] Ibid. Drafts of proceedings, 1738–84.
[58] Ibid. Ct. bk. of Chiseldon manor, 1738–61.
[59] W.R.O. 374/96. [60] Ibid.
[61] Ibid. and ex inf. Mrs. Joyce, Chiseldon.
[62] W.R.O. 569/49.
[63] *Placita de Quo Warrento* (Rec. Com.), 802, and see p. 4.
[64] These are among a large collection of ct. r. at Longleat House for all the Glastonbury Abbey manors. Material from these has been used by I. J. E. Keil, 'The Estates of Glastonbury Abbey in the Later Middle Ages' (Bristol Univ. Ph.D. thesis, 1964), and see p. 16.
[65] W.R.O. 117.
[66] Ex inf. the Revd. J. F. Collins, Chiseldon.
[67] W.R.O. 569/2.

Some kind of provision for the poor of the parish was apparently made early in the 17th century, since five two-roomed thatched cottages, which survived in Strouds Hill until the 20th century, carried a tablet inscribed: 'These houses were built by the parish of Chiseldon 1616'.[68] A poor-rate assessment for Chiseldon survives for 1649[69] and later assessments cover the period 1825–34, during which time either five or six rates a year at 1s. in the £ were levied, although seven such rates were collected in 1833–4.[70] Overseers' accounts run from 1780–9 and list sums laid out monthly in payments and the buying of clothes.[71] These monthly sums varied and in 1781 the amount paid out by the overseers during the past year amounted to c. £209, while in 1784–5 the total paid out was c. £399.[72] Various other accounts of the Chiseldon overseers run to 1834 with gaps of a few years at intervals and lists of those employed as overseers exist for 1779–1834.[73] Various poor-house accounts, including lists of inmates, cover the years 1786–1804. Work provided there at that time included spinning, weaving, and sewing. In 1786 43 people, excluding the children taken in, were admitted.[74] The early-17th-century poor house was replaced in 1818 by a range of cottages for the use of the poor built on waste land.[75] In 1968 these cottages, which were presumably converted into private dwellings after 1834, were represented by a range of stone and brick cottages with a thatched roof, then Nos. 3–6 Station Road.

During the 16th, 17th, and 18th centuries a church ale was held at Chiseldon to raise money for the clerk's wages.[76] The custom survived into the 19th century when the parish clerk was expected to provide a dinner for the principal parishioners.[77]

CHURCH. According to a charter of Edward the Elder the church of Chiseldon was granted in 903 to the New Minster, Winchester, later Hyde Abbey.[78] The patronage of the church was probably included in the grant, although the first reference found to the abbey as patron occurs in 1259. That year the Precentor of Chichester, Geoffrey de Ferynges, later Abbot of Hyde (1304–17), was presented to the rectory.[79] He was still rector in 1281[80] and it is probable that he presented William de Penes as vicar at some time during the later 13th century.[81]

Although in 1330 the abbey was given leave to appropriate the church,[82] it took no advantage of the grant but continued to present rectors until 1416. On about a dozen occasions the rectors, who

were presumably sinecurists, presented vicars, one of whom subsequently became rector.[83] Some tithe and land were available for their support (see below). In 1425 Hyde formally appropriated the church, the appropriation was confirmed four years later by Bishop Nevill,[84] and in and after 1435 the abbey presented to the vicarage.[85] Henceforth until the Dissolution the abbots of Hyde continued to present vicars.[86]

In 1540 the rectory and advowson were granted to Sir John Bridges,[87] although in 1544 John Barnabe, to whom Hyde Abbey had apparently assigned the presentation for one turn, presented.[88] Sir John Bridges presented in 1546[89] and died seised of the rectory and of the advowson of the vicarage in 1558.[90] Hereafter the descent of the rectory and advowson followed that of Chiseldon manor until 1578–9 when Giles, Lord Chandos, conveyed both to Thomas (II) Stephens,[91] who had previously held a lease of the rectory.[92] From Thomas (II) the rectory descended to his second son, Thomas (III) Stephens,[93] who conveyed it in 1623 to William Calley the elder and his son William.[94] The advowson, however, did not pass with the rectory from Thomas (II) to Thomas (III), but to Thomas (II)'s eldest son Nicholas, who died seised of it in 1611.[95] Nicholas was succeeded by his son Thomas (IV), who in 1620 conveyed the advowson to trustees for William Calley the elder and his son.[96] The rectory was conveyed to the Calleys in 1623 and thenceforth both rectory and advowson remained in the Calley family and their descent followed that of the main manor.[97] In 1967 the impropriate rector and patron of the vicarage was Miss J. M. Calley.[98] So far as is known, the patrons only once delegated their right of presentation to the vicarage; this was in 1616 when Aaron Nashe presented to the vicarage with the permission of Thomas (IV) Stephens.[99]

The church was valued for the taxation of 1291 at £20.[1] In 1341 its value, including tithes and glebe, was reckoned at £26 4s. 4d., and that of the vicarage at £5.[2]

In 1259 the rector had the small as well as the great tithes of Badbury.[3] Besides the great tithes of the whole parish, he was also entitled to the tithe of the mill and certain small tithes in 1341. He then also had 2 carucates in demesne. By the same date, the vicar was entitled to the small tithes from a virgate belonging to the church.[4] He had also been granted some land in the parish by Hyde Abbey during the abbacy of Roger of St. Valery (1248–63).[5] By 1341 he held a virgate in demesne.[6] The Bishop of Salisbury confirmed the right of Hyde Abbey

[68] Ex inf. Mr. E. Hughes, Parsonage Farm, who has preserved the tablet.
[69] W.A.M. xxx. 311.
[70] W.R.O. 569/3.
[71] Ibid. 569/4.
[72] Ibid.
[73] Ibid. 569/6, 7, 8, 9, 10, 11.
[74] Ibid. 569/5.
[75] M.H. 12/13754/1849/17588.
[76] V.C.H. Wilts. iii. 46.
[77] W.A.M. ii. 197–8.
[78] Cod. Dipl. ed. Kemble, ii, p. 145.
[79] Hist. MSS. Com. Wells, i. 140–1; V.C.H. Hants ii. 121.
[80] Glaston. Cartulary (Som. Rec. Soc. lxiv), iii. 683.
[81] B.M. Harl. MS. 1761, ff. 99v, 104.
[82] Cal. Pat. 1327–30, 536.
[83] Phillipps, Wilts. Inst. i. (index in W.A.M. xxviii. 216).
[84] Sar. Dioc. Regy. Reg. Nevill, ff. 84–85.
[85] Phillipps, Wilts. Inst. i. 126.
[86] Ibid. i. (see n. 83 above).
[87] L. & P. Hen. VIII, xv, p. 295.
[88] Phillipps, Wilts. Inst. i. 211.
[89] Ibid. 212.
[90] C 142/114/71.
[91] C 66/1175 mm. 23–24.
[92] C.P. 40/1365, Carte rot. 16.
[93] Req. 2/153/37.
[94] C.P. 25(2)/372/20 Jas. I. Trin.
[95] C 142/325/203.
[96] C.P. 25(2)/371/7 Jas. I. Trin.; W.A.M. xxxi. 175–6.
[97] See p. 10.
[98] Crockford (1963–4).
[99] Phillipps, Wilts. Inst. ii. 9.
[1] Tax. Eccl. (Rec. Com.), 192.
[2] Inq. Non. (Rec. Com.), 162.
[3] Hist. MSS. Com. Wells, i. 140–1.
[4] Inq. Non. (Rec. Com.), 162.
[5] B. M. Harl. MS. 1761, f. 99v.
[6] Inq. Non. (Rec. Com.), 162.

to certain tithes in Chiseldon in 1397, presumably because of the unexecuted licence to appropriate.[7] This confirmation seems to have led to a dispute which was heard in the consistory court in 1412. It was then ordained that the rectors were to have all tithes of corn and hay within the parish, all tithes of lambs and wool, except those arising from the vicar's land, and certain small tithes. The vicar was to have all the small tithes in the parish, except those from the rectory estate, and in lieu of these he was to receive a pension of £3 6s. 8d.[8] The award of 1412 presumably formed the basis of the arrangements made for the support of the vicar when the church was finally appropriated by Hyde Abbey in 1425.

After the Dissolution the rectorial tithes, with the exception of those of Badbury, descended in the same manner as the impropriate rectory (see above). The great tithes of Badbury seem to have been acquired at various dates by the landowners there. By the inclosure award of 1780 360 a. were allotted to the rector in place of the great tithes due to him from the rectorial glebe in the open fields.[9] In 1845 remaining rights of tithe were extinguished and a rent charge of £57 13s. was made to John James Calley in lieu thereof.[10]

After the dissolution of Hyde Abbey, the rectorial lands passed to the lay rectors and the estate was somewhat enlarged by the Inclosure Act of 1779 when land was allotted in lieu of tithe.[11] Thus in 1845 the estate comprised some 25 a. and as Parsonage Farm became merged in the Calley estate.[12]

In 1535 the vicarage was worth £8 12s. 10d.[13] No more is known of the value of the living until 1757 when Thomas Calley made a grant of £200 to which another £200 was added by the Governors of Queen Anne's Bounty.[14] By 1800 its yearly value was reckoned at £202 2s. 5d. This sum included the value of some land, tithes, and a vicarage house.[15] In 1812 the value of the vicarage was given as £125.[16] Its income was augmented in 1817 by small gifts from the then vicar and from the trustees of a Mrs. Horner and a Mrs. Pyncombe. In the same year a grant of £300 was made from Queen Anne's Bounty.[17] The vicarage was valued at £173 net in 1835, and at £207 6s. 6d. net in 1865.[18]

The vicar still received the pension of £3 6s. 8d. in lieu of small tithes from the rectorial lands (see above) in 1705.[19] By 1738[20] the small tithes of Badbury had been commuted for money payments. In 1780, when the open fields of Chiseldon were inclosed, the vicarial tithes were extinguished and

39 a. of land were awarded instead.[21] By 1786 the small tithes due from Burderop tithing had been commuted for an annual payment of 15s.[22] Between 1780 and 1831 the vicars disputed certain arrangements, which had been made for money payments in lieu of payments in kind.[23] But in 1845 all remaining vicarial tithes in the parish were commuted for a rent-charge of £106 1s. 8d. which included the £3 6s. 8d. due from the rector for the small tithes of the rectorial glebe.[24]

In 1608 the vicarage glebe was estimated at some 18 a.[25] Like the rectory estate it was enlarged by the inclosure award of 1780 when land was allotted in place of tithes (see above).[26] In 1786 the estate amounted to 56 a.[27]

A vicarage house is mentioned in 1705 and 1786.[28] It may have been derelict in 1812 when the vicar lived in Swindon (see below), and in 1841 the vicar lived in the parsonage house.[29] In 1887 the vicarage lay to the east of the church.[30] It was sold as a private residence in 1953 and a new vicarage, built of local brick, was erected in 1954 at the corner of Butts Road.[31]

In 1291 a portion of £3 13s. 4d. was paid by the church to the abbots of Hyde.[32] In 1389 the abbot maintained that he was entitled to an annuity of 20s. from the rector.[33] Litigation arose over the payment between rector and abbot and in 1390 the case was decided in favour of the abbot who was to receive the arrears.[34] In 1397 the payment was confirmed by the Bishop of Salisbury.[35]

The Rector of Ashbury (Berks.) was apparently entitled to a portion of the tithes of Badbury. Some time in the 13th century the Bishop of Salisbury ordained that the Rector of Chiseldon was to pay a pension of 50s. to the Rector of Ashbury in place of these.[36] A dispute evidently arose and papal judges-delegate repeated the Bishop of Salisbury's ordinance in 1259.[37] Records of subsequent payments occur in 1291 and 1540.[38] In the 16th century Dr. Walter Bayley, under-tenant of Ashbury rectory since 1591, claimed that Thomas (II) Stephens had refused to pay the pension ever since he had bought the rectory of Chiseldon in 1578-9.[39] The outcome of the dispute is unknown and no more is heard of the annuity. The rectors of Chiseldon presented by Hyde Abbey during the 13th, 14th, and early 15th centuries were probably non-resident. As has been shown, Geoffrey de Ferynges was Precentor of Chichester[40] and his successor at Chiseldon, Master Gilbert of Popham, obtained licence to study abroad

[7] Winch. Coll. Mun. Hyde Abbey 12171/62A, Cal. *penes* N.R.A.
[8] *W.A.M.* xxx. 328.
[9] W.R.O. Chiseldon Inclosure Award, 1780.
[10] Ibid. Tithe Award, 1845.
[11] Chiseldon Incl. Act, 19 Geo. III, c. 95 (priv. act).
[12] W.R.O. Tithe Award.
[13] *Valor Eccl.* (Rec. Com.), ii. 152.
[14] C. Hodgson, *Queen Anne's Bounty* (2nd edn. & supp.), clx, cccxxxv.
[15] W.R.O. 212B/Ch. 27, Valuation of vicarial lands and tithes in Chiseldon, 1800.
[16] *W.A.M.* xli. 132.
[17] C. Hodgson, *Queen Anne's Bounty* (2nd edn. & supp.), cxciii, cccxxxv.
[18] *Rep. Com. Eccl. Revenues*, H.C. 54, pp. 828-9 (1835), xxii; W.R.O. 374/25, Particulars of Chiseldon vicarage, 1865.
[19] *W.A.M.* xxx. 318.
[20] W.R.O. 374/14, Tithe Acct. Bk. 1738.
[21] Ibid. Chiseldon Inclosure Award, 1780.
[22] *W.A.M.* xxx. 326.
[23] Ibid. 327, 329: W.R.O. 374/41.
[24] W.R.O. Tithe Award, 1845.
[25] *W.A.M.* xxx. 309-11.
[26] W.R.O. Chiseldon Inclosure Award, 1780.
[27] *W.A.M.* xxx. 326.
[28] Ibid. 318, 326.
[29] Ibid. xli. 132; xxx. 332.
[30] O.S. Map 6″, Wilts. XV, XVI, XXII, XXIII (1st edn.).
[31] *Church Guide*, Holy Cross, Chiseldon, 9.
[32] *Tax. Eccl.* (Rec. Com.), 192.
[33] B.M. Harl. MS. 1761, f. 118.
[34] Ibid.
[35] Winch. Coll. Mun. Hyde Abbey 12171/62A, Cal. *penes* N.R.A.
[36] Hist. MSS. Com. *Wells*, i. 140-1.
[37] Ibid.
[38] *Tax. Eccl.* (Rec. Com.), 189; Req. 2/179/27.
[39] Req. 2/179/27.
[40] See p. 19.

for 2 years in 1298[41] and on his return he received permission to go to Oxford for a year in 1300.[42]

There seems to have been a certain amount of unrest in the parish during the Interregnum. In 1648 John Stevens, presumably the vicar, signed the Concurrent Testimony of Ministers in Wiltshire.[43] Puritan sympathies were also evident in 1650 when a dispute arose over the position of the pulpit and the provision of seats within the church.[44] The chief objector to the new arrangements was William (II) Calley,[45] who in 1658 presented John Baker to the vicarage.[46] Baker was ejected in 1662.[47]

In 1783 the Vicar of Chiseldon was also incumbent of Liddington.[48] It had then long been customary to hold services at Chiseldon on a Sunday alternately in the morning and afternoon. Services were held on Holy Days and on Wednesdays and Fridays in Lent, likewise alternately in Chiseldon and Liddington. Holy Communion was celebrated at the four customary seasons and there were generally fewer than 20 communicants at these services. The vicar at this time had lived in the parish for the past 20 years.[49] In 1812 the vicar lived at Swindon and services were still held on Sundays alternately in the morning and evening. Holy Communion was celebrated four times a year and there were 30 communicants.[50] On Census Sunday 1851 average attendance at morning service over the past year was estimated at 210 persons and in the afternoon at 260.[51] In 1864 services were held twice on a Sunday, and the Sacrament was administered 12 times a year. There was an average of 50 communicants.[52]

The church of *HOLY CROSS* consists of a chancel, a clerestoried nave with north and south aisles, a south tower, the base of which serves as a porch, and a north vestry. It is apparent from the interior that the fabric dates largely from soon after 1200. An even earlier origin for the church is suggested by the head of a small Saxon window which has been built into a pier near the south-west corner of the nave. The nave arcades have pointed arches supported on circular piers, the carved capitals showing a transition from Norman scallops to the 'stiff-leaved' foliage of the 13th century. The arcades are of five bays, but two substantial piers which stand one bay from the west end may indicate the position of the west wall of an earlier and shorter church. The chancel may be slightly later in date than the arcades and its east window consists of three graded lancets; below them externally is a circular recessed panel containing a much-weathered carving of the Crucifixion. There are several 14th-century windows in the church and the south doorway, which retains its ancient oak door, may be of the same date. The embattled south

tower, of three stages, was added in the 15th century. Also of the 15th or early 16th century are the nave roof and clerestory. The north, or Draycot, aisle was reputed to have been repaired with material from Draycot Foliat church, demolished in 1572.[53] A parish rate for the repair of the church was levied in 1691.[54] In 1892 a restoration was carried out by C. E. Ponting,[55] but a view of the building in 1810[56] suggests that little alteration was made to the exterior except for the replacement of some of the windows and the addition of a more steeply-pitched roof to the chancel. The vestry, which stands to the north of the chancel, was built in 1895 and also serves as an organ chamber.[57]

The church contains part of a 13th-century coped coffin lid with a foliated cross, fragments of mid-16th-century carving in the choir stalls, the remains of a screen, and a carved Jacobean pulpit. There are also two 18th-century commandment boards; one was formerly above the chancel arch, but both may originally have formed a reredos.[58] The church is particularly rich in monuments. They include a 15th-century tomb-chest in the chancel and brasses commemorating Francis Rutland (d. 1592) and his wife, the daughter of Thomas Stephens.[59] Also in the chancel is an altar tomb with a blank escutcheon, described by Aubrey as that of 'Ridforn, lord of Badbury'.[60] A mural tablet in the north aisle to Edward Mellish (d. 1707) has kneeling figures of a man and his wife with their numerous children behind them — an unusual grouping for so late a period. There are also many Georgian memorials to members of the Calley family.

In 1553 the king's commissioners left the church a chalice weighing 12 oz.[61] In 1770 Arabella Calley presented the church with a silver paten, hallmarked 1768.[62] This was still among the church plate in 1967, when there were also a chalice with its original paten cover, hallmarked 1625, a flagon hallmarked 1885, an almsdish of 1808, a silver standing pyx given in 1958, and a small silver chalice and paten given in 1960.[63]

In 1553 the church had 4 bells and a sanctus bell.[64] One of these, of 14th-century date, has survived.[65] The church had a peal of 6 bells, including the medieval bell, in 1967: four bells were of 17th-century date,[66] while a 6th bell was hung in 1937.[67] On the east buttress of the tower of the church is a scratch dial.[68] Registrations of baptisms run from 1641 but are lacking between 1669–1708. Marriage entries run from 1654 but are lacking from 1668–1713. Burial entries begin in 1641 but are lacking between 1659–1713. There are separate entries for baptisms and marriages in Draycot Foliat from 1817–19 and for burials in 1817 and 1830.[69]

[41] *Reg. Ghent* (Cant. and York Soc.), ii. 835.
[42] Ibid. 843.
[43] *Calamy Revised*, ed. A. G. Matthews, 557.
[44] Hist. MSS. Com. *Var. Coll.* i. 120.
[45] Ibid.
[46] Lambeth Palace MS. Com. III/1, f. 134.
[47] *W.N. & Q.* viii. 14.
[48] Sar. Dioc. R.O. Vis. Queries, 1783.
[49] Ibid.
[50] *W.A.M.* xli. 132.
[51] H.O. 129/250/2/5/9.
[52] Sar. Dioc. R.O. Vis Queries, 1864.
[53] Soc. Ant. Libr., Jackson MSS. Vol. ii. Chiseldon.
[54] Burderop MSS.
[55] *W.A.M.* xlv. 616; W.R.O. 569/14, Burial Bd. Min. Bk. 1876–1930.

[56] There is a S.E. view of the church by John Buckler in W.A.S. Libr., Devizes.
[57] *Church Guide*, Holy Cross, Chiseldon, 7.
[58] Pevsner, *Wilts.* (Bldgs. of Eng.), 157–8; *W.A.M.* xxxiv. 11.
[59] Pevsner, op. cit. 158; Aubrey, *Topog. Coll.* ed. Jackson, 162.
[60] Aubrey, op. cit. 163.
[61] Nightingale, *Wilts. Plate*, 155.   [62] Ibid.
[63] *Church Guide*, Holy Cross, Chiseldon, 9.
[64] Walters, *Wilts. Bells*, 56–57.
[65] Ibid. 251.
[66] Ibid. 56–57.
[67] *Church Guide*, Holy Cross, Chiseldon, 8.
[68] *W.A.M.* xlv. 294.
[69] W.R.O. 639.

In 1865 a building at Coate, which had formerly been a schoolroom, was licensed as a chapel of ease for Chiseldon church and from 1956 was known as the chapel of the Ascension. In 1958 it was so dilapidated that it was closed but was still standing in 1967.[70]

NONCONFORMITY. John Baker, the Vicar of Chiseldon who was ejected from the living in 1662, remained in Wiltshire and preached in the area around Berwick Bassett, Avebury, and Winterbourne Monkton.[71] In 1668 Richard Morse of Chiseldon was presented for holding a conventicle at his house at which four people were present.[72] The census of Bishop Compton in 1676 recorded 11 nonconformists in the parish. These, it has been suggested, were either Baptists, or both Quakers and Baptists.[73] Seven years later six people were presented for refusing to attend church or to receive the Sacrament, while one had refused to have his child baptized.[74] Chiseldon, in common with most of north-east Wiltshire, remained largely uninfluenced by nonconformity until the evangelical movement of the late 18th century. Methodism was brought to this corner of the county by George Pocock, one of Wesley's Bristol friends, who visited the area with a large tent mounted on a machine drawn by paper kites.[75] One of Pocock's first missions brought him to Hodson,[76] where, as a result of his evangelizing activities, a Methodist chapel was registered in 1789 by Thomas Wheeler.[77] The house was then said to be but lately erected and constructed of wattle and daub with a thatched roof.[78] This building was presumably the one which James Looker conveyed for purposes of worship in 1800.[79] There were said to be 21 members in 1823.[80] In 1828 services were held on alternate Sundays at the Hodson chapel, in the morning and afternoon respectively.[81] On Census Sunday 1851 the general congregation over the past year was reckoned at 65 in the morning and at 92 in the afternoon.[82] The chapel remained in use until 1895 when it was replaced by a small red-brick chapel built on land given by Gen. T. C. P. Calley.[83] Services were discontinued for a period of 8 years, which included the years 1914–18, and the chapel became derelict.[84] Subsequently the old thatched chapel, which had reverted to the Looker estate, was rented again and after repairs had been carried out services were held there.[85] The chapel was demolished in 1964.[86] The newer brick chapel, too, was renovated and re-opened in 1924,[87] but was closed by 1954.[88]

Premises occupied by William King were registered for worship at Chiseldon by an unspecified denomination in 1829.[89] Primitive Methodism appeared at Coate early in the century, since in 1828 a building occupied there by Joseph Smith was registered for worship by this denomination.[90] Later in the century it was said that for many years services had been held in the cottages of Messrs. Webb and Gregory,[91] but in 1888, largely as a result of the activity of the newly-formed Swindon Circuit,[92] a chapel for Primitive Methodists was built at a total cost of £117.[93] By 1964 the low brick chapel at Coate was no longer used for worship. The Primitive Methodist movement was also active at Badbury at an early date, and a building occupied by William Cox was registered there in 1828.[94] This congregation was still flourishing in 1851 when the average congregation over the past year was reckoned at 41 each Sunday afternoon.[95] Primitive Methodism at Badbury probably did not flourish for very long and there was apparently only a Wesleyan chapel in the 20th century.[96]

In Chiseldon itself a Wesleyan chapel was registered for worship in 1809.[97] On Census Sunday 1851 there was said to have been a general congregation of 43 people in the morning, 86 in the afternoon, and 102 in the evening over the past year.[98] Chiseldon retained a Wesleyan chapel in the 20th century.[99] This chapel, used as store in 1967, was a tall brick building which stood behind the Post Office and bore the date 1861. In 1835 Primitive Methodists at Chiseldon registered a building.[1] In 1851 average attendance there on a Sunday was reckoned to be 121 people in the morning and 120 in the afternoon.[2] A new chapel appears to have been built in 1853,[3] although it was not registered until two years later.[4] This building in its turn proved inadequate by the end of the 19th century and a new chapel and school were built in 1896.[5] The new chapel had 36 members, while the school could accommodate 90 children.[6] This building, which stood in Turnball, was still used by the Methodists of Chiseldon in 1967.

EDUCATION. In 1808 there was a charity school for 40 children, supported by the vicar and inhabitants, and a dissenters' Sunday school for 30 pupils.[7] There was also a day school for about 15 children,

[70] *Church Guide*, Holy Cross, Chiseldon, 10.
[71] *V.C.H. Wilts.* iii. 104–5, and see p. 21.
[72] Sar. Dioc. R.O. Chwdns.' Pres. 1668.
[73] *V.C.H. Wilts.* iii. 115.
[74] Sar. Dioc. R.O. Chwdns.' Pres. 1683.
[75] *V.C.H. Wilts.* iii. 142, and see p. 152.   [76] Ibid.
[77] G.R.O. Retns. to Places of Religious Worship Certifying Act, 1852, iv.
[78] B. Bailey, *Story of the Hodson Wesleyan Chapels 1800–1927*, (Swindon Pub. Libr.).
[79] Ibid.
[80] Ibid.
[81] Ibid.
[82] H.O. 129/250/2/5/10.
[83] Bailey, op. cit.
[84] Ibid.
[85] Ibid.
[86] Ex inf. the Revd. J. F. Collins, Chiseldon.
[87] Ibid.
[88] G.R.O. 34756.
[89] W.R.O. Retn. of Regns.

[90] Ibid.
[91] *Prim. Meth. Ch. Souvenir Handbk.* (1910), (Swindon Pub. Libr.).
[92] Ibid.; G.R.O. Worship Reg. ix, and see p. 155.
[93] *Prim. Meth. Ch. Souvenir Handbk.* (1910), (Swindon Pub. Libr.).
[94] W.R.O. Retn. of Regns.
[95] H.O. 129/250/2/5/12.
[96] *Kelly's Dir. Wilts.* (1903 and later edns.).
[97] H.O. 129/250/2/5/13.   [98] Ibid.
[99] *Kelly's Dir. Wilts.* (1903 and later edns.).
[1] H.O. 129/250/2/5/11.
[2] Ibid.
[3] *Prim. Meth. Ch. Souvenir Handbk.* (1910), (Swindon Pub. Libr.).
[4] G.R.O. Worship Reg. iii.
[5] *Prim. Meth. Ch. Souvenir Handbk.* (1910), (Swindon Pub. Libr.).
[6] Ibid.
[7] Lambeth Palace MS. 1732, Retn. of schools in Salisbury Dioc.

who were taught to read at their parents' expense.[8] In 1819 the only means of education for the poor was a school supported by voluntary contributions, at which about 90 children were taught by a master, whose salary depended upon subscriptions.[9] Two day schools, kept by a master and mistress, were maintained by subscription in 1835. One was attended by about 30 boys each day and by some 17 girls.[10] New school buildings were provided in 1837 with financial aid from the National Society. Buildings, and the land on which they stood, which was part of the Workhouse Close, were conveyed by John James Calley to trustees in the following year.[11] The school was to provide for the children of the poor inhabitants of Chiseldon, Badbury, Burderop, and Hodson, who were to be taught in accordance with the principals of the Church of England.[12] Some 40 to 50 boys were taught by a master, who was also parish clerk, but neither instruction nor discipline were considered satisfactory.[13] About the same number of girls were taught by the master's wife, and although the instruction was said to be of an elementary kind, the girls were thought to be cleanly and well-mannered.[14] In 1864 the Vicar of Chiseldon, assisted by the curate, ran a small school.[15] In 1868 a new National school was built on land from the Workhouse Close, given by Henry Calley.[16] The infants there were taught by a certificated teacher, a probationer, and a monitress in 1902, while the older children were taught by a head teacher and three assistants.[17] In 1906 the school, graded as Class 'A', had an average attendance of 186 children.[18] By 1909 average attendance had risen to 205,

but by 1938 it had dropped to 169.[19] In 1930 the school was transferred to the county.[20] It occupied three buildings in 1967 and was attended by some 200 juniors and infants.[21]

An emergency teachers' training college for 250 men was opened in Burderop Park in 1947 and was closed in 1951.[22] Buildings in Burderop Park also housed a secondary modern school for the area from 1948 to 1967,[23] when a new school at Wroughton was opened.[24]

CHARITIES. Richard Harvey, by his will proved in 1669, gave £100 to the parish of Chiseldon to be invested in lands worth £5 yearly, so that 20 poor persons might receive 5s. each from the income.[25] In 1677 the money was invested in about 5 a. in Chiseldon known as the New Mead purchased from Elizabeth Calley, widow of Sir William Calley.[26] The lands produced £8 in 1786, but no more was known about the charity at this date. By 1834 the lands, then known as the Poor's Mead, were let at a yearly rent of £12. This sum was distributed on 21 December to 20 of the most deserving men of the parish, not in receipt of parish relief. The recipients were chosen by the vicar and churchwardens and once nominated were entitled to receive the charity until death or disqualification. In 1903 the Poor's Mead was let for a yearly rent of £10, which was distributed in sums of 10s. to 20 poor persons, who must live in the ancient parish of Chiseldon. In 1964 the income of the charity was still about the same and was similarly distributed yearly among 20 poor persons.

CLYFFE PYPARD

CLYFFE PYPARD lies about 7 miles south-west of Swindon and on the north adjoins the parish of Wootton Bassett.[1] In spite of its proximity to Swindon the parish in 1968 seemed remarkably remote and undeveloped and was without main drainage. The modern parish, which is roughly rectangular in shape, with an extension at the south-east corner, stretches about 3 miles from north to south and is roughly 2 miles broad.[2] As will be shown below, it is made up of a number of scattered hamlets. Until created a civil parish in 1884, Broad Town was one of these hamlets, lying along the eastern boundary of Clyffe Pypard.[3] This boundary, which divided Clyffe Pypard from Broad Hinton, was extremely irregular in its course, zig-zagging from side to side along Broad Town village street.[4]

The manor of Broad Town, in fact, lay just to the east of the boundary, and so geographically was in Broad Hinton. For this reason, the lands of the two farms attached to the manor, namely Broad Town Farm, and Upper Ham Farm, although they lay on the Clyffe Pypard side of the boundary, were reckoned to be detached parts of Broad Hinton. In 1884 when the civil parish of Broad Town was created out of part of Clyffe Pypard and part of Broad Hinton, these anomalies were removed.[5] Before the creation of Broad Town Clyffe Pypard comprised 3,985 a.[6] Afterwards the area was 3,271 a.[7]

The most striking topographical feature of Clyffe Pypard is the north-west facing chalk escarpment, which stretches right across the parish, dividing the

[8] Ibid.
[9] *Digest of Retns. to Cttee. of Educ. of Poor*, H.C. 224, p. 1022 (1819), ix (2).
[10] *Educ. Enq. Abstract*, H.C. 62, p. 103 (1835), xliii.
[11] *Acct. of Wilts. Schools*, H.C. 27, p. 79 (1859 Sess. 1), xxii (2).
[12] *Endowed Char. Wilts.* (1908), p. 279.
[13] *Acct. of Wilts. Schools*, (1859 Sess. 1), xxi (2), p. 79.
[14] Ibid.   [15] Sar. Dioc. R.O. Vis. Queries, 1864.
[16] *Endowed Char. Wilts.* (1908), p. 279.
[17] W.R.O. List of Schools, 1902.
[18] *Retn. of Non-Provided Schools*, H.C. 178–xxxi, p. 827 (1906), lxxxviii.
[19] *Bd. of Educ. List 21, 1909, 1938.*   [20] Ibid. *1909–38.*
[21] Ex inf. Chief Education Officer, County Hall, Trowbridge.

[22] Ex inf. Dept. of Education and Science.
[23] Ex inf. Chief Education Officer.
[24] Ex inf. Miss J. M. Calley.
[25] All inf. unless otherwise stated from *Endowed Char. Wilts.* (1908), pp. 277–8 and Char. Com. File 238608.
[26] B.M. Add. MS. 17456.
[1] Much research for this article was undertaken by Dr. Colin Shrimpton who also wrote the preliminary draft for it.
[2] Maps used include O.S. Map 1/2,500, Wilts. XXI. 4, 8, 12, 16, XXII. 1, 2, 5 (1st and later edns.); 6″, Wilts. XXI, XXII (1st and later edns.).
[3] See p. 26.   [4] See p. 26.
[5] See p. 26.
[6] *Census*, 1881.
[7] Ibid. 1891.

clay vale to the north from the Lower Chalk below the Marlborough Downs to the south.[8] It is this steep escarpment, or cliff, which has given the parish, and several other places in the neighbourhood, their names. A local rhyme runs:

White Cleeve, Pepper Cleeve, Cleeve, and
    Cleveancy,
Lyneham and lousy Clack, Cris Mavord, and
    Dauntsey.[9]

The first three are all references to Clyffe Pypard: the fourth is a farmstead in Hilmarton.[10] On the Kimmeridge Clay to the north of the escarpment the land of the parish is flat and lies at levels of mostly around 350 ft. The Clay gives way towards the foot of the escarpment first to a belt of Gault, and then to the Greensand. Above, on the chalk downland, heights of over 700 ft. are reached. About two-thirds of the parish lies on the Clay and a third on the Chalk.

Many springs and streams rise from just above the foot of the escarpment. One of these, running north-westwards through the parish, joins with other small streams to form the Brinkworth Brook, a headwater of the Bristol Avon. Another, rising about ½ mile south-west of the parish church, supplied Wootton Bassett with water from the later 19th century until 1962.[11] In 1968 Clyffe Pypard Manor House and several nearby cottages still drew their water supply from a spring coming from the escarpment.[12] Much of the northern part of the parish was undoubtedly formerly undrained marsh. In 1334 there was a pasture at Broad Town called 'la lake', which was particularly valued as summer grazing.[13] In the 16th century a piece of ground, also at Broad Town, was described as lying 'beyond the water',[14] and one of two commons at Bushton was called the Marsh.[15] In 1968, although drained by deep ditches, the land was still fairly heavy and wet in places, and many willow trees flourished in the hedgerows.

The parish has always been well wooded. There were extensive stretches of woodland at the time of Domesday,[16] and the scattered pattern of settlement is no doubt partly due to the way in which clearance progressed. The two largest woods in the parish in 1968 were Cleeve (or Clyffe Pypard) Wood in the north and Stanmore Copse in the south. In 1762 Holloway Coppice stretched along 7½ a. of the cliff-hanging above the village of Clyffe Pypard, and there were at least 4 willow-beds in the parish.[17] In the 19th century beech trees were planted along what was called the 'cock-walk' on the side of the hill.[18] The avenue, which they formed, still, in 1968, flanked the descent into the village from Broad Hinton.

Archaeological finds, such as arrowheads, coins, jewellery, and skeletons, are evidence of a period of early settlement, extending from Neolithic to Pagan-Saxon times.[19] At the foot of the escarpment, at Woodhill and Bupton, numerous mounds and earthworks are possibly of medieval date.[20] The ancient parish was made up of five tithings, each with its own centre of settlement. These were: Clyffe Pypard, Broad Town, Bushton, Thornhill, and Woodhill, which included Bupton. All, except Woodhill and Bupton, were still settlements in 1968. The nucleus of the village of Clyffe Pypard lies immediately beneath the steep, thickly-wooded slope of the escarpment and forms a small, rather picturesque group of buildings. Besides the parish church with manor-house and vicarage closely adjoining on either side,[21] there are a few thatched, timber-framed cottages, and the 'Goddard Arms'. This stands on the site of an earlier public house of the same name, burnt down in 1961.[22] The village school lies a little to the west and beyond this is a group of terraced council houses, built after the Second World War.

Broad Town, which is described below, also stands at the foot of the escarpment, about 1½ mile east of Clyffe Pypard, but cut off from direct communication with it by a protrusion of the cliff face.[23] The third settlement just below the hill was Woodhill, which included Bupton. Bupton, as is shown above, belonged probably from 1086 to the Bishop of Salisbury's hundred of Cannings.[24] In 1968 Woodhill consisted of one large farm[25] and the area known as Bupton of a newly-built farm house, close by the road to Calne, and another new farm on top of the hill. But there was undoubtedly once a larger settlement here, some traces of which remain above the ground, although some of the earthworks are thought to be only the boundaries of abandoned closes, drainage channels, and shallow surface quarrying.[26] A medieval settlement at Bupton may have declined during the late 16th and early 17th centuries, when the lords of the manor, the Quintins, were evidently in financial difficulty.[27] A farm at Lower Bupton, just below the cliff, was used during the Second World War to house German prisoners,[28] but nothing of this remained above ground in 1968. The buildings of Bupton Farm, a little to the south-west and higher up the cliff, had likewise entirely disappeared.

The two other settlements in the parish lie to the north, away from the escarpment. One of these, Bushton, belonged by the 16th century to the hundred of Elstub and Everley.[29] In 1968 it was the largest settlement in the parish, comprising three or four small farms, a number of cottages and a public house, all strung out along the road between Clyffe Pypard and Tockenham. The 18th-century manor-house stands on the east side of the road.[30] In 1968 Clyffe Pypard post office and general store was at Bushton, so that the distance between Clyffe Pypard village and the only shop in the parish was nearly

---

[8] For some acct. of the geology of the region, see Fry, *Land Utilization Wilts.* pp. 157 sqq.
[9] *P.N. Wilts.* (E.P.N.S.), 266.
[10] See p. 51.
[11] *Water Supply Wilts.* (H.M.S.O. 1925), 36–37 and see p. 200.
[12] Local inf.
[13] *Wilts. Inq. p.m.* 1327–77 (Index Libr.), 104.
[14] W.R.O. 192/51, Survey Bk.
[15] See p. 34.
[16] See pp. 33–34.
[17] W.R.O. 110/5, Titles to Manor.
[18] W.A.S. Libr., Devizes, 'Goddard Papers', f. 26.

[19] *V.C.H. Wilts.* i (1), 58.
[20] Ibid. 264; *W.A.M.* xxxviii. 227.
[21] See pp. 28, 40.
[22] Local inf.
[23] See p. 26.
[24] See p. 3.
[25] See p. 32.
[26] Ex inf. Mr. D. J. Bonney of R.C.H.M. (Eng.). For the assessment of Bupton for taxation, see below.
[27] See p. 35.
[28] Ex inf. Mr. R. E. Sandell.
[29] See p. 3.
[30] See p. 30.

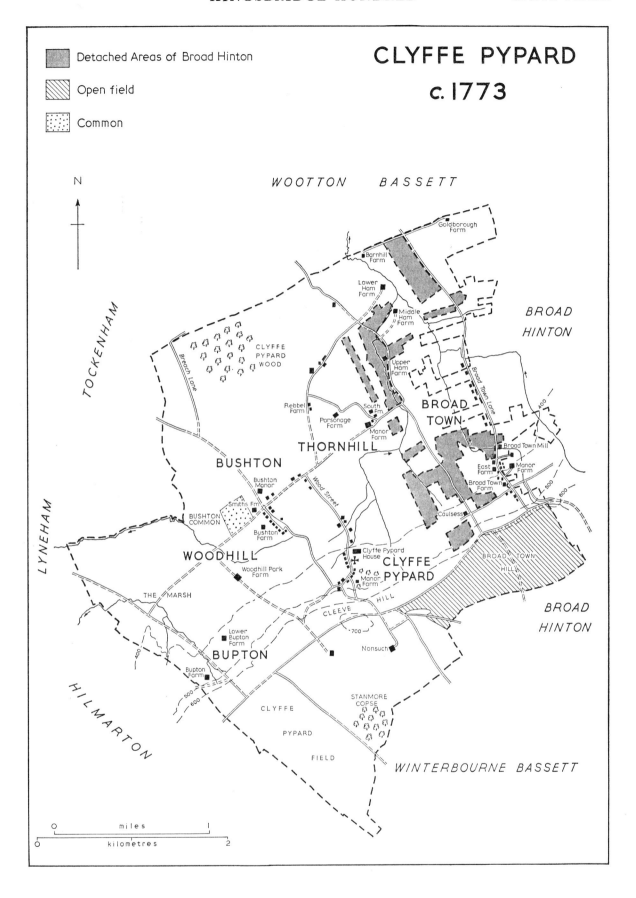

CLYFFE PYPARD
c.1773

Detached Areas of Broad Hinton

Open field

Common

two miles. There is a small Methodist chapel at the north end of Bushton. A few council houses have been added to the hamlet since the Second World War. The tithing of Thornhill lies to the east of Bushton but after the creation of the civil parish of Broad Town in 1884 the greater part of Thornhill came within the new parish.[31]

The tithings were once linked by a network of tracks. Along the roads, which now connect the hamlets, there has been a certain amount of peripheral settlement. Small wayside cottages stand along the road to Calne, especially along that part of it known as the Barton, and along the road called Wood Street, which leads north from the village of Clyffe Pypard.

No main roads run through the parish. A minor road, which leads through Bushton and skirts the village of Clyffe Pypard, links the parish eventually with the main road from Wootton Bassett to Chippenham in the north and the main road from Swindon to Marlborough in the south. Besides this road, which climbs the escarpment beyond Clyffe Pypard village, another road up the hill was made a little to the west in 1862.[32] Numerous rough tracks also ascend the hill, leading to the chalk downland where, until finally inclosed in the 19th century, the open fields of Clyffe Pypard, Thornhill, and Broad Town lay. The only houses in the upland part of the parish are the two or three farms, presumably created during the 18th century when the inclosure of the open fields was in progress. Nonsuch Farm was formed out of open-field land in this way, as is shown below.[33] Nebo Farm, another downland farm, was obliterated during the Second World War when an airfield was made in this part of the parish.[34] Since the war, however, this land has again become farm land.

In 1334 the largest contribution from the parish to the fifteenth levied that year came from the tithing of Thornhill, which contributed 42s., Broad Town made the next highest contribution (40s.), followed by Clyffe Pypard, and Bushton (both 34s.), followed by Woodhill (22s.)[35] In 1377 there were 54 poll-tax payers in Clyffe Pypard, 44 in Broad Town, 42 in Thornhill, 40 in Bushton, and 21 in Woodhill.[36] A place called 'Boreton', in Cannings hundred, possibly identifiable as Bupton, had 30 taxpayers at this date.[37] To the Benevolence of 1545 there were 4 contributors in Bushton, 3 in Clyffe Pypard, and 2 in both Thornhill and Broad Town.[38] Bupton on this occasion was assessed under the hundred of Potterne and Cannings with Highway and Clevancy and its separate contribution cannot be calculated.[39] To the subsidy of 1576 Clyffe Pypard made a contribution of £5 17s. 8d. and Bushton of £5 os. 2d.[40] Bupton was again assessed with Highway and Clevancy.[41] The other tithings in the parish liable for taxation in 1576 were presumably included either under Clyffe Pypard or Bushton. In 1801 the population of the parish was

624. In 1841 it was 933. In 1851 it had dropped to 890 and although it rose to 910 in 1861 it dropped in the next two decades and was 777 in 1881. In 1891, after the creation of the civil parish of Broad Town, the population of Clyffe Pypard fell to 427. It continued to decline until 1911 when it was 342, but then began to rise and in 1951 was 519. In 1961, however, it had fallen to 481.[42]

Several members of the Goddard family, which has been connected with the parish as rectors and lords of the manor for over 400 years, have also played important parts in the affairs of the county. Horatio Nelson Goddard (1806–1900) was active as a J.P. in dealing with the agricultural riots in north Wiltshire in 1830, and in 1860 was High Sheriff.[43] Edward Hungerford Goddard (1854–1947) was presented to the living by his uncle, Horatio Nelson Goddard, in 1883 and held it for 52 years. In 1890 he became honorary secretary of the Wiltshire Archaeological and Natural History Society and editor of its magazine. In 1909 he became the society's honorary librarian and held all three offices until 1942. Among his many writings on Wiltshire subjects his *Wiltshire Bibliography*, issued by the county council in 1929, deserves special mention.[44] Thomas Stephens (1549?–1619), Jesuit missionary and author, was the son of Thomas Stephens of Bushton. He is not known, however, to have had any influence in the parish.[45] Sir Edward Nicholas (1593–1669), secretary of state to Charles I and Charles II, was educated for four years in the house at Bushton of his uncle Richard Hunton.[46]

The civil parish of *BROAD TOWN* was created in 1884 out of parts of Clyffe Pypard and Broad Hinton. Until then Broad Town had been a tithing of Clyffe Pypard, although some of it was situated geographically in Broad Hinton. As explained above,[47] Broad Town manor in fact lay in the Broad Hinton part of the tithing, but its descent is traced below along with the descents of those manors actually situated within the parish of Clyffe Pypard.[48] The manors of Cotmarsh and Bincknoll, however, which were brought within the new parish of Broad Town in 1884, were not part of the former tithing of Broad Town and their histories are reserved for treatment with the parish of Broad Hinton, in which they originally lay.

The parish of Broad Town is roughly rectangular in shape and stretches about 2 miles from north to south and approximately the same distance from east to west.[49] Its area is 2,040 a. Almost the whole parish lies on the Kimmeridge Clay, although its southern boundary runs along the top of the north-west facing escarpment of the Lower Chalk Terrace, thus bringing within the parish the steep slope of the chalk escarpment and the belts of Gault and Greensand, which run beneath it. Below the escarpment the land lies at around 300 ft. Above it reaches over 600 ft. The only woodland in the parish is Binck-

---

[31] See below.   [32] *W.A.M.* xliv. 145.
[33] See p. 36.
[34] Local inf.
[35] *V.C.H. Wilts.* iv. 300.
[36] Ibid. 309, 311.
[37] Ibid. 307, n. 4.
[38] *Taxation Lists* (W.A.S. Rec. Brch.), 3, 20, 21.
[39] Ibid. 16.
[40] Ibid. 107, 122.
[41] Ibid.

[42] All figures from *Census*.   [43] *W.A.M.* xxxi. 244–5.
[44] Ibid. lii. 117–20.
[45] *D.N.B.* Supplement and see p. 30.
[46] *Nicholas Papers*, *vol. i* (Camd. Soc. N.S. xl), p. xiii; *D.N.B.*; and see p. 29.
[47] See p. 23.
[48] See p. 28.
[49] Maps used include: O.S. Map 1/2,500, Wilts. XXI. 4, 8, 12, 16, XXII. 1, 2, 5 (1st and later edns.); 6″, Wilts. XXI, XXII (1st and later edns.).

noll Wood, situated in the south-east corner on the slope of the escarpment. One of the streams, later forming the Brinkworth Brook, rises at the foot of the escarpment and flows through Broad Town village and northwards out of the parish.

Only two roads run through the parish, both on an approximately north-south course. The larger is the secondary road between Wootton Bassett and Broad Hinton, which for nearly a mile forms the village street of Broad Town. At its southern end in 1773 it took a sharper easterly turn before climbing the hill than it does in 1968, and left the parish by the now disused Horn Lane.[50] The northern end of the same road was called Broad Town Lane at the earlier date and is still so-called. The smaller road runs on an almost parallel course roughly ½ mile to the west, turning eastwards at its southern end to join the secondary road in Broad Town village.

Little evidence of prehistoric settlement has been found, although an axe, thought to date from the Neolithic period or the Bronze Age, was found on Broad Town Hill.[51] A large earthwork, known as Bincknoll Castle, situated on a chalk promontory in the south-east corner of the parish, is thought to be of medieval date and was possibly once a motte-and-bailey castle.[52] A white horse cut in the chalk above Little Town Farm dates from 1863.[53] Broad Town village is situated immediately below the hill. Most of its houses are small and undistinguished. A few are timber-framed and thatched but none appears to date from before the 17th century. Broad Town Farm and East Farm lie just to the west of the village street and Broad Town Manor Farm is situated on the east side. Christ Church, built in 1846, is towards the northern end of the street on the east side with the village school almost opposite.[54] The two Primitive Methodist chapels were also built at this end of the village.[55] Broad Town's more recent building, including a number of council houses, has been at this end of the village, particularly towards and at Broad Town Lane. The former Wesleyan Methodist chapel at the other end of the village has been converted into a private house and stands at the bottom of Chapel Lane.[56] Springfield House, almost the only house of any size or pretensions in Broad Town, stands about ¼ mile to the east of the village and dates from c. 1800. In 1773 a house called Caulsess stood on the site.[57]

Most of Thornhill, a former tithing of Clyffe Pypard, came within the civil parish of Broad Town after 1884, although Thornhill Manor Farm remains just within Clyffe Pypard.[58] Thornhill lies to the north-west of Broad Town village and in 1968 comprised a few humble dwellings lying along the minor road, known for part of its course as White Way, and leading eventually to the village. This region was in the earlier 20th century settled by a number of families of gipsy origin, who made encampments and later built more permanent shacks and bungalows by the roadside.[59]

The eastern half of the parish is remarkably unoccupied and is virtually inaccessible by road. Almost the only houses are those belonging to the farms of Little Town, Cotmarsh, and Bincknoll. Bincknoll Farm, an apparently 18th-century house, lies in an extremely isolated position in the south-east corner of the parish. By field paths it is only about 1½ mile from Broad Town village but by road the distance is some 4 miles.

In 1891 the population of the recently-formed civil parish of Broad Town was 483. Over the next 40 years there was little significant change, although the figures tended to drop slightly. In 1951 the number rose to 543 from 441 in 1931. In 1961 it was 503.[60]

MANORS AND OTHER ESTATES. There are no fewer than 13 references to 'Clive' in the Domesday Survey of Wiltshire, but it has not been established precisely how many relate to estates situated in Clyffe Pypard.[61] T.R.E. an estate at 'Clive' was held by Alfric, Burgel, and Godeve.[62] After 1066 this may have been held by William FitzOsbern, Earl of Hereford, and may have passed to William's son Roger, Earl of Hereford, who forfeited his lands in 1074. Either William or Roger possibly enfeoffed Gilbert de Breteuil in the estate and it is probable that after Earl Roger's forfeiture Gilbert held in chief.[63] By 1086 Gilbert de Breteuil certainly held the estate, which may be identified with the later main manor of *CLYFFE PYPARD*, of the king. At the time of the Domesday Survey Ansfrid held 11 hides of the estate of Gilbert.[64]

At an unknown date the overlordship of the estate apparently passed to the Reviers family, whose founder, Richard, was a kinsman of William (Fitz Osbern), Earl of Hereford.[65] In 1242 Baldwin (de Reviers), Earl de Lisle (d. 1245), held the estate, reckoned at 1½ knight's fee, in chief.[66] No more is known of the Reviers overlordship, and it seems that it passed to either Walter Marshal, Earl of Pembroke, or to his successors.

In 1242 the estate was held of Baldwin, Lord de Lisle by Walter Marshal, Earl of Pembroke and Marshal of England (d. 1245).[67] Either he or his successors subsequently became overlords. Thereafter the estate at Clyffe apparently descended in the same way as that of Hampstead Marshall (Berks.), the chief manor of the Marshals of England.[68] The last mention of the overlordship occurs in 1428 when Clyffe Pypard was held by Queen Joan (d. 1437), consort of Henry IV.[69]

Matthew Columbers held the estate of the Earl de Lisle in 1242, and Richard Pipard held of Matthew Columbers at the same date.[70] Matthew Columbers died childless in c. 1272–3 and was succeeded by his brother Michael.[71] By c. 1285 Michael was dead and his widow, Joan, surrendered to her father, John de Cobham (d. 1300), all her rights in

50 *Andrews and Dury, Map* (W.A.S. Rec. Brch.), pl. 14.
51 *V.C.H. Wilts.* i (1), 50.
52 Ibid. 263; Pevsner, *Wilts.* (Bldgs. of Eng.), 134.
53 Pevsner, op. cit. 134.
54 See pp. 41, 42.   55 See p. 41.
56 See p. 41.
57 *Andrews and Dury, Map* (W.A.S. Rec. Brch.), pl. 14.
58 See p. 31.
59 Local inf.
60 All figures from *Census*.

61 *V.C.H. Wilts.* ii, pp. 120, 133, 142, 144, 146, 147, 152, 156, 164, 167.
62 Ibid. p. 147.   63 *V.C.H. Berks.* iii. 268.
64 *V.C.H. Wilts.* ii, p. 147.
65 *Complete Peerage*, iv. 310.
66 *Bk. of Fees*, ii. 727.   67 Ibid.
68 For a descent of the manor of Hampstead Marshall, see *V.C.H. Berks.* iv. 179–80.
69 *Feud. Aids*, v. 277.   70 *Bk. of Fees*, ii.727.
71 *Collect. Topog. et Gen.* vii. 148.

dower to her former husband's land.[72] At about the same date Matthew's widow, Maud, who had married Henry, eldest son of John de Cobham, conveyed to her father-in-law certain lands and rents which she held in dower within the manor of Clyffe Pypard.[73] In this way John de Cobham acquired the whole manor. Before his death in 1300 John de Cobham apparently conveyed Clyffe Pypard to Roger de Cobham, his third son. Roger was described as lord of Clyffe Pypard in 1297[74] and had a grant of free warren there in 1304.[75] He must have died soon afterwards, however, and the manor reverted to his eldest brother Henry (cr. Lord Cobham 1335–6), second husband of Maud Columbers.[76] In 1306 Henry granted the manor, on terms that are not clear, to a younger son Thomas, who was founder of the Beluncle (Hoo, St. Werburgh, Kent) branch of the Cobham family.[77] The date of Thomas's death is unknown, but he was still living in 1343 when he presented to the church (see below). Henry, Lord Cobham died in 1339 and was followed by a son (d. 1355), and grandson (d. 1408), both called John.[78] John, Lord Cobham, the grandson, was impeached in 1397, at which date yet another John Cobham, who was styled 'esquire', possibly a son or grandson of Thomas was holding the manor.[79] The fee simple of the manor, however, was found to rest with John, Lord Cobham at the time of his impeachment and was claimed by the Crown.[80] The keepership of Clyffe Pypard was then granted by the king to Thomas Percy, Earl of Worcester, who was executed for treason in 1403.[81] John, Lord Cobham was pardoned in 1399, but he died in 1408 without surviving issue[82] and Clyffe Pypard continued to be held by the Beluncle branch of the family, the descendants of Thomas mentioned above. A John Cobham, possibly the same as the John Cobham of 1397 (see above), held it in 1428.[83] He had two sons, Thomas and Henry,[84] and presumably one of them succeeded his father at Clyffe Pypard. In 1510 William Cobham, whose relationship to Thomas and Henry is not known, held the manor[85] and in 1525 Edward Cobham, presumably his son, sold it to William Dauntsey.[86]

In 1530 William Dauntsey sold the manor to John Goddard of Aldbourne (d. 1542), who was succeeded by his son John Goddard the younger.[87] On his death in 1567 John the younger was succeeded by his son Thomas (d. 1610). Thomas Goddard's heir was his son Francis, upon whose death in 1652 Clyffe Pypard passed to his son Edward Goddard (d. 1684), who in turn was succeeded by his son and heir Francis (II) Goddard.

On his death in 1724, Francis (II)'s son and heir Edward (II) Goddard was a minor and until 1742 his estate was supervised by George Goddard, Francis's bastard son, who lived at Clyffe Pypard.[88] Edward (II) Goddard died in 1791 and was succeeded by his son Edward (III) Goddard, upon whose death in 1839 the estate passed to his son and heir Horatio Nelson Goddard (d. 1900). He was succeeded by his daughter and heir Frances, the wife of William Wilson. On the death of Frances Wilson in 1940, Clyffe Pypard passed to her son and heir William Werden Wilson (d. 1950), who was in turn succeeded by his son Mr. Peter Werden Wilson, who held the manor in 1968.

After the sale of their Standen Hussey (Berks.) estate in 1719,[89] the Goddards apparently lived at Clyffe Pypard. The present (1968) manor house, a gabled building of brick, lies in a secluded position just to the north of the church. It was largely rebuilt by H. N. Goddard soon after he succeeded to the manor in 1839. During the rebuilding of the front in 1840 some timber framing of an earlier house was discovered.[90]

In 1086 Miles Crispin (d. 1107) held a 5-hide estate at 'Clive', which had been held T.R.E. by Harold.[91] This estate may be identified with the later manor of Broad Town. In a way that has been traced elsewhere the estate became part of the honor of Wallingford (Berks.)[92] and the overlordship followed the descent of that honor.[93] The last mention of the Wallingford overlordship occurs in 1385.[94]

Broad Town was held of Miles Crispin in 1086 by Humphrey.[95] In 1206 it was held of the honor of Wallingford by Alan Basset (d. 1232–3), who was also lord of the manor of Wootton Bassett.[96] For the next 120 years the manor of *BROAD TOWN* passed like Wootton Bassett in the Basset family and came in the same way to Hugh le Despenser, the elder.[97] On his death in 1326 Broad Town, like Wootton Bassett, was forfeit to the Crown. In 1330 Gilbert of Berwick was appointed keeper and the following year Edward III granted the manor to his kinsman Edward de Bohun (d. 1334).[98] After Bohun's death it was held in dower by his widow, Margaret (d. 1341),[99] but in 1337 the manor was regranted to Hugh (IV) Despenser (d.s.p. 1349), grandson of Hugh the elder (see above).[1] Before his death Hugh (IV) Despenser granted his brother Gilbert Despenser (d. c. 1382) a life interest in the manor.[2] On the death of Hugh (IV) without issue Broad Town passed to his nephew and heir Edward, Lord Despenser (d. 1375), son of his brother Edward. Edward, Lord Despenser was succeeded by his son

[72] Ibid. 327.
[73] Cal. Close, 1279–88, 161; Cal. Pat. 1281–92, 178.
[74] Wilts. Inq. p.m. 1242–1326 (Index Libr.), 220; Holinshed, Chronicles, iv. 782.
[75] Cal. Chart. 1300–26, 47.
[76] Complete Peerage, iii. 343.
[77] Collect. Topog. et Gen. vii. 333; Hasted, Kent, iv. 9.
[78] Complete Peerage, iii. 344–5.
[79] Ibid. 344; Cal. Inq. Misc. 1392–9, p. 149.
[80] Cal. Inq. Misc. 1392–9, p. 149.
[81] Cal. Pat. 1396–9, 215; Complete Peerage, s.v. Worcester.
[82] Complete Peerage, iii. 344–5.
[83] Feud. Aids, v. 277.
[84] Collect. Topog. et Gen. vii. 334.
[85] W.A.M. xliv. 157.
[86] W.N. & Q. ii. 423.

[87] W.A.M. xliv. 158; for a descent of Goddard of Clyffe Pypard, see Burke, Commoners, (1833–8), iv. 329; Land. Gent. (1952), s.v. Wilson.
[88] W.R.O. 110/19, Marriage Settlement, Edward Goddard, Joanna Read, 1754.   [89] V.C.H. Berks. iv. 196.
[90] W.A.S. Libr., Devizes, 'Goddard Papers', f. 61.
[91] V.C.H. Wilts. ii, p. 146.   [92] See p. 44.
[93] For a descent of the honor of Wallingford, see V.C.H. Berks. iii. 523–7.
[94] Cal. Fine R. 1383–91, 86–87.
[95] V.C.H. Wilts. ii, p. 146.
[96] Cal. Feet of F. Wilts. 1195–1272, ed. Fry, 9.
[97] See p. 190.
[98] Cal. Fine R. 1327–37, 214; Cal. Chart. R. 1327–41, 468.
[99] Wilts. Inq. p.m. 1327–77 (Index Libr.), 104, 142–3.
[1] Complete Peerage, iv, pp. 259 sqq.
[2] Cal. Close, 1381–5, 167–8.

LAWRENCE HYDE, EARL OF ROCHESTER (d. 1711)

SARAH, DUCHESS OF SOMERSET (d. 1692)

CLYFFE PYPARD: MONUMENT TO THOMAS SPACKMAN (d. 1786)

RICHARD JEFFERIES (1848–87)

Thomas, Lord Despenser (cr. Earl of Gloucester in 1397 and executed 1400).[3] Thomas, Lord Despenser, granted the manor to Thomas Percy, Earl of Worcester, in 1398,[4] but the estate was forfeit to the Crown after Worcester's execution in 1403.[5] At some date after this Broad Town was apparently granted to Edward, Duke of York (d. 1415), the father-in-law of Thomas, Lord Despenser (executed 1400). On his death the estate was again forfeit to the Crown and in 1415 was restored to Isabel, daughter and heir of Thomas, Lord Despenser, jointly with her husband, Richard Beauchamp, Lord Bergavenny (d. 1422).[6] Isabel married secondly Richard Beauchamp, Earl of Warwick. Both Isabel and her second husband died in 1439.[7] Isabel's coheirs were George Nevill, Lord Bergavenny (d. 1492), her grandson by her first marriage, and Anne, *suo jure* Countess of Warwick (d. 1490), her daughter by her second marriage.[8] The Broad Town estate apparently formed part of the portion of Anne, Countess of Warwick, since in 1487 she conveyed it to Henry VII.[9] Thereafter it was leased out by the Crown (see below) until 1536 when it was granted to Edward Seymour, later Duke of Somerset (executed 1552).[10] Thenceforward the manor, like that of Thornhill, descended with the Somerset and Hertford titles until the death of Sarah, Duchess of Somerset in 1692.[11] By the duchess's will, dated 1686, the manor was devised to trustees for the purpose of creating a charity to provide apprenticeships for poor children born and living in Wiltshire. The estate was made up of four farms, Manor Farm, Ham Farm, Goldborough Farm, and Broad Town Farm.[12] In 1920 the trustees of the Broad Town Charity sold all 4 farms.[13]

Broad Town Manor Farm lies to the east of the village street and is a mid-19th-century red-brick house. Broad Town Farm, on the other side of the road, has a date stone on a chimney inscribed '1668 R S'. The house has been subsequently extended and in the mid 20th century was re-roofed.

In 983 land in Clyffe Pypard was granted in quick succession by Ethelred to two thegns, Aethelwine and Aethelmaer.[14] This land is almost certainly to be identified with the estate later known as *BUSHTON*, since the inclusion of the above grants in the *Codex Wintoniensis* leads to the presumption that it was subsequently given to the cathedral priory of Winchester.[15] In 1086 Bushton was one of the Wiltshire estates of the Bishop of Winchester, which had been allotted for the support of the monks of the cathedral priory.[16] It was subsequently assigned to the anniversarian of that house and remained among the priory's possessions until the Dissolution.[17]

In 1541 Bushton was granted to Thomas, Lord Seymour of Sudeley, brother of the Protector Somerset and uncle of Edward VI.[18] After his attainder and execution for treason in 1549 it reverted to the Crown and was eventually sold in 1553 to William Richmond *alias* Webb.[19] Bushton was settled on William's second son Edmund, who succeeded to it in 1580.[20] Edmund Richmond *alias* Webb sold it in 1591 to Richard Hunton, the son of William Hunton, of East Knoyle.[21] In 1622 it was settled upon Richard's son William on the occasion of William's marriage to Elizabeth, daughter of Henry Jaye, alderman of the city of London.[22] Owing to serious financial difficulties William Hunton appears to have mortgaged it to his brother-in-law Henry Cusse in 1625.[23] Its subsequent descent is somewhat obscure but in 1638 it was conveyed by Cusse and his wife to Hugh Audley, presumably a trustee.[24] By *c.* 1650 Bushton had passed to Francis Wroughton, who still held it in 1657.[25]

Some time in the 1730s or early 1740s Ralph Broome of Cowage (then a detached part of Compton Bassett) acquired Bushton and settled there.[26] By his will, dated 1767, he divided his Bushton property amongst his sons, Richard and Francis.[27] Bushton manor then apparently descended, like Woodhill, to Christopher Edmund Broome (d. 1886), grandson of Francis Broome but was sold soon afterwards and has subsequently had many owners.[28]

Francis Goddard, lord of the main manor of Clyffe Pypard (d. 1652), apparently acquired part of the Bushton estate some time in the earlier 17th century,[29] possibly from William Hunton (see above). This small estate, said to be a part of the manor of Bushton, had passed to the Holles family by 1669, when it was settled on the marriage of Francis Holles (later Lord Holles) and Anne Pile.[30] Francis, Lord Holles died heavily in debt in 1692, and since his son and heir Denzil died before his father's will was proved, his estates were settled in 1697–8 on a cousin, John Pelham, Duke of Newcastle (d. 1711), for payment of his debts.[31] John, Duke of Newcastle devised the estate at Bushton and other Holles properties to his nephew Thomas Pelham (d. 1768) in 1707.[32] Thomas Pelham, who assumed the additional surname of Holles, was created Duke of Newcastle in 1715,[33] and in 1743 he sold the estate, then known as Bushton Farm and reckoned at 80 a., to John Walker of Lyneham.[34] The farm then descended with the manor of Lyneham until the 19th century.[35] In *c.* 1854 the Revd. George Ashe Goddard (d.s.p. 1873), acquired Bushton

---

[3] Burke, *Ext. & Dorm. Peerages* (1883), 166–7.
[4] *Cal. Pat.* 1396–9, 430.
[5] *Cal. Fine R.* 1399–1405, 230, 317.
[6] *Cal. Close*, 1413–19, 241.   [7] *Complete Peerage*, i. 28.
[8] Ibid.   [9] *Cal. Close*, 1485–1500, 90.
[10] *L. & P. Hen. VIII*, x, p. 526.
[11] *Complete Peerage*, xii(1), 59–76.
[12] *Endowed Char. Wilts.* H.C. 196 ii, pp. 1–8 (1907), lxi, and see p. 42.
[13] W.A.S. Libr., Devizes, Sale Cat. and see p. 42.
[14] *Cod. Dipl.* ed. Kemble, iii, pp. 192, 195.
[15] *V.C.H. Wilts.* ii, p. 86.
[16] Ibid. p. 120.
[17] *Valor Eccl.* (Rec. Com.), vi, App. ix; *V.C.H. Hants* ii. 60, and see p. 34.
[18] C 66/708 m. 2. This grant is not included in the calendar printed in *L. & P. Hen. VIII*, xvi, pp. 462–3.
[19] C.P. 25(2)/65/533; C 142/187/118.

[20] C 60/389 no. 26.
[21] C.P. 25(2)/241/33 Eliz. 1 Hil.; *Wilts. Visitation Pedigrees* (Harl. Soc. cv, cvi), 95–96.
[22] C 142/423/70.
[23] C.P. 25(2)/508/1 Chas. I East, and see p. 35.
[24] C.P. 25(2)/510/13 Chas. I Hil.
[25] E 134/1657/Chas. II Trin. 12.
[26] *W.A.M.* xliv. 147, 192–3.   [27] Ibid. 193.
[28] W.A.S. Libr., Devizes, Sale Cat. xi. 13 (1912), and see p. 32.
[29] S.R.O. Button-Walker-Heneage Mun. 997, Abstract of title to Bushton Farm.
[30] Ibid. and see p. 31.
[31] S.R.O. Button-Walker-Heneage Mun. 997.
[32] *Complete Peerage*, ix. 529–31.   [33] Ibid.
[34] S.R.O. Button-Walker-Heneage Mun. 998, Bargain and sale, Newcastle to Walker.
[35] See p. 94.

Farm.[36] Its subsequent descent is obscure but the farm may have been acquired by Christopher Edmund Broome (d. 1886), and at a later date passed to the Buxtons of Tockenham.[37]

According to the tithe award Sir John Jacob Buxton (d. 1842), lord of the manor of Tockenham, had in some way before his death acquired an estate of some 345 a. at Bushton.[38] In 1864 what was apparently the same estate was held by his son Sir Robert Jacob Buxton (d. 1888).[39] It was presumably this estate, together with Bushton Farm, which was sold in 1913. That year land including Bushton Farm, Smith's Farm, Holly House Farm, and Bellecroft Cottages was sold in lots.[40] Bushton Farm, Smith's Farm, and Bellecroft were acquired by the county council as smallholdings and in 1968 these still belonged to the county council.[41]

In the 14th century the manor seems to have been leased by the Anniversarian of St. Swithun's Priory (see above) for terms including one of 12 years.[42] The priory granted a lease of Bushton to Richard Stephens (d. 1551), Thomas his son, and Richard his grandson in 1533. Richard and Thomas Stephens still farmed at Bushton in 1549.[43]

The manor-house at Bushton was built by Ralph Broome and has a date-stone on the façade inscribed 1747.[44] It is a square brick house with stone quoins and moulded architraves. It has a steep pitched roof covered with stone slates. The south front of 5 bays has a central doorway with a semi-circular hood on brackets, surmounted by a round-headed window.

In 1086 3 hides, which formed part of the Bishop of Salisbury's estate at Bishop's Cannings, were held by Quintin.[45] These 3 hides probably represent the origin of the estate, which eventually became known as the manor of GREAT BUPTON. Bupton continued to be regarded as part of the manor of Bishop's Cannings, and thus held of the Bishop of Salisbury, until the bishop lost Bishop's Cannings in the 17th century.[46] It also formed part of the bishop's hundred of Cannings.[47] By 1166 an unidentified estate, reckoned at 2 knights' fees, was held of the bishop by John de Mellepeis.[48] In 1242–3 John's heir is known to have held land in Clyffe Pypard of the bishop, although the holding was then reckoned to be only 1 knight's fee.[49] It seems safe to assume, therefore, that the Mellepeis holding was Bupton, although there is no later connexion between the family and the manor.

In 1242–3 the Mellepeis estate in Clyffe Pypard seems to have been held by two men, possibly father and son, both called William Quintin.[50] In 1255 it was held by William Quintin and William Bubbe, who together owed castle guard service at Devizes

castle for the knight's fee they held jointly in Clyffe Pypard.[51] Some time after this the estate seems to have been split into two distinct parts. One part, which may be identified with the estate known in the 20th century as Lower Bupton, continued to descend in the Quintin family, although the descent is for many years obscure. In 1387 Alice Grandon granted certain lands, which she held in Bupton and Woodhill, to her son Thomas Quintin.[52] In 1418 John Clyne, presumably a trustee, conveyed to Thomas Quintin certain lands in Bupton, Woodhill, and Corton.[53] Thomas Quintin conveyed the estate to his son Thomas (II) in 1438.[54] By 1497 the estate had passed to John Quintin, possibly the son or grandson of Thomas (II). In this year John Quintin conveyed it to his son Walter.[55] From Walter the estate passed to John (II) Quintin, whose heir was his son John (III). Both Johns died at unknown dates and the land passed to John (III) Quintin's son Michael, who died seised of an estate at Bupton in 1576.[56] Michael Quintin was succeeded by his son Henry, who in 1600 conveyed an estate described as the manor of Bupton to Gabriel Pile (see below).[57]

The second estate at Bupton probably originated in that part of the Mellepeis estate held in 1242–3 by William Bubbe (see above). In 1387 Thomas Fraine and Isabel his wife were seised of an estate known as the manor of Bupton.[58] After the death of Thomas and Isabel Bupton passed to their daughter Alice, wife of Thomas Horne.[59] Alice Horne was succeeded by her son William Horne (d. 1488), who in turn was succeeded by his son Thomas (d. 1527).[60] On Thomas's death without issue Bupton was divided among 3 coheirs. These were his sister Elizabeth, wife of Richard Pile, Margaret, possibly a sister or niece, the wife of Robert Edge, and another Elizabeth, again perhaps a sister or niece, the wife of Robert Duckett.[61]

In 1527 Margaret and Robert Edge conveyed their third to Ambrose and William Dauntsey.[62] In 1531 William Dauntsey reconveyed it to John Goddard.[63] This third then passed with the main manor of Clyffe Pypard until 1601, when John's grandson Thomas Goddard conveyed it to Gabriel Pile.[64] Elizabeth and Richard Pile were succeeded in their third by their son William, who was at an unknown date succeeded by his son Thomas (d. 1561).[65] Thomas Pile acquired the Duckett third in 1550, held at that date by Owen Duckett, presumably the son of Elizabeth and Robert Duckett.[66] Thomas Pile was succeeded by his son and heir Gabriel, who in 1601 acquired the Edge third (see above). In this way the estate was reunited.

In 1600 Gabriel Pile acquired the other manor of Bupton (Lower Bupton) from Henry Quintin (see

[36] Aubrey, *Topog. Coll.* ed. Jackson, 166.
[37] W.A.S. Libr., Devizes, Sale Cat. xi. 7.
[38] W.R.O. Tithe Award, 1844.
[39] *W.A.M.* xliv. 146.
[40] W.A.S. Libr., Devizes, Sale Cat. xi. 7 (1913).
[41] Ex inf. Smallholdings dept. Wilts. County Council.
[42] *Obedientiary Rolls of St. Swithun's, Winchester,* (Hants Rec. Soc.), 205.
[43] *W.A.M.* xliv. 148–9. For Thos. Stephens (d. 1619), see p. 26.
[44] *W.A.M.* xliv. 146; Pevsner, *Wilts.* (Bldgs. of Eng.), 140.
[45] *V.C.H. Wilts.* ii, p. 121.
[46] *W.A.M.* vi. 127; B.M. Add. Ch. 37571; *V.C.H. Wilts.* vii. 189.
[47] See p. 3. [48] *Red Bk. Exch.* (Rolls Ser.), i. 236.

[49] *Bk. of Fees,* ii. 736.
[50] Ibid. [51] *Rot. Hund.* (Rec. Com.), ii (1), 236.
[52] *W.A.M.* xxxv. 461.
[53] Ibid. [54] Ibid.
[55] Ibid. 462.
[56] For a descent of the Quintin family, see *Genealogist* (N.S. xii), 237–8; C 142/175/107.
[57] C 142/175/107; *W.A.M.* xxxv. 462.
[58] *W.A.M.* xxxv. 461.
[59] *Wilts. Visitation Pedigrees* (Harl. Soc. cv, cvi), 236.
[60] *Cal. Inq. p.m. Hen. VIII,* i, p. 173.
[61] *W.A.M.* xxxv. 476–9. [62] C.P. 25(2)/46/319.
[63] *W.A.M.* xxxv. 462.
[64] Ibid. 463, and see p. 28.
[65] *Wilts. Visitation Pedigrees* (Harl. Soc. cv, cvi), 236.
[66] *W.A.M.* xxxv. 479.

above), and this estate, together with that formerly held by the Horne family, became known in the 17th century as the manor of Great Bupton.[67] Gabriel Pile (d. 1626) was succeeded by his son and heir Francis (d. 1648), whose coheirs were his three daughters, Anne, wife of Francis, Lord Holles, Elizabeth, wife of Thomas Strickland, and Jane, wife of Edward Richards.[68] The manor of Great Bupton seems to have passed to Elizabeth Pile and her husband Thomas Strickland, who in c. 1665 conveyed it to Thomas Benet (d. 1670).[69] Thomas Benet was succeeded by his son Thomas (II), described as of Salthrop (in Wroughton).[70] A Thomas Bennet, presumably either Thomas (II) or his son, conveyed the manor to Edward Northey in 1743, presumably in trust.[71] By 1787 the manor had passed to George St. John, Lord Bolingbroke (d. 1824).[72] By 1844 Great Bupton had passed to Sir Richard Simeon, who in 1860 sold it to Richard Stratton of Broad Hinton, a well-known cattle breeder.[73] Stratton's trustees administered the estate in 1903 and by 1927 it was owned by Victor Carr.[74] A brief description of the sites of Bupton and Lower Bupton farms is given above.[75]

T.R.E. Stremi held an estate at Thornhill. In 1086 the land had passed to William FitzAnsculf, who also held a nearby estate reckoned at 2 hides, one of which was attached to Gilbert de Breteuil's manor of Clyffe Pypard and the other to Edward of Salisbury's estate at 'Stoche' (the later manor of Bradenstoke).[76]

It seems probable that the estate held in 1086 by William FitzAnsculf passed in some way to Edward of Salisbury, and he apparently settled it on his daughter Maud and her husband Humphrey (II) de Bohun. The Bohuns and their descendants, the Bohun earls of Hereford and Essex,[77] remained overlords of *THORNHILL*. The last mention of the overlordship occurs in 1373 when Humphrey de Bohun, Earl of Hereford and Essex (d. 1373), was overlord of the estate, then reckoned at $\frac{1}{2}$ knight's fee.[78]

In the early 12th century Maud de Bohun and her son Humphrey (III) de Bohun endowed their newly-founded Cluniac house at Monkton Farleigh with lands including the Thornhill estate. In 1131 Innocent II confirmed the gift of Thornhill and other lands.[79] The Thornhill estate continued to be held by the Prior and convent of Monkton Farleigh until the dissolution of the house in 1536.[80]

In 1536 the manor of Thornhill was granted to Edward Seymour, later Duke of Somerset (executed 1552).[81] Thenceforth until 1692 it descended like that of Broad Town.[82] In 1686 Sarah, Duchess of

Somerset (d. 1692), devised Thornhill to Brasenose College, Oxford, in order to increase the number of scholarships she had already founded there. The Thornhill scholars were to be elected in turn from Manchester, Marlborough, and Hereford schools.[83] Thornhill, which comprised four farms,[84] was still held by Brasenose in 1968.

Thornhill Manor Farm is a **T**-shaped house built of chalk-stone faced with brick. The oldest part of the house forms the trunk of the **T** and may originate from 1596, the date on a plaque discovered in an outbuilding and set in the wall of the house in the 20th century.[85] The plaque, which appears to be inscribed 'Comes de Hertford 1596', was placed in a stable wall in 1724,[86] the date when the house was probably being restored and the tall cross-wing was built on to the south-east end. The house is known to have been in need of repair in 1696 when it was reckoned that £200 would have to be spent on it before any tenant would take it.[87] The new cross-wing may have replaced the solar of the earlier house and a small sketch of this house as it was in 1706 supports the suggestion.[88] The new wing has a south-east elevation of five bays with mullioned and transomed windows and a coved cornice. Within are some contemporary panelled rooms and a central staircase. Accounts for the building works of 1723–4 survive.[89] The architect was a Mr. Townsend.[90] Wood in various forms came from Wootton Bassett, Tockenham, and Cricklade, and paving stone from Swindon. The older house may have been faced with brick at this date to match the new building, although no references to brick in large quantities have been noticed among the accounts. Among the windows made were 13 casements for the new wing, then called the 'best end of the house'. A parlour and hall were panelled, as were two rooms above.[91] These may possibly have been the parlour and hall said in 1726 to be reserved for holding the manorial courts.[92] A new garden, enclosed by a ditch, was made in 1724 and many trees were planted.[93]

In 1086 an estate at Woodhill, which T.R.E. was held by Eddulf, formed part of the estates of the Bishop of Bayeux and was held of the bishop by his tenant Odo.[94] Part, at least, of the estate eventually passed to William Marshal, Earl of Pembroke (d. 1231), since in 1233 his widow Eleanor was granted dower rights in an estate at Woodhill, which at that date was in the hands of a royal keeper, Michael son of Nicholas.[95] The overlordship of the Marshals is last mentioned in 1242–3 when Walter Marshal, Earl of Pembroke (d. 1245), was lord.[96]

By the early 13th century Woodhill was held of the Earl of Pembroke by a number of tenants.

[67] Ibid. 464.
[68] Burke, *Ext. & Dorm. Baronetcies* (1844), 413–14.
[69] *W.A.M.* xxxv. 465.   [70] *D.N.B.*
[71] C.P. 25(2)/1233/16 Geo. II East.
[72] C.P. 43/817B/27.
[73] W.R.O. Tithe Award; *W.A.M.* xliv. 147.
[74] *Kelly's Dir. Wilts.* (1903, 1927).   [75] See p. 24.
[76] *V.C.H. Wilts.* ii, p. 167.
[77] *Complete Peerage*, vi. 447–77.
[78] *Wilts. Inq. p.m.* 1327–77 (Index Libr.), 371.
[79] *V.C.H. Wilts.* iii. 262.
[80] *Valor Eccl.* (Rec. Com.), ii. 143.
[81] *L. & P. Hen. VIII*, x, p. 526.   [82] See p. 29.
[83] B.N.C. Oxford, Thornhill 13; *W.A.M.* xliv. 145–6. For a fuller acct. of these scholarships, see A. R. Stedman, 'Hist. Marlborough Grammar School' (Lond. Univ. M.A. thesis, 1945), 25, 26, 60.

[84] See p. 36.
[85] Ex inf. Mrs. Hammond, Thornhill Manor Farm.
[86] B.N.C. Oxford, Estates Thornhill 18. The inscription has been read 'Comes de Hereford' (*W.A.M.* xliv. 146), but since the Earl of Hertford was lord of the manor in 1596, this is likely to be a mistake.
[87] B.N.C. Oxford, Thornhill 11.
[88] Ibid. Map of 1706.
[89] Ibid. Estates Thornhill 18.
[90] Ibid.
[91] The above details from the accounts in B.N.C. Oxford, Estates Thornhill 18.
[92] B.N.C. Oxford, Thornhill 29.
[93] Ibid. Estates Thornhill 18.
[94] *V.C.H. Wilts.* ii, p. 122.
[95] *Close R.* 1231–4, 257, 267, 275.
[96] *Bk. of Fees*, ii. 712.

By 1233 Richard Suard held land there of the earl,[97] and in 1242–3 John St. Quintin held a fifth of a knight's fee in Woodhill of the same overlord.[98] The bulk of the estate, however, appears to have been held by the Escorcheville family. Richard Escorcheville (fl. 1204), of Hintlesham (Suff.), apparently held the lands, but at an unknown date forfeited them to the king.[99] In 1248 the king granted the manor of *WOODHILL* to Theobald de Engleschevill.[1] He enfeoffed his son William in the estate in 1250[2] but evidently retained rights in the manor. On Theobald's death Woodhill apparently escheated to the Crown, but in 1262 the manor was restored to his son William.[3] William de Engleschevill was dead by 1269 when his widow Alice had dower rights in the estate. At this date Matthew Besil, evidently a kinsman of William de Engleschevill, died seised and was succeeded by his son John.[4] John, who died some time after 1280, was succeeded by his son Edward (d. 1304), who was in turn succeeded by his son Peter (d. 1327).[5] The estate was then held in turn by Peter's son Matthew (II) (d. 1361),[6] and grandson Peter (II), who in 1381 conveyed the estate to William Wroughton and his son William.[7]

The elder William Wroughton died in 1392, and was succeeded by his son William.[8] William (II) Wroughton died in 1408 and in 1409 the manor was delivered to his widow Margaret.[9] It eventually passed to William (II)'s son John (d. 1496).[10] Woodhill was then held successively by John's son Christopher (d. 1515),[11] grandson William (III) (d. 1558),[12] and great-grandson Thomas (d. 1597).[13] On the death of Thomas Woodhill presumably passed to his son Giles, who in c. 1640 sold his Broad Hinton estate.[14] It may have been at this date that he sold Woodhill.

In 1656 Woodhill Park, as the estate was then called, was held by Hugh Audley, presumably a trustee who had acquired it from the Wroughtons.[15] Woodhill eventually passed to Ralph Broome the elder (d. 1768), who by his will of 1767 devised it to his son Francis (d. 1795).[16] Francis apparently settled the land on his son Richard Pinniger Broome (d. 1836).[17] He was succeeded by his nephew Christopher Edmund Broome (d. 1886), who in turn was succeeded by his son Edmund Broome, Vicar of Hurst (Berks.), who held the estate in 1903.[18] By 1923 the Broomes had sold Woodhill to their tenant, Ernest Pritchard,[19] who lived there until his death in 1963.[20]

The house of Woodhill Park consists of two ranges built back to back, the older and lower being an 18th-century house of red brick. The later and higher range, which faces south-east, was designed and built by Richard Pace of Lechlade (Glos.) in 1804[21] when Christopher Broome acquired the estate (see above). It has a mansard roof and is of red brick with stone dressings. It has a central classical porch with flanking Venetian windows. At eaves level there is a central gable containing a semi-circular window and a shaped parapet has vases at either end.

The descent of a number of smaller estates in Clyffe Pypard can be partially traced. T.R.E. an estate, which paid geld for 8 hides, was held by Edwin. By 1086 the same lands were held by Humphrey Lisle.[22] Subsequently the lands passed to the Dunstanvilles on the marriage of Adeliza, daughter of Humphrey Lisle, to Reynold de Dunstanville, lord of the barony of Castle Combe.[23] The estate at Clyffe was thenceforth held under the barony of Castle Combe and descended with it until at least the 15th century. The last mention of the overlordship occurs in 1454.[24]

In 1086 Humphrey Lisle's tenant was Robert.[25] By 1242–3 Ralph Lovel held a knight's fee at Clyffe of Walter de Dunstanville (d. 1269).[26] The estate apparently remained in the Lovel family and in 1330 was held by the heirs of Ralph Lovel.[27] The subsequent descent is obscure but it seems that the estate was acquired at some date by the Cobhams. In 1454 the heirs of Agnes, Lady Cobham, second wife of Lord Cobham (d. 1355), held an estate at Clyffe of the barony of Castle Combe.[28] The land evidently remained in the Cobham family and eventually passed to their successors the Brookes, descending with the barony of Cobham of Kent,[29] and was held in 1547 by George Brooke, Lord Cobham (d. 1558).[30] The descent has not been traced further and it must be presumed that the lands merged with others in the parish.

As well as the main manor of Clyffe Pypard Gilbert de Breteuil also held Stanmore in the southeast of the parish.[31] His tenant in 1086 was Ansfrid. Before the Conquest Stanmore had been held by Bruning, who paid geld for 2½ hides. Hamon of Beckhampton held it along with Beckhampton (in Avebury) of Matthew Columbers in 1242–3.[32] Like the manor of Clyffe Stanmore seems to have passed to a younger branch of the Cobhams. In 1323 Thomas Cobham acquired a small estate which had been in the possession of John of Stanmore.[33] Whether this little estate became part of the larger one which passed from the Cobhams to the Goddards is not clear, but it seems likely.

[97] *Close R. 1231–4*, 257, 267, 275.
[98] *Bk. of Fees*, ii. 725.
[99] *Cal. Chart. R. 1226–57*, 331; *Pipe R. 1204* (P.R.S. N.S. xviii), 233.
[1] *Cal. Chart. R. 1226–57*, 331.
[2] *Cal. Feet of F. Wilts. 1195–1272*, ed. Fry, 44.
[3] *Close R. 1261–4*, 81–82.   [4] *Cal. Inq. p.m.* i, p. 229.
[5] *V.C.H. Wilts.* vii. 102; *Cal. Inq. p.m.* iv, p. 152.
[6] *Cal. Inq. p.m.* vii, p. 6.
[7] *Cal. Inq. p.m.* xi, p. 17; C.P. 25(1)/256/54/32.
[8] C 136/78/4.
[9] C 137/74/50A; *Cal. Close R. 1405–9*, 425.
[10] *Cal. Inq. p.m. Hen. VII*, i, pp. 505–6.   [11] C 142/30/27.
[12] C 142/124/192; *Wilts. Visitation Pedigrees* (Harl. Soc. cv, cvi), 219–20.
[13] C 142/249/81.
[14] Aubrey, *Topog. Coll.* ed. Jackson, 334.
[15] W.R.O. 161/Bdle 49, Copy of Release to Hugh Audley, 1656. This document had in 1968 been returned to the owner, Capt. A. D. C. Francis of Cole Park.
[16] W.R.O. Will of Ralph Broome; Wilts. Tracts, 166.
[17] For a descent of the Broome family, see *W.A.M.* xliv. 191–3; Foster, *Gray's Inn Admissions 1521–1889*, 405; Wilts. Tracts, 166.
[18] W.R.O. Tithe Award; *Kelly's Dir. Wilts.* (1903).
[19] *Kelly's Dir. Wilts.* (1923).   [20] *W.A.M* xliv. 151.
[21] H. M. Colvin, *Dict. Brit. Architects*, 427.
[22] *V.C.H. Wilts.* ii, p. 144.
[23] For a descent of the family of Dunstanville, see G. P. Scrope, *Barony of Castle Combe* (1852, priv. print.), 19.
[24] Ibid. 221.   [25] *V.C.H. Wilts.* ii, p. 144.
[26] *Bk. of Fees*, ii. 726.
[27] *Cal. Inq. p.m.* vii, p. 96.
[28] Scrope, *Castle Combe*, 221, and see p. 28.
[29] For a descent of Cobham of Kent, see *Complete Peerage*, iii, pp. 343 sqq.
[30] Scrope, *Castle Combe*, 317.
[31] *V.C.H. Wilts.* ii, p. 147.
[32] *Bk. of Fees*, ii. 749.
[33] *Feet of F. Wilts. 1272–1327* (W.A.S. Rec. Brch.), 110.

The lands of the Barnard family at Broad Town were among the more important of the lesser estates. The estate may have originated in the additional hide at Broad Town held in 1086 by Miles Crispin.[34] By 1242–3 the overlordship of the estate was held by William Marshal, Earl of Pembroke (d. 1245).[35] Thenceforth the overlordship descended like that of the main manor of Clyffe Pypard (see above), and is last expressly mentioned in 1428.[36]

During the later 12th century Robert Barnard held an estate at Broad Town.[37] By 1201 he had been succeeded in the lands by his son Hugh, who granted ½ hide at Broad Town to Alan Basset (d. 1232–3), who held the main estate there.[38] Michael Barnard, perhaps Hugh's son, held land at Broad Town reckoned at ⅓ knight's fee of the Earl Marshal in 1242–3.[39] The estate remained in the Barnard family. At some date before his death in 1348 John Barnard the elder seems to have enfeoffed his son John in the estate. The younger John subsequently regranted his father and mother, Agnes (d. 1349), a life estate in the lands.[40] By 1366 Robert (II) Barnard held ⅓ knight's fee in Broad Town of the Earl Marshal.[41] By 1428 the lands had passed, presumably by marriage, to William Horne (d. 1488), who in that year held lands formerly of John Barnard at Broad Town in right of his wife.[42] The lands then descended like the Horne estate at Bupton and eventually passed to their successors, the Pile family.[43] The last mention of the manor of 'Barnards', as it was then known, occurs in 1561 when Thomas Pile died seised of it.[44]

The Paryses, like the Barnards, were another family that for long held lands in Broad Town under the overlordship of the earls of Pembroke.[45] In 1225 Grace, the wife of Thomas de Parys, claimed dower against Richard de Parys for lands at Littleton in Broad Town.[46] William de Parys held part of a fee 'in the marsh' (i.e. Cotmarsh) of the Earl Marshal in 1242–3,[47] and the estate was held by Thomas, a descendant, in 1306.[48] William Parys had lands in Broad Town and Cotmarsh in 1428.[49] John Parys of Cotmarsh was listed among the freeholders of Kingsbridge hundred in 1607–8,[50] but no subsequent reference to the family or their lands can be traced.

Besides the manor of Broad Town Hugh Despenser the elder (executed 1326) also had a small estate, which lay partly in Bupton and partly in the neighbouring parish of Berwick Bassett. This was forfeited with the rest of Despenser's estates at the time of his attainder. Later, in 1344, the lands were leased to the king's yeoman, William de Beauvoir, for 10 years.[51] William de Beauvoir died in 1346 and

William of Farleigh became lessee in his place;[52] in the following year he was made a grant for life.[53] In 1371 the estate was granted to Stanley Abbey in return for prayers for Queen Philippa's soul.[54] The estate was held by the abbey until its dissolution in 1536.[55]

In 1617 Richard Hunton and his son William conveyed a small estate at Upper Woodhill to Thomas Baskerville.[56] The land remained in the Baskerville family and in 1652 Francis Baskerville, possibly either the son or grandson of Thomas, conveyed Upper Woodhill to John Northover, who in 1659 enfeoffed John Foyle.[57] By his will of 1671 John Foyle left his land called Woodhill Farm to his daughter Joan Foyle.[58] By 1732 the land had passed to Edward Foyle, a kinsman and presumably the heir of Joan Foyle, and in this year Edward conveyed land at Upper Woodhill to Ferdinando Gorges, who died in 1737 and devised his land at Woodhill to his kinsman John Beresford.[59] By 1755 Upper Woodhill had passed to John's brother Richard Beresford, who in 1755 conveyed the land to Ralph Broome (d. 1768),[60] whose family acquired Woodhill Park later in the 18th century (see above).

ECONOMIC HISTORY. Six estates recorded in Domesday can be identified with certainty as lying in Clyffe Pypard. Two were at Clyffe, and the others at Bushton, Thornhill, Woodhill, and Broad Town.[61] The largest was Gilbert de Breteuil's of about 16 hides at Clyffe. Here on the entire estate, the larger part of which was held under Gilbert by Ansfrid, there was land for 7 ploughs, 66 a. of meadow, 87 a. of pasture, and 18 a. of woodland. The estate supported 26 servile tenants. Gilbert's part was worth 35s. and Ansfrid's £6.[62] The other estate at Clyffe was that of 8 hides, belonging to Humphrey Lisle. Here there was land for 4 ploughs, and 20 a. each of meadow and pasture. There were 13 servile tenants and also 3 burgesses in Cricklade, who were in some way attached to this manor, which was worth £4.[63] At Bushton there was the 10-hide estate belonging to the Bishop of Winchester. There was land for 5 ploughs, 30 a. of meadow, and woodland 2 furlongs long by one furlong broad. It had 13 servile tenants. Its value had increased from £3 T.R.E. to £6 in 1086.[64] A 7½-hide estate at Thornhill, belonging to William FitzAnsculf, had land for 5 ploughs, 11 a. of meadow, pasture 2 furlongs by 2 furlongs, and 10 a. of woodland. There were 15 tenants here and the estate was worth £5.[65] At Woodhill the Bishop of Bayeux's 6-hide estate had land for 3

[34] V.C.H. Wilts. ii, p. 146. This was one of the few estates in Wiltshire for which it was recorded that its holder, T.R.E., might commend himself to a lord of his own choice: ibid. p. 64.
[35] Bk. of Fees, ii. 725.
[36] Feud. Aids, v. 278.
[37] Cur. Reg. R. ii. 86.
[38] Ibid; Cat. Anct. D. iii, A 4631, and see p. 28.
[39] Bk. of Fees, ii. 725.
[40] Wilts. Inq. p.m. 1327–77 (Index Libr.), 187–8, 208–9.
[41] Ibid. 340–1.
[42] Feud. Aids, v. 278.
[43] See p. 30.
[44] C 142/132/34.
[45] See p. 27.
[46] Cur. Reg. R. xii, p. 310.
[47] Bk. of Fees, ii. 725.
[48] Wilts. Inq. p.m. 1242–1326 (Index Libr.), 337.
[49] Feud. Aids, v. 277.

[50] W.A.M. xix. 261.
[51] Cal. Fine R. 1337–47, 377.
[52] Ibid. 476.
[53] Ibid. 494.
[54] Cal. Pat. 1370–4, 59.
[55] Valor Eccl. (Rec. Com.), ii. 114; V.C.H. Wilts. iii. 274.
[56] W.R.O. 212B/Cl. 19, Feoffment, Hunton to Baskerville.
[57] Ibid. 212B/Cl. 27, Final concord, Baskerville and Northover; ibid. 212B/Cl. 33, Feoffment, Northover to Foyle.
[58] Ibid. 212B/Cl. 35, Will of John Foyle.
[59] Ibid. 212B/Cl. 74, Final concord, Foyle and Gorges; ibid. 212B/Cl. 77, Abstract of Title of John Beresford.
[60] Ibid. 212B/Cl. 95, Deed, Beresford to Broome.
[61] V.C.H. Wilts. ii, pp. 120, 122, 144, 145, 147, 167.
[62] Ibid. p. 147.
[63] Ibid. p. 144.
[64] Ibid. p. 120.
[65] Ibid. p. 167.

ploughs, 12 a. of meadow, pasture 1 furlong by 1 furlong, and woodland 1 furlong by 3 a. There were 11 servile tenants and the estate was worth £4.[66] At Broad Town there was land for 2 ploughs on Miles Crispin's 5-hide estate, 20 a. of meadow, and 12 a. of pasture. It had been worth 30s. T.R.E. but in 1086 was worth 50s.[67] Taking these 6 estates together, therefore, there was in Clyffe Pypard in 1086 land for 26 ploughs, 148 a. of meadow, over 100 a. of pasture, and some 28 a. of woodland. But these 6 estates certainly do not represent the entire parish. At least some of the other estates, all called Clive in the Domesday Survey, must have been situated in the parish, later called Clyffe Pypard, although they cannot now be identified with a specific part of it.[68]

Early in the 13th century Bushton manor was valued at £8. Assized rents produced £2 0s. 2d. and there were 16 oxen on the demesne.[69] Thornhill, at the same date, was valued at £5 with assized rents worth £3. Here there were 3 cows and 16 oxen.[70] In 1282 Clyffe manor was valued at £11 4s. 11¾d.[71] The manor of Broad Town was extended in 1271[72] and in 1334.[73] In 1271 it was valued at £8 19s. 11d. and in 1334 at £8 14s. 6d. At the earlier date there were said to be 154 a. of arable, 12 a. of meadow, together with pasture for 12 oxen and 150 sheep. Arable was valued at 5d. an acre and meadow at 1s., while grazing per head of stock was 6d. for an ox and ½d. for a sheep. Assized rents were valued at £2 14s. In 1334 120 a. of arable were worth 6d. an acre when sown, but otherwise nothing because they lay in common. There were 6 a. of meadow worth 2s. 6d. an acre and another 6 a. worth only 2s. an acre. A pasture called 'la lake' was valued at 9s. during the spring and summer months and at 3s. 4d. during the winter. There was a sheep pasture worth 6s. 8d. There were two free tenants paying rents, and one virgater who held a virgate for which he paid rent and either performed certain mowing and reaping services or made payments in lieu. There were 10 customary tenants, who held ½ virgate each and also paid rent and owed the same services as the virgater. There were 10 cottars who paid rent in lieu of all services. On the same manor in 1341 a money value was given to all customary works. Assized rents at the same date were reckoned to be £3 a year.[74]

The manor of Bushton, which in 1086 was allotted to St. Swithun's Priory, Winchester, for the support of the monks,[75] was by the end of the 14th century assigned to the anniversarian of that house.[76] The profits of Bushton were apparently the anniversarian's only source of income and in the 1390s these profits consisted of the rent of the farm, the proceeds of two views of frankpledge, and the pannage of

pigs.[77] The manor was at this time held on a 12-year lease at an annual rent of £16. Total annual profits in 1394–6 were about £17. Out of these, the anniversarian, who was also styled keeper (custodis) of Bushton, had to meet all the expenses of his office. While these were mainly concerned with the celebration of the anniversaries of founders and benefactors of St. Swithun's, they also included certain administrative costs, such as visits by the anniversarian and his servants to Bushton. In 1395 the anniversarian seems to have spent 10 weeks there.[78] In 1534–5 total income was about £18, made up in much the same way as in the later 14th century, but including an annual payment of 12d. called Monken Eve.[79]

In 1549 when Bushton was in the keeping of Sir John Thynne, receiver for crown estates, the manor was surveyed.[80] Profits were still worth £18. The site of the manor was let to Richard Stephens, who had right of common for 200 sheep. There were 5 copyholders and 7 customary tenants, but no freeholders. There were 2 commons called the Hurst and the Marsh, totalling 60 a. The arable lay in an East and a West Field, which later evidence shows lay at the top of the cliff, usually described as being 'above the hill'. Monken Eve was still payable.

In 1542 when both Thornhill and Broad Town manors formed part of the Seymour estates, the demesne farms of both were leased to John Garrard.[81] For Thornhill Garrard paid a fine of £26 16s. and undertook to provide Seymour's steward and other officers with food, lodging, and fodder when they came to hold the manor courts and inspect the farm. At Broad Town in the later 16th century there were 161 a. of demesne leased to Garrard. In the open fields above the hill there were 34 a. of arable in the West Field and 17 a. in the East Field. But most of the land lay below the hill, where some inclosure of both pasture and arable had taken place.[82] A two-acre piece of pasture had recently been inclosed at Kedmeade, and another ten-acre piece next to Lake Hedge. Sixteen acres of arable called 'Craskine' had also been inclosed, and another 7 a. near Calcroft corner.[83]

A survey of Broad Town and Thornhill made in 1587 and revised in 1601 shows that at Broad Town, in addition to the leaseholder of the manor farm, there were 7 customary tenants with holdings ranging from 17 half-acres to 138 a.[84] There were 2 freeholders, one with 30 a., the other, who was the lord of the neighbouring manor of Clyffe Pypard, with 22 a. Meadowland had been inclosed at Ham Marsh, in the north of Thornhill tithing, in Woodmeade, Homemeade, and the Overclose. Pasture had been inclosed in Thornhill Marsh, and Cotmarsh

[66] Ibid. p. 122.
[67] Ibid. p. 145.
[68] Ibid. pp. 21, 67, 110, 111n., 217, 220.
[69] Interdict. Doc. (P.R.S. N.S. xxxiv), 24.
[70] Ibid. 25–26.   [71] Cal. Close, 1279–88, 161.
[72] Wilts. Inq. p.m. 1242–1326 (Index Libr.), 65.
[73] Ibid. 1327–77, 104.
[74] Ibid. 143.
[75] See p. 29.
[76] G. W. Kitchin in Obedientary Rolls of St. Swithun's Winchester (Hants Rec. Soc.), says that the manor assigned to the anniversarian was Bishopstone in Wilts. (pp. 53, 202, n.3). Neither of the places in Wilts. called Bishopstone were manors of the priory, and there is no doubt that the manor in question was Bushton, the early forms of

which were Bissopeston, Bushepeston, or Bishopeston (P.N. Wilts. (E.P.N.S.), 266–7). In the acct. r. it is Busshopestone.
[77] Two anniversarian's acct. rolls and the fragment of a third are printed in Obedientiary Rolls St. Swithun's (Hants. Rec. Soc.), 202–9.
[78] Obedientiary Rolls St. Swithun's (Hants Rec. Soc.), 207.
[79] B.M. Add. Ch. 26872, which is an anniversarian's acct. for 1534–5.
[80] W.A.M. xliv. 148–50, and see p. 29.
[81] W.R.O. 192/51, Survey Bk.
[82] Many of the fields mentioned below can be located on the Tithe Map of 1844.
[83] W.R.O. 192/51, Survey Bk.
[84] Ibid.

(which lay to the east), and in Redhill, which had inclosed arable as well. Arable had also been inclosed in Whitelands. In all some 109 a. of inclosure are mentioned in the survey of 1587.

Acreage inclosed at Thornhill at this date was almost three times as much, namely 282 a. Meadow had been inclosed at Galworth and 'Brandier' and in the fields next to Thickthorn and above Thornhill. Inclosed pasture lay in Cotmarsh and Thornhill Marsh. Arable had been inclosed at Gableworth, Lynehill, Whiteland, and Cleyfield. Other inclosed land lay in 'le Mores', above Deacons Mills, next to 'Gouldeborowe', and in separate fields *sub montem*, that is at the base of the slopes of the escarpment. There were also 6 a. of inclosed land in Elstub furlong, possibly an instance of inclosure already having been made in the common fields above the hill. The only tenant at will had recently erected a dwelling on the manorial waste. Roger Garrard held the manor farm on long lease; this comprised 198 a., 61 of which lay inclosed just below the hill. Sheep stint at Thornhill was 2 to the acre. It was the same in the open fields of Broad Town, while in the pasture grounds on the hillside it was 2 sheep to the yardland, or one per half-yardland. The custom of both Thornhill and Broad Town manors forbade the leasing of tenements for more than a year and a day without permission of the court leet. Customary lands were let for 1, 2, or 3 lives, according to the agreement made between tenant and lord. Heriots were the best beast for a yardland, 3s. 4d. for half a yardland, and 20d. for a quarter of a yardland or a cottage. Receipts from Thornhill amounted to £13 2s. 4d. in 1588, and included £5 3s. 3d. customary rents and £6 for the leasehold of the manor farm. Those from Broad Town totalled £10 13s. 9d., and included £6 15s. 10d. in customary rents and £3 9s. 2d. for leaseholds.

During the 16th and 17th centuries some of the principal landowners in the parish met with financial difficulties. The Quintins of Bupton, who were more highly assessed than many other local families to the subsidy of 1576,[85] had by 1617 been forced to part with all their lands.[86] It is not unlikely that their ruin played some part in the decay and depopulation of Bupton.[87] Moreover, evidence suggests that the financial difficulties of the Huntons of Bushton, most acute in the third and fourth decades of the 17th century, forced not only them, but also their neighbours, the Wroughtons, of Broad Hinton, who stood bondsmen for them, to sell off their lands.[88] Financial distress entailed the spoliation and decay of the family property at Bushton and Woodhill. The plight of William Hunton, which led eventually to a debtor's gaol, is described in his correspondence with his cousin Sir Edward Nicholas.[89] Timber was felled to pay debts in 1632,[90] and two years later it was proposed to sell a sheep-house and some additional timber on the hill above Bushton.[91] Throughout the years of indebtedness and legal wrangle the

Hunton estate declined through neglect and mismanagement.[92] The financial difficulties of the Goddards were less severe, although they occurred at the close of the 17th century. During the lifetime of Francis Goddard (d. 1724) the family's Berkshire estates were sold off and the Clyffe Pypard property mortgaged and continually re-mortgaged.[93] At least until the mid 1730s a receiver of rents, appointed by one of the mortgagees, had surveillance of the Clyffe Pypard estate.[94]

Clyffe Pypard manor was surveyed in 1684.[95] There were 6 leasehold and 7 copyhold tenants. The principal farm of the estate comprised 172 a., much of which lay in small strips in the furlongs of the open fields. It was held by John Pyke, whose family had been tenants since 1634. Other leaseholds were small. They included 24 a. of pasture called 'Rosyers' and a 5-acre coppice near Cleeve Wood. Four copyholders occupied yardlands, or parts of yardlands, and one held a watermill. Fines for the leaseholds ranged from £3 to £43 and for the copyholds from £2 to £100. In 1699 the annual value of the leaseholds was £443 and the copyholds £61 10s.[96]

Little information survives about the other estates in the 17th century. The size of Bupton Farm can be estimated from the fact that in 1601 a third share, owned by Thomas Goddard, amounted to 112 a.[97] The annual value of the whole estate was reckoned by its owner, Gabriel Pile, to be £200 in 1634.[98] At the end of the century trustees appointed to administer the Duchess of Somerset's Broad Town Charity were responsible for an estate of about 575 a., divided into 4 farms (Manor Farm, Broad Town Farm, Goldborough, and Ham Farms), ranging in size from 33 a. to 250 a.[99] Significant innovations took place in the management of this estate, the most notable being the ending of leases for lives. This was replaced by a lease of 21 years, and the farms let at rack-rents.[1]

No mention is made of inclosure on Clyffe Pypard manor before the beginning of the 17th century, but on the evidence of what had taken place on the manors of Thornhill and Broad Town (see above) the movement was probably already well under way. A lease of Warrens, on Clyffe Pypard manor, in 1603 included a close of pasture 'late divided and severed from part of the common ground of the manor'.[2] This inclosed pasture was to compensate for the loss of rights of common pasture for feeding 6 beasts. Another lease of 1634 included a parcel of meadow recently taken out of a pasture ground called Layfield.[3] The manor's open-field arable on the chalk uplands was in process of being inclosed as the century drew on: a late-17th-century particular mentions that Clyffe Farm included 12 a. of arable inclosed in Clyffe field.[4] In 1711 a tenant farmer surrendered to Francis Goddard 55 a. of common-field arable above the hill, and received £40 as compensation.[5] The taking

[85] *Taxation Lists* (W.A.S. Rec. Brch.), 90, 122.
[86] See p. 30.   [87] See p. 24.
[88] E 134/1657/Chas. II Trin. 12.
[89] *Cal. S.P. Dom.* 1619–38 contains relevant correspondence, *passim*.
[90] *Cal. S.P. Dom.* 1631–3, 283.
[91] Ibid. 1634–5, 41–42.
[92] E 134/1657/Chas. II Trin. 12.
[93] W.R.O. 110/1, contains mortgages of this period.
[94] W.R.O. 110/19, Legal documents.

[95] W.R.O. 110/11, Survey of Manor.
[96] Ibid. Mr. Forster's Acct. of Manor.
[97] W.R.O. 130/42, Deed Goddard to Pile.
[98] B.M. Add. Ch. 37571.
[99] *Endowed Char. Wilts.* H.C. 196-ii (1907), lxi.
[1] Ibid.   [2] W.R.O. 110/1, Deed Hore to Church.
[3] W.R.O. 110/12, Deed Goddard to Pyke.
[4] W.R.O. 110/11, Particular of Clyffe and Parsonage Farms.
[5] W.R.O. 110/13, Deed Hopkins to Goddard.

of land in hand appears to have been another step towards the inclosure of the chalk upland. It was a piecemeal operation which took time to complete, but in the 1730s and 1740s the process was well on the way. In 1733 Nonsuch Farm was leased for 7 years.[6] Nonsuch was a new farm created out of the lands owned by the Goddards above the hill, and presumably included the 55 a. surrendered to Francis Goddard twenty years before (see above). In 1742 the lands of this farm apparently lay in two compact blocks,[7] and the following year its new buildings had been completed and 500 chains of hedge set.[8]

As shown above, a considerable amount of land had been inclosed at Thornhill by 1588, and it must be presumed that the process continued steadily during the 17th century. In 1706, some twenty years after the manor had been given to Brasenose College, Oxford, the total of all inclosure was 616 a. while 113 a. still lay dispersed in the common fields of the manor.[9] There were three fields, situated on the chalk uplands, named the Little or East Field, the Middle Field, and the West Field. All three were divided into furlongs (5 in the Little or East Field, 7 in the Middle Field, and 10 in the West Field) and within the furlongs tenants had small scattered pieces, known as ridges, mostly ranging from ¼ a. to 1 a.[10] By an Inclosure Act of 1822 the open fields of Thornhill and Broad Town were inclosed.[11] These were divided into eight parcels. The trustees of the Broad Town Charity were allotted 104 a., Brasenose College 132 a., and Edward Goddard 30 a., 16 of which he received as tithe-owner, while the remainder he bought from the other allottees.

In 1702 the Goddard estate in Clyffe Pypard totalled 753 a., and included 13 properties between 2 a. and 195 a. in size.[12] Lands called the Farm and the Demesne together totalled 310 a. There were 21 a. of woodland. In the time of Edward Goddard (d. 1839) there were nearly 200 a. in hand, three-quarters being recently inclosed arable above the hill.[13] The remainder of his lands were let at rack-rents for £490, which together with revenue from other sources, gave him an income of £870 in 1799, not including the profits of his own farming.[14] Outgoings took over £540, including £293 in interest to sundry creditors. The Goddard farming venture suffered a setback in 1779 when buildings and ricks of corn were burned down at Nonsuch.[15] Farming, however, continued to be one of the principal interests and chief sources of income to the family until the death of Horatio Nelson Goddard in 1900. This member of the family farmed over 500 a. and also held the beneficial lease of the Brasenose estate at Thornhill.[16]

The Brasenose estate was made up of four farms:

Thornhill Manor Farm, and South, North, and East Farms. In 1734 the Manor Farm comprised 265 a. with 35 a. of arable above the hill; South Farm had 117 a. with 41 a. of arable above the hill; North Farm 112 a. with no arable above the hill; East Farm had 118 a. with 36 a. of arable above the hill.[17] East Farm was valued at some £117 in 1734, South Farm and North Farm at £110 and £90 respectively in 1736.[18] In c. 1752 Manor Farm was valued at some £152 with half of all its arable land lying above the hill.[19]

Dairy farming was established as the chief enterprise in the farming of the clay lowlands of the parish at least by the early 18th century. In 1734 at Rebbel Farm (145 a.) there was a herd of 20 cows and heifers producing 20 score of cheeses.[20] At Thornhill Farm (301 a.), in 1752, it was reckoned that 19 cows ought to produce 2 tons of cheese.[21] At Bushton Farm (298 a.), valued in 1781 at £235 a year, there was in 1795 a dairy of 37 cows and heifers, which by August of that year had produced 37 cwt. of cheese.[22] Both Rebbel and Bushton Farms carried flocks of sheep: at Rebbel there were 46 sheep and lambs, and at Bushton 187.[23] When Richard Stratton bought Woodhill Park in 1861, he used the traditional sheep grounds on the slopes of the escarpment for running the young stock of his pedigree Shorthorn herd, although he was scorned for this by the local farmers.[24] In 1966 at Woodhill and Bupton young stock and store cattle continued to graze the steeper slopes, but throughout the parish sheep numbers were few. Dairying was the mainstay of most farmers. The distinction between upland arable and lowland grazing was still apparent, although crops of corn and potatoes were to be seen among the lower pasturelands.

Since the 19th century most of the larger estates have been divided up or have lost some of their land. The Broad Town farms were sold off in 1920.[25] Bushton Farm, with one or two other small farms, was bought by the county council in 1913 and converted into small holdings.[26] Part of the Goddard estate was sold off in 1901 and in the 1940s Parsonage Farm and Wood Street Farm, belonging to the same estate, were sold. The three remaining farms, namely Home Farm, Rosyiers, and Nonsuch were in the 1960s all let to one tenant.[27] All the Brasenose College lands were likewise farmed by one tenant.[28] Some owner-occupied farms, namely Woodhill Park, Lower Bupton, and the former airfield were large, but for the most part the farms of Clyffe Pypard in the 1960s were small, specializing in dairy farming.

Two of the six estates mentioned above had mills at the time of the Domesday Survey:[29] those of Gilbert de Breteuil and William FitzAnsculf.[30]

[6] W.R.O. 110/14, Deed Goddard to Millington.
[7] Clyffe Pypard Manor, map of 1742, *penes* Mr. P. W. Wilson, Clyffe Pypard Manor.
[8] W.R.O. 110/11, Acct. of Robt. Weeks with Edw. Goddard.
[9] B.N.C. Oxford, Thornhill 16 and Map.
[10] Ibid.
[11] W.R.O. Inclosure Award.
[12] W.R.O. 110/11, Particular of Clyffe and Parsonage Farms.
[13] Ibid. Schedule of income of Edw. Goddard, 1799.
[14] Ibid.
[15] Ibid.
[16] W.R.O. Tithe Award.

[17] B.N.C. Oxford, Thornhill 30 and Map.   [18] Ibid.
[19] Ibid. Thornhill 31.
[20] W.R.O. 110/11, Inventory of Stock.
[21] B.N.C. Oxford, Thornhill 31.
[22] W.R.O. 212B/Cl. 105, Inventory.
[23] W.R.O. 110/11, Inventory of Stock and 212B/Cl. 105, Inventory.
[24] J. Stratton, *The Wilts. Strattons*, 63, 73.
[25] See p. 42.
[26] See p. 30.
[27] Ex inf. Mr. P. W. Wilson, Clyffe Pypard Manor.
[28] Local information.
[29] See p. 33.
[30] *V.C.H. Wilts.* ii, pp. 147, 167.

Each was worth 5s. Two other estates which may have been situated in Clyffe Pypard also had mills worth 5s. at that time.[31] On Sir Philip Basset's manor of Broad Town in 1271 a water mill was worth 13s. 4d.[32] In the 14th century there was a windmill at Woodhill, which by the middle of the 17th century had fallen into decay.[33] A water mill at Thornhill was held by Thomas atte Mulle in 1440, and the mill site was held by John Bundeysden, who paid £3 for it.[34] In 1586 Thornhill mill was held by Thomas Lane, who paid 4s.[35] A deed of 1616 mentions a water mill belonging to Francis Goddard's estate.[36] Later evidence reveals that this mill was situated at Broad Town, and may have been the property which Thomas Goddard held in 1586 as a freeholder of the manor of Broad Town.[37] In 1684 Spackman's 'liveing', a copyhold of Clyffe manor, included a water mill.[38] A copyhold, including a mill, called Watson's Mill, millhouse, and meadow, situated at Broad Town was conveyed in 1709 by Francis Goddard to Thomas Garlick of Thornhill for a peppercorn rent.[39] By 1734 this mill was known as Broad Town Mill and a lease of it that year included the toll and custom due for grinding corn in the tithing of Thornhill.[40] Some time in the 19th century the mill was converted into a brewery. In 1885 it was owned by Samuel Hart and was in the hands of his executors in 1903. It was closed soon after this.[41]

LOCAL GOVERNMENT. A few court rolls and papers survive for the manors of Thornhill, Broad Town, and Clyffe Pypard. For Thornhill there is a broken series of rolls of the view of frankpledge held there, apparently twice-yearly, between 1427 and 1452.[42] There is also a court roll of 1493 for the same manor in which certain tenants of Marston Farm, which formed part of the manor, are shown to be liable for annual contributions to the larder of the lord of the manor.[43] There are also a few 18th-century court rolls for this manor among the records of Brasenose College, Oxford.[44] For the manor of Broad Town there is a court book for 1587–1614, showing the court meeting once a year and concerning itself chiefly with the condition of roads and ditches on the manor.[45] So far as is known the earliest records to survive for the capital manor of Clyffe Pypard are a court book of 1727–1808 and some accompanying papers.[46] By this date the court was held at irregular intervals, often only once in two years. Presentments of minor agrarian offences

continued to be made and the ending of lives in copyhold tenancies were recorded.

The surviving parish records begin in the mid 17th century and contain a detailed picture of parish government from that date.[47] Their contents can only be summarized here. By the 17th century the large and widely scattered parish was divided for administrative purposes into the four tithings of Clyffe Pypard, Bushton with Bupton and Woodhill, Thornhill, and Broad Town.[48] Rates were levied on these four tithings separately. Responsibility for providing the parish's two churchwardens apparently fell in the earlier 18th century upon certain farms. In 1720, for example, one churchwarden was said to be elected for Bushton Farm, the other for Broad Town Farm.[49] Only after the middle of the 18th century was one churchwarden said to be elected for the vicar and the other for the parish.[50] A considerable number of churchwardens' accounts survive, beginning in the mid 17th century.[51] The office of overseer of the poor seems likewise in the earlier 18th century to have been attached to certain farms in the parish. In 1720 one overseer was elected for Thornhill Farm, the other for Broad Town Farm.[52] In 1825 a salaried general overseer was appointed for seven years at the annual wage of £21 to be paid from the parish poor rates together with £2 from each of the two unpaid overseers.[53] Two years later the contributions from the overseers were discontinued and the salaried overseer's wage raised to £27, all to come from the poor rates.[54] A number of overseers' accounts survive, showing the same poor families to have continued year after year in the direst need of assistance.[55]

There was evidently a church house in which the poor were housed in the earlier 17th century.[56] In 1662 this was in a ruinous condition and in 1673 the overseers received £5 towards building a new one.[57] In 1699 over £18 was spent on building a church house and in 1709 the remainder of the 'Church House money' was used to erect three more dwellings for the poor.[58]

Waymen were appointed at least as early as 1666. Four were appointed that year for the tithings mentioned above.[59] They were nominated by the churchwardens and elected by the vestry and after 1718 were given the title of supervisor of the highways.[60] In the course of the 19th century many of the tracks and lanes connecting the scattered farmsteads, and previously maintained by the farmers concerned, were transferred to the care of the supervisors.[61] A supervising waywarden for the

---

[31] Ibid. pp. 142, 167.
[32] *Wilts. Inq. p.m.* 1242–1326 (Index Libr.), 65.
[33] E 134/1657/Chas. II Trin. 12.
[34] W.R.O. 192/16, Ct. R. 1427–52.
[35] W.R.O. 192/51, Survey Bk.
[36] W.R.O. 212B/Cl. 17, Deed Hungerford to Goddard.
[37] Cf. W.R.O. 192/51, Survey Bk.
[38] W.R.O. 110/11, Survey of Manor.
[39] W.R.O. 110/3, Titles to Manor.
[40] B.N.C. Oxford, Thornhill 35.
[41] Cf. O.S. Map 1″, Sheet 34 (1928 edn.), and O.S. Map 6″, Wilts. XXI, XXII (1888 edn.); *Kelly's Dir. Wilts.* (1885, 1903).
[42] W.R.O. 192/16.
[43] W.R.O. 192/17.
[44] B.N.C. Oxford, Thornhill 18.
[45] W.R.O. 192/2.
[46] W.R.O. 110/11.

[47] Deposited in W.R.O.
[48] W.R.O. 895, Poor Bk. 1648–1820.
[49] Ibid.
[50] Ibid.
[51] The earliest are included in Poor Bk. 1648–1820. There is also a separate series 1780–1886.
[52] W.R.O. 895, Poor Bk. 1648–1820.
[53] Ibid. Vestry Min. Bk. 1820–72.
[54] Ibid.
[55] The earliest are in Poor Bk. 1648–1820. There is also a separate series 1718–40 and some for the earlier 19th century.
[56] W.A.S. Libr., Devizes, 'Goddard Papers', f. 26.
[57] Sar. Dioc. R.O. Chwdns'. Pres.; W.A.S. Libr., Devizes, 'Goddard Papers', f. 26.
[58] W.A.S. Libr., Devizes, 'Goddard Papers', f. 90.
[59] W.R.O. 895, Poor Bk. 1648–1820.
[60] Ibid.
[61] Ibid. Vestry Min. Bk. 1820–72.

whole parish was appointed in 1866.[62] In 1842 eight parish constables were appointed.[63]

The first minutes of vestry meetings begin in 1820.[64] At this date the vestry met in the belfry of the parish church and seems to have comprised the more substantial ratepayers. Throughout the earlier 19th century, besides meeting to elect the parish officers, the vestry was much concerned with the state of employment and the level of agricultural wages. Attempts were made to deal with unemployment among the agricultural labourers by a system of billeting subsidized from the poor rates. In the summer of 1821 the vestry fixed the wage of mowers at 10s. a week, that of other labourers at 8s. and those of women at 3s. In 1827 the ordinary labourers' wages were fixed by the vestry at 7s. weekly. At the same time the billeting system was ended and the vestry decided that farmers should employ a certain number of men allotted to them. In 1842 a fund was raised to assist parishioners wishing to emigrate and the vestry appointed a committee to manage it. A salaried vestry clerk was appointed in 1846.

After the creation of the consolidated chapelry of Christ Church, Broad Town, in 1844 Clyffe Pypard and Broad Town were divided into five tithings, namely Clyffe Pypard, Bushton, Thornhill (St. Peter's district), Thornhill (Christ Church district), and Broad Town (Christ Church district).[65] These last two tithings were formed into the civil parish of Broad Town in 1884 and after 1893 Clyffe Pypard and Broad Town were governed by separate parish councils.[66]

CHURCHES. The church of Clyffe Pypard is first mentioned in 1273 in terms which imply that it was then well established.[67] In 1400 Lacock Abbey was granted licence to appropriate it,[68] since when the living has been a vicarage. As will be shown below, there was probably a chapel at Woodhill in 1340 and another at an unknown date at Bushton. Apart from these two chapels, which were clearly very small and about which very little is known, the large and scattered parish was served by a single church until 1846 when the consolidated chapelry of Broad Town was created and Christ Church, Broad Town, was built. In 1954 the benefices of Clyffe Pypard and Tockenham were joined to be held in plurality.[69]

The advowson of the rectory seems to have belonged to the lords of the capital manor by 1273, for in that year Matthew Columbers and his wife Maud successfully defended their right to the next presentation against Robert Pipard, their immediate overlord.[70] It is not known when a vicarage was ordained

but vicars were presented by the rectors in 1304, 1328, and 1334[71] and it seems likely that the vicarage was always presentative. In 1333 Thomas Cobham, who had a grant of the manor from his father, presented John de Hoby as rector but the next year the king presented to the vicarage and Hoby did not present as rector until 1342.[72] In the mean time, in 1340, the advowson had been disputed between Thomas Cobham and his elder brother John.[73] Thomas, however, retained it and in 1342 pledged it to William of Derby as security for a debt of £100.[74] In 1343 Thomas again presented a rector,[75] but in 1381 the advowson of the rectory seems to have been leased out, for in 1381 William Wroughton, who in that year acquired the manor of Woodhill,[76] presented twice.[77] After John, Lord Cobham's impeachment in 1397, the advowson was not restored to the Cobhams but shortly afterwards passed to John of Maidenhead, Canon of Salisbury and later Dean of Chichester, who in 1399 granted the reversion of it after his death to Lacock Abbey.[78] Licence for Lacock to appropriate the church was granted in 1399 and received papal confirmation in 1400.[79] Thereupon the presentation of rectors ceased and the abbesses of Lacock presented to the vicarage.[80]

From 1421 until the Dissolution vicars were presented by the Abbess of Lacock except in 1435 when John Herring presented.[81] After the dissolution of Lacock the advowson was acquired in 1540 by John Goddard who had purchased the manor of Clyffe Pypard in 1530.[82] In 1541 John was licensed to grant the advowson to his eldest son Thomas.[83] The first presentation to the vicarage by the Goddards, however, does not appear to have been before 1660.[84] In 1544 Thomas Tymmes, a kinsman of the last Abbess of Lacock, presented; in 1562 Thomas Halknight, notary public; in 1582 the queen; in 1614 Richard Hunton of Bushton; in 1620 the king.[85] In 1660 Edward Goddard, lord of the manor, presented[86] and from this date the advowson followed the same descent as the manor of Clyffe Pypard.

The rectory was granted with the advowson in 1540 to John Goddard (d. 1542), and like the advowson was conveyed by John to his son Thomas.[87] Thomas then apparently leased it to his younger brother Anthony, who lived at Clyffe Pypard and died in 1606.[88] Anthony's widow married secondly Launcelot Humber, who claimed the rectory in her right and continued to do so after her death.[89] This led to a long legal tussle in which Humber was eventually defeated and in 1648 the rectory was restored to Francis Goddard (d. 1652), lord of the manor.[90] Thenceforth the rectory

[62] Ibid.
[63] Ibid.
[64] Ibid. All subsequent information in this paragraph comes from this source.
[65] W.A.M. xliv. 152-3.
[66] W.R.O. 895, MSS. notes.
[67] Genealogist, xxi. 25.
[68] See below.
[69] Ex inf. the vicar.
[70] Genealogist, xxi. 25.
[71] Phillipps, Wilts. Inst. i. 5, 24, 25.
[72] Ibid. 28, 29, 38.
[73] B.M. Harl. R. c. 27.
[74] Cal. Close, 1341-3, 530.
[75] Phillipps, Wilts. Inst. i. 38.
[76] See p. 32.

[77] Phillipps, Wilts. Inst. i. 65.
[78] V.C.H. Wilts. iii. 306.
[79] Cal. Papal Reg. 1396-1404, 327-8; Cal. Pat. 1396-9, 447.
[80] Phillipps, Wilts. Inst. i. 65.
[81] Ibid. 126.
[82] L. & P. Hen. VIII, xv, p. 296, and see above p. 28.
[83] L. & P. Hen. VIII, xvi, p. 277.
[84] Phillipps, Wilts. Inst. ii. 23.
[85] Ibid. i. 211, 221, 231; ii. 11.
[86] Ibid. ii. 23.
[87] L. & P. Hen. VIII, xv, p. 296; ibid. xvi, p. 277.
[88] MS. Pedigree of Goddard Family compiled c. 1965 by Capt. John Goddard.
[89] W.R.O. 212B/Cl. 21.
[90] Ibid.; C.P. 25(2)/512/24 Chas. I Mich.

descended with the manor, although in the later 17th and in the 18th centuries it was frequently leased out.[91]

The church was valued for taxation in 1291 and 1341 at £10.[92] In 1291 the Prioress of Amesbury had a portion of £2 from the church.[93] This portion is not heard of again, but from the end of the 12th century Amesbury had the tithes of Woodhill (see below). When the rectory was appropriated to Lacock in 1399 its revenues were assigned to the clothing of the nuns. An annual payment of 6s. 8d. was also to be made to the poor and pensions were assigned to the Bishop of Salisbury, the cathedral chapter, and the Archdeacon of Wiltshire.[94] In 1535 the rectory was let for £10, the sum at which it was valued in 1291 and 1341 (see above). Expenditure on clothing for the nuns was £8 and the pensions were still being paid to the bishop, chapter, and archdeacon.[95]

The great tithes due from various parts of the parish were from time to time assigned to certain religious houses. Those at Thornhill were confirmed to the Prior of Monkton Farleigh by Henry I some time between 1129 and 1133.[96] The tithes of Woodhill were granted to Amesbury Priory in c. 1199 and an annual standing charge of 5s. upon them probably maintained a chantry chapel at Woodhill in the 13th and 14th centuries (see below). At an unknown date the tithes of Broad Town were assigned for the maintenance of a chantry in Wallingford (Berks.).[97] It is possible that the tithes of Bushton were appropriated by St. Swithun's Priory, Winchester. The rectors, therefore, received tithe from only a fairly small area of the parish. In 1341 a ninth of the corn, wool, and lambs due to the church was reckoned at £7 13s. a year and the tithe of hay at 17s. 4d.[98]

After the Dissolution, as a result of these early grants, the great tithes continued to be dispersed among a number of owners besides the Goddards, the lay rectors. The stages by which they eventually came into the hands of the Goddards have not been fully traced. Amesbury's tithes at Woodhill passed in 1544 to John Barwicke and in 1562 to John Ayliffe.[99] These were still held by the Ayliffe family in 1718–19.[1] In 1596 a third of the tithes of Broad Town was settled on Susan, daughter of Edward Garrard of Trowbridge, on her marriage with John Hodnett of Devizes.[2] In 1688 another third was purchased by John Atkyns of Sutton Benger from John Carpenter of Clyffe Pypard and two years later Atkyns sold his tithes to William Grinfield of Marlborough.[3] These were acquired by Edward Goddard in 1772.[4] Before 1724, however, the

Goddards, as lay rectors, had acquired the great tithes from Bushton, Woodhill, and Bupton, worth £81 13s. 6d. a year, and from Broad Town, Thornhill, and Clyffe Pypard, worth £28 1s. annually.[5] In 1844, when the tithe award was made, the only impropriator of tithe besides the lay rector, Horatio Nelson Goddard, was the Earl of Clarendon. He was awarded a rent charge of 18s. for the tithes of 17 a. in Cleeve Wood and Goddard a rent charge of £435 for all other rectorial tithes.[6] In 1901 the rent charge was acquired from H. N. Goddard by Thomas Arkell for £5,250.[7]

In 1341 the church had a messuage and a virgate of land worth 6s. 8d.[8] By the late 16th century the rectory estate, known as Parsonage Farm, which lay in the north of the parish, was being farmed with the rest of the Goddard lands. It then included 27 a. of meadow, 52 a. of pasture, and 22 a. of woodland.[9] Another survey, possibly of a little later date, gives the size of the Parsonage Farm as 200 a.[10] The farm was sold by the Goddards in the 1940s.[11]

No evidence has been found of the provisions made to support a vicar after Lacock appropriated the church in 1399. But these had presumably been made at a much earlier date since vicars were serving the church at least as early as 1304. In 1341 they were entitled to certain small tithes (see below). In 1535 the vicar reckoned the value of his vicarage to be £8 14s. 4d.[12] In 1831 the average net income of the benefice over the past three years was £279.[13]

The small tithes due to the vicar in 1341 were worth 3s. a year.[14] In 1671, besides the usual vicarial tithes, the incumbent also received the tithe of hay from certain land in the eastern and northern parts of the parish.[15] He was still entitled to this in 1783.[16] In 1799 the vicarial tithes were estimated at £174 18s.[17] In 1844 these, together with the tithe of hay mentioned above, were commuted for a rent charge of £590.[18]

Very little land was attached to the vicarage. When John of Maidenhead gave the advowson to Lacock in 1399 he included ⅓ a. of land in Clyffe Pypard.[19] This may have provided additional land for the site of the vicarage, for attached to it in 1671 were a little court, gardens, and orchard, measuring ½ a. in all.[20] After Edward Goddard, lay rector and lord of the manor, presented himself to the living in the later 18th century, the vicarage house was not required as a residence for many years (see below) and fell into disrepair. In c. 1839 the house, which stood immediately south of the church, was pulled down and another one built on an adjoining site by George Ashe Goddard (vicar 1839–63). A few cottages were removed to make way for its garden

[91] See p. 28.
[92] Tax. Eccl. (Rec. Com.), 189; Inq. Non. (Rec. Com.), 161.
[93] Tax. Eccl. (Rec. Com.), 189.
[94] Cal. Papal Reg. v. 327–8.
[95] Valor Eccl. (Rec. Com.), ii. 116, 118.
[96] Johnson and Cronne, Regesta Regum Anglo-Normannorum, ii. 382.
[97] C 66/1288 m. 16.
[98] Inq. Non. (Rec. Com.), 161.
[99] L. & P. Hen. VIII, xix (1), p. 382; Cal. Pat. 1560–3, 239–40.
[1] C.P. 25(2)/1078/5 Geo. I Hil.
[2] W.R.O. 110/1, Deed Hodnett to Garrard.
[3] Ibid. Deeds Carpenter to Atkyns and Atkyns to Grinfield.
[4] W.R.O. 110/5, Deed Grinfield to Goddard.

[5] W.R.O. 110/11, An old valuation of the manor.
[6] W.R.O. Tithe Award.
[7] W.A.S. Libr., Devizes, 'Goddard Papers', f. 77.
[8] Inq. Non. (Rec. Com.), 161.
[9] W.R.O. 110/11, An old valuation of the manor.
[10] Ibid. Particular of Clyffe Farm and Parsonage.
[11] Ex inf. Mr. P. W. Wilson, Clyffe Pypard Manor.
[12] Valor Eccl. (Rec. Com.), ii. 830.
[13] Rep. Com. Eccl. Revenues, H.C. 54, p. 830 (1835), xxii.
[14] Inq. Non. (Rec. Com.), 161.
[15] Sar. Dioc. R.O. Glebe Terrier, 1671.
[16] Ibid. 1704, 1783.
[17] W.R.O. 110/11, Schedule of income of Edw. Goddard.
[18] W.R.O. Tithe Award.
[19] Cal. Papal Reg. v. 328.
[20] Sar. Dioc. R.O. Glebe Terrier, 1671.

and stable yard.[21] In *c.* 1956 part of the vicarage was pulled down to make a smaller more convenient house.[22]

Of the early rectors and vicars connected with Clyffe Pypard church, John Campden, rector in 1381, played some part with William of Wykeham in the founding of his colleges at Winchester and Oxford.[23] Nicholas Kempston (vicar 1439–41) was an Oxford scholar, who at one time rented a 'schola astronomie' in the city, and was the owner of books and manuscripts, some of which he bequeathed to Eton College.[24] In the 17th century there were a number of incumbents with unorthodox views. Philip Hunton, later ejected from Westbury, served Clyffe Pypard for a time.[25] Daniel Reyner, Fellow of New College, Oxford, was vicar from 1657 until ejected in 1659.[26] He was followed by another dissenter, Henry Blake, vicar in 1662.[27]

In 1745 Edward Goddard, as rector, presented to the living, but it is alleged that he was so dissatisfied with the incumbent's performance, that he took holy orders and in 1780 presented himself to the benefice.[28] There followed a period of more than 150 years during which the cure was held by members of the Goddard family. Edward Goddard was succeeded in 1791 by his son Edward, who was also curate of Winterbourne Bassett, and likewise presented himself to Clyffe Pypard. George Ashe Goddard, a younger son, was the next vicar. He was followed by Charles Bradford, son of his sister, Annica. The last member of the family to serve the cure was Edward Hungerford Goddard (vicar 1883–1935).[29]

On Census Sunday in 1851 it was estimated that 110 attended church.[30] In 1864 there were morning and evening services on Sundays. Services were also held on two weekdays when from 10 to 15 people attended. Holy Communion was celebrated about every sixth or eighth Sunday. The average number of communicants was about 30.[31] In 1932 average attendance at morning service was said to be 32, and at evening service 28. The average number of communicants at the early morning service was 7, and at 11 o'clock, 5.[32]

The church of *ST. PETER* stands in a sheltered position at the foot of the steep thickly-wooded slope of the escarpment. It was much restored in the 19th century but before then most of the fabric dated from the late 15th century. The tower is embattled with a stair-turret rising above the battlements. The lofty nave has a waggon roof with arch-braced tie beams and the piers of the five-bay arcade are octagonal. Both piers and arches were once painted

to represent marble, but the marbling on the piers was painted over during the 19th-century restorations.[33] Until the time of Edward Goddard (vicar 1791–1839) there was a rood loft approached by a stair in the north jamb of the chancel arch.[34] The north and south upper doorways to the loft remain and the two openings are occupied by kneeling figures, made of hard chalk, sometimes said to be taken from one of the Goddard tombs in the church.[35]

The late-15th-century chancel screen is extended so that the eastern ends of both the north and south aisles are enclosed. At this end of the south aisle there are several memorials to the Broomes of Bushton and Woodhill.[36] A few fragments of 15th-century glass have survived and in the later 19th century some pieces of foreign glass, probably Flemish, were given by J. E. Nightingale and inserted in the windows of the north aisle.[37] The pulpit is dated 1629 and has a sounding board and an attached pierced-iron book-rest. The font, a copy of one at Over (Cambs.), was carved in 1840 by Canon Francis Goddard.[38] In a tomb recess in the wall of the north aisle is a stone effigy of the later 14th century, possibly of a member of the Cobham family.[39] In the north aisle, behind the organ, a brass of about the same date may be to a member of the Quintin family.[40] At the west end of the south aisle there is an outstanding memorial by John Deval, the younger, to Thomas Spackman (d. 1786), a native and benefactor of the parish.[41] The display of tools on the monument commemorates Spackman's trade as a carpenter.

The chancel, reported to be in need of repair in 1662,[42] was rebuilt in 1860 in a largely Early English style and at a cost to the rector, H. N. Goddard, of nearly £700.[43] In 1874 the rest of the church was restored by William Butterfield.[44] The railings enclosing the churchyard on the west were erected in memory of Lola Pevsner (d. 1963).

In 1553 there were 3 bells. These were subsequently replaced by a peal of 6, the oldest being cast in 1604. The bells were repaired in 1880.[45] Edward VI's commissioners took $3\frac{1}{2}$ oz. silver for the king, leaving a chalice of 14 oz.[46] In 1966 the plate included a chalice and paten, dated 1682, and given by William Stamp (vicar 1662–83), and a paten cover, dated 1576.[47] The registers begin in 1576 and are complete.[48]

In 1341 the annual standing charge of 5s. upon the tithes of Woodhill was said to be applied by the Prioress of Amesbury to the maintenance of a chantry there,[49] and it seems likely that there was a

[21] *W.A.M.* xliv. 153.
[22] Ex inf. Mr. P. W. Wilson, Clyffe Pypard Manor.
[23] Emden, *Biog. Reg. Oxon.* i. 343.
[24] Ibid. ii, p. 1034.
[25] *Calamy Revised*, ed. A. G. Matthews, 285–6; *V.C.H. Wilts.* viii. 177.
[26] *Calamy Revised*, ed. A. G. Matthews, 407–8.
[27] Ibid. 60.
[28] *W.A.M.* xliv. 155.
[29] List of vicars in ch.
[30] H.O. 129/251/1/1/1.
[31] Sar. Dioc. R.O. Vis. Queries, 1864.
[32] W.R.O. 895, MS. Statistics.
[33] *W.A.M.* xliv. 166.
[34] One explanation for its removal is given in 'Goddard Papers', f. 33, where it is related that Edw. Goddard did not wish his children, who used the rood loft as a family pew, to see him reading lithographed sermons when in the pulpit.

[35] *W.A.M.* xxxvii. 424, 427.
[36] See pp. 29, 32.
[37] W.A.S. Libr., Devizes, 'Goddard Papers', f. 101; *W.A.M.* xxvii. 179.
[38] *W.A.M.* xxxvii. 425; Pevsner, *Wilts.* (Bldgs. of Eng.), 163.
[39] W.A.S. Libr., Devizes, 'Goddard Papers', f. 89.
[40] Formerly in S. aisle; E. Kite, *Wilts. Brasses*, 19–20 and pl. II.
[41] R. Gunnis, *Dict. Brit. Sculptors, 1660–1851*, 129 and see p. 43, and pl. facing p. 29.
[42] Sar Dioc. R.O. Chwdns'. Pres. 1662.
[43] *W.A.M.* xliv. 166.
[44] Ibid. xxxvii. 422.
[45] Walters, *Wilts. Bells*, 59.
[46] Nightingale, *Wilts. Plate*, 140.
[47] Local inf.
[48] All early regs. in W.R.O.
[49] *Inq. Non.* (Rec. Com.), 162.

chapel at Woodhill between 1268 and 1361, when references to the charge occur.[50] A ninth of the great tithes of Woodhill were reckoned to be worth 14*s.* in 1341 and of the small tithes 11*s.*[51] A lease of 1533 mentions a former chapel at Bushton and lists a number of goods belonging to it.[52] These included a pair of vestments, a missal, a chalice with silver ornamentation, and 2 stoles. Nothing more is known of the chapel.

In 1846 the consolidated chapelry of Broad Town was formed out of parts of Clyffe Pypard and the neighbouring parish of Broad Hinton.[53] Its creation arose from the need to serve more adequately the inhabitants of the hamlet of Broad Town, most of whom lived more than a mile from any church. The desire to check the strong growth of nonconformity there was undoubtedly another reason.[54] The first curate was presented by the Bishop of Salisbury in 1846. Thereafter the vicars of Broad Hinton and Clyffe Pypard presented alternately.[55] The perpetual curate, whose living in 1864 was worth £124, received £30 from the benefice of Clyffe Pypard and £10 from that of Broad Hinton; the remainder was provided by the Ecclesiastical Commissioners and the Bounty Board.[56] A vicarage house was built in *c.* 1860.[57] Since 1951 the benefice has been combined with that of Wootton Bassett.[58]

CHRIST CHURCH, Broad Town, was built in 1846 to the design of W. Hinton Campbell, on a site provided by H. N. Goddard. Much of the cost was met by the Marchioness of Ailesbury, who also provided the church near Tottenham House (Savernake).[59] It is in an Early English style. It has one bell in a western bellcote. Besides a 19th-century chalice, there is a paten, dated 1782.[60]

NONCONFORMITY. In 1674 Frances, wife of John Church, was presented as a papist.[61] She may have been the recusant in the parish returned in Bishop Compton's census of 1676.[62] In 1782 a house, probably that belonging to Abel Greenaway, was licensed for Baptist teaching.[63] In the earlier 19th century 3 houses at Clyffe and 3 at Bushton were licensed as dissenters' meeting places.[64]

It was at Broad Town that nonconformity was most active during the 19th century, owing in large measure, no doubt, to the distance at which the hamlet lay from the parish church.[65] The strength of nonconformity there was indeed the main reason given for the creation of the new ecclesiastical district of Broad Town in 1844. A society of Primitive Methodists was formed in the hamlet as part of the Brinkworth Mission in 1824 and a chapel built in 1827.[66] By 1835 the Broad Town society had 78 members and more than 100 children attended the Sunday school, at which 39 teachers taught.[67] In 1840–1, as the result of renewed missionary activity, it was claimed that 'the greatest drunkards and Sabbath breakers were brought in' and 40 members were added to the society.[68] By this date the original chapel building was inadequate and a new chapel was built in 1842.[69] Twenty years later the incumbent of Broad Town regarded the obstacle which Primitive Methodism presented to his cure as insurmountable, and complained that the 'systematic combination' of dissenters against him had arisen from their 'long possession of the district'. He reckoned that there were some 400 nonconformists in the area, and that, among his own congregation, half attended both chapel and church.[70] A third chapel was built towards the northern end of the street in 1866 and the second (1842) chapel, which stood nearly opposite, was thenceforth used as a Sunday school.[71] In the first years of the 20th century both buildings were renovated.[72] By 1953 the chapel of 1866 was closed and in 1968 stood derelict beside its overgrown graveyard.[73] The chapel of 1842 was in 1968 in use as a garage.

By the middle of the 19th century Primitive Methodism had spread to Thornhill, although nothing is known of its progress there.[74] From Thornhill its influence spread to Bushton, where the first meetings were held in some cottages along the road called the Barton, and a society was formed in 1843.[75] In 1856–7 a cottage was bought and converted into a chapel. A new red brick chapel was built at the north end of the hamlet in 1874 and was enlarged in 1894[76]. This was still being used in 1968.

In 1784 the Vicar of Clyffe Pypard reported that Wesleyan Methodists were active in the area and named 7 of their leaders.[77] A Wesleyan Methodist chapel was built at Broad Town in 1868.[78] It was closed in *c.* 1938 and has subsequently been converted into a dwelling house.[79]

EDUCATION. Probably as a result of the scattered nature of settlement in the parish a number of small schools flourished there at various times in the earlier 19th century. Besides the free school (see below) there was a 'petty school' in Clyffe Pypard in 1808.[80] In 1819 some 50 children attended a Sunday school supported by the vicar, while an unspecified number attended two Sunday schools in the parish supported by Primitive Methodists.[81] Another school, at which

---

[50] *Wilts. Inq. p.m.* 1242–1326 (Index Libr.), 51; *Cal. Inq. p.m.* iv. 152; ibid. xi. 17.
[51] *Inq. Non.* (Rec. Com.), 162.
[52] *W.A.M.* xliv. 149.
[53] *Lond. Gaz.* July–Nov. 1846 (pp. 2669–70).
[54] W.A.S. Libr., Devizes, 'Goddard Papers', f. 65.
[55] *Crockford* (1896).
[56] Sar. Dioc. R.O. Vis. Queries, 1864.
[57] *W.A.M.* xliv. 144.
[58] A. R. J. Horn, *Guide to Wootton Bassett Ch.* (1960), 23, and see below, p. 202.
[59] Pevsner, *Wilts.* (Bldgs. of Eng.) 133 and *W.A.M.* xliv. 143.
[60] Nightingale, *Wilts. Plate*, 138.
[61] Sar. Dioc. R.O. Chwdns.' Pres. 1674.
[62] *W.N. & Q.* iii. 536.
[63] *V.C.H. Wilts.* iii. 137; Sar. Dioc. R.O. Vis. Queries, 1784.
[64] W.R.O. Retn. of Regns.

[65] A similar state of affairs existed at Goatacre in the parish of Hilmarton, see p. 64.
[66] W. C. Tonks, *Victory in the Villages*, 76.
[67] *V.C.H. Wilts.* iii. 146.
[68] Tonks, op. cit. 73–4.
[69] Ibid. 125–7.
[70] Sar. Dioc. R.O. Vis. Queries, 1864.
[71] Tonks, *Victory in the Villages*, 125–7.
[72] Ibid.
[73] G.R.O. 18028.
[74] Tonks, *Victory in the Villages*, 162–3.
[75] Ibid.   [76] Ibid.
[77] Sar. Dioc. R.O. Vis. Queries, 1784.
[78] Inscription on building.
[79] Local information.
[80] Lambeth MS. 1732, Retn. of Schools in Dioc. of Salisbury.
[81] *Digest of Returns to Cttee. of Educ. of Poor*, H.C. 224, p. 1023 (1819), ix (2).

25 children were educated at their parents' expense, was begun in 1825.[82] In 1859 a small dame school, where 10 children were 'kept out of mischief', was held at Bushton.[83]

The first successful attempt to provide adequate education for the poor children of the parish was made by Thomas Spackman, who, by his will dated 1782, endowed a free school. This was to be held in a house he had provided for the purpose at Thornhill. The endowment amounted to £30 yearly, which was used principally to support a master, who was employed to teach reading, writing, and arithmetic to poor children.[84] In 1819 between 60 and 70 children attended.[85] This number had decreased to some 40 to 50 pupils in 1859.[86] After elementary schools had been built at Broad Town and Clyffe Pypard (see below), it was felt that the house at Thornhill was no longer needed and it was sold in 1875.[87] The funds of the charity (known from 1904 as Spackman's Educational Foundation), were, after 1873, administered by a newly-constituted board of 8 governors. The fund, which had an income of £26 in 1905, was thenceforth distributed as money prizes to pupils at the Clyffe Pypard and Broad Town schools. Money from the fund was also used to maintain lending libraries in the schools and, occasionally, to buy scientific equipment.[88]

In 1850 a schoolroom, with a teacher's house attached, was built by the Vicar of Clyffe Pypard, and was aided by grants from the National Society and the Diocesan Board. There were 60 pupils taught by a mistress in 1859 and children from most nonconformist families were reported to attend.[89] In 1906 average attendance was 47,[90] and in 1938 there were 51 pupils.[91] In 1968 there were 40 children in the Clyffe Pypard Primary School.[92]

By 1819 a school, probably begun by the Primitive Methodists active in Broad Town, had some 20 pupils.[93] The school seems to have been closed by 1858, when the only means of education open to children in Broad Town was a dame school of 'very bad character', where 20 children were taught. The following year a new school was built on land given by the trustees of the Broad Town Charity.[94] About 81 children attended in 1908, and in 1938 the number was 89.[95] Broad Town Primary school had 69 children in 1968.[96]

CHARITIES. Among the numerous benefactions of Sarah, Duchess of Somerset (d. 1692), was that later known as the Broad Town Trust. By her will, proved in 1704, the duchess devised to trustees her manor of Broad Town to provide funds for apprenticing boys, born in Wiltshire and, at the time of their application to the charity, resident there.[97] She also stipulated that part of the rent of Broad Town Farm should be used each year to apprentice 8 boys born

on her Wiltshire manors of Broad Town, Thornhill, Froxfield, Wootton Rivers, and Huish. Another estate at Cotmarsh (in Broad Hinton), was devised to enable a further 4 boys from the same manors to be apprenticed.

The sole surviving original trustee of this charity, Sir Samuel Grimston (d. 1700), died without having made any disposition of the trust lands. Subsequently, in 1711, the number of trustees was fixed at 17, with a proviso that once numbers had fallen to 9, the surviving trustees were to elect others. Trustees were generally notable Wiltshire landowners, and in 1903 included the Marquess of Lansdowne and the Earl of Cardigan.

In 1834 the charity lands comprised Manor Farm, Broad Town Farm, Ham, and Goldborough Farms (all in the tithing of Broad Town), which totalled some 577 a. and were worth £597 yearly. The Broad Town and Cotmarsh lands had become intermixed by this date. The charity was then reported to be applied in strict conformity with the duchess's will, except that if insufficient boys from the manors mentioned above (who came to be known as 'manor boys') came forward, the deficiency was supplied from the county at large. The steward of the trustees reported that he frequently had to prevent encroachments upon the manors by parents, who hoped thereby to make their sons eligible for apprenticeships. Manor boys generally chose their own masters subject to the approval of the steward of the trustees. In 1811 the apprenticeship premium was raised from £10 to £15 for both manor and county boys, who must be at least 13 and not more than 17 years of age. During 1714–1833 582 manor boys and 1,717 county boys were apprenticed.

In 1849 it was reaffirmed that preference in the allotment of apprenticeships was to be given to not more than 12 manor boys, who were henceforth to receive a premium of £20 each. The remaining funds were to be used to apprentice county boys at the same premium. In 1906–7 one manor boy and 5 county boys were apprenticed and it was observed that this ratio was indicative of the tendency for the number of applications from manor boys to decrease. The apprenticeship system was then said to work satisfactorily and the trades most frequently chosen by the boys were those of engineer, builder, carpenter, and printer. At this date the acreage of the charity lands was 547 a. and the total gross income of the charity amounted to £644.

In 1920 the charity lands were sold and over £20,000 invested. The apprenticeship premiums payable were, from 1920 onwards, increased at the discretion of the Charity Commissioners. In 1923 the Commissioners approved a special arrangement whereby 20 apprenticeship premiums of not more than £100 were to be payable over a period of 5 years. The charity was further regulated by a scheme

[82] Educ. Enq. Abstract, H.C. 62, p. 103 (1835), xliii.
[83] Acct. of Wilts. Schools, H.C. 27, p. 80 (1859 Sess. 1), xxi (2).
[84] Endowed Char. Wilts. (1908), p. 282.
[85] Returns to Cttee. on Educ. of Poor (1819), p. 1023.
[86] Acct. of Wilts. Schools, H.C. 27, p. 80 (1859 Sess. 1), xxi (2).
[87] Endowed Char. Wilts. (1908), p. 284.
[88] Ibid. pp. 284–7.
[89] Acct. of Wilts. Schools, H.C. 27, p. 80 (1859 Sess. 1), xxi (2).
[90] Return of Non-Provided Schools, H.C. 178–xxxi, p. 827 (1906), lxxxviii.
[91] Bd. of Educ. List 21, 1938.
[92] Ex inf. the Head mistress, Broad Town Primary School.
[93] Returns to Cttee. on Educ. of Poor (1819), p. 1023.
[94] Acct. of Wilts. Schools, H.C. 27, p. 27 (1859 Sess. 1), xxi (2); W.A.M. xliv. 144.
[95] Bd. of Educ. List 21, 1907, 1908, 1938.
[96] Ex inf. the Head mistress, Broad Town Primary School.
[97] For an acct. of the Broad Town Charity, see Endowed Char. Wilts. H.C. 196–ii (1907), lxi; an acct. is also given in James Bradford, Particulars of Broad Town Char. Trust (1808), (copy in W.A.S. Libr., Devizes). For the duchess's portrait, see pl. facing p. 28.

of 1947, which extended charity funds to assist boys under 21 years, who had lived in Wiltshire for at least 5 years, to buy outfits or tools or to meet travelling expenses.[98] In the 1960s the bulk of the charity funds, which at this time amounted to over £2,000 yearly, were applied to enable boys, most of whom were then drawn from the county at large, to buy tools. In 1961 86 boys, including 6 receiving some kind of further education, who were given grants towards maintenance and books, benefited from the charity, by then known as the Broad Town Trust.[99]

There were two Spackman charities in Clyffe Pypard. Funds for the earlier charity, which was created by the will of Thomas Spackman, dated 1675, were derived from a rent-charge of 21s. on 6 a. of meadow.[1] These funds went to purchase bread which was distributed at the discretion of the Vicar of Clyffe Pypard to the poor. No more is known of this small charity.

The later Spackman charity was endowed with £1,000 bequeathed by the will of another Thomas Spackman, dated 1782.[2] Spackman had been born locally and had been a carpenter before becoming a wealthy Londoner. His monument in Clyffe Pypard church was maintained out of charity funds.[3] Otherwise part of the fund was used to establish and maintain a school, an endowment later called the Spackman Educational Foundation,[4] and another part was used to provide bread for distribution to poor each Sunday after church. By 1904 the distribution of bread had lapsed and at this date the income from £360, which formed the endowment of Spackman's Non-Educational Charity, was given as a subscription to a parish coal club available for residents in Clyffe Pypard and in that part of Broad Town formerly situated in the parish of Clyffe Pypard. In 1961 Thomas (II) Spackman's tomb was repaired, and in 1964 donations of £5 were made to the Broad Town and Clyffe Pypard coal clubs.

By his will proved in 1876 Jacob Pinniger Broome

left £100 to be distributed to the poor, in an unspecified manner, by his executor, Christopher Broome.[5] In 1887 the Charity Commissioners established a Scheme whereby the income of the charity was thenceforth to be distributed in subscriptions or donations in aid of the funds of any provident club or society in Clyffe Pypard for the supply of blankets, bedding, or clothing.

Elizabeth Malpass by her will proved in 1884, settled in trust £100, the income on which was to provide bread, coal, blankets, or clothing for deserving poor parishioners.[6] In 1885 the Charity Commissioners ordered that the income should be applied in subscriptions to any provident club within the parish for the supply of blankets, coals, bedding, and other necessaries. In 1905 the incomes of the Broome and Malpass charities were paid to the Clyffe Pypard bedding club. In 1955 and subsequent years an annual £1 payment of unexplained origin was made to the Malpass Charity from Brasenose College, Oxford. In 1962 the Malpass Charity had an income of £3 10s., while in 1965 Broome's Charity had an income of £9. In 1963 and 1964 the proceeds of both were used to buy groceries to distribute to the poor and aged.

The civil parish of Broad Town (cr. 1884) received funds from a charity established in 1627 by Henry Smith (d. 1628) for the benefit of the poor of the parish of Broad Hinton and certain other places.[7] In 1884 the newly-created civil parish was allotted three-elevenths from the £11 18s. then received from the Smith charity by the parish of Broad Hinton. Inhabitants living in that part of Broad Town formerly situated in Clyffe Pypard were also eligible to benefit. The share received by Broad Town was used in 1905 to increase bonuses paid to subscribers to the coal and clothing clubs of the parish. The parish of Broad Town still shared in the £17 10s. allotted to Broad Hinton from the charity in 1962 and in 1960–1 £7 14s. was disbursed in vouchers of varying amounts to enable certain poor people in Broad Town to buy coal.

DRAYCOT FOLIAT

THE ANCIENT PARISH of Draycot Foliat lies 1 mile from Chiseldon village immediately below the scarp of the Marlborough Downs, and is surrounded on the east, north, and west by the modern civil parish of Chiseldon.[1] The parish was estimated at 706 a. in 1887 and at that time measured 2 miles in length and ¾ mile in width. In 1894 the whole parish became part of the civil parish of Chiseldon.[2] It was known by 1309 as Draycot Foliat,[3] because of its connexions with the Foliot family, who held the manor in the later 13th century.[4]

Draycot Foliat lies entirely on the Lower Chalk Terrace[5] at a height varying between 550 and 575 ft. and presents an open and treeless landscape. The soil is on the whole free from flints, while fairly rapid drainage renders it suitable for arable farming.[6] In the 19th century the land was mainly under arable cultivation,[7] but in 1967 there was a considerable amount of pasture.[8] A large bowl barrow lies within the south-west corner of the ancient parish north of Gipsy Lane.[9]

A settlement at Draycot apparently flourished in

[98] Ed. Char. File L 121583 (pts. 1 and 2), at Lansdowne House, Berkeley Sq., London, W.1.
[99] Ex inf. Legal Branch, Min. of Educ. and Science, Curzon St., London, W.1, and Mr. J. O. A. Arkell, Receiver, Broad Town Trust.
[1] Endowed Char. Wilts. (1908), p. 283, and see Char. Com. File 215540/A1.
[2] Endowed Char. Wilts. (1908), pp. 282, 287; Char. Com. Files 215540, 215540/A1.
[3] See p. 40. [4] See p. 42.
[5] Endowed Char. Wilts. (1908), p. 288.
[6] Ibid. p. 289; Char. Com. Files 204231, 204231/A1, 202081.

[7] For an acct. of Henry Smith's Charity, see Endowed Char. Wilts. pp. 751, 733–4 (1908), lxxxi; ibid. p. 567 (1908), lxxx; Char. Com. File 201040.
[1] The maps used include: O.S. Map 1/25,000, SU 17 (1953 edn.); O.S. Map 6", Wilts. XV, XVI, XXII, XXIII (1st edn.).
[2] V.C.H. Wilts. iv. 347.
[3] C.P. 40/279 m. 174d. [4] See p. 44.
[5] Geolog. Survey Eng. and Wales (Drift), 1925, sheet 266.
[6] Fry, Land Utilization Wilts. 162. [7] See p. 47.
[8] Ex inf. Miss J. M. Calley.
[9] V.C.H. Wilts. i (1), 165.

the early 14th century when 12 customary tenants and their families inhabited the parish.[10] Only a minimal contribution was made to the 15th of 1334 compared with other parishes in Kingsbridge hundred, as then constituted.[11] There were 47 poll-tax payers in 1377.[12] In 1523 seven people were able to contribute to the royal loan of that year,[13] while only two were assessed for the Benevolence of 1545.[14] It is probable that the community had decayed considerably by the 16th century when the church was ruinous.[15] There were 38 inhabitants in 1801. Thereafter the number of those living in Draycot fluctuated and at the time of the transfer to Chiseldon in 1894 forty people lived there.[16]

The ancient track known as the Ridge Way transects the parish diagonally from north-east to south-west. The southern boundary of Draycot Foliat is formed by Gipsy Lane, which runs westwards to Burderop Down. From the Ridge Way southwards to Gipsy Lane the eastern boundary of the ancient parish is formed by the secondary road which runs from Chiseldon to Ogbourne St. George.

In 1967 the site of the former village was marked by a few buildings grouped round a lane which followed a semi-circular course to the west of the road from Chiseldon to Ogbourne St. George. The church stood to the north of this lane. Existing buildings include the farm-houses of Sheppard's Farm and Draycot Farm. The former is a stone building, probably of 17th-century origin with later alterations. The latter is a more pretentious house with a symmetrical brick front of the earlier 18th century; several windows have been blocked or altered, but the central doorway, flanked by columns and surmounted by a scrolled pediment, survives. In 1967 it was possible to detect, from air photographs, house-sites of the former village on either side of a short length of disused trackway running north-eastwards from the bend in the present lane towards the road from Chiseldon to Ogbourne.[17]

In 1634 John Evered *alias* Webb of Draycot Foliat emigrated to America and in 1659 was granted a substantial holding on the north bank of the Merrimack river. This settlement became known as Draycot (later Dracut, Mass.), and gave its name in American geology to Dracut Diorite.[18]

MANOR AND OTHER ESTATES. Before the Conquest Levenot held an estate at Draycot.[19] By the time of the Domesday Survey this estate had passed to Miles Crispin[20] together with other estates in Wilt-

shire held T.R.E. by Levenot.[21] Miles Crispin later acquired the honor of Wallingford, as has been explained elsewhere,[22] and Draycot was apparently held of Wallingford from this time, although the first mention found of it as a fee of the honor does not occur until 1235-6.[23] The overlordship is last mentioned in 1477 when the manor was still parcel of the honor.[24]

In 1086 Reynold, possibly the son of Croc the huntsman,[25] held an estate at Draycot of Miles Crispin.[26] Reynold's heirs were his two daughters,[27] one of whom may have been the Maud of Chilton, who held unspecified lands at Draycot in 1194.[28] Before 1207 Hawise, wife of Walter Brito, granted to her nephew by marriage, Walter Croke, 2½ hides in Draycot.[29] By 1214 Walter Croke, possibly a collateral descendant of Croc the huntsman,[30] held land there assessed at 2 knights' fees,[31] an estate which may be identifiable with Reynold's Domesday holding. Walter Croke became a monk in c. 1219-1220.[32] Before then he subinfeudated the manor to Henry Foliot (see below), but he was succeeded as mesne lord by his brother Thomas.[33] In 1241 Thomas had been succeeded as mesne lord in the manor of *DRAYCOT* by his nephew Henry,[34] the son of his brother Humphrey, who had renounced his rights in the estate.[35] Henry still held Draycot in 1275.[36] He died at an unknown date and was succeeded by his son Reynold (II) Croke, who died in 1297.[37] Reynold (II) was succeeded by his son and heir Richard, who died in 1310.[38] Richard's heir was his son Reynold (III) Croke,[39] who died apparently before 1350, by which date he had been succeeded by his son John.[40] Hereafter the descent of the mesne lordship is obscure but it seems likely that John Croke was succeeded at an unknown date by his cousin Nicholas, the grandson of Reynold (III) Croke's sister Alice.[41] Nicholas probably adopted the surname of Croke and at some date was succeeded by his son Nicholas (II) Croke.[42] Nicholas (II)'s heir was his son Robert Croke who had succeeded as mesne lord by 1412.[43] By 1428 the Croke family had ceased to hold the mesne lordship (see below).

In 1214 Walter Croke subinfeudated to Henry Foliot all his lands in Draycot.[44] By 1235-6 Henry had been succeeded in the estate by his son Sampson Foliot,[45] who, in 1242-3, held 1½ knight's fee of Henry Croke.[46] Sampson still held the manor in 1274.[47] He was pardoned for the murder of his son Roger in 1281.[48] The manor had passed by 1284-5, whether by forfeiture or by inheritance is not known,

10 *Wilts. Inq. p.m.* 1242-1326 (Index Libr.), 351.
11 *V.C.H. Wilts.* iv. 302, and see p. 1.
12 *V.C.H. Wilts.* iv. 309.
13 *L. & P. Hen. VIII,* iii (2), pp. 1489-90.
14 *Taxation Lists* (W.A.S. Rec. Brch.), 20.
15 See p. 48.
16 All inf. about population from *V.C.H. Wilts.* iv. 347.
17 Ex inf. Mr. D. J. Bonney of the R.C.H.M. (Eng.).
18 *W.A.M.* xliv. 190-1.
19 *V.C.H. Wilts.* ii, p. 146.   20 Ibid.
21 Ibid. pp. 146-7.
22 Ibid. pp. 102, 111. For a descent of the honor of Wallingford see *V.C.H. Berks.* iii. 523-8.
23 *Bk. of Fees,* i. 423.
24 C 140/56/42.
25 G. J. Kidston, *Hist. Manor of Hazelbury,* Croke Pedigree, 1086-1351.
26 *V.C.H. Wilts.* ii, p. 146.
27 Kidston, *Hazelbury,* Croke Pedigree, 1086-1351.
28 *Pipe R.* 1194 (P.R.S. n.s. v), 201.

29 Kidston, *Hazelbury,* 54-55.
30 Ibid. Croke Pedigree, 1086-1351.
31 *Pipe R.* 1214 (P.R.S. n.s. xxxv), 45.
32 Kidston, *Hazelbury,* Croke Pedigree, 1086-1351.
33 Ibid. 57-58.
34 *Cal. Feet of F. Wilts.* 1195-1272, ed. Fry, 32.
35 Kidston, *Hazelbury,* 57-58.
36 *Rot. Hund.* (Rec. Com.), ii (1), 260.
37 Kidston, *Hazelbury,* 68-69.
38 Ibid.
39 Ibid. Croke Pedigree, 1086-1351.
40 B.M. Add. Ch. 47145.
41 Kidston, *Hazelbury,* Croke Pedigree, 1351-1482.
42 Ibid.
43 Ibid; C 137/87/41.
44 *Pipe R.* 1214 (P.R.S. n.s. xxxv), 45.
45 *Bk. of Fees,* i. 423.
46 Ibid. ii. 727.
47 *Rot. Hund.* (Rec. Com.), ii (1), 276.
48 *W.A.M.* xxxi. 49-68.

to Henry Tyeys the elder (d. 1308).[49] He was succeeded by his son Henry the younger, who assigned the manor to his mother Hawise, who then released Draycot to her son in return for a yearly payment.[50] Henry the younger was beheaded in 1321[51] and the manor was forfeit to the Crown.[52] Hawise survived her son only a short time and at an unknown date the manor was restored to her daughter Alice, wife of Warin de Lisle and sister and heir of Henry Tyeys the younger.[53] Alice de Lisle was seised of Draycot in 1336.[54] The date of Alice's death is unknown. Her heir was her son Gerard de Lisle (d. 1360),[55] who was succeeded by his son Warin (II) de Lisle (d. 1381).[56] Warin (II)'s son and heir Gerard (II) de Lisle predeceased his father, but before his death had married Anne de Pole in 1373.[57] In accordance with the marriage settlement Anne had a life estate in Draycot manor on the death of her husband.[58] Warin (II)'s next heir was his daughter Margaret, wife of Thomas, Lord Berkeley,[59] and the reversion of the manor was confirmed to her and her husband in 1383–4.[60] Margaret predeceased her sister-in-law Anne in 1392[61] and on Anne de Lisle's death in 1412[62] the estate passed to Thomas, Lord Berkeley (d. c. 1417).[63] Thomas's heir was his daughter Elizabeth, wife of Richard Beauchamp, Earl of Warwick (d. 1439).[64] Elizabeth died in 1422, leaving three daughters,[65] and was succeeded by her husband Richard Beauchamp who held Draycot for life immediately of the honor of Wallingford in 1428.[66] Beauchamp died in 1439 and his coheirs in lands previously held by his first wife Elizabeth were his daughters, Margaret, Countess of Shrewsbury (d. 1467), Elizabeth, Lady Latimer (d. c. 1480), and Eleanor, successively Lady Ros and Duchess of Somerset.[67] Draycot was apparently allotted to the second daughter, Eleanor, who died seised of it in 1467.[68] On the death of Eleanor, Duchess of Somerset, it is probable that the manor escheated to the Crown, since Eleanor's son and heir, Thomas, Lord Ros (d. 1464), had been attainted in 1461.[69] Thomas, Lord Ros's heir was his son Edmund[70] but his father's attainder was not immediately reversed in Edmund's favour. At an unknown date after Eleanor's death the Crown appears to have made a grant of the manor, possibly for life, to William Yorke.

William Yorke held directly of the honor of Wallingford.[71] It is possible that William Yorke had previously held some form of life interest in the manor, an interest probably inherited from his father-in-law, Nicholas Wootton.[72] William Yorke died seised of the manor in 1477[73] and Draycot Foliat seems to have reverted to the Crown, since William Yorke's son and heir John, although possessed of land in the parish in 1513, did not hold the manor.[74] In 1485 the attainder of Thomas, Lord Ros, was reversed in favour of his son Edmund, a lunatic. Edmund, Lord Ros (d. 1508), and his lands, which were now to remain with the Crown during pleasure, were placed in the custody of Sir Thomas Lovel.[75] In 1509 Joan St. Lawrence, Lady Howth (d. 1518), the daughter of Eleanor, Duchess of Somerset, received a Crown grant for life of the manor of Draycot Foliat.[76] The Crown in 1553 made a grant of the manor to Edmund Mordaunt and Edward Langley.[77] In the earlier 16th century the manor of Draycot Foliat formed part of a parcel of estates known as the 'coparceners' lands'.[78] The coparceners were probably the four daughters of Thomas, Lord Ros (see above), of whom only one, Eleanor, wife of Robert Manners of Etal (Northumb.), left issue.[79] In 1563 her great-grandson, Henry Manners, Earl of Rutland (d. 1563), successfully vindicated his claim to Draycot Foliat.[80] Previously in 1556–7 Henry, Earl of Rutland and his wife had conveyed the manor to Thomas Bowtell and in 1563 this grant was confirmed.[81] In 1564–5 Thomas Bowtell and his wife granted the manor of Draycot Foliat to Thomas Chaddington.[82] Thomas Bowtell possibly retained an interest in the manor, however, since in 1572 he was associated with Thomas Chaddington and his wife in a mortgage of the manor to William Bowerman and others.[83]

In 1572 William Read (d. 1593) had a leasehold interest for a term of 21 years in the manor of Draycot Foliat[84] and it is possible that either he or his son Edward acquired the freehold of the estate in the later 16th century. In the early 17th century Edward Read broke up the manor into various smaller estates (see below).[85] What may represent the remnant of the earlier manor was held in 1670 by Thomas Richmond alias Webb,[86] whose family had held a lease of the manor as early as 1528.[87] In 1692 the estate was held by Mary Richmond alias Webb, the widow of Thomas.[88] The descent has not been traced further, but it is probable that this estate became the property of the Ewen family by the early 18th century. In 1773 Michael Ewen of Marlborough, great-nephew of John Ewen (d. c. 1705), gave his paternal estate at Draycot, including that once held by John Phelps, to his cousin Samuel

[49] E 179/242/112; Burke, Ext. & Dorm. Peerages, 542.
[50] Wilts. Inq. p.m. 1242–1326 (Index Libr.), 8–9.
[51] Burke, Ext. & Dorm. Peerages, 542.
[52] Cal. Fine R. 1319–27, 427.
[53] Burke, Ext. & Dorm. Peerages, 542; Wilts. Inq. p.m. 1242–1326 (Index Libr.), 8–9.
[54] Cal. Chart. R. 1327–41, 357.
[55] Burke, Ext. & Dorm. Peerages, 326–7.
[56] Ibid.
[57] Cal. Close, 1369–74, 557.
[58] C 137/87/41.
[59] Burke, Ext. & Dorm. Peerages, 326–7.
[60] C.P. 25(1)/256/55/9.
[61] Complete Peerage, viii. 54.
[62] C 137/87/41.
[63] Burke, Ext. & Dorm. Peerages, 44.
[64] Ibid. 32, 326–7.
[65] Complete Peerage, viii. 54.
[66] Feud. Aids, v. 278.
[67] Complete Peerage, viii. 54–55.
[68] C 140/24/20.

[69] Complete Peerage, xi. 104–6.
[70] Ibid.
[71] C 140/56/42.
[72] C 139/154/27.
[73] C 140/56/42.
[74] C 142/135/28.
[75] W.A.M. xxxi. 49–68.
[76] L. & P. Hen. VIII, i (1), p. 69.
[77] W.A.M. xxxi. 49–68.
[78] Ibid.
[79] Ibid.
[80] Ibid.
[81] Ibid.
[82] C.P. 25(2)/239/7 Eliz. 1 East.
[83] C.P. 25(2)/239/14 Eliz. 1 Trin.
[84] C.P. 40/1305 Carte rot. 2d.
[85] See p. 46.
[86] W.R.O. 212A/36/7, Mortgage, Richmond alias Webb to Greenfield.
[87] C 66/652 m.7.
[88] E 134/6 & 7 Wm. III Hil. 14.

Hawkes. Samuel Hawkes's co-heirs were his daughters, one of whom was the wife of John Ward of Marlborough. John Ward purchased his sister-in-law's moiety and thus reunited the estate, said to represent the manor, once held by Ewen.[89] Michael Foster Ward, the grandson of John Ward, owned the estate, then augmented by the addition of Jefferies' Farm[90] and reckoned at 577 a., in 1867, in which year he conveyed it to Henry Calley of Burderop Park.[91]

Several smaller estates existed within Draycot in the Middle Ages. In the later 12th or early 13th century Walter (III) Croke granted his brother Humphrey 2½ hides in Draycot.[92] Before 1207 Humphrey Croke conveyed 4 a. in Draycot to Bradenstoke Priory.[93] At an unknown date Prior Simeon (1215-41) leased these 4 a. to Hugh of Ogbourne for a yearly rent of 2s.[94] and Prior Geoffrey (1261–85) leased the same land to Roger Styne for the same rent.[95] The land was leased again to an unknown person in 1365.[96]

Before 1308 Henry Tyeys the elder granted land in Draycot to Roger Styne.[97] Also before this date Roger Styne died, leaving a widow Gillian and an idiot son John.[98] His lands escheated to the Crown and in 1308 two thirds of the estate were granted in custody to Ralph de Sharpenham,[99] while the remaining third was allotted to Gillian in dower.[1] In 1309 John Styne's lands were reckoned at 60 a. and his heir was Ralph Styne, his father Roger's brother.[2] In 1311 Ralph de Sharpenham established his right to two thirds of an estate in Draycot over Robert Styne, to be identified with Ralph Styne, who also acknowledged Sharpenham's right to the reversion of the third held by Gillian Styne in dower.[3] In 1322 Ralph de Sharpenham was still accounting to the Crown for this small estate.[4]

In the 15th century there was a small estate, later known as *DRAYCOT YORKE*, within the parish. This may have originated in a grant of 1417 by Robert Croke to Nicholas Wootton of a toft and croft in Draycot known as 'Bacon's'.[5] By 1509 Nicholas Wotton's grandson, John Yorke (d. 1513), had acquired a capital messuage there which he held of the Abbot of Hyde, and of which he died seised.[6] Before his death, however, John Yorke had enfeoffed his son and heir, Thomas, of an estate in the land in 1509.[7] Since Thomas Yorke held no land in Draycot at his death in 1542,[8] it is probable that he had alienated the estate by this date and its descent is obscure until 1614 when Edward Read,

his daughter Elizabeth, and son-in-law William Huntly, sold a capital messuage and farm in Draycot Foliat *alias* Yorke, Chiseldon, Wanborough, and Swindon to Thomas Buckeridge.[9] In 1626 Thomas Buckeridge settled the estate on his son Anthony, and daughter-in-law, Constance.[10] Anthony and Constance Buckeridge reconveyed the estate to Thomas Buckeridge and his son Arthur, Anthony's brother, in 1648 and in the same year Thomas and Arthur Buckeridge sold it to Edmund Fettiplace.[11] At an unknown date Edmund Fettiplace sold the estate to Roger Ewen, who was the owner of Draycot Farm, as it was then known, by 1663.[12] Roger Ewen had been succeeded there by his brother John by 1693[13] and before his death in 1705, John Ewen devised his land in Draycot Foliat to his nephew Roger, son of his brother Thomas.[14] The descent thereafter is obscure until 1746–7 when Ambrose Goddard settled the estate on his daughter, Mary and her husband, Thomas Vilett.[15] By 1816 Thomas Neale had acquired the estate and retained it in 1843.[16] By 1845 the estate, which lay partly in Draycot and partly in Chiseldon, was owned by Henry Sheppard.[17]

In 1534 Thomas Yorke leased to Thomas Richmond *alias* Webb and Joan his wife, together with other members of the same family, Yorke's Farm, which comprised land in both Draycot and Chiseldon.[18] In 1572 Joan Richmond *alias* Webb was still possessed of Yorke's Farm by virtue of the lease made to her husband Thomas,[19] and succeeded in vindicating her right in the estate against her sons Robert and Nicholas in 1574.[20] In 1601 Edward Read, who at some date had acquired the freehold of the estate, leased what may be identified as Yorke's Farm to Thomas Buckeridge, to whom he later conveyed the freehold interest (see above).[21] After acquiring the freehold estate Thomas Buckeridge leased the estate to his son Arthur in 1626.[22]

At a date before 1616 Edward Read and others sold specified lands once part of the manor of Draycot Foliat to Noah Evered *alias* Webb the elder.[23] The estate lay in the northern half of the parish of Draycot Foliat above the Ridge Way.[24] In 1616 Noah Evered *alias* Webb granted a moiety of his estate to his son John,[25] and before his death in 1641 he had assigned the other moiety to his son Stephen (d. *c.* 1667).[26] No more is known of Stephen's moiety, but that conveyed to John Evered *alias* Webb the elder passed to his son and heir John the younger, from whom it passed to Stephen

[89] Soc. Ant. Libr., Jackson MSS. vol. ii, Chiseldon.
[90] See p. 47.
[91] W.R.O. 374/180, Terrier of Burderop Estate.
[92] Kidston, *Hazelbury*, 258.
[93] *Rot. Chart.* (Rec. Com.), 170.
[94] B.M. Stowe MS. 925, ff. 80v–81.
[95] B.M. Cotton MS. Vitellius A xi, f. 76.
[96] *V.C.H. Wilts.* iii. 280.
[97] *Wilts. Inq. p.m.* 1242–1326 (Index Libr.), 373.
[98] *Feet of F. Wilts.* 1272–1327 (W.A.S. Rec. Brch.), 79; *Cal. Fine R.* 1307–19, 22.
[99] *Cal. Fine R.* 1307–19, 22.
[1] *Feet of F. Wilts.* 1272–1327 (W.A.S. Rec. Brch.), 79.
[2] *Wilts. Inq. p.m.* 1242–1326 (Index Libr.), 373.
[3] *Feet of F. Wilts.* 1272–1327 (W.A.S. Rec. Brch.), 79.
[4] S.C. 6/1145/12.
[5] *Cat. Anct. D.* vi, C 5941.
[6] C 142/135/28.　　　　　　　　[7] Ibid.
[8] C 142/70/42.
[9] W.R.O. 84/47, Abstract of Title of Edmund Fettiplace.
[10] Ibid.

[11] Ibid.
[12] E 134/6 & 7 Wm. III Hil. 14; E 134/34 & 35 Chas. II Hil. 5.
[13] W.R.O. Land Tax Assessments.
[14] W.R.O. Arch. Wilts. Will of John Ewen, 21 July 1705.
[15] Cal. of Goddard MSS. (TS in Swindon Pub. Libr.), p. 76.
[16] W.R.O. 374/41; W.R.O. Draycot Foliat Tithe Award, 1843.
[17] W.R.O. Chiseldon Tithe Award, 1845.
[18] *Cat. Anct. D.* vi, C 7341.
[19] Req. 2/262/30.　　　　　　[20] Req. 2/288/16.
[21] W.R.O. 84/47, Abstract of Title of Edmund Fettiplace.
[22] Ibid.
[23] W.R.O. 212B/Ch. 1 F, Agreement between Noah Evered *alias* Webb and son John.
[24] W.R.O. 569/48, 19th-cent. Estate Map.
[25] W.R.O. 212B/Ch. 1 F (see n. 23 above).
[26] W.R.O. Arch. Wilts. Will of Noah Evered *alias* Webb, 1641; Will of Stephen Evered *alias* Webb, 1667.

Evered *alias* Webb, eldest son of John the younger.[27] By 1698 the moiety was held by Mary Webb (d. 1706),[28] possibly either the mother or wife of Stephen Evered *alias* Webb, and her son Daniel (d. *c.* 1714).[29] In that year they conveyed their moiety to Noah Evered *alias* Webb of Marlborough.[30] At an unknown date Noah Evered *alias* Webb sold the moiety to John Phelps *alias* Bromham.[31] Phelps's heirs were his daughters Hester and Anne, who married Thomas Jones and Edmund Chapp respectively, and in 1754 they conveyed their lands to Prince Sutton.[32] The descent is obscure until 1843 when George and Jemima Jefferies, whose family had earlier leased the farm (see below),[33] held the estate, reckoned at 280 a., which covered the entire parish north of the Ridge Way,[34] and it seems likely that by this date the moieties of the 17th-century estate may have been reunited. In 1849 it was ordered that George Jefferies's estate, made up of two undivided third shares, should be sold.[35] It is likely that this land was acquired by Michael Foster Ward and formed part of the estate which he sold to Henry Calley in 1867.[36]

ECONOMIC HISTORY. In the time of King Edward Draycot paid geld for 10 hides. In 1086 there was sufficient land to support 6 ploughs. At this time there were two ploughs and a serf on the 5 hides held in demesne, while the remaining hides supported 3 ploughs with 4 villeins and 7 bordars. At the time of the Domesday Survey there were 40 a. of pasture and 18 a. of meadow. The land was worth £5 T.R.E. and in 1086.[37]

In 1307 the manor of Draycot had 100 a. of arable land in demesne, valued at 4*d.* an acre, and 6 a. of meadow land, worth 1*s.* an acre. As in 1086 there were 12 tenants on the manor. Of these 8 customers paid 10*s.* yearly, while 4 cottars paid 3*s.* yearly. The manor was estimated to be worth £6 12*s.* at this date.[38] In 1322 the manor was worth £7 12*s.* 4½*d.*, a total which included a sum of £5 14*s.* 9*d.* in assessed rents.[39]

The parish of Draycot Foliat lies entirely on the Lower Chalk Terrace, an area of heavy but easily-drained soil.[40] The sheep-and-corn husbandry typical of this region was employed within the parish until fairly recent times. In 1327 the lands of the Styne family, administered in the early 14th century by Ralph de Sharpenham, supported 250 sheep.[41] This estate also had 32 a. under corn,

valued at 3*s.* an acre, and 13 a. under barley, valued at 2*s.* an acre in 1322.[42] Sheep were still reared in Draycot Foliat in the 17th century. In 1683 there were 410 sheep on Draycot (later Sheppard's) Farm,[43] while at some date between 1696 and 1699 the same farm supported 200 sheep and during this time 90 lambs a year were produced.[44] During these years John Ewen claimed to have produced and sold 268 fleeces on Draycot Farm and King's Farm.[45]

In 1843 there were 605 a. of arable land, 76 a. of meadow land and pasture land as well as 2 a. of woodland in the parish subject to tithe.[46] There were then 3 farms,[47] all of which may be identified with earlier estates in Draycot. An arable farm of 280 a., owned by George Jefferies,[48] lay between the northern boundary of the parish and the Ridge Way and included several large arable fields known as Broad Field, Lower Field, West Field, and House Field.[49] Thomas Neale's farm,[50] 113 a. of which lay in Draycot and the rest in Chiseldon, was situated in the south-east corner of the parish and mainly consisted of a large parcel of arable land estimated at 98 a. and called the Great Field.[51] The third farm, formerly owned by John Ward,[52] was made up of 295 a. of chiefly arable land, which included King's Field, Honey Down, Bourn Mead, and Coppice Field.[53] In 1849 George Jefferies's farm was offered for sale[54] and probably at this date was acquired by the trustees of John Ward. The two farms were amalgamated in this way and became known as Draycot Farm, reckoned at 577 a. in 1867 when it became part of the Calley estate.[55] Draycot Farm remained part of the estate in 1967, when the tenant was Mr. Charles Frederick Butcher.[56] The third farm in the parish, Draycot *alias* Neale's (later Sheppard's) Farm, was farmed by John Green in 1939.[57] In 1967 mixed farming prevailed throughout the parish.[58]

LOCAL GOVERNMENT. The manor of Draycot Foliat was held of the honor of Wallingford from the 12th century until 1540 when this honor was merged in that of Ewelme, held by the Crown.[59] Draycot Foliat formed part of a group of manors held of Wallingford and administered from Ogbourne St. George, where a yearly manorial court was held. Court rolls for this group of manors are extant for the years 1422,[60] 1437,[61] 1520,[62] 1536,[63] 1538,[64] 1541,[65] and 1546,[66] but record only view of frankpledge for Draycot Foliat. In 1672–3 Roger Ewen

[27] W.R.O. 212B/Ch. 9 C, Deed to lead the uses of a fine, Evered *alias* Webb.
[28] Ibid; W.R.O. Arch. Wilts. Will of Daniel Webb, 1714.
[29] W.R.O. 212B/Ch. 9 C (see n. 27 above); W.R.O. Arch. Wilts. Will of Daniel Webb, 1714.
[30] W.R.O. 212B/Ch. 9 C (see n. 27 above).
[31] W.R.O. 212B/Ch. 17 A, Copy of recovery, Jones and Chapp.
[32] Ibid.
[33] W.R.O. Draycot Foliat Tithe Award.   [34] Ibid.
[35] W.R.O. 374/128/73, Sale Cat. 1849.
[36] See p. 46.
[37] *V.C.H. Wilts.* ii, p. 146.
[38] *Wilts. Inq. p.m.* 1242–1326 (Index Libr.), 351.
[39] S.C. 6/1145/12.
[40] Fry, *Land Utilization Wilts.* 162.
[41] *Cal. Pat.* 1327–30, 220.
[42] S.C. 6/1145/12.
[43] E 134/35 & 36 Chas. II Hil. 11.
[44] E 134/1 Anne Trin. 4.

[45] E 126/17/1 Anne Hil. f. 310.
[46] W.R.O. Tithe Award, 1843.   [47] Ibid.
[48] See above.
[49] W.R.O. Tithe Award, 1843.
[50] See p. 46.
[51] W.R.O. Tithe Award, 1843.
[52] See p. 46.
[53] W.R.O. Tithe Award, 1843.
[54] See above.
[55] See p. 46.
[56] Ex inf. Miss J. M. Calley.
[57] *Kelly's Dir. Wilts.* (1939).
[58] Ex inf. Miss J. M. Calley.
[59] G. J. Kidston, *Hist. Manor of Hazelbury*, 12, 13.
[60] S.C. 2/212/2.
[61] S.C. 2/212/9.
[62] S.C. 2/212/14.
[63] S.C. 2/212/18.
[64] S.C. 2/212/19.
[65] S.C. 2/212/20.
[66] S.C. 2/212/24.

and other landholders in Draycot Foliat still owed suit of court at Ogbourne St. George.[67] After the union of the benefices of Draycot Foliat and Chiseldon in 1572 (see above), Draycot was regarded as part of the parish of Chiseldon for purposes of parochial administration, although it was not until 1894 that Draycot Foliat officially became part of the civil parish of Chiseldon.[68]

CHURCH. At some time between 1208 and 1214 a rector served the church of Draycot Foliat.[69] The benefice remained a rectory[70] but no further mention of it has been found until the 16th century. By the later 16th century the church was apparently ruinous and in 1572 it was ordered that the benefice should be united with that of Chiseldon and the church of Draycot demolished.[71] Henceforth the inhabitants of Draycot Foliat were regarded as parishioners of Chiseldon and attended church there. In 1581 a presentation to the united benefice was made[72] but after this, as is shown below, rectors of Draycot continued to be presented separately. In 1923 the union of the rectory of Draycot Foliat and the vicarage of Chiseldon was reaffirmed and the respective patrons made a joint presentation to the living.[73]

No mention of the advowson of the rectory during the Middle Ages has been found, but it seems likely that it followed the descent of the manor of Draycot Foliat. In 1556–7 Henry, Earl of Rutland, and his wife Margaret, who at that date claimed the manor as descendants of Thomas, Lord Ros, also claimed the advowson of the rectory of Draycot Foliat, and in that year conveyed it to Thomas Bowtell, who purchased the manor at the same date.[74] Bowtell was confirmed in the manor in 1563, but the Crown retained the advowson and in 1564 granted it to Richard Pipe and Francis Bowyer[75] who in the same year conveyed it to Thomas Chaddington, who had also acquired the manor at the same date.[76] In 1572 the benefice was united with that of Chiseldon and the first presentation to the united benefice was made in 1581 by the patron of Chiseldon church, Robert Stephens.[77] Afterwards Thomas Chaddington seems to have regained the advowson, although whether it was of the united benefice, or only of the rectory of Draycot, is not clear. Chaddington conveyed it with the tithes of the parish of Draycot (see below) to William Read (d. 1593).[78] No record of any presentation by either Chaddington or Read survives and in 1611 the king, by reason of lapse, presented John Gallimore as Rector of Draycot,[79] although Gallimore had been presented to the combined benefice in

1581[80] and was thus presumably already both Vicar of Chiseldon and Rector of Draycot. In spite of this presentation by the king the advowson passed from William Read to his son Edward, who in 1614 conveyed it to Thomas Buckeridge.[81] No record of any presentation by Buckeridge survives and once more in 1664 the king presented a rector of Draycot by reason of lapse, and he again presented the Vicar of Chiseldon, Thomas Twittee.[82] In 1711 Twittee died and for the first time, so far as is known, different persons were presented to the vicarage of Chiseldon and the rectory of Draycot. The presentation to the sinecure rectory of Draycot was made by William Bryan of Hodson.[83] In 1722 Thomas Smith exercised the patronage.[84] By 1737 the advowson had passed to Pleydell Goddard of Swindon[85] and on his death in 1742 it passed with his other estates to his kinsman and heir Ambrose Goddard (d. 1815).[86] In 1780 Ambrose Goddard presented a kinsman, Edward Goddard (d. 1791) to the rectory and on his death presented a nephew, Thomas Goddard Vilett.[87] On the death of Ambrose Goddard the advowson passed to his son and heir, Ambrose the younger (d. 1898), who in 1817 presented his brother Richard to the rectory.[88] In 1858 Ambrose Goddard presented George Eastman, and at an unknown date presumably also conveyed the advowson to him, since in 1898 and again in 1912 Eastman's trustees presented rectors.[89] In 1923, when the benefices of Chiseldon and Draycot Foliat were reunited, the patronage of both remained separate and in this year General T. C. P. Calley joined with the Eastman trustees to make a joint presentation to the vicarage of Chiseldon with Draycot Foliat.[90] Joint patronage rights were exercised until c. 1947.[91] In this year the patron of Chiseldon vicarage, Miss J. M. Calley, was allowed to make two presentations to every one made by G. R. T. Eastman.[92] Some time before 1961–2 the separate patronage rights were finally merged and vested in Miss Calley, who at this time made the first presentation as sole patron to the united benefice.[93]

In 1535 the rectory was valued at £6 12s. 7d. out of which 9s. were paid in procurations.[94] At the union of the two benefices in 1572 Thomas Chaddington acquired all the tithes of Draycot Foliat, including those from an estate which lay partly in Chiseldon, and which was known in the 17th century as Draycot Farm.[95] In return Chaddington and his successors were to pay the Vicar of Chiseldon and his successors £7 a year.[96] The tithes then passed, as did the manor, to Edward Read, who leased some of them to Thomas Buckeridge.[97] In 1622–3 Read and his wife Elizabeth, together with Thomas Stephens, conveyed the tithes to William

[67] E 134/23 & 24 Chas. II Hil. 2.
[68] See p. 43.
[69] E 179/242/104.   [70] Ibid.
[71] W.A.M. xxx. 46–48.
[72] Phillipps, Wilts. Inst. i. 231.
[73] Crockford (1926).
[74] C.P. 25(2)/81/694/3 & 4 Ph. & M. Trin. and see p. 45.
[75] Cal. of Goddard MSS. (TS in Swindon Pub. Libr.), p. 70.
[76] W.R.O. 212B/Ch. 1 G, Abstract of title to advowson of rectory of Draycot Foliat, 1624, and see p. 45.
[77] W.A.M. xxx. 46–48; Phillipps, Wilts. Inst. i. 231.
[78] W.R.O. 212B/Ch. 1 G (see n. 76 above).
[79] Phillipps, Wilts. Inst. ii. 6.
[80] Ibid. i. 231.
[81] C.P. 25(2)/371/12 Jas. I East.

[82] Phillipps, Wilts. Inst. ii. 27.   [83] Ibid. 51.
[84] Ibid. 57.
[85] Ibid. 67.
[86] Burke, Commoners (1833–8), iv. 326–7.
[87] Phillipps, Wilts. Inst. ii. 90, 96.
[88] Clerical Guide (1822).
[89] Clergy List (1859); Crockford (1907); Clergy List (1915).
[90] Crockford (1926).
[91] Ibid. (1935 and later edns.).
[92] Ibid. (1947).
[93] Ibid. (1961–2).
[94] Valor Eccl. (Rec. Com.), ii. 150.
[95] W.A.M. xxx. 46–48, and see p. 46.
[96] W.A.M. xxx. 46–48.
[97] Burderop MSS. Lease, Read to Buckeridge, 1604–5.

Calley and his son William.[98] For some years after this the descent of the tithes is obscure. In about 1672 the Rector of Draycot, Thomas Twittee, who was also Vicar of Chiseldon, claimed the tithes from the Chiseldon lands of Draycot Farm[99] and in the course of a lengthy law-suit, this issue became subordinate to the wider question of the right to take tithes, both great and small, from the whole parish.[1] Twittee denied all knowledge of the £7 composition payment, which had been agreed upon in 1572, and it seems that some time before 1660 a modus of £30 in lieu of all tithes had been substituted,[2] although it is not clear to whom this was payable. In 1672, as a result of Twittee's legal proceedings, it was decreed that the rector was entitled to all tithes in the parish of Draycot and that these were to be commuted for an annual payment of £65.[3] In 1683–4 the settlement was reaffirmed.[4] In 1812 the value of the rectory was reckoned at £200,[5] a sum, for the most part, presumably, still made up of tithe. In 1843 the great and small tithes of the parish were commuted for £180, which was payable to the Rector of Draycot Foliat.[6] Thereafter the net value declined from £165 in 1835 to £108 in 1897, while in 1915 the rectory was valued at £100 net.[7] In 1867 it was noted that the Vicar of Chiseldon, also licensed curate of Draycot Foliat, was assigned a stipend by the Bishop of Salisbury and that this was paid by the sinecure rector,[8] but the amount of the stipend is not known.

At some date between 1208 and 1214 the Rector of Draycot Foliat had a hide of land in demesne.[9] The rectorial glebeland was reputedly divided amongst the landholders of Draycot Foliat in 1572, when the church was closed, and in 1694–6 was said to have contained two yardlands.[10] At the end of the 17th century 4 a. of the former glebe lay in the Great Field of Draycot, which was a large parcel of arable in the south-eastern corner of the parish, and part of Draycot alias Neale's (later Sheppard's) Farm.[11] In 1699 the Rector of Draycot

attempted to recover these 4 a.,[12] but the outcome of his claim is unknown.

In 1550 the parishioners reported that the rector, Thomas Parham, was unable to discharge the cure, and three years later complained that no quarterly sermons were preached.[13] The rector employed curates in 1550 and 1553.[14]

The church at Draycot was apparently demolished soon after 1572[15] and the materials of the former church used to repair the parish church of Chiseldon, where the north aisle subsequently became known as the Draycot aisle.[16] Twittee, on becoming Rector of Draycot Foliat in 1664, was inducted on the site of the former church,[17] which lay close to the ancient nucleus of the parish, near the track which formerly ran north-westwards to meet the Ridge Way. In 1857 it was still possible to discern the ground plan of the church, the nave of which was 60 ft. long and 20 ft. broad, while at the eastern end lay a chancel, which measured 15 ft. in length and 15 ft. in breadth.[18] A parsonage house was said to have been acquired by Thomas Chaddington in 1572 and in 1694–6 was reputed to stand on land once held by Thomas Webb, the windows of whose house contained glass from the demolished church.[19] In 1553 a chalice and two bells were left for the use of the parish by the king's commissioners, while plate weighing 5 oz. was taken for the king's use.[20]

NONCONFORMITY. No evidence of dissent in Draycot has been found.

EDUCATION. Children living in Draycot Foliat have always attended school at Chiseldon.

CHARITIES. No charities applicable to the ancient parish are known to exist.

HILMARTON

THE PARISH of Hilmarton adjoins the borough of Calne on the south and the parish of Lyneham on the north. The parish church, which lies roughly in the middle of the parish, is about 3 miles from the centre of Calne and 7 miles from Wootton Bassett. Beversbrook, in the south of the parish, was probably a detached part of the hundred of Calne in 1084 and remained part of that hundred.[1] A later-19th-century map shows two small portions of land in Hilmarton, one including Middle Beversbrook Farm, as belonging to Calne.[2] Catcomb in the north-

west of the parish was considered to be in Selkley hundred after 1841.[3] In 1883 the western boundary of the parish was extended to bring in Cowage Farm and 316 a. of land, until then a detached part of Compton Bassett.[4] In 1890 the southern boundary was redrawn to embrace the whole of the civil parish of Highway (813 a.).[5] The area of the parish after these changes was 5,311 a.[6]

The irregularly shaped parish touches upon several clearly defined geological regions. From north to south through its western side runs the

[98] C.P. 25(2)/372/20 Jas. I Trin.
[99] W.A.M. xxx. 51–54.
[1] E 126/14 f. 48.
[2] E 134/34 & 35 Chas. II Hil. 5.
[3] E 126/14 f. 48.
[4] Ibid.
[5] W.A.M. xli. 133.
[6] W.R.O. Tithe Award, 1843.
[7] Rep. Com. Eccl. Revenues, H.C. 54, pp. 832–3 (1835), xxii; Crockford (1907); Clergy List (1915).
[8] Soc. Ant. Libr., Jackson MSS. vol. ii, Chiseldon.
[9] E 179/242/104.
[10] E 134/6 & 7 Wm. III Hil. 14.
[11] Ibid.; W.R.O. Tithe Award, 1843.
[12] E 126/17 ff. 53v–54.

[13] Sar. Dioc. R.O. Bp's Detecta Bk. 1550–8, ff. 33, 140.
[14] Ibid.
[15] W.A.M. xxx. 46–48.
[16] See p. 21.
[17] Phillipps, Wilts. Inst. ii. 27; E 134/23 & 24 Chas. II Hil. 2.
[18] W.A.M. iii. 280.
[19] E 134/6 & 7 Wm. III Hil 14; E 134/7 Wm. III Trin. 3.
[20] W.A.M. i. 93; xii. 367.
[1] V.C.H. Wilts. ii, p. 182.
[2] O.S. Map Index to the Tithe Survey.
[3] Census, 1841.
[4] Ibid. 1891.
[5] Ibid. 1901. For Highway, see V.C.H. Wilts. vii. 197–8.
[6] Census, 1901.

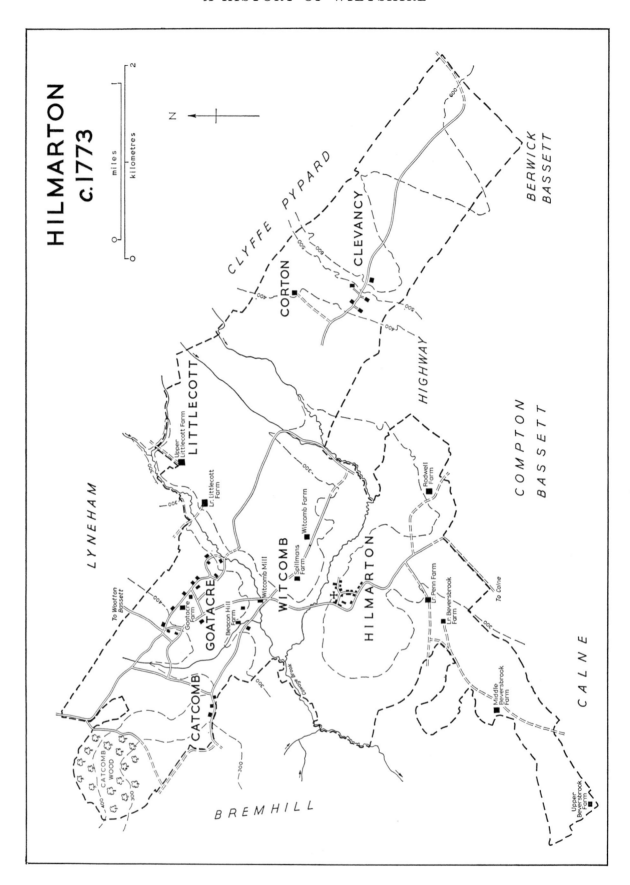

HILMARTON
c.1773

Corallian ridge, which extends from Oxford to Calne.[7] To the west of the ridge the parish just touches upon the Oxford Clay Vale of north and mid-west Wiltshire. To the east of the ridge it crosses the vale of Kimmeridge Clay and extends eastwards over belts of Gault and Upper Greensand to the Lower Chalk of the Marlborough Downs.[8]

On the western side of the parish, along the Corallian ridge, the ground is fairly high, reaching about 400 ft. near Catcomb.[9] The soil here is light and sandy and the frequent exposures of Coral Rag have been extensively quarried, especially at Catcomb and Goatacre.[10] The stone thus obtained has been much used locally for building and road making. On its north-western side the ridge drops fairly steeply to the heavy Oxford Clay. South-eastwards it descends more gently with undulating folds to the low-lying clay land, which in some places is below 300 ft., and near the site of Witcomb Mill is marshy. Beyond the Kimmeridge Clay the land rises steeply up a bank, or cliff of chalk, which forms the lower shelf of the Marlborough Downs. This cliff is responsible for the names of several places in the district, including Clevancy.[11] At Corton the cliff is breached by a small cutting or 'corf'. Above the cliff the ground rises gradually to the highest point in the parish which is about 600 ft.

Cowage Brook runs south-westwards through the parish and forms part of the western boundary. Another stream, coming from the chalk escarpment, crosses the parish roughly from east to west, and joins Cowage Brook just north-west of Hilmarton village. The largest wood in the parish is Catcomb Wood in the north-west corner and there has been a certain amount of afforestation on the lands of the former Poynder estate. There is a belt of scrubby woodland on the lower slopes of the downs and tall trees in thick hedgerows help to create an impression of a well-wooded landscape.

A map of 1773 shows that the road from Calne in the south approached Hilmarton village on a more easterly course than it does today.[12] The stretch of the present main road between Beversbrook and Hilmarton probably became the high road after it was turnpiked between 1776 and 1800.[13] From the village, which is on the Corallian ridge, this road drops to one of the lowest points in the parish and then rises steeply up Snow Hill to Goatacre, also on the ridge. The other roads in the parish have been developed from the many tracks and lanes needed to connect the various scattered areas of settlement (see below). The road under the downs, connecting Corton and Clevancy with Hilmarton and Bushton (in Clyffe Pypard), was made in c. 1863.[14]

The ancient parish was made up of a number of scattered hamlets, some of which may once have been fair-sized centres of settlement and apparently of considerable antiquity. A well at Corton bears witness to Roman occupation there and Roman coins have been found at Goatacre and elsewhere in the parish.[15] Of the hamlets within the parish assessed for taxation in 1334, Hilmarton, which lies roughly in the centre, had by far the largest assessment (130s.), but this probably included Goatacre, lying over a mile to the north and not separately assessed. Clevancy and Corton, about 2 miles east of Hilmarton, were assessed at 43s. and 36s. respectively. Witcomb, about ½ mile north-east, was assessed at 35s., and Littlecott, about a mile north, at 26s. Beversbrook, in the south of the parish, was assessed as part of the hundred of Calne at 26s.[16] In 1377 Hilmarton, again probably including Goatacre, had 92 poll-tax payers, Clevancy and Littlecott together 30, Witcomb 20, and Corton 18. The number of poll-tax payers in Beversbrook at this date is unknown, since on this occasion Beversbrook was combined for purposes of taxation with Whitley, also part of the hundred of Calne.[17] In 1428 Corton, presumably because there was a chapel there, was included in a list of Wiltshire parishes having fewer than 10 households.[18] To the Benevolence of 1545 Hilmarton, Clevancy, and Corton all had three contributors, Witcomb but one.[19] In 1576 the parish as a whole had 15 tax-payers.[20]

A map of 1773 shows that by then only Hilmarton and Goatacre could be described as hamlets, although there was a cluster of cottages around the farms at Clevancy.[21] In the 20th century, besides the village of Hilmarton, Goatacre is the only hamlet of any size in the parish. Witcomb consists of two farms and a couple of cottages.[22] Littlecott is represented by two farms. Corton consists of a single farmstead.[23] Clevancy comprises two farms, a few farm cottages, and a small undenominational chapel.[24] Here in a field below Cliffansty House some irregularity of the ground probably marks the the site of some former closes and both at Clevancy and Corton the slope beneath the cliff is here and there scarred where there has been digging for iron pyrites nodules, used locally for hard core. The moated site south-east of Corton Farm may have been made to provide a dry enclosure, possibly for an orchard. Townsends Knoll, a large mound standing by the roadside below Cliffansty House at the edge of a field once called Culverhays, has never been excavated, and its origin is unknown.[25] At Beversbrook air photography has revealed traces on the ground of a small settlement, probably of medieval date and now quite deserted.[26]

The area around Catcomb Farm in the north-west of the parish was returned as a tithing with 68 inhabitants in the census of 1841. But, as far as is known, Catcomb was not assessed separately for taxation in the Middle Ages. In 1801 the population

[7] Some account of this ridge is given in W. J. Arkell, 'Geology of the Corallian Ridge near Wootton Bassett and Lyneham', W.A.M. liv. 1–18.
[8] For further description of the region, see Fry, Land Utilization Wilts. 151, 160.
[9] Maps used include O.S. Map 6″, Wilts, XXI, XXII, XXVII (1st edn.); 1/25,000, 41/07, 31/97; Geolog. Survey Eng. and Wales (Drift), 1925, sheet 266.
[10] See p. 60.
[11] P.N. Wilts. (E.P.N.S.), 266, 268.
[12] Andrews and Dury, Map (W.A.S. Rec. Brch.), pl. 14.
[13] V.C.H. Wilts. iv. 257.
[14] W.A.M. xliv. 147.
[15] V.C.H. Wilts. i (1), 77.
[16] Ibid. iv. 298, 300.
[17] Ibid. 307, 309.
[18] Ibid. 314. For chapel, see below, p. 63.
[19] Taxation Lists (W.A.S. Rec. Brch.), 21–22.
[20] Ibid. 107.
[21] Andrews and Dury, Map (W.A.S. Rec. Brch.), pl. 14.
[22] See p. 56.
[23] See p. 55.
[24] See p. 64.
[25] Advice on topographical features mentioned above was given by Mr. D. J. Bonney of the R.C.H.M. (Eng.).
[26] W.A.S. Libr., Devizes, Air Photo. A/92.

of the entire parish was 717. It rose to 828 in 1851, but thereafter it began to decline. In 1891, after the addition of Cowage Farm and Highway, the population was 810. In 1961 it was 743.[27]

The village of Hilmarton lies just to the east of the Calne-Lyneham road. It is compact with the parish church, school, village shop, and the Poynder almshouses all lying close together. Its most notable feature is the number of buildings of more or less the same style and date. These were all built in the 19th century, between 1832 and 1877, by members of the Poynder family and mostly to the design of Henry Weaver, an architect, who was for a time agent for the Hilmarton estate.[28] Besides the school built in 1851 and the almshouses built in 1878,[29] there are a number of cottages, mostly in pairs, built for employees on the estate. Apart from the school, which is of brick with stone dressings, all are built of local stone with slate roofs and have leaded windows with diamond panes. The later cottages have certain decorative features, such as ornamental barge-boards to gables and porches. There is little in the village of earlier date, except at the east end, where there are two thatched houses, one partly timber-framed, which probably date from the 17th century. A third house, apparently of the same date, standing close to the small stream, was burnt down in the early 1960s.[30] At the extreme east end of the village there are a few council houses built soon after the Second World War.

To the south of the church the former Parsonage Farm, called Manor Farm in the 20th century, has a wing added in the typical Poynder style.[31] Most of the farm-houses of the Hilmarton estate were either rebuilt or much restored by Thomas Henry Allen Poynder (d. 1873).[32] They include the Manor, called Hilmarton Lodge for a time in the 20th century, and Goatacre, Beversbrook, and Catcomb Farms. The Duke Inn, standing on the west side of the main road, was also rebuilt in the mid 19th century.[33]

The hamlet of Goatacre lies on high ground over a mile from Hilmarton village. In 1846 it was the scene of one of the largest anti-corn-law meetings in Wiltshire.[34] The agricultural population of Hilmarton was reckoned scarcely to exceed 200 at the time, but the parish lay at the heart of a wide area where similar conditions of distress prevailed. Moreover, the fact that Goatacre was a strong centre of religious dissent is probably significant. The meeting was organized by a body known as the Goatacre Reform Society. It was held at night by lantern-light at the crossroads in Goatacre and was attended by nearly 1,000 people. The lengthy proceedings were reported fully in *The Times* two days later.

The houses in Goatacre are mostly strung out for about a mile along a minor road which crosses the main road between Calne and Lyneham. A few are thatched, including a 17th-century stone farmhouse which has been divided into two cottages. The centre of the village may be said to be at the crossroads and here are the Methodist chapel and the village shop. A few old peoples' bungalows were built closeby early in the 1960s.

MANORS AND OTHER ESTATES. In 962 10 *mansae* at Hilmarton and Littlecott were granted by King Edgar to Wulfmaer, a thegn.[35] In the Domesday Survey there are 3 estates called Hilmarton, amounting together to 11 hides, and thus possibly representing roughly the land granted in 962. An estate of 1 hide, which had been held T.R.E. by Aschil, belonged to Ernulf of Hesdin and was held of him by Robert.[36] It is not possible to identify this holding certainly with any later estate in the parish. Another one-hide estate was held by Alfric the little, a king's thegn, and may, it has been suggested, have descended to Walter Spileman, who held land in Hilmarton by serjeanty in 1198.[37] The largest of the 3 Domesday holdings was assessed at 9 hides and formed part of the fief of William of Eu.[38] Many of William's estates are known to have passed to the Earl Marshal and in 1242–3 *HILMARTON* was among the nine Wiltshire holdings of the earl, which in 1086 had belonged to William of Eu.[39] From Walter, Earl of Pembroke, the Earl Marshal of 1242–3,[40] the overlordship descended in the same way as Hampstead Marshall (Berks.), the chief manor of the Marshals, to the Bigods, earls of Norfolk, and from them in 1306 to the king.[41] In 1348 Goatacre, which by this date was parcel of the manor of Hilmarton, was held in chief as of the manor of Hampstead Marshall,[42] but Hilmarton was said to be held of the manor of Chepstow,[43] another manor belonging to the Bigods, which had come in the same way as Hampstead Marshall to the Crown in 1306.[44] In 1428 Hilmarton was said to be held of the queen as of her manor of Hampstead Marshall.[45] In 1501 it was said to be held of the manor of Chepstow, which by this date had passed from the Crown to the Herberts, earls of Pembroke.[46] Thereafter, however, so far as it can be traced, it was said to be held of the manor of Hampstead Marshall. The last reference to the overlordship found occurs in 1576 when Hilmarton was said to be held of Thomas Parry (d. 1616) as of his manor of Hampstead Marshall.[47]

Under William of Eu Hilmarton was held in 1086 by one, Ralph.[48] By 1242–3 Roger Bluet was holding it of Ralph de Wancy, who held it of the Earl Marshal.[49] By 1297 John Bluet, possibly Roger's son or grandson, was presenting to the rectory of Hilmarton[50] and two years later was granted an annual fair at his manor there and free warren in all

[27] *Census.*
[28] Henry Weaver, *Hints on Cottage Architecture* (1848). This has plans and pictures of some of the Hilmarton cottages.
[29] See p. 65.
[30] Local information.   [31] See p. 58.
[32] Francis Goddard, *Reminiscences of a Wilts. Vicar, 1814–1893* (copy in W.A.S. Libr., Devizes).
[33] The earlier building is just visible in a painting of the church by John Buckler, 1810 (W.A.S. Libr., Devizes).
[34] *The Times*, 7 Jan. 1846.
[35] Birch, *Cart. Sax.* no. 1081 ; *V.C.H. Wilts.* ii, p. 97.
[36] *V.C.H. Wilts.* ii, p. 140.

[37] Ibid. p. 161, and see below.
[38] Ibid. p. 149.
[39] Ibid. p. 111.
[40] *Bk. of Fees*, ii. 712, 724.
[41] *V.C.H. Berks.* iv. 179–80.
[42] See p. 57.
[43] *Wilts. Inq. p.m. 1327–77* (Index Libr.), 189.
[44] I. J. Sanders, *English Baronies*, 110–11, 46–47.
[45] *Feud. Aids*, v. 277.
[46] *Cal. Inq. p.m. Hen. VII*, ii. 317.
[47] C 142/175/101, see also *V.C.H. Berks.* iv. 181.
[48] *V.C.H. Wilts.* ii, p. 149.
[49] *Bk. of Fees*, ii. 724.   [50] See p. 61.

his demesne lands.[51] In 1306 John Bluet held the manor directly of Roger Bigod,[52] and two years later settled it upon himself and Margery his wife.[53] John's successor, Sir John (II) Bluet, likewise settled the manor upon himself and his wife Eleanor with contingent remainder to his daughter Margaret.[54] Eleanor died, a widow, in 1348 holding the manor, and her heir was Peter, son of her daughter Margaret, who had married William de Cusance.[55] Peter was of age in 1350 when he did homage for all the lands Eleanor held at her death.[56] He held Hilmarton in 1369 and presented to the rectory in 1380, but probably died soon after.[57] He was succeeded by his cousin Philip Baynard, son of Edmund Baynard and his wife Eleanor, another daughter of Sir John (II) Bluet.[58] Philip Baynard died seised of the manor in 1415 and was succeeded by his son Robert.[59] Robert died in 1437,[60] having settled the manor upon his son Philip.[61] Thenceforth for about 170 years the manor passed from father to son in the Baynard family. Philip was succeeded by Robert (d. 1501),[62] Robert's son Philip was succeeded in 1521 by Robert;[63] Robert was succeeded in 1535 by Edward[64] and Edward in 1575 by Robert.[65] This Robert conveyed the manor in 1607 to Robert Sadler, son of William Sadler, who was leasing part of the manor at the time of his death in 1600.[66] Robert was granted livery of the manor with the fair there in 1611.[67] In 1616 Robert Sadler sold Hilmarton to John Norborne, who that year was granted the right to hold a court leet for the manor.[68] The sale was disputed by Edward Baynard, possibly a brother of Robert Baynard, and Edward seems to have remained for a time in occupation of the main farm-house of the manor.[69]

John Norborne died c. 1635[70] and was succeeded by his son Walter, of Calne, a royalist, who was fined for his loyalty to the king.[71] Walter died in 1659 and was followed by his son, another Walter, who was killed in a duel in 1684, leaving two daughters, Elizabeth and Susan, between whom Hilmarton was equally divided.[72] Elizabeth married first Edward Devereux, Viscount Hereford (d. 1700), and Susan married Sir Ralph Hare.[73] The two parts of the manor were re-united in 1728 when Susan died and her moiety passed to her sister Elizabeth.[74] Elizabeth married secondly John Symes Berkeley of Stoke Gifford (Glos.) who died in 1736.[75] Their son Norborne Berkeley recovered the ancient barony of

Botetourt, then in abeyance, but died without surviving issue in 1770.[76] He was succeeded by his sister Elizabeth, who was the widow of Charles Noel Somerset, Duke of Beaufort (d. 1756).[77] She died in 1799 and her son Henry Somerset, Duke of Beaufort (d. 1803), sold the Hilmarton estate piecemeal in 1802.[78] The manor was purchased by Samuel Hale, who sold it c. 1809 to Benjamin Ansley.[79] Ansley sold it in 1813 to Thomas Poynder.[80] Thomas Poynder died in 1856 and was followed by his two sons successively, Thomas Henry Allen Poynder (d. 1873), and William Henry Poynder (d. 1880).[81] During the lordship of these three Poynders the estate was built up again. In 1880 it passed to John Poynder Dickson, who was the son of Thomas Poynder's daughter Sarah Matilda, wife of Rear-Admiral J. B. Dickson.[82] In 1888 John Poynder Dickson assumed the additional surname of Poynder.[83] He was created Baron Islington in 1910, G.C.M.G. in 1913, and was Governor of New Zealand 1910–12. He died in 1936.[84] He sold the Hilmarton estate in lots in 1914.[85]

For much of its history the Hilmarton estate has been but part of a larger estate and the manor-house has probably been seldom occupied by the lords of the manor. The house, which stands close to the main road between Calne and Lyneham, was called for a time in the early 20th century Hilmarton Lodge. It appears to have been very thoroughly remodelled in the 19th century by T. H. A. Poynder (d. 1873).

Of the fourteen estates called Clive in Domesday, that held by Alfred of Marlborough and reckoned at four hides has been identified as the estate later called CLEVANCY.[86] In the time of King Edward these four hides had been held as separate manors by Godric, Tedgar, Alfric, and Ulfric.[87] As has been shown elsewhere, much of Alfred's fief passed to Harold of Ewias and from Harold to the family of Tregoze.[88] In 1242–3 Robert Tregoze (d. 1265) held a knight's fee in Clevancy in chief.[89] This fee then passed to Robert's son John (d. 1301) and then to John's grandson Roger le Warre.[90] Roger died in 1370 seised of the overlordship, which has not been traced further.[91]

In 1086 Clevancy was held of Alfred of Marlborough by Roger.[92] By c. 1230 land in Clevancy was held by William de Dodeford and in 1242–3 the fee of Robert Tregoze there was held by Thomas de

[51] Cal. Chart. R. 1257–1300, 481.
[52] Wilts. Inq. p.m. 1242–1326 (Index Libr.), 337.
[53] Cal. Pat. 1307–13, 145; Feet of F. Wilts. 1272–1327 (W.A.S. Rec. Brch.), 77.
[54] Feet of F. Wilts. 1272–1327 (W.A.S. Rec. Brch.), 85.
[55] Wilts. Inq. p.m. 1327–77 (Index Libr.), 189–90.
[56] Cal. Close, 1349–54, 161.
[57] Ibid. 1364–8, 502; Phillipps, Wilts. Inst. i. 65.
[58] Cal. Pat. 1399–1401, 368; Cal. Close, 1349–54, 37; W.N. & Q. iii. 52.
[59] Cal. Fine R. 1413–22, 112.
[60] W. N. & Q. iii. 53.
[61] Ibid. viii. 38.
[62] Wilts. Visit. Pedigrees, (Harl. Soc. cv, cvi.), 14; Cal. Inq. p.m. Hen. VII, ii. 317.
[63] C142/37/143.
[64] C 142/58/10.
[65] C 142/175/101.
[66] C.P. 25(2)/369/5 Jas. I Mich.
[67] C 60/459 no. 41.
[68] Badminton MSS. 110.5.10 and K.21.
[69] C.P. 25(2)/372/19. Jas. I East; C 2/Jas. I/N3/40.
[70] Badminton MS. K. 29.
[71] Genealogist, xxiii. 64; W.A.M. xxiv. 218.

[72] W.A.M. xxiv. 218; Badminton MS. 110.5.12.
[73] Badminton MS. 110.5.12.   [74] Ibid.
[75] Complete Peerage, Botetourt.
[76] Ibid.   [77] Ibid.
[78] Ibid. Beaufort; W.R.O. 498/14, Sale Cat. 1802; Francis Goddard, Reminiscences of a Wilts. Vicar 1814–93 (copy in W.A.S. Libr., Devizes).
[79] W.R.O. 498/14, Sale Cat. 1802; ibid. 498/9, 10, Ct. Bks. 1789–1890.
[80] W.R.O. 498/9, 10, Ct. Bks. 1789–1890.
[81] Gent. Mag. 1856 (2), 127; W.A.M. xviii. 7; xix. 180 and memorials in ch.
[82] W.A.M. xlviii. 119.
[83] W.R.O. 498/5, Note from London Gaz.
[84] Complete Peerage, xiii. 115.
[85] W.A.S. Libr., Devizes, Sale Cat.
[86] V.C.H. Wilts. ii, p. 142.   [87] Ibid.
[88] See p. 78.
[89] Bk. of Fees, ii. 712.
[90] Wilts. Inq. p.m. 1242–1326 (Index Libr.), 253. For more detailed account of descent in Tregoze family see p. 78.
[91] Wilts. Inq. p.m. 1327–77 (Index Libr.), 360.
[92] V.C.H. Wilts. ii, p. 142.

Dodeford.[93] A Thomas de Dodeford still held it in 1268,[94] but he was apparently succeeded soon afterwards by Hugh de Dodeford, who conveyed land in Clevancy *c.* 1270 to his son Robert de Dodeford.[95] Robert had a brother William,[96] and in 1294 William de Dodeford conveyed his holding in Clevancy, which, as the result of several earlier conveyances comprised some 40 a., to Roger of Corton and Roger's son William.[97] This Roger was Roger Fitz-Ellis (d. 1302), lord of the manor of Corton, and henceforth this estate in Clevancy, usually known as Corton Clevancy, was attached to the manor of Corton.[98]

In 1242–3 a ½ fee in Clevancy was held in chief by the Earl Marshal.[99] The overlordship of this then passed like that of the manor of Hilmarton and in 1428 was held by the queen as of her manor of Hampstead Marshall (Berks.).[1] In 1472, however, when the overlordship is last heard of, Clevancy was said to be held of George Nevill, Lord Bergavenny (d. 1492).[2]

In *c.* 1220 William de Wancy and Ralph de Wancy, members of the family which later gave the place part of its name, held land in Clive,[3] and the Earl Marshal's ½ fee there was held of him in 1242–3 by Geoffrey de Wancy.[4] Geoffrey may have been the brother and heir of William de Wancy.[5] In 1249 Christine, widow of Ralph de Wancy, conveyed a ½ hide in Clevancy to Adam of Littlecott,[6] but Geoffrey de Wancy seems to have been still holding the manor in 1254–5 when it was found that he had withdrawn the suit due by his men to the hundred court for the past ten years.[7]

In 1283 Edmund Mortimer held land at Clevancy[8] and was probably lord of the manor, for in 1305 Elizabeth Pedwardine claimed that this had been granted to her and her late husband Walter by Mortimer.[9] Her claim was disputed by Mortimer's wife Margaret, but by 1306 the manor was held by Elizabeth and her son John.[10] John Pedwardine held it in 1316,[11] but by 1380 it had passed to Sir Philip FitzWaryn and his wife Constance, who conveyed it that year to John of Stanshawe and Henry Warner and the heirs of John.[12] In 1412 John (II) Stanshawe was a minor and the manor was consequently in the queen's hands.[13] In 1428 John (II) had been succeeded by Robert Stanshawe[14] who was succeeded as lord of the manor by his son, also called Robert, but the younger Robert died in 1472 without heirs, and the manor passed to his brother Thomas Stanshawe.[15] In 1478 Thomas Stanshawe sold

Clevancy, with the manor of Highway, which he also held, to Thomas Leckhampton.[16]

The next mention of the manor occurs in 1542 when it was held by John Calley and his wife Isabel.[17] It may have been acquired by John's father William Calley, draper of London, for William had land in Clevancy at the time of his death in *c.* 1515.[18] Ralph Calley (d. *c.* 1582), son of John and Isabel, settled the manor in 1580 upon his eldest son by his first marriage, John (d. 1595).[19] By his will, proved 1598, this John devised his estate at Clevancy to his wife Martha for life and thereafter to his younger son Roger, expressly excluding his eldest son Christopher.[20] The descent of the manor over the next 40 years is obscure. In 1603 Christopher Calley, in spite of the terms of his father's will, conveyed it to William Calley, who may have been William Calley (d. 1630), third son of Christopher's grandfather, Ralph Calley, by his second wife.[21] But in 1606 Christopher's mother, Martha, was still alive and holding the manor.[22] It may not, however, have passed from her to her younger son, Roger, and is not among the property settled by him in 1659 upon his daughter and heir, Martha, wife of John Jacob.[23] In 1640 Richard Turner, Lucy his wife, who may have been a Calley, and William Turner sold Clevancy to John Glanville, of Broad Hinton, serjeant-at-law (d. 1661), and to William Glanville.[24] The manor then passed in the Glanville family until *c.* 1789 when Lady Glanville was succeeded by Henry Merewether of Calne.[25] The estate at this date comprised two adjoining farms both leased to tenant farmers.[26] In 1809 the estate was acquired from Henry Merewether by Richard Large.[27] In 1866 William Abbot Large was the owner of the Clevancy estate.[28] In 1901 Clevancy was purchased by Magdalen College, Oxford, to add to the small estate the college already held there.[29] In 1921 Magdalen sold all its Clevancy lands to a Mr. Bolt.[30]

Clevancy Farm stands on an elevated site on the slopes of the downs. It appears to date from the late 18th or early 19th century and may have been largely rebuilt when Richard Large bought the estate in 1809. Cliffansty House, which stands to the northeast, and is the farm-house of the second of the two farms at Clevancy, was probably rebuilt at the same time.

Corton cannot be certainly identified with any entry in Domesday, although it has been conjectured that the 'Corstone' held by Alfred of Marlborough

93 *Cal. Feet of F. Wilts.* 1195–1272, ed. Fry, p. 21; *Bk. of Fees,* ii. 712. Elsewhere it says Thos. only held ½ and 1/10th knight's fee of Robt: ibid. 725.
94 *Close R.* 1264–8, 487.
95 Magdalen Coll. Oxford, Macray Cal. 6.
96 Ibid. 11.
97 Ibid. 18, 19. For earlier conveyances to Wm. see ibid. 9, 10, 11.
98 See p. 55.
99 *Bk. of Fees,* ii. 725.
1 See p. 52.   2 C 140/562/18.
3 Magdalen Coll. Oxford, Macray Cal. 1.
4 *Bk. of Fees,* ii. 725.
5 Magdalen Coll. Oxford, Macray Cal. 9.
6 *Cal. Feet of F. Wilts.* 1195–1272, ed. Fry, p. 42.
7 *Rot. Hund.* (Rec. Com.), ii. 233.
8 *Wilts. Inq. p.m.* 1242–1326 (Index Libr.), 150.
9 C.P. 40/153 m. 188.
10 *Wilts. Inq. p.m.* 1242–1326 (Index Libr.), 337.
11 *Feud. Aids,* v. 207.
12 C.P. 25(1)/256/54/18.

13 *Feud. Aids,* vi. 529.
14 Ibid. v. 277.
15 C 140/562/18.
16 C 54/330 m. 17; C.P. 25(1)/257/65/40 see also *V.C.H. Wilts.* vii. 198.
17 C.P. 25(2)/322/33 Hen. VIII East.; *W.A.M.* xxxi. 146.
18 *W.A.M.* xxxi. 142.
19 Ibid; C.P. 25(2)/240/22 Eliz. I Trin.
20 *W.A.M.* xxxi. 155.
21 C.P. 25(2)/369/1 Jas. I Trin.; *W.A.M.* xxxi. 173–4.
22 *W.A.M.* xxxi. 157–61.
23 Ibid. 161–2.
24 C.P. 25(2)/511/16 Chas. I Mich. For Sir John Glanville, see *D.N.B.* and *W.A.M.* xxiv. 73.
25 W.R.O. For some acct. of Merewether family. See A. E. W. Marsh, *Hist. Calne,* 196–9.
26 W.R.O. 415, Map of Manor of Clevancy.
27 W.R.O. Land Tax.
28 *W.A.M.* xliv. 151.
29 See p. 55.
30 Ibid.

may be that estate.[31] By 1242–3 it belonged to the honor of Gloucester[32] and was still held of the Earl of Gloucester in 1428.[33]

William FitzEllis was seised of Corton in the earlier 13th century.[34] In 1242–3 it was held by Roger Waspail of William FitzEllis, who held of the chief lord.[35] FitzEllis was succeeded by a son William (d. 1262), and this son granted Corton to his younger son Roger FitzEllis.[36] Roger, who died in 1302, also acquired an estate in Clevancy and henceforth the manor of CORTON and these lands in Clevancy, sometimes known as Corton Clevancy, followed the same descent.[37] Roger was succeeded by his son William (d. 1318), and William's heir was his daughter Elizabeth. Elizabeth married John Russell of Bradenstoke, usually called simply John of Bradenstoke, who presented to the free chapel of Corton in 1344, 1350, and 1354.[38] John Russell, son of John of Bradenstoke and Elizabeth, both of whom died in 1363, married first Alice Elkested and by her had a son Nicholas. He married secondly Agnes and they had a daughter Joan. After John Russell's death Agnes married secondly Walter Botiller and Corton was held by her and her husband during the minority of Nicholas Russell. On coming of age Nicholas granted Corton to Agnes and Walter but shortly afterwards he made a similar grant to John Dauntsey and great confusion ensued. After the death of Agnes, Corton should have passed by settlement to William, son of Nicholas, with remainder to John, son of Agnes and Walter Botiller. Both William and John died, however, before Agnes, and so the manor passed to Joan Russell, daughter of Agnes by John Russell of Bradenstoke.

Joan Russell married Thomas Quatremains and they were succeeded by a son Richard.[39] Richard died childless in 1477 and Corton passed to Thomas Danvers, son of Joan Danvers, who was the daughter of Richard's sister Maud. In 1482 Thomas Danvers sold the manor to Bishop William of Waynflete, who devised it to Magdalen College, Oxford, recently founded by him.

Magdalen College retained Corton until 1921 when it was sold to a Mr. Ferris.[40] The lands known as Corton Clevancy had been enlarged in 1901 when the college purchased Clevancy Farm and in 1921 they were sold with this farm to a Mr. Bolt.[41] Corton Farm is a brick house of the late 18th century.

Before the Conquest Brictric held 2 hides in WITCOMB, which by 1086 had passed to Ernulf of Hesdin.[42] The overlordship of this land passed in

the same way as Ernulf's estate at Great Chalfield to the earls of Salisbury[43] and was held as a knight's fee of the earl in 1242–3 as of the honor of Trowbridge.[44] It then descended like the earldom of Salisbury[45] and the last reference to it found occurs in 1570 when Witcomb was said to be held of the queen as of her manor of Great Amesbury, which was an integral part of the Salisbury Earldom.[46]

In 1086 Robert held Witcomb under Ernulf of Hesdin.[47] When it is next heard of, in 1242–3, it was held by William of Bingham of the Earl of Salisbury.[48] In 1305 Clemence, widow of William of Bingham, perhaps the son of the above William, conveyed the manor to Walter du Punt of Langford and in 1316 Walter Hervy conveyed it to John of Langford and Ellen his wife.[49] John of Langford, or another of the same name, held the manor in 1332 and 1339 and presented to the chapel at Witcomb in those years.[50] The manor is next heard of in 1428 when it was held by William of Witcomb,[51] who in 1433 was committed to prison charged with various debts and misdemeanours.[52] In 1447 it had passed to John Lowys and his wife Joan, possibly daughter of William of Witcomb, and that year they conveyed it to Walter, Lord Hungerford, Sir Robert Hungerford, Sir Edmund Hungerford, and others.[53]

In 1512 Walter Mervyn died seised of the manor, which may have been acquired by his father, John Mervyn, who bought the manor of Fonthill Giffard from the Hungerfords.[54] Witcomb then passed in the Mervyn family like Fonthill Giffard until 1609 when Sir James Mervyn settled it upon his daughter, Lucy, her husband, George Tuchet, Lord Audley, and their heirs.[55] Lord Audley was created Earl of Castlehaven in 1616 and Witcomb then descended with that title to James Tuchet, Lord Castlehaven.[56] Before his death in 1684 Lord Castlehaven must have conveyed Witcomb to his brother and eventual heir, Mervyn Tuchet, for Mervyn conveyed it in 1658 to Walter Norborne.[57] Norborne was lord of the capital manor of Hilmarton and after his death in 1684, Witcomb, like Hilmarton, was divided between his two daughters, Elizabeth, wife of Viscount Hereford, and Susan, wife of Sir Ralph Hare.[58] In 1709 Ralph and Susan conveyed their share of Witcomb to Elizabeth, by then dowager Viscountess of Hereford.[59] In 1717 Elizabeth and her second husband, John Symes Berkeley, conveyed Witcomb to Dr. George Clarke, who, with other benefactions, gave it to Worcester College, Oxford.[60] It was sold by the college in 1919.[61]

[31] Dom. Bk. Wilts. ed. Jones, 210, but see V.C.H. Wilts. ii, p. 141, n. 69.
[32] Bk. of Fees, ii. 724.
[33] Feud. Aids, v. 277.
[34] Magdalen Coll. Oxford, Corton MS. 94.
[35] Bk. of Fees, ii. 724.
[36] Magdalen Coll. Oxford, Corton MS. 94. This is a full descent of the manor based on deeds penes the college, which have been calendared in TS by W. D. Macray. F. N. Macnamara, Memorials of the Danvers Family also contains a descent based on the deeds.
[37] Magdalen Coll. Oxford, Corton MS. 94. The subsequent descent until 1482 is based on this MS. unless otherwise stated. For the Clevancy lands see p. 54.
[38] Phillipps, Wilts. Inst. i. 39, 49, 52.
[39] For Quatremains, see W. F. Carter, Quatremains of Oxford.
[40] Magdalen Coll. Oxford, Bursary, Index to Coll. Orders.
[41] Ibid. and see p. 54.
[42] V.C.H. Wilts. ii, p. 139.

[43] Ibid. vii. 59.
[44] Bk. of Fees, ii. 721.
[45] G. Ellis, Earldoms in Fee, 202.
[46] C 142/154/116; Antrobus D. (W.A.S. Rec. Brch.), p. viii.
[47] V.C.H. Wilts. ii, p. 139.
[48] Bk. of Fees, ii. 721.
[49] Feet of F. Wilts. 1272–1377 (W.A.S. Rec. Brch.), 54, 93.
[50] Phillipps, Wilts. Inst. i. 27, 34, 35.
[51] Feud. Aids, v. 278.
[52] Cal. Pat. 1429–36, 329.
[53] C.P. 25(1)/257/64/9.
[54] C 142/27/74; Misc. Gen. et Herald. (N.S. i), 358.
[55] Misc. Gen. et Herald. (N.S. i), 358; C 142/352/130.
[56] Complete Peerage.
[57] C.P. 25(2)/609/Trin. 1658.   [58] See p. 53.
[59] Worcester Coll. Mun. Abstract of Mr. Clarke's Title to Witcomb and Spillman's Farms.
[60] Ibid.; V.C.H. Oxon. iii. 300.
[61] Ex inf. Mr. J. Campbell, Worcester Coll.

The Witcomb estate included two farms, Witcomb Farm and Spillman's Farm. Spillman's Farm may derive from the hide in Hilmarton held in 1086 by Alfric the little, a king's thegn,[62] for this, it has been suggested elsewhere, may be the origin of the carucate in Hilmarton held in serjeanty by Walter Spileman in 1198.[63] No further reference to Spileman's holding has been found, and it presumably became merged in the Witcomb estate where the name is preserved in the farm called Spillman's.

The farm-house at Witcomb is an L-shaped building with a stone slated roof. Structurally it is of stone rubble with a brick facing. The house may have been largely rebuilt in 1740–1 when there is evidence that Worcester College spent considerable sums on building works there.[64] Spillman's Farm appears to date from the 17th century but much rebuilding was done there, too, in 1740–1.

Two estates at Beversbrook are recorded in Domesday Book.[65] One of ½ hide was held by Niel the physician. The other, which T.R.E. had paid geld for 2½ hides, was part of the fief of William of Eu, as was the main manor of Hilmarton. The descent of Niel's estate has not been traced and it may have become merged in the larger estate belonging to William of Eu. The overlordship of William of Eu's estate passed, like that of Hilmarton, to the Earl Marshal, by whom it was held in 1242–3.[66] It then descended like the overlordship of Hilmarton and was said in 1409 to be held of the queen as of her manor of Hampstead Marshall.[67]

Beversbrook was held in 1086 of William of Eu by William de Mara.[68] In 1242–3 Robert de Mare, presumably a descendent of William de Mara, held ½ a knight's fee there of Andrew Blunt, who held of Peter la Mare, who held of the Earl Marshal.[69] In 1247 Walter de la Mare, perhaps the son of the above Robert de Mare, conveyed to Robert le Blunt land in Beversbrook.[70] This was probably one of a number of conveyances which brought the manor of *BEVERSBROOK* to the family of Blunt. In 1298 Hugh le Blunt presented to the manorial chapel there.[71] In 1337 Andrew le Blunt was lord of Beversbrook.[72] By 1377 he had been succeeded by Sir John Blunt, who may have been the Sir John Blunt who died holding the manor in 1383–4.[73] He was followed by another Sir John Blunt, who was holding the manor in 1398 and it was presumably he who conveyed Beversbrook in 1406 to William and Thomas Wroughton.[74] The manor then passed in the Wroughton family in the same way as Woodhill in Clyffe Pypard to Sir William Wroughton.[75] Sir William died in 1559 and was succeeded by his son, Thomas.[76] Thomas died in 1597 and his son

Giles conveyed Beversbrook in 1612–13 to Mervyn Audley, who succeeded his father in 1617 as Earl of Castlehaven.[77] After Lord Castlehaven's execution in 1631 Beversbrook passed to his son and heir James Tuchet, Earl of Castlehaven (d. 1684), and at an unknown date, but perhaps in 1654, Lord Castlehaven conveyed it to Walter Norborne (d. 1659),[78] who held it by 1657.[79] Thenceforth Beversbrook descended with the main manor.[80]

As mentioned above, land in Littlecott was included in the grant of 962 of 10 *mansae* in Hilmarton by King Edgar to Wulfmaer, a thegn.[81] Part of Littlecott may still have been included in the returns for Hilmarton in the Domesday Survey,[82] but another part was reckoned separately. This was the estate of 1 hide and 1 virgate held immediately before the Conquest by Godric[83] and in 1086 by Miles Crispin.[84] By 1242–3 the overlordship was divided between the Earl of Salisbury, who held a knight's fee, and the Earl of Hereford, who held ⅓ fee. Both were held of the honor of Trowbridge, which at that time was divided between the two earls[85] and, so far as is known, the overlordship then descended with the honor.

Under Miles Crispin Littlecott was held by Turchetil.[86] In 1242–3 the Earl of Salisbury's fee there was held by Adam of Littlecott and the Earl of Hereford's ⅓ fee was held by Robert Mauduit.[87] In 1316 Ralph Bluet was said to hold Littlecott,[88] but it is not known how it came to him, nor how it descended from him for the next 60 years.

In 1377 John of Littlecott, conceivably a descendant of Adam of Littlecott (see above), had an estate in Littlecott.[89] This, reckoned at ½ knight's fee, and said to have once been held by William of Littlecott, was held in 1428 by Thomas Quintin in right of his wife Alice, probably a daughter, or granddaughter of John of Littlecott.[90] In 1448 Thomas and Alice Quintin conveyed the estate to three persons, presumably trustees.[91] This may have been followed by a grant to Bradenstoke Priory, which already held lands in Littlecott.[92]

On the eve of the Dissolution land in Littlecott formed part of the manor of Lyneham, one of Bradenstoke's largest estates.[93] It was probably this part of Littlecott which was granted with Lyneham in 1559 to William Button.[94] Button's holding in Littlecott, later evidence shows, is represented in modern times by Upper Littlecott Farm.[95] It passed, like the manor of Lyneham, in the Button family until 1707 when Sir John Button (d. 1712) conveyed it to Thomas Cromwell and another.[96] By 1714 Upper Littlecott Farm had been acquired by Thomas Benet of Salthrop (Wroughton), who con-

[62] *V.C.H. Wilts.* ii, p. 161.
[63] Ibid. pp. 77–78.
[64] Worcester Coll. Mun. Building Accts. for work undertaken at Witcomb and Spillman's.
[65] *V.C.H. Wilts.* ii, pp. 158, 149.
[66] *Bk. of Fees*, ii. 724 and see p. 52.
[67] *Cal. Fine R.* 1405–13, 153.
[68] *V.C.H. Wilts.* ii, p. 149.
[69] *Bk. of Fees*, ii. 724.
[70] *Cal. Feet of F. Wilts.* 1195–1272, ed. Fry, p. 37.
[71] *Reg. Ghent* (Cant. and York Soc.), ii. p. 580.
[72] Aubrey, *Topog. Coll.* ed. Jackson, 43.
[73] *Cal. Close*, 1377–81, 98; C 131/31/4.
[74] *Cal. Pat.* 1396–9, 303; C.P. 25(1)/256/58/47.
[75] See p. 32.
[76] C 142/124/192.
[77] C 142/249/81; C.P. 25(2)/370/10 Jas. I Mich.; *Complete Peerage.*

[78] Badminton MS. K. 29.
[79] Ibid. 110. 5. 12.
[80] See p. 53.
[81] See p. 52.   [82] See p. 52.
[83] *V.C.H. Wilts.* ii, p. 146.   [84] Ibid.
[85] *Bk. of Fees*, ii. 721, 723; *V.C.H. Wilts.* ii, p. 110 n.; I. J. Sanders, *English Baronies*, 91.
[86] *V.C.H. Wilts.* ii, p. 146.
[87] *Bk. of Fees*, ii. 721, 723.
[88] *Feud. Aids*, v. 207.
[89] *Wilts. Inq. p.m.* 1327–77 (Index Libr.), 400.
[90] *Feud. Aids*, v. 207.
[91] C.P. 25(1)/257/64/4.
[92] See p. 94.
[93] *Valor Eccl.* (Rec. Com.), ii. 123, and see p. 93.
[94] *Cal. Pat.* 1558–60, 300.
[95] W.R.O. 529/8, Release to Robt. Neale, 1732.
[96] C.P. 25(2)/980/6 Anne East. and see p. 94.

veyed it in 1732 to Robert Neale.[97] It then descended in the Neale family until 1856 when it was sold by the trustees of John Corbett Neale (d. 1853) to Gabriel Goldney of Chippenham.[98]

Besides the estate acquired by William Button other land in Littlecott, also said to have belonged previously to Bradenstoke, was granted in 1541 to Edward Seymour, Earl of Hertford (cr. Duke of Somerset 1546–7, executed 1552).[99] Somerset's son Edward, Earl of Hertford (d. 1621), settled his Littlecott lands in 1612 upon his grandson Francis Seymour.[1] In 1647 Francis, by then Lord Seymour of Trowbridge, and his son, Charles, conveyed Littlecott to John Romen, clothier.[2] Two years later John Romen and his wife, Mary, settled the estate upon their only daughter Ruth and her husband Jacob Selfe of Beanacre.[3] Jacob and Ruth Selfe had three daughters upon whom, in 1685, the estate was settled in three parts, namely $\frac{1}{3}$ to Margaret, who married Daniel Webb, $\frac{1}{3}$ to Ruth, who married Roger Spackman, and $\frac{1}{3}$ to Mary, wife of John Tuck.[4] Margaret and Daniel Webb had one child, Elizabeth, who married Thomas Smith of Shaw House, Melksham.[5] In 1698 Roger and Ruth Spackman conveyed their third to Thomas Smith, who also acquired later the share of John Tuck.[6] Thomas Smith died in 1723, leaving as heirs to his Littlecott lands his son Walter and daughter Elizabeth.[7] On the death of Walter Smith in 1732 Elizabeth acquired her brother's share and in the same year she acquired the share, which had been settled upon Margaret Webb, her grandmother, in 1685.[8] In 1735 Elizabeth Smith married Robert Neale (d. 1776)[9] who had already acquired Upper Littlecott Farm. All the Littlecott lands then passed in the Neale family until sold in 1853 (see above).

A rent of 50s. at Catcomb was among the endowments given in 1114 to the Abbey of St. Georges de Boscherville, near Rouen (Seine Maritime) by William de Tancarville to found a priory at Avebury.[10] Catcomb then became attached to the manor of Avebury and passed in 1411 with that manor to Fotheringhay College (Northants.), which held it at the Dissolution.[11] After the Dissolution Catcomb continued to pass with Avebury first to William Sharington in 1548,[12] and from Sharington to William Dunch in 1551.[13] Still as part of the manor of Avebury, it was sold in 1633 by William Dunch's

grandson, also called William, to Sir Edward Baynton.[14] Baynton's eldest son, Robert, sold CATCOMB in 1682[15] now detached from Avebury and called a manor, to Matthew Barlow of Lockerley (Hants), M.D., and henceforth Catcomb descended as a separate estate.

Matthew Barlow in 1686 settled Catcomb upon his wife for her life and after her death upon his nephew, also called Matthew Barlow, and his heirs.[16] Matthew (II) Barlow died in 1723 and devised Catcomb to his nephew, John Barlow, watchmaker, of London.[17] John Barlow's daughter, Eleanor, married John Cowper[18] and their son John (II) Cowper settled Catcomb upon his wife, Anne.[19] John (II) Cowper was dead by 1786 and Anne had married Wade Toby Caulfield. Catcomb was then settled upon Anne and W. T. Caulfield and their issue.[20] By 1802 W. T. Caulfield was dead and Anne married thirdly Charles Francis de Chartier de Bolleville.[21] As Madame de Bolleville, Anne held Catcomb Farm in 1842.[22] But soon afterwards it became part of the Poynder estate and the farm house was rebuilt by Thomas Henry Allen Poynder (d. 1873).[23]

It has been suggested that the hide at 'Gategram' held in 1086 by Saulf, a king's thegn, may refer to Goatacre.[24] But the first certain reference to Goatacre found occurs in 1242–3 when the Earl Marshal held $\frac{1}{8}$ fee there.[25] This was held of the earl by Ralph de Barneville and of Ralph by Roger Bluet.[26] Roger was also holding the main manor of Hilmarton at this date as terre tenant of the earl, and presumably the two estates became amalgamated.[27] On the death of Eleanor Bluet in 1348 Goatacre was described as parcel of the manor of Hilmarton. It was, however, said to be held in chief as of the manor of Hampstead Marshall, while Hilmarton at that date was held of the manor of Chepstow.[28] No further reference to a separate overlordship for Goatacre has been found, however, and it remained part of the main manor of Hilmarton until the beginning of the 19th century. At the sale of 1802 Goatacre Farm was sold with Hilmarton to Samuel Hale,[29] but, unlike Hilmarton, it then passed to Anne de Bolleville, who owned it in 1838 and 1842.[30] Soon after this, however, it was bought by Thomas Poynder, and thus restored to the Hilmarton estate.[31] The farm-house was remodelled by his son T. H. A. Poynder (d. 1873).[32]

[97] W.R.O. 529/8, Deeds.
[98] W.R.O. Sale Cat. For the Neale family see J. A. Neale, *Charts. and Recs. of Neales of Berkeley etc.* (priv. printed, 1906).
[99] *L. & P. Hen. VIII,* xvi, p. 381.
[1] *Wilts. Inq. p.m.* 1625–49 (Index Libr.), 25.
[2] J. A. Neale, *Neales of Berkeley, etc.* 135.
[3] Ibid. 131.
[4] Ibid. 132.
[5] Ibid. 214, 215.
[6] Ibid. 135.
[7] Ibid. 133.
[8] Ibid. 136, 214.
[9] Ibid. 32.
[10] *V.C.H. Wilts.* iii. 392.
[11] Ibid. The manorial descent of Avebury, to which Catcomb was attached from the 12th to the 17th centuries, is reserved for treatment in another volume of the *History.* It will, therefore, only be summarized here.
[12] *Cal. Pat.* 1547–8, 401.
[13] Ibid. 1550–3, 84.
[14] W.R.O. 248/161, Deed of purchase Sir Edw. Baynton from Sir Wm. Dunch.
[15] W.R.O. 248/161, Deed of purchase Matthew Barlow from Robt. Baynton.

[16] W.R.O. 248/161, Settlement Mat. Barlow upon Mat. Barlow.
[17] W.R.O. 248/161, Copy of will of Mat. Barlow.
[18] W.R.O. 248/161, Promissory Note Mat. Barlow to John Cowper, 1763.
[19] W.R.O. 402/35, Marriage settlement for Mrs. Anne Caulfield, 1802.
[20] Ibid.
[21] Ibid.
[22] W.R.O. Tithe Award.
[23] Francis Goddard, *Reminiscences of a Wilts. Vicar, 1814–93* (copy in W.A.S. Libr., Devizes). Catcomb was included in the sale of the Hilmarton Estate in 1914: W.A.S. Libr., Devizes, Sale Cat.
[24] *Dom. Bk. Wilts.* ed. Jones, p. 217.
[25] *Bk. of Fees,* ii. 724.
[26] Ibid.
[27] See p. 52.
[28] *Wilts. Inq. p.m.* 1327–77 (Index Libr.), 189.
[29] W.R.O. 498/14, Sale Cat.
[30] Ibid. 498/40/1–3, Poor Rate Assessmt; Tithe Award.
[31] W.R.O. 498/61/1b, Estate Map, 1855.
[32] Francis Goddard, *Reminiscences of a Wilts. Vicar, 1814–93* (copy in W.A.S. Libr., Devizes).

The rectory acquired by John and Martha Calley in 1590 included a farm known as Parsonage Farm.[33] This passed with the rectory, as shown below, and came in 1752 to Norborne Berkeley, lord of the capital manor.[34] At this date the farm was leased to Joseph Hopkins and comprised some 67 a. of arable and pasture, scattered in small pieces throughout the common fields of Hilmarton.[35] From 1752 the farm followed the same descent as the capital manor and became merged in the Hilmarton estate.[36] In the 20th century its name was changed to Manor Farm.[37]

The farm-house stands in the middle of the village just south-west of the church. It is an **L**-shaped building of two stories the north wing being timber-framed and probably dating from the 16th century. The east wing is in the mid-19th-century Tudor style of the Poynders. Stone gate piers supporting vases in front of the house are of the 18th century.

By 1232 Bradenstoke Priory had a rent of 2s. in Clevancy, the gift of Muriel, late wife of Robert de Dodeford, and a meadow, which had been granted by Muriel, daughter of Ralph Lovel.[38] Other rents were conveyed to the prior by Thomas de Dodeford in 1249.[39] At the Dissolution Bradenstoke had a house, a virgate with common of pasture, some meadow, and 2s. rent in Clevancy.[40] Assized rent there was valued at 40s. 8d.[41] In 1560 these lands were granted to Thomas Reve and George Evelyn.[42] Their subsequent descent has not been traced.

ECONOMIC HISTORY. The largest of the three estates called Hilmarton in 1086 was assessed at 9 hides in 1066 and was valued then and in 1086 at £7.[43] In 1086 there was land for 8 ploughs. The demesne contained 3 hides and had on it 2 ploughs. Seven villeins and 10 bordars had 6 ploughs. There were 50 a. of meadow and 40 a. of pasture. The one-hide estate belonging to Ernulf of Hesdin had increased in value from 15s. in 1066 to 30s. in 1086.[44] There was land for 1 plough and there were 3 coscez on the estate. There were 6 a. of meadow, 1 a. of pasture, and 8 a. of wood. The other one-hide estate was valued at 1s. in 1086 and on it were a plough and a serf.[45]

Five other entries in Domesday refer certainly to lands in Hilmarton. An estate in Littlecott was assessed in 1066 at a hide and a virgate.[46] In 1086 it was valued at 10s. There was land for ½ a plough and on it was a bordar. There were 4 a. each of meadow and pasture and 4 a. of bramble wood. The larger of the two Beversbrook estates was assessed in 1066 at 2½ hides and valued then and in 1086 at 30s.[47] In 1086 on the demesne of 1½ hide there were 2 ploughs and 2 serfs, and elsewhere on the estate

there were 1 villein and 8 bordars. The half-hide estate in Beversbrook was worth 7s. in 1086 and on it were a villein and a bordar.[48] There was woodland 1 furlong long by ½ furlong broad. Clevancy was assessed at 4 hides in 1066 and valued at 40s.[49] But by 1086 its value had increased to 50s. There was then land for 2 ploughs. On the demesne there were 3 serfs and 2 coscez with 1 plough. There were 24 a. of meadow, 20 a. of pasture, and 6 a. of woodland. Witcomb assessed at 2 hides in 1066 and valued at 20s. was worth 30s. in 1086.[50] There was land for 2 ploughs, but only 1 is returned for the estate on which there were 7 coscez. There were 12 a. of meadow, 6 a. of pasture, and 12 a. of wood.

By the 14th century the main manor of Hilmarton included two farms, namely Hilmarton and Goatacre. When the manor was extended in 1348[51] there was at Hilmarton a messuage with garden and curtilage, and a dovecot. There were 3 carucates of arable land containing 180 a. Of these 120 a. could be sewn every year, and were worth 6d. an acre, while 60 a. lay fallow. The pasture was said to be worth nothing because it lay in common. But 20 a. of meadow were worth 1s. 4d. an acre and an inclosed pasture was valued at 6s. 8d. A wood, in which there was no underwood, lay in common. Assized rents and labour services were worth £16. Goatacre was worth 15s. 6d. in all its issues and comprised 2 messuages and 18 a. A West Field and an East Field of Goatacre are mentioned at about this date,[52] so apparently Hilmarton and Goatacre each had its own set of common fields.

From the mid 13th century until the beginning of the 17th century the main manor of Hilmarton belonged to the lords of Lackham (in Lacock) and was probably farmed as an adjunct of that estate.[53] A considerable number of manorial account rolls survive for the later 14th and early 15th centuries and these show that in this period all but 9 a. of the Hilmarton demesne was in hand and they contain some evidence of a traffic in produce between Hilmarton and Lackham.[54]

In 1588 a three-year rotation was followed in the arable fields of the main Hilmarton manor, which permitted the land to be tilled for two years and then left fallow for the third year when no common grazing was allowed upon it. A North Field of Hilmarton is mentioned at this date.[55] The three-year course is mentioned again in 1671.[56] In 1716 East, West, and South Fields are recorded.[57] In 1752, when Parsonage Farm was acquired for the estate, all its arable lay scattered in quite small pieces throughout the common fields of Hilmarton.[58] Fields and furlongs expressly named as common were Cowage Field, Mead Furlong, Crates Furlong, Black Furlong, and Swillfield. The pasture belong-

[33] See p. 61.   [34] See p. 53.
[35] Worcester Coll. Mun. Release John Jacob to Norborne Berkeley.
[36] See p. 53.
[37] Ex inf. Mr. H. C. Taylor, Hilmarton.
[38] Cal. Chart. R. 1226–57, 160, 162.
[39] Cal. Feet of F. Wilts. 1195–1272 ed. Fry, p. 40. Fry has de Bodeford but this is an error.
[40] V.C.H. Wilts. iii. 280.
[41] Valor Eccl. (Rec. Com.), ii. 124.
[42] Cal. Pat. 1558–60, 315.
[43] V.C.H. Wilts. ii, p. 149.
[44] Ibid. p. 140.
[45] Ibid. p. 161.
[46] Ibid. p. 146.

[47] Ibid. p. 149.   [48] Ibid. p. 158.
[49] Ibid. p. 142.
[50] Ibid. p. 140.
[51] Wilts. Inq. p.m. 1327–77 (Index Libr.), 189–90.
[52] Badminton MS. 110. 5. 3. Acct. R. 1337–8.
[53] See p. 53.
[54] Badminton MSS. 110. 5. 3, and 110. 5. 4. These accts., together with the other Badminton MSS., came to light as this article was nearing completion. They could, therefore, only be used superficially.
[55] Sar. Dioc. R.O. Glebe Terrier, 1588.
[56] Ibid. 1671.
[57] Badminton MS. 110. 5. 9. Survey.
[58] See above, and Worcester Coll. Mun. Release John Jacob to Norborne Berkeley.

ing to Parsonage Farm lay in three closes called Upper Close, Lower Marsh, and New Leaze. Presumably when this and other farms were added to the estate (see below), a re-allotment of the arable lands would be made, whereby the scattered strips were exchanged for more conveniently situated compact blocks. On a large estate, made up of several farms, all under one owner, the benefits of inclosure could be thus achieved without the authority of an inclosure award. Record survives of some exchanges of small quantities of land in the mid 18th century.[59] There is no inclosure award for Hilmarton.

In 1627 the Hilmarton estate comprised three farms, namely Hilmarton, Goatacre, and Penn.[60] In the mid 17th century the farms at Beversbrook and Witcomb were added,[61] and although early in the 18th century Witcomb was sold, that century also saw a building up of the estate. By the beginning of the 19th century, besides the farms already mentioned, it included Rodwell Farm, Beacon Hill Farm, and Catcomb Farm as well as a number of smaller unnamed farms.[62] All the farms were let to tenant farmers and the estate was managed as part of the larger Norborne estate. In the later part of the century the steward visited Hilmarton about three or four times a year to collect rents, order and pay for repairs, and once a year to hold a dinner for the tenant farmers.[63] During the 1790s considerable sums were spent on draining operations at Rodwell Farm.[64] In 1787 the expense of cropping an acre of corn on the estate, from the time of ploughing until delivery at the market, was reckoned at £3. The produce of the acre was valued at £4 15s., thus making the value of the acre £1 15s.[65]

In 1802 the estate covered some 3,000 acres and extended from the extreme north of the parish to its southern boundary.[66] All farms were let and the total rental was £1,512, exclusive of the manor, on which 27 copy- and leasehold tenants paid some £4 in rent. The estate was broken up at the sale of that year and the farms sold piecemeal.[67] But after the manor was bought by Thomas Poynder in 1813 the estate was built up again and a period of reconsolidation and improvement began. By 1880 it comprised some 3,500 a. and included besides Hilmarton Farm, Parsonage Farm (later called Manor Farm), Rodwell Farm, Penn Farm, Lower Littlecott Farm, Beversbrook Farm, Goatacre Farm, Catcomb Farm, and Cowage Farm.[68] It also included 106 a. in Catcomb Wood, part of which had been planted in 1876.[69] In the later part of the century 108 a. of the estate were in hand and 3,486 a. were let.[70] A policy of spending most of the income upon improvements was pursued by all the Poynders.[71] Piped water and drainage were laid on and most of the farmhouses were rebuilt. In 1883 £1,051 was spent on new buildings and £1,176 on improvements.[72] The

appearance of the village in 1967 bears witness to the number of estate cottages built. In 1914 the estate was again broken up at a sale when many of the tenant farmers bought the farms they were occupying.[73]

Of the other farms in the parish, which were not, or were for only a short time, part of the Hilmarton estate, those at Corton and Clevancy on the east, at Littlecott in the north, and at Witcomb, roughly in the middle, were the largest. But little is known of their history. In the later 13th century Clevancy had a West Field and an East Field.[74] These lay above the farmsteads on the chalk uplands of Clevancy Hill and were reached by steep tracks running up the hillside from the farms. A holding granted in 1345 consisted of some 6 a. of arable distributed in small pieces among 5 furlongs in the East Field, about the same amount lying in 4 furlongs in the West Field, and 2 small pieces of land, presumably pasture, situated 'below the hill'.[75]

In c. 1483 the arable of the farm known as Corton Clevancy, which was a detached part of the manor of Corton, lay scattered in small strips in the two fields of Clevancy. Corton's arable also lay on Clevancy Hill, and its common pasture was at Corton Marsh to the north-west of the farmstead and adjoining a common known as Goatacre Common. Here the tenants of Corton Clevancy, as well as those of Corton, had grazing rights, and rights of way existed so that they could cross the lands of the intervening Clevancy manor to reach the marsh.[76] There were also rights of way enabling them to reach the market and mill in Hilmarton.[77] In 1768 the land of Corton Farm was divided about equally between pasture and arable. The arable of Corton Clevancy still lay in a field marked as open-field land on a map of this date and its pasture lay in two separated blocks.[78] This small farm belonging to Corton Farm, but surrounded by the lands of Clevancy Farm, was farmed by the two tenant farmers, who farmed the Clevancy manor lands in 1787.[79] But in 1901 Magdalen College, Oxford, the owners of Corton, bought Clevancy Farm and thus enlarged and consolidated its holding in Clevancy.[80]

The two farms at Witcomb lay mostly on the Oxford Clay and here dairy farming predominated. In 1724 Witcomb Farm had 48 a. of arable lying in 5 fields, 31 a. of meadow in 7 fields, and 118 a. of pasture in 5 fields.[81] Spillman's Farm at the same date had 16 a. of arable in 2 fields, 45 a. of meadow in 2 fields, and 31 a. of pasture in 4 fields.[82] In the early 20th century a special kind of cheese was made at Spillman's Farm which was said to be in high repute locally.[83]

As shown above stone suitable for building and road-making, could be had from numerous small quarries, particularly on the western side of the

[59] Badminton MS. Farming Acct. Bk. 1748–57.
[60] Ibid. 110. 5. 8. Rental.   [61] See pp. 55, 56.
[62] W.A.S. Libr., Devizes, Sale Cat. 1802.
[63] Badminton MSS. Farming Acct. Bks. 1748–57 and 1758–70.
[64] Ibid. Farming Acct. Bk. 1748–57.
[65] Ibid. 110. 5. 23. Memo. Bk.
[66] W.A.S. Libr., Devizes, Sale Cat. 1802.
[67] See p. 53.
[68] W.R.O. 137/128 Rental n.d.   [69] Ibid.
[70] Rep. Asst. Com. Agric. Depression [C. 8125], pp. 24–25, H.C. (1896), xvi.
[71] Francis Goddard, Reminiscences of a Wilts. Vicar, 1814–95 (copy in W.A.S. Libr., Devizes).

[72] Rep. Agric. Depression (1896), xvi, 24–25.
[73] W.A.S. Libr., Devizes, Sale Cat. 1914.
[74] These are frequently mentioned in the 13th-century deeds penes Magdalen Coll. Oxford.
[75] Magdalen Coll. Oxford, Corton MS. 39.
[76] Ibid. 52.
[77] Ibid.
[78] Ibid. Bursary, Map of 1768.
[79] W.R.O. 415/95, Map of Clevancy, 1787.
[80] Magdalen Coll. Oxford, Bursary, Map of 1914, and see p. 54.
[81] Worcester Coll. Mun. Map of 1724.
[82] Ibid.
[83] Ibid. Memo. by Bursar.

parish.[84] An early 19th-century Highways Book shows quarries being worked and then filled in as need for stone arose.[85] Considerable quantities of stone came from quarries at Goatacre, Catcomb, and Littlecott. Farmers were compensated from the highway rates for damage done to their land when stone was hauled across it.[86] Local stone was used in 1833 for repairing the bridge, called the Arch Bridge, by Witcomb Mill, for building 161 yds. of causeway in Hilmarton Street, and for a wall in Catcomb Street.[87] In 1840 stone from a quarry in Goatacre Field was used for the turnpike road from Calne to Lyneham Green.[88]

Two mills in Hilmarton are mentioned in 1086. One was on the estate of 9 hides held in chief by William of Eu, the other on the one-hide estate of Ernulf of Hesdin.[89] In 1348 there was a windmill worth 13s. 4d. on the manor of Hilmarton,[90] but, as far as is known, the only watermill in the parish was Witcomb Mill, which was part of the Witcomb estate and so passed to Worcester College, Oxford, in the 18th century. It was then a flour mill.[91] At the beginning of the 19th century it was leased from Worcester by Robert Stiles and his son Edward.[92] By 1899 it was described as useless, since the supply of water was inadequate during more than half the year.[93] In 1903 it was falling into disrepair and some time before 1915 it was pulled down.[94] In 1967 its site and some of the hatches could be clearly seen.

An annual fair to be held on the manor of Hilmarton on the eve and feast of St. Lawrence (10 and 11 Aug.) was granted to John Bluet in 1299.[95] Its tolls are mentioned in the extent of the manor in 1348 and with the pleas and perquisites of the manor court amounted to 20s. a year.[96] The fair was confirmed to Philip Baynard in 1401,[97] and in 1407–8 its tolls were worth 3s. 6d.[98] It seems that the fair was still being held in 1621, but nothing more is known about it.[99]

Almost no evidence of the clothing industry has been found. In 1349 there were 2 tailors in the parish,[1] and as is mentioned below, some people closely connected with the industry were active among the nonconformists at Goatacre in the 17th and 18th centuries.[2]

LOCAL GOVERNMENT. A considerable number of records of the manorial court survive. Beginning in 1337 there are court rolls for some years in the 14th, 15th, and 16th centuries.[3] From the beginning of the 18th century there is a complete set of court books, ending in 1890 when the last court was held.[4] In the earlier period, besides Hilmarton and Goatacre, the tithings of Witcomb, Clevancy, in which

Littlecott was sometimes expressly said to be included, and Clyffe Pypard sent tithingmen to the court.[5] So far as is known, the only other manor court in the parish was one for the manor of Corton, and there is only evidence for this for one year in the 15th century.[6] In the 18th century Corton sent its tithingman to the Hilmarton court.[7]

In the 14th century the court probably met four times a year.[8] In 1616 John Norborne, who had recently acquired the manor, had a re-grant of a court leet within it.[9] At first this met separately but by the 18th century the view of frankpledge and court baron were held together.[10] By the later date the court met twice a year. It was presided over by the steward of the estate, and at it a constable of Hilmarton and a hayward of Hilmarton and Goatacre were appointed. The court dealt with admissions to the manor of Hilmarton and the presentment of nuisances for the whole parish.[11] In 1738 the tithings of Witcomb and of Littlecott and Clevancy were ordered to erect stocks in the usual places.[12] Throughout the century nuisances continued to be presented, although the court probably had little authority to insist upon their remedy, since the same complaint is presented over and over again. The court, however, survived the break-up of the Hilmarton estate in 1802,[13] and when Thomas Poynder became lord of the manor in 1813, rules of procedure for holding it were laid down.[14] These dealt with the appointment of the constable, hayward, jury, and homage. In the 19th century courts were usually held annually, although for a time they were held only once every two years.[15]

Although the manor court survived so long, its function was limited to the matters mentioned above, and it is not known to have played any other part in parish affairs. In the later 17th century there were 2 churchwardens, 2 overseers, and 2 waywardens.[16] Liability to serve in these offices was evidently imposed upon specified estates or farms in the parish.[17] A few cases occur of women being elected to the office of overseer, presumably because they owned or occupied premises liable for this duty.[18] At the end of the 18th century the vestry, at least when important matters were under discussion, seems to have been composed of the principal paymasters of the parish.[19] In 1784 this body and the parish officers agreed to pay a doctor £12 12s. a year to attend the sick suffering from smallpox.[20] A similar arrangement was made in 1786, but a limit was then set upon the number and type of cases the doctor need attend for this salary.[21] As will be shown below, the vicarage house was used in the earlier 19th century to accommodate a few pauper families.[22] In 1805 the vestry decided to make 'the

84 See p. 51.
85 W.R.O. 718, Highways Bk. 1820–40.   86 Ibid.
87 Ibid. 796/46, Surveyors' Accts. 1810–42.   88 Ibid.
89 See p. 52.
90 Wilts. Inq. p.m. 1327–77 (Index Libr.), 189.
91 C.P. 25(2)/1077/4 Geo. I East.
92 Worcester Coll. Mun. Schedule of lands in Hilmarton.
93 Ibid. Memo. by Bursar.   94 Ibid.
95 Cal. Chart. R. 1257–1300, 481.
96 Wilts. Inq. p.m. 1327–77 (Index Libr.), 190.
97 Cal. Pat. 1399–1401, 368.
98 Badminton MS. 110. 5. 4. Acct. R.
99 C 2/Jas. I/N3/40.
1 W.A.M. xxxiii. 409.   2 See p. 64.
3 Badminton MSS. 110. 5. 3, and 110. 5. 4.
4 Ibid. 110. 5. 5 and W.R.O. 498/8, 9, 10.

5 Badminton MSS. 110. 5. 3, and 110. 5. 4.
6 Magdalen Coll. Oxford, Corton MS. 53 (2).
7 W.R.O. 498/8, 9, 10.
8 Badminton MS. 110. 5. 3.
9 Ibid. K. 21, Grant of Ct. Leet.
10 Ibid. 110. 5. 5.   11 Ibid.
12 Ibid. Ct. Bk. 1726–48.
13 See p. 53; W.R.O. 498/11, Deeds relating to cts. of Manor of Hilmarton.
14 W.R.O. 498/10 Ct. Bk. 1810–90.   15 Ibid.
16 W.R.O. 796/47, Overseers Accts. etc. 1669–1787.
17 Ibid. and 718, Highways Bk. 1820–40.
18 Ibid. 796/47, Overseers Accts. 1669–1787.
19 Ibid. 718, Poor Relief Bk. 1782–8.
20 Ibid.   21 Ibid.
22 See p. 62.

west corner' of the church a place suitable for paying the poor. The floor was to be boarded, and a small fire-place provided. Coal when required was to be paid for by the parish at large.[23] In the autumn of 1811 the vestry fixed the price of men's labour until the following haymaking time at 10s. a week.[24]

CHURCHES. The church of Hilmarton is first mentioned in 1291 when it was valued for the taxation of Pope Nicholas.[25] Besides the parish church there were in the 14th century two free chapels, one at Corton and another at Witcomb. Corton chapel survived until the Reformation, that at Witcomb is heard of only for a few years (see below). There was also a chapel attached to the manor of Beversbrook (see below). In 1952 Highway church, until then a chapelry in Bremhill parish, was united with Hilmarton and a few years later Highway was closed.[26]

Although the church was not at that time appropriated, a vicarage had been ordained by 1291,[27] presumably because the rector could not reside or at some period had not done so. The advowson of the rectory belonged to the lords of the capital manor. The rector presented to the vicarage in 1301, 1342, and 1361,[28] but perhaps the vicarage was not always presentative for the institution of the vicar who held the cure in 1321–5 has not been traced.[29] The vicar instituted in 1361 had become rector by 1380.[30] His successor, instituted in 1380, was apparently reinstituted in 1395.[31] In 1386 Philip Baynard, lord of the manor, conveyed the advowson to three persons, presumably trustees.[32] In 1396 three other persons conveyed the advowson to Bisham Priory (Berks.), who the same year was given leave to appropriate the church.[33] Thereupon the presentation of rectors ceased and the priors of Bisham presented to the vicarage.[34] After the Dissolution rectory and advowson were granted in 1540–1 to Anne of Cleeves.[35] William Cavendish presented in 1546 under a grant from the priory.[36] The queen presented in 1552[37] and from that time the advowson belonged to the Crown.

In 1291 the church, apart from the vicarage, was valued at £20.[38] At the time of the appropriation by Bisham it was reckoned at a sum 'not exceeding 30 marks'.[39] A re-allotment of the revenues between rector and vicar was probably made at this time whereby the vicar received a larger share.[40] In c. 1535 the value of the rectory was reckoned to be £9 19s. 3d.[41]

In 1590 the rectory, which had passed to Anne of

Cleeves in 1540–1, was acquired by Sir Walter Hungerford and Edward Hungerford.[42] The Hungerfords sold it immediately to John and Martha Calley, who had been leasing it since 1583.[43] Like the manor of Clevancy, the rectory was settled in 1595 by John Calley upon his wife Martha and their youngest son Roger.[44] Roger's heir was his daughter Martha, who married John Jacob in 1649, and in 1659 her father's estate, including the rectory, was settled upon her and her heirs.[45] By 1752 the rectory had passed to John Jacob, grandson of John and Martha, and that year he sold it to Norborne Berkeley, lord of the manor of Hilmarton.[46] John Jacob, however, retained for himself and his heirs responsibility for the upkeep of the chancel of the church and the right to be buried there.[47]

All the great tithes belonged to the rectory except those of Clevancy, which belonged to the vicarage,[48] and those of Corton, which belonged to the free chapel there until its suppression (see below). After the dissolution of Bisham Priory, the great tithes passed with the rectory in 1540–1 to Anne of Cleeves. They then descended with the rectory (see above) and so came in 1752 to Norborne Berkeley, lord of the manor of Hilmarton.[49] They followed the same descent as that manor until its sale in 1802.[50] At that sale the great tithes due from certain lands at Witcomb were acquired by Robert Stiles.[51] Thus at the time of the tithe award in 1842 Thomas Poynder, lord of the manor of Hilmarton, and Edward Stiles, son of Robert, were the impropriators of the great tithes.[52] The tithes due to Poynder were that year commuted for a rent-charge of £83 4s. 6d., and those due to Stiles for a rent-charge of 16s. 8d.[53] A number of other landowners, including Worcester and Magdalen Colleges, had by this date acquired the great tithes due from certain lands. All these were extinguished by the tithe award.

In 1341 the church had an estate comprising a messuage, a carucate of land, some 14 a. of meadow, and certain rights of pasture.[54] When Bisham Priory appropriated the rectory in 1396 an acre of land accompanied the grant.[55] An estate, known as Parsonage Farm, descended with the rectory, as shown above, and so came in 1752 to Norborne Berkeley.[56]

In 1291 the vicarage was valued at £6 13s. 4d.[57] After the appropriation of the church by Bisham Priory in 1396 the endowment of the vicarage was probably increased and in c. 1535 it was reckoned at £19 8s. 9d. net.[58] In 1835 the average net income of the benefice was £399.[59]

[23] W.R.O. 718, Poor Relief Bk. 1805–10.
[24] Ibid. 1811–17.
[25] *Tax. Eccl.* (Rec. Com.), 190.
[26] *V.C.H. Wilts.* vii. 198; W.R.O. 796.
[27] *Tax. Eccl.* (Rec. Com.), 190.
[28] Phillipps, *Wilts. Inst.* i. 3, 37, 55.
[29] *Reg. Martival* (Cant. and York Soc.), iii. 21.
[30] Phillipps, *Wilts. Inst.* i. 55, 65.
[31] Ibid. 65, 79.
[32] *Cal. Close,* 1385–9, 144.
[33] *Cal. Pat.* 1391–6, 706; *Cal. Papal Lett.* v. 162–3.
[34] Phillipps, *Wilts. Inst.* (index in *W.A.M.* xxviii. 222).
[35] *L. & P. Hen. VIII,* xvi, p. 717.
[36] Phillipps, *Wilts. Inst.* i. 212.
[37] Ibid. 215.
[38] *Tax. Eccl.* (Rec. Com.), 190.
[39] *Cal. Papal. Lett.* v. 162–3.
[40] W.R.O. 212 B/3501/7/1, Impropriation of Rectory. The original has not been found in the Bishop's Register.
[41] Dugdale, *Mon.* v. 534.
[42] W.R.O. 212B/7/34, Abstract of Title of John Jacob to rectory.
[43] Ibid.
[44] See p. 54.
[45] *W.A.M.* xxxi. 161–2.
[46] Worcester Coll. Mun. Release John Jacob to Norborne Berkeley.
[47] Ibid.
[48] Sar. Dioc. R.O. Glebe Terrier, 1671.
[49] See p. 53.
[50] See p. 53.
[51] Worcester Coll. Mun. Abstract of title of Edw. Stiles to great tithes of certain lands.
[52] W.R.O. Tithe Award.
[53] Ibid.
[54] *Inq. Non.* (Rec. Com.), 161.
[55] *Cal. Pat.* 1391–6, 706.
[56] For Parsonage Farm after 1752, see p. 58.
[57] *Tax. Eccl.* (Rec. Com.), 190.
[58] *Valor Eccl.* (Rec. Com.), ii, 131.
[59] *Rep. Com. Eccl. Rev.* H.C. 54, p. 836 (1835), xxii.

The vicar had the tithes both great and small from Clevancy and the small tithes from the rest of the parish.[60] By 1588 certain farms and holdings had commuted their tithes for money payments. One of the farms at Littlecott (William Button's) paid 14s. 4d., the other (Lord Hertford's) paid 10s. A holding called 'Arterells' paid 3s. 4d., and another called 'Tarrants Trowghe' paid 1s.[61] There was some dispute in the earlier 16th century about the tithes from Corton Farm, formerly belonging to the free chapel of Corton.[62] But in 1704 a modus of 1s. was being paid to the vicar for the Corton tithes.[63] In 1842 the vicarial tithes were commuted for a rent-charge of £493 12s. 2d.[64]

In 1588 the vicarial glebe comprised 3 a. of meadow and 3 a. of arable, which lay scattered in the common fields of Hilmarton, and had to be tilled according to the custom of the manor.[65] It was estimated at about 5 a. in the glebe terriers of 1671 and 1704.[66] The vicar also had the right of pasturing 6 oxen at Great Beversbrook Farm in the summer.[67] In 1841 the detached pieces of glebe were exchanged with Thomas Poynder for land nearer the vicarage, thus making a more compact holding.[68] In 1887 it comprised some 3 a.[69]

A vicarage house is mentioned in 1588, 1671, and 1704.[70] In 1835 it was described as unfit for habitation.[71] It stood on a small piece of glebe almost opposite the eastern end of the present (1967) Poynder almshouses.[72] Since in the 18th and earlier 19th centuries the vicars were usually, if not always, non-resident, the vicarage house was used as a workhouse for paupers, and in the 19th century was described as a mere dilapidated cottage.[73] A new house was built in c. 1844 by John Henry Hume (vicar 1835–8) on a site to the south-west of the church.[74] This was much added to by Francis Goddard (vicar 1858–92).[75] In 1961 a smaller vicarage was built in the grounds of the previous one.

In 1291 the church was charged with the payment of a portion of £2 a year to the Prior of Ewias (Herefs.).[76] This payment may originate in a grant by Harold of Ewias, overlord of parts of Hilmarton, and founder and benefactor of the priory in c. 1100.[77] The portion is mentioned in 1341 and 1428.[78] After the dissolution of Ewias the portion, by then only 6s. 8d., was transferred to St. Peter's Abbey, Gloucester, the parent house of the priory.[79] It continued to be paid to Gloucester Cathedral until 1876 when it was extinguished.[80] In 1301 tithes valued at 70s. were due to Ewias Priory from the parishes of Hilmarton and Lydiard Tregoze.[81] But no other references to these have been found. At the

time of the appropriation of Hilmarton by Bisham payments of 3s. 4d. to the Bishop of Salisbury and 2s. to Salisbury Chapter were imposed upon the church.[82] Only that due to the chapter is heard of again and that was still being paid in 1535.[83]

There was considerable religious dissent in the parish in the 17th century. In 1650 James Wealsh, the incumbent, vigorously resisted attempts by a group of parishioners to introduce lay preachers into the church. He refused to contribute towards the maintenance of a lecturer and was threatened with imprisonment.[84] He was ejected from the living in 1657, presumably for his failure to comply with Parliament's orders, and at the Restoration petitioned the king to re-instate him.[85] His petition was unsuccessful and he was followed in 1660 by Robert Rowswell, who was, however, also ejected two years later for his Puritanical and Independent views.[86] Nonconformity continued to be active in the parish, particularly at Goatacre, which lay a considerable distance from the parish church. At the end of the 17th century the incumbent had difficulty in extracting tithes from certain dissenters there.[87]

In 1783 the incumbent also served the churches of Lyneham and Tockenham.[88] A service was held at Hilmarton only once on Sundays and attendance was considered poor because some parishioners were occupied about the farms and others failed to attend because of 'profaneness and irreligion'. Holy Communion was celebrated at Christmas, Easter, and Whitsun, and there were about 10 communicants in the parish. Plain English and the Christian religion were taught in a Sunday school.[89] John Henry Hume (vicar 1835–8) built the first substantial vicarage house in the parish and installed in it a curate to serve the cure.[90] Hume was succeeded in 1838 by David James Stewart, who himself lived in the parish, the first incumbent, it was thought, to do so for a long time.[91] But upon Stewart's arrival, certain members of the congregation left the church to form a group led by the former curate. From this group grew the Particular Baptist church opened in 1849.[92] Since Stewart's time all vicars have resided. In 1861 weekly services were held in private houses in Goatacre and Clevancy. Attendance at Goatacre was about 60 and at Clevancy about 40.[93] In 1864 there were two services in the parish church on Sundays and the total congregation over the year was about 600. There was one weekday service with an attendance of about 60. Holy Communion was celebrated once a month as well as at the usual festivals. There were 48 communicants and the church was said to be

[60] Sar. Dioc. R.O. Glebe Terriers.
[61] Ibid. 1588.
[62] Ibid. 1588, 1671, and see below, p. 63.
[63] Sar. Dioc. R.O. Glebe Terrier, 1704.
[64] W.R.O. Tithe Award.
[65] Sar. Dioc. R.O. Glebe Terrier, 1588.
[66] Ibid. 1671, 1704.
[67] Ibid. 1588, 1671, 1704.
[68] W.R.O. Tithe Award.
[69] Rtn. of Glebe, H.C. 307, p. 164 (1887), lxiv.
[70] Sar. Dioc. R.O. Glebe Terriers.
[71] Rep. Com. Eccl. Rev. H.C. 54, p. 836 (1835), xxii.
[72] Francis Goddard, Reminiscences of a Wilts. Vicar, 1814–1893 (copy in W.A.S. Libr., Devizes).
[73] Ibid.
[74] Ibid.
[75] Ibid.
[76] Tax. Eccl. (Rec. Com.), 190.
[77] See p. 86.
[78] Inq. Non. (Rec. Com.), 161; Feud. Aids, v. 285.
[79] Valor Eccl. (Rec. Com.), ii. 131.
[80] W.R.O. 796/21, Notice from Eccl. Commrs.
[81] Reg. Ghent, (Cant. & York Soc.), ii. 847.
[82] W.R.O. 212 B/3501/7/1.
[83] Valor Eccl. (Rec. Com.), ii. 81.
[84] C 3/467/3.
[85] Cal. S.P. Dom. 1660–1, 176.
[86] V.C.H. Wilts. iii. 104–5; Calamy Revised, ed. Matthews, 418.
[87] See p. 64.
[88] See pp. 102, 172.
[89] Sar. Dioc. R.O. Vis. Queries, 1783.
[90] Francis Goddard, Reminiscences of a Wilts. Vicar, 1814–1893 (copy in W.A.S. Libr., Devizes).
[91] Ibid.
[92] See p. 64.
[93] W.R.O. 796/26, MS. Diary. Later volume with the vicar.

HILMARTON: CHURCH OF ST. LAWRENCE IN 1806

WOOTTON BASSETT: CHURCH OF ST. BARTHOLOMEW AND ALL SAINTS IN 1806

1. Lyneham: Bradenstoke village street

2. Clyffe Pypard

3. Chiseldon: cottage at Hodson, dated 1714, associated with *The Gamekeeper at Home* by Richard Jefferies

4. Hilmarton: Poynder estate cottages of the mid 19th century

VILLAGE STREETS AND COTTAGES

always full.[94] In 1955–6 Sunday attendances over the year were calculated to average 25 persons.[95]

In 1662 Lancelot Addison, father of Joseph Addison, the essayist, was presented to the vicarage. But since in the same year he was appointed chaplain to the new dependency of Tangier, he cannot have resided.[96] Between 1858 and 1892 Francis Goddard, a member of the Goddard family of Clyffe Pypard, was vicar. In 1850 the Revd. Francis Fisher started a diary of parish events, which has been kept rather intermittently until the present day (1967).[97]

The church of *ST. LAWRENCE*, so called by the earlier 15th century,[98] comprises a chancel with vestry on the north and organ chamber on the south, nave of four bays, north aisle, south porch, and embattled west tower. The church was so thoroughly restored in the 19th century that the date of the original fabric is not immediately obvious. A view painted in 1810 shows the battlemented tower rising in two stages with, at its south-east corner, a small turret with conical-shaped roof.[99] The simple south porch had a barge-boarded gable-end and there were then, as now, two three-light windows in the south wall of the nave. There was a similar window on the south side of the chancel and another at the east end. Chancel, nave, and tower were all buttressed.

The oldest feature of the restored church is the north arcade of c. 1200. The chancel arch is probably of the 15th century and across it is a stone screen in Perpendicular style. After the closure of Highway church the beam from the chancel screen there was removed and placed along the top of the Hilmarton screen. In the north jamb of the chancel arch a little passage leads from the north aisle to the chancel, a feature which occurs in a few other Wiltshire churches, e.g. Avebury, and Bremhill. Just inside the passage is the entrance to a rood stair. The chancel walls may date from the 14th century and the nave, with its waggon-type roof, is probably of the 15th century. In the nave hang five hatchments of arms and in the south wall are the remains of a piscina. On the east wall of the north aisle there is a memorial tablet to William Quintin (d. 1651), and Margaret his wife (d. 1647). A Lady Chapel was formed at this end of the aisle in 1955.[1]

Repairs were required in 1804 when the rural dean visited the church and minor ones were carried out.[2] More substantial restoration was undertaken by Thomas Poynder towards the middle of the century. The tower was partly rebuilt in 1840 and the chancel restored. A little later the south porch was rebuilt to the design of Poynder's agent, Henry Weaver, who supervised the restoration of this period.[3] In 1879 a complete restoration of the whole church was begun at the expense of William Henry

Poynder and under the superintendence of G. E. Street.[4] Among the larger structural alterations made were the building of the organ chamber and the removal and rebuilding of the north wall of the aisle nearly 2 ft. to the north. Internally the church was restored throughout.

In 1553 there were three bells.[5] In 1874 there were five and a sixth was added that year by W. H. Poynder. The fourth from the Bristol foundry, c. 1400, is dedicated to the patron saint. Its inscription is preceded by a cross of unusual design. The bells were re-hung and retuned in 1885 and a chiming apparatus was added.[6] They were again re-hung in c. 1933.[7]

The commissioners of 1553 took 11 oz. of silver from the church for the king and left a chalice of 10½ oz.[8] In 1848 Thomas Poynder presented a large chalice, paten, flagon, and almsdish, all with the hall mark 1847.[9] In 1909 a smaller chalice was bought and in 1961 the Revd. K. S. Rich bequeathed to the church his own communion set and a silver-gilt baptismal shell.[10] The registers date from 1645 and are complete. A black letter chained bible, found in the parish chest in 1857, is kept in a glass case in the church.[11]

The free chapel of Corton is first mentioned in a deed of c. 1250–60.[12] The advowson belonged to the lords of the manor of Corton and all recorded presentations are by them, except once in 1507 when the bishop presented.[13] In 1434 the chapel was conveyed by Joan Quatremains to Walter Lord Hungerford, who in 1442 was granted licence to annex it to the chantry of St. Mary in Heytesbury church.[14] But no further reference to any connexion between Corton and the chantry has been found. In 1524 John Bryssett was instituted to the chapel in place of James Bromwich.[15] Bryssett was one of the first canons appointed by Wolsey to Cardinal College, Oxford,[16] and so far as is known, his only interest in Corton was his dispute with the Vicar of Hilmarton over the tithes there (see below). As late as 1548 Magdalen College presented to the chapel, but clearly no incumbent had been resident for many years. In 1549 the king granted the late free chapel, as it was called, to George Owen, one of his physicians, and to William Marten.[17] In 1556 the site of the chapel was acquired by Magdalen College.[18]

In 1291 the chapel was valued at £5.[19] The tithes of Corton Farm belonged to it. In 1341 a ninth of the tithe of sheaves, fleeces, and lambs was estimated at 14s. a year. Small tithes were reckoned at 13s. 4d. An estate of 1 messuage and 2 virgates belonged to the chapel.[20] In 1428 the value was again said to be £5.[21] In the earlier 16th century the right to the Corton tithes was disputed between John Bryssett,

[94] Sar. Dioc. R.O. Vis. Queries, 1864.
[95] Vicar's Rep. *penes* the vicar.
[96] *W. N. & Q.* iii. 42; *D.N.B.*
[97] W.R.O. 796/26, Diary.
[98] Walters, *Wilts. Bells*, 101–2.
[99] By John Buckler, water colour in W.A.S. Libr., Devizes. See pl. facing p. 62.
[1] Dedication Service Leaflet, *penes* the vicar.
[2] W.R.O. 796/26, Diary.
[3] Ibid.; *W.A.M.* xxxvii. 432.
[4] *W.A.M.* xxxvii. 431–6 gives full account of restorations.
[5] All information about bells, unless otherwise stated, from Walters, *Wilts. Bells*, 101–2.
[6] Kelly, *Wilts. Dir.* (1939).
[7] Ex inf. the vicar.
[8] Nightingale, *Wilts. Plate*, 143.
[9] Ibid.
[10] Ex inf. the vicar.
[11] W.R.O. 796/26, Diary.
[12] Magdalen Coll. Oxford, Corton MS. 85.
[13] Phillipps, *Wilts. Inst.* i. 184.
[14] *W.A.M.* x. 274.
[15] Magdalen Coll. Oxford, Macray Cal. 93.
[16] W. D. Macray, *Reg. Magdalen Coll.* i. 152–3.
[17] *Cal. Pat.* 1548–9, 194.
[18] Magdalen Coll. Oxford, Macray Cal. 105.
[19] *Tax. Eccl.* (Rec. Com.), 190.
[20] *Inq. Non.* (Rec. Com.), 161.
[21] *Feud. Aids.* v. 285.

the non-resident incumbent (see above), and the Vicar of Hilmarton. The dispute dragged on over several years but in 1547 Bryssett renounced all claim to tithe from Corton, accepting instead an annual pension of £1 a year.[22] In 1535 the annual value of all tithes great and small and of other dues was £3 6s. 8d.[23]

The only reference found to the chapel's dedication occurs in 1588–9 when it was said to have been dedicated to St. Mary Magdalen.[24] The site of the chapel is traditionally said to be in a field to the south of Corton Farm on the slope of the downs.[25] It is marked on Ordnance Survey maps of the 19th and 20th centuries.

Record survives of three presentations to a chapel at Witcomb. These are in 1332 and twice in 1339. On all three occasions presentation was by the lord of the manor of Witcomb.[26] Nothing more is known about this chapel.

A chapel at Beversbrook is first mentioned in 1298 when the lord of the manor presented John Chyriel to it.[27] So far as is known, no record of any other presentations has survived. The advowson was conveyed with the manor in 1406.[28] The last mention of it found occurs in 1438.[29]

NONCONFORMITY. After his ejection from the living for his Independent views in 1662 Robert Rowswell continued to live in Hilmarton, preaching to dissenters there and in the neighbourhood.[30] In 1676 there were said to be 17 nonconformists in the parish.[31] These were probably mostly Quakers, who had a strong centre at Goatacre, led by members of the Harris family.[32] The families of Wakeham and Baily at Catcomb and Romen at Littlecott were also active dissenters and were connected by marriage with some of the other prominent Wiltshire Quaker families. Most had connexions with the cloth trade.[33] Some of the dissensions in the parish caused by the presence of these nonconformists have been touched upon above.[34] At the end of the 17th century John Harris of Goatacre was imprisoned for withholding his tithes and after his death Mary, his widow, was distrained to the value of about £150 upon items including yarn and cloth as well as farm produce.[35]

A Quaker burial ground was opened in 1678 in a remote place at the extreme east end of the hamlet of Goatacre. But in spite of the early activity of the Friends, especially at Goatacre, no settled Quaker meeting was established in the parish. In 1867 the burial ground was procured as a site for a Primitive Methodist chapel by a Mr. and Mrs. Harris of Goatacre, who were still Quakers.[36]

Goatacre stands out as a centre of nonconformity within the parish. Its rather isolated position at the top of a hill over a mile from the parish church undoubtedly had much to do with this. A chapel for Independents, later the Congregational Chapel, was licensed there in 1824 and was built with assistance from the Congregational Association.[37] On a Sunday in 1851 attendances here were 68 in the morning, 40 in the afternoon, and the same in the evening.[38] The chapel was closed in c. 1917 and for a time the building was used as a club-room.[39] In 1967, much converted, it housed a village shop.

The house of Frederick Taylor at Goatacre was licensed as a meeting-place for Primitive Methodists in 1825.[40] Owing largely to the exertions of Elizabeth Blackman a small chapel was built on the site of the Friends' burial ground in 1867.[41] In c. 1907 the church had 30 members and its week-night congregations were said to be among the largest in the Brinkworth Circuit.[42] But its situation at the east end of Goatacre was considered too remote, and in c. 1909 a new red-brick chapel was built on the main road where it passed through the centre of Goatacre.[43] The old chapel was then pulled down[44] and in 1967 only its foundations could be seen, lying in a little enclosure of trees and undergrowth, which contained also the remains of the former Quaker burial ground. The Methodist chapel on the main road was still in use in 1967.

A group, which left the parish church in 1838,[45] formed the nucleus of the Little Bethel Strict Baptist chapel, which was opened in Hilmarton in 1849.[46] On a Sunday in 1851 63 attended morning service, 39 came in the afternoon, and 55 in the evening. The average number attending over the year was said to vary from 55 to 120.[47] The chapel, a small corrugated iron building not far from the parish church, was still in use in 1967.

A cottage at Clevancy was used in the 19th century as a place for religious worship. This was replaced in 1881 by a small corrugated iron structure, which in 1967 was known as the Mission Hall and was in regular use for undenominational services.[48]

Besides the chapels mentioned above four houses were licensed as dissenters' meeting-places during the earlier 19th century: at Goatacre the house of Mary Greenaway in 1816, at Hilmarton the houses of Isaac Clifford in 1821, of William Goodwin in 1827, and of James Rumming in 1848.[49]

EDUCATION. In the early 18th century an annual rent-charge of £4 from land in Kenn (Som.) was granted to pay a schoolmistress to teach 5 poor children of Hilmarton to read. The origin of the rent-charge is obscure, but it is thought to have been granted by Ann Jacob in 1709.[50] Later when a village school

[22] Magdalen Coll. Oxford, Macray Cal. 95, 96, 99.
[23] Valor Eccl. (Rec. Com.), ii. 132.
[24] C 66/1324 m.22.
[25] W.A.M. x. 274.
[26] Phillipps, Wilts. Inst. i. 27, 34, 35.
[27] Reg. Ghent (Cant. and York Soc.), ii. 580.
[28] See p. 56.
[29] Cat. Anct. D. i. C, 1011.
[30] V.C.H. Wilts. iii. 104–5, see above p. 62.
[31] W.N. & Q. iii. 536.
[32] V.C.H. Wilts. iii. 116.
[33] See 'Quaker Marriage, Birth, and Burial Recs.' in W.N. & Q. ii–vii.
[34] See p. 62.
[35] W.N. & Q. ii. 169.

[36] Partics. of Charitable Trusts . . . of Bristol and Som. Quart. Meeting of Friends (1870), 71.
[37] W.R.O. Retns. of Regns. 1813–51; V.C.H. Wilts. iii. 140.
[38] H.O. 129/254/1/9/26.
[39] Ex inf. Mr. E. V. Iles, Goatacre.
[40] W.R.O. Retns. of Regns. 1813–51.
[41] W. C. Tonks, Victory in the Villages, 154–5.
[42] Ibid. 155.
[43] Ex inf. Mr. E. V. Iles, Goatacre.   [44] Ibid.
[45] See p. 62.
[46] H.O. 129/254/1/9/27.   [47] Ibid.
[48] Ex inf. Miss O. M. Pinniger, Hilmarton.
[49] W.R.O. Retns. of Regns. 1813–51.
[50] Endowed Char. Wilts. H.C. 218, p. 546 (1908), lxxx.

had become well established, the money was used to buy prizes.[51] In 1819 the £4 was paid to a mistress, who taught 7 or 8 children. Four other schools existed at this date, but were probably very small, and the poor were said to be 'very desirous of possessing more sufficient means of education'.[52] There were 7 children in the school in 1835. Another school, begun in 1826, had from 6 to 28 children, and a third, opened by a group of Independents in 1830, had 12 children. All three were mixed schools. There was a fourth school, run at the expense of the parents, and both Anglicans and Independents had Sunday schools.[53] The Independents still had a school at Goatacre in 1859. It was held in their chapel there, and in warm weather about 30 children were taught by a motherly middle-aged woman, who also managed the village shop. In winter 10 or 20 children were taught in the parlour at the back of the shop.[54]

A new school was built in Hilmarton in 1851, entirely at the expense of Thomas Poynder.[55] The old one, which had stood at the east end of the village street, was converted into a cottage.[56] A committee of farmers was formed to manage the new school, but it had few functions, and in 1857 was replaced by the vicar.[57] Two mistresses were appointed in 1855, and a few years later a master also.[58] In 1859 the school comprised two good schoolrooms and had 70 children.[59] The building was handed over to the county council in 1914.[60] In 1902 there were, besides the head master, an infants' teacher, 2 pupil teachers, and 2 monitors, aged 14. There were 31 infants and 95 boys and girls in the school.[61] In 1938 average attendance was 60.[62] In 1968 it was a primary school with about 80 children.[63]

In c. 1850 a night school was started by the vicar and had an average attendance of 40 men and boys.[64] In 1860 there were 26 attending night classes, which were held in the vicarage.[65] The following year the number was about 50 and classes in reading, writing, and arithmetic were popular.[66]

CHARITIES. Ann Jacob by her will, dated 1780, gave £500 to be invested for charitable purposes in Hilmarton and Tockenham. From the interest on this an annual sum of approximately £10 was allotted to Hilmarton. Part was to be used to keep the family monuments in the church in good order, and the rest was to be distributed among the unrelieved poor. In 1905 the whole of the £10 was used to pay a bonus to all subscribers to the parish coal club. There were then between 60 and 70 subscribers. No more is known of that portion of Ann Jacob's Charity allotted to Hilmarton.[67]

In 1878 William Henry Poynder settled in trust a piece of ground, on which he had built five almshouses. He also invested £3,000 to provide for the maintenance of the property and to allow small pensions for the almspeople. These could be either married men over 65 years and their wives or single men or women over 65. The almspeople were to be former employees on the Hilmarton estate, preferably members of the congregation of the parish church, and they were not to be already in receipt of parish relief. In 1905 a doctor was paid £2 2s. a year from the charity's funds to attend the inmates and about £50 had accumulated as a repairing fund.

The pensions allotted to newly-appointed almspeople were reduced to 4s. in 1938 and in 1952 these payments ceased. In 1961 almspeople were appointed only if they agreed to contribute a sum of not more than 10s. weekly to the cost of maintaining the almshouses, and in 1962 this contribution was raised to 15s. a week. Since 1938 the property of the charity has been maintained partly by means of an extraordinary repair fund.[68]

The almshouses lie to the south-east of the church and are built of stone in the rather ornate style of the later Poynder buildings in the village. They are all on one floor and comprise living room, bedroom, kitchen, and the usual offices.

LIDDINGTON

THE PARISH of Liddington lies to the south-east of Swindon and is a narrow rectangle in shape. It measures c. 4½ miles in length and in width varies between c. ¾ mile at its northern and c. 1½ mile at its southern end. It is bounded on the north by a small stream which flows south-westwards from the River Cole and then turns sharply south to form the eastern boundary of Coate tithing before flowing into Coate Water. At its north-east tip it is bounded by the Roman road to Mildenhall and further to the south the eastern boundary is formed by a stream

anciently called the 'Liden Brook', whence the parish derives its name. The eastern boundary takes a sharp bend eastwards after leaving the 'Liden' to join the ancient trackway known as 'Lyde Cumb'.[1] It continues south-eastwards along a track called 'Sugar Way', while the southern boundary follows that known as the 'Thieves Way'.[2] In 1881 the area of the parish was reckoned at 2,767 a.[3] while ten years later the land acreage was 2,535.[4] The reason for the decreased acreage was the transfer in 1884 of a detached portion of the parish, the tithing of Coate,

[51] W.R.O. List of Schools, 1902.
[52] Digest Retns. Cttee. of Educ. of Poor, H.C. 224, p. 1028 (1819), ix (2).
[53] Educ. Enquiry Abstract, H.C. 62, p. 109 (1835), xliii.
[54] Acct. of Wilts. Schools, H.C. 27, p. 90 (1859 Sess. 1), xxi (2).
[55] W.R.O. 796/26, Diary.
[56] Ibid.
[57] Ibid.
[58] Ibid.
[59] Acct. of Wilts. Schools (1859 Sess. 1), xxi (2), p. 90.
[60] W.R.O. 796/39, Memo on Hilmarton School.
[61] W.R.O. List of Schools, 1902.
[62] Bd. of Educ. List 21, 1938.

[63] Ex inf. the head master.
[64] W.R.O. 796/26, Diary.
[65] Ibid.
[66] Ibid.
[67] Endowed Char. Wilts. p. 546 (1908), lxxx; Char. Com. File 204382, and see p. 173.
[68] Endowed Char. Wilts. (1908), pp. 548, 550; Char. Com. File 200943/A1.
[1] O.S. Map 1/25,000, 41/28 and SU 18 (1959 edn.).
[2] For some discussion of this boundary, see T. R. Thomson, 'The Early Bounds of Wanborough and Little Hinton', W.A.M. lvii. 207, 208.
[3] Census.
[4] Ibid.

to the civil parish of Swindon.[5] Coate, part of which is within the parish of Chiseldon, lies immediately south-east of Swindon and c. ½ mile west of the northern part of Liddington, and is made up of 232 a. bounded on the south by the main Swindon-Chiseldon road and on the east by a tributary of the River Cole. It was part of the parish by the 12th century and continued to be a tithing until 1884 when it was transferred to Swindon. More recently, as a result of this transfer, the eastward expansion of Swindon has completely absorbed the tithing. The house formerly belonging to Prince's Farm in Coate, and now surrounded by a housing estate, was used in 1966 as the Common Room of the Park Boys' Club in Cranmore Avenue.

Liddington is characteristic of the long narrow parishes of the Wiltshire chalk country. From the low-lying clays in the north, the land rises gradually across the Upper Greensand to the Marlborough Downs in the south. In the north, around Liddington Wick, the clay soil is pre-eminently suited to dairy farming. The Upper Greensand belt which flanks the clay on the south is porous and fairly resistant to weathering, and this combination has produced more suitable conditions for the growth of settlements.[6]

The main settlement of Liddington is situated below the chalk scarp but the parish also contains two outlying hamlets: Liddington Wick c. 1½ mile north-west of the main village and Medbourne c. ¼ mile to the south-west. Both these hamlets were once the centres of small estates within the parish. Both Liddington itself and Medbourne are situated on the gently rising Upper Greensand ridge just above the spring-line, whence they draw their water supply. To the south of these settlements the chalk scarp rises sharply and at its highest point, Liddington Castle, just south-west of the village, reaches a height of 910 ft.[7]

The parish, bounded by ancient lines of communication such as 'Sugar Way' and 'Lyde Cumb', and traversed by the Ridge Way, has been an area of settlement since the earliest times. The site was occupied in Mesolithic times and a number of pits have been claimed as Neolithic flint-mines. The discovery of 28 loomweights and 4 pits of the early Iron Age suggests considerable activity in the growing of wool and weaving of woollen cloth in the area at this time.[8] The outstanding archaeological feature of the neighbourhood is the univallate Iron Age hill-fort known as Liddington Castle which covers some 7½ a.,[9] while to the east of this is a roughly rectangular system of earth-works covering c. 10 a.,[10] and between the Ridge Way and Liddington Castle there is possibly an 80-acre field system of early date.[11]

From place-name evidence the main settlement west of the brook known by the pre-Saxon name of

'Liden'[12] may be attributed a Saxon origin.[13] Liddington Wick, like the main settlement, formed part of the lands of Shaftesbury Abbey by the mid 12th century,[14] although the larger hamlet of Medbourne is not mentioned until the 13th century.[15] The prosperity of the parish must have been fairly considerable, since in 1334 the contribution of Liddington to the 15th of that year was second only to that of Wanborough, the most highly-rated fiscal unit in Thornhill hundred.[16] Again, in 1377, 174 persons in the parish were qualified to pay the poll tax, a number second again only to Wanborough.[17] There were only two contributors to the Benevolence of 1545, a fairly low number compared with the other parishes of the hundred.[18] The number of contributors to the Subsidy of 1576 was similarly low.[19] In 1801 the total population of the parish was estimated at 337 and thenceforth rose steadily to 454 in 1841 and included 43 persons who lived in Coate tithing, but thereafter the population gradually declined and in 1961 stood at 346.[20]

The parish, as shown above, was served by a good number of ancient trackways, one of which, the Ridge Way, traversed the parish from east to west just north of the village and has been metalled in modern times.[21] A map of 1773 shows numerous tracks traversing the parish. One of these ran from Aldbourne Chase and entered Liddington in its south-west corner, whence it ran north-eastwards past Liddington Castle to join the Swindon-Hungerford road south of its junction with the Ridge Way. Another track ran from the Ridge Way north to Medbourne.[22] These tracks no longer had any importance in the 20th century. In the 18th century a lane following a semi-circular course ran off the village street to give access to Upper Mill, which stood north-west of the manor house. The lane curved north-westwards to join the road from Badbury to Wanborough.[23] It had disappeared in 1967. The main roads in Liddington have changed little since the 18th century. The Swindon-Wanborough road was turnpiked by 1841,[24] the Swindon-Hungerford road, which passed through Liddington, in 1813–14 and the Coate-Marlborough road, which joins the latter just north of Common Head, in 1819.[25] In 1939 the Swindon-Hungerford road was diverted to by-pass Liddington and became the trunk road to Aldbourne and Newbury.[26]

The village of Liddington is arranged in a triangular pattern around the green. To the south-west of the by-pass road lies the parish church, the Parsonage Farm, and the school, unoccupied since 1962. The main nucleus of the village lies to the north of the road with the manor-house on its eastern outskirts.[27]

In 1583 some kind of ale-house was kept by a tailor, Thomas Gilbert,[28] and by the middle years of the 18th century the number of ale-houses in the

5 Ibid.
6 For an account of the geology and land utilization of the area, see Fry, *Land Utilization Wilts.* 215–16, 219.
7 Ibid.
8 *V.C.H. Wilts.* i (1), 81–82.
9 Ibid. 267 and see pl. facing p. 15.   10 Ibid.
11 Ibid.
12 *W.A.M.* xli. 338.
13 *V.C.H. Wilts.* ii, p. 11.
14 See p. 70.
15 See p. 67.
16 *V.C.H. Wilts.* iv. 302.

17 Ibid. 311.
18 *Taxation Lists* (W.A.S. Rec. Brch.), 22.
19 Ibid. 104.
20 *Census*, 1961.
21 O.S. Map 1", sheet 157 (1958 edn.).
22 *Andrews and Dury, Map* (W.A.S. Rec. Brch.), pl. 15.
23 Ibid.
24 W.R.O. Tithe Award, 1841.
25 *V.C.H. Wilts.* iv. 263.
26 Ibid. 266.
27 See p. 67.
28 *Sess. Mins.* (W.A.S. Rec. Brch.), 88.

parish had increased to three, although their location is unknown.[29] In 1753 a complaint was received by the Justices of the Peace that disorderly ale-houses kept by Thomas Hatt and Robert Berry were disturbing the parish.[30] It is possible that the complaint was partly justified since in 1761 only two of the three ale-houses in the village were still licensed, including the one kept by Thomas Hatt.[31] These two remaining ale-houses were probably the 'Sun' and the 'Bell', mentioned by name for the first time in 1822[32] and which in 1966 were still serving the parish. The village contains several thatched cottages of various periods, one of the most recent having a date tablet of 1827. The development of Liddington in modern times has been confined to the building of a number of private houses in large gardens to the east of the manor-house and along the Wanborough road. Several older houses have also been modernized as middle-class residences. Council houses have been built in the centre of the village. At Medbourne there is a stone farm-house probably of late-17th-century origin[33] and in recent times a number of council houses have been built. The hamlet of Liddington Wick has a farm-house and several cottages.

The parish of Liddington will always be associated with Richard Jefferies (d. 1887), the poet-naturalist.[34] Although he was born at Coate Farm, then in Chiseldon, two of his works, *The Story of My Heart* (1883), and *Wild Life in a Southern County* (1885), draw much of their inspiration from the area around Liddington Castle. In 1938 a memorial plate to Richard Jefferies and to another Wiltshire poet Alfred Williams (d. 1930), was affixed to the O.S. Triangulation Pyramid on Liddington Castle.[35]

MANORS AND OTHER ESTATES. By the time of the Domesday Survey the manor of *LIDDING-TON*, assessed at 38 hides, belonged to Shaftesbury Abbey,[36] but it is not known at what date the abbey had acquired it. A grant in 940 by King Edmund to his man Adulf of 10 *mansae* at Liddington is included in the abbey's 15th-century cartulary,[37] but these, it has been suggested,[38] may not have been held by Shaftesbury at the time of Domesday and may represent the 5-hide estate, called the Burgate and previously held by Picote de Burgate, which Henry I granted to the abbey in 1121–2.[39]

Liddington remained among the possessions of Shaftesbury Abbey until the house was dissolved in 1539.[40] In 1542 lands in Coate and Medbourne, both in Liddington, which had previously belonged to Shaftesbury, were granted to Sir William Sharington of Lacock[41] and in 1543 Sharington received a grant

of the manor of Liddington.[42] On his attainder a few years later Sharington forfeited all his lands but these were restored to him in 1550.[43] He died without issue in 1553 and was succeeded by his brother Henry.[44] Henry's heirs were his three daughters and on his death in 1581[45] Liddington passed to the youngest, Olive, who married John Talbot. Olive died in 1646 and was succeeded by her grandson Sharington Talbot (d. 1677). His heir was his son John (d. 1714)[46] who sold the manor to the Duke of Marlborough (d. 1722).[47] It then descended with the Marlborough title until 1877 when the Liddington estate, including Medbourne Farm, Liddington Upper Farm, and Parsonage Farm, was sold in lots.[48]

The manor-house at Liddington stands to the east of the village just above the source of the 'Liden' brook. Here a spring, rising from below the Greensand, supplies a pond or small lake which may formerly have served Upper Mill.[49] The house, approached by a bridge across the lake, is a building of stone rubble dating from the late 16th or early 17th century. It consists of two stories and attics, having stone mullioned and transomed windows and a three-gabled front; internally there is a contemporary stone fireplace on the upper floor.

Lands in Medbourne probably formed part of Shaftesbury Abbey's estate in Liddington from at least the 13th century. John of Earlscourt and Alice his wife subinfeudated a messuage and 2 virgates of land in Medbourne to William Giffard in 1270.[50] The lands may have already been held in chief by Shaftesbury Abbey, since in 1301–2 William of Earlscourt, presumably the son of John, regranted them to the abbess.[51] Shaftesbury also appears to have been granted a small amount of land in Medbourne in the early 14th century by William Giffard.[52]

In 1392 the manor known as that of *MEDBOURNE DOYNEL* and *MEDBOURNE STOKE* was held of the abbey by William Wroughton (d. 1392) and his wife Isabel.[53] The lands were presumably connected with the Doygnel family at an earlier date, but it is not known exactly when the Wroughtons acquired them. The estate then descended in the Wroughton family until the 16th century in the same way as the manor of Woodhill (in Clyffe Pypard).[54]

Medbourne did not pass to Sir William Sharington with the rest of the Shaftesbury Abbey lands in Liddington but was granted to him in 1547–8 by William (III) Wroughton.[55] On the death of Sir William Sharington in 1553[56] the Medbourne estate presumably passed to his brother, Sir Henry,[57] who, in c. 1556–7 enfeoffed his brother John and

[29] W.R.O. Aleho. Kprs. Recogs.
[30] Blenheim MSS. Petition to J.Ps. for Kingsbridge hundred.
[31] Ibid.   [32] W.R.O. Aleho. Kprs. Recogs.
[33] See p. 68.
[34] D.N.B. and see pl. facing p. 29.
[35] *The Liddington-Barbury Memorial* (Wilts. Tracts cxlix), 11.
[36] *V.C.H. Wilts.* ii, p. 128.
[37] *Cart. Sax.* ed. Birch, no. 754; B.M. Harl. MS. 61, f. 9v.
[38] In an unpublished study by Lydia M. Marshall, 'The Early Economic History of Shaftesbury Abbey'. Thanks are due to Miss Marshall for lending the TS.
[39] *Regesta Regum Anglo-Normannorum*, ii, p. 346 (ed. C. Johnson and H. W. C. Cronne).
[40] *V.C.H. Dors.* ii. 79.
[41] *L. & P. Hen. VIII*, xvii, pp. 630–1.
[42] Ibid. xviii (2), p. 280.
[43] *Cal. Pat.* 1549–51, 188–9.
[44] C 142/101/121.
[45] C 142/193/91.
[46] Burke, *Land. Gent.* (1937), s.v. Talbot.
[47] Schedule of Marlborough Deeds, *penes* N.R.A.
[48] *Complete Peerage*, s.v. Marlborough; W.A.S. Libr., Devizes, Sale Cat. 1877.
[49] See p. 71.
[50] C.P. 25(1)/252/22/16.
[51] *Cal. Inq. Misc.* 1307–49, p. 159.
[52] *Wilts. Inq. p.m.* 1242–1326 (Index Libr.), 341–2.
[53] C 136/78/4.
[55] E 210/9755.   [54] See p. 32.
[56] C 142/101/121.   [57] Ibid.

the latter's wife, Anne, with lands known as Medbourne Farm.[58] It is not known when John Sharington died, but, after his death, Anne married a second husband, Nicholas Stephens of Chiseldon.[59] Anne died c. 1577[60] and the estate passed to her eldest son Edward Sharington, who died seised of Medbourne Farm c. 1583.[61] The Medbourne property then passed to William Sharington, Edward's son,[62] who died seised of the farm in 1610.[63] After William's death the Medbourne lands passed, in part, at least, to his sister Anne, wife of William Saule,[64] although her sister-in-law, Elizabeth, widow of William and later the wife of Thomas Farwell, had an interest in the estate.[65] The history of the estate then becomes obscure, but in 1617–18 the lands at Medbourne were said to be held of the lord of the capital manor of Liddington.[66] By the 18th century the estate had become broken up into at least four small freehold estates, and at the end of the century three of these were held by the Eycott family. Two parcels of land were bought by the Duke of Marlborough from S. and J. Eycott in 1771, while a third, called Larges Close, was purchased from J. Eycott in 1772. In 1776 land which probably represents the remnant of the estate known as Medbourne Farm, was sold by Thomas Warman to the Duke of Marlborough.[67] Henceforward the estate was let to farm by the Duke of Marlborough, and at the end of the 18th century was said to be made up of 255 a.[68] Medbourne Farm, the house of which is probably of late-17th-century construction, was reckoned at 223 a. in 1877, and was sold in that year,[69] together with other estates held by the Duke of Marlborough in Liddington.

There appears to have been a smaller estate within Medbourne, which is first mentioned in 1412, when John Blakett was said to hold the manor of Medbourne.[70] This estate was certainly not the main manor, which was held by the Wroughtons at this date. What was probably the same land was still part of the farm at Medbourne in 1617–18, when the estate was said to include 2 yardlands known as 'Blaks'.[71]

The estate, sometimes called the manor of *LIDDINGTON WICK*, formed part of the main manor[72] until 1543[73] when Sir William Sharington conveyed the lands to William Fisher (d. 1585).[74] A water-mill and other tenements in Liddington Wick were conveyed to Fisher in 1578–9 by John Purlyn.[75] William Fisher died seised of 9 messuages in Liddington Wick,[76] and this estate passed to his son Thomas, who died seised in 1598 of c. 294 a. in Liddington Wick and Moor, which included

pastures called Burlands and Ellonds Mead.[77] Thomas's son Henry was seised of 9 yardlands in 1617–18,[78] and was still styled of Liddington Wick in 1623,[79] but by the time of his death he was said to be of Westlecott (in Wroughton),[80] and had apparently sold Liddington Wick. Henry was succeeded by his son William, who died in 1663, leaving a widow Jane, a son Henry, and a brother John. William devised his lands to Henry and John for the payment of his debts. The will was disputed by Jane, who claimed that she had surrendered part of her marriage jointure to enable her husband to buy the manor of Liddington Wick, possibly from his father, and that in return William had agreed to settle the manor on her for life if she survived him. William had, however, in 1636, settled the manor upon his brother John, for the payment of his debts.[81] The outcome of this involved dispute is not known, but by 1643 the estate included lands in Liddington Wick, Liddington Moor, and Medbourne,[82] and by 1652 Liddington Down had been acquired.[83] William Fisher was a Royalist but his estate, said to be worth £200 a year, was not sequestered.[84] In 1695 Frances Fisher, widow of Henry, William's son, was seised of the manor and after her death the estate passed to her oldest daughter Henrietta (d. 1742), who married Stephen Gythens of Gloucester. Their daughter Henrietta (d. 1756) devised the property to her cousin Rachel Gythens of Bristol and to Samuel Commeline in equal parts. In 1760 Rachel sold her share to Commeline for £2,000.[85] No more is known of the estate until 1794 when Liddington Wick Farm, reckoned at c. 164 a., was held by Ambrose Goddard, who at this date was arranging to exchange it with the Duke of Marlborough for Walcot in Swindon.[86] The exchange must have taken place, as Liddington Wick Farm was part of the Duke of Marlborough's Liddington estate in the 19th century.[87]

In 1567 William Fisher and Thomas Fisher his son leased 3 messuages and lands including Ellonds Mead to John, William's younger son.[88] The next year John was leasing a further 2 messuages in Liddington Wick.[89] In 1578–9 John was granted a long lease of the estate conveyed to his father William and brother Thomas by John Purlyn.[90] It is possible that the 4 yardlands, held in 1617–18 by a William Fisher, represent this estate, and that William was the son of John.[91] In 1652 William Fisher, the Royalist, leased the site of the farm and manor of Liddington Wick, and lands including Liddington Down, to William Button of Lyneham and West Tockenham (d. 1654–5).[92] In 1695 the capital

[58] C 3/217/84.
[59] Ibid.
[60] R. M. Glencross, *P.C.C. Admins. 1572–80*, 81.
[61] *W.A.M.* l. 466.
[62] C 142/203/33.
[63] C 142/680/25.
[64] Ibid.
[65] C.P. 25(2)/370/11 Jas. I Mich.
[66] Lacock MSS. Survey of Liddington Manor, 1617–18.
[67] Schedule of Marlborough Deeds, *penes* N.R.A.
[68] Blenheim MSS. Undated Survey of Liddington Manor.
[69] W.A.S. Libr., Devizes, Sale Cat. and see p. 67.
[70] *Feud. Aids*, vi. 530.
[71] Lacock MSS. Survey of Liddington Manor, 1617–18.
[72] Ibid.
[73] C 3/24/27.
[74] C 142/193/47.
[75] C.P. 25(2)/240/20, 21 Eliz. I Mich.

[76] C 142/193/47.
[77] C 142/258/139.
[78] Lacock MSS. Survey of Liddington Manor, 1617–18.
[79] *Wilts. Visitation Pedigrees* (Harl. Soc. cv, cvi), 63.
[80] [J.S.] 'Lydham Weeke, in Liddington', *W.N. & Q.* viii. 458–64.
[81] Ibid.
[82] W.R.O. 56/2, Fisher Deeds.   [83] Ibid.
[84] *W.A.M.* iv. 152.
[85] *W.N. & Q.* viii. 458–64.
[86] Blenheim MSS. Letters of Ambrose Goddard, and see p. 123.
[87] W.A.S. Libr., Devizes, Sale Cat. 1877.
[88] W.R.O. 56/2, Fisher Deeds.
[89] Ibid.
[90] C.P. 25(2)240/21 Eliz. I Mich.
[91] Lacock MSS. Survey of Liddington Manor, 1617–18.
[92] W.R.O. 56/2, Fisher Deeds. For the Button family, see p. 94.

messuage of Liddington Wick was leased to Henry Harding by Frances Fisher, widow of Henry, the great-great-grandson of William Fisher (d. 1585).[93]

The later history of the estate of Liddington Wick is obscure but in 1877 the land there, reckoned at *c.* 171 a., was sold[94] with other of the Duke of Marlborough's Liddington estates.

In 1543, when Sir William Sharington acquired the manor of Liddington, it was in the tenure of the former bailiff of the Abbess of Shaftesbury, Thomas Bristowe,[95] who was recorded in 1535 as farming the manor for a rent of 13*s.* 4*d.*[96] In 1543–4 Sir William Sharington conveyed the site of the manor and certain of the demesne lands, which included 400 a. called Farmer's Down, to William Bristowe,[97] who died in 1568 holding the site of the manor,[98] which then passed to his son Anthony Bristowe.[99] On Anthony's death in 1591 the estate passed to his grandson William, a boy of six.[1] In 1615 William Bristowe conveyed the site of the manor of Liddington to Richard Younge.[2] The subsequent descent of this small estate has not been traced but it seems subsequently to have been re-united with the capital manor, since in 1768 the Duke of Marlborough was leasing out land there.[3]

Immediately upon receiving the grant of the site of the manor from Sir William Sharington in 1544 William Bristowe (see above) obtained licence to alienate the land known as Liddington or Farmers' Down to Thomas Stephens of Chiseldon,[4] who died seised of it in 1553.[5] Also known as Leferves or Bristowe's Down,[6] this small estate of *c.* 600 a.[7] remained in the Stephens family until *c.* 1607. On the death of Thomas Stephens the elder it passed to his son Thomas Stephens the younger[8] (d. 1596).[9] On the death of Thomas (II) Stephens the Down passed to his heir Nicholas Stephens (d. 1611),[10] who sold it to Richard Goddard (d. 1615),[11] probably just before 1607 when Goddard settled it as part of a marriage jointure on his wife Jane Fettiplace.[12] On Goddard's death it probably passed to his son Thomas,[13] but by 1652 had been acquired by William Fisher (d. 1663).[14] The estate remained only a short time with the Fishers and was acquired by the dukes of Somerset at some date during the later 17th century when they were said to hold a considerable freehold estate within the parish,[15] and the duke certainly held Liddington Down in 1707.[16] In 1715 the Down, together with 110 a. known as Farringcombe Down was held by Charles, Duke of Somerset (d. 1748). On his death the estate passed to his son Algernon, on whose death in 1749 it passed to a grandson, Charles Wyndham, Earl of Egremont

(d. 1763). Liddington and Farringcombe Downs were inherited by his third son, Charles Wyndham, who was confirmed in these and other lands by Act of Parliament in 1779.[17] In 1817 the estate, then estimated at 613 a., was held by William Wyndham.[18] By 1893 John Heath had succeeded him. He sold it in that year, under the name of Liddington Warren, for £3,300.[19]

In 1341 the rector held 2 virgates and a meadow.[20] This small estate had increased considerably by 1677 when the rectorial glebe consisted of *c.* 42 a. situated in Liddington Breach, the field next to Wanborough, Middle Down Field, the Down Field next to Badbury, South Down, West Field, Middle Field, and Farm Fields.[21] In 1716 the rectorial estate was estimated at *c.* 36 a.,[22] and the same amount of glebe was recorded in 1731 and 1776.[23] By the inclosure award of 1777 some 190 a. were allotted to George, Duke of Marlborough, as the impropriator, in lieu of tithes.[24] In 1817 the rectory estate, estimated at *c.* 143 a. and valued at *c.* £68 a year, formed part of the demesne lands of the Duke of Marlborough.[25] The estate was made up of Home Farm, which covered *c.* 73 a. to the south of the church, and 2 smaller areas of *c.* 24 a. and *c.* 46 a. respectively, which lay in Liddington Mead, a large area of meadow land in the north-east corner of the parish.[26] In 1887 the total area of glebe belonging to the benefice was estimated at *c.* 186 a.,[27] a figure which probably included both rectorial and vicarial glebe. The rectorial estate, both before and after the Dissolution, was probably often let to farm by the rectors, as in the early 16th century when the parsonage estate was farmed by Thomas Appryce and William Stradlyng.[28]

ECONOMIC HISTORY. At the time of the Domesday Survey the parish, which contained meadow land 4 furlongs in length and 3 furlongs in breadth, and pasture land measuring ½ league by 4 furlongs, was assessed at 38 hides, of which 24 were held in demesne; the remaining 14 were farmed by tenants of the abbess. There were 6 serfs on the demesne, which contained land enough for 4 ploughs, while the remaining land contained land for 7 ploughs and supported 23 villeins and 17 bordars. The land T.R.E. was worth £18, but by the time of the Domesday Survey its value had risen to £22.[29]

A survey of the lands of Shaftesbury Abbey, which has been dated *c.* 1160, shows the parish as made up of three distinct agrarian units, which were subject to an economy typical of the lowland clays

[93] *W.N. & Q.* viii. 458–64.
[94] W.A.S. Libr., Devizes, Sale Cat. 1877.
[95] *L. &. P. Hen. VIII*, xviii (2), p. 280.
[96] *Valor Eccl.* (Rec. Com.), i. 277.
[97] C 54/434 nos. 50, 51.
[98] C 142/152/169.
[99] C 60/390/34.
[1] C 142/231/85.
[2] C.P. 43/127 rot. 38.
[3] See p. 71.
[4] *L. & P. Hen. VIII*, xix (1), p. 287.
[5] C 142/97/130.   [6] Ibid.
[7] C 142/351/115. In 1543–4 the estate is estimated at *c.* 400 a.: C 54/434 nos. 50, 51.
[8] *W.A.M.* xxx. 134–6.
[9] C 142/247/101.
[10] C 142/325/203.
[11] C 142/351/115.
[12] Cal. of Goddard MSS. (TS in Swindon Pub. Libr.), 56.
[13] C 60/473/37.
[14] W.R.O. 56/2, Fisher Deeds.
[15] Lacock MSS. Late 17th-cent. Survey of Liddington Manor.
[16] C.P. 43/496 rot. 136.
[17] Partitition of Estates of Algernon, 7th Duke of Somerset, 19 Geo. III, c. 46 (priv. act).
[18] Blenheim MSS. Survey of Liddington Manor, 1817.
[19] W.A.S. Libr., Devizes, Sale Cat. 1893.
[20] *Inq. Non.* (Rec. Com.), 162.
[21] Sar. Dioc. R.O. Glebe Terrier, 1677.
[22] Blenheim MSS. Survey of Liddington Manor, 1716.
[23] Liddington Incl. Act, 16 Geo. III, c. 20 (priv. act).
[24] W.R.O. Inclosure Award, 1777.
[25] Blenheim MSS. Survey of Liddington Manor, 1817.
[26] Ibid.
[27] *Retn. of Glebe*, H.C. 307, p. 54 (1887), lxiv.
[28] C 3/6/113.
[29] *V.C.H. Wilts.* ii, p. 128.

and the higher chalk scarps of downland country, and which no doubt were organized much as were the lands of other Benedictine communities.[30] Coate, a detached part to the north-west, contained 5 hides which supported 10 holdings, for the most part of ½ hide in area. Services here laid stress on work with the flock and at haymaking. In Liddington there were 29 holdings of varying amounts, including one of 3 hides held by Everard of Medbourne, for a rent of 30s. The ploughmen in Liddington held by virtue of the same services as the men of Coate, except that they were bound to send 2 measures of grain to Shaftesbury Abbey at Martinmas, as were the men of Wick. There were 19 cotsetlers and 1 crofter in Liddington. In Wick, to the north of Liddington, there was pasture for 30 cows and 9 a. of meadow land. There were 4 smallholdings there, each amounting to no more than a few acres. One of the cotsetlers of Wick, to be chosen by the abbess's bailiff, tended the abbess's cattle and had to render 10 cheeses of Winchester measure to the abbess, a service for which he was granted certain privileges, such as the right to pasture his beasts with those of the abbess.[31]

In the 12th-century survey of the Shaftesbury lands the duties and services of both lord and tenant are described in detail. Without exception small amounts of rent, normally no more than a few shillings or pence varying with the amount of land held, were payable to the abbey in addition to services due.[32] Little can be said of the pattern of land tenure within the parish before the Dissolution, but by the 17th century the number of holdings seems to be fewer perhaps as a result of the accumulation of more land in the open fields by individual tenants. In the late 16th century there were 3 leaseholders and 49 copyholders, of whom 4 and possibly a fifth were tenants at will on the manor, according to a survey of this date.[33] A few years later in 1617–18 there were some 43 tenants, of whom 3 were leaseholders, 29 copyholders, and 11 cottagers, and who together owed a rent of c. £27.[34] Henceforward the number of copyholders declined and the number of those holding by lease gradually increased; in 1672 there were 20 leaseholders in Liddington and 11 in Coate, and 6 copyholders in Liddington.[35] This development continued into the 18th century and in 1731 the manor contained 30 leaseholdings, including those in Coate and Medbourne, together with 7 copyholdings and 10 customary holdings.[36] Nineteenth-century surveys of Liddington manor show no copyholding,[37] and in 1817 there were said to be 12 leaseholdings and 17 freeholdings within the manor.[38]

In 1617–18 there were 4 arable fields in the parish, 2 called Overfields and 2 called Lower Fields, a meadow known as Liddington Mead, which lay in

the north-east corner of the parish, once open but now farmed in several allotments, and three pastures, Liddington Down, Marsh Leaze, and Ox Leaze.[39] It seems likely that some of these open lands lay in the north-west of the parish on either side of the Swindon-Hungerford road east of Common Head, since this area was known as Liddington Common in 1773.[40] By 1776 the number of open fields had increased to 6, Upper and Lower East Fields, Upper and Lower Middle Fields, and Upper and Lower West Fields, covering a total of c. 639 a. There were 3 commons, Cow Common, Sheep Down, and Sheep Pasture, with an overall acreage of c. 421 a.[41] According to a survey of 1617–18, 30 sheep could be kept on each yardland and 15 on each 'corcytrell' on Liddington Down, while a horse and 2 cows might be kept on each yardland and a horse and cow on each 'corcytrell' in Marsh Leaze, while in Ox Leaze an ox could be pastured on a yardland and on a 'corcytrell'. In Coate there was a marsh containing leaze for 60 beasts together with 2 'slades' of c. 50 a. and a fallow field, where there was leaze for 30 horses. At this date it was estimated that there were 37 yardlands and 15 'corcytrells' within the manor of Liddington, while the 'manor' of Coate was said to be made up of 20 yardlands.[42] In the late 17th century arable land in three upper fields was valued at 4s. 6d. an acre, and in the three lower fields at 5s. 6d. an acre. Pasture land and meadow in the open fields was worth 16s. an acre yearly, while land in Liddington Meadow was valued at 20s. an acre, the Horse Common at 12s., and the Beast Common at 6s. yearly.[43]

The economy of the parish was until recent times largely devoted to the rearing of sheep on the downs in the south of the parish.[44] Towards the middle of the 17th century it was estimated that Liddington Down contained common grazing for 14,000 or 15,000 sheep, and in addition there was a large beast common of some 110 a.,[45] probably at this time, and certainly by the 18th century, known as Farringcombe Down.[46] In 1731 the total amount of sheep pasture within the manor of Liddington was 423 a., while 118 a. were given over to cow commons.[47] On Spring, or Liddington Farm in 1746, the tenant farmer had 163 sheep and lambs but only 17 cattle.[48] The best pasture land was in the more northerly part of the parish away from the chalk escarpment. Here some meadows may have been laid out as water-meadows. Bee Leaze, comprising about 26 a., was so described in the late 18th or early 19th centuries. This was part of Medbourne Farm and lay below Common Head to the southeast of the Coate-Marlborough road.[49] The arable land also lay in the north of the parish. About 1746 the amount of acreage devoted to the growing of wheat on Liddington Farm was some 80 a., while

[30] B.M. Harl. MS. 61, ff. 80, 80v, 82; Lydia M. Marshall, 'Early Economic History of Shaftesbury Abbey'.
[31] B.M. Harl. MS. 61, ff. 80, 80v, 82; Lydia M. Marshall, op. cit.
[32] B.M. Harl. MS. 61, ff. 80, 80v, 82.
[33] Lacock MSS. 16th-cent. Survey of Liddington Manor.
[34] Ibid. Liddington Services, 1617–18.
[35] Ibid. Survey of Liddington Manor, 1672.
[36] Blenheim MSS. Survey of Liddington Manor, 1731.
[37] Ibid. Surveys of Liddington Manor, one of 1817, the other undated.
[38] Ibid. Survey, 1817.
[39] Lacock MSS. Liddington Services, 1617–18.
[40] Andrews and Dury, Map (W.A.S. Rec. Brch.), pl. 15.
[41] Liddington Incl. Act, 16 Geo. III., c. 20 (priv. act).
[42] Lacock MSS. Survey of Liddington Manor, 1617–18.
[43] Ibid. Late 17th-cent. Survey of Liddington Manor.
[44] Lacock MSS. and Blenheim MSS. Manorial Surveys.
[45] Lacock MSS. Late 17th-cent. Survey of Liddington Manor.
[46] Partition of Estates of Algernon, 7th Duke of Somerset 19 Geo. III, c. 46 (priv. act).
[47] Blenheim MSS. Survey of Liddington Manor, 1731.
[48] Ibid. Effects of Spring Farm in 1746.
[49] Ibid. Undated Survey of Liddington Manor.

about 45 a. were given over to barley.[50] There is no further evidence of barley, but in 1801 the average wheat yield was 40 bushels an acre.[51]

As in neighbouring parishes a certain amount of inclosure was being carried out in the early 17th century. In 1641 the tenants and freeholders of the manor of Liddington were allowed to choose 8 men to arrange exchanges of arable and pasture between tenants, so that they might be able to inclose land as they wished.[52] At the same time there were said to be a number of freehold estates within the parish not intermixed with the open fields but inclosed.[53] By 1766 many small inclosures of land at Coate had been made: all tenants there had small amounts of inclosed arable, pasture, and meadow, while the holdings grouped together and known collectively as Coate Farm amounted to some 137 a. of inclosed land in 1766. In Liddington 19 lease-holders had small amounts of inclosed land.[54] But even in Coate the land was by no means completely inclosed, since a meadow, Coate Lot-Mead, was held in common and divided by lot amongst the tenants there.[55] In 1776 these old inclosures were said to amount to some 206 a.,[56] and these were allowed to remain when allotments of land in the open fields were made the following year. The main allotment of some 900 a. was made to the Duke of Marlborough as impropriator and lord. The lands lay chiefly in the Upper East and Upper Middle Fields, and in Liddington Common, and were bounded by Liddington Wick in the north and by Stephen's Down in the south.[57]

In the early 18th century the numerous freehold estates, which were being formed from the early 17th century onwards, begin to emerge as distinct farms. Some 41 a. were farmed by Robert Webbe, who appears as a leaseholder in the late 17th or early 18th century, while another farm, Ile's, was estimated at c. 32 a., and another, farmed by Richard Pierce, was reckoned at c. 141 a.[58] The land farmed by Robert Webbe was estimated at c. 95 a. in 1731 and at this date was said to be part of Liddington Farm, itself part of the demesne lands of the manor[59] and otherwise known as Bacon's or Spring Farm.[60] At the same date the land at Coate, which also formed part of the demesne lands of Liddington manor, was largely occupied by some 152 a. farmed by John Prince.[61] The farm was tenanted by William Prince in 1794[62] and, as a result of its associations with the family, became known as Prince's Farm, a name which it retained into the 20th century. A survey made after the Inclosure Act lists 4 farms held by tenants of the Duke of Marlborough: of these, Liddington Commons was

estimated at 101 a., Liddington Meadows at 70 a., while Medbourne Farm and Upper Farm were reckoned at 255 a. and 520 a. respectively.[63] In 1817 the two latter farms were merged to form some 776 a. known as Liddington and Medbourne Farm.[64] Other farms at this date included Liddington Commons, now called Common Farm and reckoned at 102 a., and the Parsonage Farm, which covered an area of some 143 a. and included 73 a. known as Home Farm.[65] In the 20th century there were at least 7 farms,[66] including the farms at Coate, Medbourne, Liddington Wick, and Liddington Warren, all of which were representative of earlier freehold estates within the parish.

There were 2 mills within the manor of Liddington at the time of Domesday Survey, which together paid 5s.[67] In the mid 12th century one of these mills was held by Edward the miller, who paid a rent of 30d., while the other was held by a widow, Maud, for a rent of 6d.[68] The former was probably attached to the manor and was known as Liddington Mill, the wheel of which tore Thomas Chauler to pieces in 1249.[69] This mill was situated just north-west of the manor-house and it is likely that it remained part of the site of the manor, since in 1543-4 a water-mill was included in a grant of the site of the manor to William Bristowe by William Sharington.[70] This mill was still attached to the manor in 1591 when William Bristowe's son, Anthony, died seised of the site of Liddington manor,[71] and remained so in 1768 when the lord of the manor, the Duke of Marlborough, leased a messuage, tenement, and water-mill with their tolls and profits to the miller, Edward Cripps of Liddington.[72] By 1773 this mill was known as Upper Mill, and was fed by a large pond which fronted the manor-house.[73] It remained in use until the 20th century.[74]

A second mill, possibly that rented by the widow Maud, was attached to the estate at Liddington Wick by the 16th century, although it was situated just north of Liddington village and was fed by the same stream as Liddington Mill. It may have been this mill that was held by John Wroughton in 1496,[75] but a mill is seen certainly to be part of the Wick estate by 1577-9 when tenements and lands there, including a water-mill, were conveyed to William and Thomas Fisher.[76] This mill, still part of the estate in 1689[77] and 1762,[78] was known as Lower Mill[79] and remained in use until the 20th century.[80]

LOCAL GOVERNMENT. In 1967 no parish records other than registers (see below) were known to exist for Liddington.

[50] Ibid. Effects of Spring Farm in 1746.
[51] *W.A.M.* liv. 91.
[52] Lacock MSS. Court Bk. of Liddington Manor, 1641-1650.
[53] Ibid. Late 17th-cent. Survey of Liddington Manor.
[54] Blenheim MSS. Wilts. Rental, 1766.
[55] Ibid. Survey of Liddington Manor, 1731.
[56] Liddington Incl. Act, 16 Geo. III, c. 20 (priv. act).
[57] W.R.O. Inclosure Award, 1777.
[58] Lacock MSS. Late-17th-cent. survey of houses and lands in possession in Liddington, Coate, and Medbourne.
[59] Blenheim MSS. Survey of Liddington Manor, 1731.
[60] Ibid.
[61] Ibid.
[62] Ibid. Note of Prince's Farm, 1794.
[63] Ibid. Undated Survey of Liddington Manor.
[64] Ibid. Survey of Liddington Manor, 1817.
[65] Ibid. and for parsonage estate see above.
[66] *Kelly's Dir. Wilts.* (1939).
[67] *V.C.H. Wilts.* ii, p. 128.
[68] B.M. Harl. MS. 61, f. 81.
[69] *Crown Pleas Wilts. Eyre, 1249* (W.A.S. Rec. Brch.), 216.
[70] C 54/434 nos. 50, 51.
[71] C 142/231/85.
[72] Blenheim MSS. Lease, Marlborough to Cripps, 1768.
[73] *Andrews and Dury, Map* (W.A.S. Rec. Brch.), pl. 15.
[74] Anon. MSS. notes *penes* the Revd. H. R. Rogers.
[75] *Cal. Inq. p.m. Hen. VII,* i, pp. 505-6.
[76] C.P. 25(2)/240/20, 21 Eliz. I Mich.
[77] C.P. 43/426 1 Wm. and Mary Mich.
[78] C.P. 43/718 3 Geo. III Mich.
[79] *Andrews and Dury, Map* (W.A.S. Rec. Brch.), pl. 15.
[80] Anon. MSS. notes *penes* the Revd. H. R. Rogers.

CHURCH. The church of Liddington is first mentioned in 1291 when it was valued for the taxation of Pope Nicholas.[81] Probably long before that date, and certainly a few years later it was attached to Shaftesbury Abbey as a prebend. This meant that in return for certain services to the community at Shaftesbury, the prebendaries or rectors of Liddington enjoyed the profits and perquisites of the rectory, which was not appropriated to Shaftesbury.[82] To serve the church of Liddington the prebendaries or rectors appointed vicars. The earliest known presentation of a vicar to serve the church is that of John of Coate, who was presented by the rector, Walter Burdoun, in 1297.[83]

The Abbess of Shaftesbury presented to the prebend throughout the Middle Ages, except in 1368–1369 when the king presented by reason of an alleged voidance.[84] In 1371–2 Robert Walsham, Canon of Salisbury Cathedral, and William Walsham, Prebendary of Liddington, were granted a royal pardon for in some way disputing the king's right to present.[85] By 1389 the abbess was presenting again,[86] and continued to do so until 1537 when Sir Thomas Arundel presented with her consent.[87] The prebendaries or rectors presented to the vicarage without exception, so far as is known, throughout the Middle Ages.[88]

In 1543 Sir William Sharington, who also acquired the manor that year, was granted the advowson of the rectory and of the vicarage of Liddington.[89] His brother, Henry Sharington, to whom the manor passed, presented to the rectory in 1554.[90] Thenceforth throughout the 17th and 18th centuries the advowson of the sinecure rectory or prebend as it began sometimes to be called again towards the end of the 17th century, descended with the lordship of the manor of Liddington.[91] On at least two occasions, however, the right of presentation was leased out: in 1591 when Nathaniel Torperley, a prominent mathematician, presented,[92] and in 1632 when Sir John St. John presented.[93] The advowson of the vicarage continued to belong, as it had before the Dissolution, to the rectors or prebendaries,[94] who appear to have leased their right of presentation frequently in the 16th and 17th centuries. In 1583 the queen presented, apparently because there was no rector to provide a vicar.[95]

The rectors were sometimes laymen, but in 1695 Sir John Talbot (d. 1714) presented his cousin William Talbot (d. 1730), then Dean of Worcester, and later successively Bishop of Oxford, Salisbury, and Durham.[96] On the death in 1759 of Matthew Tate, John Talbot's successor as lord of the

manor, the Duke of Marlborough presented John Moore (d. 1805), the tutor of his younger sons, Lords Charles and Robert Spencer. Like all the rectors he did not live at Liddington and, while still rector of the church there, became successively Prebendary of Durham (1763) and Dean of Canterbury (1771). He relinquished the rectory of Liddington on becoming Bishop of Bangor in 1775 and subsequently became Archbishop of Canterbury in 1783.[97]

Soon after the beginning of the 19th century the institution of incumbents was simplified: the rectors, having been presented by the Duke of Marlborough (as lord of the manor) began presenting themselves to the vicarage.[98] The advowson of the church was then said to rest jointly with the Duke of Marlborough and the Prebendary (or rector) of Liddington, while the incumbent was styled the Prebendary, Rector, and Vicar of Liddington, and the benefice was called a rectory and a vicarage.[99] In 1951 C. W. Francis, who had been Prebendary, Rector, and Vicar of Liddington since 1936, left Liddington for another living, but remained prebendary and as such presented his successor to the vicarage.[1] On Prebendary Francis's death, the vicar, the Revd. H. R. Rogers, who had been presented by him in 1963, was presented to the prebend by the Duke of Marlborough, who in 1966 still retained his right of patronage.[2]

The church was valued at £13 6s. 8d. for the taxation of Pope Nicholas in 1291,[3] 1308–9,[4] and 1341.[5] In 1772 sums totalling £200 were received from the trustees of Lord Crew, Bishop of Durham, and from those of a Mrs. Horner and a Mrs. Pyncombe respectively.[6] A further £200 was added from the Royal Bounty and the benefice was endowed in 1773.[7] It had a net income of £325 in 1835.[8]

The prebend, probably at the time of its foundation, was endowed with certain portions, presumably at first in the form of tithes, from the churches of Chesilbourne, Compton Abbas, and Melbury Abbas, all of which lay in Dorset. By 1291 Chesilbourne was making a yearly payment of £3 6s. 8d.,[9] Compton Abbas £3 10s.,[10] and Melbury Abbas £3 3s. 4d.[11] These portions were extracted with some difficulty and the Rector of Liddington made repeated and probably unsuccessful attempts in 1324, 1325, and 1326 to secure arrears of £28 from Compton Abbas[12] and of £25 6s. 8d. from Melbury Abbas.[13] These portions, which formed part of the gross value of the rectory, continued to be made throughout the Middle Ages and similar amounts were still paid in 1535,[14] although by this date

[81] *Tax. Eccl.* (Rec. Com.), 190.
[82] For an essay on prebends in nunnery churches see A. Hamilton Thompson: 'Abp. of Canterbury's Cttee. on the Ministry of Women', *App. viii.*
[83] *Reg. Ghent* (Cant. and York Soc.), 559.
[84] *Cal. Pat.* 1367–70, 170.
[85] Ibid. 1370–4, 44.
[86] Phillipps, *Wilts. Inst.* i. 74.
[87] Ibid. 206.
[88] Ibid.
[89] *L. & P. Hen. VIII*, xviii (2), p. 280.
[90] Phillipps, *Wilts. Inst.* i. 218.
[91] Ibid.
[92] Ibid. 232. For Torperley, see *D.N.B.*
[93] Phillipps, *Wilts. Inst.* ii. 16.
[94] Ibid.
[95] Ibid. i. 231.
[96] Ibid. ii. 43; Burke, *Land. Gent.* (1937), s.v. Talbot; Burke, *Peerage* (1959), s.v. Shrewsbury.
[97] *D.N.B.*
[98] *Crockford* (1896 and later edns.).
[99] Ibid. (1907 and later edns.).
[1] Ibid. (1951–2).
[2] Ex inf. the Revd. H. R. Rogers; *Brist. Dioc. Dir.* (1966–7).
[3] *Tax. Eccl.* (Rec. Com.), 190.
[4] *Reg. Ghent* (Cant. and York Soc.), 237.
[5] *Inq. Non.* (Rec. Com.), 162.
[6] Hodgson, *Queen Anne's Bounty* (2nd edn.), p. clxx.
[7] Ibid. (1st edn.), p. ccccxvii.
[8] *Rep. Com. Eccl. Revenues*, H.C. 54, p. 840 (1835), xxii.
[9] *Tax. Eccl.* (Rec. Com.), 179.
[10] Ibid. 177.
[11] Ibid.
[12] *Reg. Martival* (Cant. and York Soc.), iii. 139, 157, 159, 177, 171.
[13] Ibid. 139, 157, 159, 178.
[14] *Valor Eccl.* (Rec. Com.), i. 288, 290.

Chesilbourne, in lieu of giving all its tithes to Liddington, paid £6,[15] a sum agreed upon by the respective rectors in 1438.[16] These portions continued to be paid after the Dissolution, and in the 17th century were said to belong to the prebend and to be worth £12 10s.[17]

In 1341 the rectory was valued at £13 6s. 8d., of which the great tithes amounted to £9 and those small tithes, which the rector had in certain meadows, to 40s.[18] In 1535 the rectory was valued at £24 gross, less 7s. 5½d. for synodals. Its value was made up of the portions paid by Chesilbourne, Compton Abbas, and Melbury Abbas, all great tithes, certain small tithes, and a landed estate.[19] It is possible that this sum represents a miscalculation based on the assumption that Chesilbourne was still paying £3 6s. 8d. instead of £6, and that the value of the rectory was c. £27.

After the Dissolution there is no mention of any small tithes being due to the rector, but, with the exception of those from the glebe-lands and from Liddington Meadows, all the great tithes belonged to the rectory.[20] By 1705, and probably at an earlier date, the rectorial tithes were impropriated by the lords of the manor,[21] who then presumably granted them to the successive rectors, whom they appointed. In 1731 all great tithes from Liddington, Stephen's Down, Medbourne, and Coate belonged to the rectory,[22] with the exception of the great tithes from the rectorial glebe which belonged to the vicarage.[23] After the inclosure award of 1777 right to certain great tithes was extinguished,[24] although 1,501 a. of land in the parish remained subject to tithe.[25] In 1841 the great tithes in Coate were commuted for a rent-charge of £42 9s., which was paid to the rector and his lessee, Elizabeth Henrietta Crowdy.[26] At the same date the rectorial tithes in Liddington were commuted for a rent-charge of £174 7s., which was paid to the rector's lessees, the Earl of Shaftesbury, Sir Edward Stracey, and Sir James Graham.[27] Together, therefore, the surviving rectorial tithes in the whole parish were commuted in 1841 for £216 16s.[28] The rectors leased out their tithes in the 16th century on at least two occasions.[29] The great tithes were also leased from time to time in the 18th century.[30]

The rector's house was described in 1677 as a building of 4 bays with a barn, stable, and outhouses standing in a small garden.[31] It is likely that as the rectors did not live in Liddington, the parsonage or prebendal house was occupied as a farmhouse from an early date. It was used as such in 1812 when it was described as a mean stone and thatched building standing between the churchyard and the vicar's house.[32] The Parsonage House, still so-called, stands immediately south of the churchyard. It is of chalk-stone and retains some 17th-century features, but was evidently altered and enlarged in the early 19th century and later.

No ordination of a vicarage has been found. In 1535 the vicarage was worth £12 9s. 6d., less 4s. 2d. for synodals. Its value consisted of certain great tithes, all small tithes, except some which the rector had, and other emoluments.[33] In 1677[34] and 1704[35] the vicar had the tithes both great and small of all the glebe-land belonging to the rector, as well as all the small tithes. In 1705 the vicar maintained that he had only the small tithes[36] but at this date, as in 1731[37] and 1775,[38] he also had the tithes both great and small from the rectorial glebe. By the inclosure award of 1777 the rectorial and vicarial glebe were freed from tithe and the vicar, in lieu of the great tithes from the rectorial and vicarial glebe, was compensated with 53 a. of land.[39] In 1841 the vicarial tithes were commuted for a rent-charge of £221.[40]

In c. 1634 the vicar had an estate of about 2 a.,[41] which remained unchanged until 1777 when under the inclosure award of that year he received an allotment of land in the open fields of Liddington, in lieu of tithes.[42] In 1786 this new estate was estimated at c. 53 a. and most of the land was situated in the Lower East Field.[43] In 1817 the vicar's estate was estimated at c. 64 a., and was made up of two closes, one south-east and the other north-east of the church, while the third and largest part of the estate, now known as Parson's Field, lay north of the main settlement to the east of the Newbury road.[44]

There was also a vicarage house in 1677, then described as a building of 4 bays with a barn and stable attached.[45] The house is often mentioned in the 18th century.[46] By the early 19th century the incumbents no longer occupied it, since in 1783 the Vicar of Liddington was also incumbent of Chiseldon where he lived,[47] and in 1812 the vicar lived at King's Somborne (Hants).[48] In the same year it was noted that the vicarage house had once contained a library, or collection of books, which had long since disappeared because the house was unguarded and open to marauders.[49] In 1824 Prebendary Michael Hare, who was both rector and vicar, built a new house and henceforth the incumbents lived there.[50] After 1835 the house was known for a time as the Glebe House,[51] but it subsequently became known as the Rectory. The Rectory is a

[15] Ibid. 259.
[16] W.A.M. xlvii. 517–18.
[17] Lacock MSS. Survey of Liddington Manor, in a 17th-century hand.
[18] Inq. Non. (Rec. Com.), 162.
[19] Valor Eccl. (Rec. Com.) ii. 127; for the estate, see above p. 69.
[20] Sar. Dioc. R.O. Glebe Terrier, 1677.
[21] W.R.O. 413/450, Valuation of Wilts. Livings, 1705.
[22] Blenheim MSS. Survey of Liddington Manor, 1731.
[23] Ibid.
[24] W.R.O. Inclosure Award, 1777.
[25] Ibid. Tithe Award.
[26] Ibid.   [27] Ibid.
[28] Retn. of Tithes Commuted, H.C. 214, p. 230 (1887), lxiv.
[29] C 3/6/113; C 2/Jas. I/F 11/18.
[30] There are several such leases surviving among records at Blenheim Palace.
[31] Sar. Dioc. R.O. Glebe Terrier.

[32] W.A.M. xli. 136.
[33] Valor Eccl. (Rec. Com.), ii. 127.
[34] Sar. Dioc. R.O. Glebe Terrier, 1677.   [35] Ibid.
[36] W.R.O. 413/450.
[37] Blenheim MSS. Survey of Liddington Manor, 1731.
[38] Ibid. Letter of the Revd. W. R. Stock, Vicar, to T. Walker.
[39] W.R.O. Inclosure Award, 1777.
[40] Ibid. Tithe Award.
[41] Sar. Dioc. R.O. Glebe Terrier.
[42] W.R.O. Inclosure Award, 1777.
[43] Sar. Dioc. R.O. Glebe Terrier, 1634.
[44] Blenheim MSS. Survey of Liddington Manor, 1817.
[45] Sar. Dioc. R.O. Glebe Terrier, 1677.
[46] Ibid. 1709, 1786; Blenheim MSS. Survey of Liddington Manor, 1731; W.R.O. Inclosure Award, 1777.
[47] Sar. Dioc. R.O. Vis. Queries, 1783.
[48] W.A.M. xli. 136.   [49] Ibid.
[50] Ibid. xlvii. 519.
[51] Rep. Com. Eccl. Revenues, H.C. 54, p. 840 (1835), xxii.

large house of rough-cast brick, standing in a garden to the south-east of the church, and may possibly occupy the same site as the former vicarage house.

At the end of the 18th century, services were held in the morning and in the afternoon alternately with those at Chiseldon. Holy Communion was celebrated at the four customary seasons, and there was an average of 12 communicants. Services were held on Wednesdays and Fridays in Lent, again alternately with those at Chiseldon. Children of the parish were catechized on Sundays, Wednesdays, and Fridays in Lent, and sermons were preached on the catechism every other year during that season. The congregation was said to be fairly numerous.[52] Over half a century later, on Census Sunday 1851, 100 people were present at morning service, while 140 attended the afternoon service, although one service was presumably held at Chiseldon.[53]

The church of *ALL SAINTS* consists of chancel, nave, north aisle, north vestry, and west tower. There may originally have been a narrow south aisle, as the chancel and chancel arch are not centrally placed in relation to the present nave. A severe restoration of the church by C. E. Ponting in the late 19th century makes it difficult to distinguish how many of its features are original.[54] The chancel and north aisle date from the 13th century, the former having two lancet windows in the south wall and one in the north; the east window is a 19th-century insertion. The north aisle appears to have been little altered;[55] there are two lancets and a trefoil-headed doorway in the north wall and its east window consists of three graded lancets beneath a rear arch which is supported on corbelled shafts. The aisle's west window has a cusped rear-arch and curious star-shaped tracery, apparently of the early 14th century. The windows in the south wall of the nave, which date from the 19th-century restoration, have similar tracery and possibly replace original windows of the same design. The north aisle contains two tomb-recesses of c. 1300. The embattled west tower, of three stages with diagonal buttresses to its western angles, dates from the late 15th or early 16th century.[56] Most notable among the church furnishings is the circular font bowl of c. 1200 which has tapered sides and bands of pellet and zig-zag ornament.[57] Other furnishings, including the sanctuary rail, pulpit, lectern, and choir stalls, were installed during the 19th-century restorations.[58] The vestry was added outside the north doorway of the aisle in 1900.[59] The glass in the east window of the aisle was placed there in 1914 by Prebendary and Mrs. Pitt in memory of their son, Clifford George Pitt.[60]

Three bells were noted by the king's commissioners in 1553[61] but their fate is not known. The church has 5 bells (in 1966): the first three, made by

Roger and William Purdue, are inscribed with the churchwardens' names and date from 1663, while the fourth and fifth date from 1786 and 1849 respectively and bear the makers' names, Robert Wells of Aldbourne and William Taylor.[62] In 1553 the king's commissioners left a silver chalice weighing 6 oz. for the church:[63] this was still among the church plate in 1812 but had disappeared by 1920.[64] A paten was given by Prebendary George May in 1859. All other plate dates from 1886 when a chalice, paten, flagon, and spoon were provided by subscription.[65] The church also possesses a pewter flagon, possibly of 18th-century date, of a type which is found comparatively rarely in Wiltshire.[66] A barrel organ, given by Prebendary May in 1846, was restored to the church in 1891.[67] Outside the church, near the chancel door, is the stump of an ancient churchyard cross, and on one of the tower buttresses is a medieval scratch dial. The registers are complete from 1692.[68]

NONCONFORMITY. Bishop Compton's census recorded no dissenters in the parish in 1676.[69] By the 1680s there may have been a group of Anabaptists in the village, although the movement was slow to establish itself in this part of the county.[70] In 1699 the house of John Warman in Coate was certified as a meeting-house for protestant dissenters.[71] This meeting may not have lasted long and by 1783 there were again said to be no dissenters in the parish.[72] In 1822 a building belonging to Thomas Besant was registered as a meeting-place for Independents,[73] although no more is heard of it. By the mid 19th century both Primitive Methodists and Wesleyan Methodists used the village green for meetings.[74] In 1842 a chapel and premises, belonging to and occupied by James May, were registered for the use of protestant dissenters,[75] most probably Primitive Methodists. On Census Sunday in 1851 it was estimated that over the past year an average of 38 people had attended morning service in this chapel, while there was an average of 42 in the afternoon, and 60 in the evening.[76] Wesleyan Methodists in the village registered a chapel in 1870[77] and this was still in use in 1966.[78]

EDUCATION. By 1819 a group of dissenters in Liddington supported a school 'for want of contributions from the parishioners', at which about 20 children were taught.[79] A Sunday school, which began in 1823, was supported by the parishioners and had 50 pupils. A daily school was opened in 1825, where 10 pupils were taught at the expense of their parents.[80] A school with a teacher's house attached was built in 1851 at a cost of £400, the

[52] Sar. Dioc. R.O. Vis. Queries, 1783.
[53] H.O. 129/250/2/4/7.
[54] *W.A.M.* xlvii. 519.
[55] An early-19th-century view by John Buckler shows the aisle from the north-west: W.A.S. Libr., Devizes, vol. vii. 14.
[56] *W.A.M.* xlvii. 519.
[57] Ibid. liii. 468.
[58] Ibid. xlvii. 519.
[59] Date on wall.
[60] *W.A.M.* xlvii. 519.
[61] Ibid. i. 93.
[62] Walters, *Wilts. Bells*, 121.
[63] *W.A.M.* i. 93.
[64] Ibid. xli. 136.
[65] Nightingale, *Wilts. Plate*, 183.
[66] *W.A.M.* xxv. 350.
[67] Ibid. xliv. 302.
[68] Ibid. xlvii. 520.
[69] *W. N. & Q.* iii. 535.
[70] *V.C.H. Wilts.* iii. 115.
[71] W.R.O. Certs. of Dissenters' Meeting Houses.
[72] Sar. Dioc. R.O. Vis. Queries, 1783.
[73] W.R.O. Certs. of Dissenters' Meeting Houses; G.R.O. Retn. of Regns.
[74] Wilts. Cuttings, xii. 200.
[75] Glouc. City Libr. Hockaday Abstracts, 350, pp. 298–9.
[76] H.O. 129/250/2/4/8.
[77] G.R.O. Worship Register.
[78] *Kelly's Dir. Wilts.* (1939).
[79] *Digest of Retns. to Cttee. of Educ. of Poor*, H.C. 224, p. 1031 (1819), ix (2).
[80] *Educ. Enq. Abstract*, H.C. 62, p. 112 (1835), xliii.

money being provided by the rector and public sub-scription. By 1859 there were about 20 children being taught by a 'dame' from Chiseldon.[81] In 1896 the school received a parliamentary grant[82] and sub-sequently became united with the National Society.[83] The average attendance was 56 in 1910, but by 1938 had dropped to 29,[84] although in 1950 attendance had risen again to an average of 55 children.[85] The school was closed in 1962 and the pupils were trans-ferred to Wanborough.[86]

CHARITIES. By his will proved in 1876 William Brind bequeathed £100 in trust, the income of which was to be used to provide an evening school for boys employed in farm labour.[87] In 1884 the Charity Commissioners were informed that the income had been used to maintain a reading room, since a night school was said to be no longer required. The charity was extended in 1887 to enable books to be purchased for a lending library or for distribution as prizes for farm-labouring boys. The income from the invest-

ment was about £2 in 1903 and the money was gen-erally used to buy books for distribution as prizes in the village school. In 1968 it was about the same.

As is explained below, Liddington was supposed to have a share in the apprenticing charity founded by William Savage of Wootton Bassett in 1882.[88] But in 1903 no child of Liddington had benefited from this and the rector complained to the Charity Commissioners that it was difficult to obtain infor-mation about the fund. The charity still existed in 1963 when the income was about £2.

Jonathan Gosling, by his will proved in 1915, bequeathed £250, the profits of which were to be distributed annually to the sick and poor of the hamlet of Coate, which then lay partly in Liddington and partly in the neighbouring parish of Chiseldon.[89] During 1962–6 the Gosling Bequest Fund yielded about £9 yearly. In 1966 the Vicar of Chiseldon complained of a lack of adequately qualified bene-ficiaries in Coate which, since 1915, had been en-gulfed in the south-eastward expansion of Swindon (see above).

LYDIARD TREGOZE

THE NORTH-EASTERN CORNER of the parish of Lydiard Tregoze adjoins the western boundary of the borough of Swindon, but it is some 3 miles from the outskirts of Swindon to the centre of the parish. The parish may be described very roughly as **T**-shaped, the top of the **T**, the northern part of the parish, stretching about 5½ miles from east to west, and the trunk of the **T** extending about 4 miles from north to south.

Until the end of the 19th century there were two detached parts of the parish, both lying to the south in Wroughton. One was the Basset Down estate (approx. 192 a.), and the other was a field of 18 a., lying further south still.[1] The situation of the Basset Down estate led to some confusion as to the boundary, and consequently the exact area of the parish in the later 19th century. In 1831 and 1841 the area was said to be 5,930 a.[2] Between 1851 and 1881 it was given as 5,142 a.[3] In 1885, when the first ordnance survey maps to mark parish boun-daries were made, the area was said to be 5,327 a., including the 18 detached acres, but excluding Basset Down, which was shown as part of Wrough-ton.[4] An enquiry by a Local Government Board Commission in 1899, however, found that histori-cally Basset Down belonged to Lydiard Tregoze and the boundary was redrawn on later editions of the maps to bring Basset Down within the parish of Lydiard Tregoze.[5] In 1901, after this correction had

been made, the area was 5,430 a., still including the detached 18 acres in Wroughton.[6] In 1928 the parish lost 95 a. in the east to the borough of Swindon, thus reducing the area to 5,335 a.[7]

The 18 detached acres in Wroughton lay about ¾ mile south of the southern end of Lydiard and represented part of the land which until 1660 had belonged to the estate called Can Court (see below). That year Richard Spenser of Quidhampton acquired three fields, called Overfields and the Croft, comprising 64 a., from the owner of Can Court, since they could more conveniently be farmed with Quidhampton.[8] These fields then apparently became merged in the parish of Wroughton, in which Quidhampton lies, but a fourth field of 18 a., also belonging to Can Court, and not conveyed to Spenser, continued to be regarded as a detached part of Lydiard Tregoze until 1934 when it, too, was transferred to Wroughton.[9] In 1951 the area of the parish was 5,316 a.[10] The southern boundary of the parish even after the confusion of the late 19th century had been cleared up, remains remarkably irregular, undoubtedly owing to conveyances of land between the owners of the various manors.

For the most part the soil of the parish is Kim-meridge Clay, but roughly in the middle there is an inlier of Corallian rocks, some 2 miles in length. Wheatley Limestones predominate at the north-east end of this inlier and have been quarried there,

[81] *Acct. of Wilts. Schools*, H.C. 27, p. 95 (1859 Sess. 1), xxi (2).
[82] *Schools in receipt of Parl. Grants, 1896* [C. 8174], H.C. (1896), lxv.
[83] *Min. of Educ. List 70, 1950.*
[84] *Bd. of Educ. List 21, 1938.*
[85] *Min. of Educ. List 70, 1950.*
[86] Ex inf. Chief Education Officer, Trowbridge.
[87] All inf. about Brind's charity from *Endowed Char. Wilts.* (1908), p. 647 and Reg. Educ. Char. Lansdowne House, Berkeley Sq. London W.1.
[88] See p. 204. All other inf. from *Endowed Char. Wilts.* (1908), pp. 648–9 and Reg. Educ. Char. (see n. 87 above).
[89] All inf. about this charity is from Char. Com. Files 201053, 201053/A1.

[1] W.R.O. Tithe Map (Elcombe) and O.S. Map 6", Wilts. XV, XXII (1st edn.).
[2] *Census*, 1831, 1841.
[3] Ibid. Relevant years.
[4] O.S. Maps 6", Wilts. XV, XXII (1st edn.); 1/2,500 Wilts. XVI. 15, 22 (1st edn.).
[5] T. Story-Maskelyne, *Notes on Maskelyne Family and their Home* (pamphlet in W.A.S. Libr., Devizes), 29; W.R.O. 675, Par. Council Min. Bk. 1894–1936; O.S. Map 6", Wilts. XV, XXII (1922 edn.).
[6] *Census*, 1901.   [7] Ibid. 1931, table 4.
[8] *W.A.M.* xxxvi. 214–21.
[9] Story-Maskelyne, *Maskelyne Family*, 30; *V.C.H. Wilts.* iv. 282–3.
[10] *Census.*

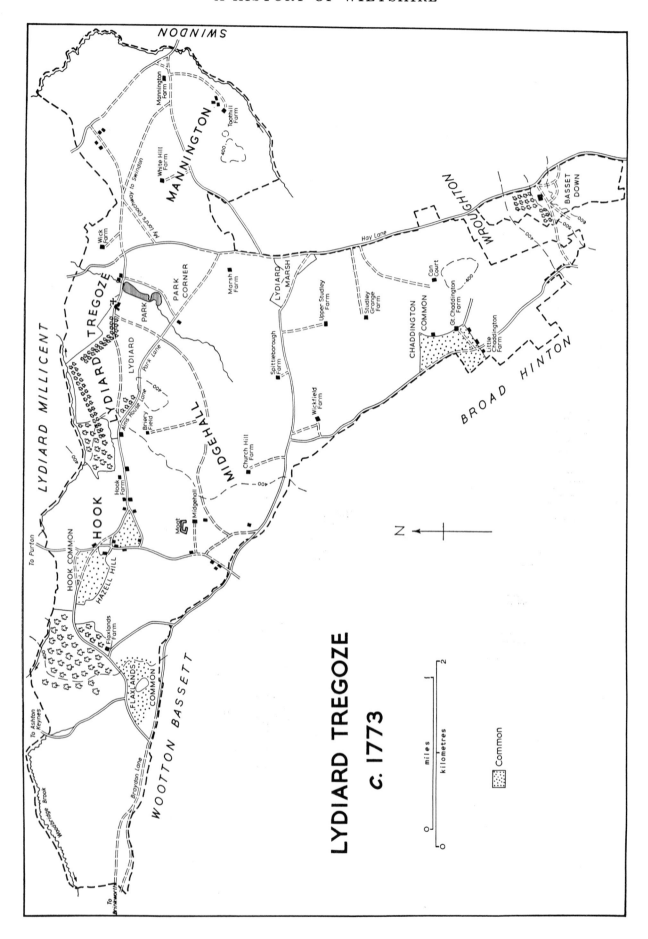

LYDIARD TREGOZE
c. 1773

Common

but coral rag covers most of the rest of the surface and has been dug from various small quarries.[11] In the extreme south the parish just touches upon the Lower Chalk Terrace of the Marlborough Downs. The general impression of the parish is one of flatness, the land hardly anywhere rising above 400 ft., but in the south, where it reaches up to the Chalk, there is a steep rise up Basset Down to 600 ft.

Aubrey, writing in the mid 17th century, mentions a mineral spring in Lydiard called 'Antiock's Well', which once, he says, was famous for its miraculous and healing properties.[12] The exact site of this well is no longer known, there are, however, several possible locations, including Toothill, where, in the early 19th century a small chalybeate spring, 42 ft. down, was found while the Wilts. and Berks. Canal was being made.[13]

Small streams form the northern boundary of the parish for much of its course, and another stream entering on the north was dammed to form the lake in Lydiard Park. On the heavy clay lands, particularly towards the south of the parish, deep drainage ditches divide the fields.

Domesday records extensive woodland at Lydiard[14] and the parish came within the royal forest of Braydon at its greatest extent in the 12th century. Frith Copse, in the north of the parish, lay within the forest in the 13th century. But by perambulations of 1279 and 1300 both Lydiard and Midgehall tithings were disafforested.[15] As has been shown elsewhere, Robert Tregoze had his own park within the forest by 1256,[16] and this was probably enlarged in 1270 when leave was given to inclose and impark a wood called Shortgrove.[17] A map of c. 1700 shows the woodland in the north-west corner of Lydiard Park to be divided into three distinct parts: Old Park Coppice (30 a.), Park Coppice (14 a.), and New Coppice (16 a.).[18] Two narrow plantations of trees bordering the road, east of Hook Gate, were called Castle Break and Oak Plantation. In 1964 the parish was still well-wooded in the north-west with numerous copses, and a thick belt of trees covered the slopes of Basset Down in the south.

A Pagan-Saxon cemetery was uncovered at Basset Down in 1822. There have also been a few finds of Roman date in the same region.[19]

In the 14th century Lydiard Tregoze was divided into three separate tithings of Lydiard Tregoze, Mannington, and Midgehall.[20] The first presumably covered the area roughly speaking in the north of the parish, the second the lands on the eastern side, and the third those on the west. There can be little doubt that there was once a village settlement in the tithing of Lydiard Tregoze somewhere near the parish church, which contains traces of 13th-century work.[21] Probably the track, overgrown and disused in 1964, formerly the drive-way to Lydiard Park, and just south of the present drive, marks the

line of a former village street, leading up to the church. Taxation assessments made in the 14th century show Lydiard Tregoze to have been then a more populous tithing than either Midgehall or Mannington, and in the 16th century there were more tax-payers in Lydiard Tregoze than in Midgehall (see below). But at some later date the tithing of Lydiard Tregoze drops out and a tithing of Hook emerges, possibly suggesting a shifting of population to that area, and a de-population of the area around the church. Hook and Midgehall were the two tithings into which the parish was divided in the 19th century. No reference to Mannington as a tithing has been found after the 14th century, but since most of the lands comprising the tithing were acquired by the Charterhouse in the 17th century, they retained a collective identity and were known as the Charterhouse lands.

In the 20th century there is no immediately obvious centre of settlement in the parish and the isolation of the parish church within Lydiard Park emphasizes the fact that the parish lacks any real village nucleus. Only at Hook do houses cluster and they lie along the main road between Wootton Bassett and Cricklade, and for a short distance along Hook Street. Here is the school, Methodist chapel, post office, a public house, and a few council houses built after the Second World War. About a mile along Hook Street the grass verges widen out to form greens on either side of the road. This area was known in the 18th century as Lower Marsh and a few cottages bordered the green on the south side.[22] Apart from this small settlement at Hook the parish consists of a fair number of scattered, medium-sized farms and of Lydiard Park, which lies in the north of the parish and is described below.[23]

Hay Lane, which, for about two miles, forms the parish boundary between Lydiard and Wroughton, is part of a prehistoric north-south track running between Cirencester and Avebury.[24] It is undoubtedly the way called 'Saltharpesweye' and known as the 'ancient way' in the 14th century.[25] The present main road between Swindon and Wootton Bassett, which crosses the parish from east to west, was turnpiked some time between 1751 and 1775.[26] A map of 1773 shows only some sections of the present route to have been roadway then, and part of it was unfenced.[27] The section running between the turnings to Blagrove and Upper Studley Farms may have been made in 1790–1 under an Act of that year for amending and improving the route between Swindon and Wootton Bassett and beyond.[28] This section of the road is not marked on the map of 1766 and at that date the way taken from Lydiard Park to Swindon ran north of the present road and was known as 'My Lord's Coachway'.[29] The road from Cricklade to Wootton Bassett running from north to south through the parish was turnpiked between 1776 and 1800.[30] The only other

[11] W. J. Arkell, 'Corallian Beds around Purton', *W.A.M.* xlix. 274–82.
[12] Aubrey, *Nat. Hist. Wilts.* 23.
[13] W. Whitaker and F. H. Edmunds, *Water Supply of Wilts.* (H.M.S.O. 1925), 22.
[14] *V.C.H. Wilts.* ii, p. 141.
[15] Ibid. iv. 402 and map on p. 445.
[16] Ibid. 404.   [17] Ibid.
[18] Warws. R.O., Map of Lydiard Pk. (Boughton-Leigh MSS.).
[19] *V.C.H. Wilts.* i (1), 83–84.

[20] Ibid. iv. 297, 306, 309.   [21] See p. 88.
[22] W.R.O. 305/11, Survey of Manor of Lydiard Tregoze 1766 (map).
[23] See p. 80.
[24] *W.A.M.* lvi. 271.
[25] *Cal. Pat.* 1350–4, 148.
[26] *V.C.H. Wilts.* iv. 257.
[27] *Andrews and Dury, Map* (W.A.S. Rec. Brch.), pl. 14.
[28] 31 Geo. III, c. 121.
[29] W.R.O. 305/11, Survey of Lydiard Tregoze, 1766.
[30] *V.C.H. Wilts.* iv. 257.

road in the parish is that running east from Hook; in 1766 the section east of Lower Marsh was called Almshouse Lane and a section east beyond this was Park Lane.[31]

The section of the Wilts. and Berks. Canal which crosses the parish from west to east was opened in 1804 and a small wharf was made at Hay Lane.[32] In 1964 the canal was thickly overgrown with weeds and bushes, and the stretch just outside the parish between Lydiard and Swindon had been filled in. The railway line from London to Bristol, opened in 1841,[33] runs through the parish just north of the canal.

In 1334 Lydiard Tregoze, Mannington, and Midgehall contributed 80s., 18s., and 12s. respectively to the fifteenth.[34] In 1377 there were 65 taxpayers in Lydiard Tregoze, 46 in Midgehall, and 21 in Mannington.[35] To the Benevolence of 1545 there were 4 contributors in Midgehall and 8 in Lydiard Tregoze; to the subsidy of 1576 there were 17 contributors in the two tithings combined.[36] In 1801 the population of the parish was 576.[37] Thereafter it rose to 807 in the middle of the century. In 1841 it was as high as 960 but this was due to the presence of many labourers working on the railway line opened that year. In 1871 it was 832 but was down ten years later to 660, although in 1891 it had risen again to 731. From 1901 onwards the figure dropped steadily until 1951 when there was a steep rise to 772 persons from 543 in 1931. This rise was, however, partly due to the hutted camp in Lydiard Park, which provided temporary dwellings for Polish refugees for some years. In 1961 the population was 525.

The best known name associated with Lydiard Tregoze is that of Henry St. John, Viscount Bolingbroke, the Tory statesman. But his connexion with the parish is remote. He was almost certainly born there, since his mother, who died soon after his birth, was buried in the parish church.[38] But, so far as is known, he was very rarely at Lydiard in later life. He was there for a short time in the summer of 1701,[39] but no other reference to his presence there has been found and in c. 1742 he renounced all his rights in his estate there to his half-brother, John, Viscount St. John (d. 1748).[40] Oliver St. John, who was the second son of Nicholas St. John (lord of the manor, d. 1589), became Lord Deputy, and later Lord High Treasurer, of Ireland and in 1623 was created Viscount Grandison. But although born at Lydiard, he had, so far as is known, no connexion with it in adult life.[41] Grandison's nephew, Sir John St. John (lord of the manor, d. 1648), worked for the royalist cause, and three of his sons died of

wounds received when fighting for the king.[42] Sir John's sixth son, Sir Walter St. John, who became lord of the manor in 1656 and died in 1708, was founder of the Sir Walter St. John School at Battersea.[43] John St. John, third son of John, 2nd Viscount St. John (d. 1748), was the author of a treatise called *Observations on the Land Revenues of the Crown*, and wrote a play about Mary Queen of Scots which was performed at Drury Lane. He died in 1793.[44] His elder brother, Henry, who became a General died in 1818.[45]

MANORS AND OTHER ESTATES. In 1086 South Lydiard, later to be called *LYDIARD TREGOZE*, was held by Alfred of Marlborough.[46] Alfred also held Ewias Castle and land in Herefordshire and it is likely that Lydiard passed like Ewias Castle to Harold, son of Ralph, Earl of Hereford (d. 1057).[47] Harold certainly held Lydiard by 1100, for that year he gave the church there to Gloucester Abbey.[48] He was succeeded by a son Robert of Ewias, who had a son of the same name. One of the two Roberts was holding the Ewias fief in 1166.[49] The younger Robert of Ewias died in 1198[50] and the honor of Ewias, including Lydiard, apparently passed to his second daughter, Sybil, wife of Robert Tregoze, Sheriff of Wiltshire, 1191–2.[51]

Robert Tregoze died before 1215[52] and was succeeded by his son, who is presumably the Robert Tregoze, lord of the honor of Ewias, who held a knight's fee in Lydiard in chief of the king in 1242.[53] In 1256 the king gave Robert some deer from Braydon Forest to restock the park at Lydiard.[54] Robert Tregoze was killed at Evesham in 1265 and was succeeded by a son, John,[55] who had a grant of free warren at Lydiard in 1274,[56] and died in 1300.[57] John's heirs were his grandson, John la Warre, son of his daughter Clarice, and Sybil, his daughter, who had married William de Grandison.[58] Lydiard is not mentioned among John's lands in the inquisition made on his death in 1300, and it may have been settled on Sybil and William earlier, for in 1299 the park at Lydiard was restored to William, having been taken into the king's hands for an offence committed by William.[59] In 1323, in exchange for the release of their son Peter,[60] held as a prisoner since the battle of Boroughbridge (1322), William and Sybil, under duress, conveyed the manor of Lydiard to Hugh le Despenser, the elder.[61] After the fall and death of Despenser in 1326 Lydiard was restored to William and Sybil de Grandison.[62]

Sybil de Grandison died in 1334 and William in 1335.[63] William's heir was his son, Peter, but in

[31] W.R.O. 305/11, Survey of Lydiard Tregoze, 1766.
[32] *V.C.H. Wilts.* iv. 273.
[33] Ibid. 282.
[34] Ibid 297.
[35] Ibid. 306, 309.
[36] *Taxation Lists* (W.A.S. Rec. Brch.), 21, 108.
[37] This and subsequent figures from *Census*.
[38] Frank T. Smallwood, 'Bolingbroke's Birthplace', *W.A.M.* lx. 96–99.
[39] Hist. MSS. Com. *Devonshire*, i (2), 804, 806.
[40] See p. 79.   [41] Britton, *Beauties of Wilts.* iii. 33.
[42] G. J. Taylor, *Our Lady of Batersey*, 158–66.
[43] Ibid. passim.
[44] *D.N.B.*   [45] Ibid.
[46] *V.C.H. Wilts.* ii, p. 141.
[47] Ibid. p. 110; *Herefordshire Domesday* (P.R.S. N.S. xxv), 111.
[48] See p. 86.

[49] *V.C.H. Wilts.* ii, p. 110; *Herefordshire Domesday* (P.R.S. N.S. xxv), 111.
[50] *Pipe R.* 1198 (P.R.S. N.S. ix), 70.
[51] *Herefordshire Domesday* (P.R.S. N.S. xxv), 111; Burke, *Dormant and Extinct Peerages*, p. 537 (Tregoze).
[52] *Herefordshire Domesday* (P.R.S. N.S. xxv), 111.
[53] *Bk. of Fees*, ii. 712.
[54] *V.C.H. Wilts.* iv. 404.
[55] Burke, *Dormant and Extinct Peerages*, p. 537.
[56] *Rot. Hund.* (Rec. Com.), ii. 244.
[57] *Cal. Inq. p.m. Edw. I*, iii, pp. 453–6.   [58] Ibid.
[59] *Cal. Close*, 1296–1302, 281.
[60] S.C. 8/49/2437.
[61] *Cal. Pat.* 1321–4, 285; *Feet of F. Wilts.* (W.A.S. Rec. Brch.), 110; *Cal. Pat.* 1327–30, 245.
[62] *Cal. Pat.* 1327–30, 245.
[63] *Complete Peerage*, Grandison; *Wilts. Inq. p.m.* 1327–77 (Index Libr.), 110.

1331, William and Sybil had leased Lydiard to their daughter, Agnes, widow of John de Northwood, for her life.[64] In 1347 Peter de Grandison granted the reversion of the manor, after the death of Agnes, his sister, to Roger de Beauchamp and Roger's wife, Sybil, who was the daughter of Mabel, wife of Sir John Patshull of Bletsoe (Beds.), another sister.[65] Agnes de Northwood died in 1348 and Peter conveyed the manor to Roger and Sybil and their heirs male.[66] Peter de Grandison died without issue in 1358.[67]

Roger Beauchamp died in 1380 and was succeeded by his grandson, also called Roger.[68] The younger Roger died in 1406 and was succeeded by his son John.[69] John Beauchamp died in 1412, having settled Lydiard upon his wife, Edith, for life.[70] John's heir was his infant son, John, but this John died in 1420, still a minor, before his mother.[71] Edith, who married as her second husband Robert Shottesbrook, died in 1441, and was succeeded at Lydiard by her daughter, Margaret, sister and heir of the John who had died in 1420.[72] Margaret Beauchamp married first Oliver St. John, who died in 1437, and secondly John Beaufort, Duke of Somerset, by whom she had a daughter, Margaret, who became the wife of Edmund Tudor, Earl of Richmond, and the mother of Henry VII.[73] Margaret Beauchamp died in 1482, having settled the manor upon Oliver St. John, her second son by her first husband, and upon Oliver's wife, Elizabeth.[74]

Oliver St. John died in 1497 and Elizabeth in 1503 and were succeeded by their son, John.[75] John, who was knighted by his cousin, Henry VII, died in 1512 and was succeeded by his son, another John, who at the time of his father's death was eleven years old.[76] This John was followed on his death in 1576 by his son Nicholas,[77] who died in 1589, and was succeeded by his son, another John St. John.[78] John died in 1594 when his heir, Walter, was ten years old.[79] Walter survived his father by three years only, and was succeeded by his brother, John, a boy of about eleven.[80]

John St. John came of age in 1606 and in 1611 was made a baronet.[81] In 1630 the manor of Battersea (Surr.) was devised to him by his uncle, Oliver St. John, who had been created Viscount Grandison in 1620.[82] Thereafter Battersea provided another home for the family, although Sir John continued to live chiefly at Lydiard.[83] Sir John, who was predeceased by five of his sons, three of them dying of wounds sustained while fighting on the king's side

in the Civil War, was succeeded in 1648 by his grandson, John, son of his eldest son, Oliver (d. 1641).[84] The younger John died unmarried in 1656, and Lydiard and the baronetcy passed to his uncle, Walter St. John, a younger brother of his father.[85]

Sir Walter St. John, who was apparently already occupying the manor-house at Battersea, continued to live mostly there.[86] In 1673 he settled both Lydiard and Battersea upon his son, Henry, then about to marry Lady Mary Rich, and upon the heirs male of the marriage.[87] Lady Mary died five years later giving birth to her only child to survive infancy, a son, Henry, the future Viscount Bolingbroke, Secretary of State to Queen Anne.[88] When in 1701 the younger Henry married Frances Winchcombe Lydiard and Battersea were settled upon him and the male heirs of the marriage by his grandfather, Sir Walter St. John, and his father, Henry St. John.[89] Sir Walter died in 1708 and was succeeded by his son, Henry, who in 1716 was created Viscount St. John with remainder to his sons by his second wife, Angelica Magdalena Pelissary.[90] Thus when Lord St. John died in 1742, the heir to his estates, including Lydiard Tregoze, but not to his title, was his son by his first marriage, Henry. Henry, created Viscount Bolingbroke in 1712, had been attainted and impeached in 1715,[91] but his right to inherit and acquire real estate had been restored to him by a private Act of Parliament of 1725.[92] At an unknown date, however, presumably about the time of his father's death, and certainly before 1743, Bolingbroke had renounced all his right to Lydiard, but not to Battersea, in favour of his half-brother John St. John, eldest son of his father's second marriage,[93] and from about this time John probably made Lydiard his home. Thus John St. John succeeded in 1742 to his father's title in accordance with the special remainder, and probably also to Lydiard Tregoze in consequence of his half-brother's renunciation.[94] John died in 1748 and was succeeded by his son, Frederick, who on his uncle Henry's death in 1751, succeeded also to Battersea and, again according to a special remainder, to the viscounty of Bolingbroke, forfeited by Henry in 1715, but revived on his death.[95]

Thenceforth the lordship of the manor passed with the titles of Bolingbroke and St. John from father to son until the death of Lord Bolingbroke in 1899 when the legal estate passed in accordance with Lord Bolingbroke's will to his widow, Mary

[64] Cal. Pat. 1330–4, 234; Wilts. Inq. p.m. 1327–77 (Index Libr.), 110.

[65] Cal. Pat. 1345–8, 438; Complete Peerage, Grandison.

[66] Wilts. Inq. p.m. 1327–77 (Index Libr.), 188–9; C.P. 25(1)/255/47/32; Cal. Close, 1346–9, 583.

[67] Cal. Inq. p.m. x. 347.

[68] C 136/8(3)/5.

[69] C 137/53/22.

[70] C 137/89/10; C 138/46/47.

[71] C 138/46/47.

[72] Complete Peerage, Beauchamp.   [73] Ibid.

[74] C 140/82/7; Cal. Inq. Hen. VII, ii, p. 111.

[75] Cal. Inq. Hen. VII, ii, p. 111; C 142/17/47.

[76] C 142/29/52.

[77] C 142/175/99.

[78] C 142/227/208.

[79] C 142/239/119.

[80] C 142/249/82.

[81] G. J. Taylor, Our Lady of Batersey, 159–60; Burke, Peerage and Baronetage (1949), Bolingbroke.

[82] Taylor, op. cit. 153, 67; Oliver's title was limited, in

failure of male issue, to the heirs of his niece, Barbara St. John, m. Sir Edw. Villiers. On Oliver's death, childless, therefore, the title passed to Sir Wm. Villiers, Barbara's eldest son: ibid. 69; Complete Peerage, Grandison.

[83] Taylor, Our Lady of Batersey, 81.

[84] Ibid. 164 and App. C3, table vi.

[85] Ibid. 74, 78, 164.

[86] Ibid. 74, 81–82.

[87] C 54/4873 no. 7.

[88] Complete Peerage, Bolingbroke; D.N.B. and see p. 78.

[89] C 54/4873 no. 7.

[90] Burke, Peerage and Baronetage (1949), Bolingbroke.

[91] D.N.B.

[92] 11 Geo. I c. 40 (priv. act).

[93] The only evidence found for this renunciation is in a letter from Bolingbroke to his half-sister, dated 1745: B.M. Add. MS. 34196, f. 147; Burke, Peerage and Baronetage (1949), Bolingbroke.

[94] Burke, op. cit.

[95] Complete Peerage, Bolingbroke.

Emily Elizabeth, Viscountess Bolingbroke.[96] Lady Bolingbroke died in 1940 and three years later the house and 147 a. were purchased from her executor by the Corporation of Swindon.[97] Throughout the 19th century the house was in the hands of mortgagees.[98]

LYDIARD PARK. Seen from the south Lydiard Park appears to be a rather grand house of the 18th century. Built of Bath stone ashlar, the south-west front has two stories and eleven bays.[99] The three central bays project slightly and those at either end are raised an additional story to form two towers with pyramidal roofs. Between the towers runs an ornamental stone balustrade, which is interrupted by a large central pediment. In the tympanum is a cartouche carved with the St. John arms with an escutcheon of Furnese. The entrance door and two of the ground-floor windows are also pedimented. The south-east front is of similar design but without the pedimented centrepiece.

An inscription in the attics of the house records that it was rebuilt in 1743 by John, Viscount St. John (d. 1748), who married Anne Furnese, a wealthy heiress. But in fact the house was only in part remodelled at this date, as is immediately seen by looking at it from the back, where building of various earlier dates is visible. A small drawing of the house as it was in c. 1700,[1] coupled with examination of the interior structure, confirms that this was so and that the remodelling was applied to a house with a basically late-medieval plan, which had been extensively altered and enlarged in the 17th century. The original house consisted of a central hall block with screens passage flanked by projecting kitchen and solar wings to the west and east respectively. Small additions at either end of the house in order to enlarge the two wings were apparently made in the 17th century, and in the same century the kitchen quarters were further extended by a range of buildings at the back. By c. 1700 there was also a substantial service wing running south-westwards from the west side of the house. This has entirely disappeared. In 1743 by building a new south-west front, which filled in the recessed central part of the earlier house, Sir John St. John provided a much grander entrance and an enlarged hall. The hall rises through one and a half stories so that the three central windows above it serve no function but to complete the regularity of the façade. By adding a new south-east front in the same style, Sir John ensured that his house, when seen from the park, had all the appearance of a building in the classical style of his time. The name of Sir John's architect is unknown, although Roger Morris has been suggested. The only addition made to the house since 1743 is a kitchen wing to the west, built in the mid 19th century. In the 1960s this was converted into sleeping accommodation in readiness for the use of Lydiard Park as a conference centre.

Most of the valuable contents of the house were sold in 1824 and the rest in 1943 when the house was acquired by the Corporation of Swindon. Only a bust of Henry St. John, Viscount Bolingbroke (d. 1751), by Michael Rysbrack, seems to have escaped the sales and remains in the house. But the internal decoration and fittings, all dating from the 1740s, have survived and are of an outstanding standard of elegance and craftsmanship. Extensive restoration of the house was undertaken by the corporation in the 1950s and 1960s. The corporation also furnished some of the rooms and brought back many of the St. John family portraits.

In c. 1700 three long avenues of trees crossed the park and vestiges of these remained in 1964.[2] Before the remodelling of 1743 there was a formal garden enclosed by railings immediately in front of the house and there appears to have been a large walled garden to the east. Also on the east there was a small lake and immediately south of this was an irregularly shaped fishpond. Some new landscaping was probably done after the remodelling of the house in 1743. A map of 1766 marks the lake as the 'new pond or canal', and calls the former fishpond the 'old pond'.[3] A plantation of trees to the south-west of the house is shown on the same map, and perhaps the large ice-house situated on this site may have been built about this time. The present (1964) walled garden to the west of the house is marked. The approach to the house from the east in 1766 ran south of the drive of 1964, passing between Brook Cottage and the lake. It was not until after 1830, when Lord Bolingbroke acquired some glebe land lying immediately north of the church, that the present drive could be made. The wych elms lining this drive were planted in 1911.[4]

The manor of MIDGEHALL was among the estates granted to Stanley Abbey between 1151 and 1154 by Henry Duke of Normandy, later Henry II.[5] At least from about the time of this grant, Midgehall was considered to be a member of the manor of Shrivenham (Berks.) and between 1168 and 1242 the Sheriff of Berkshire claimed £7 for the holding of the monks of Stanley in Midgehall.[6] Stanley continued to hold Midgehall until the Dissolution.

In 1536 Midgehall was granted to Sir Edward Seymour, Viscount Beauchamp (cr. Duke of Somerset 1546–7).[7] After the duke's execution in 1551 and attainder in 1552 Midgehall passed to his son Edward (cr. Earl of Hertford 1558–9), who died seised of the manor in 1621.[8] The earl was succeeded by his grandson William who was restored to his great-grandfather's dukedom of Somerset.[9] He died in 1660 and was succeeded by his grandson, also called William.[10] William, Duke of Somerset, died unmarried in 1671 and the title passed to his father's brother, John, who died childless in 1675.[11] Midgehall then apparently passed to John's sisters, Frances,

[96] Ibid.; records in possession of borough of Swindon.
[97] Conveyance 9 Oct. 1943 penes the borough of Swindon.
[98] W.R.O. 305/7, Schedule to conveyance of property at Hook.
[99] Except where otherwise stated, all information about the house and park comes from the accounts of these by Mr. A. R. Dufty, in the Guide to Lydiard Park and Church, printed in 1967.
[1] This picture is on a map of Lydiard Park, c. 1700, in Warws. R.O. (Boughton-Leigh MSS.), see pl. opposite.

[2] Description of park and gardens before the remodelling of the house from map cited in n. 1 above.
[3] W.R.O. 305/11, Map of Lydiard Tregoze, 1766.
[4] See n. 99 above.   [5] V.C.H. Wilts. iii. 269.
[6] Red. Bk. Exch. (Rolls Ser.), ii. 673 where 'Migehald' is wrongly identified as Midgham; Pipe R. 1168–1242 (P.R.S.), see indexes; Bk. of Fees, i. 107.
[7] L. & P. Hen. VIII, x, p. 526.
[8] Wilts. Inq. p.m. 1625–49 (Index Libr.), 29.
[9] Complete Peerage, Hertford.   [10] Ibid.   [11] Ibid.

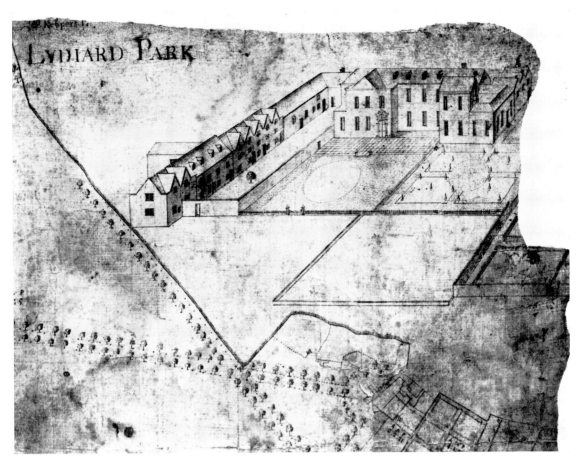

Lydiard Park, south-west front, detail from a map of *c.* 1700

Lydiard Park, south-west front, as rebuilt in 1743

LYDIARD TREGOZE

wife of Conyers Darcy, later Earl of Holderness (d. 1692), and Jane, wife of Charles Boyle, Viscount Dungarven (d. 1694), for they conveyed the manor to trustees in 1677.[12] Jane died in 1679 and Frances in 1680 and before then Midgehall had passed to their niece Elizabeth, sister of William Duke of Somerset (d. 1671).[13] In 1685 Elizabeth and her husband Thomas Bruce, later Earl of Ailesbury (d. 1741), conveyed Midgehall to Lawrence Hyde, Earl of Rochester (d. 1711).[14] The earl had bought the manor of Wootton Bassett in 1676 and thenceforth Midgehall followed the same descent as that manor.[15]

Stanley Abbey was given licence to let the manor to farm for 20 years in 1324.[16] But no names of any lessees have been found before the 16th century. In 1534 the abbot and convent leased the manor to William Pleydell for 95 years. By his will, proved 1556, William devised the remaining years of the lease to his wife, Agnes, for her life, and after her death to his fourth son Gabriel Pleydell and his heirs male.[17] Agnes died in 1567[18] and Gabriel in in 1590.[19] Gabriel was succeeded by his son Oliver, and Oliver, the date of whose death is unknown, by his son Charles.[20] Charles was knighted in 1618 and died in 1642.[21] Sir Charles's son by his first wife, John Pleydell, was M.P. for Wootton Bassett and styled himself of Midgehall. He died without surviving issue in 1692.[22] Midgehall then passed to Sir Charles's descendants by his second wife. His grandson Edmund was styled of Midgehall and several of his children were born there.[23] His wife Anne was buried at Lydiard in 1723, although Edmund was buried in 1726 at Milborne Port, the family home in Dorset.[24] Shortly after this date the Pleydells apparently left Midgehall, and the family of Bradford became tenants under the Earl of Clarendon.[25]

Midgehall is an **L**-shaped farm-house, standing at the south-east corner of a large rectangular moat. It dates from c. 1800 but has quite extensive later additions.

In 1242½ a knight's fee in *MANNINGTON* was held of the king by Baldwin (de Reviers), Earl of Devon (d. 1244–5). The Earl of Pembroke, the Earl Marshal (d. 1245), held this of the Earl of Devon, Matthew Columbers held it of the Earl of Devon, and Richard Pipard held it of Matthew.[26] In 1274 the overlordship had passed to the Earl of Devon's daughter, Isabel Countess of Devon (d. 1293), of whom the heirs of the Earl Marshal held, and Matthew Columbers held of these heirs.[27] No more is heard of the overlordship of the Earl of Devon, nor of the lordship of the Earl Marshal. In a way

traced elsewhere,[28] the lands of Matthew Columbers passed to John de Cobham (d. 1300) and in 1331–2 the overlordship of Mannington was apparently held by John's grandson, also called John (d. 1354–1355), who succeeded his father as Lord Cobham in 1339.[29] The overlordship then descended with the Cobham title and in 1428 was held by Thomas Brooke, who was *jure uxoris* Lord Cobham (d. 1439).[30]

In 1304 Mannington was held of the Cobhams by Walter Pavely (d. 1323), for that year Walter was granted free warren in his demesne lands there.[31] Walter was succeeded by a son Reynold, and in 1331–2 John de Cobham was claiming wardship of Reynold on the ground that Walter had held the manor of him.[32] Nothing more is known of the manor until 1414 when John Lovel, Lord Lovel, died holding a third and the reversion of the rest which Parnel de Knolle held for life.[33] Lord Lovel was succeeded by a son William, who died in 1455 and was succeeded by his son John.[34] John died in 1464–5 and his widow Joan was holding Mannington at her death in 1466.[35] Joan was succeeded by her son Francis, who was only nine at the time of his father's death.[36] Francis was created Viscount Lovel in 1482–3 and held high office under Richard III, but in 1485 he was attainted and all his honours were forfeited.[37]

Mannington, with Lord Lovel's other Wiltshire manors, was granted to Sir John Cheney but upon Sir John's death in 1499 was resumed by the Crown.[38] In 1512 the manor was granted to Sir William Compton.[39] Sir William died in 1528 and was succeeded by his son Peter.[40] Peter died in 1544 and was succeeded by his son Henry, then aged one.[41] Henry was created Lord Compton and on his death in 1589 was succeeded by his son William (d. 1630).[42] In 1605 William conveyed Mannington, with some other Wiltshire manors, to Thomas Sutton, the founder of the London Charterhouse.[43] Mannington thus became one of the manors with which Sutton endowed his foundation.[44] Mannington, which included the farms of Toothill and Whitehill, remained part of the Charterhouse estate until 1919 when it was sold to the Wiltshire County Council to provide small-holdings for discharged soldiers of the First World War.[45]

Mannington farm-house, which dates from the late 18th century, stands on the north side of the main Swindon-Chippenham road close to the boundary between Lydiard Tregoze and Swindon. It is roughcast with stone dressings and has a hipped mansard roof. Three-light casement windows flank the central doorway.

[12] C.P. 25(2)/762/29 Chas. II East.
[13] For Jane see *Complete Peerage*, ii. 431; for Frances see ibid. vi. 536.
[14] C.P. 25(2)/369/1 Jas. II Trin. and see pl. facing p. 28.
[15] See p. 191.
[16] *Cal. Pat.* 1324–7, 11.
[17] P.C.C. 5 Ketchyn. Printed in *W.N. & Q.* v. 131–4.
[18] Will proved 1567: P.C.C. 35 Stonard. Printed in *W.N. & Q.* v. 134–5.
[19] *Wilts. Visitation Pedigrees* (Harl. Soc. cv. and cvi), 133.
[20] Ibid.
[21] Aubrey, *Topog. Coll.* ed. Jackson, 185.
[22] Hutchins, *Dors.* i. 197.
[23] Lydiard Tregoze church, Reg. of Births.
[24] Hutchins, *Dors.* i. 197.
[25] W.R.O. Land Tax Assessments.
[26] *Bk. of Fees*, ii. 724.
[27] *Rot. Hund.* (Rec. Com.), ii. 243.

[28] See p. 27.
[29] C.P. 40/284 m. 11; *Complete Peerage*.
[30] *Complete Peerage*; *Feud. Aids*, vi. 279.
[31] *Cal. Chart. R.* 1300–26, 42.
[32] C.P. 40/284 m. 11.
[33] C 138/239/30.
[34] *Complete Peerage*; *Feud. Aids*, v. 279.
[35] C 140/487/20.
[36] *Complete Peerage*.
[37] Ibid.
[38] E 150/968/7.
[39] Ibid.
[40] C 142/48/158.
[41] C 142/72/105.
[42] *Complete Peerage*.
[43] C.P. 25(2)/369/3 Jas. I Mich.
[44] *W.A.M.* xxxvii. 412.
[45] Ibid. xli. 460.

By 1242–3 ½ knight's fee in *CHADDINGTON* belonged to Walter of Dunstanville's barony of Castle Combe.[46] It has been suggested that Chaddington is the place called in the Domesday Survey 'Schetone' and held at that date by Humphrey de Lisle.[47] If this is so, then Chaddington would presumably have descended to Walter of Dunstanville in the same way as the rest of Humphrey's estates.[48] But more recently 'Schetone' has been identified as Ashton Giffard in Codford St. Peter.[49] It cannot, therefore, be said for certain how Walter acquired Chaddington. The overlordship descended with the barony of Castle Combe until the death of Giles Badlesmere in 1339.[50] On the partition of Giles's estates Chaddington, then reckoned as a whole fee, was among the lands allotted to his sister Margaret and her husband John Tibetot.[51] It seems, however, to have been alienated shortly afterwards, like the other lands that had been allotted to Margaret and John,[52] and was not among John's possessions at his death.[53] No more is known of the overlordship.

In 1242–3 Chaddington was held of Walter of Dunstanville by William of Burdeville.[54] Soon after this, however, William and a number of other persons by a succession of grants conveyed their lands in Chaddington to the prior and convent of Bradenstoke.[55] In 1274–5 the jurors in the hundred court asserted that the holding, formerly held by William of Burdeville and known as East Chaddington, had been held for the past ten years by the Prior of Bradenstoke.[56]

The priory's estate in Chaddington was enlarged somewhat in 1303 when Thomas of Chiseldon was granted licence to alienate to it a messuage and ½ virgate there.[57] In 1339 the holding, held of the barony of Castle Combe, was reckoned as a whole fee.[58] In 1535, however, Bradenstoke appears to have been receiving only a portion of tithes from Chaddington.[59] By 1562 Chaddington had become annexed to the manor of Bincknoll, in Broad Hinton, and was sold with it that year by William Lord Cobham (d. 1596–7) to John St. John (d. 1576).[60] Its subsequent descent, therefore, follows the main manor of Lydiard Tregoze. In 1900 Great and Little Chaddington farms still formed part of Bincknoll manor, one of the two manors into which the St. John estate was divided for administrative purposes.[61] The two farms were thus sold at the same time as Bincknoll in *c.* 1920.[62]

Great Chaddington Farm is a timber-framed house with a thatched roof, which has been considerably altered. It dates from the 17th century. Little Chaddington, which was derelict in 1968, is of red brick with a thatched roof and is of 19th-century date.

By 1460 Stanley Abbey had a grange in Lydiard Tregoze, which was sometimes called the manor of Studley by Midgehall *alias* Studley Grange. That year the Abbot of Stanley obtained licence to alienate an annual rent of 10 marks issuing from the grange and from land in Heywood (in Westbury) to the chaplain of the chantry of William Ingram in Highworth church.[63] Studley Grange remained among the possessions of Stanley Abbey until the Dissolution.[64] After the Dissolution it passed like Midgehall to Sir Edward Seymour, Viscount Beauchamp (cr. Duke of Somerset 1546–7).[65] It then descended like Midgehall to Somerset's son, Edward, Earl of Hertford, who held it at his death in 1621.[66] Hertford's heir, his grandson William (d. 1660), sold Studley in 1648 to William Yorke and Yorke's son-in-law, Henry Kemp. Thereupon the estate was split up, the southern part being taken by Yorke and becoming the later Basset Down estate, and the northern part becoming the share of Henry Kemp.[67] The subsequent descent of the part belonging to Henry Kemp has not been traced. The Basset Down estate was sold by William Yorke's grandson, also called William, in 1709 to John Coxe and in 1764 Coxe's son, John Hippisley Coxe, sold it to Edmund Maskelyne.[68] Edmund Maskelyne (d. 1775), devised the estate to his brother Nevil, the Astronomer Royal (d. 1811), who continued, however, to live at Purton Stoke.[69] After the death of Nevil Maskelyne, Basset Down passed to his daughter Margaret, who married Anthony Mervyn Story.[70] The family then took the name of Story-Maskelyne. Basset Down passed to Margaret's son, Mervyn Herbert Nevil Story-Maskelyne (d. 1911), and then to his daughter Mary, who married H. O. Arnold-Forster, Secretary of State for War, 1903–1906.[71] Basset Down passed to their son, John A. Arnold-Forster, who died in 1958.[72] His son, Nigel M. Arnold-Forster, demolished the house a few months later.[73]

A history and description of Basset Down House have been written by Mary Arnold-Forster.[74] It apparently dated from the 15th century but was partially rebuilt at the end of the 17th century. It was extensively altered again in the later 19th century in order to make it a smaller house.

The first mention found of the estate called Can Court occurs in 1564 when the lordship belonged to Henry Compton (d. 1589), who held it as part of his manor of Elcombe in Wroughton.[75] Henry's son, William, Lord Compton (d. 1630), sold Elcombe in 1605 to Thomas Sutton, but Can Court does not seem to have been included in the sale.[76]

[46] *Bk. of Fees*, ii. 726.
[47] 'Manors subordinate to Barony of Castle Combe', G. Poulett Scrope, *W.A.M.* ii. 283; *Dom Bk. Wilts.* ed. Jones, 231.
[48] *V.C.H. Wilts.* ii, pp. 110–11.
[49] Ibid. p. 144.
[50] G. Poulett Scrope, *Hist. Castle Combe*, 12–84; *Wilts. Inq. p.m.* 1327–77 (Index Libr.), 133.
[51] *Cal. Close*, 1339–41, 283; Poulett Scrope, op. cit. 70.
[52] Poulett Scrope, op. cit. 73–74.
[53] *Cal. Inq. p.m.* xii, p. 151.
[54] *Bk. of Fees*, ii. 726.
[55] B.M. Stowe MS. 925, ff. 41–43.
[56] *Rot. Hund.* (Rec. Com.), ii. 244.
[57] *Cal. Pat.* 1301–7, 131–2.
[58] *Wilts. Inq. p.m.* 1327–77 (Index Libr.), 133.
[59] *Valor Eccl.* (Rec. Com.), ii. 123.
[60] C.P. 25(2)/239/4 Eliz. I Trin.

[61] W.R.O. 305/24, Estate papers.
[62] W.R.O. 305/18, Sale particulars.
[63] *Cal. Pat.* 1452–61, 640.
[64] *Valor Eccl.* (Rec. Com.), ii. 114.
[65] *L. & P. Hen. VIII*, x, p. 526 and see above.
[66] *Wilts. Inq. p.m.* 1625–49 (Index Libr.), 23.
[67] W.A.S. Libr., Devizes, Story-Maskelyne Papers, Box N.
[68] Ibid.
[69] Mary Arnold-Forster, *Basset Down: An Old Country Home*, 28, 31.
[70] Ibid. 31.
[71] Ibid. 62.
[72] *W.A.M.* liv. 118.
[73] *Wilts. Herald*, 26 June, 28 Aug. 1958.
[74] See n. 69. above.
[75] C 142/140/201.
[76] C.P. 25(2)/369/3 Jas. I Mich.

Under Henry Compton Can Court was held by George Prater, who died in 1564 and was succeeded by his son George.[77] In 1586 John Weare, *alias* Browne, and Thomas Weare, *alias* Browne, seem to have been farming Can Court, but whether as tenants or owners is not clear.[78] By 1607 the farm had passed to Thomas Hutchins, who settled it upon himself for life and then upon Thomas Baskerville and his heirs.[79] In 1616 Baskerville sold it to Sir John Benet, who conveyed it to Pembroke College, Oxford.[80] In 1965 the farm still belonged to the college.[81]

The farm-house is a tall stone building of four stories dating from the 17th century. There are three rooms to each floor, separated by stud partitions, and a massive oak staircase reaching from basement to attics. The twin-gabled front is flanked by projecting chimneys with tall diagonally-set stacks; in the centre is a timber-framed porch of two stories with a hipped roof. The stone windows, most of which have survived, have ovolo-moulded mullions and are surmounted by relieving arches. The ground floor contains a hall and parlour with a smaller room and the staircase at the rear. Oak panelling in the hall is framed in tall narrow panels and there is an arcaded overmantle. The unusual plan of the house and the workmanship of its fittings may indicate that it was not designed as an ordinary farm-house, while its architectural character suggests a building date of *c.* 1650. In front of the house is a small enclosed forecourt. At the entrance to this there is a stone slab on which an inscription was still legible in the later 19th century. It apparently commemorated Cornelius Bradford (d. *c.* 1750).[82] The Bradford family were tenants of Can Court for most of the 18th century before leaving it for Midgehall.

In 1307 Henry de Tyeys died holding ¼ knight's fee in Lydiard of the lords of the main manor, William and Sybil de Grandison.[83] Henry's son, also called Henry, was executed in 1322 and at the time of his death was said to be holding ⅓ knight's fee of William and Sybil, which included land in Lydiard and Hook.[84] In 1330 this had apparently passed to Alice, sister and heir of Henry, and widow of Warin de Lisle,[85] and in 1336 she was granted free warren in her demesne lands in Lydiard.[86] Alice died in 1347 and was succeeded by her son Gerard.[87] The estate, which was sometimes called the manor of Lydiard Tyeys, descended to Gerard but was subsequently resumed by the lords of the main manor, for in 1428 Gerard's lands in Lydiard were held by Robert Shottesbrook, husband of Edith, upon whom the manor had been settled by her first husband, John Beauchamp (d. 1412).[88] Besides the part held by Alice de Tyeys in 1330 another part of the manor was held that year by Thomas de Monthermer (d. 1340) and Margaret his wife.[89] In

1343 Margaret de Monthermer held a third of the manor and had leased it to John de Wyk for three years.[90] John Wyk, possibly a son of this John, had lands in Lydiard in 1412.[91]

In addition to holding, for a time, the manor of Lydiard Tregoze, the elder Despenser also held some land at Hook.[92] After the forfeiture of his lands in 1326 the land in Hook (la Hoke) was granted to William Strut to hold for seven years.[93] The same estate was granted in 1340 by the king to William Dale, his yeoman, but it seems that the overlordship of the estate had by this time been assumed by Agnes de Northwood who was holding the manor of Lydiard for life.[94] In 1358, ten years after the death of Agnes, William Dale died holding the estate of Roger Beauchamp, lord of the manor of Lydiard Tregoze.[95] After William's death, the Hook estate appears to have been resumed by the lords of the manor of Lydiard.[96]

ECONOMIC HISTORY. In 1086 Alfred of Marlborough's estate at Lydiard Tregoze paid geld for 7 hides and there was land for 7 plough-teams. Three hides were in demesne, leaving 4 hides for tenant farming. On the demesne there were one plough and three serfs, while elsewhere 8 villeins and 10 coscez had 4 ploughs. There were 40 a. of meadow, 30 a. of pasture, and woodland 1 league long by ¼ league broad. T.R.E. the manor had been worth £10 but in 1086 it was only worth £6.[97] Lydiard was one of the nine rural estates in Wiltshire which, at the time of Domesday, had burgesses of Cricklade appurtenant to them. There were seven such burgesses at Cricklade, who were attached to Alfred's estate at Lydiard and contributed 5s. to it.[98]

A grant of land in Chaddington by William of Burdeville to Bradenstoke Priory in the later 13th century mentions an East Field and a West Field there.[99] The grant, which conveyed rather more than 9 a. in all, was made up mostly of half-acre pieces widely scattered throughout the fields. Some are described as lying upon the hill, suggesting that here, as in other parishes in the region, at least some of the arable lands were situated on the higher ground in the south of the parish. A furlong called Cliffurlong presumably lay on the chalk escarpment. Besides the pieces of arable, 2 separate half-acres of meadow were included in the grant. Also included were pasture for 1 ox in a place called 'Heya' and common pasture for 5 cattle, 25 sheep, and 1 draught-beast. The prior at this time had a meadow called 'le Hay' at East Chaddington and surrendered all pasture rights in two other meadows called Medcroft and Wykecroft on condition that he should have unrestricted access to it along a causeway through Medcroft 16½ ft. broad.[1]

The earliest surviving extent relates to the estate

---

[77] C 142/140/201.
[78] *W.A.M.* xxxvi. 214–19.
[79] C 142/297/161
[80] W.A.S. Libr., Devizes, Story-Maskelyne Papers, Box C.
[81] Ex inf. the Bursar.
[82] S. J. Elyard, *Some Old Wilts. Homes*, 50.
[83] *Wilts. Inq. p.m.* 1242–1327 (Index Libr.), 350–1.
[84] Burke, *Dormant and Extinct Peerages*, 542; *Wilts. Inq. p.m.* 1327–77 (Index Libr.), 8.
[85] C.P. 40/283/229.
[86] *Cal. Chart. R.* 1327–41, 257.
[87] *Cal. Inq. p.m. Edw. III*, ix. 394.

[88] *Feud Aids*, v. 279 and see above p. 79.
[89] C.P. 40/283/229.
[90] *Wilts. Inq. p.m.* 1327–77 (Index Libr.), 154–5.
[91] *Feud. Aids*, vi. 537.
[92] E 142/33 m. 5.
[93] *Wilts. Inq. p.m.* 1327–77 (Index Libr.), 139.
[94] Ibid.
[95] Ibid. 252.
[96] *Cal. Pat.* 1358–61, 89.
[97] *V.C.H. Wilts.* ii, p. 141.
[98] Ibid.
[99] B.M. Stowe MS. 925, ff. 41r–42v.
[1] Ibid. ff. 42r–43v.

which Henry Tyeys held of the lords of the capital manor at the beginning of the 14th century.[2] In *c.* 1307 there were said to be 40 a. of arable in demesne here as well as 5 a. of several meadow. There were an unspecified number of freemen and 11 cottars who paid rent but apparently owed no services for their holdings. Seven other customary tenants, who also paid rent, were liable for labour services between the end of August and Michaelmas. Some 20 years later the same estate was reckoned as having 300 a. of arable in Lydiard and 100 a. in Hook.[3] At Lydiard there was pasture for 100 sheep. Rents of free tenants there were valued at 30s. while at Hook one free tenant paid 10s. a year.[4]

A little information about the value of the main manor comes in 1326 when the elder Despenser forfeited his estates in Lydiard Tregoze along with all his other lands.[5] The manor of Lydiard was said to be worth £10 a year, and the estate at Hook £2. Goods and chattels at Lydiard were valued at £29 8s. 4d., and those at Hook at 12s. 6d. Among the goods and chattels were stock, valued at £8 6s. 8d., which had been taken for the queen, upon whom the forfeited estates were settled, and corn valued at £14 4s. 2d. which had been sold. The estate at Hook eventually passed to William Dale. By the time of William's death in 1360 50 out of 70 a. of demesne arable on his estate were inclosed and were for that reason more highly valued.[6] There were also 2 a. of inclosed meadow, which were of more value than the remaining 5 a., which lay in common after the hay was lifted. The estate had in addition common pasture for 12 oxen and an unspecified number of other animals.

The parish lies at the heart of the pasture and dairy farming region of north-west Wiltshire, where until the 19th century farms were primarily concerned with the production of cheese and butter and the fattening of cattle. Aubrey, writing in the later 17th century, remarked that the fat cattle from Lydiard Tregoze shared the renown of those from Dauntsey at Smithfield markets.[7] He also observed that round about Lydiard butter, as good as any in England, was made, although the same pastures did not produce an entirely satisfactory cheese.[8]

In the 16th century the tenants of the main manor had common of pasture in three grounds called High Mead, Eastleaze, and Cowleaze.[9] Early in the 1520s, when the lord of the manor, Sir John St. John (d. 1576), was still a minor and the manor was being farmed, disagreement arose over these pasture rights and a reassessment was made of the number of beasts every tenant could pasture. Later when Sir John came of age and farmed the demesne lands himself, fresh disputes arose and St. John excluded his tenants altogether from the two leazes. The quarrel was eventually taken to Chancery by Thomas Pleydell, brother of Gabriel Pleydell, farmer of the manor of Midgehall. Thomas claimed in respect of the few acres he held of the St. Johns the right to pasture 6 oxen in the mead and leazes mentioned above. Gabriel Pleydell was involved in

a similar dispute with St. John when he claimed that the manor of Midgehall had certain pasture rights in a ground called Flaxlands.[10]

As in other parishes in this grassland region of Wiltshire inclosure took place early in Lydiard. As shown above, a considerable amount of arable was inclosed on William Dale's estate at Hook in the mid 14th century. In the 16th century, during the lordship of Nicholas St. John (d. 1589), the common fields, commons, and marshes of the main manor were inclosed by agreement made between lord, freeholders, and tenants of the manor.[11] The only land to be excluded were the two common pastures of Eastleaze, and High Mead, mentioned above, and another common pasture called the Green. Lord, freeholders, and tenants combined to pay William Garrard, of Shaw in Lydiard Millicent, and two others to make the survey and award the allotments. The task was evidently carried out with care, exact measurements being made and records kept of the allotments awarded.[12]

There was apparently, however, some opposition, for in *c.* 1579 Quarter Sessions ordered that the land in Lydiard, which had been staked out and measured, should remain as it was until the next assizes when 11 persons, all of Chaddington, were due to appear on a charge of riot, rout, trespass, and battery.[13] Although inclosure was probably virtually complete by the end of the 17th century, a map of the St. John estate of 1766 shows commons at Flaxlands in the north-west corner of the parish, at Hazel Hill to the east of this, at Hook, and at Chaddington in the south.[14] In the mid 20th century part at least of the common at Hook was still to be seen and the wide verges along the road to Chaddington bore witness to the former common there.

By 1616 the lands of Mannington manor situated within the parish were farmed as three several farms by tenant farmers.[15] Mannington itself comprised 203 a. and was farmed by Thomas Sadler, a member of a family closely connected with Lydiard and the neighbouring parish of Wroughton. Toothill comprised 188 a. and was leased to Robert Cole, while Whitehill had 65 a. and was farmed by John Lane. All were pasture farms. Only a small area of meadow belonging to this manor lay in common and was divided into some 17 small strips. This lay in the extreme north-east corner of the parish.

In the mid 19th century of the land of the parish subject to tithe there were 1,762 a. of meadow and pasture and only 200 a. of arable.[16] By far the largest estate in the parish was that belonging to the Bolingbrokes which covered some 3,000 a.[17] For administrative purposes the estate was divided into two manors, namely Lydiard Tregoze and Bincknoll (Broad Hinton).[18] Belonging to the manor of Lydiard Tregoze were the farms of Parkside, Wick, Marsh, Flaxlands, Windmill Leaze, East Leaze, Hook and Franklins, Hook, and Purley. There were also a few cottages and small holdings, unattached to any farm, and certain cottages at Hook. The only farms belonging to the Bincknoll manor, which

[2] *Wilts. Inq. p.m.* 1242–1326 (Index Libr.), 350–1.
[3] Ibid. 1327–77, 8. [4] Ibid.
[5] E 142/33, m.5 and see p. 78.
[6] *Wilts. Inq. p.m.* 1327–77 (Index Libr.), 262–3.
[7] Aubrey, *Nat. Hist. Wilts.* 37.
[8] Ibid. 105.
[9] C 3/137/40.
[10] C 3/138/17.
[11] Req. 2/56/18.
[12] Ibid.
[13] *Sess. Mins.* (W.A.S. Rec. Brch.), 46.
[14] W.R.O. 305/11.
[15] W.R.O. 631/1/1/1.
[16] W.R.O. Tithe Award.
[17] W.R.O. 305/24.
[18] Ibid.

lay within the parish, were Great and Little Chaddington.

When Cobbett visited Lydiard Park in 1826 he observed an appearance of neglect, 'if not abandonment', although the land he thought to be good.[19] Nineteenth-century particulars show that this state of affairs applied not only to the park, but existed on many of the farms too.[20] At Windmill Farm, for example, in 1866 it was considered that drainage would have to be undertaken before the farm could be let.[21] In 1900 the estate was described as chiefly fairly good pasture: houses were mostly old, and cottages and buildings had been so neglected that a large expenditure was required to make them tenantable.[22] The gross rental of the whole estate, excluding Lydiard Park, was reckoned at about £5,000. The rental value of the house, land in hand, some 50 a , and sporting rights over the entire estate was estimated at some £700 only, because of the dilapidated condition of the house. In 1920 something over 1,000 a. of the estate, including some of the outlying farms, were sold.[23] Ten years later another 1,800 a., including Marsh, Windmill Leaze, Hook, Flaxlands, Wick, Parkside, and Eastleaze farms, were put up for sale.[24] What remained of the land, about 750 a. including Lydiard Park, was sold in 1943.[25]

The lands belonging to the manor of Midgehall formed the next largest estate in the parish and in the mid 19th century covered between 1,000 and 2,000 a.[26] For about 200 years from 1534 this manor was farmed as tenants by members of the Pleydell family,[27] who no doubt occupied the large family pew in the Midgehall, or north aisle of the church.[28] The chief farms belonging to the Midgehall estate, beside that at Midgehall itself, were Spittleborough, Wickfield, Church Hills, and Ballard's Ash. Throughout the 19th century the Midgehall farms in Lydiard were farmed by tenant farmers as part of the large estate extending over several parishes and belonging first to the earls of Clarendon and then to the Meux family. The whole estate was broken up and sold in lots in 1906.[29]

Besides the Bolingbroke and Midgehall estates, the three farms belonging to Charterhouse, namely Mannington, Toothill, and Whitehall had a combined acreage of nearly 500 a. in the 19th century.[30] These farms were sold in 1919 and the greater part of their lands were acquired by the Wiltshire County Council and converted into smallholdings for ex-service men.[31] Of the other farms of any considerable size in the parish in 1966, Can Court had over 200 a. and the two Studley farms well over 100 a. each.

There is almost no evidence of any occupation in the parish other than farming. In the later 14th century linen and woollen cloths were stolen from a house in Midgehall, suggesting a possible connexion with the cloth trade.[32] But no other evidence of a concern with this trade has been found. After the construction of the Wilts. and Berks. Canal across the parish in c. 1804 a wharf was made at Hay Lane. But it was very small and could never have been very busy. The wharf seems to have been chiefly important for the public house built beside it which attracted a little trade but mostly apparently from undesirable characters.[33] In the 20th century the proximity of Swindon has provided the parish with ample opportunities for employment there. In spite of this, however, the parish has been very little built-up and retains a remarkably rural and unsophisticated appearance.

LOCAL GOVERNMENT. Towards the end of the 17th century, when the earliest surviving parish records begin, there were two overseers for the whole parish.[34] As in some other parishes in the region, liability to serve in this office was for a time attached to certain farms. In 1674, for example, one overseer was appointed for Chaddington, and in 1708 one was said to serve for Can Court.[35] Sometimes in the 19th century there were four overseers. In 1856 there were two for the tithing of Midgehall and two for the tithing of Hook.[36] In 1881 a salaried assistant overseer was appointed.[37] In the mid 19th century the parish had two constables.[38] At about the same date there were four surveyors of the high-ways, two for each of the two tithings mentioned above.[39]

The earlier 19th-century vestry records show that body to have been active and responsible in its attempts to deal with the widespread unemployment and distress which prevailed in the parish. In 1821 a plan devised by the magistrates for dealing with unemployment having failed, the vestry decided to subsidize to some extent the wages of those not in regular employment.[40] In the summer months of the following year, however, the vestry decreed that farmers should pay the full wage.[41] For the next few years rates of pay for mowers during the summer months were agreed in vestry meetings.[42] In 1825 the vestry ordered that all employers of regular labour were to accept a certain number of unemployed and rates of pay were fixed.[43] The vestry was still occasionally regulating wages in 1853 at meetings to which all the paymasters of the parish were summoned.[44]

In spite of these measures, there was much distress in the parish. In 1823 Lord Bolingbroke and Lord Clarendon gave £5 each to buy coal for the poor.[45] In 1845 the vestry held a special meeting of all rate-

[19] Cobbett's Rural Rides, ed. G. D. H. and M. Cole, ii. 406.
[20] W.R.O. 305/15.
[21] Ibid.
[22] W.R.O. 305/24.
[23] W.R.O. 305/18.
[24] W.R.O. 305/26.
[25] See p. 80.
[26] W.R.O. Tithe Award and Par. Rate Bks.
[27] See p. 81.
[28] See p. 88.
[29] W.R.O. 106, Sale Cat.
[30] W.R.O. Tithe Award.
[31] W.A.M. xli. 460.
[32] J.I. 3/156.
[33] Alfred Williams, Villages of the White Horse, 18.
[34] W.R.O. 674, Chwdns.' Acct. Bk. 1668–1828 and Overseers' Accts. 1674–1766.
[35] Ibid.
[36] W.R.O. 675, Vestry Min. Bk. 1845–61.
[37] Ibid. 1873–1903.
[38] Ibid. 1845–61.
[39] Ibid.
[40] W.R.O. 675, Vestry Min. Bk. 1818–81 and Vestry Mins. 1821–5.
[41] Ibid.
[42] Ibid.
[43] Ibid.
[44] Ibid. Vestry Min. Bk. 1845–61.
[45] Ibid. Overseers' Accts. and Vestry Mins. 1821–5.

payers to consider the cases of young men wishing to emigrate to America, and as a result the church-wardens and overseers were authorized to raise £8 towards expenses.[46] The following year it was decided to raise money on the poor rates to assist emigration to Australia, and in 1851 £200 were borrowed for the same purpose.[47]

The early meetings of the parish council, formed in 1894, were very largely concerned with a dispute over responsibility for the new burial ground at Hook.[48] By 1880 the need for a new ground was urgent. It was impossible to enlarge the parish churchyard since it lay so close to Lydiard Park and Lord Bolingbroke refused to permit it.[49] In 1888 the churchyard was closed and the vestry set up a committee to deal with the problem.[50] Eventually in 1891 an offer from Lord Bolingbroke of a field at Hook called 'Ables' was accepted and the new burial ground was made there.[51]

CHURCH. The church of Lydiard Tregoze is first mentioned in 1100 when Harold of Ewias gave it to St. Peter's Abbey, Gloucester, along with other endowments, to found a cell at Ewias (Herefs.).[52] The benefice was not, however, appropriated to St. Peter's and has always been a rectory. In 1956 it was united with that of Lydiard Millicent.[53]

Harold's gift evidently conveyed the advowson to the Abbot of Gloucester, but in 1280 the abbot granted it to John Tregoze (d. 1300), in exchange for that of the church of Burnham (Som.).[54] The advowson thus became re-attached to the lordship of the Tregoze manor.[55] In 1331 when William and Sybil de Grandison demised the manor to their daughter, Agnes de Northwood, for life, the advowson was included, and Agnes presented in 1342 and 1348.[56] But when in 1347 Peter de Grandison, heir of William and Sybil, granted the reversion of the manor, after Agnes's death, to Roger and Sybil de Beauchamp, the advowson was expressly excluded from the grant, and Peter presented in 1349, although by then the manor had passed to Roger and Sybil.[57] On Peter's death in 1358 the advowson, unlike the manor, passed to his brother, John de Grandison, Bishop of Exeter, who presented in 1362.[58] Two years later, however, the bishop conveyed the advowson to Roger and Sybil, and so advowson and lordship again came into the same hands.[59]

Thenceforth until the 19th century the lords of the Tregoze, later St. John, manor nearly always exercised the patronage.[60] In 1430 and 1431 Robert Shottesbrook, whose wife, Edith, was the widow of John Beauchamp and held the manor for life, presented, and in 1486 Oliver Seymour was patron.

Oliver's identity has not not so far been established. In 1498 Elizabeth Bigod, widow of Oliver St. John (d. 1497), presented, and in 1513 Nicholas Saunders presented in the right of his wife, Jane Iwardby, widow of John St. John (d. 1512). In 1612 presentation was by the President of Magdalen College, Oxford. In 1780 the patronage was exercised by George Watson, to whom it was sold for one turn. In the 19th century it was again sold for single turns, in 1839 to Mrs. Martha Collins,[61] and in 1878 to Francis Sharp Powell.[62] Thereafter the patronage was exercised by the lord of the manor until 1944 when it was transferred to the Bishop of Bristol.[63]

In 1291 the church was assessed for taxation at £11 10s., including an annual pension (30s.) paid to the Prior of Ewias.[64] In 1341 it was claimed that the earlier assessment was too high, since allowance had to be made for the glebe estate, valued at just over £4.[65] In 1535 the net value was £10 5s. 5d., after the deduction of the pension and an annual payment of 11s. 3d. to the Archdeacon of Wiltshire.[66] In 1835 the average gross income was £651 and £23 were deducted for permanent, unspecified, annual payments.[67] When the possibility of selling the advowson was being considered in 1868, the living was said to be worth £889 16s. 10d. This was made up of £639 16s. 10d. for commuted tithe, glebe valued at £200, and a parsonage house reputed to be worth £50. Set against this were outgoings calculated at £100.[68]

The land of the manor of Midgehall was held to be exempt from the payment of tithe on the grounds that it belonged to Stanley Abbey, a Cistercian house.[69] But in 1228 an agreement was reached whereby the abbey agreed to pay 8s. annually in lieu of all tithes in kind due from its lands in the tithing of Midgehall.[70] In 1341 great tithes reckoned to be worth 6s. 8d. were also owed by the Abbot of Stanley from 2 virgates of land at Studley. In the same year the Prior of Bradenstoke owed great tithes worth 20s. from 8 virgates, presumably at Chaddington.[71]

By 1677 the governors of the Charterhouse had compounded with a money payment for the tithes due from their estates within the parish. For Mannington and Toothill they paid 16s. annually; for Whitehill 8s.[72] The sum paid for Midgehall was by this date 50s. and included contributions from all copyholders on the manor.[73] Studley Farm paid 4 nobles and Can Court 5 nobles. A payment of £20 was made for lands described as 'the ancient demesnes of Lydiard Tregoze'. The rest of the parish paid tithes in kind.[74] By 1783 the tithes due from the tithing of Chaddington had been commuted. In Midgehall tithing exemption was still claimed in some cases on the grounds that the land

[46] Ibid. Vestry Min. Bk. 1845–61.   [47] Ibid.
[48] Ibid. Par. Council Min. Bk. 1894–1936.
[49] Ibid. Vestry Min. Bk. 1873–1903.
[50] Ibid. Papers relating to burial ground.
[51] Ibid. Vestry Min. Bk. 1873–1903.
[52] Dugdale, Mon. i. 546, iii. 628.
[53] Ex inf. Dioc. Regy., Bristol.
[54] Feet of F. Wilts. 1277–1327 (W.A.S. Rec. Brch.), 64.
[55] See p. 78.
[56] See p. 79, and Phillipps, Wilts. Inst. i. 38, 42.
[57] Cal. Pat. 1345–8, 438, and Phillipps, op. cit.
[58] Phillipps, op. cit.
[59] Cal. Pat. 1361–4, 522.
[60] See above pp. 79–80 and Phillipps, Wilts. Inst. (index in W.A.M. xxviii. 224).
[61] Ex inf. Dioc. Regy., Gloucester.
[62] Ex inf. Dioc. Regy., Bristol.
[63] Ex inf. the rector.
[64] Tax. Eccl. (Rec. Com.), 190.
[65] Inq. Non. (Rec. Com.), 162.
[66] Valor Eccl. (Rec. Com.), ii. 127.
[67] Rep. Com. Eccl. Revenues, H.C. 54, p. 840 (1835), xxii.
[68] W.R.O. 305/12, Partics. of Rectory of Lydiard Tregoze.
[69] See p. 87.
[70] W.R.O. 212B/5856, Agreement concerning tithes.
[71] Inq. Non. (Rec. Com.), 162.
[72] Sar. Dioc. R.O. Glebe Terrier, 1677.
[73] Ibid.
[74] Ibid.

had once belonged to a Cistercian abbey. But Lord Clarendon, lord of the manor, paid the 8s. which had been agreed upon in 1228.[75] Thus when the tithe award was made in 1841 no tithes were being paid in kind. That year a gross rent-charge of £630 18s. 5d. was substituted for the various compositions then in force and from this £27 were deducted if the glebe was occupied by the rector.[76]

In 1341 there was one carucate of land attached to the church. It was valued then at £2 17s. 4d. and rents and services due from tenants were worth 6s. 8d.[77] In 1677 the glebe estate comprised some 87 a. This lay mainly in two blocks. One, of about 42 a. divided between two meadows called Parsonage Close and the 'Hamme', lay immediately north of the church. The other, of about 30 a. divided between three arable fields called Prinnells, Claypiece, and Blacklands, lay about ¼ mile east of the church.[78] In 1830 the rector exchanged the block of glebe north of the church, and the fields called Prinnells and Claypits, estimated in all at 61 a., with Lord Bolingbroke for 73 a. lying in a compact block south of the house which was between c. 1830 and 1956 the rectory.[79] The glebe estate after this exchange had been made and at the time of the tithe award comprised 90 a.[80] In 1868 the land was partly in hand and partly let.[81]

At the time of the exchange the rector conveyed to Lord Bolingbroke the parsonage house and its grounds.[82] This lay immediately east of the church. In 1783 it was described as a stone-built house, roofed with slate.[83] That year the rector found the house to be 'indifferent' and lived in Wootton Bassett.[84] Four years later the house was still in need of repair, but it was said that it could have been made 'a decent house'.[85] It was, however, abandoned in 1830 and a new one built outside the park on the east side of the road running north to Lydiard Millicent.[86] This remained the rectory house until the union of the benefices of Lydiard Tregoze and Lydiard Millicent in 1956 when the rector went to live in Lydiard Millicent.

In addition to the glebe the rector was entitled to the first crop of hay from two meadows belonging to Lord Bolingbroke called Brook, or High Mead, and Parsonage Mead.[87] In 1704 an alternative name for both meadows was Cut and Go Mead and they lay on either side of the way to Swindon. In 1844 the rector surrendered his rights in these meadows in exchange for a meadow called East Freshbrook belonging to Lord Bolingbroke.[88]

The gift of the church of Lydiard in 1100 to endow a cell of Gloucester Abbey at Ewias resulted in an annual payment from the church of Lydiard Tregoze to the Prior of Ewias. In 1291 this pension was £1 10s.[89] But in 1359 Gloucester Abbey withdrew the monks from Ewias on the plea that the revenues of the cell no longer sufficed even for the maintenance of a prior.[90] Thenceforth and until the Dissolution the pension was paid to Gloucester, the parent house, although in 1428 it was still said to be for the Prior of Ewias.[91] By 1535 the amount paid was £1.[92] After the Dissolution the pension was granted to the newly created Dean and Chapter of Gloucester,[93] and was paid to them until extinguished in 1886.[94]

Edward VI's commissioners reported a piece of land for the maintenance of a lamp in the church in 1548.[95] In 1563 the land, with more elsewhere, was granted to Cecily Pickerell of Norwich in part payment of a debt owed to her late husband by the late Duke of Somerset.[96] Nothing more is known of the lamp in the church. No evidence has been found to support Aubrey's suggestion that there was once a hermitage in Lydiard.[97]

Little is known of any of the rectors of Lydiard. In 1304 licence was granted for William of Radnor, presented to the living that year, to study in Oxford for two years.[98] Two rectors, Walter Elyot in 1445, and Alexander Thornton in 1576, were deprived of their living, but it is not known why.[99] Timothy Dewell, who was presented in 1645 and was rector until his death in 1692, had sympathy with Presbyterianism and was one of the Wiltshire signatories to the Testimony of Ministers of 1648.[1] He seems to have been on friendly terms with his patron, Sir Walter St. John (d. 1708), and when some of the St. John children were ill with smallpox they were sent to lodge with Dr. Dewell and his wife at Lydiard.[2] Dewell's memorial stone in the church records his fluency as a preacher.[3] Richard Miles, presented in 1780 and rector for 59 years, lived, at least during the early part of his incumbency, in Wootton Bassett, but by 1783 had a curate residing in the parish.[4] In 1831 the curate was paid an annual salary of £75.[5]

The exemption from tithe claimed by the tithing of Midgehall on the grounds that its lands belonged to a Cistercian house (see above) gave rise to a custom known locally as the 'Word Ale'.[6] This was a court held annually just after Michaelmas, usually in the manor-house, and attended by tenants of the manor. At it were recited the words: 'You are to pray for the Abbot of Stanley and all the monks of the Cistercian Order by whom we are all tithe free, tithe free.' The court, held in great secrecy, was followed by a feast. The custom persisted until 1939, but has been held only once (in 1948) since the Second World War.[7]

The church has stood for so long so far from any

[75] Ibid. 1783.
[76] W.R.O. Tithe Award.
[77] Inq. Non. (Rec. Com.), 162.
[78] Sar. Dioc. R.O. Glebe Terriers, 1677, 1704, 1783 and W.R.O. 305/11, Map, 1766.
[79] W.R.O. 305/6, Agreement for an Exchange.
[80] W.R.O. Tithe Award.
[81] W.R.O. 305/12, Partics. of Rectory.
[82] W.R.O. 305/6, Agreement for an Exchange.
[83] Sar. Dioc. R.O. Glebe Terrier, 1783.
[84] Ibid. Vis. Queries, 1783.
[85] Ibid. Vis. Churches and Parsonage Houses, 1787.
[86] W.R.O. 305/12, Partics. of Rectory.
[87] Sar. Dioc. R.O. Glebe Terriers.
[88] W.R.O. 305/6, Agreement for an Exchange.
[89] Tax. Eccl. (Rec. Com.), 190.
[90] V.C.H. Gloucs. ii. 58.
[91] Feud. Aids v. 286.
[92] Valor Eccl. (Rec. Com.), ii. 127.
[93] L. & P. Hen. VIII, xvi, p. 573.
[94] Lond. Gaz. 29 June, 1886 (p. 3106).
[95] W.A.M. xxxvi. 539.
[96] Cal. Pat. 1560–3, 566.
[97] Aubrey, Topog. Coll. ed. Jackson, 183.
[98] Reg. Ghent (Cant. and York Soc.), ii. 869.
[99] Phillipps, Wilts. Inst. i. 136, 228.
[1] W.A.M. xliii. 170; W.N. & Q. viii. 437; Calamy Revised, ed. A. G. Matthews, 557.
[2] G. J. Taylor, Our Lady of Batersey, 313.
[3] W.A.M. xliii. 170.
[4] Sar. Dioc. R.O. Vis. Queries, 1783, and ex inf. the rector.
[5] Rep. Com. Eccl. Revenues (1835), xxii, p. 840.
[6] An account of this custom is contained in W.N. & Q. vi. 331–6 and W.A.M. ii. 394, 400.
[7] Records penes Mr. J. Cooper, Midgehall.

village that it may well have played a somewhat restricted part in the life of the parish. With its wealth of St. John family monuments it tends to give the impression of a private chapel rather than of a parish church. Little can be said of the influence upon church life of the patrons of the living, although their mark is left so clearly upon the furnishings of the church. John St. John (d. 1576) was accused by the churchwardens in 1556 of detaining certain church goods.[8] Sir Walter St. John (d. 1708) was accused of being 'a rogue and a rebel, an anabaptist and a quaker'.[9] But the accusation probably derived more from Sir Walter's political sympathies than from his religious ones, although he was apparently the friend as well as the patron of the nonconformist, Timothy Dewell.

In 1668–9 Holy Communion was celebrated six times — on Whit Sunday, All Saints' Day, Christmas Day, Palm Sunday, Easter Day, and Low Sunday. Four quarts of wine were used for each of the first four celebrations and five quarts each for Easter Day and Low Sunday. Twopence was spent on bread on every occasion.[10] In 1676 there were 139 communicants.[11] In 1783 a service was held every Sunday, but only in the mornings. An afternoon service was considered quite impracticable because of the demands of the local dairy farms. Holy Communion was said to be celebrated four times a year when there were 16 or 18 communicants.[12] On 30 March 1851 150 people attended church in the morning and the congregation over the past year was thought to have averaged between 150 and 200. Attendance, it was pointed out, depended greatly upon the weather, since the church was so far from any village. On a fine day in summer the church was said to be quite full.[13] In 1964 there was either a morning or an evening service every Sunday.[14]

The church of ST. MARY lies within a stone's throw of Lydiard Park and the churchyard adjoins the back premises of the house. The church comprises a chancel with south chapel, a nave with north and south aisles, the north aisle sometimes being called the Midgehall aisle,[15] a west tower, a south porch, and a south-west vestry. The tower has a parapet with pierced quatrefoils and 4 pinnacles. The south chapel, south aisle, and south porch are all battlemented. There are 3 dormer windows in the south side of the nave roof and at the east end of the roof there is a small sanctus-bell turret.

Externally the church appears to date from the 15th century, but close examination of the interior shows that it is of 13th-century origin.[16] The nave, the second and third arches of the north arcade, and the eastern three-quarters of the north aisle date from that century. The three-bay south arcade and the south aisle were added in the later 14th century. A scheme of enlargement and general improvement was begun in the 15th century, probably at the instigation of Oliver St. John

(d. 1437) and Margaret Beauchamp his wife, who succeeded to Lydiard in 1420 and died in 1482.[17] The chancel was rebuilt, the south chapel, west tower and south porch added, the north aisle extended westward to the full extent of the nave, and the windows of the aisles completely remodelled. Somewhat later, in c. 1500, two small windows were inserted high in the east wall of the nave, and in the later 17th century the easternmost arch of the north nave arcade was formed.

In 1633 Sir John St. John (d. 1648) re-designed the south chapel to form a mortuary chapel for his family. Only the 15th-century east wall and window were retained. The south wall was rebuilt and Sir John's work was commemorated above the entrance to the chapel from the outside on a stone panel carved with his and his wives' arms. Between the chapel and the chancel an open Tuscan screen was built. About the same time the round-headed windows flanking the east window of the chancel were inserted, as were the clerestory windows in the north wall of the nave, which were remodelled in the 19th century. In the 18th century two dormer windows were inserted in the south side of the nave roof and a third was added in the 19th century. The vestry is also a 19th-century addition. At the beginning of the 20th century the church was restored under the direction of C. E. Ponting, who uncovered a number of medieval wall-paintings.[18] Some idea of the appearance of the church at the beginning of the 19th century may be had from a south-east view painted by John Buckler in 1810,[19] and from an early 19th-century model preserved in Lydiard Park.

John Aubrey, writing c. 1670, remarked of the church 'for modern monuments it exceeds all the churches in this county'.[20] The number and richness of the furnishings are scarcely less impressive in the 20th century. This is almost entirely due to one man Sir John St. John (d. 1648),[21] the designer of the south chapel. The most elaborate of the monuments is the so-called triptych standing against the north wall of the chancel. This comprises a series of painted panels, four of which are hinged to open and two of which are removable. They stand upon a carved stone plinth and above is a pedimented entablature of painted wood. In the tympanum of this is a portrait of Margaret Beauchamp (d. 1482) through whom the St. Johns claimed common ancestry with the sovereign. The triptych was erected, although not exactly in the form it takes today, in 1615 by Sir John to commemorate his parents. The two central doors open to reveal the life-size painted figures of Sir John St. John (d. 1594) and his wife Lucy Hungerford (d. 1598) kneeling upon a tomb. To the left stands Sir John, the younger (d. 1648), the erecter of the monument, and his first wife Anne Leighton; to the right are his six sisters with shields of arms at their feet. When the central leaves are closed, their outer surfaces and the panels and leaves flanking them bear an

[8] Sar. Dioc. R.O. Detecta Bk. 1556, f. 18.
[9] V.C.H. Wilts. iii. 31.
[10] W.R.O. 674, Chwrdns.' Accts. The author is indebted to the rector, the Revd. B. G. Carne, for this reference and much other help.
[11] W.N. & Q. iii. 535.
[12] Sar. Dioc. R.O. Vis. Queries, 1783.
[13] H.O. 129/251/1/5/11.   [14] Ex inf. the rector.
[15] Aubrey, Topog. Coll. ed. Jackson, 171–2.

[16] The architectural description of this church is based upon the account by Mr. A. R. Dufty in the Guide to Lydiard Park and Church (1967).
[17] See p. 79.
[18] For some account of these paintings, see W.A.M. xxxvii. 441–4.
[19] In W.A.S. Libr., Devizes.
[20] Aubrey, Topog. Coll. ed. Jackson, 171.
[21] See p. 79.

Detail from triptych. Sir John St. John
(d. 1648) and his wife Anne Leighton
(d. 1628)

Effigies of Sir John St. John (d. 1648) and his wives,
Anne Leighton (d. 1628) and Margaret Whitmore
(d. 1637)

Chancel, showing windows and glass installed by Sir John St. John (d. 1648) and altar rails
probably commissioned by Sir Walter St. John (d. 1708)

LYDIARD TREGOZE CHURCH

elaborate display of painted heraldic genealogical tables of the St. John family. These tables were originally based upon the genealogical work of Sir Richard St. George, Clarenceux King of Arms,[22] and Sir John's uncle by marriage, but many additions were made subsequently.

Having remodelled the south chapel, Sir John erected within it in 1634 a large canopied monument to himself and his two wives, Anne Leighton (d. 1628) and Margaret Whitmore, who did not die until 1637. In her arms Anne clasps her thirteenth child at whose birth she died. Sir John died in 1648 at Battersea, where he lay in state amid circumstances of great pomp, before his body was brought to Lydiard for burial in the vault he had prepared beneath the south chapel there.[23] The interment at Lydiard was probably also accompanied with some ceremony. Aubrey visiting the church only about twenty years later, remarked upon the numerous pennons, standards, and banners, as well as other trappings of knightly prestige, which then decorated the chancel and St. John chapel.[24] In 1964 three helmets and a number of iron brackets from which pennons were once suspended remained on the walls of the chancel and the south aisle.

Sir John is also responsible for the glass, probably Flemish, in the east window of the chancel, which shows the descent of the manor of Lydiard to himself. The olive tree in the centre light and the flanking figures of St. John the Baptist and St. John the Evangelist, are a rebus on the name Oliver St. John. Sir John's last monument stands against the north wall of the chancel and is to his fourth son Edward, who died in 1645 of wounds received when fighting for the king at the second battle of Newbury.[25] This is sometimes called the 'golden cavalier'.

Among other St. John monuments is that in the south aisle erected by Sir John's father to his parents Nicholas (d. 1589) and Elizabeth (d. 1587). Also on the south side of the church are the monument erected by Sir Giles Mompesson to his wife, Katherine (d. 1633), eldest sister of Sir John St. John (d. 1648), and one by Michael Rysbrack to John, Viscount St. John (d. 1748), the rebuilder and embellisher of Lydiard Park.[26]

The elaborate coloured and gilded wrought-iron communion rails date from c. 1700 and were probably commissioned by Sir Walter St. John (d. 1708). Sir Walter may also have installed the curved ceiling of the chancel painted with sun, moon, and stars. The coloured and gilded oak chancel screen is surmounted by a carving of the Stuart royal arms. The font dates from the 13th century. New box pews were placed in the nave in the 19th century but some of the earlier ones survive, including the St. John and Midgehall family pews. The pulpit is Jacobean.

In 1553 there were four bells.[27] By 1670 there were five.[28] Numbers 1, 2, and 3 are dated 1635, and thus date from the time of Sir John St. John's works

within the church. Number 4 was recast by Abraham Rudhall, of Gloucester, in 1757. Number 5, by William and Robert Cor, is dated 1701, and bears the elaborate ornamentation characteristic of the work of those founders.[29] In 1964 the tower was stripped and the bells rehung in a new frame. The old 4th bell was recast, and a new treble added in memory of Canon W. H. Willetts (rector 1936–55) and Mrs. Willetts. The ring was retuned to the key of F sharp.[30]

'A great clock', presented by 'Lady — ' belonged to the church in 1670 and may have been the clock in the tower which was there in 1783.[31] A clock in the tower is shown in the model of the church mentioned above, but it does not appear in the painting of the church done by John Buckler in 1810.

A chalice (14 oz.) was left for the church by Edward VI's commissioners and 8 oz. of plate removed for the king's use.[32] In 1964 all the church plate dated from the 17th century. There were two large flagons with domed covers. One is hall-marked 1650 and the cover is inscribed 'The gift of Deborah Culme, Daughter of Sir Charles Pleydell of Midghall'. Deborah Culme was the second daughter of Sir Charles Pleydell and wife of Benjamin Culme, sometime Dean of St. Patrick's Dublin, who died at Midgehall in 1657 and was buried at Lydiard. The second flagon, similar in design, is hall-marked 1663, and inscribed on the cover 'The gift of Lady Eliz. Newcomen Daughter of Sir Charles Pleydell of Midghall'. Elizabeth Newcomen was an elder sister of Deborah Culme. There are also a paten, hall-marked 1669, and likewise the gift of Deborah Culme, and a chalice and paten hall-marked 1649, both engraved with the St. John crest.[33] The registers begin in 1666 and are complete.

In 1645 Sir John St. John created a trust to administer an annual rent-charge of £10 from land which he had acquired from Edward Pleydell. By his will dated the same year Sir John directed that this money should be spent upon the upkeep of the chapel he had reconstructed, then called the 'new aisle', and also upon the maintenance of the 'old aisle', the chancel, and all his family monuments and vaults. Aisles and vaults were to be inspected every Easter Monday when £1 was to be spent on providing dinner or supper for the inspectors.[34]

In 1834 the rent-charge had not been paid for more than 50 years. Such repairs as had been done had been paid for by Lord Bolingbroke, but monuments and aisles were said to be in much need of attention. After 1834 the arrears were made good and payments resumed for a time, but by 1901 they had lapsed again. At some time before 1880 £100, made up of unapplied income, had been invested,[35] but accounts had been kept irregularly and it was impossible to trace the regular receipt and application of the income. In 1964 the income, which consisted of the interest on an investment of £50, was spent on insuring the monuments.[36]

[22] The inscription on the triptych wrongly calls him Garter King.
[23] Taylor, *Our Lady of Batersey*, 186–8. It seems that *V.C.H. Surr.* iv. 12 is wrong in saying that he was buried at Battersea.
[24] Aubrey, *Topog. Coll.* ed. Jackson, 171–2.
[25] Ex inf. Brigadier Peter Young.
[26] See p. 79.
[27] *W.A.M.* xii. 367.
[28] W.R.O. 674, Chwrdns.' Bk.

[29] Walters, *Wilts. Bells*, 127.
[30] Ex inf. the rector.
[31] W.R.O. 674, Chwrdns.' Bk.; Sar. Dioc. R.O. Vis. Queries, 1783.
[32] *W.A.M.* xii. 367.
[33] Nightingale, *Wilts. Plate*, 184–5.
[34] Except where otherwise stated, this and next paragraph based upon *Endowed Char. Wilts.* (1908), 659–61.
[35] W.R.O. 305/24, Memorandum on Church Fund.
[36] Ex inf. the rector.

NONCONFORMITY. One dissenter was reported in the parish in 1676.[37] In 1822 the house of John Ferris was licensed as a place of worship for nonconformists.[38] The denomination of this group is not known, but in 1827 a Primitive Methodist church was formed in the parish and became part of the Brinkworth Circuit.[39] The early 1830s was a time of great activity for this circuit and in 1832 the Revd. S. Turner conducted a remarkable missionary service at Hook.[40] By the end of it 20 people had professed conversion. The next year premises at Hook, held and occupied by William Ind, were licensed for use as a chapel.[41] This may have been superseded by a house belonging to Richard Wolford, for in 1837 this also was licensed as a chapel.[42] A chapel was built in 1840 but Lord Bolingbroke claimed as his the land upon which it stood and the building had to be surrendered to him at valuation.[43] Thenceforth for many years the congregation met in a cottage which was partially converted to form a chapel.[44] In 1886 a small iron chapel was built and was enlarged three years later.[45] By 1907 the debt on this had been paid, but a local Primitive Methodist minister described the village as 'somewhat derelict materially' and as 'presenting great problems'.[46] The same chapel was still in use in 1964.

A site in Hay Lane was acquired in 1887 and a small Primitive Methodist chapel was built and licensed for worship the following year.[47] This became part of the Swindon Circuit and in 1964 a service was held once a month.[48]

EDUCATION. There was no school in the village in 1819.[49] By 1835 there was a day school with 50 children, of whom 26 were paid for by Lord Bolingbroke and the rest by their parents. There was also a Sunday school with 50 boys.[50] In 1859 the school, which stood in the south-west corner of Lydiard Park in Hook Street, consisted of one small room with flagged floor and bare walls, which had been added on to a cottage.[51] Here 30 children were taught by an elderly man and his daughter. In 1860 the site of the present (1965) school at Hook was acquired and a school built with aid from the National Society.[52] In 1906 average attendance was 75.[53] In 1938 it was 47.[54] In 1965 the Lydiard Tregoze Junior and Infants' School was closed and the children transferred to Lydiard Millicent.[55] The cottage school of 1859, although derelict, still stood in 1965.

CHARITIES. In c. 1692 Thomas Hardyman and Timothy Dewell (rector 1645–92) gave £20 each to be invested for the benefit of the poor of the parish.[56] The rector and churchwardens decided to use this money to build some cottages 'for the use and benefit of the parish'. In 1733 Viscount St. John gave some land at Hook Common as a site and here the cottages were built. It is probably because of these cottages that part of Hook Street was called Almshouse Lane in 1766, although they were not, in fact, almshouses.[57] In c. 1800 the cottages were let for £3 each a year, £1 of which was paid to Lord Bolingbroke and £2 to the poor. In 1834 the payments to the poor had lapsed and in 1901 the charity was reported to be irretrievably lost.

Richard Miles (rector 1747–1839) gave £700 for investment so that blankets and bedding could be distributed every Christmas to the poor, not already receiving parochial relief. In 1901 the interest on this was £19 and the year before 68 people had received a blanket. The income of the charity was about £17 in 1960, and in that year most of it was distributed to the poor in vouchers, but a small amount was used to buy various small comforts.[58]

LYNEHAM

LYNEHAM LIES 3¾ miles south-west of Wootton Bassett and 5½ miles north of Calne.[1] The parish covers 3,442 a.[2] and is roughly rectangular in shape. It measures 4 miles from east to west at its widest point and 2¾ from north to south.[3]

Lyneham is made up of 4 scattered hamlets and the evidence suggests that in 1086 the main area of settlement lay at the present hamlet of Bradenstoke in the north-west corner of the parish.[4] Known then as 'Stoche' (settlement), this area was then well wooded[5] and had probably once lain within Braydon Forest, since the settlement was called 'Bradenstoke' by the 12th century.[6] It was here that Bradenstoke Priory was founded in the 12th century.[7] Probably throughout the Middle Ages, and certainly in the earlier 16th century, the name 'Bradenstoke' seems to have been applied to the area immediately around the priory, including its demesne lands.[8] The name 'Clack' (hill), a word of uncertain origin, first occurs in the parish in 1310,[9]

[37] W.N. & Q. iii. 535.
[38] W.R.O. Retn. of Regns. 1813–51.
[39] W. C. Tonks, Victory in the Villages, 76.
[40] Ibid. 70.
[41] W.R.O. Retn. of Regns. 1813–51. [42] Ibid.
[43] Tonks, Victory in the Villages, 145. [44] Ibid.
[45] Ibid. [46] Ibid. 146.
[47] Ex inf. the rector.
[48] Notice on chapel.
[49] Digest of Returns to Cttee. of Educ. of Poor, H.C. 224, p. 1031 (1819), ix (2).
[50] Educ. Enq. Abstract, H.C. 62, p. 112 (1835), xliii.
[51] Acct. of Wilts. Schools, H.C. 27, p. 95 (1859 sess. 1), xxi (2).
[52] Retn. of Non-Provided Schools, H.C. 178–xxxi, p. 831, (1906), lxxxviii.
[53] Ibid. [54] Bd. of Educ. List 21, 1938.
[55] Ex inf. the rector.

[56] Information about both these charities mentioned here is from Endowed Char. Wilts. (1908), pp. 659–61.
[57] See p. 78.
[58] Endowed Char. Wilts. (1908), pp. 661–2; Char. Com. File 201518.
[1] Grateful thanks are due to the Officer Commanding, R.A.F. Station Lyneham, the Chief Surveyor of Defence Lands, Tolworth Tower, Surbiton, and to Mr. W. E. A. Salter, Ministry of Defence, for help during the preparation of this article.
[2] Census, 1961.
[3] Maps used include: O.S. Maps 6", Wilts. XIV, XX (1st edn.); 1/25,000, SU 07 (1959 edn.); 1", sheet 157 (1958 edn.).
[4] V.C.H. Wilts. ii, p. 137.
[5] Ibid. [6] P.N. Wilts. (E.P.N.S.), 270.
[7] V.C.H. Wilts. iii. 276. [8] E 318/863.
[9] P.N. Wilts. (E.P.N.S.), 271.

and evidently refers to the large mound north-east of Bradenstoke Farm (see below). The name was thereafter until the later 19th century generally applied to the hamlet which flanked the road leading to the priory.[10] The area was also known by the reduplicative name of 'Lousy (teutonic 'lloew' = hill) Clack', a tradition perpetuated in the local rhyme, which is quoted above.[11] The earlier name of 'Bradenstoke' was revived in the 20th century and the whole hamlet was known by that name in 1968. Lyneham, about a mile east of Bradenstoke, is mentioned for the first time in 1224, and was probably included in the Domesday holding of 'Stoche'.[12] West Tockenham, which lies a mile south-west of Lyneham village, was known in 1198 simply as 'Tockenham',[13] but by 1293 the area, which contained several small estates, was also known as West Tockenham to distinguish it from East Tockenham.[14] Preston, marked only by two farms, a few cottages, and a Methodist chapel in 1968, lies 1¼ mile south-east of Lyneham village. This hamlet formed part of the manor of Lyneham in 1557[15] and remained such until the 20th century.[16]

The western and southern areas of the parish are situated on the Corallian ridge which runs south-westwards from Wheatley (Oxon.) to Calne. Within an area bounded to the north by the Chippenham-Swindon road, to the east by the Hilmarton-Lyneham road, and to the south by the Preston-Lyneham road, beds of Red Down Clay alternate with beds of Red Down Iron Sand. East of a line from Church End to Trow Lane the clay gives way to the Coral Rag of the ridge again. In the extreme south-eastern corner of the parish around Thickthorn Farm a belt of Red Down Clay, which runs south-westwards from Greenway to the boundary with Hilmarton, is succeeded by a bed of Red Down Iron Sand. In the most south-easterly corner of the parish Thickthorn Farm stands on an extensive bed of Kimmeridge Clay.[17]

The northern limits of the Corallian ridge determine the northern, western, and part of the southern, boundaries of Lyneham. Bradenstoke, Lyneham, and Preston all lie on the Coral Rag of the ridge, while West Tockenham and Shaw Farm are situated on the Red Down Iron Sand. In the west and south of the parish the Corallian ridge reaches a height of c. 400 ft., and rises gradually to over 475 ft. west of Bradenstoke. The dip slope of the ridge falls gently away south-eastwards to the clays and sandy soils in the east of the parish, where, at Thickthorn, on the Kimmeridge Clay, the land drops away to 350 ft. For the most part, by virtue of its somewhat exposed position on the Corallian ridge, the parish presents an open and treeless landscape, except in the north, where the spring action of Lilly Brook has caused the erosion of sand beneath the Coral Rag at Blind

Mill. Here this process has resulted in the incision of a steep-sided and thickly-wooded gully. North and east of Preston the parish is traversed by a network of streams and the soil there is wet and heavy. These streams are tributaries of Cowage Brook and meet above Littlecott (Hilmarton). One stream has gorged a narrow, curving valley, now flanked by trees and known as the Strings, through which it flows southwards from Freegrove. Another tributary forms the eastern part of the southern boundary of the parish, while a third flows south-westwards from Middle Hill, past Preston, and thence to Littlecott. Most of the land was under pasture in 1968, although there was some arable cultivation on the lighter, sandier soils, especially around Shaw Farm.[18]

There is little visible evidence of early settlement in the parish, although the name 'Barrow End', applied to an area immediately north-west of Lyneham village, suggests prehistoric activity there.[19] Roman coins have been found near the site of Bradenstoke Priory and a hoard of Constantinian coins appeared at an unlocated area in the parish. An extended skeleton of unknown date was found near West Preston Farm.[20] Lyneham Camp, a motte-and-bailey earthwork of possibly Norman date, lies in the north of the parish by Hillocks Wood.[21] Clack Mount, a Norman earthwork, rises on the Corallian ridge at its highest point behind Bradenstoke Farm.[22]

In 1334 Lyneham paid the second highest contribution in Kingsbridge hundred to the 15th of that year.[23] The parish had 227 poll-tax payers in 1377, a number which constituted the highest in the hundred. West Tockenham was assessed separately at this date and had 24 contributors.[24] In 1523 54 people from Lyneham and Clack made contributions to the royal loan. The prior's household at Bradenstoke, assessed separately, provided 20 contributors.[25] Five people in Lyneham and one in West Tockenham contributed to the Benevolence of 1545, the average for the parishes in the hundred.[26] In 1576 21 people in Lyneham, Clack, and Preston contributed to the subsidy of that year, a number second only to Wootton Bassett.[27] Thereafter little is known of the population of the parish until 1801 when there were 833 people in Lyneham and its hamlets.[28] Thenceforth the population rose gradually until in 1841 there were 1,317 people in the parish,[29] a number which included 179 labourers employed in laying the G.W.R. line in the neighbouring parish.[30] After this date the population declined again until in 1921 there were only 836 inhabitants in the parish.[31] The establishment of R.A.F. Lyneham in 1940 (see below) resulted in a sharp increase in population. In 1951 there were 2,430 inhabitants,[32] and by 1961 this number had increased to 3,688.[33]

[10] For e.g. see *Andrews and Dury, Map* (W.A.S. Rec. Brch.), pl. 14 and Sar. Dioc. R.O. Vis. Queries, 1864.
[11] See p. 24.
[12] *P.N. Wilts.* (E.P.N.S.), 270-1.
[13] *Bk. of Fees*, i. 12.
[14] *Wilts. Inq. p.m.* 1242-1326 (Index Libr.), 196-7, and see p. 168.
[15] *Cal. Pat.* 1555-7, 463.
[16] See p. 94.
[17] For an account of the geology of the parish see W. J. Arkell, 'Geology of the Corallian Ridge near Wootton Bassett and Lyneham', *W.A.M.* liv. 1-18.
[18] For an account of farming practices in the region see Fry, *Land Utilization Wilts.* 213-14.

[19] *V.C.H. Wilts.* i (1), 181.
[20] Ibid. 84.
[21] Ibid. 267.
[22] Ibid. 181.
[23] Ibid. iv. 300.
[24] Ibid. 309.
[25] *L. & P. Hen. VIII*, iii (2), p. 1490.
[26] *Taxation Lists* (W.A.S. Rec. Brch.), 21.
[27] Ibid. 106-7.
[28] *V.C.H. Wilts.* iv. 352.
[29] Ibid.
[30] Ibid. 320.
[31] Ibid. 352.
[32] Ibid.
[33] *Census*, 1961.

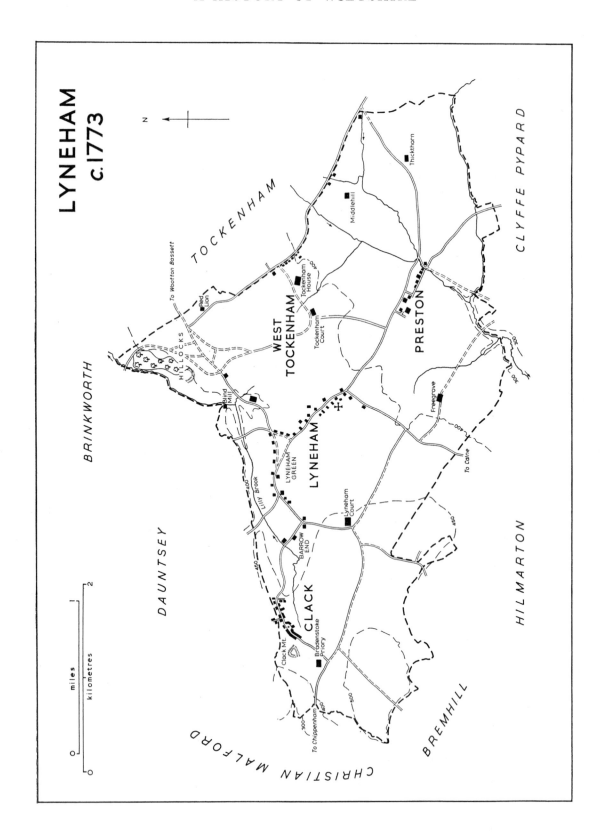

LYNEHAM
c.1773

Roads in the parish have changed comparatively little since the 18th century. The junction of all roads, then as now, was Lyneham Green. The Calne-Lyneham road followed its present (1968) course as early as 1736, and at that time was known as Even Lane where it ran through the village.[34] Although a secondary road, it carried a considerable amount of traffic in 1968. In 1773 the Swindon-Chippenham road entered the parish from Dauntsey to the east of Bradenstoke Priory and ran eastwards forming the village street of Bradenstoke. This road was probably of some importance during the Middle Ages, when it led to the priory and to Clack spring and fall fairs. On leaving Bradenstoke the road skirted Lyneham Green and thence ran north-eastwards to Tockenham, leaving the parish to the north of Shaw Farm.[35] By 1887 a bypass to the north of Bradenstoke was built and henceforth that part of the road which formed Bradenstoke high street became relatively unimportant. In 1968 the Swindon-Chippenham road was the only main road in the parish. Two small roads in the parish have been entirely obliterated with the coming of the airfield. One of the these led to Lyneham Court Farm and on to Stockham Marsh (Bremhill), while the other ran from Lyneham Court towards Free-grove.[36] The eastern boundary of the parish in 1968 ran along the west side of the minor road known north of West Tockenham as Trow Lane, and to the south as Greenway, thus bringing the west side of Tockenham village street, which lay along this road, into Lyneham. In 1968 a proposal to move the boundary westwards and thus to include West Tockenham in the parish of Tockenham was being discussed.[37] From this road a small lane turns back westwards past Thickthorn and Preston to Church End. An early-19th-century toll-house stood at this junction and survived until c. 1960.[38] Tockenham Reservoir, constructed in c. 1810 to feed the Wilts. and Berks. Canal, which had been constructed north of the parish by 1801, lay partly within the parish north-east of Blind Mill. The reservoir was abandoned when the Swindon section of the canal was closed in 1914.[39] In 1968 it was used for boating and fishing.

Although flanked to the south by the airfield, the hamlet of Bradenstoke remained relatively unchanged in 1968, still resembling the compact medieval village which had been dominated by the buildings of Bradenstoke Priory to the south-west. Most of the priory buildings were removed c. 1930.[40] The village consists of a single narrow street, closely built up on both sides. In a widening near the middle of the street on its south side stands the base and part of the shaft of an ancient cross first mentioned in 1546-7.[41] South of this the church of St. Mary was built in 1866.[42] On the opposite side of the street is Providence Chapel, dating from 1777.[43] A few of the houses have exposed timber-framing while others, although altered and refronted, show traces of their timber construction. It is probable that several are of medieval origin, among them a partly refronted house at the corner of the road to Dauntsey, which has heavy curved braces to its framing. A house to the west of Providence Chapel, now three dwellings, has a jettied upper story with a continuous moulded bressummer, probably dating from the early 16th century. Two brick houses carry date-stones of 1762 and 1788. Several thatched roofs, and others of stone slate, add to the picturesque appearance of the street.

The two farm-houses at Preston are largely of early 18th-century date although Preston East Farm incorporates a 17th-century building. To the south of Preston West Farm is an older house, now two cottages, of which the principal range was formerly timber-framed and of medieval cruck construction; the remains of two cruck trusses dividing its three bays have survived. A small group of timber-framed thatched cottages stands near the ford at the east end of Preston. Shaw Farm, which lies east of Trow Lane, is an 18th-century building.

The arrival of the R.A.F. Station in 1940 and its consequent housing development have partly obscured the former village of Lyneham which straddled the Hilmarton-Lyneham road. The nucleus of the village lay to the north, where a few houses of various periods were still grouped around an extensive green in 1968. At this time the green was crossed by the Hilmarton and main Chippenham-Swindon roads. There were also some older houses scattered along the Hilmarton road between the green and Church End. Lyneham's development since the Second World War has been limited for the most part of an area directly west of Church End. Here, in 1968, stood the new schools surrounded by an R.A.F. housing estate. An extension of the estate lay in the apex of the Preston and Hilmarton roads.

West of the Calne-Lyneham road the parish is now covered by the airfield of R.A.F. Station Lyneham, which stretches the width of the Corallian ridge from Bradenstoke in the north to the northerly edge of Catcomb Wood (Hilmarton), in the south. R.A.F. Station Lyneham, opened in 1940, assumed full status as a station in 1942.[44] The airfield covered over 1,200 a. in 1968 and was made up of land formerly belonging to Lyneham Court Farm, Church Farm, Cranley Farm, and Bradenstoke Abbey Farm.[45] In 1968 the station was the principal employer of labour within the parish.[46]

MANORS AND OTHER ESTATES. It is probable that at the time of the Domesday Survey the estate later known as Lyneham was included in Edward of Salisbury's holding at 'Stoche', and presumably passed with it to Bradenstoke Priory in c. 1139.[47] By 1316 the Prior of Bradenstoke held *LYNEHAM*, then described as a vill.[48] The manor continued to be held by the priory until the house was dissolved in 1539.[49]

Lyneham apparently remained with the Crown

[34] *Q. Sess. and Ass.* 1736 (W.A.S. Rec. Brch.), 60.
[35] *Andrews and Dury, Map* (W.A.S. Rec. Brch.), pl. 14.
[36] Ibid.
[37] Ex inf. Clerk of County Council, Trowbridge and see p. 168. It was moved in 1969.
[38] Ex inf. Mrs. Margaret Tomlinson.
[39] *V.C.H. Wilts.* iv. 273; Wilts. and Berks. Canal Abandonment Act, 4 & 5 Geo. V, c. 108 (local and personal act).

[40] Pevsner, *Wilts.* (Bldgs. of Eng.), 115–16; see p. 95.
[41] E 318/863.   [42] See p. 102.
[43] See p. 103.
[44] Ex inf. Mr. W. E. A. Salter, Min. of Defence.
[45] Ex inf. Chief Surveyor of Defence Lands, Tolworth Tower, Surbiton.
[46] See p. 98.   [47] See below.
[48] *Feud. Aids*, v. 207.
[49] *V.C.H. Wilts.* iii. 287.

until 1557 when Thomas Matson received a royal grant of the manor including land at Littlecott (in Hilmarton), Preston, and Thickthorn, to be held by service of $\frac{1}{20}$ knight's fee.[50] It is likely that this grant was revoked, since in 1559 the queen granted the manor of Lyneham to William Button,[51] who died seised of it in 1591.[52] He had previously settled the manor on his second son, William (II) Button,[53] who entered and died seised in 1599.[54] His heir was his son, William (III) Button (d. 1654–5), who in turn was succeeded by his son William (IV) Button (d. 1659–60). William (IV)'s heir was his brother Robert (d. c. 1679).[55] Robert Button's heir was his brother John, who was certainly seised by 1679.[56]

John Button died without issue in 1712, and his heir was his great-nephew Heneage Walker, grandson of his sister Mary, who had married Clement Walker.[57] During the lifetime of John Button, the land at Littlecott, until then part of the manor of Lyneham, was sold as a separate farm.[58] Heneage Walker died in 1731 and was succeeded by his brother John (d. 1758). John Walker's heir was his son, another John, who in 1777 adopted the name Walker-Heneage.[59] In 1793 his estate at Lyneham comprised 9 substantial farms, including East Preston, West Preston, and Thickthorn.[60] John Walker-Heneage died without issue in 1806 and was succeeded by his great-nephew George Wyld, son of his niece Mary.[61] George Wyld subsequently adopted the name of Walker-Heneage, and on his death in 1875 was succeeded by his son Clement Walker-Heneage (d. 1901).[62] Clement Walker-Heneage was succeeded by his son Godfrey Walker-Heneage (d. 1939).[63] In 1905 the Lyneham estate, reckoned at 2,016 a., was offered for sale. At this date it comprised most of Lyneham village as well as various farms which included the Preston and Thickthorn Farms.[64] Godfrey Walker-Heneage remained lord in 1931, but by this date the estate had been sold in lots.[65] In 1951 Church Farm, previously part of the Lyneham estate of the Walker-Heneage family, and then estimated at 120 a., was bought by the Air Ministry from the trustees of William Miflin for the enlargement of the airfield at Lyneham.[66]

In the time of King Edward Stremi held 'Stoche',[67] an estate which probably included the later manors of Bradenstoke and Lyneham. Edward of Salisbury held the estate in 1086.[68] Edward was succeeded by his son Walter, and the estate at 'Stoche' subsequently formed one of the chief en-dowments of the house of Augustinian canons which Walter founded at Bradenstoke in c. 1139.[69] In 1207 King John confirmed the manor of *BRADEN-STOKE* to the convent.[70] Thenceforth the estate remained with the priory until the house was dissolved in 1539.

In 1546 the king granted Richard Pexsall the site of the priory, the prior's lodging, and certain specified lands in Bradenstoke, Clack, and Lyneham,[71] most of which had previously formed part of the priory demesne lands.[72] After the Dissolution until at least the later 17th century the manor was frequently known as that of Bradenstoke with Clack.[73] In 1540–1 the lands had been leased to Henry Long (d. 1556) for 21 years.[74] Shortly before his death in 1571 Sir Richard Pexsall devised his estates, including Bradenstoke, to his second wife Eleanor (née Cotgrave) for 13 years until his grandson Pexsall Brocas, son of his daughter Anne, came of age. The will was invalid as to a third of the estate, and this part descended to 4 coheirs, daughters of Sir Richard Pexsall. These were Anne, wife of Bernard Brocas; Margery, who married, first Oliver Beckett, and secondly Francis Cotton; Elizabeth, who married John Jobson, and Barbara, the wife of Anthony Bridges.[75] It seems that Eleanor Pexsall still retained the two thirds due to Pexsall Brocas in 1590.[76] By this date, besides the twelfth she had inherited, Anne Brocas had also acquired her sister Barbara's twelfth and thus held a sixth of the estate.[77] In c. 1572–3 Elizabeth Jobson and her husband granted their twelfth to Eleanor Pexsall, who, by this date, had married John Savage.[78] Eleanor and John Savage settled this twelfth on Edward Savage, second son of John Savage, in 1573,[79] and he retained it in 1590.[80] In 1609 Pexsall Brocas was apparently entitled to a life estate in the manor of Bradenstoke,[81] but it seems likely that his stepmother, Eleanor Savage, continued to hold two thirds until her death in 1617–18. Pexsall Brocas, who by this date had also inherited his mother's sixth, died seised of ten twelfths of his estate in 1630.[82] He was succeeded by his son Thomas in 1630 and Thomas Brocas conveyed some form of interest in the manor of Bradenstoke to his son Robert in 1635.[83] It was presumably Robert Brocas who sold ten twelfths of the manor to Henry, Earl of Danby, in c. 1640.[84]

By the time of his death in 1594 Sir John Danvers had acquired, either from Edward Savage or Francis Cotton, a twelfth of the manor of Bradenstoke.[85]

[50] *Cal. Pat.* 1555–7, 463.
[51] Ibid. 1558–60, 300–1.
[52] C 142/239/123.
[53] Ibid.
[54] C 142/260/156.
[55] G.E.C. *Baronetage*, i. 193.
[56] C.P. 25(2)/747/31 Chas. II East.
[57] G.E.C. *Baronetage*, i. 193; C.P. 25(2)/1077/1 Geo. I Trin.; 'Cat. Button-Walker-Heneage Mun.', pp. 28–29 (TS in S.R.O.).
[58] See p. 56.
[59] Burke, *Land. Gent.* (1952), s.v. Walker-Heneage.
[60] S.R.O. Button-Walker-Heneage Mun. Add. 21, Lyneham Farms.
[61] 'Cat. Button-Walker-Heneage Mun.', p. 29 (TS in S.R.O.).
[62] Ibid.
[63] Burke, *Land. Gent.* (1952), s.v. Walker-Heneage.
[64] Wilts. Cuttings, xvi. 260.
[65] *Kelly's Dir. Wilts.* (1931).
[66] Ex inf. Chief Surveyor of Defence Lands, Tolworth Tower, Surbiton. The first substantial purchases of land to form the airfield came from Lyneham Court Farm and the former Bradenstoke estate.
[67] *V.C.H. Wilts.* ii, p. 137.
[68] Ibid.
[69] Ibid. iii. 276.
[70] *Rot. Chart.* (Rec. Com.), 169b.
[71] *L. & P. Hen. VIII*, xxi (2), p. 157; E 318/863.
[72] See p. 98.
[73] For e.g. see S.C.6/Hen. VIII/3985; B.M. Add. Ch. 26579; C.P. 25(2)/747/35 Chas. II Trin.
[74] E 210/10515.
[75] *V.C.H. Hants* iv. 166.
[76] B.M. Add. Ch. 26579.
[77] Ibid.; *V.C.H. Hants* iv. 166.
[78] C 2/Eliz. I/S 15/55.
[79] Ibid.
[80] B.M. Add. Ch. 26579.
[81] Sta. Cha. 8/82/3.
[82] Montagu Burrows, *Hist. of Family of Brocas of Beaurepaire*, 223.
[83] C.P. 25(2)/510/11 Chas. I Mich.
[84] Aubrey, *Topog. Coll.* ed. Jackson, 189.
[85] C 142/247/100.

His heir was his son Charles (d. 1601), who was succeeded by his brother Henry (cr. Earl of Danby 1626),[86] who probably acquired the Brocas ten twelfths in c. 1640 (see above). Henry (d. 1644) was succeeded by his brother John (d. 1655).[87] The estate held by the Danverses at this date was still reckoned to consist of a twelfth of the manor of Bradenstoke, but there is no doubt that they had acquired the manor itself by 1655. John Danvers's heirs were his daughters, Elizabeth (d. 1709), wife of Robert Wright alias Villiers alias Danvers, and Anne, wife of Sir Henry Lee.[88] In 1677 Elizabeth Danvers and her husband were seised of half of the manor.[89] Presumably Anne Lee and her husband held the other moiety. Eleanor (d. 1691), daughter of Henry and Anne Lee, married James, Lord Norreys, later Earl of Abingdon (d. 1699),[90] and had inherited her mother's moiety of the Bradenstoke estate by 1678, when James, Lord Norreys, leased out land there.[91] In 1683 Elizabeth Danvers, now the wife of John Duvall, conveyed her moiety to James, Lord Norreys,[92] and he thus acquired the whole manor. The estate presumably passed to his son Montagu, 2nd Earl of Abingdon (d. 1743), and during his ownership the Bradenstoke estate was sold to Germanicus Sheppard, who was in possession by 1738.[93] At an unknown date Sheppard sold the manor to Paul Methuen (d. 1795),[94] who was succeeded there by his son Paul Cobb Methuen (d. 1816). He in turn was succeeded by his son Paul, Lord Methuen (d. 1849), whose estate was made up of lands which included Bradenstoke Farm and Cranley Farm in 1846.[95] Paul, Lord Methuen, was succeeded by his son Frederick, Lord Methuen (d. 1891), who sold the estate to Gabriel Goldney (d. 1900) in 1863.[96] From Gabriel Goldney the estate passed to his son Gabriel Prior Goldney (d. 1925), who sold it to Francis, Baron de Tuyll in 1917.[97] Baron de Tuyll sold the manor to J. A. A. Williams in 1920 and he in turn sold it in 1921 to H. Lushington Storey.[98] In 1923 the estate was offered for sale[99] and it was presumably bought at this date by H. Fry, who was owner in 1926.[1] Shortly afterwards it was apparently broken up. Donald and Hannah Bridges owned Cranley Farm, estimated at 133 a., in 1942, at which date the farm was bought by the Air Ministry. By 1946 Bradenstoke Abbey Farm was owned by Maria Cole, who that year sold 235 a. of it to the same purchaser.[2]

The 19th-century farm-house attached to Bradenstoke Abbey Farm, built on the site of the former priory, may contain some of the masonry of the conventual buildings, most of which, together with the tithe barn, were demolished in c. 1930. The

buildings of the former priory have been outlined elsewhere.[3] In 1968 little remained on the priory site except the vaulted undercroft of the cloister's western range and a square turret which had stood at its north-west angle; both date from the 14th century.[4]

During the 13th, 14th, and early 15th centuries the priors of Bradenstoke consolidated their holding in West Tockenham by the acquisition of a number of small estates there. These, together with estates granted by the families of Bohun and Mortimer, and the manor known as Little Tockenham or Tockenham Doygnel, formed the later manor of *WEST TOCKENHAM*.

In 755-7 Aethelbald granted Abbot Eanberht of Malmesbury 10 cassati at 'Toccansceaga',[5] an area later known as West Tockenham. King Ethelwulf may have granted 5 mansiones there to Malmesbury in 854, although this grant is suspect.[6] By the time of King Edward an estate at 'Tockenham' was certainly held by Malmesbury Abbey, but by the time of the Domesday Survey the abbot and convent had apparently relinquished their rights in it.[7] By 1086 the estate had passed to Durand of Gloucester.[8] At his death his lands passed to his son Roger (d.s.p. 1106). Roger's heir was his cousin Walter, who was in turn succeeded by his son Miles (d. 1143), who was created Earl of Hereford in 1141. Miles's coheirs were his two daughters, one of whom, Margaret, wife of Humphrey de Bohun, secured most of Durand's Wiltshire fief.[9] Margaret de Bohun's grandson Henry was created Earl of Hereford and thenceforth the overlordship descended with the earldom.[10] The last recorded mention of the Bohun overlordship occurs in 1384 when, after the death of Humphrey de Bohun, Earl of Hereford (d. 1373), his daughter Mary and her husband Henry, Earl of Derby, were confirmed in the overlordship of an estate in West Tockenham.[11]

In 1066 Doun held the 'Tockenham' estate of Malmesbury Abbey. By 1086 Roger held it of Durand.[12] No more is known until the 13th century, when part at least of the estate was apparently held under the Bohuns by the Baynton family. In 1242-3 Walter Baynton held $\frac{1}{5}$ knight's fee in 'Tockenham' of Humphrey de Bohun, Earl of Hereford (d. 1275), as of his honor of Trowbridge.[13] It was presumably this small estate which Henry Baynton and his wife Joan granted to Bradenstoke Priory in 1262.[14] At a date before 1373 Humphrey, Earl of Hereford (d. 1373), granted an estate in West Tockenham to the priory.[15]

In 1066 Alwin held an estate, reckoned at $2\frac{1}{2}$ hides, in 'Tockenham'.[16] In 1086 the overlord of the estate,

[86] C.P. 43/107 rot. 34.
[87] C.P. 25(2)/512/23 Chas. I East.
[88] Burke, *Dorm. & Ext. Peerages* (1883), s.v. Danvers.
[89] C.P. 25(2)/746/29 Chas. II East.
[90] Burke, *Peerage* (1959), s.v. Abingdon.
[91] W.R.O. 529/45, Lease, Jas. Lord Norreys to Matthew Smith.
[92] C.P. 25(2)/747/35 Chas. II Trin.
[93] W.R.O. 529/47, Lease, Germanicus Sheppard to Goddard Smith.
[94] Ibid. 529/30, Proposal for the sale of the manor of Clack.
[95] Ibid. Tithe Award.
[96] J. Badeni, *Wilts. Forefathers*, pp. 11 sqq.
[97] Wilts. Cuttings, xiv. 113.
[98] *W.A.M.* xlii. 76; J. Badeni, *Wilts. Forefathers*, pp. 11 sqq.

[99] *W.A.M.* xlii. 400.
[1] Ibid. xliii. 447.
[2] Ex. inf. Chief Surveyor of Defence Lands, Tolworth Tower, Surbiton.
[3] *V.C.H. Wilts.* iii. 288.
[4] Pevsner, *Wilts.* (Bldgs. of Eng.), 115-16.
[5] *V.C.H. Wilts.* ii, p. 5 n.
[6] Ibid. p. 90.
[7] Ibid. p. 148.   [8] Ibid.
[9] Ibid. p. 108.
[10] G.E.C. *Complete Peerage*, pp. 451 sqq.
[11] *Cal. Close*, 1381-5, 514-15.
[12] *V.C.H. Wilts.* ii, p. 148.
[13] *Bk. of Fees*, ii. 723.
[14] B.M. Stowe MS. 925, f. 173r.
[15] Ibid. f. 39r and v.
[16] *V.C.H. Wilts.* ii, p. 152.

which may have included land previously held by Malmesbury Abbey, was Ralph Mortimer of Wigmore.[17] The overlordship of this small estate remained in the family of Mortimer of Wigmore until the 14th century.[18] It is last mentioned in 1425 when Edmund Mortimer, Earl of March (d. 1425), was overlord.[19]

In 1086 Oideland held the estate at 'Tockenham' of Ralph Mortimer.[20] No other mesne tenants are known until 1242–3 when Thomas of Tockenham held ½ knight's fee in 'Tockenham' of Brian of Branton, who held it of the overlord Ralph Mortimer (d. 1246).[21] Some time before 1265 Thomas of Tockenham granted the estate to Bradenstoke Priory, who thenceforth apparently held it of the Mortimers.[22] The holding was estimated at 1 knight's fee in 1360.[23]

In 1198 William Spelman held an unspecified amount of land in West Tockenham,[24] which cannot be identified with any Domesday estate. At an unknown date between 1198 and 1293 this estate had passed to Nicholas Spelman.[25] By 1293 it had passed to Christine Spelman,[26] although her relationship to Nicholas Spelman is unknown. The estate is perhaps the same as that held in chief in 1344 by Gilbert Testwood, the grandson of Catherine Spelman.[27]

By 1198 William Spelman had subinfeudated ½ carucate in West Tockenham to Richard Spelman.[28] Their relationship is unknown. Before 1293 Nicholas Spelman, as overlord, granted Guy Doygnel 1 hide in West Tockenham, a holding which included ½ hide held by Nicholas Spelman in demesne, 1 virgate held by Henry Forde, and 1 virgate held by Humphrey FitzPayne.[29] In 1293 Silvester Doygnel, presumably the son of Guy Doygnel, died seised of 3 virgates in West Tockenham, which he had held since c. 1269.[30] The estate, reckoned in 1313 to contain 1 messuage and 4 virgates,[31] passed to his son Peter, who in 1332–3 conveyed a life estate in the manor of Little Tockenham to John of Cricklade, bailiff of Lyneham.[32] The manor was known alternatively as Tockenham Doygnel in the later 14th century.[33] In 1334 Peter Doygnel conveyed the manor to Bradenstoke Priory.[34] With this grant, together with that made in the 13th century by Thomas of Tockenham and that made by Humphrey, Earl of Hereford (d. 1373), the manor of West Tockenham finally emerged. It was further augmented in 1412 when John Elcombe and his wife Joan gave the priory land in Lyneham, Littlecott, and West Tockenham, amounting to about 100 a.[35] The manor remained with Bradenstoke until the house was dissolved in 1539.

The manor remained in hand until 1560 when William Button (d. 1591) and Thomas Estecourte were granted the reversion.[36] In the same year Estecourte relinquished his rights.[37] The manor, known from the 17th century as Tockenham Court Farm, descended in the same way as the manor of Lyneham (see above) and passed from the Buttons in 1712 to their successors, the Walker-Heneages, who remained lords in 1900.[38]

Tockenham Court Farm is a stone house apparently of 18th-century date, but incorporating an L-shaped building of the late 16th or early 17th century. The only visible features of the older house are its heavy chamfered ceiling beams which retain carved stops of several different designs. The house, then owned by Sir William Button (d. 1654–5), was looted by Parliamentary troops in 1643 and 1644.[39]

The house known in 1773 as Tockenham House[40] and in 1968 as Meadow Court, which stands about 500 yards north-east of Tockenham Court Farm, is a building of two distinct periods. The southern part represents the two-storied hall range and service cross-wing of a stone house of c. 1630, partly remodelled in the 18th century. Alterations to the service wing in the 20th century included the removal of a massive chimney at its east end. Externally on the west wall are inscribed the words 'Levavi Oculos'. It has been suggested that the house was occupied by the Walker family after the death of the last Button in 1712.[41] If so Heneage Walker (d. 1731) must have been responsible for the building or rebuilding of the northern part of the house on a grand scale between 1720 and 1730.[42] The brick addition, which is probably on the site of a former solar wing, is only one room deep but is of considerable height and has an impressive entrance facing north. This elevation is of seven bays, the three central bays being surmounted by a pediment; stone dressings include moulded window-heads with carved keystones and a central doorway with an open segmental pediment on brackets. Internally there are panelled rooms and a contemporary staircase. A brick orangery or coach-house to the south-east of the house also dates from the earlier 18th century. Tockenham Manor Farm lies further east and has a stone farm-house probably of 18th-century origin.

In 1341 the glebe attached to the church of Lyneham amounted to 1 carucate of land, worth £2 yearly.[43] It is probable that this small rectorial estate had increased considerably by 1541–2, when Henry Long (d. 1556) received a royal grant of an estate of c. 315 a. in Lyneham and Littlecott, previously held by Bradenstoke Priory.[44] This estate represents the glebe-lands of the impropriate rectory of Lyneham.[45] On Henry Long's death the estate apparently

[17] Ibid.; see p. 101: as early as 1291 the Abbot of Malmesbury farmed out the great and small tithes from lands once held in demesne by Thos. of Tockenham to the Prior and convent of Bradenstoke.
[18] For the descent of Mortimer of Wigmore, see G.E.C. Complete Peerage, pp. 266 sqq.
[19] C 139/18/15.
[20] V.C.H. Wilts. ii, p. 152.
[21] Bk. of Fees, ii. 300.
[22] Cal. Close, 1264–8, 148–9; Cal. Inq. p.m. x, p. 537.
[23] Cal. Inq. p.m. x, p. 537.
[24] Bk. of Fees, i. 12.
[25] B.M. Stowe MS. 925, f. 157r.
[26] Wilts. Inq. p.m. 1242–1326 (Index Libr.), 196–7.
[27] Ibid. 1327–77, 165.
[28] Bk. of Fees, i. 12.
[29] B.M. Stowe MS. 925, f. 157r.
[30] Wilts. Inq. p.m. 1242–1326 (Index Libr.), 196–7.
[31] Feet of F. Wilts. 1272–1327 (W.A.S. Rec. Brch.), 84.
[32] B.M. Stowe MS. 925, ff. 157v–158v.
[33] Ibid. ff. 161r–162r.
[34] Ibid. f. 159v.
[35] Cal. Pat. 1408–13, 366.
[36] S.R.O. Button-Walker-Heneage Mun. 1445.
[37] Ibid. 1444.
[38] Ibid. Add. 21, Lyneham Farms.
[39] J. Badeni, Wilts. Forefathers, pp. 146 sqq.
[40] Andrews and Dury, Map (W.A.S. Rec. Brch.), pl. 14.
[41] J. Badeni, op. cit.
[42] It is thought that work was started c. 1720: ex inf. the Hon. Mrs. J. M. Manningham-Buller, occupier in 1968. A rainwater head is dated 1730.
[43] Inq. Non. (Rec. Com.), 161.
[44] E 318/722.
[45] E 315/446.

passed to his fifth son, Richard, who died in 1558 seised of a capital messuage belonging to the rectory of Lyneham.[46] He was succeeded there by his son Edmund.[47] In 1571 the estate contained a holding known as 'Freth Grove' (Freegrove),[48] and in 1617–1619 included the parsonage house and a small park stocked with deer.[49] Edmund Long died seised in 1635, and by virtue of a settlement made in 1619 the rectorial estate was divided between his sons Richard and Walter. The bulk of the estate, reckoned at c. 289 a., passed to his elder son Richard, but some 80 a. were settled on his younger son Walter,[50] who predeceased his father in 1630. The smaller estate passed to Walter's widow, Mary, as her jointure, and she was still seised in 1636.[51] No more is known of this small estate. On Richard (II) Long's death in 1639 his estate at Lyneham passed to his eldest son Edmund (II) Long (d. 1664), who was thus entitled to most of the glebe-lands.[52] Edmund Long sold off the estate in lots at an unknown date.[53]

By 1667 Oliver Pleydell (d. 1680) was seised of the largest portion of the former rectorial lands, known by this date as the Lyneham Court estate.[54] He was apparently succeeded by his grandson Thomas Pleydell, who in turn was succeeded by his son Thomas (II) Pleydell (d. 1727),[55] who held the estate in 1704.[56] Thomas (II) Pleydell was succeeded by his son Sir Mark Stuart Pleydell (d. 1768), whose daughter and heir Harriet married William Bouverie, 1st Earl of Radnor (d. 1765).[57] Their son Jacob, Earl of Radnor (d. 1828), was seised of Lyneham Court in 1800.[58] The estate then descended with the Radnor title until the early 20th century.[59] It was sold to the tenant, Frank Fry, in 1920.[60] In 1940 Lyneham Court Farm, estimated at 292 a., and owned by Frank Fry, was bought by the Air Ministry.[61]

Before his death in 1664 Edmund (II) Long sold part of the estate of the impropriate rectory of Lyneham to either Adam or Robert Tuck.[62] The estate remained in the Tuck family and by 1719 Robert Tuck was seised of Freegrove Farm.[63] In 1744 he devised Freegrove to his son Adam.[64] No more is known of the estate until 1846 when it was owned by Jacob Large.[65] By 1880 Freegrove, at this date leased to Arthur Pocock, had been acquired by William Henry Poynder (d. 1880), and by 1885 had passed to William Dickson-Poynder.[66]

ECONOMIC HISTORY. T.R.E. an estate at 'Stoche' paid geld for 16 hides and 1 virgate and was worth £6. The size of the estate suggests that it included the later manor of Lyneham. At the time of the Domesday Survey the estate contained enough land for 10 ploughs, and 7½ hides were held in demesne. There were 4 ploughs and 2 serfs on the demesne hides. Elsewhere on the estate there were 16 bordars, 16 cottars, and 8 villeins with 6 ploughs. At this date there were 4 a. of meadow and 12 a. of pasture, while the woodland was estimated to be ½ league long and 3 furlongs broad. The value of the estate had risen to £10 in 1086.[67] There was an additional half-hide holding in 'Stoche' in 1086, which contained land for half a plough and was worth 10s.[68]

During the Middle Ages the manor of Lyneham comprised the property of Bradenstoke Priory in Lyneham, Clack, Littlecott (in Hilmarton), and Preston, and was worth £18 6s. in 1291.[69] In 1535 the manor of Lyneham, which still included Littlecott and Preston, but which by this date excluded Bradenstoke (see below), was valued at £40 17s., of which £27 represented the rents of an unspecified number of customary tenants and £6 the farm of the rectory of Lyneham. There were 211 a. of arable land and 78 a. of pasture and meadow in demesne at this date.[70] During the years 1538–40 the manor was valued at £14 0s. 1d., an estimate which probably did not include the farm of the rectory lands. At this date the rents of customary tenants in Lyneham were reckoned at £18 19s. 10d., while those of customary tenants in Preston were reckoned at £8 3s.[71] In 1545–6 the overall value of the estate was £46 4s. 3d. and in 1546–7 £48 17s. 8d., while the rents of customary tenants were reckoned at £27 2s. 9d. There were apparently no freeholders on the manor at this date.[72] The total rents paid by tenants there in 1563 amounted to £23 13s. 1d.[73]

In the later 16th century Preston Leynes, a pasture ground, was leased to the tenants of Lyneham manor at Littlecott.[74] Traces of this common pasture survived in 1968 as an extremely wide verge on either side of the road at Preston, just west of Thickthorn Farm. Nothing is known of any open fields within the manor and it is likely that most of the estate was farmed in consolidated holdings from an early date. In a survey of the manor of Lyneham dating from the earlier 18th century there were 10 copyhold tenures within the manor and 53 leasehold tenures.[75] In 1793 the manor of Lyneham included 9 farms, namely, Thickthorn (163 a.), Preston East and West Farms (134 a. and 127 a.), Lyneham Church Farm (107 a.), Lyneham Pound Farm (108 a.), Lyneham Green Farm (116 a.), Barrow End Farm (151 a.), Mansion House Farm (151 a.), and Middle Hill Farm (162 a.). All these farms consisted of practically equal amounts of

[46] E 150/999/14.
[47] C 66/1168 m. 5.
[48] E 178/3139.
[49] Sta. Cha. 8/194/25.
[50] *Wilts. Inq. p.m.* 1625–49 (Index Libr.), 390–2.
[51] Ibid. 213.
[52] Ibid. 277; C 78/1940 Entry 3.
[53] C 78/1940 Entry 3.
[54] W.R.O. 118/Bdle. 132, Lease and release, Pleydell to Ash.
[55] Burke, *Ext. & Dorm. Baronetcies* (1844), s.v. Pleydell.
[56] Sar. Dioc. R.O. Glebe Terrier.
[57] Burke, *Peerage* (1959), s.v. Radnor.
[58] C.P. 43/868 rot. 124.
[59] W.R.O. Tithe Award; *Kelly's Dir. Wilts.* (1903).
[60] Longford Castle MSS. Rental (N. Wilts.), no. 61.
[61] Ex inf. Chief Surveyor of Defence Lands, Tolworth Tower, Surbiton.

[62] C 78/1940 Entry 3.
[63] C.P. 25(2)/1078/5 Geo. I Hil.; C 78/1854 Entry 6.
[64] C 78/1854 Entry 6.
[65] W.R.O. Tithe Award.
[66] Ibid. 498/66, Lease, Wm. Hen. Poynder to Arthur Pocock; ibid. Renewal of lease, Wm. Dickson-Poynder to Arthur Pocock.
[67] *V.C.H. Wilts.* ii, p. 137.
[68] Ibid. p. 168.
[69] Ibid. iii. 280.
[70] *Valor Eccl.* (Rec. Com.), ii. 123.
[71] S.C. 6/Hen. VIII/3985.
[72] E 315/446.
[73] S.R.O. Button-Walker-Heneage Mun. 3100, Rental of Lyneham.
[74] E 315/446.
[75] S.R.O. Button-Walker-Heneage Mun. 3104, Survey of the manor of Lyneham with Preston.

arable, pasture, and meadow.[76] In 1896 all these farms remained within the Walker-Heneage estate at Lyneham.[77]

In 1291 land at Clack was included for purposes of assessment as part of the manor of Lyneham (see above). Little distinction seems to have been made between the Lyneham and Bradenstoke estates for administrative purposes until 1535, when for the first time, so far as is known, the manor of Bradenstoke was assessed separately. The manor there was then valued at £12 19s. and the Prior of Bradenstoke held 270 a. of arable land and 90 a. of pasture and meadow in demesne.[78] During 1538–40 the manor itself was valued at £13 13s. 9d., while manorial rents totalled £23 19s. 10d. The manor at this date included a park, and the demesne arable of the Prior of Bradenstoke, now reckoned at 81 a., included Prior's Field, Faircroft, Sheepleaze, Longmead, Bryerclose, and Butteclose, while the demesne pasture, now reckoned at 193 a., included Grange Pasture, Cosyners Leaze, Windmill Field, and Woodfield.[79] In 1545–7 manorial rents totalled £24 3s. 10d. At this time there were 8 copyholders, at least 4 leaseholders, and a similar number of tenants-at-will within the manor.[80] The demesne lands at Bradenstoke held by Sir Richard Pexsall were let to farm at £5 5s. 4d. in 1549 (see above) and supported 5 tenants. There were 15 tenants on the rest of the manor, and unspecified rents there totalled £5 12s. 8d.[81] In 1590 manorial rents totalled £33 16s. 4½d., and the demesne lands, farmed by Sir John Danvers, were valued at £16 10s. 2d. There were 23 tenants within the manor of Bradenstoke at this date, but it is not known how they held their land.[82] The estate was frequently leased out after the Dissolution. In the 17th and early 18th centuries it was leased successively by Thomas Crompton, Henry Pinnell, and Goddard Smith.[83]

An estate at 'Tockenham', held at that date by Bradenstoke Priory, was worth £4 6s. 8d. in 1291.[84] Another estate also held by Bradenstoke, was taxed at £2 10s. at the same date.[85] Little is known of the manor of West Tockenham before the later 14th century. By this time the Prior of Bradenstoke had received grants of estates there from Thomas of Tockenham and from the Doygnel family[86] and had consolidated his holding by the acquisition of several smaller estates.[87] A survey of West Tockenham made shortly after this period of consolidation shows the manor once held by the Doygnels there to have contained 3 open fields, North Field, West Field, and East Field. The West Field contained about 54 a. of arable land, the East Field about 81 a., and the North Field 38 a. Four tenants held land in the

East and West Fields, together with small appurtenant parcels of meadow land, but only three of these held land in the North Field.[88] In 1532 Anne Danvers (d. 1539), widow of Sir John Danvers (d. 1514), leased the farm of 'Tockenham' from Badenstoke Priory for an 82-year term.[89] She was succeeded in the lease by her son John (d. 1556),[90] grandson Richard (d. 1604),[91] and great-grandson William.[92] Thereafter the estate continued to be leased out until the 20th century. By 1535 the enlarged manor of 'Tockenham' was worth £15.[93] In 1535–7 the estate was valued at £17 16s. 11½d. The assessed rents and those of the free tenants were reckoned at 2s. 11½d., while the rents of customary tenants totalled £8 14s.[94] In 1563, shortly after the Button family acquired the estate, the manorial rents totalled £9 9s. 5½d. and there were 3 free tenants and 10 other tenants.[95] In the earlier 17th century the manor apparently covered a total acreage of 265 a., which included 126 a. of meadow, 54 a. of pasture, and 85 a. of arable.[96] Inclosure within the manor appears to have taken place at an early date. In 1609 the lessee of the Tockenham estate, Timothy Stampe, agreed not to plough up Tockenham Marsh, which had been 'lately laid in severalty'. Stampe further agreed not to plough up ley grounds or lawns beside certain arable lands in West Tockenham, 'which were lately also inclosed'.[97] By 1673 the manor, known as Tockenham Court Farm, was farmed in conjunction with Shaw Farm, also part of the Button estate. In this year a total of 557 sheep and lambs was kept at Tockenham Court Farm, besides 55 beasts and cattle.[98] By 1793 the farm contained 412 a., including a park of 20 a. The general increase in acreage was the result of increased pasture land, which now covered some 211 a.[99]

Little is known of economic conditions within the parish during the 19th century. In 1968, despite the large acreage of R.A.F. Station Lyneham, there were 10 farms in the parish, mostly devoted to mixed farming.

Much agricultural land within the parish was purchased by the Air Ministry during the period 1940–58 for the initial establishment, and later enlargement, of R.A.F. Station Lyneham,[1] which, since its establishment in 1940–1, has been the largest employer of labour in the parish. In 1940 No. 33 Maintenace Unit, which was still based at Lyneham in 1968, was opened on part of the present airfield. A year later control of Lyneham passed to Flying Training Command and in 1942 Lyneham, by then part of Ferry Command, assumed full status as a station. The chief function of R.A.F. Lyneham during the Second World War was the dispatch of most outward-bound, non-combatant aircraft from

[76] Ibid. 3100, Particulars of farms in Lyneham, Tockenham, and Preston.
[77] Ibid. Add. 21.
[78] Valor Eccl. (Rec. Com.), ii. 123.
[79] S.C. 6/Hen. VIII/3985.
[80] E 315/446.
[81] B.M. Add. Ch. 26560.
[82] Ibid. 26579.
[83] W.R.O. 529/44, Lease, John and Hen. Danvers to Thos. Crompton; ibid. 529/46, Lease, Jas. Earl of Abingdon to Hen. Pinnell; ibid. 529/47, Lease, Germanicus Sheppard to Goddard Smith.
[84] V.C.H. Wilts. iii. 280.
[85] Tax. Eccl. (Rec. Com.), 192b.
[86] See p. 96.
[87] See pp. 95–96.

[88] B.M. Stowe MS. 925, ff. 161r–162r.
[89] E 315/446.
[90] F. N. Macnamara, Memorials of the Danvers Family, pp. 274 sqq.; Aubrey, Topog. Coll. ed. Jackson, 188.
[91] C 142/289/81.
[92] C 2/Jas. I/B 39/58, and see p. 170.
[93] V.C.H. Wilts. iii. 280.
[94] E 315/446.
[95] S.R.O. Button-Walker-Heneage Mun. 3100.
[96] Ibid. 1482, Survey of Tockenham Court Farm, temp. Chas. I.
[97] Ibid. 1471, Articles of agreement, Wm. (III) Button and Tim. Stampe.
[98] Ibid. 3114, Wages and Cattle Bk.   [99] Ibid. 3110.
[1] Ex inf. Chief Surveyor of Defence Lands, Tolworth Tower, Surbiton.

Britain. In 1942 an Air Dispatch and Reception Unit began to function and since that time many distinguished people have flown from Lyneham. At the end of the war Lyneham became part of Transport Command and in 1967 became part of the newly-formed Air Support Command.[2] In 1965 the station was reported to employ some 3,400 personnel, including about 500 civilians who lived in the parish.[3] At about the same date some 400 flights, 2,000 aircraft movements, 8,000–10,000 passengers, and $1\frac{3}{4}$ million lb. of freight were handled monthly. In 1968 the station was served principally by a newly-formed squadron of C–130K Hercules transports.[4]

MILLS. In 1086 a mill on the 'Tockenham' estate of Durand of Gloucester paid 50d.[5] Between 1189–94 Bradenstoke Priory built a mill on an estate, presumably recently acquired, at 'Tockenham'.[6] In 1301–2 Robert Brut and others granted a mill in West Tockenham to Bradenstoke Priory.[7]

At the time of the Domesday Survey a mill at 'Stoche', an area which at this date probably included the modern settlements of Bradenstoke and Lyneham, was assessed at 30d.[8] In 1538 a horse-mill, with two appurtenant closes of pasture, all part of the manor of Bradenstoke, was leased to William Towresley for 40 years by Bradenstoke Priory.[9] No more is known until 1649 when Thomas Crompton's lease of the Bradenstoke estate included a 'newly-built' grist-mill near the farm-house.[10] In 1692 James, Earl of Abingdon, leased a grist-mill at Bradenstoke to Henry Pinnell, who agreed to keep it in repair.[11] After Henry Pinnell's death, Goddard Smith became entitled to the unexpired term of the lease formerly held by Pinnell, but by 1738 he had let the mill fall into disrepair.[12]

No record of a mill on the Lyneham estate survives until the 18th century. In 1718 James and Mary Baker were granted a lease of Blind Mill, although the lease did not include the right to take fish from the mill-pond.[13] In 1773 Blind Mill, fed by Lilly Brook, lay to the north of Lyneham village.[14] It was presumably the same mill, then known as Lyneham mill, which was tenanted by James Hiskins in 1885.[15] He remained tenant in 1903.[16] In 1968 the site of the mill, then derelict, could be seen beside Lilly Brook to the south-west of Hillocks Wood.

MARKET AND FAIRS. The two annual fairs and the weekly market granted to Bradenstoke Priory in the 13th and 14th centuries have been mentioned in another volume of the *History*.[17] They presumably brought a considerable amount of trade to the parish. It is probable that the fairs were held on the ground

called Faircroft in 1538–40.[18] Presumably the fairs continued on this site, which may possibly be identified with the part of Clack known as Horse Fair, which lay to the south-east of the hamlet in 1887.[19] Nothing is known of the weekly market which was granted to Bradenstoke Priory in 1361.[20] It may, however, have flourished for a time. In 1628 Clack was described as a 'market town' and delinquency there was such that it was necessary to suppress 4 alehouses.[21] Before 1827, Clack spring and fall fairs, as they were called, were well-attended for such purposes as the sale of livestock, the hiring of servants, and for entertainment.[22]

LOCAL GOVERNMENT. In 1513–14 the Prior of Bradenstoke granted land called 'Harvies' for the building of a house, later known as the church house of Lyneham, for meetings of the parishioners. The site proved to be too far from the church and an alternative site called 'Weekemeade' was granted in 1530 for the erection of 'a very good and meet house', which, when built, cost *c.* £100. William Button, lord of the manor of Lyneham, subsequently claimed the house as parcel of the manor there. The claim was allowed in 1611, provided that the yearly rent from the premises was paid to the churchwardens of Lyneham, but it is not known whether the parishioners of Lyneham continued to meet there.[23]

Before the dissolution of Bradenstoke Priory manorial courts for the manors of Lyneham and West Tockenham were held in Lyneham Court.[24] After the Dissolution the courts of both manors continued to be held by the king's officials either at Lyneham Court or in the church house at Lyneham.[25] There is a court roll for Lyneham manor for 1567,[26] and a record of view of frankpledge for 1647, at which a constable and a tithingman were elected.[27] After 1560, when William Button purchased the reversion of West Tockenham manor (see above), courts for West Tockenham were apparently held separately there. Court rolls survive for West Tockenham manor for 1560,[28] 1561, 1562, 1563,[29] 1567, in which year two courts were held,[30] and for 1584.[31] At these courts manorial officials were appointed and copyholders admitted; in 1562 various presentments concerning the necessity of repairing the lane between West and East Tockenham, and between Tockenham Marsh and Marrow Ash, were recorded.[32] Very little can be said of the government of the parish after this date. Apart from the parish registers the only surviving parish records are a vestry book for 1863–81, which deals with the levying and administration of poor rates, and a vestry minute book for 1888–1923.[33]

[2] Ex inf. Mr. W. E. A. Salter, Min. of Defence.
[3] Lyneham W. I. Scrapbk. 1965 (Microfilm in County Libr., Trowbridge).
[4] Ex inf. Mr. W. E. A. Salter.
[5] *V.C.H. Wilts.* ii, p. 148.
[6] Ibid. iii. 280.
[7] C 143/39/19.
[8] *V.C.H. Wilts.* ii, p. 137.   [9] E 315/446.
[10] W.R.O. 529/44.
[11] Ibid. 529/47, Lease, Sheppard to Smith.   [12] Ibid.
[13] S.R.O. Button-Walker-Heneage Mun. 3104.
[14] *Andrews and Dury, Map.* (W.A.S. Rec. Brch.), pl. 14.
[15] S.R.O. Button-Walker-Heneage Mun. Add. 21.
[16] *Kelly's Dir. Wilts.* (1903).
[17] *V.C.H. Wilts.* iii. 278; *Cal. Chart. R.* 1341–1417, 169.

[18] S.C. 6/Hen. VIII/3985.
[19] O.S. Map 6″, Wilts. XIV, XX (1st edn.).
[20] *Cal. Chart. R.* 1341–1417, 169.
[21] *Wilts. Q. Sess. Rec.* ed. Cunnington, 90.
[22] Hone, *Every Day Book*, ii. 686.
[23] C 2/Jas. I/ P 10/55.
[24] S.R.O. Button-Walker-Heneage Mun. 1454.
[25] Ibid.   [26] Ibid. 1450.
[27] Ibid. 1481.
[28] Ibid. 1442.
[29] Ibid. 1446.
[30] Ibid. 1451.
[31] Ibid. 1459.
[32] Ibid. 1446.
[33] In 1968 in Lyneham Par. Ch.

CHURCHES. Lyneham church is first mentioned in 1182 when it belonged to Bradenstoke Priory.[34] It is likely that the church, together with estates in Bradenstoke and Lyneham, were among the original endowments of the house in c. 1139.[35] The appropriation of the church by Bradenstoke was confirmed by Pope Lucius III in 1182.[36] After the Dissolution the benefice became a perpetual curacy and after 1868 was deemed to be a vicarage. In 1864 the need was felt for a church to serve the hamlet of Clack, which lay over a mile from Lyneham parish church.[37] As a result the consolidated chapelry of Bradenstoke-cum-Clack was formed in 1866 (see below). In 1924 the consolidated chapelry of Bradenstoke-cum-Clack, the vicarage of Lyneham, and the rectory of Tockenham were all united to form one benefice.[38] In 1954 Tockenham was separated from the other two churches,[39] which thenceforth became the united benefice of Lyneham with Bradenstoke-cum-Clack.

The church of Lyneham was probably served by canons of Bradenstoke from earliest times and no vicarage was ordained. A canon was described as curate of Lyneham in 1538.[40] After the dissolution of Bradenstoke the Longs, as lay rectors (see below), were responsible for appointing and paying a curate to serve the church, but apparently frequently neglected to do so. In the mid 17th century Edmund Long's failure to make an appointment[41] led to the presentation by the king in 1678 of an incumbent, who was duly instituted by the bishop, the only occasion before the 19th century when this procedure was adopted.[42] After the break-up of the rectory estate in the mid 17th century the responsibility for providing and paying a curate was said to be divided between the various holders of the parts of the estate.[43] But no appointments seem to have been made by them and throughout the 18th century the church was served by the incumbents of either Hilmarton or Tockenham, or by the curate of Hilmarton.[44] After the beginning of the 19th century, when the benefice had been endowed by a grant from Queen Anne's Bounty (see below), the lay rectors, who were also lords of the manor, began to present incumbents regularly, who were licensed, or after 1868, instituted by the bishop. The first such presentation occurs in 1826 when G. H. W. Heneage presented.[45] Thenceforth the advowson followed the descent of the manor.[46] After the union of the benefices of Lyneham, Bradenstoke-cum-Clack, and Tockenham in 1924 the patrons of the three livings retained for a time their rights to present in turn.[47] But after the rectory of Tockenham had been separated from the combined benefice in 1954, the patronage of the united benefice of Lyneham and Bradenstoke-cum-Clack passed to the Lord Chancellor, with whom, in theory, it remained in 1966.[48] In practice, however, early in the 1960s existing patronage rights were suspended and an agreement reached between the Bishop of Salisbury and the Chaplain-in-Chief R.A.F., whereby R.A.F. chaplains were to serve the churches of Lyneham and Bradenstoke-cum-Clack.[49]

After the dissolution of Bradenstoke Priory the rectory of Lyneham was granted by the king in 1541–2 to Henry Long (d. 1556).[50] He was succeeded as lay rector by his son Richard (d. 1558), who was in turn succeeded by his son Edmund Long (d. 1635).[51] In 1619 Edmund Long had settled the rectory on his second son Richard (d. 1639),[52] and he succeeded his father as lay rector. On Richard (II) Long's death his eldest son Edmund (II) was entitled to the rectory.[53] Edmund Long died in 1664 and was succeeded by his half-brother Humphrey Long as lay rector.[54] Humphrey died in 1679 without heirs and the rectory passed to Robert Compton and his wife Susanna (née Long), sister of Edmund and Humphrey Long.[55] After the death of Robert Compton, Susanna married a second time in 1690 and in her marriage settlement she directed that after her death her trustees should dispose of her estate.[56] She died before 1698–9 when her trustees, in accordance with her instructions, conveyed the rectory of Lyneham to Henry Danvers, who made his future wife, Mary Wolnall, joint purchaser of the property.[57] Henry Danvers died without heirs at an unknown date. His wife Mary died in 1736 and devised the rectory to Elizabeth Warwick, Hannah Hylton, and Robert Fransham, as joint tenants. In 1743 Thomas Hylton and his wife Hannah acquired the thirds held by Elizabeth Warwick and Robert Fransham, and thus became entitled to the whole rectory of Lyneham.[58] Thomas Hylton died shortly before 1758, in which year John and Robert Hylton, kinsmen and devisees of Thomas Hylton, together with William Hylton, Thomas Hylton's son, conveyed the rectory to Jeremiah Berry.[59] In 1765 Berry conveyed it to John Walker (later Walker-Heneage).[60] Thereafter the rectory remained with the Walker-Heneage family and descended as the manor of Lyneham.[61]

In 1291 the church of Lyneham was valued for taxation at £10.[62] It was estimated to be of the same value in 1341.[63] At the beginning of the 18th century the endowments to which the incumbent was said to be entitled, besides a stipend of £13 a year, were

[34] V.C.H. Wilts. iii. 278.
[35] Ibid. 276.   [36] Ibid. 278.
[37] Sar. Dioc. R.O. Vis. Queries, 1864.
[38] Ex inf. Sar. Dioc. Regy. Although the benefices were in theory united at this date, in practice they remained separate since the incumbents then serving the churches were allowed to retain their cures.
[39] See p. 171.
[40] S.C. 6/Hen. VIII/3985.
[41] C 78/1940 Entry 3.
[42] Phillipps, Wilts. Inst. ii. 35.
[43] C 78/1940 Entry 3. For rectory estate, see p. 97.
[44] This statement is based on an examination of the Subscription Bks. and Bp's Transcripts in Sar. Dioc. R.O.
[45] Sar. Dioc. Regy. Reg. Burgess.
[46] See p. 94.
[47] Lyneham Par. Ch. Proceedings of Ch. Council, 1926–1958, and see n. 38 above.

[48] Crockford (1955–6 and later edns.).
[49] Ex inf. Officer Commanding, R.A.F. Station Lyneham.
[50] E 318/722.
[51] Wilts. Inq. p.m. 1625–49 (Index Libr.), 390–2.
[52] Ibid.
[53] C 78/1940 Entry 3.
[54] Sar. Dioc. R.O. Glebe Terrier, 1671.
[55] C.P. 25(2)/747/32 Chas. II East.
[56] S.R.O. Button-Walker-Heneage Mun. 1862, Marriage settlement, 1690.
[57] Ibid. 1864, Bond, 1698.
[58] E 126/28 Mich. 1753 Entry 7.
[59] S.R.O. Button-Walker-Heneage Mun. 1883.
[60] Ibid. Add. 124–5, Lease and release, Berry to Walker.
[61] See p. 94.
[62] Tax. Eccl. (Rec. Com.), 190.
[63] Inq. Non. (Rec. Com.), 161.

a house, the herbage of the churchyard, and the Easter offerings.[64] In 1813 a grant of £1,400 from the Royal Bounty was made to endow the benefice.[65] In 1835 the average net income over the past three years was estimated to be £58.[66] In 1910 a grant of £74 was made to the church by the Ecclesiastical Commissioners from the Common Fund.[67]

The Abbot of Malmesbury had a portion payable out of the church of Lyneham, assessed for taxation in 1291 at 10s.[68] In 1364 a dispute arose over this portion, which was payable in lieu of the right of the Abbot of Malmesbury to take tithes from lands granted by Thomas of Tockenham to Bradenstoke Priory at some date before 1265. An agreement was reached whereby Malmesbury Abbey allowed Bradenstoke Priory to take the tithes in return for a yearly payment of 20s.[69] In 1535 the abbot was still receiving this payment.[70]

In 1341 the great tithes of Lyneham were due to Bradenstoke Priory as rector, while those arising from the rectory estate (see below) were reserved for the sole use of the prior.[71] In 1364 the prior and convent also established their right to certain tithes, both great and small, in West Tockenham[72] and at the time of the Dissolution all the tithes in the parish belonged to Bradenstoke.[73] After the dissolution of Bradenstoke these tithes were included in the grant of the rectory to Henry Long (see above).[74] In 1629 Edmund Long (d. 1635) settled certain of the great and small tithes, presumably those arising from the rectorial estate (later known as Lyneham Court), on his son Richard (II), Richard's second wife, Susanna, and their heirs.[75] Richard (II) Long died in 1639 and the tithes of the estate apparently passed to his son by his first marriage, Edmund (II) Long, as guardian of his half-brother Humphrey Long.[76] Edmund (II) Long (d. 1664) then conveyed all the tithes of Free-grove, formerly a part of the rectorial estate, to either Adam or Robert Tuck.[77] Humphrey Long died in 1679 and his heir was his sister Susanna, wife of Robert Compton.[78] Thereafter the remaining tithes both great and small from the rectory estate continued to belong to the lay rectors of Lyneham, who have been traced above.

Edmund (II) Long (d. 1664) also conveyed certain of the great and small tithes in Lyneham, Preston, and West Tockenham to William (III) Button, lord of the manors of Lyneham with Preston and West Tockenham.[79] These tithes then followed the descent of those manors and so came in 1712 to Heneage Walker.[80] In 1753 the lay rectors, who, as shown above, had only the tithes of the rectory estate, claimed unsuccessfully the West Tockenham tithes belonging to John Walker, brother and heir of Heneage Walker.[81] Twelve years later, in 1765,

John Walker acquired the rectory and so added to the tithes of Lyneham, Preston, and West Tockenham, those of the rectory estate.

There was an estate belonging to the church by 1341, which was subsequently enlarged and held by Bradenstoke Priory, as rector, until the Dissolution.[82] After the Dissolution it was granted with the rectory to Henry Long. Its subsequent descent has been traced above.[83]

Since no vicarage was ordained, the small as well as the great tithes of the parish were due to the rectors and in 1341 small tithes, including the tithe of fowls and young deer, belonged to Bradenstoke Priory.[84] After the Dissolution James Cole, the curate of Lyneham, had apparently received at least some of the small tithes of the parish as well as a stipend of £6 13s. 4d.[85] This arrangement did not last, and in 1678 Daniel Salway, then curate of Lyneham, was unsuccessful in his claim to the small tithes.[86] Certain small tithes were included in the grants mentioned above of great tithes made by members of the Long family in the 17th century. Like the great tithes, however, most of the small tithes eventually came into the hands of John Walker (later Walker-Heneage) in 1765 (see above).

In 1775 and 1782-3 tenants on Lyneham manor compounded their tithes for £71 9s.[87] By 1846 most of the tithes in the parish had been declared to be merged in the lands from which they were due. Only those arising from 161 a. were still due in kind and in 1846 a rent-charge of £37 was awarded to G. H. W. Heneage in respect of these.[88]

After the Dissolution the practice whereby the lay rectors paid someone to serve the cure evidently led to the church being frequently without any incumbent at all, or else resulted in the appointment of some unsatisfactory person. The canon of Bradenstoke who served the church at the Dissolution was still curate in 1553,[89] but thereafter there is no record of a curate at Lyneham until the later 17th century when Edmund (II) Long allowed John Hayes, described as his servant, £13 to read divine service in the church.[90] Hayes, who was reported to be 'defective through age',[91] died before 1674, and no one apparently succeeded him, although previously Humphrey Long, half-brother of Edmund (II) Long, had, as lay rector, allotted £13 for the maintenance of a curate.[92] The only incumbent to be episcopally instituted before the 19th century, Daniel Salway, successfully established his right to the arrears of a salary of £13, chargeable on all the holders of the rectorial estate.[93] In the later 18th century, when the church was served by the Rector of Tockenham, a service was held at Lyneham early on Sunday afternoons. At this time there were 10 or 12 communicants in the parish.[94]

[64] Sar. Dioc. R.O. Glebe Terrier, 1705.
[65] Hodgson, *Queen Anne's Bounty* (2nd edn.), p. cccxxxvi.
[66] *Rep. Com. Eccl. Revenues*, H.C. 54, pp. 840-1 (1835), xxii.
[67] Sar. Dioc. Regy. Index of Deeds, ii.
[68] *Tax. Eccl.* (Rec. Com.), 190.
[69] B.M. Stowe MS. 925, f. 40 and v; and see pp. 95-96.
[70] *Valor Eccl.* (Rec. Com.), ii. 125.
[71] *Inq. Non.* (Rec. Com.), 161.
[72] *V.C.H. Wilts.* iii. 280 n.
[73] S.C. 6/Hen. VIII/3985.   [74] E 318/722.
[75] C 78/1940 Entry 3.   [76] Ibid.
[77] C.P. 25(2)/745/18 & 19 Chas. II Hil.
[78] See above.
[79] C.P. 25(2)/508/1 Chas. I Mich.

[80] See pp. 94, 96.
[81] E 126/28 Mich. 1758 Entry 7.
[82] See p. 96.   [83] See p. 96.
[84] *Inq. Non.* (Rec. Com.), 161.
[85] *V.C.H. Wilts.* iii. 288.
[86] C 78/1940 Entry 3.
[87] S.R.O. Button-Walker-Heneage Mun. 1885, Lyneham Rectory Deeds.
[88] W.R.O. Tithe Award.
[89] Sar. Dioc. R.O. Bp's Detecta Bk. 1550-8.
[90] C 78/1940 Entry 3.
[91] Sar. Dioc. R.O. Chwdns.' Pres. 1662.
[92] Ibid. 1674.
[93] C 78/1940 Entry 3.
[94] Sar. Dioc. R.O. Vis. Queries, 1783.

By 1783 the Vicar of Hilmarton was undertaking the customary afternoon service.[95] Early in the 19th century the parishioners informed the bishop that they had resolved to raise among themselves an annual stipend and provide a comfortable residence in order to secure the full-time services of a certain curate, who had served the church in the past.[96] It was presumably shortly after this that incumbents began to be regularly presented and paid from the endowment granted in 1813 (see above). On Census Sunday in 1851 it was reckoned that the average congregation at morning service over the year had been 95 and at afternoon service 105.[97] The distance at which many of the congregation lived from the parish church was remarked upon at this time and it was stated that many people found it more convenient to attend church in Tockenham.[98] In 1864 morning and evening prayers were said in Lyneham church and in addition evening prayers were said at a licensed schoolroom in Clack. Services were held at Lyneham on festivals and on Wednesdays and Fridays, but weekday attendance was reported to be poor. Holy Communion was administered at Christmas, Easter, Whitsun, on Trinity Sunday, and on the first Sunday in every month. There were about 37 communicants at this date.[99]

The Prior of Bradenstoke evidently provided a house, at least in the earlier 16th century, in which the curate of Lyneham lived.[1] There was evidently a house available in the early 18th century but it was not required until the 19th century when incumbents began to be regularly presented.[2] In 1864 the curate, John Duncan, lived in the glebe house.[3] This is probably to be identified with the vicarage house, an 18th-century building with a 19th-century 'Gothic' frontage, which stood south of the road from Lyneham to Wootton Bassett in 1887,[4] and in 1968 was used as a private house.

The church of *ST. MICHAEL*, dating largely from the later 14th and 15th centuries, consists of chancel, nave, north aisle, south porch, and embattled west tower. Both the tower, which has belfry windows containing early Perpendicular tracery, and the nave, were probably rebuilt late in the 14th century; the north aisle may be slightly later in date. The chancel, shown in a watercolour of 1806[5] to have had 15th-century features, was out of repair in 1662 and again in 1674.[6] A new chancel was built by William Butterfield in 1860[7] and the nave appears to have been reroofed and thoroughly restored at the same time; a single Perpendicular window in the south wall[8] was replaced by two windows of similar design. An ancient yew which stands near the south porch is shown in 1806 as an already well-established tree.[9]

Fittings in the church include a re-set 15th-century chancel screen and a carved Jacobean screen

below the tower arch. Among memorials to the Walker and Walker-Heneage families is a large wall monument of veined marble commemorating Heneage Walker (d. 1731). It stands in the north aisle and consists of an inscribed tablet flanked by Corinthian pilasters and surmounted by an open segmental pediment, *putti*, and a cartouche of arms.

There were three bells in 1553.[10] It may have been one of these which was reported broken in 1662.[11] In the 20th century there was a peal of 5 bells, including one of *c.* 1450 from the Bristol foundry.[12] One bell was recast and the whole peal rehung in 1926.[13]

The commissioners of Edward VI took 2 oz. plate for the king's use, but left a chalice weighing 7 oz. for the use of the parish. A cup, dated 1811, and an 18th-century paten, were sold to the parish of Seagry in the 19th century, and a new chalice, flagon, and paten, all hall-marked 1863, were bought.[14] In 1682 it was noted that the parish register of Lyneham had been lost in 'the late troubles', and that another had been begun.[15] The registers of baptisms in 1968 dated from 1708, those of marriages from 1709, and those of burials from 1708. Baptisms are wanting between 1754 and 1761, and marriages between 1736 and 1754.[16]

The consolidated chapelry of Bradenstoke-cum-Clack was formed in 1866 out of parts of Lyneham and Christian Malford.[17] In 1924 it was united with the benefices of Lyneham and Tockenham (see above). Gabriel Goldney, lord of the manor of Bradenstoke, was the first patron of the consolidated chapelry.[18] He was succeeded by his son Gabriel Prior Goldney in 1900,[19] but by 1926 the advowson had passed to the Bishop of Salisbury.[20] After the benefices were united in 1924 the three patrons had the right to present in turn (see above).

Shortly after its creation the consolidated chapelry received endowments which consisted of certain tithe commutation rent-charges worth £27 6s. This sum, together with a benefaction of £1,000, provided a yearly income of £33 6s. 8d., to which the Ecclesiastical Commissioners added an additional stipend of £50 from the Common Fund.[21] The former vicarage, which stands in the village street opposite the church, is a stone house with a date tablet of 1710; it was evidently converted into a vicarage, enlarged, and given lavish red brick dressings *c.* 1866.

In 1866 the church of *ST. MARY* at Bradenstoke, designed by C. F. Hansom in the Decorated style,[22] was built in stone at the expense of Gabriel Goldney (d. 1900). It consists of chancel, nave, and north aisle, with a stone bell-cote at the west end of the nave. The interior is enriched with carved stonework and the carved font is said to have been exhibited at the Exhibition of 1862.[23]

The church plate, dated 1862, comprises a

95 Ibid.
96 Ibid. Curates Nominations.
97 H.O. 129/251/1/2/2.   98 Ibid.
99 Sar. Dioc. R.O. Vis. Queries, 1864.
1 S.C. 6/Hen. VIII/3985.
2 Sar. Dioc. R.O. Glebe Terrier, 1705.
3 Ibid. Vis. Queries, 1864.
4 O.S. Map 6″, Wilts. XIV, XX (1st edn.).
5 By John Buckler: W.A.S. Libr., Devizes, vol. iv. 48.
6 Sar. Dioc. R.O. Chwdns.' Pres. 1662, 1674.
7 Pevsner, *Wilts.* (Bldgs. of Eng.), 286.
8 W.A.S. Libr., Devizes, vol. iv. 48.   9 Ibid.
10 Walters, *Wilts. Bells*, 127–8.

11 Sar. Dioc. R.O. Chwdns.' Pres. 1662.
12 Walters, *Wilts. Bells*, 127–8.
13 *Kelly's Dir. Wilts.* (1939).
14 Nightingale, *Wilts. Plate*, 143, 224.
15 *W.A.M.* xlv 103.
16 In 1968 in Lyneham Par. Ch.
17 *Lond. Gaz.* 29 June 1866 (p. 3722).   18 Ibid.
19 *Clergy List* (1915).
20 *Crockford* (1926).
21 *Lond. Gaz.* 24 Mar. 1868 (p. 1836).
22 Pevsner, *Wilts.* (Bldgs. of Eng.), 115; *Kelly's Dir. Wilts.* (1939).
23 Pevsner, *Wilts.* (Bldgs. of Eng.), 115.

flagon, paten, and plate, all presented by Mrs. Gabriel Goldney at the opening of the church in 1866.[24]

NONCONFORMITY. After his ejection from Hilmarton the former vicar, Robert Rowswell, preached in Lyneham and Clack.[25] He was licensed to preach at his house in Clack in 1672.[26] Independency flourished in the parish in the 18th century. In 1739 John Cennick, the disciple of George Whitefield, preached at Lyneham and in c. 1741–3 a society, regarded at first as an offshoot of Whitefield's Tabernacle, was formed there.[27] This society had possibly moved towards congregationalism by 1773, when a licence was granted to a group of Independents at Lyneham.[28]

In 1777 Isaac Turner of Calne built a Particular Baptist chapel at Clack,[29] later known as the Providence Chapel. The chapel is a high building of red brick with stone dressings and a roof of stone slates. A hipped gable-end facing the street contains a segmental-headed window and is surmounted by a wooden bell cupola. Similar windows below appear to have been enlarged and a porch has been added. The minister's house is attached. In 1851 it was reckoned then that the average congregation over the past year had numbered 110 persons in the morning, 112 in the afternoon, and 50 in the evening. The chapel was served by lay ministers.[30] By 1934 a baptistry beneath the floor of the chapel had been added. Previously baptisms had taken place in 'Adam's Dam', a pond near Bradenstoke, or in disused clay-pits at Old Dauntsey brickyard.[31] Services were still held at the chapel in 1968.

In 1783 it was reported that some 'Methodists,' belonging to 'the lowest class of people', had recently built a chapel at Clack, together with a house for the minister.[32] It seems likely, however, that this is in fact a reference to the Particular Baptists at the Providence Chapel. Wesleyan Methodism, if indeed it ever appeared in the parish, apparently had little lasting influence there, but that of Primitive Methodism lasted throughout the 19th century. As a result of Samuel Heath's evangelizing activities in the early 19th century around Brinkworth, many chapels were built, including a Primitive Methodist chapel at Clack in 1827,[33] which was registered a year later.[34] The members of this chapel were taunted by fellow villagers in 1837 until the trouble was suppressed by the incumbent of Lyneham.[35] In 1851 this chapel, a low brick building standing on the north side of the village street, had 50 free and 40 other sittings. On a certain Sunday in that year it was estimated that the average general congregation over the past year had numbered 40 in the afternoon and 100 in the evening, while those who occupied separate

sittings averaged 30 persons at both afternoon and evening services.[36] In 1887 a larger and more substantial building, able to accommodate 150, was built to the east of the former chapel.[37] Seventeen members attended in 1907,[38] and services were still held at the chapel in 1968.

Primitive Methodism also flourished at Preston, where a society was formed in 1830, and until 1906 services were held in cottages.[39] In c. 1907 the new chapel of corrugated iron had 7 members.[40] Services were still held in this chapel once on alternate Sundays in 1968. A society of Primitive Methodists, made up of 9 members, was formed at Lyneham in 1906 and services were held in cottages.[41] In 1934 the Gaisford Memorial Methodist chapel was built in the centre of Lyneham village, and in 1968 was used by Presbyterians and other denominations. At this date the chapel was served by chaplains from R.A.F. Lyneham.

EDUCATION. In 1716 Ralph Broome of Lyneham bequeathed £450 to the parish to provide for a school master, to be appointed by the trustees of the charity. The master was to teach 30 poor children of Lyneham reading, writing, arithmetic, and the Christian religion according to the Church of England.[42] No more is known of the free school until 1819 when 41 children, some of whom boarded in the master's house, attended. The master was assisted by a 'very old and infirm man', and it was feared that the charity children were greatly neglected.[43] By 1834 the improved premises contained a schoolroom and 4 other rooms, where an average attendance of 20 pupils in the summer and of 40 in the winter, was usual. Pupils, both day children and boarders, were generally admitted at 6 years and remained in the school until they were 12 years old.[44] In 1835 it was reported that, besides the charity children, additional fee-paying pupils, presumably the boarders, were taught in the school.[45] By 1861 the free school was united with the National Society and in this year new buildings were provided.[46] These stood at Church End in Lyneham, opposite St. Michael's church.[47] An average number of 27 infants and 76 mixed juniors attended Lyneham National School in 1902. The infants were taught by an articled teacher, while the juniors were taught by a head teacher and two assistants.[48] By 1905 the school was administered by the Wiltshire County Council.[49] In 1953 a new county primary school was built on adjoining land but the old buildings remained in use.[50] A new infants' school was built in 1965. In 1968 the two schools had a total attendance of c. 860 from Lyneham and Bradenstoke, 90 per cent of whom were children of R.A.F. personnel.[51]

In 1859 the older children from the hamlet of

[24] Nightingale, *Wilts. Plate*, 135.
[25] *V.C.H. Wilts.* iii. 105.
[26] *Calamy Revised*, ed. Matthews, 418.
[27] *V.C.H. Wilts.* iii. 130–1.　　　[28] Ibid. 134 n.
[29] Ibid. iii. 137.
[30] H.O. 129/251/1/2/5.
[31] *W.A.M.* xlvi. 657.
[32] Sar. Dioc. R.O. Vis. Queries, 1783.
[33] *V.C.H. Wilts.* iii. 143–4.
[34] W.R.O. Retns. of Regns.
[35] W. C. Tonks, *Victory in the Villages*, 138–9.
[36] H.O. 129/251/1/2/4.　　　[37] Tonks, op. cit. 138–9.
[38] Ibid.　　　[39] Ibid. 156–7.

[40] Ibid. 24.　　　[41] Ibid. 170–1.
[42] *W.A.M.* xliv. 33–34.
[43] *Digest of Retns. to Cttee. of Educ. of Poor*, H.C. 224, p. 1031 (1819), ix (2).
[44] *Endowed Char. Wilts.* (1908), pp. 662 sqq.
[45] *Educ. Enq. Abstract*, H.C. 62, p. 111 (1835), xliii.
[46] *Endowed Char. Wilts.* (1908), p. 665.
[47] O.S. Map 6", Wilts. XIV, XX (1st edn.).
[48] W.R.O. List of Schools, 1902.
[49] *Endowed Char. Wilts.* (1908), p. 670.
[50] Wilts. Cuttings, xxi. 227.
[51] Ex inf. the head master, County Junior School, Lyneham.

Clack attended school at Lyneham, while the younger children were taught in a cottage by a young woman. A few children from the hamlet went to school at Christian Malford.[52] In 1860 a National school was built in the hamlet,[53] and in 1875 part of the income of the Broome charity at Lyneham was allotted to the school,[54] which stood opposite the church of St. Mary.[55] Owing to the cost of new buildings at Lyneham school charity funds were applied to Bradenstoke only once, in 1889. In 1899 it was agreed that when the cost of building at the Lyneham school had been discharged, three quarters of the income of the Broome charity was to apply to Lyneham, while a quarter was to be known as Broome's Bradenstoke Charity. Trustees, who were to receive payment from the Lyneham trustees, were appointed to administer the new charity.[56] In 1902 an average of 69 boys and girls were taught by a head teacher and an assistant in two rooms.[57] In 1905 it was reported that for 2 or 3 years past Broome's Bradenstoke Charity had been used for school prizes, but that in this year it was used to maintain an evening school in the buildings of the National school.[58] The school, then known as Bradenstoke C.E. Controlled Primary School, was closed in July 1966,[59] and pupils henceforth attended the schools at Lyneham.

In 1831 a school for 24 boys was supported by 'the lady of the manor', while in 1835 20 or 30 girls in the parish were taught at the expense of their parents.[60]

CHARITIES. Lyneham shared equally with Wootton Bassett in the charity created by Charles Compton in his will, dated 1700.[61] Lyneham's share, which amounted to £50, was at first distributed to the poor of the parish on Tuesday in Easter week. The charity was further regulated in 1726 as the result of a lawsuit and reinvested in land at Badbury (Chiseldon). A moiety of the profits was then distributed among the poor of Lyneham, according to the size of their families, at Midsummer.[62] The charity lands at Badbury were sold and the proceeds invested in stock in 1961.

In the early 18th century Dame Eleanor Button, Sir Robert Button, and John Still made various bequests to the poor of Lyneham. These charities were known jointly as 'The Poor's Land'.[63] This was, together with Charles Compton's and Thomas Burchall's charities (see below), vested in the Charity Commissioners in 1862.

Thomas Burchall (d. 1734) devised land in Bushton (Clyffe Pypard) to the poor of Lyneham.[64] The income was to be used to keep his tomb in repair, to provide bread for the poor on the day of his funeral, and for the endowment of 6 sermons, one to be preached on the anniversary of his death, and the others at appointed times. The ministers who preached these sermons were to be paid 10s. each. Apparently the sermons soon lapsed and the charity was distributed in bread. By 1834 money payments were made to the poor of Lyneham at Christmas.

In 1862 the incomes of all the above-mentioned charities were amalgamated, provision being made for the maintenance of Thomas Burchall's tomb. Ninety-seven persons received 13s. 6d. each from the income of the Button and kindred charities in 1956. In 1962 the total income of the amalgamated charities was about £75.

By his will, proved in 1865, Robert Henley bequeathed £200, the profits of which were to provide coals for the poor of the parish of Lyneham, excluding Bradenstoke, on 21 December.[65] By 1905, however, it was usual for money to be distributed. In 1956 36 persons received payments of 3s. each.

SWINDON

SWINDON, the largest town in Wiltshire, lies near the north-eastern boundary of the county.[1] The geology of its site has been discussed at length by W. J. Arkell,[2] and need only be summarized here. The site of Old Swindon, the ancient centre of the parish, is at the eastern side of a hill rising to almost 500 ft. above sea level.[3] Apart from a small outlier of Wealden Beds, the summit of the hill, somewhat over a mile long from east to west, consists of successive exposures of Purbeck and Portland Beds. Below these beds, round the slopes of the hill, are narrow exposures of Swindon Clay and Pectinatus Sand. These two formations are more extensively exposed on a ridge about 400 ft. high, extending south-eastward from Old Swindon to the borough boundary near Broome Farm. On the eastern side of this ridge a smaller area of Portland Beds is exposed, while the ridge is overlaid by con-

[52] Acct. of Wilts. Schools, H.C. 27, p. 95 (1859, Sess. 1) xxi (2).
[53] Endowed Char. Wilts. (1908), p. 670. [54] Ibid. p. 665.
[55] O.S. Map 6", Wilts. XIV, XX (1st edn.).
[56] Endowed Char. Wilts. (1908), p. 665.
[57] W.R.O. List of Schools, 1902.
[58] Endowed Char. Wilts. (1908), p. 667.
[59] Ex inf. Chief Education Officer, Trowbridge.
[60] Educ. Enq. Abstract, H.C. 62, p. 111 (1835), xliii.
[61] See p. 204.
[62] All inf. from Endowed Char. Wilts. (1908), pp. 663-4 and Char. Com. File 201408/A1.

[63] Endowed Char. Wilts. (1908), pp. 663-4, 668.
[64] This and all subsequent inf. from Endowed Char. Wilts. (1908), p. 664 and Char. Com. File 203586.
[65] All inf. from Endowed Char. Wilts. (1908), p. 671 and Char. Com. File 203586.
[1] This article was written between 1964 and 1965. Any reference to later years is dated.
[2] W. J. Arkell, 'A Geological Map of Swindon', W.A.M. lii. 195-212.
[3] The following maps were used generally: O.S. Maps 1/2,500, Wilts. XV. 3, 4, 7, 8 (all edns.); 1", sheet 34 (1828 edn.).

siderable areas of Lower Greensand. North and east of the slopes of Swindon Hill the land drops more gradually from about 375 ft. to below 300 ft. near Rodbourne Cheney. Much of New Swindon is built on Kimmeridge Clay, but in the north of the borough are Corallian outcrops on which the Pinehurst and Penhill estates are built, and beyond them the Oxford Clay appears. The River Ray forms the western boundary of the borough, and a tributary of the River Cole runs from Coate Reservoir on the south-eastern boundary through Coate and Walcot before turning away eastwards.

The ancient parish of Swindon is of an irregular shape, about three miles from north to south and the same distance from east to west; it contained 3,136 acres.[4] Swindon Hill lies near its centre. The hill was clearly a place of resort for men since Neolithic times, for many scattered finds, including some burials, have been made there. The earliest evidence of continuous occupation is from Roman times. A Roman building near the west end of Westlecott Road was excavated in 1897.[5]

Swindon is first mentioned by name in Domesday Book.[6] Very little is known of it during the Middle Ages, but it is probable that the growth of an urban settlement on the hill is due to the powerful de Valence family, lords of High Swindon in the 13th century. In 1274 it was said that William de Valence had been holding a market at Swindon for 15 years,[7] and in 1289 it was distinguished as Chipping Swindon.[8] Later references to burgages,[9] and to the town as a 'borough',[10] suggest that deliberate steps were taken to foster urban growth, probably in the 13th century. The name of Newport Street, first mentioned in 1346,[11] adds weight to this supposition. That the attempt was not unsuccessful may be inferred from 14th-century assessments. In 1334 High Swindon was assessed at 133s. 4d., considerably more than the adjoining rural manors, and comparable to the assessments of, for instance, Devizes, Westbury, and Warminster.[12] In 1377 its figure of 248 poll-tax payers[13] indicates more than a rural manor, and compares with several of the smaller market towns in the county.

Very little more is known of Swindon until the 17th century, and the only inference from the lack of references to it must be that it remained a very small market town of little importance. In 1627 the constables of Kingsbridge hundred considered that nine licensed alehouses were too many for a place which did not contain 300 communicants and was on no through road.[14] Somewhat later in the century, however, Swindon's fortunes took an upward turn when a quarry of white smooth stone suitable for paving the insides of houses was found,[15] and there is evidence of considerable quarrying activity in Swindon in the late 17th century.[16]

Aubrey records the increased prosperity of the market, dating from the Civil War.[17] It was in the 17th century, too, that much of the lower land of the parish was inclosed and converted from arable to pasture.[18]

A picture of the parish at the end of the 17th century is provided by a list of inhabitants made in 1697.[19] Its population was then 791. Most of the retail trades and handicrafts of a small country town were represented and 40 labourers are recorded. There were also 14 men described as yeomen and 4 others owning land worth £50 a year. At least five inns and an alehouse existed. The lord of the manor, the lay rector, two other members of the Vilett family, a 'gentleman', the vicar, and two other clergymen formed the core of the polite society of the town.

Just over a century later it was the politeness of society in Swindon which struck John Britton. 'The pleasantness of its situation', he wrote, 'combined with other circumstances, may have induced many persons of independent fortune to fix their residence at Swindon; and their mansions contribute as much to ornament the town as their social intercourse may be said to animate and enliven it.'[20] He considered that Swindon had advanced both in prosperity and in 'liberality of mind' over the past century, alluding to the savage persecution of nonconformists which had taken place in the 1740s.[21] The population had certainly increased, for in 1801 it was 1,198.[22] The opening of the Wilts. and Berks. Canal in 1810 and the North Wilts. Canal in 1819 increased the general trade of the town.[23] The market and fairs seem to have been well attended[24] and the population increased at each census until it was 1,742 in 1831.[25] Yet this was a town on the smallest scale. As telling a reference as any to its lack of importance occurs in a newspaper of 1798, when the inhabitants of Wroughton referred to their village as 'near Marlborough'.[26] William Morris, Swindon's first historian, has left a vivid description of the air of activity which arose in the quiet little town when a blacksmith bonded a wheel, and of the sport of backsword-playing for which the town was noted.[27]

In 1840 the Great Western Railway Company's line reached Swindon and almost immediately the company decided to build its railway works there.[28] With this decision a completely new course of development began for Swindon. The railway works were built to the north of the line and in 1842 the first estate of some 300 cottages for employees was laid out on the southern side. From these beginnings grew the town of New Swindon which only about ten years later had, with the hamlet of Eastcott which it had engulfed, a population of 2,468, slightly larger than that of the old town.[29] Nearly a

[4] W.R.O. Tithe Award.
[5] *V.C.H. Wilts.* i (1), 111–13, and see p. 126.
[6] See pp. 119, 121–4.
[7] *Rot. Hund.* (Rec. Com.), ii. 261, and see p. 132.
[8] *P.N. Wilts.* (E.P.N.S.), 276.
[9] e.g. Goddard MSS. 127, 154; *Cal. Close,* 1405–9, 435.
[10] Goddard MS. 1147, *passim.*
[11] Ibid. 1.
[12] *V.C.H. Wilts.* iv. 296–302.
[13] Ibid. 306, 312.
[14] *Wilts. Q. Sess. Rec.* ed. Cunnington, 86.
[15] Aubrey, *Nat. Hist. Wilts.* ed. Britton, 43.
[16] See pp. 126–7.

[17] Aubrey, op. cit. 115, and *Topog. Coll.* ed. Jackson, 191–2.
[18] See pp. 124–5.
[19] W.R.O. 212B/W.G.8/9, List of inhabitants of Swindon, 1697.
[20] Britton, *Beauties of Wilts.* iii. 6–7.
[21] See p. 151.
[22] *V.C.H. Wilts.* iv. 358.
[23] See p. 128.
[24] Morris, *Swindon,* 298–9, 302, 310–11.
[25] *V.C.H. Wilts.* iv. 358.
[26] *Salisbury and Winchester Jnl.* 9 Apr. 1798.
[27] See p. 141.
[28] See p. 128.
[29] H.O. 107/1833.

mile of open country separated the works and the first housing estate from the town on the hill, but as the works expanded the intervening land was hurriedly built over with streets of workers' houses. Throughout the 19th century, however, Old and New Swindon remained physically separate and were under separate authorities from 1864 until 1900.[30] But by 1900 with the rapid expansion of New Swindon southwards and the slower growth of Old Swindon northwards the two towns had virtually merged on Swindon Hill and their physical junction was crowned that year by their incorporation into one municipal borough.[31]

From 1900 until the end of the Second World War the history of Swindon is one of slowly increasing population, gradual diversification of industry, and, because of changing standards of housing, of some outward expansion. After the end of the Second World War a programme of greatly accelerated expansion was planned in order to attract new industry to the town and so avoid too great a dependence upon the railway works for employment. This programme was well under way when in 1952 Swindon became one of the towns approved under the Town Development Act to receive overspill population and industry from London.[32] Thereupon building and re-development proceeded at such a pace that by c. 1960 all land suitable for building within the borough boundary had been covered. Permission was then given for building beyond the boundary to the east and here in the early 1960s housing and industrial estates built by Swindon Corporation were being laid out.

The following study of the growth of the town is divided roughly into four periods: before 1840, from 1840 to 1864, from 1864 to 1900, and after 1900.

GROWTH OF THE TOWN. Little is known of the topography of Swindon before the 18th century. Newport Street, first mentioned in 1346, Wood Street in 1599, High Street in 1645, the principal streets of the town,[33] seem to have been fairly continuously built up by 1773.[34] The topography of the town and parish can best be studied by a survey of the town as it was just before the railway came.[35] Its centre was High Street, where lived the rather large number of people in easy circumstances for which the town was still remarkable in 1838.[36] Here too were the principal inns of the town, of which the 'Goddard Arms' remains little altered, a late-18th-century building of brick with a long frontage of nine bays, a Doric porch, and a stone-tiled mansard roof. It had replaced a thatched building called the 'Crown', the history of which can be traced to the 16th century.[37] The 'Bell', the other posting house in Swindon in the early 19th century, occupies a building with a Victorian frontage from which hangs a huge metal bell. There are traces of a galleried upper story in the yard at

the rear and the inn is reputed to date from 1515.[38] The former 'King of Prussia', now no. 4 High Street,[39] is a low stone building which may be of 17th-century origin. The houses on the west side of High Street, including the 'Bell' and no. 4, form the most substantial range of old buildings in the town. Several, however, have been faced with stucco or altered by the insertion of shop fronts. No. 2, at the corner of Wood Street, carries a date tablet of 1708 and until the late 19th century had two gables facing High Street. Nos. 6 and 8 are late-18th-century houses retaining their original pedimented doorways. The rainwater-heads of no. 16 are dated 1631; this is a timber-framed building with a twin-gabled front in which sash windows have been inserted. Nos. 18 and 20 both date from c. 1700. A block of six bays near the corner of Newport Street called Manchester House was of the same period and had a shell hood over its door. It was demolished in 1964.

Opening out of the east side of High Street is the small Market Square. On its south side, where the town hall now stands, were stables for the horses of the London stage waggon, with stores above for cheese and other goods awaiting transit.[40] In the centre once stood a small circular market cross on oaken pillars, which existed in 1662,[41] but was removed in 1793. Nearby stood the stocks and pillory.[42] On the north side were two stone-tiled cottages,[43] replaced in the later 19th century by John Toomer's corn store.[44] Next to this stands Square House, an 18th-century brick building of two stories with a symmetrical front and an original doorway; the gable-end of its adjoining outhouse is surmounted by a weather-cock and has an inserted Victorian window with Gothic shafts. Set back in its garden on the east side of the Square stood the Rectory House, a large brick building of the early 19th century.[45]

The other principal street of the town, Wood Street, was colloquially known as Blacksmiths' Street from the three forges which stood there, or Windmill Street from the windmill which once stood on the site of the 'Kings Arms'. About 1840 it contained a number of poor thatched cottages occupied by labouring people,[46] but Richard Jefferies spoke of it as a pleasant street in which vines were trained against several houses on the sunny side.[47] In 1964 two dignified houses of c. 1800 survived at the west end of the street — no. 31 and, opposite to it, no. 32. Elsewhere the frontages had mostly been rebuilt in the later 19th and 20th centuries. Like Wood Street, Newport Street was the home of many of the lesser tradesmen of the town, shoemakers, bakers and the like, but was reckoned more humble. It was generally called Bull Street from a public house called the 'Bull' opposite the present Railway Hotel, and consisted chiefly of thatched and whitewashed cottages, many of which survived into the present century.[48] In

[30] See pp. 135–8.
[31] See p. 138.
[32] See pp. 139–40.   [33] Goddard MSS. 1, 9, 10, 41.
[34] *Andrews and Dury, Map* (W.A.S. Rec. Brch.), pl. 15.
[35] Based on H.O. 107/1179 (1841 Census returns) and W.R.O. Tithe Award, which shows only part of the parish.
[36] Robson, *Com. Dir.* (1838).
[37] Morris, *Swindon*, 225; see below, p. 123.
[38] Inscription on building.

[39] W.A.S. Libr., Devizes, Sale Cats. v, no. 32; F. Large, *A Swindon Retrospect*, 36–37.
[40] Morris, *Swindon*, 228.   [41] Goddard MS. 1147.
[42] Jefferies, *Swindon*, 74.   [43] Morris, *Swindon*, 228.
[44] See p. 115.   [45] See p. 146.
[46] Morris, *Swindon*, 1–2, 248.
[47] Jefferies, *Swindon*, 74–75.
[48] Morris, *Swindon*, 1, 4–5; photograph c. 1905 in W.A.S. Libr., Devizes (Prints AA 78); Large, *Swindon Retrospect*, 38.

1964 there was no visible work earlier than the 16th century. At the western end stood the parish lock-up, called the 'black hole', removed *c.* 1853,[49] while the Independent chapel, the earliest nonconformist meeting in Swindon, was built in Newport Street in 1804.[50]

These three streets form three sides of a square of which the fourth, now called Devizes Road, was known as Short Hedge.[51] There were apparently no houses there in 1773,[52] and none on the west side in 1811;[53] by 1828 a few had been built on the east side

house, a brick building which stood at the corner of the road to the quarries, now Springfield Road.[56] Westward a lane to the quarries ran unfenced through Okus Great Field past a few cottages, while near the centre of the field stood the pest house which had been there since at least 1773.[57] The road through Wroughton to Beckhampton was turn-piked in 1761–2.[58]

From High Street southwards the present Marlborough Road was known as Lower Town. There were a few houses on it as far as its junction with the

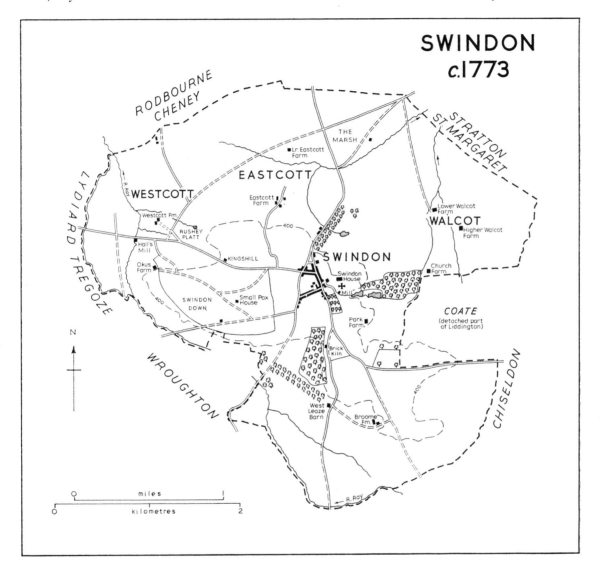

and one or two on the west,[54] and there were 12 houses there in 1841. Some still existed in 1964, such as no. 13 (Canford House), with a wrought iron porch, and nos. 15–16, 19–21, smaller houses. The date 1818 on a house in Britannia Place may indicate the first growth of this part of the town, although most houses there are later. This part of the town was also known as Horse Fair.[55] Southward from Short Hedge the road to Wroughton ran through open country, past the old parish work-

lane to the mill; one thatched house still survived in 1964. The 'Bell and Shoulder of Mutton', which was here in 1830,[59] was in 1964 housed in an elaborate brick building of the late 19th century. On to the south-east the road ran through country, which had long been inclosed, on its present course past Coate Water. The main way to Marlborough in 1773 was a road, now partly lost, running along Marlborough Lane and thence southwards down the western boundary of Chiseldon.[60] The southern part of

[49] Morris, op cit. 465–6; Jefferies, *Swindon*, 77–78.
[50] See p. 153.
[51] Morris, *Swindon*, 4.
[52] *Andrews and Dury, Map* (W.A.S. Rec. Brch.), pl. 15.
[53] W.R.O. Q. Sess. High Diversions, no. 37.
[54] O.S. Map 1″, sheet 34 (1828 edn.).

[55] Morris, *Swindon*, 311.
[56] Ibid. 81.
[57] *Andrews and Dury, Map* (W.A.S. Rec. Brch.), pl. 15.
[58] *V.C.H. Wilts.* iv. 262.
[59] Pigot, *Nat. Com. Dir.* (1830).
[60] See p. 6.

Swindon parish, the former manor of Broome, remained largely rural in 1964. Besides the farm-
house the only other houses in this neighbourhood
in 1841 were three or four labourers' cottages and
the house of the keeper of Coate reservoir.[61]

Immediately east of High Street stood the house
and park of the Goddards; early-19th-century gate
piers and stone walls still flank its approach from
High Street but its two single-storied lodges have
disappeared. The house, known as the Lawn by
1830, was demolished in 1952,[62] but the grounds,
stretching down the hill to the south and east, have
been retained as an open space. Adjoining the site of
the house on the south are the remains of the old parish
church.[63] In front of the churchyard was formerly a
pond, while a water-mill stood in the hollow below
until c. 1850.[64] Eastward from the park to the parish
boundary stretched the inclosed land belonging to
Church and Park Farms, both of which lay at the
edge of the park. Eastward from High Street and
Marlborough Road run three lanes; Mill Lane has a
stone lodge at its western end, and at the park end
three stone cottages with stone-tiled roofs and
hipped dormers, and one larger house of similar
design. The Planks leads from the Square to the site
of the Lawn, named no doubt from the flags which
paved it.[65] On its south side are the stables which
formerly belonged to the Lawn, a long stone range
dating from the 18th century, and on its north side
the former vicarage now converted to industrial
use.[66] Dammas Lane, a cul-de-sac, was so named
in 1684[67] and contained 19 houses in 1841; few are
left now. The Sanctuary is a small stone house of the
early 19th century; adjoining is the neo-Tudor house
called the Hermitage, described in 1848 as a pretty
residence[68] and since extended.

The chief road out of the town northwards was
Cricklade Street, or Brock Hill, continuing the line
of High Street. It was turnpiked in 1755–6,[69] but
even in the early 19th century it remained very
steep, rising at the top to the level of the high pavement behind which Christ Church now stands.
Extra horses were needed to bring up heavy loads.
At the bottom of the hill a stream ran across the
road and formed a water supply for that end of the
town.[70] In 1773 the road was lined with trees which
remained a feature of this way out of Swindon until
the present century.[71] Half way down, Brock Hill
was joined by Little London, or Back Lane, a
narrow lane running from the west end of Wood
Street. In 1964 it was largely a neglected backway;
almost the only house remaining was a thatched
cottage near the top end. This and Brock Hill were
in 1841 the poor quarter of the town; in Brock Hill
stood a common lodging house. Yet at the top on
the east side stands no. 42 Cricklade Street, built in
1729, the finest surviving 18th-century house in
Swindon. It was occupied by Robert Harding

(d. 1770) and then by 1773 by Thomas Vilett.[72]
The front is of five bays and two stories, of brick
with elaborate stone dressings, which include a
central doorway surmounted by a segmental pediment and flanked by pilasters, a Venetian window
above, grotesque masks on the keystones of the
other windows, and broad pilasters at the angles.
The whole is crowned by a wide dentil cornice and
a central pediment flanked by balustraded parapets.
Internally there is a contemporary staircase. Bow
windows on the side walls were added in c. 1800.

Northwards the Cricklade road ran through inclosed ground on its present course, now called
Drove Road. At the north end it crossed the Wilts.
and Berks. Canal at Swindon Wharf, where was the
house of the manager, 'a villa, surpassing the second
and approaching the first class' as Cobbett described
it in 1826.[73] Beyond the canal the road towards
Stratton St. Margaret turned off; it was turnpiked
in 1757–8.[74] East of the Cricklade road were only
the two farms at Walcot and one at Swindon Marsh.

The fields of Eastcott manor occupied much of the
lower ground to the north of the town. From the
town the hamlet of Eastcott was reached by a lane
which followed the course of Eastcott Road and
Eastcott Hill. Along this were scattered some twenty
cottages; six thatched cottages in two groups of three
stood on a bank on the side of the entrance to
Crombey Street.[75] Northwards the road ran between
high stone walls to a small open space on the site of
Regent Circus. On its east side were Upper Eastcott Farm and the manorial pound, and some ten or
a dozen other houses were scattered near at hand;
orchards occupied the area later covered by Regent
Place. Here the ways branched; northwards a lane
followed the course of the southern part of Princes
Street then wound round Cow Lane, now a back way
to the west. At the northern end of Cow Lane was a
swing bridge over the canal, beyond which an unfenced track led along the edges of fields to Lower
Eastcott Farm, on a site occupied in 1964 by the
omnibus depot.

North-westwards from Upper Eastcott another
track ran through fields on the course of Regent
Street, again crossing the canal by a swing bridge, to
the point now the crossing of Bridge and Fleet
streets. Here it met an ancient lane which ran south-
westward toward Rushey Platt. This track was in
existence and called 'le flet' in 1600;[76] it was hedged
for most of its length. Northwards from there a lane
to Rodbourne Cheney ran along the present Park
Lane and Rodbourne Road. Rushey Platt at the
western end of Fleetway was probably the area
called Rushmore in 1657.[77] It was one of the bogs
which the inhabitants called 'quaring gogs',[78] and
caused great difficulties when the Wilts. and Berks.
Canal was made across it.[79] Here were one or two
poor cottages and a turnpike-gate house; in the part

[61] Jefferies, *Swindon*, 54–57, and see p. 139.
[62] See p. 120. [63] See p. 147.
[64] See p. 131.
[65] Goddard and Dartnell, *Wilts. Words*, 119.
[66] See p. 146.
[67] W.R.O. 700, Deed, Heath to Thorne, 1684.
[68] *P. O. Dir. Wilts.* (1848).
[69] *V.C.H. Wilts.* iv. 260.
[70] Morris, *Swindon*, 225–6.
[71] *Andrews and Dury, Map* (W.A.S. Rec. Brch.), pl. 15;
Morris, *Swindon*, 225; Large, *Swindon Retrospect*, pl. opp.
p. 69.

[72] Morris, *Swindon*, 88; *Swindon Studies*, 162; *Andrews
and Dury, Map* (W.A.S. Rec. Brch.), pl. 15 and see pl.
facing p. 138.
[73] Morris, op. cit. 121–2.
[74] *V.C.H. Wilts.* iv. 270.
[75] Large, *Swindon Retrospect*, 14; for a photograph of a
thatched cottage on Eastcott Hill, see *Prim. Meth. Ch.
Souvenir Handbk.* (1910), 5.
[76] W.R.O. 2/3, Ct. proceedings manor of Nethercott.
[77] Morris, *Swindon*, 518.
[78] Britton, *Beauties of Wilts.* iii. 8.
[79] Morris, *Swindon*, 199.

Parish church of Holy Rood in 1850. Swindon House, later called the Lawn,
is seen on the left

Town Hall, Old Swindon, built in 1852 as a market-house with room above for public functions

SWINDON

of the parish north-west of Fleetway and the Wootton Bassett road were the farms at Westcott, and at North Laines, the site of which is now occupied by Horace Street, and a cottage near the parish boundary, whose site is included in the railway yards. South of the Wootton Bassett road stood a water-mill close to the 'Running Horse', with a few cottages adjoining, and southwards beyond the canal Okus Farm lay at the western end of Swindon Hill. Eastwards from Rushey Platt the road to Swindon ran up the steep Kingshill, past some half dozen cottages on the north side, to the western end of Wood Street. This way out of Swindon was turnpiked in 1757-8.[80]

The view of the town c. 1840 must be completed by mentioning its recent suburban growth. Apart from Croft House, a large villa just east of the Devizes road built by 1841, this was confined to the north-west of the town. By 1841 eleven middle-class houses stood in Bath Road, then commonly called the Sands. One house at least stood there in 1830,[81] probably Apsley House (now Swindon Museum), a plain stone house of three bays with a Greek Doric porch, banded rustication, and acroteria above the parapet. Further west nos. 8-14 Bath Road comprise one detached house and three double-fronted terrace houses of red brick, dating from c. 1835;[82] all have wide eaves and cast-iron trellis porches of intricate design. Opposite, on the south side of the road, were no houses, only a high stone wall and a belt of fir trees.[83] Just down the hill Prospect Place was also begun by 1830;[84] this was the area known in the mid 20th century as Prospect, where double-fronted stone houses remained. By 1841 there were 21 houses.

The railway made an impact on Swindon before it actually arrived. Thus in 1836, when three fields in Eastcott were offered for sale, the vendors pointed out that they were bounded by the proposed lines of the Great Western and Cheltenham and Great Western Union Railways, and added that since the important depot for the junction of the lines was 'not unlikely to be actually upon, and must at all events be very near this property, its future value was incalculable'.[85] The works were built on land which belonged to the Cheltenham Railway just north of the line, and opened in 1843.[86] Their history is traced elsewhere,[87] and can only be mentioned here as it affected the growth of a new town. In 1843 the establishment at the works was 423 men and by 1848 had risen to 1,800.[88] The company's decision to provide accommodation was acted upon immediately and in 1842 it was said that a scheme of about 300 houses was begun.[89] To save the company from capital expenditure the actual building of the cottages and of permanent station buildings was undertaken by Messrs. J. & C. Rigby of London who were to be compensated by the tenants' rents and

a 99-year lease of the profits of the refreshment room; a ten-minute stop at Swindon was compulsory until 1895, making the lease very profitable.[90] The station buildings were opened in July 1842 and still existed in 1964. They consist of two three-storied stone blocks, one on each side of the line, built in a plain Georgian style. The estate of houses is thought to have been designed by Sir Matthew Digby Wyatt, architect of Paddington Station.[91] It was laid out on a symmetrical plan about a central square originally called High Street, later Emlyn Square. In High Street provision was made for some half dozen shops.[92] From it ran four parallel streets on each side, the southernmost almost on the line of Fleetway, and the northernmost parallel to and facing the railway. They were named after stations on the line; the western ones were Bristol, Bath, Exeter, and Taunton Streets, and the eastern ones London, Oxford, Reading, and Faringdon Streets. Bath Street was changed to Bathampton Street c. 1902.[93] Along these streets were built the stone terraces which still remained in 1964.

Although the individual houses were cramped by modern standards, some having only one bedroom, the terraces were attractively designed and sturdily built of local stone.[94] In general the style still followed the Georgian tradition but the façades facing London Street and Bristol Street were embellished with small gables. Each house had a small front garden and a yard at the rear containing a wash-house and a privy; back alleys gave access to the yards. Facing Emlyn Square a few larger gabled houses, some incorporating ground-floor shops or public houses, accommodated the better-paid employees. In the 1850s similar houses were built in Church Place to mask the western end of the terraces. A block of houses which later included the G.W.R. hospital was also added across the south end of Emlyn Square.[95] Between London Street and the railway stood two large villas in extensive grounds for managers at the works. By 1885 their site had been taken into the works, as had the company's school at the western end of Bristol Street.[96] St. Mark's Church, opened in 1845, the adjoining vicarage, and a sports ground on the site of the Park, bought in 1844, completed the planned scheme.[97]

With the expansion of the works mentioned above, it could hardly be supposed that the original scheme as laid down in 1841 would be adequate to house the greatly increased number of employees. Indeed it is clear that in 1851 the G.W.R. estate was seriously overcrowded and many houses were subdivided.[98] These were ideal conditions for the speculative builder. The first considerable area of working-class housing was built on the line of Fleetway, and was known by its present names of Westcott Place and Westcott Street. Many of the long terraces of houses, which in 1964 still lined the

[80] V.C.H. Wilts. iv. 260.
[81] Pigot, Nat. Com. Dir. (1830).
[82] Swindon Studies, 163 and see pl. facing p. 117.
[83] Morris, Swindon, 248.
[84] Pigot, Nat. Com. Dir. (1830).
[85] Wilts. Gaz. 7 Apr. 1836.
[86] V.C.H. Wilts. iv. 207-8.
[87] Ibid. 207-19.   [88] Ibid. 208-9.
[89] Pigot, Nat. Com. Dir. (1842).
[90] The history of the lease is detailed in Swindon Studies, 120-2.

[91] Swindon Studies, 100. For description of housing see ibid. 167, 170. A painting in Swindon Museum shows a bird's-eye view of the lay-out in 1849.
[92] Kelly's Dir. Wilts. (1848).
[93] North Wilts. Dirs. (1901, 1902).
[94] See pl. facing p. 116.
[95] Neither group appears on the painting in Swindon Museum.
[96] Swindon Studies, 111, for schl. see p. 161.
[97] Ibid. 111, 120, for St. Mark's Ch. see p. 148.
[98] H.O. 107/1833.

north side of the eastern end of Westcott Place, must date from the mid 1840s,[99] while on the south side, which contains fewer houses of that period, are two inscribed 'Munn's Cottages 1846'. By 1850 the group of houses could be described as 'the modern village of Westcott'.[1] On the station side of the railway estate development was slower and more informal. In 1841 it was limited to one beerhouse standing on the western bank of the North Wilts. Canal where it went under the railway.[2] Seven years later a short row of buildings on both sides of the canal had grown up there, near what was later the north end of Bridge Street.[3] These were distinguished in 1851 as Sheppard's cottages, taking their name from the owner of the fields in which they stood. They included inns or beerhouses called the 'Old Locomotive', the 'Wholesome Barrel', and the Union Railway Inn.[4] At the station itself was the Queen's Arms Inn;[5] near the Wilts. and Berks. Canal were some buildings in a close called Little Medgbury, which included the terrace of 12 houses called Cetus Buildings, erected c. 1842, and also probably the Whale beerhouse.[6] By 1849 also a small group of houses had been built at the swing bridge where the lane from Upper Eastcott crossed the Wilts. and Berks. Canal; it included the Golden Lion Inn and several cottages adjoining. Another group lay facing the part of Fleetway later called Fleet Street. Here was the Locomotive Inn, a building which still survived in 1964, and a Baptist chapel, built in 1848, beside one or two other houses.[7] Finally, standing alone on the track up to Eastcott was a Primitive Methodist chapel opened in 1849; 'it was like building a chapel on some foreign land, scarcely a house was near, there was a road through the field but not a stone was to be seen upon it', a member later wrote about the present course of Regent Street.[8]

Three years later the 1851 census reveals little change in New Swindon, perhaps a reflection of a short but severe recession of business at the works c. 1848–50.[9] The town in 1851 consisted of Westcott Place and Street, the railway estate, and the groups of houses adjoining the station, the 'Golden Lion', the 'Locomotive', the 'Union Railway', and the 'Whale'. The only significant additions since 1848 were five houses then being built in Fleetway. Further south a number of houses were built on the hill up to the old town from Eastcott between 1841 and 1851; they were mostly for working people, and included a row of eleven houses called Tarrant's Villas.[10]

The 1851 census shows that there were some

dozen inns and beerhouses in New Swindon; it was true, as Jefferies said, that 'publicans discovered that steel filings make men quite as thirsty as hay dust'. But although he went on to point out the higher needs of the mechanics in meat, groceries, other comforts, and smart clothes,[11] yet shopkeepers were at first slower to take advantage of them. By 1851 the population of St. Mark's district, which included the whole new town and the hamlet of Eastcott, was 2,468 compared with 2,411 in the remainder of the parish, yet there were not more than a dozen shops to serve the larger population.[12] This lack led to the formation in 1853 of the New Swindon Improvement Company and the building of the Mechanics' Institute with an adjoining covered market in the middle of the railway estate.[13] Even with this, however, the old town remained the chief shopping centre for some years; a weekly shopping parade took the inhabitants of New Swindon up a steep and narrow footpath, across stiles and through fields and allotments, from the end of Regent Street to the Castle Inn in Prospect.[14]

The decade 1851–61 was one of expansion at the works.[15] The population of the new town grew by 1,478,[16] an increase of 67 per cent. The period saw further provision of housing by the G.W.R.; £5,000 was allotted for that purpose in 1853–4,[17] and it was probably at this time that the original layout was amended by the addition of houses facing Church Place and East Street. A company experiment which failed was the provision of accommodation for unmarried men in a large building 'upon the plan of French lodging houses, to have a common kitchen and common entrance, with a day and night porter'.[18] The 'Barracks', as it was called, still stood in 1964 towards the west end of Faringdon Road, a large stone building in a somewhat forbidding Gothic style. It was apparently under construction in 1849,[19] but not occupied by 1851.[20] By 1867 it was derelict,[21] and after many years of use as a Methodist chapel[22] it was in 1962 opened as a railway museum.

The most important private development in the new town in this period was the building of houses along the lane from Eastcott to the end of Fleetway, and so north to the Union Railway Inn. This is now the line of Regent and Bridge Streets, but until c. 1867 the whole street on both sides of the canal was called Bridge Street.[23] The fields through which the lane ran were called Culverys, or Upper and Lower Harris's Meads.[24] They were sold in lots in 1854,[25] and by 1861 the part south of the canal contained some 50 houses. Most were clearly built in

[99] Ibid.; *Swindon Studies*, 97; *Kelly's Dir. Wilts.* (1848).
[1] G. T. Clark, *Rep. to Bd. of Health on Swindon* (1851), 5 (copy in Swindon Pub. Libr.).
[2] H.O. 107/1179; W.R.O. Tithe Award.
[3] Painting in Swindon Museum; the original shows more detail than the reproduction in *Swindon Studies*, pl. opp. p. 113.
[4] H.O. 107/1833.
[5] *Kelly's Dir. Wilts.* (1848).
[6] W.R.O. 374/128, Sale Partic. 1854, which says they were erected 12 years before. The suggestion (*Swindon Studies*, 170) that Westcott Pl. and Cetus Bldgs. are earlier than the railway is wrong: H.O. 107/1179.
[7] Painting in Swindon Museum; W.R.O. 212A, section 36, Deed of 1853, which wrongly describes chap. as Methodist.
[8] *Prim. Meth. Ch. Souvenir Handbk.* (1910), 9.
[9] *V.C.H. Wilts.* iv. 210; D.E.C. Eversley, 'Swindon Works in the Great Depression', *Univ. Birmingham Hist. Jnl.* v. 172.

[10] H.O. 107/1833; W.R.O. 700, Deeds relating to Tarrant's property, with plan of 1874.
[11] Jefferies, *Swindon*, 63.
[12] H.O. 107/1833.
[13] See p. 142.
[14] Large, *Swindon Retrospect*, 22.
[15] See p. 129.
[16] *P.O. Dir. Wilts.* (1867).
[17] *Swindon Studies*, 151.
[18] Jefferies, *Swindon*, 63–64.
[19] Painting in Swindon Museum.
[20] H.O. 107/1833.
[21] Jefferies, *Swindon*, 64.
[22] See p. 155.
[23] Jefferies, *Swindon*, 64–65; the name Regent Street occurs in *Moore's Almanack Supp.* (1865), but not in New Swindon L.B. Min. Bks. until 1869.
[24] W.R.O. Tithe Award.
[25] W.R.O. 212A, section 36, Deed of 1853.

small terraces with names such as Hope Cottages, Crimea Cottages, Ebenezer Cottages, Alliance Terrace, Mount Pleasant, and Barnes's Cottages. York Place, that part of the north side of Regent Street which faces what became Regent Circus, was also built. On the corner, about on the site in 1964 of the Post Office, stood the house reckoned to be the manor-house of Eastcott.[26] In this part of Bridge Street also were the 'Rifleman's Arms', the 'Cross Keys', behind which was the Primitive Methodist chapel of 1849.[27] North of the canal were about 50 houses in Waterloo Terrace, Bellwood Place, Alma Terrace, and Albion Terrace; the last is commemorated in the name of the Albion Club. At the canal crossing the 'Golden Lion' gave its name to the swing bridge which crossed the canal there, while further north were the 'Jolly Sailor' and the 'Foresters' Arms'. Some buildings which must date from the development of this area still stood in 1964, much obscured by shop fronts. Running off the northern part of Bridge Street was Queen Street, laid out by 1855.[28] The part of Queen Street which adjoins Fleet Street was then known as Chapel Street, from the Methodist chapel nearby. By 1861 eight houses stood in Chapel Street, while in Queen Street apparently lay the 13 houses of Breeze's Buildings.[29] Connected with this growth was some building in what was beginning to be called Fleet Street. Here the low terrace opposite the 'Locomotive' is probably Fleetway Terrace, built by 1861,[30] and remembered as a row of private houses with neat gardens in front.[31] Some other building of the period survived, derelict in 1964, between John Street and the line of the North Wilts. Canal. This growth of the Bridge Street area, although notable, was still sporadic, and confined to what were only workmen's cottages and beerhouses; the street contained only four small shops, and ran from a farmyard at the Eastcott end past a brick-field and waste ground near the canal.[32]

At the western end of New Swindon a few houses had been added in Westcott Place; nos. 1–7 Falcon Terrace must be the western end of the long stone terrace of which the pedimented Falcon Inn forms the principal feature.[33] Adjoining, the 'Wild Deer' also existed by 1855.[34] The only other significant growth in the district had been in Eastcott Lane, probably in the stretch between the site of the entrance to North Street and the 'George'. The latter was built by 1861, while almost opposite, on the site of the gardens of the houses in Warwick Road, stood Hay Lane Cottages.[35] This terrace of single-storied timber-framed houses took its name from Hay Lane Wharf in Wroughton, where it was first put up for G.W.R. workmen employed there when the line was being built. When the need for it

ended it was apparently sold, and re-erected on this site.[36]

Between 1861 and 1871 the G.W.R. works continued to expand owing to the company's policy of concentration at Swindon.[37] By 1871 the population of New Swindon was 7,628,[38] an increase of 83 per cent over 1861. Many Welsh families had moved to the town to work in the rolling mills, and for their accommodation the stone-fronted terraces at Cambria Place were built c. 1864, and the small Welsh Baptist chapel there in 1866.[39] Other growth of the early 1860s took place in two areas. On a field called Road Ground immediately east of the G.W.R. estate three streets were laid out. At first they were reckoned as parts of London, Oxford, and Reading Streets, but in 1870 J. H. Sheppard, who had owned the field, asked that they should be called Sheppard, Harding, and John Streets after his names. In fact John Street was known from the beginning as Henry Street, probably because John Street south of Fleet Street was already so named. On Sheppard's estate might still be seen in 1964 some well-built brick houses with stone window surrounds and string courses, having prominent flat hoods on elaborately shaped brackets over the doors. A few similar houses still remained in the other estate built at this time. This consisted of three streets on the south-west side of Regent Street, called Cromwell Street, Brunel Street, and Havelock Street (the north-eastern part only).[40] Havelock Street originally consisted of a row of brick cottages standing in a field in which cattle pastured close to the front and back doors.[41] The three streets were adopted by the Local Board in 1867.[42] To these developments of the early 1860s should probably be added some houses on the east side of Cow Lane. A field here was bought by John Page in 1863, and on it he must have built Page Street, which is now the western part of Beckhampton Street, and perhaps some of the houses in what became Princes Street as well.[43]

Boards of Health for Old and New Swindon were set up in 1864[44] and their records provide a more accurate picture of the growth of Swindon than is possible earlier, since the boards had to grant permission for new building.[45] Apart from the addition of small numbers of houses to streets already existing, the earliest significant development in New Swindon which they reveal dates from 1868, when 19 houses were added to complete Falcon Terrace in Westcott. A larger scheme was begun in the following year by the newly-founded Swindon Permanent Building Society, which bought a field called Great Culvery on the north-east side of the North Wilts. Canal. Here were laid out streets called Gloucester, Cheltenham, and Wellington Streets, in which over 200

[26] Jefferies, Swindon, 64–65.
[27] R.G. 9/1272.
[28] W.R.O. 700, Deed of 1855, referring to land opposite the 'Golden Lion', and with plan showing Bridge Rd. and Queen St.
[29] Ibid.; W.R.O. 212A, section 36, sale particular, 1858; R.G. 9/1272; W.A.S. Libr., Devizes, Sale Cat. ix, no. 36; Swindon Pub. Libr., New Swindon L.B. Min. Bks. s.a. 1868 (Breeze's Bldgs.), 1871 (Queen St. alias Chapel St.).
[30] R.G. 9/1272.
[31] Large, Swindon Retrospect, 16.
[32] Ibid. 14–15.
[33] R.G. 9/1272.
[34] Moore's Dir. Swindon (1855).
[35] R.G. 9/1272.

[36] W. H. Hallam, 'Notes on Swindon Street Names', W.A.M. xlviii. 526; W.A.S. Libr., Devizes, Sale Cat. ix, no. 55; W.R.O. 700, Deeds of Tarrant's property, with plan 1874.
[37] See p. 129.   [38] P.O. Dir. Wilts. (1875).
[39] Swindon Studies, 146, 170, and see p. 157.
[40] Swindon Pub. Libr., New Swindon L.B. Min. Bks.
[41] Large, Swindon Retrospect, 15–16.
[42] Swindon Pub. Libr., New Swindon L.B. Min. Bks.
[43] W.A.S. Libr., Devizes, Sale Cat. vi, no. 26.
[44] See p. 135.
[45] Only a more detailed study than is possible here would be able to show whether all houses for which permission was obtained were actually built, but in general it seems safe to assume this.

houses had been built by the time they were adopted by the board in 1871.[46] A sale of lands in Eastcott in 1869 led to the development of two new areas;[47] both were on the way to Old Swindon, probably because of the convenience for its shops and for the pleasant aspect which the slope of the hill afforded. On a field south of Upper Eastcott Farm Henry Marrin and John King laid out Rolleston Street and Byron Street. On an adjoining field to the south again the Berkshire Estates Company laid out Dover Street, Western Street, North Street, Prospect Hill, and the western part of Cross Street. On these, houses were built intermittently for a number of years, and the estate was not fully complete in 1885.[48] Perhaps the chief public work of these years was the replacement of the old wooden swing bridge over the Wilts. and Berks. Canal at the 'Golden Lion', by an iron drawbridge more suitable to the greatly increased traffic. This had been advocated as early as 1854,[49] but was not accomplished until 1870. The establishment of the New Swindon Gas Company in 1863 with works near the canal off Queen Street may also be noticed.[50]

The 1870s saw Swindon little affected by the national depression of trade, and in fact the works expanded steadily. Each year the local directory recorded the addition or extension of shops, including new carriage shops, which replaced managerial villas and gardens between Bristol Street and the railway line at this time.[51] The villas were probably replaced by others which by 1880 stood north of the station,[52] on ground later itself taken into the works. Other industries began to appear at Swindon as will be shown below.[53] The rapid expansion of the town had given rise to a considerable building industry, and bricks were made in large works at several places on the fringes of the new town.[54] In 1867 Jefferies called New Swindon the Chicago of the western counties,[55] and it was indeed the late sixties and seventies that saw New Swindon change from a large working-class suburb into a town in its own right. Almost monthly the local board sanctioned the alteration of buildings in Bridge Street and Regent Street to provide for shops, and by 1880 New Swindon had outstripped the old town in the number of its tradespeople.[56] In 1881 it was almost four times as large as its neighbour, and with a population of 17,678 was the largest town in Wiltshire.[57]

It was in this decade that a factor appeared which exerted a decisive effect on the development of New Swindon for a generation to come. This was the fact that the extensive estates of the Vilett family, which had become the property of Colonel W. V. Rolleston,[58] were involved in a Chancery suit, and could only with difficulty be offered for building by the trustees.[59] They almost encircled New Swindon, for they included much of the land between Old Swindon and the railway bounded on the west by

Eastcott Hill and the lines of Princes and Corporation Streets, and another large area north of Westcott Place and east of the railway works. The most serious impediment to the expansion of the new town was a third area which extended from Faringdon Road across to Eastcott Hill and Rolleston Street. In these circumstances builders were. driven to lay out streets where they could find land, irrespective of its convenience. What was available on the east side of the town was taken up early in the decade. Near the station Haydon Street and Mill Street (now the west end of Manchester Road) were laid out by Merrin and King in a field called Great Breach, and adjoining it on the south the Oxford Building Society squeezed Carfax, Oriel, Merton, and Turl Streets into a small and awkwardly shaped field called Briery Close. Slightly to the east Gooch Street and the northern part of Gladstone Street were laid out in a field called Martins, and the Trowbridge Building Society built a road adjoining Cetus Buildings in a narrow field near the canal called Medgbury. All these streets were considerably built up by 1875. It was probably the following year which saw the building of Princes Street between the end of Regent Place and the canal, thus reducing Cow Lane to a backway. Many of the houses, said to be in Cow Lane at this time, must be the brick terraces, which in 1964 still faced parts of Princes Street. Regent Place, demolished by 1964, may also have belonged to this period.

To the west of the town one small part of the Rolleston estate was built over by the United Kingdom Land and Building Association in the early 1870s; it included Catherine, Vilett, and Carr Streets, the east side of Farnsby Street, and the buildings on the south side of that stretch of Faringdon Road.[60] In the centre of the town small pieces of land were used. Holbrook Street, off Bridge Street, was mostly built in 1872, and College Street, Sanford Street, and Edgware Road are slightly later. In 1871 a terrace of 15 houses was put up on a narrow strip of ground between King Street and the canal. In Eastcott, Swindon Street was added to the estate at Prospect in 1878, and Carlton Street, off Wellington Street, is of about the same time. Carlton and Carfax Streets still preserved in 1964 the shape of the orchard of Lower Eastcott Farm which lay between them.

For larger schemes builders had to look further afield. Beyond the Vilett estate lay the Kingshill estate of J. H. Sheppard which first came into the market in 1870. On a large field called Gilbert's Hill two roads called Dixon and Stafford Streets were laid out, and the land adjoining them offered in plots in 1873. Further sales followed in 1877 and 1881,[61] but the estate was for some reason not popular, for the streets were only thinly built in 1885.[62] Perhaps the reserve price on the plots was high, for houses

---

[46] *Dore's Swindon Almanack* (1871); W.R.O. 700, plan of building land.

[47] W.R.O. 374/130.

[48] O.S. Map 1/2,500, Wilts. XV. 8 (1st edn.). In Swindon building societies usually laid out the streets and then offered plots of land, which were taken by individuals, singly, or by builders, usually in fairly small numbers. The effect of this can be seen in the town.

[49] *Swindon Advertiser*, Supp. 5 Feb. 1904; see also Jefferies, *Swindon*, 65.

[50] *Dore's Swindon Almanack* (1864).

[51] *V.C.H. Wilts.* iv. 214; *G.W.R. Mag.* xxvi. 152–5.

[52] O.S. Map 1/2,500 Wilts. XV. 4 (1st edn. 1879); *Kelly's Dir. Wilts.* (1880).

[53] See p. 130. [54] *Kelly's Dir. Wilts.* (1875).

[55] Jefferies, *Swindon*, 65.

[56] *Kelly's Dir. Wilts.* (1880).

[57] *V.C.H. Wilts.* iv. 358.

[58] *W.A.M.* xlii. 84; see p. 113.

[59] *North Wilts. Dir.* (1879).

[60] *Kelly's Dir. Wilts.* (1885).

[61] W.A.S. Libr., Devizes, Sale Cats. v, no. 24, ix, nos. 19–20.

[62] O.S. Map 1/2,500, Wilts. XV. 8 (1st edn. 1879).

here were more expensive than in most parts of New Swindon, and included some semi-detached 'villas'. The more westerly part of Sheppard's estate was also offered in 1870 and again in 1875, the largest part of it in one lot of 28 a. The auctioneer, pointing out the extensive prospect, remarked that 'the fortunate purchaser who may desire to exchange the busy scenes and anxieties of commercial life for the more agreeable pursuits of agriculture may find here an opportunity of exercising his taste and judgement in the erection of a suitable residence commensurate with his views'.[63] This idyllic future was not to be realized, for between 1877 and 1880 some 300 houses were built on parts of the estate, forming the eastern parts of Albion and William Streets, Redcross Street (changed to Radnor Street in 1881), Clifton and Exmouth Streets. One field became the cemetery, opened in 1881.[64] Another field adjoining Kingshill, sold separately, attracted some terrace builders to the main road there, but the most ambitious scheme on the Sheppard estate proved a failure. This was an elaborate layout of large villas in extensive grounds on the Down Field and Quarry Close, a site later occupied by Ashford and Hythe Roads; although the lots were offered in 1870 and 1875,[65] the whole was still vacant in 1885,[66] perhaps because of the stipulation that the houses to be built had to be of the villa type.

It was in the seventies also that New Swindon began to grow north of the railway. Development here was prompted no doubt partly by shortage of building land near the works, but also by the wish to avoid paying the heavier rates in the local board district. The beginning of a working-class suburb at Even Swindon in the parish of Rodbourne Cheney belongs to the period 1870–5 following sales of lands there in 1870 and 1871.[67] In 1874 some houses there were connected to the New Swindon sewers, and had to pay a special rate in consequence. They no doubt lay in William (now Manton), Charles, Thomas, and Henry (now Hawkins) Streets, east of Rodbourne Lane, and Percy and Morris Streets opposite. The extra rating presumably made it of little consequence whether the houses were inside or outside the district boundary and the next streets were built within it. They were Jennings, Linslade, and Guppy Streets, accepted by the board in 1875. To the east the history of Gorse Hill, then in Stratton St. Margaret, is similar. Where once had only been one or two houses and a public house called the 'Tabernacle',[68] grew up Avening, Chapel, Hinton, and Bright Streets, and long terraces on the west side of the Cricklade road. Both districts were taken into the local board area for public health purposes in 1880.[69]

The lack of bridges over the two canals caused great inconvenience; the Golden Lion drawbridge frequently made men late for work when it was up,[70] and in 1877 a fixed foot-bridge of the type used on railways was placed beside it by public subscription. A year later the local board gave £200 towards building a drawbridge in Fleet Street to avoid the

detours to the old fixed bridges in Sheppard Street (Union or Bullen's Bridge), and John Street (Stone Bridge). The board was, however, unwilling to help in a scheme to provide a road across part of the Rolleston estate from the end of Regent Street to Old Swindon. In spite of this the road was laid out in 1875 on the course of Victoria Road from Cannon Street to Byron Street; it became the common pedestrian way between the towns, and the old footpath to Prospect was closed.[71] The New Swindon board again refused to have anything to do with the scheme in 1884.

Between 1878 and 1887 the G.W.R. works suffered a severe depression and construction of new shops ended. Between 1881 and 1891 the population of New Swindon increased by 9,617 to 27,295. The increase was, however, largely due to transfers to the parish of parts of neighbouring parishes. In 1884 Coate, a detached part of Liddington, was added, and in 1890 Even Swindon and Gorse Hill. The populations of the last two amounted to over 6,000,[72] so that the real increase over the period was comparatively small. In such circumstances building was bound to slacken off, although fair numbers of houses were added to streets already begun, chiefly in the Kingshill and Even Swindon areas. Yet the western parts of Albion and William Streets, marked out by 1880,[73] had no houses in them five years later. Ashford Street and Hythe Road were also laid out but without houses in 1885.[74] During this pause in the expansion of New Swindon the building trade in the town was kept busy by the provision of five schools for the newly-formed school board between 1877 and 1885, St. Paul's Church in 1881, St. John's in 1883, and, among other nonconformist chapels, with which the town had always been prolific, the monumental Baptist building at the top of Regent Street in 1886.[75]

Meanwhile the most immediate bar to the further progress of the town was removed when the Rolleston estate came into the market for building in 1885.[76] The beginning of the west side of Farnsby Street in the following year[77] marked the start of a building boom such as Swindon had not yet seen. Between then and 1901 the whole of the centre part of the Rolleston estate, stretching from Faringdon Road and Cambria Bridge Road across the fields to the top end of Regent Street in the east and the back of Dixon Street in the south, was covered with streets of closely-built brick terraces. Such terraces had always been the staple product of New Swindon builders. Even Commercial Road, the axis of the whole scheme, contains only two-storied dwelling-houses which in 1964 had been variously adapted as shops and offices. At its western end a market house was built in 1892, and it is said that it was intended to replace Regent Street as the chief shopping centre of the town.[78] Only in its northern extension, Milton Road, can be seen more pretentious buildings of three stories, but in general the layout of the whole estate is that of a working-class suburb. At the eastern end of the estate the top of

[63] W.A.S. Libr., Devizes, Sale Cat. v, nos. 31–32.
[64] Kelly's Dir. Wilts. (1885).
[65] W.A.S. Libr., Devizes, Sale Cat. v, nos. 31–32.
[66] O.S. Map 1/2500, Wilts. XV. 8 (1st edn. 1879).
[67] Large, Swindon Retrospect, 19–20; W.R.O. 374/130.
[68] Large, op. cit. 19.
[69] See p. 138.
[70] Swindon Advertiser, Supp. 5 Feb. 1904.

[71] North Wilts. Dir. (1887).
[72] V.C.H. Wilts. iv. 358.
[73] W.A.S. Libr., Devizes, Sale Cat. ix, no. 29.
[74] O.S. Map 1/2,500, Wilts. XV. 8 (1st edn. 1879).
[75] See pp. 159, 149, 157.
[76] North Wilts. Dir. (1885).
[77] Ibid. (1886).
[78] W.A.M. xlviii. 524.

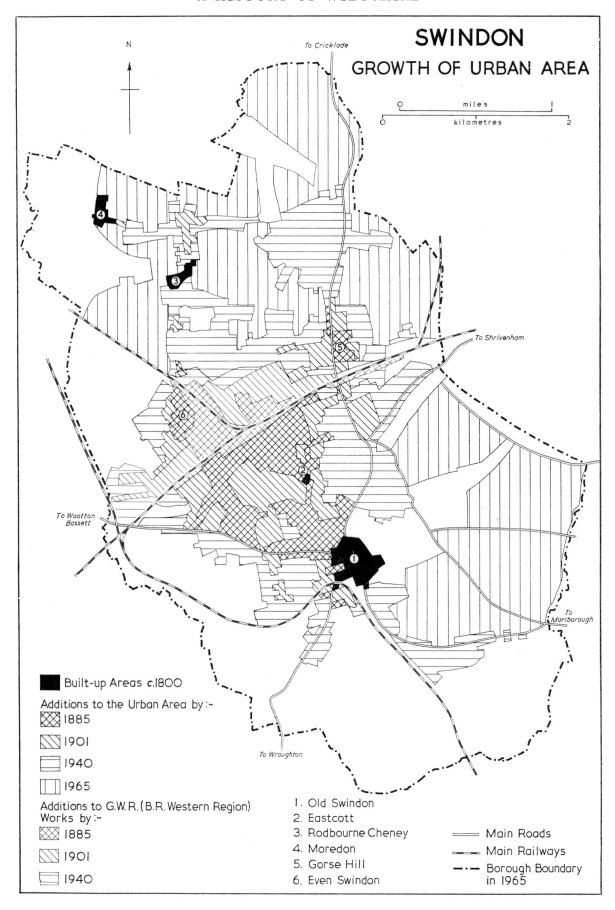

SWINDON

GROWTH OF URBAN AREA

To Cricklade

To Shrivenham

To Wootton Bassett

To Marlborough

To Wroughton

Built-up Areas c.1800

Additions to the Urban Area by :-
1885
1901
1940
1965

Additions to G.W.R.(B.R.Western Region)
Works by :-
1885
1901
1940

1. Old Swindon
2. Eastcott
3. Rodbourne Cheney
4. Moredon
5. Gorse Hill
6. Even Swindon

Main Roads
Main Railways
Borough Boundary
  in 1965

Regent Street was remodelled to form the small square known as Regent Circus, an idea proposed as early as 1883 and carried out in 1888–9. In the centre of it the local board built its offices, later known as the Town Hall. Surprisingly no opportunity was taken to line Regent Circus with large blocks of shops or offices. In the very centre of the town and facing its principal building several brick villas were built, some of which survived in 1964 and were used as offices. Nearby in Regent Street, another villa of the same period adjoining the 'Rifleman's Arms' was still in 1964 occupied as a private house.

The growth of the town in the 1890s was by no means confined to the area just described. The new road, called Victoria Road, was made up in 1888, and considerably built up by 1899. Hunt Street ran out of it to the bottom of Belle Vue Road; in it are elaborate brick terraces dated 1895 bearing the initials of Thomas Turner, a brickmaker, who also built several villas near his works in Drove Road. His name is perpetuated in Turner Street, off Westcott Place. The estate containing Ashford, Kent, Hythe, Maidstone, and Folkstone Roads was almost complete by 1899, as were the older streets north of Kingshill. North of Westcott Place the area between Dean and Birch Streets was built on part of the Rolleston estate,[79] while north of the railway Redcliffe Street was built and additions made to other streets west of Rodbourne Road. To the east of the railway works the Eastcott Lodge estate took its name from a house built c. 1860 in a field north of the station.[80] The land fronting Ferndale Road was for sale in plots as part of the Gorse Hill Farm estate by 1895,[81] and by 1900 both that road and Florence, Whiteman, Poulton, and Beatrice Streets were considerably built along. South of the railway the farm track from the Whale Bridge past Lower Eastcott Farm had been made into Corporation Street, and east of it several streets were begun, stretching from Elmina Road to Manchester Road, partly built, and so to Volta Road. The period of expansion between 1885 and 1900 was not confined to dwelling houses; the amenities of the town were increased in the same period by a new church of St. Barnabas at Gorse Hill, the town hall and market house mentioned above, general and isolation hospitals, a theatre, new baths, a recreation ground at Rodbourne, a sports ground at the County Ground, electric lighting, and a municipal water works.

The development of Old Swindon in the 60 years after the coming of the railway may be traced more briefly. In 1841 the population of the whole parish was 2,459, but this figure included 500 navvies employed on the railway. Fifty years later the old town district contained 5,545 inhabitants.[82] Although the growth was clearly to be traced to the coming of the railway, its impetus was not solely derived from the rise of New Swindon. The inhabitants of the new town long continued to rely on the old for shopping, but the influence of Old Swindon spread much

wider before it was engulfed in the growing suburb below. The days when Swindon people went to Wootton Bassett to buy groceries[83] had gone; the cattle market flourished, and when in 1867 Jefferies wrote that Swindon had become the emporium of North Wiltshire and the neighbouring counties,[84] and another writer said that its shops were equal to those of Bath or Cheltenham,[85] it was the old town that they meant. The influence of this period of unexampled prosperity can clearly be seen in its streets, where buildings of the middle decades of the 19th century outnumber earlier ones. In 1878 it was said that within a decade almost every place of business in the town had been rebuilt, enlarged, or improved.[86] In High Street nos. 10–14 formed the street frontage of the North Wilts. Brewery.[87] Nos. 9–11, 14, 24–26, and the 'Bell' frontage all appear to be of c. 1850–70. Other work of this time may be seen in Newport Street in the Railway Hotel, and the premises of Messrs. Rentaset, and in Wood Street in no. 7, the 'Cross Keys', and the National Provincial Bank. Wood Street also contains the most striking Victorian frontage in Swindon, that of the 'King's Arms', which is a three-storied building of red brick with stone dressings; it has windows with stilted arches and gothic shafts, a projecting central chimney supported at first-floor level on similar shafts, the royal arms in bold relief, and four gables containing carved roundels. Another impressive building, slightly earlier, is the corn warehouse of John Toomer at the corner of the Square, a four-storied brick building with wide eaves supported by shaped brackets.

The same period gave Old Swindon its chief public buildings. Christ Church replaced the small old parish church in 1851.[88] About the same time an assembly room used for public business was added to the 'Goddard Arms'.[89] Three years later a market house was built on the south side of the Square and the corn exchange adjoining was opened in 1866.[90] Swindon's first police station, built in 1852–3 in Devizes Road, was replaced by the present one in Eastcott Hill in 1873.[91] In 1872 the idea of making Old Swindon a railway town itself was mooted by the promoters of a line to Marlborough and Andover. After many delays the line to Marlborough was opened in 1881 with a station in the old town just south of Newport Street. The line was joined to the G.W.R. at Rushey Platt in the following year, and completed to Andover in 1883.[92] It was closed to passenger traffic in 1961.[93]

But although Old Swindon, with its market, shops, and banks, retained a certain commercial pre-eminence over the new town for many years, its growth was paradoxically connected with its position as a suburb of New Swindon. Something of the atmosphere of the genteel little town which John Britton described in 1814 has always clung to Old Swindon,[94] and made it socially acceptable as a dwelling place. In 1850 it was said that what houses had been built were of a superior class, and that the

[79] W.A.S. Libr., Devizes, Sale Cat. iii, no. 53, from which the dates of many streets on the Rolleston estate can be deduced.
[80] Ibid. Sale Cat. vi, no. 26.
[81] W.R.O. 700, Deeds of 1895 and 1897.
[82] V.C.H. Wilts. iv. 320, 358.
[83] Large, Swindon Retrospect, 107.
[84] Jefferies, Swindon, 62.
[85] Kelly's Dir. Wilts. (1867).

[86] North Wilts. Dir. (1878).
[87] Dore's Swindon Almanack (1871).   [88] See p. 144.
[89] Kelly's Dir. Wilts. (1867).
[90] See p. 132.
[91] Morris, Swindon, 465–6.
[92] V.C.H. Wilts. iv. 289.
[93] County of Wiltshire Development Plan, Swindon Central Area, 1962, 30.
[94] See e.g. John Betjeman in Swindon Studies, 171, 174.

tenants, more or less connected with the railway were a 'well-behaved and intelligent class of persons'.[95] It has been pointed out above that even before the coming of the G.W.R., Old Swindon had begun to spread slightly to the north-west. This continued to be the principal direction of growth, no doubt because land was more easily available there, the park and farms of the Goddards preventing growth on the other sides. By 1851 Bath Terrace, facing the end of Victoria Street, and Bath Buildings, on the west of the north part of Devizes Road, had been built.[96] On the opposite side of Devizes Road, most of the twenty humble cottages of Britannia Place, which were described as new-built in 1850,[97] remained in 1964, and a small terrace of stone houses on the same side may have been built then too. To the north two new streets had been built on a small field west of Little London: Albert Street, which still contains a few of its original small stone terrace houses, and Victoria Street, now the southernmost part of Victoria Road, which was the home of prosperous tradesmen and professional men.[98] Most of the long stone terrace on its east side still remained in 1964. A plaque on one of the houses records that Richard Jefferies lived here for one year. At the bottom of these streets Union Row was built, and a number of houses had been built in Prospect. Here may be seen a terrace of three houses surmounted by a large segmental pediment,[99] no doubt built by 1851. Another addition of the same period, which still remains, is the pair of suburban houses near the park entrance in Drove Road, still inscribed with their original names, Rose Cottage and Woodbine Cottage.[1]

The chief growth of the 1850s took place in the same direction. In 1852 land called the Orchard at the bottom of Victoria Street was sold,[2] and the extension of Victoria Street northwards was probably begun soon after. Adjoining it on the east another field was sold in 1854, and let in over 120 building plots.[3] On it Belle Vue Road was laid out and partly built by 1861;[4] by then it included Belle Vue Villas, a few Italianate houses still remaining in the lower part of the road. Mostly, however, the road contains terrace houses of varying design, some with flat hoods over the doors. Some larger houses probably of the 1850s remain in Devizes Road, where there are two pairs of stone villas on the east side, and in Bath Road, near the corner of the Avenue.[5] In the 1860s more houses were built in Bath Road, and north of it Lansdown Road and King William Street were laid out.[6] In the same decade Belle Vue Road and the northern part of Victoria Street were largely built upon. Union Street, leading off Victoria Street, was begun c. 1865, while South Street is slightly later. A curious feature of the 1860s was the building of a few working class terraces on waste ground near the quarries; some may still be seen in Quarry Road, but Trout's Folly, an insanitary group which caused the local board

much trouble in the 1870s has disappeared.[7] It stood near the site of the bowling green in the Town Gardens.[8]

In the later 1870s and early 1880s the growth of Old Swindon northward was prevented by the Rolleston and Sheppard estates, whose history has been described above, while the Goddard family still declined to have its land built upon. Only along Bath Road was there much building, mainly of villas and terraces of large houses.[9] It did, however, share in the building boom of the end of the century; Avenue Road was begun in 1890,[10] while Ripley and Lethbridge Roads are of about the same time. By 1900 Goddard Avenue, St. Margaret's Road, and Winifred Road were laid out and partly built, and building had just begun on Okus and Westlecott Roads.[11]

By the end of the 19th century the two towns had virtually merged and their physical junction was acknowledged in 1900 by the incorporation of the whole town into one municipal borough, whose population the following year was 45,006.[12] From that time until the end of the Second World War the town's population slowly increased. There is new building of the years before 1914 in many parts of the town. West of Old Swindon the chief growth was along Westlecott Road and Belmont Crescent, and in the northern part of the Mall and Okus Road. Much of Kingshill Road belongs to this period. Vacant places in older areas were filled up. Between Corporation Street and what was now called County Road the whole of the remaining space was built over, and encroachments were made on the area south of the canal with Newcastle, Plymouth, and Portsmouth Streets and York Road. Not far away Euclid Street and several nearby streets were begun. North of the railway the settlements at Even Swindon and Gorse Hill were extended, especially in the Ferndale Road area. The final abandonment of the Wilts. and Berks. Canal in 1914 quite soon resulted in a noticeable change in the appearance of the centre of the town, for the canal was drained and filled in although its course remained clearly visible in 1964.[13]

In the period between the two World Wars the chief expansion of the town was to the north. The large corporation housing scheme at Pinehurst was planned by Sir Raymond Unwin just after 1918, while to the west the 1920s saw the beginning of Rodbourne Cheney as a residential suburb. In 1928 the borough boundary was extended to take in the parts of Stratton St. Margaret and Rodbourne Cheney in which the new housing lay and at the same time small parts of Chiseldon, Wroughton, Lydiard Tregoze, and Lydiard Millicent were added to Swindon. With the transfer of the land in Chiseldon the whole of Coate Water was brought within the borough boundary.[14] In the 1920s the remaining area west of Drove Road was built, and

[95] G. T. Clark, *Rep. to Bd. of Health on Swindon* (1851), 5 (Copy in Swindon Pub. Libr.).
[96] H.O. 107/1833.
[97] Clark, op. cit. 11; the date 1849 is traditionally remembered: ex inf. Mrs. Ada F. Tanner.
[98] H.O. 107/1833.
[99] Pevsner, *Wilts.* (Bldgs. of Eng.), 457.
[1] H.O. 107/1833.
[2] W.A.S. Libr. Devizes, Sale Cat. ix, no. 21.
[3] W.R.O. 293, Sale, 1854.

[4] R.G. 9/1271.   [5] Ibid.
[6] W.R.O. 374/130, sale particular, 1868.
[7] Swindon Pub. Libr., Old Swindon L.B. Min. Bks.
[8] O.S. Map 1/2,500, Wilts. XV. 8 (1st edn. 1879).
[9] *North Wilts. Dirs.* (1878, 1879); W.R.O. 374/130, sale of 5 houses in Brunswick Terrace, 'newly built', 1879.
[10] *North Wilts. Dir.* (1890).
[11] O.S. Map 1/2,500, Wilts XV. 8 (2nd edn.).
[12] *V.C.H. Wilts.* iv. 358.   [13] *Swindon Studies*, 138.
[14] *V.C.H. Wilts.* iv. 358, and see p. 6.

A terrace in Emlyn Square on the railway estate, built *c.* 1842. The former lodging-house, built *c.* 1850 and called the 'Barracks', is on the left

Railway estate from Emlyn Square, showing the 'Barracks' and in the foreground one of the larger houses

SWINDON

Terrace in Bath Road, *c.* 1835

House in Bath Road, *c.* 1860

SWINDON

there was much ribbon development here and along Shrivenham, Marlborough, and Croft Roads. The 1930s saw estates of private houses grow in five main areas. At Rodbourne Cheney, Churchward Avenue, Northern Road, and associated roads were built. Off Cricklade Road areas around Headlands Grove and Malvern Road were developed. East of Drove Road the fields of Walcot were first encroached upon by the building of Burford Avenue, Walcot Road, and several other roads. Off Marlborough Road the estate south of the Lawn was built and finally some roads were laid out south of Kingshill Road. This extension of the town accommodated a population growth from 54,920 in 1921 to about 61,000 in 1939.[15]

After the Second World War besides a general shortage of housing due to war-time restrictions, houses were needed for the workers in industries which had moved to Swindon during the war, and also for workers in the new industries it was hoped would come to the town.[16] In 1952 the need to build became even greater when Swindon was approved as one of the towns to be expanded for the reception of population and industry from the Greater London area.[17] It was estimated that, as a result, housing for some additional 26,000 people would be required, all, at first, to be built within the borough boundary.[18]

To meet the immediate post-war needs some temporary houses were added to the corporation's only housing estate at Pinehurst, but this had been virtually completed in 1925.[19] Beech Avenue, leading from Pinehurst to Rodbourne Green, and some associated roads, were also built up with council houses in the first years after the war. In 1948, however, the corporation bought farms at Rodbourne Cheney and Moredon,[20] in the north-west corner of the borough, and on this land a new estate of some 1,685 houses and 12 shops was built. Post-war shortages of labour and materials are reflected in some of the houses where non-traditional materials and methods of construction were employed. Extensive use was made of the Easiform House, designed and erected by Messrs. John Laing & Son, Ltd. and of the Airey House, both built substantially of concrete. Schools for the new estate were opened between 1952 and 1955, but by 1951 almost all the land available for housing in this area had been used.

In 1951 the corporation acquired 250 a. for another housing estate by the purchase of Penhill Farm, which lay in Stratton St. Margaret just outside the borough boundary.[21] Next year the boundary was extended northwards somewhat to bring all the land acquired within the borough.[22] At Penhill use was also made of several types of partially pre-fabricated houses, but more variety was introduced than on the Moredon Estate and

as an experiment part of the Penhill Estate was laid out on Radburn lines. A small community hall, a branch library, and a parade of shops in Penhill Drive were designed to provide a focal point for the estate. St. Peter's Church nearby was consecrated in 1956 and the Free Church, built by the Congregationalists in 1959, also lies in Penhill Drive. By 1965 there were just over 2,000 dwellings, including three multi-story blocks of flats, on the Penhill estate, which occupied the whole of the northern tip of the borough. Schools for the estate were opened between 1955 and 1963.

As soon as Swindon became a receiving district for overspill population from London in 1952, over 1,000 a. were acquired by the corporation for the next big housing development.[23] This land was made up almost entirely of the farmlands of the Goddard estate, namely of Upper and Lower Walcot Farms, and of Park, Church, Manor, Coate, and Prince's Farms.[24] On it between c. 1954 and c. 1960 nearly 1,500 dwellings were built. While negotiations for the land were proceeding some houses for overspill population were built on the newly developed Penhill estate. But as soon as negotiations were complete building began on a new estate which was to be called Walcot East. It was built by the corporation with a residential density of 45 persons to the acre.[25] The need to build quickly and cheaply, which was felt when this estate was being developed, can be detected in the appearance of some of its houses and its lay-out. Walcot East has been criticized for its small houses in long, somewhat monotonous terraces and for its 'overwide avenues and aimless closes'.[26] Later, however, greater variety was introduced and improvements in design were achieved where local architects were employed. A block of flats for more prosperous tenants was included on this estate, but this experiment was not repeated on other Swindon housing estates. Building began at about the same time on the Walcot West estate which is separated from Walcot East by the Queen's Drive dual carriage-way (see below). Much of Walcot West was developed by private enterprise with a residential density of 35 to the acre.[27]

The Walcot estates were the first in Swindon to have fully developed neighbourhood centres. Sussex Square, designed by the borough architect, is a paved and arcaded shopping precinct, containing 14 shops with maisonettes above.[28] A community hall and a branch library adjoin the precinct, and nearby are a petrol station and public house, built by private enterprise. Sussex Square, opened in 1958, won a Civic Trust award.[29] In its centre stands a Sarsen stone, 8 ft. in height, which was found on the site. The church of St. Andrew, built in 1958, lies a little to the north-east of the square, but can be plainly seen from it. The Walcot schools were opened between 1957 and 1959.

[15] Ibid.; *Planning for Swindon*, 3, 21.
[16] Except where otherwise stated, information about the development of Swindon since 1945 is from material supplied by the Borough Planning and Borough Architect's offices.
[17] *Wilts. Development Plan, Swindon Central Area, 1962*, 2.
[18] *Wilts. County Council Development Plan for Swindon, 1952*, 11.
[19] *Local Government is our Business*, Handbk. issued by N.A.L.G.O. (1960), 35.
[20] Ibid.   [21] Ibid.

[22] Swindon Corp. Act, 14 & 15 Geo. VI, c. 40 (local and personal act).
[23] Wilts. Pamphlets, 3, *The Expansion Area, Handbk. for Members of the Council; Wilts. Development Plan for Swindon, 1952*, 23.
[24] Ex inf. the Town Clerk.
[25] *Wilts. Development Plan for Swindon, 1952*, 21.
[26] *Architectural Review*, cxxxiv. 365; *Sunday Times* (colour supp.), 24 Mar. 1964.
[27] *Wilts. Development Plan for Swindon, 1952*, 21.
[28] *Evening Advertiser*, 1 Oct. 1958.
[29] *Swindon Guide* (1960) and see pl. facing p. 148.

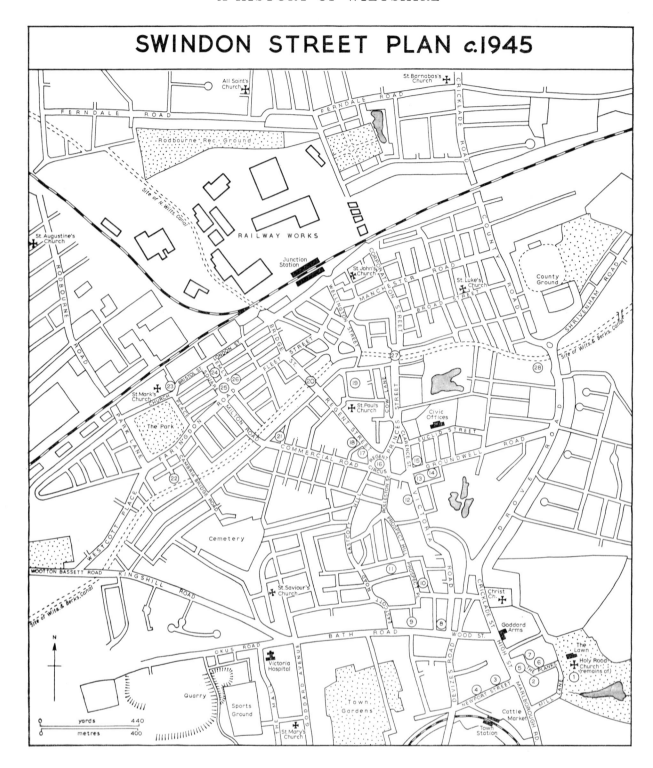

SWINDON STREET PLAN c.1945

1. Site of Mill
2. Site of Methodist Ch.
3. Site of Independent Ch.
4. Site of Free Sch.
5. Former Corn Exch. and Town Hall
6. Former Vicarage Ho.
7. Former Rectory Ho.
8. Former Congreg. Ch.
9. Methodist Ch.
10. Methodist Ch.
11. Baptist Ch., South St.
12. The College, formerly Swindon and N. Wilts. Tech. Inst.
13. Trinity Presbyt. Ch.
14. Holy Rood R. C. Ch.
15. Empire Theatre
16. Town Hall
17. Tabernacle Baptist Ch.
18. Methodist Ch.
19. Congreg. Ch., Sanford St.
20. Golden Lion Bridge
21. Covered Market
22. Baptist Ch., Cambria Pl.
23. Site of G.W.R. Sch.
24. Mechanics' Inst.
25. G.W.R. Hosp.
26. The 'Barracks'
27. Whale Bridge
28. Site of Wharf

Besides the land in Walcot West, an area, known as the Lawn, lying between the Marlborough road and Queen's Drive, was handed over by the corporation for private development. Here in the 1950s and early 1960s such roads as Sandringham Road and Windsor Road were built up with houses for private ownership.

Shortly after work on the Walcot East estate was begun, building began on the remaining land to the south-east, which was to take Swindon's housing development right up to the borough's eastern boundary. Here two estates, Park North and Park South, were laid out. They are divided from one another by Whitbourne Avenue and on them 3,670 dwellings, including three multi-story blocks of flats, were built by the corporation. Park neighbourhood centre, designed by Frederick Gibberd, provides a shopping precinct for both estates, and also a community hall and a branch library. The precinct was designed to give an effect of a tightly built-up urban core.[30] The Reuben George Hall, opened within the precinct, in 1956, provides a hall for social activities. The church of St. John the Baptist, built in 1957, faces the precinct, and schools for the Park estates were opened in 1959 and 1960.

While the Penhill estate was being developed on the north side of the town early in the 1950s, an industrial estate was being created on 75 a. of land acquired by the corporation between 1949 and 1951 in the Rodbourne Cheney district to the west. On this site between 1955 and 1964 some 20 factories and warehouses were built, either by the corporation or by the firms concerned.[31]

Since a large part of Swindon's population was to live on the estates lying to the east of Drove Road and the old town, a new direct traffic route to the centre of the town and beyond to the industries on its western side became necessary. This was provided in part by the opening in 1953 of Queen's Drive, a dual carriage-way, running between Marlborough road and Shrivenham and County Roads, and forming also an eastern by-pass for both the old and the new towns.

With the plan for the full development of the Park estates virtually all land within the borough's boundaries available for large-scale housing schemes was used up. In 1961 the corporation was authorized to develop farm-land to the east of the boundary lying in the parishes of Stratton St. Margaret, Wanborough, Liddington, and Chiseldon.[32] About 90 a. of this were allotted for industrial development and the rest was to be used for housing. In 1965 work on two housing estates, Covingham and Nythe, developed by the corporation and private enterprise respectively, was well advanced and the Greenbridge and Nythe industrial estates had advanced commensurately. But since they all lie outside the borough boundary, any further account of them is reserved for treatment with the parishes in which they are situated.

As has been shown above, New Swindon, apart from the G.W.R.'s first housing estate, was developed piecemeal, mostly by local builders in later 19th century. Already by the end of the Second World War the town, which had grown so quickly and so haphazardly, lacked any shopping, commercial, or administrative centre suited to its size and importance. With the enormous industrial and suburban expansion planned for the post-war years, the need for a completely remodelled town centre was obvious. A plan for this was prepared in 1962 and approved subject to certain amendments by the Government in 1964.[33] In 1965 there had been much clearance of the old central area but only a very small part of the plan had been carried out. Between 1960 and 1964 the site of the former Wilts. and Berks. Canal on either side of Regent Street was transformed into a pedestrian shopping precinct as part of a plan to make all Swindon's central shopping streets pedestrian ways only. This site was planned by the borough engineer and surveyor, assisted by Messrs. Shingler and Risdon, architects to the property developers, and the corporation's consultant architect, Frederick Gibberd.[34] In 1965 Fleming Way, a dual carriage-way, also following the route of the disused canal, and leading from the Drove Road roundabout to Fleet Street, was opened as the first section of a proposed inner ring-road to serve the central shopping area. Many of the streets of houses to the east and north of Regent Street had been demolished to make way for car parks and service roads, and for the public buildings it was planned to build along Princes Street. On the west side of this street the Courts of Justice, designed by the borough architect, were opened in 1965, and in the same year the first part of a new Post Office sorting office in Wellington Street came into use.

MANORS AND OTHER ESTATES. There were five holdings at Swindon in 1086, amounting to $21\frac{3}{4}$ hides; the assessment of another holding at Walcot at $3\frac{1}{4}$ hides[35] makes it seem likely that Swindon was a 25-hide estate divided between a number of lords. Apart from Walcot, only the five-hide holding of the Bishop of Bayeux can be confidently identified with any later estate,[36] but the largest of the other holdings, the 12 hides of Odin the Chamberlain, must have formed the chief part of what was known throughout the Middle Ages as the manor of *SWINDON* or *HIGH SWINDON*. From the mid 16th century the manor of West Swindon was joined to it, and the whole property was conventionally described as the manors of *OVER AND NETHER SWINDON*, or *WEST AND EAST SWINDON*.[37] Although these terms indicated a topographical division of the estate,[38] the property was treated as one manor from the 1640s onwards.[39]

Nothing is certainly known of the manor between Odin the Chamberlain's time and the early 13th century, when William de Pont l'Arche held it.[40] He was probably a descendant of a namesake who was Sheriff of Hampshire and Berkshire 1132–8, and a royal chamberlain,[41] so that the manor may have

---

[30] *Municipal Jnl.* 28 Aug. 1962.   [31] See p. 131.

[32] *Swindon 52–62*, 26.

[33] *Wilts. Development Plan, Swindon Central Area, 1962*; ex inf. Town Clerk's Dept.

[34] *Municipal Jnl.* 3 Mar. 1961.

[35] *V.C.H. Wilts.* ii, pp. 122, 141, 146, 163–4, 167.

[36] See below.

[37] e.g. Goddard MS. 3.   [38] See p. 124.

[39] Goddard MS. 1147, *passim*; cf. ibid. s.a. 1644–6, where separate courts for W. Swindon are recorded.

[40] *Cur. Reg. R.* iv. 33; *Red Bk. Exch.* (Rolls Ser.), ii. 482.

[41] *Herald and Genealogist*, v. 140–5.

descended with the office. The younger William died c. 1238 and was succeeded by his son Robert,[42] who held Swindon in 1242–3.[43] He died soon after this,[44] leaving a brother and heir William,[45] but his lands seem to have passed into the king's hands, perhaps by forfeiture because of felony.[46] The king apparently granted these lands to his half-brother William de Valence, and in 1252 William de Pont l'Arche assigned his interest in them to de Valence.[47] William de Valence married a daughter of one of the coheirs of William Marshal, Earl of Pembroke (d. 1219), and was invested with that title. He died in 1296; his son Aymer succeeded, and died without issue in 1324.[48] His third wife held Swindon in dower until her death in 1377.[49]

The inheritance passed to Aymer's niece Elizabeth, wife of Richard Talbot of Goodrich Castle (Herefs.).[50] Their son Gilbert obtained Swindon in 1377, and died in 1387 leaving a son Richard.[51] Richard died in 1396; from him the manor descended in the same way as part of the manor of Broughton Gifford to the Talbots, Earls of Shrewsbury.[52] It was among the possessions of George, Earl of Shrewsbury in 1505,[53] and it may have been after his death in 1541 that it was sold to the Tame family of Fairford (Glos.). Edmund Tame held Swindon in 1544.[54] When he died without issue in the same year, his heirs were his three sisters.[55] A partition appears to have been made among them, and Swindon must have been allotted to Elizabeth, wife of Lewis Watkins.[56] Edmund Tame's widow, however, long survived him, marrying as her second husband Sir Walter Buckle, and as her third Roger Lygon of Fairford.[57] She still held Swindon in 1562 when Rice ap Owen and William Watkins sold the reversion of the manor to Thomas Goddard of Upham in Aldbourne.[58]

Goddard, a member of a family already of some standing in the county, founded a line which remained at Swindon until the 20th century.[59] Six generations held the manor in the direct male line. Thomas, dying in 1598, was succeeded in turn by Richard (d. 1615), Thomas (d. 1641), Richard (d. 1650), Thomas (d. 1704), and Richard (d. 1732). This last Richard, a bachelor, left the estates to his unmarried brother Pleydell (d. 1742) for life and then to Ambrose Goddard of Box, who was descended in a younger line from Richard (d. 1615). Dying in 1755, Ambrose was succeeded by his unmarried son Thomas (d. 1770), from whom Swindon passed to a younger brother Ambrose (d. 1815). He was succeeded by his son, another Ambrose (d.

1854), grandson Ambrose Lethbridge Goddard (d. 1898), and great-grandson Fitzroy Pleydell Goddard (d. 1927). After the death of F. P. Goddard his widow continued to live at the Lawn, the family home in Old Swindon, until 1931.[60] But she was the last of the family to do so. In 1943 the house and its grounds were sold to Swindon corporation[61] and in 1952 the house was demolished.[62]

The Lawn, which was known until the early 19th century as Swindon House,[63] undoubtedly occupied the site of the medieval manor house. Immediately south of it stood the parish church, with, until c. 1850, a mill beyond it. The north range of the house, dating from the 18th century, was built of red brick with stone dressings and had a stone-tiled roof.[64] Several of its architectural features were similar to those found at what is now no. 42 Cricklade Street, built in 1729.[65] The long north front had a recessed central bay with a pedimented doorway flanked by windows on the ground floor and a Venetian window above. The projecting side blocks, each of four bays, were divided by stone pilasters rising the full height of the building. Above the cornice was a parapet with balustraded panels, surmounted by angle vases. Additional wings to the south and east probably dated from the early 19th century, as did two bay windows at the west end of the 18th-century range. Further extensions were made later in the 19th century, including an arcaded loggia at the south-west angle of the building. The loggia overlooked a sunk garden to the west of the house. In 1965 this garden, surrounded by stone balustrades, was all that survived to mark the site of the former mansion. The landscaped grounds to the north, east, and south of the house were preserved as a public park.

The manor of *EVEN SWINDON* is first met with in 1210–12, when the Abbess of St. Mary in Winchester (Nunnaminster) held land in Swindon worth £4 a year.[66] The house had probably had the property for many years, for in 1242–3 Philip Avenel was said to hold it of the abbess of the old feoffment.[67] Philip still held it in 1249.[68] Later in the century the rent of £4 by which the land was held became attached to the Countess of Aumale's manor of Sevenhampton, but after the disgrace of Adam de Stratton in 1289 it was restored to the abbess.[69] It was still paid at the Dissolution.[70] In 1284–5 Christine Avenel held the land,[71] and in 1313 it was settled on Robert Avenel and Christine his wife.[72] It was no doubt the same estate in Even Swindon which in 1386 was held for life by Roger Feltwell of the inheritance of John

[42] Ibid.
[43] *Bk. of Fees*, ii. 735.
[44] *Herald and Genealogist*, v. 140–5.
[45] *Cal. Chart. R.* 1226–57, 402.
[46] Hutchins, *Hist. Dors.* ii. 292–3; *Collectanea* (W.A.S. Rec. Brch.), 88, 91.
[47] *Cal. Chart. R.* 1226–57, 402; C.P. 25(1)/283/13/284.
[48] *Complete Peerage.*
[49] *Wilts. Inq. p.m.* 1327–77 (Index Libr.), 400.
[50] *Cal. Pat.* 1340–3, 200; C.P. 25(1)/287/42/372.
[51] C 136/48/4. [52] *V.C.H. Wilts.* vii. 54.
[53] C.P. 40/972 m. 449.
[54] *L. & P. Hen. VIII*, xix, p. 85.
[55] C 142/72/104.
[56] Ibid.; Atkyns, *Hist. Glos.*, 221; cf. *Glos. Visitation Pedigrees 1623* (Harl. Soc. xxi), 260, where she is said to have married Rice ap Howell.
[57] Collins, *Peerage*, ed. Bridges, ix. 508; Req. 2/33/43; Req. 2/67/47.
[58] Goddard MS. 3; see also *Cal. Pat.* 1558–60, 10.
[59] The following account is based on MS. accounts of the Goddard family by Col. R. W. Awdry and A. Story-Maskelyne in W.A.S. Libr., Devizes.
[60] *Evening Advertiser*, 11 Nov. 1950. [61] Ibid.
[62] Ibid. 2 May 1952.
[63] *Andrews and Dury, Map* (W.A.S. Rec. Brch.), pl. 14; sketch of house in W.A.S. Libr., Devizes (1801); Pigot, *Nat. Com. Dir.* (1830).
[64] The following description of the house is based on photographs taken before its demolition in 1952 and an unfinished sketch of the north front in 1801 in W.A.S. Libr., Devizes.
[65] See p. 108. [66] *Red Bk. Exch.* (Rolls Ser.), ii. 484.
[67] *Bk. of Fees*, ii. 738.
[68] C.P. 25(1)/251/17/1.
[69] *Lands Adam de Stratton* (W.A.S. Rec. Brch.), p. xxiv, 39, 50, 60, 71, 153.
[70] S.C. 6/Hen. VIII/3342.
[71] *Lands Adam de Stratton* (W.A.S. Rec. Brch.), 153.
[72] *Feet of F. Wilts.* 1272–1327 (W.A.S. Rec. Brch.), 83.

Feltwell, Rector of Chiseldon.[73] By 1458 the manor was held by Thomas Winslow, who then settled it on his daughter Elizabeth when she married John Terumber, son of James Terumber, a rich clothier from Trowbridge.[74] John must have died without issue, for Elizabeth Winslow subsequently married Humphrey, younger son of John Seymour (d. 1463), of Wolfhall (in Great Bedwyn).[75] From him must have descended Simon Seymour, whose trustees let the manor to Thomas Mill *alias* Saunders in 1510, and Alexander Seymour, party to a further lease to the same man in 1528. This leasehold interest was assigned *c.* 1572, by Edmund Mill *alias* Saunders to Edward Walrond of Aldbourne,[76] who still held it in 1582.[77] Meanwhile the freehold of the lands was sold by Simon Seymour of Chippenham to Thomas Wenman of Witney (Oxon.).[78] From him it passed, no doubt by sale, to Edward Seymour, Duke of Somerset, on whose attainder in 1552 it fell into the king's hands. In 1552 'the pasture called Even Swindon' was granted to William Herbert, Earl of Pembroke (d. 1570).[79] In 1606 William, the 3rd earl, sold the manor to Lawrence Hyde (d. 1643); the sale was the occasion of involved lawsuits about leasehold interests dating from the time of the Seymours.[80] From Hyde Even Swindon descended in the same way as Heale (in Woodford) to William Bowles, a Salisbury banker, who went bankrupt in 1813.[81]

In 1086 Wadard, a knight depicted in the Bayeux tapestry, held 5 hides in Swindon of Odo, Bishop of Bayeux; before the Conquest they had belonged to Leviet.[82] Many of the lands held by Odo before his banishment in 1088 were charged with castle guard at Dover,[83] so that lands at *NETHERCOTT* in Swindon, which did this service, may be confidently identified with this 5-hide estate. Unlike most of Wadard's estates, they are not known to have passed to the Arsic family;[84] land at Nethercott is next mentioned in 1241, when Augustus, Prior of St. John at Cricklade, acknowledged that a carucate there belonged to John Barlet.[85] In 1242–3 John Barlet held ¼ fee in Nethercott of Fulk Basset, who held of Gilbert de Hay, who held of the honor of Dover, while William Pipard held ¾ fee there of John Barlet; John held this directly of Gilbert de Hay of the same honor.[86] This division of Nethercott seems to have persisted for some time. In 1252 John Barlet leased his part of the manor to the Rector of Swindon,[87] while at another time he relinquished his intermediate lordship over William Pipard to Gilbert Basset.[88] The Basset overlordship descended

by marriage to Roger Bigod, Earl of Norfolk,[89] who in 1274 held a whole fee in Nethercott; it was held of him in two parts by Margery Pipard and John Bruton.[90]

The descent of the Pipard share of the manor can be imperfectly traced. William Pipard died in 1267 leaving a son Edmund who died without issue in 1272.[91] In the following year his widow Margery was at variance over Nethercott with his brother and heir, Thomas.[92] Thomas died in 1282 leaving a son who died under age in 1301, when his heir was his cousin, John, son of William Pipard, another brother of Edmund and Thomas.[93] John was perhaps father or brother of William Pipard, who in 1340 was entitled to the reversion of parts of the Pipard property after the death of Margery, widow of Thomas Pipard (d. 1282);[94] she survived until 1344.[95] In 1340 William Pipard had settled Nethercott and other property on himself and his wife for life, with remainders to Robert FitzEllis and Margaret his wife, and then to Stephen Pipard, his own son. Robert's wife Margaret was William's daughter; Robert himself died soon afterwards, and by 1349 when William died, Margaret had remarried Warin de Lisle.[96] William's heirs were then Margaret and her sister, Maud, wife of Osbert Hamelyn.

Margaret, the elder sister, died in 1375, leaving a son and heir Gerard,[97] who died without issue in his father's lifetime. Warin de Lisle died in 1382, when his heir was his daughter Margaret, wife of Thomas, Lord Berkeley.[98] Osbert Hamelyn and Maud still held the other moiety of Nethercott in that year.[99] By 1413–14 this moiety had passed to Julian Banister for life, with remainder to men called Trevilines and Alet; Thomas, Lord Berkeley, bought it in that year[1] and so united the manor again. It is possible that the temporary division gave rise to the practice, which first appeared at this time,[2] of calling the manor *EASTCOTT* and *WESTCOTT* or of giving the aliases of Eastcott, Westcott, Nethercott, and Overcott to it. Thomas, Lord Berkeley, died in 1417, leaving an only daughter and heir Elizabeth, wife of Richard Beauchamp, Earl of Warwick. She in turn left three daughters and coheirs, of whom the eldest Margaret, married John Talbot, Earl of Shrewsbury, as his second wife. Being the only daughter with issue, the Lisle inheritance passed to her son John Talbot, created Viscount Lisle (d. 1453). His only son, Thomas, Viscount Lisle, was killed at Nibley Green (Glos.), in 1469, fighting

[73] C.P. 25(1)/256/55/30.
[74] *Cal. Close, 1454–61*, 285, 296; for James Terumber, see *V.C.H. Wilts.* iv. 134–6.
[75] W.A.S. Libr., Devizes, Jackson's Seymour MSS.; for an unexplained reason old pedigrees of the Seymours (e.g. Banks, *Baronies in Fee*, i. 121) derive the family from Sir Roger Seymour of Even Swindon (fl. *c.* 1370), but no evidence that Seymours held there as early as that has been found, and the descent outlined here seems to explain their connexion with the manor adequately.
[76] C 2 Eliz. I/S. 23/49.
[77] W.R.O. 130, Assignment, Owen to Trusloe, 11 May 1586.
[78] C 54/422 no. 11.
[79] *Cal. Pat.* 1549–51, 430; 1550–3, 358; *Survey Lands of First Earl of Pembroke* (Roxburghe Club 1919), ed. C. R. Straton, i. 187–8.
[80] W.R.O. 130, Exemplification of Chancery Decree and Quitclaim, King to Hyde, 20 June 1608; C.P. 25(2)/385/4 Jas. I Trin.
[81] *V.C.H. Wilts.* vi. 224.

[82] Ibid. ii, pp. 107, 122.
[83] Sanders, *English Baronies*, 31, 36–37, 45, 97, 105, 151.
[84] Ibid. 36.   [85] C.P. 25(1)/251/12/9.
[86] *Bk. of Fees*, ii. 731.
[87] *Cat. Anct. D.* iii, A 4602.
[88] Ibid. A 4594, 4730, 4745.
[89] Dugdale, *Baronage*, 135.
[90] *Rot. Hund.* (Rec. Com.), ii. 243.
[91] W. A. Copinger, *Suffolk Manors*, vi. 50–52; *Cal. Inq. p.m.* i, p. 204.
[92] *Cal. Close, 1272–9*, 54.
[93] Copinger, *Suffolk Manors*, vi. 50–52; *Cal. Inq. p.m.* i, p. 286: ii, p. 14.
[94] *Cal. Pat.* 1338–40, 520.
[95] *Cal. Inq. p.m.* viii, p. 287.
[96] Ibid. xii, p. 166; *Cal. Chart. R.* 1327–41, 486; *Cal. Close, 1374–7*, 372.
[97] *Cal. Inq. p.m.* xii, p. 166.
[98] John Smyth, *Lives of the Berkeleys*, ii. 3–5.
[99] C.P. 25(1)/256/54/31.
[1] Smyth, *Berkeleys*, ii. 15.   [2] C 138/259/50.

against William, Lord Berkeley, in the protracted quarrel which followed the division of the Berkeley and Lisle estates in 1417. His heir was his sister Elizabeth, wife of Sir Edward Grey. Sir Edward was created Viscount Lisle,[3] and died holding Nethercott in 1492.[4] Their son John, Lord Lisle, also held it at his death in 1504.[5]

From this time the descent of the manor is obscure until 1600, when John Pleydell of Alderton sold it to Henry Martin of Upham in Aldbourne.[6] Martin died in 1626 and was succeeded by his son Edward.[7] In 1640–1 and 1649 Edward sold considerable parts of the manor to several purchasers.[8] By 1656–7, when the common fields were inclosed,[9] the manor was held by almost 30 small freeholders, and Gabriel Martin, son of Edward, held less than 100 a.[10] Some of this land was immediately sold, and when the manor was settled on Edward, Gabriel's son, in 1663, it consisted only of a house, 3 closes, 3 cottages, and £4 in chief rents.[11] In the 18th century the chief rents belonged to Richard Dickerson,[12] who in 1773 sold what was called the manor of Westcott to Ambrose Goddard.[13] Yet in 1840 Westcott Farm belonged to William and Elizabeth Large,[14] and when it was sold by Mrs. Mary Plummer's trustees in 1866 it was said to include the reputed manor of Westcott. No quit rents were then collected.[15]

Much of the land allotted under the inclosure award of the manor of Eastcott in 1656–7 eventually came into the hands of the Vilett family. Thomas and John Vilett received about 47 a. in lieu of rectorial tithes and a small piece of glebe which belonged to them, while Thomas Vilett received about 54 a. in lieu of his land in the fields.[16] What had probably been the demesne farm of the manor consisted of various closes called Court Knapps and Court Closes. It was sold by Edward Martin to John Yorke of Marlborough and William Yorke of Basset Down in 1640. Twenty years later the Yorke family sold it to Thomas Lawrence of London, tallow chandler, and it still belonged to the Lawrence family in 1699.[17] By 1780 it formed part of the Vilett estate.[18] Another property was the 46 a. allotted in 1657–8 to William Fairthorne,[19] and sold by Thomas Fairthorne to John Vilett in 1729.[20] By 1840 the Vilett estate in Eastcott consisted of three holdings, at Lower Eastcott, Upper Eastcott, and Court Knapps, and amounted in all to over 300 a.[21] Their position, and the sale of the estate, are described above.[22]

In 1086 Ulward, the king's purveyor, held 2 hides in Swindon.[23] By 1151 the abbey of Malmesbury

held lands there [24] and as they were often reckoned at 2 hides, it is quite likely that they had been Ulward's. Abbot Osbert (1176–82) granted these lands to Humphrey Stive (or Stine) whose father had occupied them previously, charging them with 40s. a year.[25] This rent was still paid to the abbey at the Dissolution[26] and was retained by the Crown until 1672, when it was sold to Thomas Goddard, who then held the lands.[27] The history of the tenancy thus created can be only imperfectly traced. Richard Stive was tenant c. 1220[28] and Robert Stive in 1274.[29] John Stive (fl. 1341) was probably a tenant too.[30] Thereafter nothing more is known until the 16th century. It was then said that a property known as the manor of *WEST SWINDON* was held by Sir Richard Bridges of the queen's manor Malmesbury by a rent of 40s.[31] Soon after Sir Richard's death in 1558 it is probable that his son Anthony sold the manor to the lords of East Swindon, for in 1563 the Goddard family acquired the manors of East and West Swindon, as described above.

Rotrou II, Count of Perche, in the reign of Henry I, gave land in *BROOME* to the priory of Marcigny (Saône et Loire).[32] In 1274 the prior was said to hold a carucate there,[33] but three years later the Prior of Monkton Farleigh held Broome of Marcigny at fee farm.[34] Farleigh still held Broome at the Dissolution.[35] In 1536 it was granted to Edward Seymour, later Duke of Somerset,[36] and descended in the same way as the manor of Trowbridge[37] until 1613, when it was settled on Francis Seymour, later Lord Seymour of Trowbridge, when he married Frances Prynne.[38] It descended, still in the same way as Trowbridge, to Algernon, 7th Duke of Somerset (d. 1750). On the partition of his estates made in 1779, Broome, which had long been held as a single large farm, was allotted to Charles William Wyndham, grandson of one of the duke's sisters. Wyndham died in 1828 without issue, and was succeeded by his older brother George, 3rd Earl of Egremont (d. 1837).[39] In 1840 the 4th earl offered Broome Farm for sale,[40] and it was bought by Ambrose Goddard and added to his estates.[41]

The farm-house, known in 1965 as Broome Manor, is a much altered roughcast building which incorporates at least part of a 17th-century house. The only visible features of the early house are a large projecting chimney on the north-east side and stone mullioned windows in the cellar and in one of the gables.

In 1066 Alnod and Levenot held small estates in

[3] Smyth, *Berkeleys*, ii. 28–29, 109–12; *Trans. Bristol and Glos. Arch. Soc.* iii. 305–24.
[4] *Cal. Inq. p.m. Hen. VIII*, i, p. 338.
[5] Ibid. ii, p. 506.
[6] Deed recited in W.R.O. 348/1, no. 4.
[7] *Wilts. Inq. p.m.* 1625–49 (Index Libr.), 395–6; see also settlement, 18 Jan. 1625, in W.R.O. 130.
[8] Deeds in W.R.O. 130, and W.R.O. 348/1, no. 4.
[9] See p. 124. [10] Morris, *Swindon*, 507–23.
[11] W.R.O. 130, Deeds of 1658 and 1663.
[12] Goddard MSS.
[13] C.P. 25(2)/1446/13 Geo. III East.
[14] W.R.O. Tithe Award.
[15] W.A.S. Libr., Devizes, Sale Cat. vi, no. 25.
[16] Morris, *Swindon*, 507–23.
[17] W.R.O. 348/1, nos. 4–5, 9, and 348/2, nos. 4, 12.
[18] Ibid. Land Tax Assessments and Tithe Award.
[19] Morris, *Swindon*, 507–23.
[20] W.R.O. 348/1, no. 17. [21] Ibid. Tithe Award.
[22] See pp. 112–13. [23] *V.C.H. Wilts.* ii, p. 164.

[24] *Reg. Malm.* (Rolls Ser.), i. 348–52.
[25] Ibid. ii. 4; *Interdict Docs.* (P.R.S. n.s. xxxiv), 23.
[26] S.C. 6/Hen. VIII/3986.
[27] Goddard MS. 111; see also *Cal. Pat.* 1563–6, 463.
[28] *Reg. Malm.* (Rolls Ser.), ii. 16–17.
[29] *Rot. Hund.* (Rec. Com.), ii. 243.
[30] *Inq. Non.* (Rec. Com.), 162.
[31] C 142/124/191; Goddard MS. 5.
[32] *Bk. of Fees*, ii. 738; 'The Priory of Marcigny and its Wilts. Connexion', *W.A.M.* xxxv. 93–102.
[33] *Rot. Hund.* (Rec. Com.), ii. 275.
[34] *Cal. Close*, 1272–9, 380.
[35] *Valor Eccl.* (Rec. Com.), ii. 143.
[36] *L. & P. Hen. VIII*, x, p. 526.
[37] *V.C.H. Wilts.* vii. 129.
[38] *Wilts. Inq. p.m.* 1625–49 (Index Libr.), 53.
[39] *Complete Peerage*; Partition of Estates of Algernon, 7th Duke of Somerset, 19 Geo. III, c. 46 (priv. act).
[40] W.R.O. 137, Sale Particular.
[41] *W.A.M.* vii. 123–4; Goddard MSS. 898, 906.

WALCOT. Alnod still appears to have held his in 1084, but by 1086 both estates, amounting to 2½ hides, were held by Reynold of Miles Crispin.[42] Miles's estates later formed the honor of Wallingford, of which land in Walcot was said to be held until the 16th century.[43] The honor then became merged in that of Ewelme (Oxon.); courts for the Wiltshire portion of the honor of Ewelme were held at Ogbourne St. George until 1847, and the tithingman of Walcot attended and paid 1s. 6d. a year until then.[44]

Reynold, the Domesday tenant, called Reynold Canut in the Geld Rolls, has been identified with Reynold Croc, who held land also in Hampshire and Oxfordshire. Reynold left two daughters, one of whom probably married a Foliot and gained possession of parts of Reynold's fee in Wiltshire. His other lands in the county passed to Walter Croc or Canut, who held 5 fees of the honor of Wallingford in 1166. He was the ancestor of the Croke family of Hazelbury (in Box), whose pedigree has been carefully worked out.[45] Members of that family continued to hold part of Walcot until the 14th century. Richard Croke held land there in 1300,[46] and in 1324 John Harding held ½ fee there of Reynold Croke.[47] The subsequent descent of this holding has not been traced.

What was perhaps a larger holding in Walcot was held by the Montfort family of Ashley (in Box), and so neighbours of the Crokes at Hazelbury. Robert de Montfort had some interest in Walcot in the late 12th century.[48] In 1242–3 Simon de Montfort of Ashley held ½ fee in Walcot of the honor of Wallingford.[49] In 1336 William Poyntz of Ashley held land at Walcot in right of his wife Alice, probably widow of a Montfort, and granted it for lives to Ralph de Sharpenham.[50] In 1428 John Montfort held these lands,[51] and in 1481 they were released by John Babur and Isabel his wife, also perhaps a Montfort widow, to feoffees.[52] In 1523–4 Thomas Montfort sold Walcot to Edmund Audley, Bishop of Salisbury.[53]

Audley used Walcot to endow the charity he founded in Hereford Cathedral.[54] After the chantry was dissolved the manor was granted in 1550 to Richard Roberts of London,[55] who immediately sold it to Sir William Sharington of Lacock.[56] It descended in the same way as the manors of Liddington and Coate into the Talbot family, and, like those manors, was sold to the Duke of Marlborough in 1709.[57] It descended with that title until 1796,

when it was sold to Ambrose Goddard and added to his other Swindon estates.[58] Two smaller properties in Walcot are mentioned below.[59]

In 1341 the Prior of Wallingford held certain tithes in Swindon,[60] and probably lands too. At the Dissolution lands held by the house in West Swindon were granted to Sir Richard Bridges, lord of the manor of West Swindon.[61] In 1556 Sir Richard leased the property to a man named Allworth; it then consisted of a capital messuage called the 'Crown' and certain lands belonging to it. Allworth's widow married William West,[62] who at the expiry of the lease in 1581 bought the freehold of the property from Sir Richard's son Anthony Bridges.[63] West died in 1610, and his son and heir Thomas in 1617.[64] Thomas's son William sold the estate to Thomas Goddard (d. 1641),[65] and it descended in the same way as his manor of Swindon.[66] The 'Crown' stood on the site of the present 'Goddard Arms'.[67]

By the early 13th century some part of the Croke family's lands in Walcot[68] seems to have passed to Sampson Foliot by gift of Walter Croke, who became a monk 1219–20. In 1241 the parson of Swindon was at variance with Sampson Foliot over the tithe of a meadow said to lie in Walcot, while in 1370 and 1415 lands in Walcot were associated with an estate in Draycot Foliat.[69] It is perhaps to be identified with a virgate of land in Walcot which in 1393 was delivered as dower to Isabel, widow of William Wroughton, for the Wroughtons also held land in Draycot.[70] The family retained the Walcot property until the 16th century,[71] but its further history is not known. The known history of another small estate there begins in 1634, when it was settled on Richard Organ of Lambourn (Berks.), and his wife Lucy. When Richard died childless four years later his heir was his bachelor brother John,[72] whose estates passed at his death in 1640 to his two nephews, children of his sisters.[73] The Walcot property was evidently assigned to John Hippesley, in whose family it remained until 1701, when it was sold to Richard Goddard.[74] The farm at Lower Walcot was held from at least 1780 by the Freeman family.[75] When it was offered for sale in 1805 it amounted to 50 a.[76] It was sold to the Goddards c. 1820.[77]

The origin of the farm at Okus is to be found in a sale in 1648 by Richard Goddard to Rebecca Hedges of Bourton (Berks.), of a pasture at 'Okesse' and various lands and closes in West Swindon Field.[78]

[42] *V.C.H. Wilts.* ii, pp. 146, 216.
[43] e.g. *Bk. of Fees,* i. 314, ii. 727; *Feud. Aids,* v. 279.
[44] Wilts. Cuttings, xvi. 358; see also *W.A.M.* xxiv. 207.
[45] G. J. Kidston, *History of the Manor of Hazelbury,* 15–99.
[46] *Wilts. Inq. p.m.* 1327–77 (Index Libr.), 274–5.
[47] *Feud. Aids,* v. 214.
[48] C.P. 25(1)/250/1/17.   [49] *Bk. of Fees,* ii. 727.
[50] C.P. 25(1)/254/43/17.
[51] *Feud. Aids,* v. 279.
[52] C.P. 25(1)/257/65/46.
[53] *W.N. & Q.* ii. 422.
[54] *Valor Eccl.* (Rec. Com.), iii. 13.
[55] *Cal. Pat.* 1549–51, 5–6.
[56] C.P. 40/1143 m. 11.
[57] See p. 67; Catalogue of Deeds at Blenheim (copy in W.R.O.).
[58] Catalogue of Deeds at Blenheim; *W.A.M.* xlv. 462; W.R.O. Land Tax Assessments.
[59] See below.   [60] *Inq. Non.* (Rec. Com.), 162.
[61] Goddard MS. 5; *L. & P. Hen. VIII,* xviii, p. 281.

[62] C 3/6/55.   [63] Goddard MSS. 5, 8.
[64] C 142/330/26; C 142/371/94.
[65] Goddard MSS. 11–13.
[66] See p. 120; for later leases, see Goddard MSS. 21, 215.
[67] See p. 106.   [68] See above.
[69] C. W. Hughes, 'Draycot Foliat', *Marlborough College Nat. Hist. Soc. Rep.* lxxvi, pp. 50–62; C.P. 25(1)/255/52/2; *Cat. Anct. D.* vi, C 5362.
[70] *Cal. Close,* 1392–6, 161.
[71] Ibid. 1405–9, 425; C 139/42/16; *Cal. Inq. p.m. Hen. VII,* i, p. 505; C 1/477/22.
[72] *Wilts. Inq. p.m.* 1625–49 (Index Libr.), 312–17.
[73] Ibid. 401–6; for the family see *Wilts. Visitation Pedigrees* (Harl. Soc. cv–cvi), p. 146.
[74] Goddard MSS. 73, 195, 202, 209, 664–7, 820; for a small property in Walcot sold by T. S. Hippesley to Pleydell Goddard in 1733 see ibid. 310–11, 320–2, 342–3.
[75] W.R.O. Land Tax Assessments.
[76] W.A.S. Libr., Devizes, Sale Cat. ix, no. 41.
[77] W.R.O. Land Tax Assessments.
[78] Goddard MS. 50.

She married Thomas Blagrove of Watchfield (Berks.), who at his death in 1682 devised his lands to John, son of his daughter Sarah by Thomas Saunders. He sold Okus Farm to Richard Goddard in 1724, and it was added to the Goddard estates.[79]

In 1086 Ulvric held a hide and a virgate at Swindon, and Alfred of Marlborough held 1½ hide there.[80] One of these estates is probably to be identified with the ¾ carucate held in 1198 by Everard of William Spileman by serjeanty.[81] Later tenants of this holding were perhaps the William Everard who acquired land in Westlecott in 1312,[82] and John Everard who died holding lands in West Swindon in 1414.[83] Another serjeanty in Swindon was that in Walcot held in 1198 by Maurice *serviens*.[84] In 1226–8 it was described as a virgate held by Maurice *clericus* by service of making summonses.[85]

AGRICULTURE. As has been shown, there were five separate estates in Swindon, excluding Walcot, at the time of the Domesday Survey.[86] The largest was the 12-hide estate of Odin the Chamberlain, which probably was merged eventually in the manor of High Swindon. Its demesne was worked by 2 serfs with 2 ploughs. On the rest of the estate 6 villeins and 8 bordars had 3 ploughs, making a total of 5 ploughs on the whole estate, although it was reckoned that there was land for six. On this estate there were 30 a. of meadow and 20 a. of pasture.[87] On the Bishop of Bayeux's 5-hide estate, which may have descended to the lords of the manor of Nethercott (later called the manor of Eastcott, Westcott, and Nethercott), there was 1 hide in demesne, on which 4 serfs and 1 plough were occupied. On the rest of the estate there were 5 villeins and 2 bordars with 2 ploughs. There were 30 a. each of meadow and pasture.[88] A connexion with later manors cannot be established for the other three Domesday estates, and the Survey gives little information about them. On Ulward's 2-hide estate and on Alfred of Marlborough's 1½-hide estate it was estimated that there was land for 6 plough-teams,[89] and on Ulvric's estate of 1 hide and 1 virgate there was only land for half a plough.[90] Thus in Swindon in 1086 on the two estates for which the information exists there were 27 servile tenants with 5 ploughs, while there were 3 ploughs for demesne working. For Miles Crispin's estate of 2½ hides at Walcot Domesday Book offers no information about tenants or ploughs.[91]

By the 13th century the land of Swindon was divided between five manors.[92] Walcot lay in the east, largely upon heavy clay-land; Broome occupied all the south of the parish where stretches of lighter soils are to be found; High or West Swindon occupied the top of Swindon Hill, where, besides the beds of Purbeck and Portland stone, there was a mixture of clay and sandy soils; Low or East Swindon stretched from near Gorse Hill in the north to Piper's Corner in the south, thus lying to

a large extent upon the clay, but also taking in some of the lighter soil of Swindon Hill; the manor of Nethercott, Eastcott, and Westcott covered all the north-western part of the parish between the Wootton Bassett and Cricklade roads, and so was situated mostly on the low-lying clay-lands, but extended southwards up the slopes of Swindon Hill nearly to the Bath road.

No information has been found to make possible any account of the rural economy of these manors in the Middle Ages. There was, apparently, at High Swindon in the 13th century a park stocked with deer for the lord's hunting,[93] and there is reference to overstocking the common at Broome with 100 sheep in the early 14th century.[94]

At the beginning of the 17th century there were 13 free tenants on the manor of Nethercott, Eastcott, and Westcott.[95] Their arable holdings, which varied in size from 1 rood to 16 acres, lay scattered throughout three fields, namely, West, East, and North Field, and also in a region described as 'on the hill'. This last place may possibly represent a recent conversion of grazing land to arable. With the aid of the tithe map of 1840 it is possible to locate roughly on the map of modern Swindon the three arable fields of this manor.[96] North Field lay approximately in the angle formed by the junction of the Gloucester railway line with the main line to Bristol. East Field lay south-east of this to the south of the modern Fleming Way as it runs between Princes Street and York Road. The site of West Field is not so certainly known, but it probably lay north of Westcott Place. 'The hill' may be the region, later called Lapper's Hill, lying just north of the railway station.

Between 1640 and 1649 the manor of Eastcott (*alias* Nethercott, Eastcott, and Westcott) was dismembered and its lands sold to some 30 small freeholders.[97] The holdings so created, however, still lay dispersed in the common fields and meadows of the manor. One holding, sold in 1641, included, for example, 3 half-acres lying in 4 ridges in middle furlong, 1 yard in Long Lands, 3 separate yards in Chesly Furlong, and 1 yard in Hollow Chesly, all of which were within the West Field.[98] In the Breach this same freeholder had two separate acres. In the East Field he had a half-acre, another half-acre and a yard in Wool Lands, and a half-acre in Rushmore. On Eastcott Down he had 2 separate half-acres and a yard. In Eastcott Meadow he had a yard and a half-acre in Hill Mead, a half-acre in Long Hides, which was moveable every year, and a yard in North Groves, also moveable every year. With this holding went common of pasture for 3 rother beasts, a horse, 15 sheep, and a calf.

Farming these holdings made up of parcels so widely scattered obviously presented great difficulties. To overcome these, and to facilitate the conversion of more arable to pasture, which it was considered most desirable to do, the common fields of this manor were inclosed in 1656–7.[99] A surveyor

[79] Ibid. 135, 275–8, 280–2, 293–6, 787, 837–8, 1052.
[80] *V.C.H. Wilts.* ii, pp. 163–4, 141.
[81] *Bk. of Fees*, i. 12.
[82] *Feet of F. Wilts.* 1272–1327 (W.A.S. Rec. Brch.), 80.
[83] C 139/118/13.
[84] *Bk. of Fees*, i. 12.
[85] Ibid. 380.
[86] See p. 119.
[87] *V.C.H. Wilts.* ii, p. 167.
[88] Ibid. p. 122.
[89] Ibid. pp. 141, 164.
[90] Ibid. p. 163.
[91] Ibid. p. 146.
[92] See pp. 119–22.
[93] *Close R.* 1247–51, 249, 509.
[94] W.R.O. 192, Broome Ct. r.
[95] Ibid. 2/3, Cts. baron manor of Nethercott, 1600–1.
[96] Ibid. Tithe Map and Award.
[97] See p. 122.
[98] W.R.O. 130, Sale, Martyn to Lawe, 1 May 1641.
[99] 'Decree for the Enclosure of Eastcott, dated 23 Sept. 1657', printed in Morris, *Swindon*, 507–23.

was employed to measure up all the dispersed holdings, and in their stead consolidated blocks of land, both in the former open arable fields and in the meadows, were awarded. Blocks were allotted in all the former arable fields and on Lapper's Hill, and in a field called Down Field, which may originally have been rough downland grazing, but which by 1641 contained at least some arable.[1] Allotments were similarly made in Eastcott Mead, Great and Little Breach, Eastcott Marsh, and North Breach. One allotment in Benbrook, which had once been the lord's meadow within the common meadow of the manor, was made to Gabriel Martin, son of the last lord of the manor.[2] All these had probably been at one time meadow lands, but were now, like the arable, to be divided into small inclosed fields. Already by the year of the inclosure a pasture ground, called New Ground, had been made within the north arable field.[3]

In all 668 a. were inclosed. But, divided among some 31 landowners, the individual holdings so formed were mostly quite small. The largest holding was 81 a. lying in 3 compact blocks, allotted to Gabriel Martin (see above). Of the other holdings 2 were just over 50 a., 4 between 40 a. and 50 a., 4 between 20 a. and 40 a., 3 between 10 a. and 20 a., and 16 under 10 a., 8 of which were under 5 a. An allotment of about 46 a. at the south end of Eastcott Mead was also made to Thomas and John Vilett in lieu of rectorial tithes.[4] With the award went the stipulation that the lands allotted should be satisfactorily inclosed with mounds and ditches. Footpaths and ways of access were provided for, and it was ordered that springs and watercourses should be maintained and allowed to flow freely.

Although the evidence is lacking, it is most likely that the low-lying lands of the manors of Walcot and East Swindon, in the north-eastern part of the parish, were similarly inclosed in the course of the 17th century. Their cold clay-lands were eminently suited to pasture farming, for which small inclosed fields were required. They were particularly suited to dairy farming, but beef, bacon, mutton, and wool were produced as well.[5] On the manor of East or Lower Swindon much of the land in the north lay in Swindon Marsh.[6] But it stretched southwards up Swindon Hill and beyond towards the manor of Broome. The lower arable field of East Swindon lay in the north, and mention of grounds within it called New Closes in 1642 suggests that it was at least partly inclosed.[7] There was also in the 17th century another arable field in the southern part of the manor with land in it abutting upon the highway to Wroughton and in the neighbourhood of Westlecott Way.[8]

On the manor of West Swindon there was little early inclosure of arable. Here in the 17th century there was one large arable field known as West Swindon Field, which extended approximately from the Devizes road in the east to Okus on the west,

and from the Sands (later the Bath road) in the north to Mill Lane and Westlecott Road in the south.[9] Within it lay the Swindon quarries,[10] which must have added considerably to the difficulties of cultivating the scattered strips into which the field was divided.

A sale of nearly 65 a. in 1648 shows how dispersed a single holding might be.[11] About 32 a. lay in two fields, themselves but subdivisions of West Swindon Field. But within these two fields the 32 a. were distributed in quite small portions among the furlongs and pieces into which the fields were divided. The portions ranged in size from ½ to 8 acres. Even where the land lay within one furlong, the most usual subdivison of the arable field, it could be scattered, as, for example, the three half-acres 'in several pieces in the furlong against the linches'. The other 32 a. of the holding were similarly widely dispersed. The largest portion was a block of 11 a. lying between 'the scrags and the quarry'. With the entire holding went common of pasture for 80 sheep in the fields and wastes of the manor.

In 1798 the great field of West Swindon measured about 237 a., including 22 a. of waste ground, which could not be used for agricultural purposes.[12] That year the field was divided into 18 furlongs, the largest containing 19 a. and the smallest 3 a. In addition to the furlongs there were 3 small pieces, 3 linches, 4 a. at Brinchcomb Bottom and Common Hill, which had recently been converted into arable, and 25 a. of inclosed land called the New Inclosure. Only on the inclosed land was wheat grown. Of the 3 pieces one (about 2 a.) was rough fallow, another (about 1 a.) had late-sown barley, and the third (about 3 a.) was partly rough and partly plain fallow. East Linch (about 6 a.), which lay north of Okus Road, was upland pasture; Middle Linch (about 1 a.) grew vetches and clover grass, and West Linch (about 2 a.) was sown with barley. The land in the various furlongs was used as follows: barley, late and early sowings 57 a.; fallow 23 a., including 7 a. on which sheep were penned; hops and broad clover 19 a.; cinquefoil 18 a.; beans 11 a.; oats 9 a.; vetches and clover grass 8 a.; peas 5 a.

The common pasture of West Swindon manor lay on the southern slopes of Swindon Hill, roughly along the line of the modern borough boundary as it runs from the Wootton Bassett road towards Westlecott Stalls.[13] Here were three common pasture grounds—Siddowne, Mandowne, and West Swindon Mead.[14] Siddowne and Mandowne probably remained open downland grazing until well into the 19th century. West Swindon Mead, however, seems to have contained a number of inclosed meadows, certainly by the end of the 17th century.[15] Meadows there called Foremead,[16] Two Lights,[17] and Six Lights[18] are mentioned at that time and throughout the 18th century. By the time of the tithe award in 1842 West Swindon Mead appears to have been divided into West, South, and Long Mead.[19] In

[1] W.R.O. 130, Sale, Martyn to Savidge, 1 May 1641.
[2] W.R.O. 348/4, 27 Mar. 1640.
[3] W.R.O. 130, Sale, Martyn to Dewell, 19 Mar. 1657–8.
[4] See p. 145.
[5] V.C.H. Wilts. iv. 44.
[6] Goddard MS. 96.
[7] Wilts. Inq. p.m. 1625–49 (Index Libr.), 378–9.
[8] Ibid. 377–80.
[9] Swindon deeds among Goddard MSS. For e.gs. see nos. 19, 53.

[10] See p. 127.
[11] Goddard MS. 798.   [12] Ibid. 872.
[13] It is clearly marked on the Tithe Map.
[14] Frequently referred to in Swindon deeds among Goddard MSS. For e.gs., see nos. 211–18, 222, 224–6, 183–5.
[15] Goddard MSS. 131, 150, 86.
[16] Ibid. 131.   [17] Ibid. 335.
[18] Ibid. 210.
[19] W.R.O. Tithe Award.

addition to the common pasture a number of in-closed meadows had been made on this manor by the 17th century. A meadow called Tismead was described as a new inclosure in 1642.[20] By the end of the century there were certain closes of meadow known as West Swindon Closes, which from the tithe map seem to have been situated just south of the Bath road.[21] Closes named in the 18th century include Stone Close, Pounds Close, Kembles Close, Kingshill Close, Holloways Close, and Martin's Close.[22]

Leases of holdings consisting of parcels of land scattered about West Swindon Field continued to be made throughout the 18th century.[23] An early-19th-century lease of 6 a. within the New Inclosure was accompanied by the stipulation that the scattered parcels should be inclosed with a double quickset mound.[24] But since most of the holdings on this manor were in the hands of two or three families only, it is likely that little but piecemeal inclosure took place. In 1822 a lease of Okus Farm by Ambrose Goddard for 7 years included, among other lands, 166 a. in West Swindon Field, 71 a. in in West Swindon Mead, the Closes, Siddowne, Mandowne, and Brenchcomb.[25] Thus a large part of West Swindon manor came to be farmed by the tenants of Okus Farm.

At the beginning of the 19th century the land of the parish was chiefly meadow and pasture. Of the crops grown in 1801 wheat covered 122 a.; barley 138 a.; oats 62 a.; potatoes 24½ a.; peas 25 a.; beans 43 a.; turnips and rape 57 a. The poor at this date were encouraged to cultivate all waste ground with potatoes, which were said to be abundant.[26] But it was for pasture that the land as a whole was best suited and in 1830 it was said that some of the best grazing land in the kingdom lay in this parish.[27] In 1842 it was reckoned that meadow and pasture covered 2,261 a. and arable 739 a.[28]

In 1842 there were 11 farms in the parish. These included Upper Eastcott Farm (160 a.), Lower Eastcott Farm (93 a.), and Court Knapps.[29] These three holdings may be said to have been working the land of the former manor of Nethercott, East-cott, and Westcott. On the manorial lands of West and East Swindon, which came into the hands of the Goddards in the 16th century,[30] there were in 1842 Church Farm (144 a.), Lower Town Farm (83 a.), Marsh Farm (179 a.), and Okus Farm (339 a.) all of which were at that date being farmed by tenant farmers.[31] On the manor of Walcot, acquired by the Goddards towards the end of the 18th century,[32] there were Upper Walcot Farm (247 a.) and Lower Walcot Farm (128 a.), both likewise let to tenant farmers.[33] The farm of the manor of Broome was not acquired by the Goddards until 1840 when it comprised some 674 a.,[34] and was thus the largest farm

in the parish. The absorption of some of these farms for the extension of Swindon in the later 19th century has been dealt with above.[35] Until the mid 20th century the farms on the east side of the town continued to be worked. But in 1954 the two Walcot farms were acquired by the corporation for housing estates, and their purchase was followed the next year by that of all the other farms on this side of the town.[36] By 1965 the only farm-land remaining within the borough boundary was that belonging to the two farms at Broome, which were formed out of Broome Manor Farm.

TRADE AND INDUSTRY. Until the establishment of the G.W.R. works in the mid 19th century Swindon was a small market town of no more consequence than many others in Wiltshire. The main local industry was quarrying. In all probability the Roman camp at Wanborough was built of Swindon stone,[37] and in 1301 roofing tiles of Swindon stone were being used at Sevenhampton.[38] The meadow lands to the north of the town and the downlands to the south carried the cattle and sheep which provided the raw material for local leather and wool trades. A skinner named John Oryot lived in Swindon in 1354.[39] In 1451 two Swindon woolmongers, John and Walter Morleys, were robbed of 2,500 woolfells at Salisbury.[40]

It was during the 17th century that, overcoming the geographical disadvantage of 'it being no thoroughfare', Swindon received its first obvious stimuli to economic growth, first, from the expansion of the weekly market which attracted local commerce,[41] and then from the discovery and working of a seam of fine Purbeck Limestone, from which arose a traffic with the London market.[42] Contemporary records reveal quite a wide range of trades and crafts, including those of clothier, shearman, tailor, mason, stonecutter, weaver, and silkweaver.[43] Further evidence of trading and commercial pursuits can be found in the instructions given in 1680 to the steward of the manor to guard against the washing of dyed wool and mats in the church well and skins in the mill-pond.[44] At the end of the century a rather more complete picture of the town's economy can be formed from the employments listed in 1697. There were then 14 masons, 4 weavers, 3 coopers, a glover, a feltmaker, a woolman, and a cheesefactor; also 4 smiths and 4 carpenters, together with 7 shoemakers, 6 tailors, 3 drapers, 2 bakers, 2 butchers, and 2 barbers. The town contained 40 labouring families as well.[45]

John Aubrey gives the year 1640 or thereabouts for the discovery of the Purbeck Limestone strata, on which the reputation of the Swindon quarries came to be based.[46] They lay only five feet under-

[20] Goddard MS. 794.
[21] Ibid. 151.
[22] Ibid. 284.
[23] Ibid. 353 for e.g., and see index to Cal. of Goddard MSS. (TS in Swindon Pub. Libr.).
[24] W.R.O. 700, Lease, Goddard to Bradford.
[25] Goddard MS. 450.
[26] H.O. 67/23.
[27] Pigot, Nat. Com. Dir. (1830).
[28] W.R.O. Tithe Award.
[29] Ibid.
[30] See p. 120.
[31] W.R.O. Tithe Award.
[32] See p. 123.
[33] W.R.O. Tithe Award.
[34] See p. 122, and W.R.O. 137/125/24.
[35] See pp. 112–13.
[36] See p. 117.
[37] V.C.H. Wilts. i (1), 112.
[38] Lands Adam de Stratton (W.A.S. Rec. Brch.), p. xxvii.
[39] V.C.H. Wilts. iv. 234.
[40] Cal. Pat. 1446–52. 443.
[41] See p. 132.
[42] Aubrey, Nat. Hist. Wilts. ed. Britton, 43.
[43] Goddard MSS. 19, 40, 42, 43, 69, 86, 88, 113, 127, 155, 172, 177.
[44] Goddard MS. 1166.
[45] W.R.O. 212 B/W.G. 8/9, List of inhabitants of Swindon, 1697.
[46] Aubrey, Nat. Hist. Wilts. ed. Britton, 43.

ground and so were dug in shallow quarries. Aubrey suggests that the stone was transported via the Thames from Lechlade to London, where it was used for interior masonry. It was, he says, especially 'excellent for paving halls, staircases, etc.', being white, taking a little polish, and remaining dry even in wet weather.[47] By Aubrey's time it had been used in a number of the town houses of the aristocracy. The limestone quarries lay to the west of the town in the West Field, surrounded by the open-field arable plots. Earlier quarrying of building stone had been on another site, for the 'old quarre', referred to in 1641, lay 'at the townes end of East Swindon'.[48] The earliest recorded quarry in the West Field was the half-acre site of which Guy Hopkins purchased the lease in 1669; it lay east and west of the road which ran to Westlecott.[49] The quarries were worked as small enterprises. One of the more substantial of the 17th-century quarriers was Rise Brown, who had interests in Windmill Quarry, Flaxlands Quarry, Westcott Quarry, and the 'old quarre'.[50] Towards the end of the century a number of quarriers purchased the leases of quarry sites; £40 was paid for a ½ a. site in 1687,[51] £25 for an acre site in 1694,[52] and £22 for ½ a. in 1697.[53] In 1695, after paying £15 for ½ a. in the West Field, John Robinson had converted it into a quarry from which he had dug and sold a quantity of stone.[54] Two years after his death in 1697 his quarry was sold for £14 and in 1705 was disposed of for £9.[55]

It was part of the duty of the steward of the manor to superintend quarrying activities. In 1680 Thomas Goddard charged his newly-appointed steward to inquire into quarrying on or near the highway, to see that the manor court viewed quarries and presented those structures where quarries were 'hazardous', and to report new quarries.[56] The terms of quarry leases likewise aimed at controlling the extraction of stone. A lease of 1687 warned against undermining adjacent land and enjoined upon the quarrier to dig 'straight and down' to prevent encroachment.[57] At the end of the lease the quarry was to be filled in so as to restore it to tillage. In the 17th and 18th centuries frequent presentments were made in the manor court of quarriers who failed to fence off their quarries by the side of the highway to Westlecott.[58]

There is record of at least 9 families of quarriers in the later years of the 18th century: those of Farmer, Archer, Ewen, Hopkins, Humphries, Bury, Cox, Jones, and Simmons.[59] Prominent among them was the Hopkins family, who had been quarry owners at least since 1669. Guy Hopkins left to his wife in 1729 all his 'quarry houses, quarries, gardens, and freehold lands lying in Swindon field'.[60] Between

1739 and 1748 the family relinquished a number of quarry sites to the lord of the manor, an indication perhaps of either the end of the working of the Purbeck seams or a contraction in the family's business.[61] The family were still quarriers late in the century. Another family, that of Humphries, had taken possession of a ½ a. quarry site in 1707.[62] In 1744 William Humphries took an apprentice,[63] in 1745 acquired a ¾ a. quarry near the Westlecott road,[64] and in 1752 was presented in the manor court for not getting the stone ready to erect a blind-house.[65]

How long the Purbeck seams continued to be worked is unknown, but in all probability the quarries in the West Field were by the end of the 18th century approaching exhaustion. In the 1790s quarries at the top of Kingshill were mentioned in the court book for the first time.[66] These were the quarries which provided so much of the undressed building stone for the 19th-century development of Swindon. About the beginning of the 19th century, when the whole of the space on the western brow of the hill towards Westlecott was excavated, quarrying was reckoned never to have been so busy.[67] A principal cause of this activity was the building of the Wilts. and Berks. Canal which used Swindon stone in the building of bridges, the erection of the canal office house at Swindon wharf, and the paving before buildings on neighbouring wharves.[68]

There is no proof that the building of the canal led to the export of Swindon stone on any large scale. The superintendent of the canal showed little interest in fostering such trade, for his own business interests were concentrated in the Monkton Farleigh quarries.[69] No record of the export of stone eastward from Swindon exists before 1852, and there was only one short period of extensive trade westward in 1840–1, when 5,500 tons of stone were transported from Swindon to Semington.[70] Between 1852 and 1860 only 440 tons of stone were recorded as shipped by canal, most of it way-stone for parishes along the canal.[71] In only five instances was paving stone exported, the largest consignment being 10 tons early in 1854. Much larger quantities of stone were, in fact, being imported into Swindon from the quarries of west Wiltshire. Between 1864 and 1878 imports of stone amounted to 29,425 tons.[72] The development of Swindon, in both the old town and the railway settlement, had outstripped the supply of stone from home sources.

In the early years of the century an estimated 300 to 400 hands were employed in the quarries,[73] and they formed a distinctive element in the town's population, 'standing about on Saturdays in scores'

[47] Ibid.
[49] Ibid. 104.
[51] Ibid. 156.
[53] Ibid. 186.
[54] Ibid. 1070.
[55] Ibid.
[56] Goddard MS. 1166.
[57] Ibid. 156.
[58] Ibid. 1147 (Ct. Bk.).
[59] Ibid.
[60] Ibid. 1087. Another reference to 3 'quarr houses' was made by John Hopkins in 1748 (Goddard MS. 393). A 'quarr' house was presumably a store-house for the finer quality limestone to prevent weathering.
[61] Cf. Goddard MSS. 363, 393–5.
[62] Goddard MS. 228.
[48] Goddard MS. 32.
[50] Ibid. 1040.
[52] Ibid. 175.
[63] *Apprentices and their Masters* (W.A.S. Rec. Brch.), 85.
[64] Goddard MS. 390.
[65] Ibid. 1147 (Ct. Bk.).
[66] Ibid.
[67] Morris, *Swindon*, 204.
[68] Ibid. Swindon Pub. Libr., Wilts. and Berks. Canal Recs. No. 8, Trade ledger, 1828–36.
[69] Cf. Swindon Pub. Libr., Wilts. and Berks. Canal Recs. No. 15, Letter bk.
[70] Ibid. No. 6, Trade ledger, 1837–60. The stone was possibly for building the workhouse at Semington: V.C.H. Wilts. viii. 202.
[71] Swindon Pub. Libr., Wilts. and Berks. Canal Recs. No. 29, Swindon wharfage accounts (exports), 1852–86.
[72] Ibid. No. 7, Trade ledger, 1861–79.
[73] *Northern Univs. Geog. Jnl.* Feb. 1961, 41.

in their flannel jackets.[74] As the century drew to a close, however, the quarry industry contracted. There had been at least 3 stone merchants and quarry owners in 1851[75] but in later decades quarrying leases were granted to outsiders, including an Oxford builder and a Manchester architect.[76] In 1899 Joseph Williams, a builder, was granted a lease to dig 62 perches on the Okus quarry site.[77] In the first decade of the 20th century 3 quarriers are known to have been working this last important Swindon site: they were Edwin Bradley, George Organ, and a Mr. Wiltshire. Between 1904 and 1922 Bradley entered upon a number of quarrying leases.[78] In 1913 he, along with Organ, entered into an agreement with Fitzroy Pleydell Goddard to fix the price of stone at 2s. 6d. a yard for building stone.[79] In 1933 the firm of Edwin H. Bradley purchased from the Goddard estate 2 a. of the Okus site, which became the headquarters of their building construction business.[80] Quarrying on the Okus site continued until the late 1950s. In 1965 the firm, specializing in the manufacture of compound building blocks, was employing 300 office staff and maintenance technicians at Swindon.[81]

In the 18th and early 19th centuries developments took place in Swindon, characteristic of those to be expected in a country market town. By 1719 an attorney had become established there who took apprentices.[82] There were two attorneys in 1784, when besides grocers, there were also the following crafts and professional men: 2 surgeon-apothecaries, a woolstapler, a brandy merchant, a saddler, a currier, 2 tallow-chandlers, 2 ironmongers, and an upholsterer.[83] The following 50 years saw some development of Swindon as a commercial centre. Three firms of attorneys were in practice in 1831, and there was a local bank, originally Strange, Garrett, Strange, and Cook, but by then known as Strange, Strange & Co., composed of a family of Swindon tradesmen.[84] In the earlier part of the century the Strange family had accumulated a large part of the town's trade, for not only were they bankers, but also grocers, cheesefactors, coal- and salt-merchants, undertakers, and drapers as well, and the owners of a ready-made clothes warehouse.[85] Between 1836 and 1839 the North Wilts. Bank opened a branch in Swindon, [86] and in 1842 Strange's was taken over by the City of Gloucester Banking Co.[87]

The remark of Richard Jefferies that the opening in 1810 of the Wilts. and Berks. Canal, which passed through the low-lying northern part of the parish, gave the 'first push' to the enormous development of Swindon in the 19th century, seems to overemphasize its contribution to the industrialization of the town.[88] The canal, however, certainly helped to increase the volume of its trade, especially before

and during the early years of the railway. Its most notable contribution lay in making Somerset coal available to the Swindon area, a factor which Brunel did not ignore when choosing Swindon as the site for a G.W.R. engine depot. But this trade dropped off sharply as the century progressed: in the period 1838–47 34,815 tons of coal were imported, but in the following two decades fell away to 25,184 and then to 14,659 tons.[89] Between 1868 and 1877 no more than 6,750 tons were imported. Tonnages of other imports carried by canal fell from 7,984 to 2,347 tons.[90] Export tonnages, never very great, similarly slumped. The canal had never been profitable, and the G.W.R. in time robbed it of the trade it had managed to establish, although figures tend to confirm the assertion that the advent of the railway and the erection of the railway works for a time stimulated canal trade.[91] In the later 19th century the Wilts. and Berks. Canal had a sorry history of decay, financial loss, and changed ownership. By 1906 all traffic had ceased and in 1914 the canal was closed.[92]

The establishment by the G.W.R. in 1841 of its engine depot and repair shops in the northern part of the parish, beyond the canal, naturally altered the whole course of Swindon's history.[93] The colossus of heavy engineering which came into being grew into one of the largest engineering units in the country, dominating the economic life of Swindon. This, of course, was not apparent at the outset, for the works and the adjacent railway settlement lay quite separate from the old town, with pasture land between and no connecting road. The two communities appear to have had little to do with one another in the early years, apart from the trade brought to the shops and beerhouses of the old town by the railway workers.[94] The newcomers were, indeed, strangers to the inhabitants of the old town, drawn from other parts of the country for their engineering crafts and skill. In 1851 more than 55 per cent of New Swindon's 2,371 inhabitants came from outside Wiltshire, having origins in the main in the counties of the West and South-West, in London, and some eastern counties, and in the North.[95] Later there came influxes of considerable size from the Midlands, and from Wales. But despite the acute shortage of accommodation in the railway settlement in the early years, railway workers apparently intermingled little with the inhabitants of Old Swindon, for no more than a handful of them had taken up residence there some eight years after the opening of the works.[96] One of the first immigrants to have an influence beyond the railway settlement was David Morrison, who became the leader of Chartism in Swindon and the neighbouring villages.[97]

An account of the Swindon railway works has

[74] R. J. Tarrant, 'Recollections of Swindon 80 odd years ago' (TS in Swindon Pub. Libr.).
[75] Slater's Dir. (1851).
[76] Goddard deeds penes Messrs. Townsends, Solicitors, Swindon.
[77] Ibid. [78] Ibid.
[79] Ibid. [80] Ibid.
[81] Ex inf. Mr. Lionel Bradley of Messrs. E. H. Bradley & Sons, Swindon.
[82] Apprentices and their Masters (W.A.S. Rec. Brch.), 25.
[83] Bailey's British Dir. (1784).
[84] Pigot, Nat. Com. Dir. (1830–1).
[85] For a description of Thomas Strange, see Morris, Swindon, 223–5.

[86] Cf. Robson, Com. Dir. (1839).
[87] Morris, Swindon, 261. [88] Jefferies, Swindon, 53.
[89] Swindon Pub. Libr., Wilts. and Berks. Canal Recs. Nos. 6, 7, Trade ledgers, 1837–60, 1861–79.
[90] Ibid. [91] C. Hadfield, Canals of Southern Eng. 287.
[92] V.C.H. Wilts. iv. 277.
[93] Cf. ibid. 208, also E. T. MacDermot, Hist. G.W.R. i, 74.
[94] Morris, Swindon, 243–7.
[95] Swindon Studies, 143–6. Since these pages contain some inaccuracies, calculations have been checked with the Census.
[96] H.O. 107/1833.
[97] Asa Briggs, Chartist Studies, 214.

been given elsewhere in the *Wiltshire History* and will, therefore, only be dealt with briefly here.[98] The reasons for Brunel's choice of Swindon as the site for a main engine depot and repair sheds are well-known: the change in gradient westwards from Swindon, the junction with the Cheltenham line, and the supply of Somerset coal.[99] The engine and repair houses came into operation in 1843 with an establishment of 423, a sixth of whom were skilled artisans.[1] With the construction of locomotives beginning in 1846, the number of employees increased more than fourfold in the space of two years.[2] This industrial explosion was the first of a series greatly to expand the size of the Swindon works and gave rise to some social problems, the most obvious being the shortage of housing.

The building of New Swindon has been described above.[3] But building could not keep pace with the expansion of the works. In 1845 Daniel (later Sir Daniel), Gooch, who as Locomotive Superintendent was in charge at Swindon until 1864, was urging the speedy completion of new cottages, since in some instances 10 or 12 people were living in 2 rooms, and when the night men got up the day men went to bed, and workers were leaving Swindon because they could not get a place of any kind to live.[4] The problem of accommodation continued for many years.

Almost from the outset additions were made to the railway shops, and for more than 60 years the works continued to expand while New Swindon grew up round them. By 1849 the original workshop space had been doubled.[5] Thereafter the erecting of new shops was almost continuous to accommodate the growing agglomeration of different kinds of railway engineering which came to be performed at Swindon during the 19th century. One main addition, built in 1861, was the rail-mill which at full capacity was reckoned capable of producing 19,300 tons of rails a year.[6] The most important addition, in terms of the increased volume of employment created, was the carriage works, transferred to Swindon in 1868.[7] By this date the inhabitants of Swindon were in little doubt about the economic advantages of having the railway works in their midst. Three years earlier a number of them, including some in the old town, had addressed a memorandum to the G.W.R. directors, expressing the view that, with the rest of the company's engineering works there, New Swindon was 'the fittest place' for the carriage works. As an added inducement they drew attention to the large population of artisans and labourers already there and the facilities of the railway town which could 'readily be extended to meet any increase'.[8] Early in the 20th century the carriage works alone were employing 5,000 workmen.[9]

Periods of industrial depression were experienced in the works. The first, and perhaps the most serious, occurred in 1849 when the number employed dropped from the 1,800 it had been the year before to 667.[10] There were also slumps between the late 1870s and mid 1880s when a lull in the demand for stock and a curb on expansion reduced wages.[11] The production of carriages was also halted for a time in the early 1890s.[12] But, on the whole, the Swindon works were not badly hit by the 'Great Depression'. Work created by the conversion from broad to narrow gauge and the introduction of new equipment to be manufactured accounted in part for this.[13] In 1875 the number employed was 4,000; by the end of the century it had risen to 11,500, and by 1905 it was over 14,000.[14]

For the first three decades of the 20th century this large labour force was engaged upon the production of locomotive engines, carriages, wagons, and fittings for rolling stock and permanent way in what by the beginning of the century had developed into one of the largest undertakings in British industry.[15] In 1924 14,369 people were employed and in 1939 the works covered more than 326 a.[16] But during the 1920s the peak in the number employed was reached and thereafter a decline began. The slump of 1930 affected the works considerably and some workers left Swindon.[17] In 1936 the number employed was 11,500 and this had dropped to 10,500 by 1939.[18] But much of this reduction was due not so much to the slump as to improved technical efficiency, and it is true to say that railway engineering in Swindon never experienced a truly severe or lasting depression.[19] Nationalization brought about some changes in the structure of the works and standardization of engines meant a reduction in some of the specialized work of the foundries and other shops.[20] In 1952 10,119 people were still employed[21] but the 1960s saw the long-expected contraction of the works so that by 1965 only 5,620 people were employed.[22]

Early in the 1950s the works had the capacity to build two or three new engines a week, and to repair over 1,000 annually.[23] In 1959, however, because of the conversion of the Western Region of British Railways to diesel motive power, the manufacture of steam locomotives ceased. The Swindon works had, therefore, during the early 1960s to change over from the 'world of steam', where the product, the steam locomotive, was almost entirely works-built, to the assembling and equipping of diesel locomotives, whose main parts had to be imported into the works. This entailed a reduction of productive capacity in certain sectors of the plant, and the re-equipping of the works for the building and maintaining of diesel engines.[24]

The scale and self-sufficiency of this heavy en-

98 *V.C.H. Wilts.* iv. 207–19.
99 Brit. Trans. Hist. R.O. HL 1/28, Gooch to I.K. Brunel, 18 Sept. 1840.
1 *V.C.H. Wilts.* iv. 208.
2 Ibid. 209.
3 See pp. 109–13, 115.
4 Brit. Trans. Hist. R.O. HL 1/1/2, Gooch to J. Hammond, 26 Nov. 1845.
5 *V.C.H. Wilts.* iv. 209.
6 Brit. Trans. Hist. R.O. HL 1/1/2, Gooch to Directors of G.W.R. 21 Dec. 1863.
7 *V.C.H. Wilts.* iv. 213.
8 Brit. Trans. Hist. R.O. G.W. 4/130.
9 *Swindon Guide* (c. 1905).
10 Brit. Trans. Hist. R.O. G.W. 8/6.

11 *V.C.H. Wilts.* iv. 215.
12 Ibid. 216.
13 Ibid. 213.
14 Ibid. 214–15.
15 Ibid. 215.
16 Ibid. 219.
17 Ibid.
18 Ibid.
19 Ibid.
20 Ibid.
21 Ibid.; *Swindon Guide* (1960), 17.
22 Ex inf. the Town Clerk's dept.
23 *Visit to the Swindon Works* (Inst. Mech. Engineers), 19 Jan. 1952.
24 *Railway Gaz.* Mar. 1963, 352.

gineering plant was a great source of strength to the Swindon economy. Part of this strength lay in bringing together many varieties of engineering skill. By 1849 there were already employed in the works draughtsmen, engine-turners, fitters, coppersmiths, brass-finishers, grinders, gas-fitters, smiths, spring-makers, and boiler-smiths.[25] A tradition of skill was created which passed from one generation of craftsmen to its successor. Despite criticisms levelled against so massive an undertaking, such as those mentioned in Alfred Williams's *Life in a Railway Factory*, the works continued to retain, at least to the outsider, the semblance of a 'complete industrial community'.[26] As such it possessed its own hierarchy, industrially significant within the works and socially significant within the town, its management and the town's leading figures were not infrequently drawn from the body of successful apprentices trained at the Mechanics' Institute.

For about a hundred years after the establishment of the railway works Swindon was practically a one-industry town. The few other 19th-century industries were all small. When the amount of building which had to be done is considered, it is not surprising that apart from the G.W.R. and the quarry owners, the largest single employer of men in 1851 was a builder, George Major, with 30 men working for him.[27] Numerous small brick-works flourished too. One between Drove Road and Victoria Road, belonging to the family of Turner, was probably started in the 18th century and its products are to be seen in many of Swindon's streets.[28] Another source of employment was cabinet-making. Charles Collier employed 13 men about the middle of the century, and shipped some of his joinery by flyboat from Swindon wharf.[29] Cabinet-making was still of some significance in Swindon in the early 20th century.[30] The connexion between Old Swindon and the neighbouring farming community was maintained by the numerous small engineering concerns specializing in the manufacture of farm machinery. One of them in mid century was owned by George Kerr, an iron and brass founder, who employed 8 men.[31] His business was later acquired by Messrs. Suter and Edwards, much of whose raw materials and equipment were brought to Swindon by barge.[32] Another local engineer was William Frampton, who specialized in cheese vats.[33] The engineering firm begun by William Affleck in the 1850s had premises at the Prospect Works and by the end of the 19th century had expanded to employ a 'large staff of men', adapting its numbers to the 'changed character of the town from an agricultural to a busy commercial centre.'[34] Besides the above-named engineers, there were others whose businesses were catalogued in local directories between the early 1840s and the late 1860s. Six are so mentioned, with such descriptions as iron and brass founder, millwright, machine

maker, agricultural implement agent, and winnowing machine maker.[35] There was also a 'working and consulting gas engineer', who supervised the gas-works, built about 1851.[36]

Some of the businesses and trades closely connected with the countryside persisted in Old Swindon: they included those of a bacon factor, corn and hop factors, and brewers.[37] There were, in addition, hat, boot, and shoe manufacturers in High Street. Old trades to continue were those of wool-stapling and currying. The Shepherd family, who had been prosperous woolmen in the 17th century, still continued their business.[38] The Reynolds family, to whom are ascribed origins of similar date, continued as curriers. Robert Reynolds was employing 10 men in mid 19th century, and began a boot manufacturing business in Mill Lane which specialized in boots and leggings for the country trade.[39]

In the later 19th century a clothing industry was established in Swindon. The clothing factories served the local community as auxiliaries to the railway works, for they could employ the female labour which was otherwise unemployed in a town of heavy engineering. One of the first factories to open belonged to J. Compton and Co., who supplied the G.W.R. with uniforms under contract, and occupied premises in Sheppard Street.[40] This became the largest clothing factory in the town, the number of employees increasing from 300 to 1,000 by the end of the century. By 1860 there was also a factory in Fleet Street, where Charles Lea operated a 'steam machine clothing manufactory'.[41] Charles Wills and Sons, a Bristol firm, opened a factory at Swindon in 1886,[42] which employed 400 work people in the early 1900s, half of whom were 'out-door' workers. Another factory, opening in 1902 with 75 employees, belonged to the Cellular Clothing Company, who specialized in undergarments and ladies' clothing.[43]

The clothing factories helped in the 19th century towards the process of diversification, chiefly by providing some employment of women. This process continued in the 20th century with the opening of a tobacco factory of W. D. & H. O. Wills in Colbourne Street in 1915, followed by the transference in 1919 of the Garrard Engineering and Manufacturing Co. Ltd. from Willesden to Newcastle Street, Swindon.[44] Both these factories depended on female labour, Garrard's employing 3,000 in 1960 and Wills' 650. Early in the Second World War the Plessey Company, makers of radio components, moved to a factory in Kembrey Street, and employed about 2,300 there in the early 1950s, again mostly women.[45] Also during the Second World War Vickers-Armstrong, aircraft manufacturers, took over an airfield at South Marston on the outskirts of Swindon, and in 1960 drew on a labour

[25] Brit. Trans. Hist. R.O. GW 8/6.
[26] *The Sphere*, 6 Nov. 1954.
[27] H.O. 107/1833.
[28] *Swindon Studies*, 166, 174, 176.
[29] Swindon Pub. Libr., Wilts. and Berks. Canal Recs. No. 29, Swindon wharfage accts. (exports), 1852–86.
[30] *Swindon Guide* (c. 1905).
[31] *V.C.H. Wilts.* iv. 202; R.G. 9/1271.
[32] *V.C.H. Wilts.* iv. 202; Swindon Pub. Libr., Wilts. and Berks. Canal Recs. No. 29. (see n. 29 above).
[33] *Moore's Almanack Supp.* (1855).
[34] *Swindon Advertiser*, Supp. 5 Feb. 1904.

[35] Cf. Pigot, *Nat. Com. Dir.* (1842); *Slater's Dir.* (1851), and *Moore's Almanack Supp.* (1852–68).
[36] Cf. *Slater's Dir.* (1851) and *Moore's Almanack Supp.* (1855).
[37] Pigot, *Nat. Com. Dir.* (1842); *Slater's Dir.* (1851), and *Moore's Almanack Supp.* (1852–68).
[38] Morris, *Swindon*, 43.
[39] R.G. 9/1271; *Swindon Advertiser*, Supp. 5 Feb. 1904.
[40] *Swindon Advertiser*, Supp. 5 Feb. 1904.
[41] *Moore's Almanack Supp.* (1860).
[42] *Swindon Advertiser*, Supp. 5 Feb. 1904.   [43] Ibid.
[44] *Swindon Guide* (1960), 24.   [45] *V.C.H. Wilts.* iv. 205.

force from the Swindon area of about 3,000.[46] R. A. Lister Ltd., taking over the former Admiralty wartime engineering workshops at Wroughton for their subsidiary, Marine Mountings, likewise drew on Swindon for workers.[47]

Some of these firms came to Swindon to escape the war-time hazards of more congested areas. After the war the corporation adopted a determined policy of encouraging such firms to remain and of attracting new and diversified industries to the town in order to avoid complete dependence upon the railway works.[48] This policy, which needed for its fulfilment an increased population drawn from elsewhere, was put into effect by means of the Town Development Act, 1952, which led to the acceptance by Swindon of industry and population transferred from the Greater London area.[49] New industries were attracted to the Cheney Manor industrial estate acquired by the corporation and developed from 1955 onwards. There a variety of firms established themselves, including specialists in precision engineering, such as member companies of the Plessey Group, the Metal Box Co., and several smaller concerns.[50] In 1965 the estate also contained some branch factories of clothing firms, small engineering and proto-type casting firms, a G.P.O. engineering depot, and distribution stores and warehouses. In 1954 the Pressed Steel Co. established a factory just over the borough boundary, in Stratton St. Margaret, which in 1965 employed 6,595 people, (about 1,000 more than the railway works at the same date).[51] Also in 1954 the corporation acquired Parsonage Farm, in the same parish, for development as an industrial estate and about eight years later, in 1962, work began on another such estate at Greenbridge, also in Stratton St. Margaret.[52]

MILLS. Domesday records the existence of two mills in Swindon in 1086. Both were valued at 4s. One was on the 12-hide estate of Odin the Chamberlain;[53] the other on the 5-hide estate of the Bishop of Bayeux.[54] The bishop's estate has been identified with the manor of Nethercott (*alias* Eastcott and Westcott);[55] that of Odin the Chamberlain probably formed part of the medieval manor of Swindon (*alias* Over and Nether, or West and East Swindon).[56] But it is impossible to connect the mills of Domesday certainly with any later mills in Swindon.

When Thomas Goddard acquired the manor of Over and Nether Swindon in 1563, two water-mills were included.[57] One of these was certainly the mill which stood south-west of the church of Holy Rood in 1773.[58] It was supplied with water from a spring called Church Well which flowed through a large

pond north of the mill. The mill had an overshot wheel, reckoned by Morris to be over 30 ft. high. Morris also affirmed that the machinery of the mill could be operated by a primitive form of turbine.[59] The mill was demolished about the middle of the 19th century, according to Morris, on the termination of a lease to a Mr. Kemble.[60] Shortly before 1867 the mill-pond was filled up,[61] but its site, marked by a shallow depression to the south-west of the ruins of Holy Rood, could still be seen in 1964.

A mill and land in Eastcott and Nethercott were conveyed to William Goldhyne and Margery his wife by Robert de Colcote, of High Swindon, and Maud his wife in 1339.[62] A mill in West Swindon belonged to William Stichell at the time of his death in 1618.[63] William's heir, John, mortgaged the mill in 1631, along with other property, to Henry Cusse.[64] In 1659 William Stichell, probably John's son, with his wife Frances, Arthur Vilett, and William Lawrence of Broome sold the mill and 5 a. of land to Timothy Dewell, the incumbent of Lydiard Tregoze.[65] At the time the mill was occupied by Thomas People.[66] From a description of the property conveyed to Dewell it is clear that this was the mill on the River Ray, just south of the road to Wootton Bassett, which went by several names, but which, by the 19th century had become known as Ladd's Mill (see below). In 1691 the mill, then called Arthur's Mill, was leased with land in Eastcott by John Cullum, a London woollen-draper, to Stephen Lawrence of Broome.[67] The mill is marked as Hall's Mill on a map of 1773.[68] In 1780 it was owned and occupied by Roger Hall, but that year was called Westcott Mill.[69] It was owned and occupied by Richard Simmonds, quarrier of Swindon, in 1805 when it was sold as Ladd's Mill to the Wilts. and Berks. Canal Company under powers enabling the company to acquire mills on streams likely to be affected by the needs of the canal.[70] It was subsequently sold by the company and in 1851 was occupied by Henry Brooks, miller.[71] It was included in the sale of property belonging to J. H. Sheppard in 1870.[72] No trace of it remained in 1964.

There was a windmill on the manor of Swindon held by Aymer de Valence (d. 1324).[73] This was possibly the mill which stood on the site of the King's Arms Hotel in Wood Street, formerly called Windmill Street.[74] It was pulled down some time before 1867, although in 1967 some traces were thought to remain in the stables behind the hotel.[75] The furlong in Swindon West Field called Windmill Furlong in the 17th and 18th centuries probably took its name from this mill.[76]

In 1849 Isaac Holdway, who had leased part of Okus Farm from Ambrose Goddard the previous

[46] Ibid. and *Swindon Guide* (1960), 23.
[47] *V.C.H. Wilts.* iv. 205.
[48] *Memo. on Potentialities of Swindon for Industrial Development* (1945).
[49] See p. 140.
[50] Cf. *Swindon Guide* (1960), 16–25.
[51] Inf. supplied by research assistant to the Town Clerk.
[52] Ex inf. the Town Clerk.
[53] *V.C.H. Wilts.* ii, p. 167.
[54] Ibid. p. 122.
[55] See p. 121. [56] See p. 119.
[57] Goddard MS. 4.
[58] *Andrews and Dury, Map* (W.A.S. Rec. Brch.), pl. 15.
[59] Morris, *Swindon*, 167–8.
[60] Ibid.
[61] R. Jefferies, *Jefferies' Land*, 80–81.

[62] C.P. 25(1)/254/44/14. [63] C 142/371/101.
[64] Ibid.; Goddard MS. 18.
[65] W.R.O. 348/2, no. 15. [66] Ibid.
[67] W.R.O. 348/1, no. 9.
[68] *Andrews and Dury, Map* (W.A.S. Rec. Brch.), pl. 14.
[69] W.R.O. Land Tax Assessment.
[70] Swindon Pub. Libr., Wilts. and Berks. Canal Recs. Ledger bk. 7 Dec. 1805.
[71] H.O. 107/1833.
[72] W.A.S. Libr., Devizes, Sale Cat. v, no. 32.
[73] *Cal. Inq. p.m.* vi, p. 328.
[74] Morris, *Swindon*, 2.
[75] R. Jefferies, *Jefferies' Land*, 74, and inf. supplied by Mr. Mark Child.
[76] Frequent references will be found among the Goddard MSS. See for e.g. nos. 204–6.

year, built a corn windmill there.[77] The mill still functioned in 1851, but shortly before 1854 was destroyed by fire.[78] A map of 1887 marks a corn-mill at Swindon Wharf on the north side of the Wilts. and Berks. Canal,[79] but this seems to have been worked for a short time only, and is not marked on maps of the 20th century. A flour-mill, known as Swindon Town Mill, was built for Ernest Clement Skurray in 1893. The mill ceased to operate as such in 1924 and was that year sold for a garage.[80]

MARKETS AND FAIRS. There was a market in Swindon in 1274 which, it was alleged, had been held for 15 years without warrant, and damaged that at Marlborough to the extent of 40s. a year.[81] Nevertheless, it clearly continued, for in 1289 the town was referred to as 'Chepyng Swyndon',[82] and in 1336 as Market Swindon.[83] A market was regularly mentioned as appurtenant to the manor,[84] so that the grant of a weekly market on Mondays to Thomas Goddard in 1626[85] must really have been a confirmation. Before the Civil War the market was a 'petty, inconsiderable one', but Aubrey said that it gained much in importance because the plague and the presence of a parliamentary garrison discouraged the graziers from going to Highworth. In 1670 Swindon continued 'a gallant market for cattle'.[86] In the early 19th century Swindon market was clearly still of some importance for cattle, although it was then held only monthly. Morris has vividly described the 'candle and lantern' market, held in the early hours of Monday morning, and over by breakfast time. The cattle were formed into two rows along High Street, occasionally reaching into Wood and Cricklade Streets, and inspected and sold by lantern light. Later in the century, however, the cattle market was not held so early in the day, so that the rows of cattle became a nuisance to the tradesmen of the town.[87] In 1848 it was said that it was tolerated only because the inhabitants feared losing the town's great reputation as a cattle market.[88] It is clear, however, that inconvenience to buyers and sellers caused a serious decline in the business, which was only halted by the enterprise of William Dore. About 1860 he began holding sales in a private yard near the Queen's Hotel at the station, generally on days other than market days and so evaded payment of toll. This did not pay, and about 1865 Dore built another yard just below Christ Church, where he held sales on market days.[89] In 1870 he moved to another yard in Lower Town where fortnightly sales were begun.[90] In 1873 Dore acquired a larger yard in Marlborough Road and by 1875 his sales were held weekly, and had almost entirely superseded the old market still held in High Street.[91] The pig market, held in the Square, had also become a nuisance,[92] and by the later 1870s Dore was selling

all kinds of stock in large numbers. Thus in 1879 2,600 cattle, 6,590 sheep, and 993 pigs were sold in his yard.[93] A public market-yard adjoining Dore's yard on the south was provided in 1887 by A. L. Goddard in an attempt to revive the old Swindon market.[94] In 1889 Goddard leased this market to the Swindon Central Market Company which thenceforth sub-let the market rights to various firms of auctioneers.[95] In 1930 the company purchased the market from the Goddard estate.[96]

After the death of William Dore in 1877 his firm of auctioneers and its successors continued to hold cattle sales fortnightly in the yard acquired by Dore. In 1949 this yard was bought by the Swindon Central Market Company and was amalgamated with the company's cattle market next door.[97] The combined cattle market and sale-yard were thenceforth managed by a firm of auctioneers called the Amalgamated Livestock Auctioneers.[98] During the Second World War the Swindon cattle market had a considerable trade and was the clearing centre for wide agricultural area. By the 1960s, however, trade was declining, although in 1965 the market was still held every week.[99]

In the early 19th century corn was sold in Swindon market by a small sample only, giving rise to a 'gin and water' market in which business was carried on over that drink in public houses. About 1840 Ambrose Goddard offered to give up tolls on corn for a number of years to persuade farmers and dealers to establish a 'pitched' market, in which the sample consisted of a whole sack out of the load. To provide for this two rows of movable posts and rails were made and put up in the Square each Monday, against which farmers placed their sacks if weather allowed. In 1852 the Swindon Market Company was formed to improve accommodation. It built a market-house facing the Square on the south side, to the design of Sampson Sage. This is a building of stone ashlar having an impressive five-bay front with classical pilasters and a central pediment. It was not, however, used for its original purpose and the arcaded lower story, evidently designed as a produce market, soon had its arcades filled in and was let to a firm of wine merchants. It had always been intended that the large upper room should be used for public purposes, thus giving rise to the building's name of the Town Hall. Only one small room was used to store the posts and rails and as a sack office, and the corn market remained in the same state as before.[1]

To remedy this the Swindon Central Market Company was founded in 1863 and built the present corn exchange, designed by Wilson and Wilcox of Bath, in 1866. A tower of four stages, built in 1864, forms a link between the corn exchange and the adjoining Town Hall; it is designed in an Italian Renaissance style, having an open top stage with

[77] Goddard MSS. 1885, 1887.
[78] H.O. 107/1833; ex inf. Mr. Mark Child.
[79] O.S. Map 6″, Wilts. XV (1st edn. 1887).
[80] Inf. about this mill supplied by Mr. Mark Child.
[81] Rot. Hund. (Rec. Com.), ii. 261.
[82] P.N. Wilts. (E.P.N.S.), 276.
[83] Cal. Pat. 1374–7, 205.   [84] e.g. Cal. Pat. 1558–60, 10.
[85] Goddard MS. 15; Cal. S.P. Dom. 1625–6, 352.
[86] Aubrey, Nat. Hist. Wilts. ed. Britton, 115; Aubrey, Topog. Coll. ed. Jackson, 191–2. R. Blome, Britannia (1673), 243, mentions a considerable market for fat cattle.
[87] Morris, Swindon, 302–4.
[88] Kelly's Dir. Wilts. (1848).

[80] Swindon Advertiser, Supp. 5 Feb. 1904.
[90] Dore's Swindon Almanack (1870, 1871).
[91] North Wilts. Dir. (1875).
[92] Swindon Pub. Libr., Old Swindon L.B. Min. Bk. 1865–77, s.a. 1868.
[93] North Wilts. Dir. (1880).
[94] Kelly's Dir. Wilts. (1899).
[95] Records of Swindon Central Mrkt. Co. penes Messrs. Fielder, Jones and Taylor, Auctioneers, Swindon. Thanks are due to Mr. Mark Child for consulting these records.
[96] Ibid.   [97] Ibid.
[98] Ibid.   [99] Local information.
[1] Morris, Swindon, 299–302 and see pl. facing p. 108.

Venetian windows, and is of Swindon stone with Bath stone dressings. Corn markets were held in the corn exchange until early in the present century; in the 1880s the trade was very large,[2] but by 1904 it had much declined, largely because of the decrease of corn growing in the district.[3] By 1910 the building had been converted to a skating rink[4] and was subsequently used as a cinema. In 1964 it was used as a dance and bingo hall.

Produce and butcher's meat were presumably always sold in the market. The cross which was mentioned as in need of seats in 1662[5] was probably for the accommodation for those that brought these goods. Late in the 17th century Thomas Goddard accepted the church-house of Swindon, previously used to house a few poor people, for conversion into a market-house.[6] It is not clear whether this was the small market-house in the centre of the Square which was pulled down in 1793.[7] About 1800 the meat market was apparently very small, only attended by one butcher who was the sole source of fresh meat in the town.[8] In 1848 poultry and butter were sold weekly and cheese monthly.[9] In New Swindon facilities for the sale of country produce were first provided in a covered market attached to the Mechanics' Institute.[10] In 1892 this was replaced by a new market off Commercial Road, provided by the local board.[11] The triangular building provided 17 shops, while the centre was an open space for country dealers. This was roofed over in 1903[12] and in 1906 was acquired by the corporation.[13] In 1965 it was used mainly for the sale of fruit and vegetables, and small items of hardware. Fridays and Saturdays were the principal market days.[14]

The market charter of 1626 also granted two fairs on the second Mondays in May and December.[15] There can be little doubt that, like the market, the right to hold these fairs was merely being confirmed. In 1775 four fairs were being held, on the Monday before 5 April, the second Monday after 11 May, the second Monday after 11 September, and the second Monday in December. All were said to be for cattle, pigs, and sheep, and the last for fat cattle as well.[16] These dates were regularly mentioned with minor variation from then on.[17] In the earlier 19th century the first fair was famous 'the country over' for the sale of in-calf heifers, and the second supplied them to those who had mistakenly bought barreners. The last was of great repute for fat cattle, while the March and September ones were hiring fairs which were well-attended. Large numbers of horses were sold at the fairs; they were lined up in what is now called Devizes Road, and gave it its former name of Horse Fair. The sales of cattle and horses dwindled later in the century before the competition of the large-scale auctions held regularly in the town. Horses in particular were sold at the White Horse

Repository of Deacon and Liddiard, founded in 1871. In the 1880s some 1,300 horses a year changed hands there.[18] The September hiring fair was still held as late as 1913, when, although it was 'an apology for the old-time function', a considerable amount of business was done.[19] As the 20th century progressed the fairs became more and more insignificant. By 1965 when the corporation acquired the right to hold them, they had become merged and amounted to no more than a few roundabouts in High Street.[20]

LOCAL GOVERNMENT AND PUBLIC SERVICES. As suggested above it appears likely that during the 13th century one of the medieval lords of Swindon may have deliberately encouraged urban growth there by granting his men the right to hold a market.[21] Nothing is known of any organ of local government formed as a result of this encouragement. But in the 17th century there was still an area of the manor recognized as the borough which had a constable, two 'carnarii', and an ale-taster, and sent a tithingman to the manorial court. The manors of East and West Swindon were also represented by tithingmen at the Goddards' court, but it is clear that by 1644, when its surviving records begin, the court had little power. Presentments of nuisances of cottages built on waste, of the lack of pillory and stocks, and of broken assizes of bread and ale, continue for numbers of years unamended, and the court seems to have been active only in the regulation of agricultural practice.[22] After 1780 it was held only every four years. It was last summoned in 1864.[23]

From the few records that survive it is clear that by the late 17th century the vestry was the only effective organ of local government within the parish. It seems, in intention at least, to have been also fairly democratic, for it was ruled that certain important parish matters could only be dealt with by the majority of parishioners at monthly meetings held after Sunday evening prayer.[24] Only with the consent of the majority at these meetings could paupers be accepted for relief; the cost of all work for the church had to be estimated and approved by the same meeting and its consent was necessary before any churchwarden could remain in office for more than a year. At the same time it was ruled that all parish officers should submit accounts, that expenses at times of visitations should not exceed £1, and that wayfarers should not be given relief.

Almost all that is known about the parish officers in the 17th century is that they were chosen from among the more substantial parishioners. In 1674 there were 46 parishioners qualified by their means to serve in person or by proxy.[25] Of these 46 16 were in West Swindon and the borough, 14 in Eastcott,

2 Ibid. 313.
3 *Swindon Advertiser*, Supp. 5 Feb. 1904.
4 *North Wilts. Dir.* (1910).
5 Goddard MS. 1147.
6 Ibid. 223.
7 Jefferies, *Swindon*, 74.
8 Morris, *Swindon*, 228.
9 *Kelly's Dir. Wilts.* (1848).
10 See pp. 110, 142.
11 Wilts. Cuttings, xii. 129.
12 *Kelly's Dir. Wilts.* (1911).
13 *Borough of Swindon Record of Administration* (1947).
14 Local information.
15 Goddard MS. 15.

16 *Traveller's Pocket Bk.* (1775).
17 e.g. *Univ. Brit. Dir.* v. 206; Lewis, *Topog. Dict. Eng.* (1838); *Kelly's Dirs. Wilts.*
18 Morris, *Swindon*, 305–12.
19 Wilts. Cuttings, xvi. 358.
20 *Evening Advertiser*, 25 Nov. 1965.
21 See p. 132. A plausible date would be c. 1259, for in 1274 a market had been held *de novo* for 15 yrs.: *Rot Hund.* (Rec. Com.), ii. 261.
22 Goddard MS. 1147.
23 Ibid. 1226, 1227.
24 Ibid. 1280.
25 Ibid. 1267.

10 in Nethercott, and 6 in Walcot—the four tithings into which the parish was divided certainly for rating, and possibly for other administrative purposes. The elective parish offices were those of constable, churchwarden, overseer of the poor, surveyor of the highways, assessor, and rate-collector.[26]

Overseers' accounts for 1669–70 and churchwardens' accounts for 1692–3 survive.[27] In that period the overseers spent £54 on the poor, disbursing a little over £2 every fortnight to 21 or 22 persons in sums ranging from 2s. 6d. to 3d. a person. The churchwardens, besides accounting for money spent upon the maintenance of the church and its services, assisted cases of unusual distress where relief from the overseers was inappropriate.[28]

For the years 1733–1824 a vestry minute book and, with some gaps, accounts of churchwardens, overseers, and surveyors of the highways survive.[29] By the time the minutes begin the vestry only met with any regularity to appoint the parish officers; every December it nominated those fit for election as surveyors of the highways, and every April it elected two churchwardens and two overseers. Meetings were held at other times to deal with important parish matters, which lay beyond the scope of the parish officers' duties. These meetings, however, seem to have decreased in frequency, the parish officers presumably assuming more responsibility for the conduct of parish affairs.

Next to appointing the officers the vestry's chief concern was poor relief. In the exceptionally severe winters of 1739 and 1768 it augmented the overseers' ordinary payments.[30] In 1755 it ordered that all paupers should wear the letters S.P. on the right shoulder of their coats. It had to repeat the order ten years later.[31]

In the later 18th century the vestry was forced to provide more adequate relief. A third overseer was elected in 1761[32] but the number of these officers was later reduced to two again. In 1786, however, a salaried assistant overseer was appointed, although it seems only temporarily.[33] In 1795 the churchwardens and overseers were authorized to sell flour to the poor at a subsidized rate of 5s. a bushel, the loss being made good from the poor rates.[34] The following year a full-time salaried overseer was appointed.[35] Besides managing the poor, the overseer was to conduct the making and selling of bread and ale for them, and a qualified person was employed by the parish to assist and instruct him in bread-making.[36]

In 1705 the church-house served as a dwelling for a few paupers in receipt of parish relief. But that year it was leased to one of the Goddards and converted into a market-house.[37] In 1767 the vestry decided to build a workhouse. It was to be 80 ft. by 20 ft. and it was hoped to borrow the money required for the building.[38] How and when the money was eventually raised is not known, but a workhouse was built, which in the mid 19th century was described as an 'old brick building' standing at the corner of the road to the quarries, now (1964) Springfield Road.[39] It was demolished in 1864 and had then recently been occupied by a few poor families.[40]

Land for a pest-house in West Swindon Field was given by Ambrose Goddard in 1753. The vestry then authorized the churchwardens and overseers to spend £100 on its building.[41] Precisely when it was built is not known, but it appears on a map of 1773.[42] A decision to build a blind-house at the corner of Short Hedge and the Sands was taken in 1762.[43]

A surgeon and apothecary to care for the poor was appointed by the vestry in 1827. His salary was to include attendance, medicines, fractures, and midwifery cases.[44]

The approach of a new era in local government was heralded in 1850 by the arrival of an inspector from the Board of Health to enquire into the sanitary condition of Swindon.[45] He came in response to a petition signed by 162 people, including the lord of the manor, the vicar, and the Wesleyan and Independent ministers, but a more numerously attended public meeting had already passed resolutions objecting to the parish being put under the provisions of the Public Health Act. He concurred with local feeling in agreeing that Old and New Swindon could not be united, and since at that time the new town was still a somewhat loosely-knit community, largely run by the G.W.R., confined his attention to the old. He found Old Swindon governed by the vestry and its officers and also, for the one purpose only, by an elected body of nine gas inspectors, three of whom retired annually. They raised rates charged on an area 200 yards beyond the furthest lamps, and paid the Swindon Gas Company to light and maintain 45 lamps situated in all parts of the town except Little London and Britannia Place. He was pleased by the general appearance of Swindon; the streets were well scavenged and lighted, in good repair, and named, and there were many large and handsome old houses. There were, however, no sewers. Some covered drains took house refuse and the washings of three slaughterhouses to pits and ditches outside the town, which soon became offensive; some, at the bottom of Victoria and Albert Streets, were very near dwelling-houses. The sewage of most houses went into cesspools called dry wells. In better houses they were covered and emptied at intervals, but those of poorer people were open and very offensive. Seepage from them caused all the wells in the town to be more or less contaminated, while the public water supply at the church pond was dirty. In these

[26] Ibid.
[27] Ibid. 1264, 1276.
[28] For some extracts from these accounts, see *Swindon Studies*, 63–66.
[29] In Christ Church, Old Swindon. Some facts from the overseers' accts. have been extracted and printed in Morris, *Swindon*, 317–18, 320.
[30] Vestry Min. Bk. 20 Jan. 1739, 25 Jan. 1768.
[31] Ibid. 8 July 1755, 4 May 1766.
[32] Ibid. 24 Mar. 1761.
[33] Ibid. 3 June 1783.
[34] Ibid. 8 Feb. 1795.
[35] Ibid. 1796 (no more exact date given), 5 Apr. 1796.
[36] Ibid. 5 Apr. 1796.
[37] Goddards MS. 223.
[38] Vestry Min. Bk. 20 Nov. 1767.
[39] Morris, *Swindon*, 81.
[40] Ibid.
[41] Vestry Min. Bk. undated entry but between entries dated Dec. 1752 and 24 Apr. 1753.
[42] *Andrews and Dury, Map* (W.A.S. Rec. Brch.), pl. 15.
[43] Vestry Min. Bk. 12 May 1762.
[44] Note in Acct. Bk. 1733–1827 in Christ Church, Old Swindon.
[45] Swindon Pub. Libr., G. T. Clark, *Rep. to Bd. of Health on Swindon* (1851).

circumstances the inspector recommended the immediate application of the Act to the old town, and the provision of sewerage and water supply.[46]

In spite of this the Act was not adopted by either town until 1864 when, it has been suggested, both feared inclusion in a rural sanitary district.[47] The history of the two boards of health then appointed, and the urban district councils which succeeded them in 1894 can be traced here separately, beginning with that of New Swindon.[48] The board there consisted of twelve members from its first election until 1895, when the number was increased to 30. The board's area covered 974 a. Clerk, surveyor, inspector of nuisances, and treasurer, all part time, were appointed, and a seal depicting a locomotive with the motto 'Ferra cuncta moventur' was adopted. The first question to receive the board's attention was that of public lighting. The G.W.R. properties in the town had long been lit by gas, but previous proposals to have public lighting had met with strong opposition. In 1864, however, the members of the Free Christian Church subscribed for a lamp to be placed by the Golden Lion Bridge, and, shamed into action, the board contracted with the New Swindon Gas Company for 25 lamps to be put in Westcott Place, Bridge Street, and Eastcott Hill.[49] This company, established in 1863, had that year opened another gas works in Queen Street.[50] The extension and supervision of the town's gas lighting remained a regular function of the board. The board also exerted its control over the town streets, other than those repaired by turnpike commissioners; continual attention was given to making builders of new roads make them up to a certain standard, and to providing lengths of footpath in frequented places. It is clear, nevertheless, that the pavements of the town still remained in a bad state in the 1880s. In 1880 the board refused to consider a general paving, in spite of many protests. In 1868 the streets were ordered to be named and the houses numbered, and street-watering was begun. The first road sign in Swindon was no doubt the 'Danger' board at the top of Prospect Hill which the Swindon Amateur Bicycle Club were authorized to put up in 1883.

The great preoccupation of the board was, however, with sewerage and sewage disposal. After a committee had enquired into the sanitary state of the district, the board began to lay sewers in 1866; these merely ran out of the town into ditches, for in 1870 the owner of an estate in Rodbourne Cheney complained of the pollution of the River Ray by sewage. The board immediately decided to buy a farm of 108 a. in Rodbourne Cheney for £7,750 and laid it out as a sewage farm, and in 1871 new and more adequate sewers were laid in the town. A further action for river pollution was begun in 1872, and large sums were spent on trying to make the farm more efficient. For a time the works were regarded as complete, but more pollution led to further extensive works in the town to separate the surface water from the sewage and so prevent the

farm from being deluged. The board managed the farm, apparently not with great success, through a bailiff, and questions of agriculture and schemes to make the farm absorb more sewage occupied much of its time.

The board was long unwilling to meddle with other public schemes. Water supply was left to private initiative. The Swindon Water Company (after 1872 called the Swindon Waterworks Company) was formed in 1857, although its waterworks at Wroughton were not begun until 1866.[51] A first attempt to bring piped water from Wroughton failed in 1867 when pipes leading to the G.W.R. cottages in New Swindon burst.[52] At first the relations between the board and the company were limited to bickering over the laying of pipes in roads, but in the 1880s the board regularly used its powers to make landlords give their tenants a proper supply. In 1894 the works were taken over by a joint water board of the Old and New Swindon Local Boards under the Swindon Water Act.[53] A scheme to take over the New Swindon Gas Works failed in 1885–6.

The board's reluctance to concern itself with road improvements, particularly with the improvements to the canal bridges and on Eastcott Hill, has been mentioned above.[54] The Eastcott Hill schemes, and the idea of a new road to the bottom of Victoria Street, involved a measure of co-operation with the Old Swindon Board, which could not be faced. In 1878 delegates from both boards agreed on a scheme to appoint a joint surveyor, but New Swindon refused to ratify it. The first signs of successful co-operation came in the matter of fire precautions. The board had entered into an agreement with the water company at its formation for the supply of water to extinguish fires, and in 1869 it bought four lengths of hose. The railway company was relied upon for engines; in 1870 it introduced a powerful steam fire-engine which was made available in the town.[55] The scheme which involved the Old Swindon Board was inaugurated two years later when each board contributed to the cost of maintaining a private telegraph line from the manager's house to the works at Wroughton, so that the supply could be turned on in case of fire at night. In 1880 the boards agreed to build a joint fire station in Victoria Street (later Road).

More important instances of co-operation came in the field of public health. The earliest arrangements in New Swindon were made by the railway when the G.W.R. Medical Fund Society was founded in 1847.[56] In 1853 an outbreak of typhus saw the company active in cleansing the town, and in 1860 baths were provided, first at the Mechanics' Institute and then behind the 'Barracks'.[57] Public arrangements began in 1871 when the local board appointed a paid medical officer of health. At the end of the year there was a small-pox epidemic, and the two boards joined to build an isolation hospital at a site in Okus Great Field, on which the pesthouse had stood for at least a century.[58] In 1873 New Swindon refused to join with neighbouring sanitary

[46] Based on the Min. Bks. of both boards in Swindon Pub. Libr.
[47] *Swindon Studies*, 130.
[48] Subsequent information about the activities of the boards and the U.D.Cs., except where otherwise stated, from Min. Bks. in Swindon Pub. Libr.
[49] *Swindon Advertiser*, Supp. 5 Feb. 1904.
[50] *Dore's Swindon Almanack* (1864).

[51] Min. Bks. of company in Swindon Pub. Libr.
[52] Ibid.
[53] Swindon Water Act, 57 & 58 Vic. c. 181 (local and personal act).
[54] *Swindon Advertiser*, Supp. 5 Feb. 1904.
[55] *Dore's Swindon Almanack* (1870).
[56] *Swindon Studies*, 114–15.   [57] Ibid. 115–16.
[58] *Andrews and Dury, Map* (W.A.S. Rec. Brch.), pl. 14.

authorities in appointing a full-time medical officer of health. In 1877 the first public urinals were placed at the station, Faringdon Road, and the Golden Lion Bridge, but in 1881 the board declined to build a public slaughterhouse. Some trouble was experienced because of the nearness of the town streets to agricultural land, and the board often had to take action against offensive ditches and overhanging trees. Towards the end of the century the canals, rapidly falling into disuse, became a nuisance through pollution. In spite of this the board opposed their closure in 1874, and its successor, the U.D.C., again did so in 1897 because it feared the loss of the towpaths as highways.[59]

The Victoria Hospital in Okus Road was built and supported by subscription in 1887–8 to the design of W. H. Read on land given by A. L. Goddard. It was extended in 1894.[60] The two boards were more concerned with the provision of better accommodation for the treatment of infectious diseases. In 1888 the old hospital in Okus Field was dismantled because the boards quarrelled over it; the New Swindon Board rented a house called the Firs at Wroughton, thereby causing a public protest meeting in the village, and received patients from Old Swindon by arrangement.[61] In 1892 the boards joined with the Highworth R.D. in building a new isolation hospital at Gorse Hill, designed by H. J. Hamp.

In 1891 the New Swindon Board built its new offices in Regent Circus on a site strategically situated between the centres of Old and New Swindon. This was a brick building with stone dressings 'in a vaguely 17th-century Dutch style', designed by Brightwen Binyon of Ipswich,[62] and later known as the Town Hall.

Towards the end of the century the boards had to co-operate in other projects. The question of a town cemetery first came to the fore in 1869, when nothing was done. In 1876, when the vestry proposed providing one for Old Swindon, one member pointed out that a joint one would be more satisfactory.[63] A public meeting in New Swindon immediately supported the idea of a burial board but the vestry disliked it, apparently on the grounds that accommodation would be provided for dissenters, and a poll of the parish was called for. This aroused violent controversy about whether the expenses of the poll could be paid for out of the poor rate or the district rate, and in these quarrels and in a new debating point over the necessity of a school board, the original proposal seems to have disappeared.[64] Four years later the matter was raised again by the Old Swindon Board, and discussed in a friendly way with the New Swindon Board.[65] The matter came to a head when St. Mark's burial ground had to be closed in 1881; the two boards agreed on action in spite of the opposition of the Vicar of St. Mark's,[66] and a burial board was set up and the cemetery off Clifton Street laid out.

The history of the Swindon School Board is dealt with below. It included many members of both local

boards, and provided a good example of how one authority could work successfully in both districts. Among other activities of the New Swindon Board, and of the urban district council which replaced it in 1894, may be mentioned the provision of allotments, begun on the Rodbourne sewage farm in 1887, and of open spaces. The first of the latter had been provided by the G.W.R. near St. Mark's church as early as 1844.[67] In 1889 the local board bought the Rodbourne recreation ground, and the U.D.C. provided other sites at Birch Street, Edinburgh Street, and Cambria Bridge Road in 1898–9.

In contrast with that of New Swindon Old Swindon Local Board had a stormy history. In 1866 the *Swindon Advertiser* wrote that 'the manner in which the first local board was elected . . . is a notoriety—a greater farce was never enacted in this or any other town, the election being nominally with the ratepayers, but in reality managed by one or two individuals'. It went on to comment on the very high rate, 2s. 3d. in the £, compared with 1s. 3d. in New Swindon, and alleged that even then it was dissipated in extravagant salaries and office expenses.[68] The board's earliest efforts were here, as in New Swindon, directed to sewerage and sewage disposal. In 1866 A. L. Goddard let to the board two areas each of 30 a. lying north and south of the town to be laid out for receiving sewage, and sewers were made in the town. In 1871, however, Goddard took advantage of a stipulation in the lease to withdraw the land to the north on the ground that it was a nuisance, and offered part of Broome Farm instead.[69] The expense of taking all the sewage through or round Swindon Hill prompted the board to reject this, but after failing to buy some of the Stratton St. Margaret glebe, they were forced to take 142 a. at Broome on a 21-year lease at £357 a year. At the same time they were granted a lease of a spring in the Wroughton road for flushing the new sewers, which they then began to construct. Even before this the local board had been the target of the *Swindon Advertiser*, which repeatedly complained of its failure to deal adequately with sanitary matters, and of the flippancy with which its proceedings were conducted. Now the management of the sewage farm and the losses in which it involved the board brought regular attacks. In 1872 its accounts were said to be much confused, and in 1877 a Ratepayers' Protection Association was formed and demanded a judicial enquiry into its affairs.[70] A year later the *Advertiser* delivered its most tremendous denunciation, not sparing New Swindon either. 'The parish was manoeuvred into its local boards in the first outset, and the ratepayers have been the victims of a series of manoeuvres ever since', wrote William Morris; 'for a succession of bungles, muddles and disappointments there has been nothing to compare with the history of our local boards'.[71] In 1882, however, the *Advertiser* reverted to its usual line of comparing the high rates of Old Swindon with the much lower ones in the new town, although it admitted that things were

[59] *Swindon Studies*, 137–8.
[60] *Swindon Advertiser*, Supp. 5 Feb. 1904.
[61] *North Wilts. Dir.* (1889); *Swindon Advertiser*, 4 Feb. 1888.
[62] Pevsner, *Wilts.* (Bldgs. of Eng.), 458; see pl. facing p. 156.
[63] *Swindon Advertiser*, 12 June 1876.
[64] Ibid. July to Sept. 1876, *passim*.

[65] Ibid. 19 July, 18 Sept. 1880.
[66] Ibid. 5 Feb. 1881.
[67] *Swindon Studies*, 120.
[68] *Swindon Advertiser*, 20 Aug. 1866.
[69] Ibid. 8 July 1872.
[70] Ibid. e.g. 22 June, 24 Aug. 1868, 3 Apr. 1872, 17 Mar. 1877.
[71] Ibid. 23 Mar. 1878.

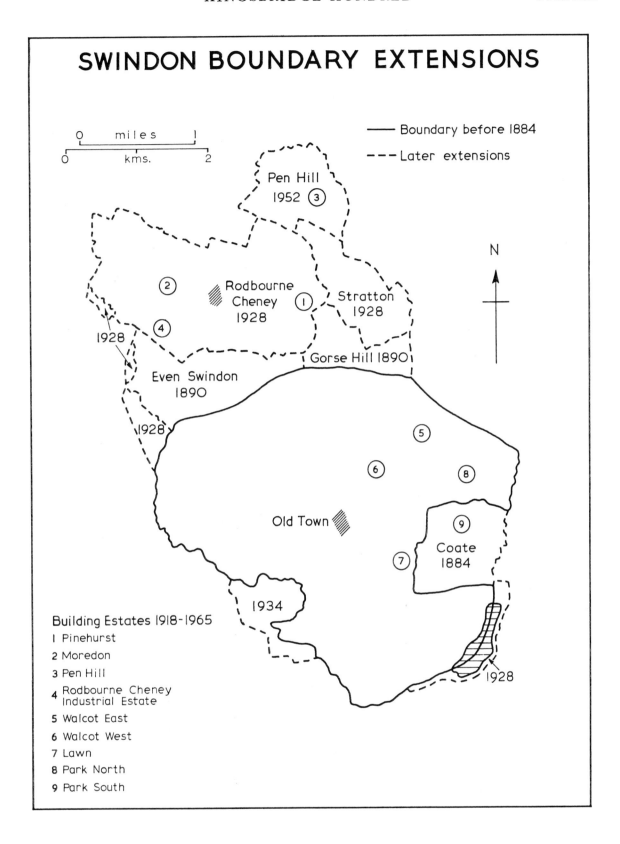

SWINDON BOUNDARY EXTENSIONS

Boundary before 1884
Later extensions

Pen Hill 1952 ③

N

② Rodbourne Cheney 1928 ① Stratton 1928

④
1928
Even Swindon 1890
Gorse Hill 1890
1928

⑤
⑥ ⑧
Old Town
⑨
⑦ Coate 1884
1934
1928

Building Estates 1918-1965
1 Pinehurst
2 Moredon
3 Pen Hill
4 Rodbourne Cheney Industrial Estate
5 Walcot East
6 Walcot West
7 Lawn
8 Park North
9 Park South

better than they had been. The ratepayers could feel relief and hope,[72] but were to beware of Stone and Sammes, two protagonists, who constituted a rowdy and unbusinesslike element.[73] In 1884 Stone and his 'myrmidons' allied themselves with the lord of the manor in a dispute with the board over an obstruction of the highway, but in the upshot Goddard pleaded guilty at Salisbury Assizes.[74] The following year Stone and his party were defeated, to the *Advertiser's* great delight.[75] In its late years, however, the Old Swindon Board showed more activity in performing its functions. Some instances have been mentioned above in the provision of hospital accommodation, water supply, and a cemetery. In 1894 it provided the Town Gardens, a recreation ground of 7 a. on the site of quarries in Okus Field.[76]

The idea that it would be better to have one local authority for the two towns was first put forward in the 1870s. The occasion was the difficulty of setting up a burial board, because the areas of the two local boards added together did not make the whole parish, so that neither board nor poor rates could fairly be used.[77] This was because the tithings of Broome and Walcot were not in either area, but were reckoned part of the rural sanitary area. Between 1857 and 1862 a series of lawsuits had established that Walcot was not liable to parish highway rates,[78] so that the parish was under three authorities for sanitation and highways, but only one for education and poor relief. In 1878 William Morris wrote optimistically that old jealousies were dying out, and the prejudices of a former day giving way to friendly feeling, and forecast that incorporation must come soon.[79] In fact it was not until the 1890s that amalgamation seemed at all likely, and even then the Old Swindon Council was very loth to agree. When it was finally won over, some voices in New Swindon had qualms that its change of heart was due to its bad drainage, poor roads, and high rates. The physical junction of the two towns had brought some disputes over the boundary between the districts, and the joint authorities which had been created for public purposes posed many financial problems, and led to suspicions that one district was paying for the other.[80] A county council enquiry on amalgamation in 1893–4 came to nothing, but in 1897 the question of the incorporation of the two districts as a borough was first put forward. The idea immediately gained much support in the town and won over the Old Swindon Council. A government enquiry revealed no considerable opposition, and a charter to take effect from 9 November 1900 was granted.[81]

The new borough consisted of the entire ancient parish and the added districts of Even Swindon and Gorse Hill, a total of 4,246 a. It was divided into six wards each returning six councillors and there were twelve aldermen, one of whom was mayor.[82] The same six wards existed in 1965. The offices built by the New Swindon Local Board in 1891 in Regent Circus became the offices of the corporation.[83] A consolidation agreement was made with the county council for policing the newly created borough by the county police force.[84] A separate magistracy for Swindon was obtained in 1906.[85] In 1962 a separate court of Quarter Sessions was granted.[86]

Until after the First World War there was but little relationship between national party politics and the affairs of the borough council. From the time of the creation of the New Town Local Board in 1864 rival groups existed, but these represented local interests rather than national party divisions. The G.W.R. was naturally strongly represented and a minority opposition soon arose. The nonconformist churches, too, which had a strong following in the town in the later 19th century, put up their own candidates. Before the end of the century candidates were also sponsored by both the Conservative Party and the Swindon and District Trades Council, which soon after its formation in 1891 revealed an affinity with the Independent Labour Party. But in so far as there was any party division during the first eighteen years of the borough council's history, this followed the national pattern of Conservative versus Liberal, without either obtruding unduly. A Labour Party group appeared on the council in *c.* 1919 and to oppose this the older parties combined to form the Citizens' League. The League lasted but a short time and thereafter the issue was a clear-cut one between Labour and Independent. In the late 1920s Labour almost gained control of the council but thereafter its influence declined for a time and it did not succeed until 1945. In 1965 Labour still controlled the council.[87]

The early years of the corporation were marked by great vigour in providing new amenities and improving existing ones. The old water supply from Wroughton was augmented by new works at Ogbourne St. George built in 1903. Already in 1895 the New Swindon U.D.C. had obtained an Electric Lighting Order, and in 1903 an electricity works was opened in Corporation Street on the site of Lower Eastcott Farm. In 1911 a new cemetery was laid out in Whitworth Road.[88] The idea of tramways in Swindon had first been considered in 1883, when steam was suggested as the motive power. An ambitious scheme was put forward soon after incorporation, providing for two routes between Old and New Swindon, and four routes to the borough boundary, a total of 8 miles. In fact the system as opened in 1904 amounted to 3 miles 5 furlongs, along which ran 9 vehicles operated by an overhead trolley system. From a centre at the junction of Fleet and Bridge Streets routes ran to the Square in Old Swindon, to Gorse Hill, and to Rodbourne Road.[89] In 1927 a few motor buses were introduced to supplement the 13 trams then operating, and two years

[72] Ibid. 18 Mar., 1 Apr. 1882.
[73] Ibid. 1 Apr. 1882, 24 Mar., 31 Mar. 1883.
[74] Ibid. 29 Mar., 19 July, 12 July 1884.
[75] Ibid. 28 Mar. 1885.
[76] *Swindon Borough Guide* (1906).
[77] *Swindon Advertiser*, 12 June, 14 Oct. 1876.
[78] Wilts. Cuttings, xvi. 358; Goddard MS. 1143. Broome and Walcot were added to the Old Swindon district in 1895.
[79] *North Wilts. Dir.* (1878).
[80] *Swindon Advertiser*, Supp. 5 Feb. 1904.

[81] *Swindon Studies*, 130–4.
[82] *Swindon Advertiser*, Supp. 5 Feb. 1904.
[83] See p. 136.
[84] Ex inf. the Town Clerk.
[85] *North Wilts. Dir.* (1908).
[86] *Swindon and District Review*, Feb. 1963.
[87] Thanks are due to Mr. D. H. MacLean of Swindon for advice on this paragraph.
[88] *Kelly's Dir. Wilts.* (1911).
[89] *Swindon Borough Guide* (1906); *Swindon Studies*, 139–40.

No. 42 Cricklade Street, built 1729

Congregational Church, Victoria Street, built 1866, demolished *c.* 1945

SWINDON

later the tramway services were entirely replaced by 38 buses.[90] In 1964 the town's bus services were still being operated by the Swindon Corporation Transport Undertaking.

In 1919 the borough council began work on its first housing estate at Pinehurst, to the north of the town.[91] Between this date and 1925 some 932 council dwellings were built, almost all on this one estate.[92] The boundary extensions of 1928 brought increased responsibilities for the council.[93] The period between the World Wars thus saw a steady expansion of the town, calling for numerous additions and improvements to the public utilities and services.

By 1925 the electricity generating station in Manchester Road had reached full capacity, and the corporation decided to supplement supply by building a new power station at Moredon, just within the borough boundary.[94] This was opened in 1929.[95] In 1936 the Moredon station became a selected station for the Central Electricity Board.[96] No new supply of water for Swindon had been added since the opening of the pumping plant at Ogbourne St. George in 1903.[97] In 1931 the first bore hole was sunk at Latton and three years later the waterworks there were opened.[98]

The period between the World Wars also saw some additions to the town's amenities. In 1914, in connexion with their promotion of a Canal Abandonment Act, the corporation acquired Coate Water and about 80 a. of land surrounding it, although part of the land and mile-long reservoir at that date lay outside the borough boundary.[99] After 1928 land and water came wholly within the borough, and subsequent improvements to the property, mostly made after the Second World War, provided Swindon with a valuable open space.[1] Coate Farm, the birthplace of Richard Jefferies, lying north of the reservoir, was opened by the corporation as a museum in 1960.[2] The original house dates from the late 17th or early 18th century but was extensively added to in the nineteenth. In the centre of the town the corporation acquired the Park recreational ground from the G.W.R. Company in 1925 in exchange for part of the Rodbourne recreation ground.[3]

Between the two World Wars Swindon continued to rely to a large extent upon the services of the G.W.R. Medical Fund Society. In 1927 the society's hospital in Faringdon Road was enlarged to accommodate 42 beds.[4] But some steps were taken to provide other hospital accommodation outside the G.W.R. scheme. The isolation hospital at Gorse

Hill, built in 1892,[5] had been somewhat enlarged soon after it was taken over by the corporation in 1900.[6] The voluntarily supported Swindon and North Wilts. Victoria Hospital, founded in 1887 in Okus Road, was extended in 1923, and in 1930 when two new wards were added.[7] The hospital was recognized as a training school for state registered nurses in 1931 and in 1939 had 90 beds.[8] Kingshill House was acquired, extended, and opened as a maternity hospital by the corporation in 1931.[9]

The history of public education in Swindon between 1902 and 1944, when the council's education committee was responsible for elementary education within the borough, is traced below.[10] To house a number of exhibits collected privately, the town's first museum was opened in 1920 by the corporation in a building in Regent Circus, formerly used as a Roman Catholic church.[11] The museum was moved in 1930 to Apsley House in Bath Road.[12] In 1964 an art gallery was built on the east side of the house.[13]

By 1936 the borough council had quite outgrown its offices in the Town Hall in Regent Circus. All departments, except those of the town clerk and borough treasurer, had to be housed in various buildings scattered about the town.[14] That year a small recreation ground in Euclid Street was used as a site and work begun on building new civic offices. The architects were Messrs. Bertram, Bertram, and Rice, of Oxford. The building, which was opened in 1938, is of brick with stone plinths and dressings to the main doors and windows. It is planned around two quadrangles and includes a council chamber 35 ft. by 50 ft.[15] By 1965 these offices in their turn had become far too small for the borough council's greatly enlarged staff, and temporary accommodation in the grounds and elsewhere in the town had to be used.

From a town of 54,000 inhabitants in 1921, Swindon grew to one of about 61,000 in 1939[16] and there was a further considerable rise in population during the Second World War.[17] Immediately the war was over the council recognised the need to plan for the town's future expansion and development. At this date more than half the male population was still employed by the G.W.R. but the council foresaw the dangers and disadvantages of continued dependence upon a single industry for employment.[18] The danger had to some extent been foreshadowed during the depression of the 1930s[19] and in 1943 the council was determined to adjust the economic and social balance of the community by attracting a far wider range of industries

[90] *Borough of Swindon Record of Administration* (1947), 109.
[91] *Local Government is our Business*, Handbk. issued by N.A.L.G.O. (1960), 35, and see above p. 116.
[92] Inf. supplied by the Borough Architect's dept.
[93] See p. 116.
[94] Wilts. Pamphlets, 70, *Official Visit to Moredon Power Station, Oct. 1929.*
[95] Ibid.
[96] *Planning for Swindon, 1945.*
[97] See p. 138.
[98] Wilts. Pamphlets, 37, *Official Opening of Latton Water Scheme, 1934.*
[99] Wilts. Pamphlets, 28, J. B. Jones, *The Coate Reservoir System,* and see p. 8.
[1] Ibid.
[2] *21 Years of Public Library Service in Swindon.*
[3] *Swindon Studies,* 120.
[4] *V.C.H. Wilts.* v. 344.

[5] See p. 136.
[6] Ex inf. the Town Clerk and *Kelly's Dir. Wilts.* (1903).
[7] *Kelly's Dir. Wilts.* (1939); *Swindon and N. Wilts. Victoria Hosp. Annual Rep. 1934.*
[8] Local information and *Kelly's Dir. Wilts.* (1939).
[9] *V.C.H. Wilts.* v. 335.
[10] See pp. 159–60.
[11] *W.A.M.* xli. 319.
[12] *Swindon Studies,* 136.
[13] *Swindon Public Librs. 1943–64* (pamphlet in Swindon Pub. Libr.).
[14] Wilts. Pamphlets, 6, *Opening of Civic Offices, 5 July 1938.*
[15] Ibid.
[16] *Census,* and see p. 117.
[17] See p. 116.
[18] *Memo. on Potentialities of Swindon for Industrial Development.*
[19] See p. 129.

to the town.[20] To do this considerable expansion was necessary and in 1945 the council produced a preliminary report upon some of the ways this might be achieved.[21] In 1951 the county council, by then the planning authority for Swindon, prepared the first development plan for the borough which allowed for an additional population of some 9,300 by 1971.[22] Before this plan was approved, however, Swindon was accepted for expansion under the Town Development Act of 1952 to receive about 20,000 people and some industries from the Greater London area.[23] At first it was proposed that all development should be within the borough boundary but in 1959 government approval was given to a plan for a total population of about 110,000 to be accommodated in Swindon and the neighbouring parish of Stratton St. Margaret.[24]

The development of the post-war housing estates has been briefly traced above.[25] A small extension of the borough boundary in 1951 brought in an area then being developed as the Penhill housing estate.[26] Between 1945 and 1965 the council built some 9,000 dwellings and 85 shops within the borough boundary.[27] In 1961 permission was given for Swindon to build outside the borough boundary on the east, and here by 1965 some 480 houses had been built, which, instead of leasing, the corporation sold to tenants of council houses, who wished to buy their own homes.[28] In c. 1955 the corporation provided its first industrial estate and on this, as on the two estates laid out later, about half the factories and warehouses were built by the corporation and leased to the various industrial concerns.[29]

To accompany these developments large-scale improvements to the public utilities were essential. In 1953-4 a central relief sewer was built and the Rodbourne sewerage works were enlarged,[30] so that the Broome works could be closed by 1962.[31] In the late 1950s a fourth bore hole was sunk at Latton waterworks, the main source of water supply in 1965,[32] although water also came from Ogbourne St. George and from Wroughton. The gas works of the South Western Gas Board in Chapel Street at Gorse Hill, were enlarged in the early 1940s.[33]

In certain spheres of local government the borough council lost powers both to the county council and to national bodies in the re-organisation that followed the Second World War. But as the only completely industrial town in a predominantly rural county Swindon had frequently to be treated as an exception and in practice continued to manage most of its own affairs. Even so, the borough council believed that the full autonomy which county borough status would give was desirable for the town

and an application under the Local Government (Boundary Commission) Act, 1945, was made in 1947. As a result county borough status was recommended, but, before the recommendation was put into effect, the commission was dissolved.[34]

Under the Education Act of 1944[35] Swindon ceased to be a Part III authority, but, as shown elsewhere, became the one 'excepted district' in the county.[36] By the Town and Country Planning Act of 1947[37] the county council became the planning authority for the whole county. But by agreements made in 1948, 1957, and 1960 wide delegation of planning power was made by the county council to the borough.[38] A special arrangement for the Swindon area was made under the National Health Service Act of 1946[39] when a sub-committee of the county health committee, composed chiefly of members of the borough council, was formed to administer almost all the personal health services within the borough and neighbouring area and the services of a full-time medical officer of health were retained. In 1961 the sub-committee was replaced by a committee of the borough council and additional powers were delegated to Swindon so that the borough administered all mental health and welfare services dealing with the blind, deaf, and handicapped.[40]

The isolation hospital at Gorse Hill and the Swindon and North Wilts. Victoria hospitals came under the Oxford Regional Hospital Board after 1946, and under the board were administered by a Swindon and District Hospital Management Committee.[41] The G.W.R. hospital was closed in 1960.[42] In 1957 work began on a large new general hospital of 800 beds on a 20-acre site at Okus.[43] The hospital, the first to be approved in the country after the Second World War, was named after Princess Margaret, who laid the foundation stone.[44] It was designed by Messrs. Powell and Moya, and the first sections came into operation in 1960.[45] The school of nursing was opened in 1962[46] and further extensions were being built in 1965.

Two important properties were purchased by the council immediately after the Second World War. In 1943 Lydiard Park was bought with the intention of converting it into a conference centre,[47] and at about the same time the council acquired the Lawn, the Goddard family home in Old Swindon.[48] A Garden of Remembrance, off Drove Road, was opened in 1950 by Princess Elizabeth (later Queen Elizabeth II) when she visited Swindon to mark the borough's jubilee year.[49] In 1953 Queen's Park, incorporating the Garden of Remembrance, was opened to commemorate the Queen's coronation and was later extended.[50]

[20] *Memo. on Potentialities of Swindon for Industrial Development.*
[21] *Planning for Swindon,* Survey and Report by W. R. Davidge.
[22] *Local Government is our Business,* Handbk. issued by N.A.L.G.O. (1960), 29.
[23] Ibid.   [24] Ibid.
[25] See p. 117.
[26] Swindon Corp. Act, 14 & 15 Geo. VI, c. 40 (local and personal act).
[27] Ex inf. Borough Architect's office.
[28] *Swindon 52–62,* 26 and ex inf. Borough Planning Dept.
[29] See p. 119.
[30] *Local Government is our Business,* Handbk. issued by N.A.L.G.O. (1960), 57.
[31] Local information.
[32] *Local Government is our Business,* Handbk. issued by N.A.L.G.O. (1960), 54.

[33] *Swindon Guide* (1950–1). For an earlier extension of the gas works see p. 135.
[34] Ex inf. the Town Clerk.
[35] Education Act, 7 & 8 Geo. VI, c. 31.   [36] See p. 160.
[37] Town and Country Planning Act, 10 & 11 Geo. VI, c. 51.
[38] Ex inf. the Town Clerk.
[39] Nat. Health Service Act, 9 & 10 Geo. VI, c. 81.
[40] Ex inf. the Town Clerk.
[41] *V.C.H. Wilts.* v. 346; *Swindon 52–62,* 21.
[42] Local information.
[43] *Swindon 52–62,* 21.
[44] *Evening Advertiser,* 16 Apr. 1957.
[45] *Swindon 52–62,* 21.   [46] Ibid.
[47] See p. 80.   [48] See p. 120.
[49] *Souvenir Programme for Opening of Queen's Park* (in Swindon Pub. Libr.).
[50] Ibid.

As happened elsewhere, war-time conditions during the Second World War revealed a lack of adequate cultural amenities in the town. In 1942 the Mayor of Swindon's Community Fund was established to give financial aid to various cultural projects.[51] Until 1943 the only public library in Swindon was that of the Mechanics' Institute.[52] That year, however, a public library was opened in a shop in Regent Street.[53] In 1949 it was moved to the Town Hall where it was still housed in 1965, awaiting a permanent home.[54] There were five branch libraries in 1965.[55] In 1946 an Arts Centre was opened in Regent Street. This was moved in 1956 to a building in Devizes Road equipped for theatricals and other social activities.[56] Aid from the Mayor of Swindon's Community Fund was extended occasionally to assist enterprises of concern to the whole county. In 1947 Swindon was the prime mover in launching the Wiltshire volumes of this *History* and in 1965 was still one of the major contributing authorities sponsoring their preparation.[57] In 1950 it assisted the publication of a volume of *Studies in the History of Swindon*.[58] After 1947 the corporation subsidized the Records Branch of the Wiltshire Archaeological and Natural History Society.[59] In 1962 a Railway Museum, maintained jointly by British Rail and the Swindon Corporation, was opened in the building once known as the 'Barracks'.[60] Here are preserved, among other objects, some of the famous engines built in Swindon in the 19th and 20th centuries.

SEAL, INSIGNIA, PLATE, ARMS, AND OFFICERS. The seal used since the incorporation of the borough in 1900 is round, 2¼ inches, of brass and bears the borough arms with the words 'Salubritas et Industria' below. Legend, humanistic:

THE SEAL OF THE MAYOR ALDERMEN AND BURGESSES OF THE BOROUGH OF SWINDON

A mayoral chain was presented in 1902 by F. P. Goddard, lord of the manor of Swindon. W. E.

BOROUGH OF SWINDON. *Quarterly, the fesswise line nebuly; the first quarter azure with a silver pile and thereon three crescents gules; the second gules with three silver castles; the third gules with a gold mitre; and the fourth azure with a gold winged wheel: on a chief argent a locomotive engine proper*

Morse gave the mayoral robes in 1927 and a mace bearing the cipher of Edward VIII in 1936. A chain for the mayoress was given in 1935 by J. L. Calderwood.

The first piece of corporation plate was a silver salver presented in 1948. Among later acquisitions are two silver bowls given in 1959 by the Wiltshire Regiment (Duke of Edinburgh's) and two silver models of aircraft given in 1964 by the R.A.F. at Lyneham. Several local industries and business firms have presented plate. In 1962 a model in silver of the King George V railway engine was given to mark the opening of the Railway Museum.

The borough arms were granted in 1901. Lists of mayors and chief officers are printed in the *Year Books* which have been issued regularly by the borough since 1900.[61]

SOCIAL LIFE. No evidence exists on which to base an account of the social life of Swindon before the arrival of the railway. Record of two pastimes only has survived. These were bull-baiting and backsword-playing, both of which took place in the Market Square.[62] Bull-baiting was dying out by the beginning of the 19th century, but experienced a brief revival when the opening of the Wilts. and Berks. Canal brought new life to the town.[63] The last bull-baiting was, however, in *c.* 1810.[64] Swindon, according to Morris, was renowned for its backsword-playing, a sport hardly less ferocious than bull-baiting.[65] The last great bout was fought in 1841 on a stage erected in the fields at the foot of Eastcott Hill. The contestants were the brothers, James and Thomas Edwards, who fought to celebrate the opening of the G.W.R. line to Swindon and their own success in a lawsuit.[66] Of the gentler pursuits of the inhabitants no evidence has survived, although Morris writes at some length about the mummers who, early in the 19th century, visited the villages and towns of north Wiltshire.[67]

The social amenities of Old Swindon could not possibly provide for the needs of the new town, so suddenly planted on its outskirts. But the immigrants, who formed the first railway colony, were without common social traditions and lacked the means to organize such amenities for themselves. It fell, therefore, to the G.W.R. Company to provide the first facilities for social life and welfare in the new town. Within five years of the erection of the first workmen's cottages, a school and a church had been built, largely with funds from the G.W.R.[68] In 1847 the G.W.R. Medical Fund Society was started.[69] Its foundation was largely due to Daniel (later Sir Daniel) Gooch, locomotive superintendent at Paddington, who was in complete charge in Swindon, although he never lived in the town. The original object of the society was to provide medicine and attendance for the men employed in the G.W.R.

[51] *Memo. on Potentialities of Swindon for Industrial Development.*
[52] See p. 142.
[53] Wilts. Pamphlets 44, *Official Opening of Public Library.*
[54] *Local Government is our Business*, Handbk. issued by N.A.L.G.O. (1960), 68.
[55] *21 Years of Public Library Service in Swindon.*
[56] *Bath Critic*, June, 1952.
[57] *V.C.H. Wilts.* vii, p. xiii.
[58] By L. V. Grinsell, H. B. Wells, H. S. Tallamy, and John Betjeman.

[59] *Swindon Studies*, 135.
[60] *Swindon 52–62*, 21; *21 Years of Public Library Service in Swindon.*
[61] All information supplied by the Mayor's Secretary.
[62] Morris, *Swindon*, 120.
[63] Ibid. 121.
[64] Ibid. 119.
[65] Ibid. 128.   [66] Ibid.
[67] Ibid. 141.
[68] For school see p. 161, for church see p. 148.
[69] The Medical Fund Soc. has been dealt with in *V.C.H. Wilts.* v. 343–4.

works and their families. Archibald Sturrock, manager of the Swindon works, was the society's first president. In the early days the society offered little more than the services of the company's salaried surgeon. But over the years it acquired practically all the facilities needed for a general health service, so that by 1948 its hospital, out-patient departments, and clinics could deal with most of the medical needs of about 40,000 Swindon people.

The first sign of a wish for some form of cultural amenity in the new town seems to have come in 1843 when a few G.W.R. employees started a very modest library among themselves.[70] The following year, with the approval of the G.W.R. Company, a Mechanics' Institution was established with the object of 'disseminating useful knowledge and en-couraging rational amusement'. Membership in the early months was 15 and the library contained 150 books. Gooch was the institute's first president. All activities took place in the works; part of 'O' shop in the locomotive department was used for theatri-cals, and dancing and other amusements were held in one of the paint shops. By the end of the first year membership was 129 and the library had 522 books, with a circulation of 80 volumes a week. In 1851 there were 500 members, over 2,000 books, and 60 pupils attending educational classes. Two years later the New Swindon Improvement Company was formed to build a centre which would include not only a library and lecture rooms, but also baths, refreshment rooms, and, at the rear of the building, a covered market and a few shops.[71] A site in the middle of the G.W.R's housing estate was leased by the company at a nominal rent, and the company agreed to subscribe £100 a year towards the im-provement company's activities. The building was completed by 1855.

When the baths were moved in 1864, and the refreshment rooms in 1890, the extra space thus gained was used by the Mechanics' Institute for its educational classes, and in 1890, by which time the market and shops had outgrown their usefulness, the property was transferred from the improvement company to the Mechanics' Institute. Between 1890 and 1893 the buildings were much enlarged. After 1891 the institute no longer had responsibility for providing technical education,[72] but it continued as a cultural and recreational centre. Until 1943 its library, which that year had branches at Rodbourne and Gorse Hill, and held over 30,000 books, was the only public library in Swindon. In 1930 the centre of the building was badly damaged by fire and was rebuilt to provide a theatre, known as the Playhouse, with a dance hall below. After the nationalization of the railways British Railways con-tinued to support the Mechanics' Institute,[73] but with the social and economic changes of the post-war period its importance in the life of the town declined markedly. In 1959 the building was adapted

to accommodate the British Rail Staff Association.[74] The library was closed in 1961.[75]

The original building erected in Emlyn Square for the Mechanics' Institute was designed in a Tudor style by Edward Roberts and was built of Swindon stone with Bath stone dressings.[76] The main block was of two stories although externally giving the appearance of a single great hall with buttressed sides of eight bays. At its north end was an arcaded porch flanked by octagonal and em-battled turrets. This part of the building, altered internally, survived in 1965. To the south was a two-storied cross-wing containing the reading room. The upper stories were altered and rebuilt after the fire of 1930. Beyond the wing was the low octagonal market, surmounted by a conical roof and spired turret. The additions of 1890–3, which extended over the site of the market, are built of darker stone and are designed in a more sophisticated Tudor style.

One of the earliest privileges offered to members of the Mechanics' Institute was a day excursion to Oxford in the summer of 1849. Each member was allowed to take a companion with him on the outing and on this occasion 500 people travelled in the special train.[77] This was the beginning of an annual event in Swindon known as 'Trip'. Until 1913 it was a day excursion, but that year the holiday, which was unpaid, was extended to one week.[78] Weymouth was a popular resort for the 'Trip' holiday-makers at this period, and it was reckoned that some 25,000 travelled somewhere on the free 'Trip' trains.[79] For weeks before money was saved for the holiday.[80] In 1939 27,000 people left Swindon for the holiday in 30 special trains.[81] In 1946 the holiday was extended to two weeks' paid holiday.[82] The 'Trip' holiday takes place during the first two weeks in July and, so long as the G.W.R. was virtually the only em-ployer of labour in the town, it meant that almost the whole of Swindon was on holiday during this time. With the arrival of other industries with different holiday arrangements, the 'Trip' holiday period lost some of its importance.

Another annual event connected with the Mechanics' Institute was the juvenile fête. This was held annually, except during the war years, between 1868 and 1939 in the Park.[83]

The amenities of the Mechanics' Institute, backed by the resources of the G.W.R., presumably tended to outshine the social activities of the old town. But no doubt the usual activities of a small country town continued, regardless of any new attractions which the railway town might have to offer. In the 1860s weekly Penny Readings were held in the Town Hall with A. L. Goddard as their patron.[84] The talent, according to Frederick Large, was almost entirely local, and proceeds went to local good causes.[85] Large also writes of numerous dramatic and other popular forms of entertainment held in the Corn Exchange in the old town.[86]

[70] G.W.R. Mechanics' Institution, Swindon, Centenary Souvenir and Prospectus, 1843–1943 (Swindon priv. print. 1943). Except where otherwise stated, information about the institute comes from this source.
[71] For market see p. 133.   [72] See p. 159.
[73] Swindon Studies, 120.
[74] Wilts. Herald, 2 Apr. 1959.
[75] Evening Advertiser, 28 Nov. 1961.
[76] The Builder, xii. 289 has description and illustrations and see Swindon Studies, 118 and pl. facing p. 129.
[77] Mechs'. Inst. Centenary Souvenir, p. iv.
[78] Ex inf. Swindon Public Libr. Thanks are due to Mr. Mark Child for research into the 'Trip' holiday.
[79] Alfred Williams, Life in a Railway Factory, 247, 248.
[80] Ibid. 247.
[81] Swindon Studies, 117.
[82] Ex inf. Swindon Pub. Libr.
[83] Mechs'. Inst. Centenary Souvenir, p. v.
[84] Notices of Meetings (Swindon Pub. Libr.).
[85] F. Large, Swindon Retrospect, 99–100.   [86] Ibid.

The G.W.R. Company, as has been shown, catered for some of the most important social and cultural needs of its first employees in Swindon, but organizations, not connected in any way with the works, quickly began to establish themselves. The various churches and chapels, which grew up as the town developed, obviously played an extremely important part in creating a sense of community and providing centres for social gatherings. The Friendly Society movement seems to have appeared in the town as early as 1840, just before the railway works were established.[87] That year a few members of the Oddfellows came to Swindon from other parts of Wiltshire to prospect. The first lodge to be opened in Swindon was the Mackies Good Intent Lodge which had nine members. A second lodge was opened in 1842 and the Ancient Order of Foresters was established in the town by 1843. From these beginnings the movement grew quickly in Swindon and by the early 20th century, besides the Oddfellows and Foresters, well over a dozen societies were active. By 1920 the Oddfellows had 19 lodges and the Foresters about the same number of courts and some 22 other societies were represented in the town.[88]

A Swindon Co-operative Society was founded in 1850 with a small shop specializing in the sale of bread.[89] Twelve years later the New Swindon Industrial Co-operative Society was formed by a group that was dissatisfied with the original society, and in 1880 a third society was formed called the Kingshill Co-operative Society.[90] In 1965 only the New Swindon Industrial Co-operative Society survived.

As far as is known, the first workingmen's club in Swindon was the Bridge Street Club which was established in 1880.[91] By 1904 this club had a membership of 1,600. Soon after the formation of the Bridge Street Club similar clubs were started at Gorse Hill and Even Swindon and by the beginning of the 20th century there were 21 clubs affiliated to the Swindon and District Branch of the London Club and Institute Union. Most of these clubs offered some sort of social security such as sickness benefit as well as the usual kinds of recreational facilities. In 1948 there were still 27 workingmen's clubs, many of which dated from the end of the 19th century.[92] In 1965 there were at least 20 clubs in the town.[93] By 1910 Swindon seems to have been fairly well supplied with those recreational and sporting clubs usual in a working-class community. The Swindon Town Football Club was formed in

1881 and the Swindon Rugby Club in 1895.[94] There was a town cricket club by the middle of the 19th century.[95] In 1910 there were also 11 cycling clubs, 2 gymnastic societies, a swimming club, and 4 brass bands.[96]

Soon after its formation in 1903 the Swindon Education Committee arranged for university extension lectures to be held in the town.[97] They were organized in conjunction with Oxford University and, in conjunction with Bristol University, were still part of the programme of adult cultural activities in 1966. A branch of the Workers' Educational Association was formed in 1908 after a visit from Albert Mansbridge.[98] The first classes were held by R. V. Lennard, of Wadham College, Oxford, in the Higher Elementary School in Euclid Street.[99] For these 26 members enrolled[1] but by 1930 membership of the W.E.A. in Swindon was 500.[2]

The early success of both the university extension lectures and the W.E.A. was very largely due to the enthusiasm of Reuben George (d. 1936).[3] George came to Swindon from Gloucester as a young man and worked there as agent for the Wesleyan and General Insurance Company for the rest of his life. His main interest, however, lay in social and political work. The formation of the Swindon Labour Party in 1916 owed much to him and he was one of the first three Labour candidates to stand for Parliamentary election in Wiltshire. He was a member of the Swindon Town Council from the time of the borough's incorporation and was mayor in 1921–2.[4] Alfred Owen Williams (1877–1930), the poet and writer, who lived and died at South Marston, was also a member of the Swindon branch of the W.E.A.[5]

A theatre for Swindon was built in 1898 at the corner of Groundwell Road and Clarence Street. Its architects were Messrs. Drake and Pizey of Bristol.[6] It was called at first the Queen's Theatre, could accommodate 1,600, and opened with a performance of 'Dick Whittington'.[7] The theatre's name was later changed to the Empire and between 1929 and 1947 it was used as a cinema.[8] It was demolished in 1959.[9] The first cinema in Swindon was the County Electric, built in 1910. Four other cinemas were opened within the next five years. Three were built between the two World Wars.[10] Only two remained open in 1966.[11]

Swindon's first newspaper appeared in 1854.[12] Its founder was William Morris (d. 1891), who was educated in the town and became its first historian. His paper, the *Swindon Advertiser and Monthly*

---

[87] Unless otherwise stated, inf. about Friendly Socs. from *Swindon Advertiser*, Supp. 5 Feb. 1904.
[88] *N. Wilts. and District Dir.* (1920).
[89] 'Work, Wages, and Pastimes, 1800–1950', a social survey undertaken c. 1960 by Burderop Pk. Training Coll. (TS in Swindon Pub. Libr.)
[90] Ibid.
[91] Unless otherwise stated, inf. about workingmen's clubs from *Swindon Advertiser*, Supp. 5 Feb. 1904.
[92] *Wilts. County Council Educ. Cttee. Draft Scheme for Further Educ. in Swindon Excepted District (1948)*.
[93] *Evening Advertiser*, 30 Apr. 1965.
[94] Ex inf. Sec. Swindon Town F.C. and for Rugby Club see pamphlet in Pub. Libr.
[95] R. J. Tarrant, 'Recollections' (TS in Swindon Pub. Libr.).
[96] *N. Wilts. and District Dir.* (1910).
[97] J. B. Lloyd, 'Development of Education in Swindon' (Bristol Univ. M.A. Thesis (Educ.), 1954), 221, 283.

[98] R. George, *The Path we Trod* (pamphlet in Swindon Pub. Libr.).
[99] Notice of Meeting (Swindon Pub. Libr.).
[1] Lloyd, 'Development of Education in Swindon', 283.
[2] Ibid.
[3] Ibid. 221; R. George, *The Path we Trod* (pamphlet in Swindon Pub. Libr.).
[4] Wilts. Pamphlets, 8, *Obituary Notice*.
[5] Leonard Clark, *Alfred Williams*, 39.
[6] Notice of Opening of Theatre in Swindon Pub. Libr.
[7] Ibid.
[8] 'Work, Wages, and Pastimes, 1800–1950' (see n. 89 above).
[9] *Evening Advertiser*, 17 Mar. 1959.
[10] 'Work, Wages, and Pastimes, 1800–1950' (see no. 89 above).
[11] Ex inf. Swindon Pub. Libr.
[12] Unless otherwise stated, inf. about Swindon newspapers from *Swindon Advertiser*, Supp. 5 Feb. 1904 and *Swindon Studies*, 140–1.

Record, was at first issued monthly. The first number contained four pages. It became a weekly paper in 1855 when the stamp duty on newspapers was repealed. In the early issues about half the space was devoted to advertising. The remainder was said to be confined to reports which 'do not partake of a political, party, or personal character'. The paper, however, consistently advocated a progressive policy and in the course of its career was involved in several libel actions. It was said that if there was anything approaching a Liberal party in Swindon it came into being with the foundation of the *Advertiser*. In 1870 it was re-named the *Swindon Advertiser and Wiltshire, Berkshire and Gloucestershire Chronicle*. It was last issued as a weekly newspaper in December 1925 and thereafter became an evening paper called the *Evening Advertiser*.[13] After the death of William Morris the paper was conducted by his sons for some years.[14] In 1920 it was acquired by the Swindon Press Ltd. and in 1956 by Wiltshire Newspapers Ltd.[15] The Swindon Press, however, remained the general printing company and both companies came under the ownership of the Westminster Press and Provincial Newspapers Ltd.

Another newspaper, the *North Wilts. Herald*, with a more conservative viewpoint, was started in Swindon in 1861.[16] It was designed to cater more for the surrounding countryside than did the *Advertiser*, and between 1866 and 1879 absorbed three small local papers.[17] In 1882 it produced a daily evening edition, and between 1865 and 1881 there was also a market edition.[18] In 1922 control of the *Herald* passed from the Piper family, who had held it since 1865, to the Swindon Press Ltd. In January 1942 the name of the *North Wilts. Herald* was changed to the *North Wilts. Herald and Advertiser*, and in April 1950 became the *Wiltshire Herald and Advertiser*. Since October 1956 it has appeared weekly as the *Wiltshire Gazette and Herald*.

A third newspaper, the *New Swindon Express*, had a short career from 1876 to 1880,[19] and the *Borough Press*, a Saturday evening sheet, reporting football news, was issued between 1904 and 1930. A weekly paper, the *Swindon Echo*, published by E. H. Perkins and Son, and printed by Papers and Publications (Printers), Ltd., was first issued in 1962. It ceased publication in 1966.[20]

As has been shown above, after about the middle of the 19th century there were two Swindons— the old market town and the new town created during the 1840s by the G.W.R. Company. Since roughly the middle of the 20th century a third Swindon may be said to have been created with the building of the suburban estates in the north and east.[21] Here, as was the case in New Swindon a hundred years earlier, the new community was largely made up of people who came from other parts of the country. Between the passing of the Town Development Act of 1952 and 1965 some 14,000 people came to Swindon from London alone, while considerable numbers came from other parts on their own initiative.[22]

CHURCHES. Until 1845 Swindon had only one parish church, namely, the church of Holy Rood, lying in the middle of what was to be called the old town. By 1845 another church was needed for the new G.W.R. housing estate situated over a mile from the parish church. That year, therefore, St. Mark's church was built and in the next the district chapelry of Swindon New Town was created out of the ancient parish of Swindon. The chapelry covered the northern part of Swindon, which in 1846 was but little built over. Even before the arrival of the railway the ancient parish church was proving to be too small for the town's population and furthermore was structurally unsound. In 1851, therefore, Christ Church, Cricklade Street, was built and the church of Holy Rood was closed and dismantled.

In 1881, when the population of St. Mark's parish was 7,628, having risen by more than 5,000 over the last 30 years, a second parish for the new town was formed out of parts of the parishes of Christ Church and St. Mark. This was the parish of St. Paul, New Swindon. Two years later the first of St. Mark's daughter churches, St. John's, was built to serve the then newly built-up Queenstown area of the parish. Two more daughter churches were needed for St. Mark's before the population began to shift away from the centre of the town to live in the suburbs on the north and east. These were St. Saviour's in the south-east, built in 1889, and St. Luke's in the east, built in 1901.

The expansion of the town north of the railway line in the 1870s created a need for churches in the Gorse Hill and Rodbourne districts. In both areas work was first conducted from mission churches, but in 1890 the parish of St. Barnabas, Gorse Hill, was created, and in 1908 that of St. Augustine, Rodbourne. In 1908 church work was also begun from a temporary building in the Southbrook district, then beginning to be developed as a suburb, but it was not until 1929 that the parish of All Saints, Southbrook, was formed.

Following the common course of urban history, the need for churches in the centre of the town subsequently declined while on the outskirts it rose. The first mission church for the parish church of Christ Church was opened on the west side of the old town in 1926. The large-scale expansion of Swindon in the Walcot area after the Second World War led to the building of Christ Church's second daughter church, St. Andrew's, which was opened in 1957 to serve the new Walcot estates. To meet the requirements of the other new estates to the north and east of the town two new parishes were formed, namely St. Peter, Penhill, in 1956, and St. John the Baptist, Park, in 1962.

In the centre of the town the church of St. John, the first of St. Mark's daughter churches, was closed in 1956. In 1965 the parishes of St. Mark and St. Paul were amalgamated and the church of St. Paul was demolished. The site of St. Paul's was then sold for commercial development except for a plot which was reserved for the building of a small chapel of ease. The clergy and funds belonging

[13] Ex inf. Swindon Pub. Libr.
[14] *Swindon Advertiser*, Supp. 5 Feb. 1904.
[15] Unless otherwise stated, all subsequent inf. about newspapers supplied by Swindon Pub. Libr.
[16] *Swindon Studies*, 141.
[17] Ibid.
[18] Ibid.
[19] Ibid.
[20] Ex inf. Borough Press Assistant.
[21] For the development of these estates see pp. 117–19.
[22] Ex inf. the Town Clerk.

to the former parish of St. Paul were transferred to provide for the conventional district of Covingham formed in 1965 to serve the latest of Swindon's new estates.

After an account of the ancient parish church, shorter accounts follow of the churches mentioned above.

The church of Swindon is first mentioned towards the end of the 12th century when it was given to the Augustinian priory of Southwick (Hants) by Robert Pont de l'Arche.[23] This church most probably stood upon the site of the parish church, later dedicated to Holy Rood, in which there are thought to have been traces of Norman work.[24]

In spite of this grant it is possible that the priory subsequently lost the church since licence to appropriate it was not granted until 1325.[25] Even then appropriation did not apparently follow immediately and licence was again granted in 1357.[26] A vicarage was not ordained until 1378.[27]

With the grant of the church to Southwick the advowson passed to the prior of that house. In 1203 and 1204, however, William Pont de l'Arche claimed it by assize of darrein presentment.[28] Pont de l'Arche sued again in 1228 and although the outcome is not known the dispute may well have been settled then.[29] The prior presented in 1302 and normally thereafter until the Dissolution.[30] In 1381 because the office of prior was vacant the king presented.[31] Nine years after the dissolution of Southwick the king granted the advowson to Thomas, Lord Seymour of Sudeley, but Seymour did not exercise the patronage before his attainder and execution two years later in 1549.[32] In 1560 when the rectory of Swindon was granted to Thomas Stephens of Inglesham,[33] the advowson was included in the grant and Stephens presented that year and in 1575, 1579, 1580, 1581, and 1584.[34] The advowson was, however, never again conveyed with the rectory, in spite of the fact that in many of the conveyances it was said to be included.[35] In 1623 Thomas White of Thornhill (in Clyffe Pypard) presented William Gallimore to the living, but there was evidently some doubt about the validity of this, for Gallimore later resigned and was presented again by the king.[36] From then on the patronage belonged to the Crown and in 1965 was exercised by the Lord Chancellor.[37]

Just before Southwick was dissolved the prior leased the rectory for 41 years to Thomas Stephens of Burderop (in Chiseldon).[38] By 1560 Thomas was dead and that year his son, also called Thomas, of

Inglesham, received a grant of the rectory, including the advowson, from the Crown.[39] Thomas Stephens the younger died in 1596, and left his possessions, including the rectory of Swindon, to his son John for six years with remainder to another son, Nicholas.[40] In 1602 John Stephens, with Bridget his wife, and Nicholas Stephens conveyed the rectory to two persons, apparently in trust for Nicholas Vilett,[41] who in the same year acquired it,[42] although a year later the vicar, Miles Kendal, disputed the right of Nicholas's wife to a seat in the chancel, even going so far as to assault her as she sat there.[43] From this date, however, the rectory remained with the Vilett family. When the new parish church was built in 1851 the vestry assumed responsibility for the fabric of the old church and the Rollestons, descendants of the Viletts, transferred their liability as rectors for the maintenance of the chancel to the new church.[44] About the middle of the 20th century the Rollestons compounded for their liability entirely.[45]

In 1291 the church was valued for taxation at £13 6s. 8d.[46] In 1341, before a vicarage had been ordained, land, tithes, oblations, and mortuaries were worth £9.[47] The rectory was valued at £10 13s. 4d. in 1538[48] and was leased for that sum,[49] although it was reckoned to be worth £40 more.[50]

In 1341 2 virgates of land belonged to the church.[51] Some of this was allotted to the vicar when a vicarage was ordained.[52] But 16 a. of arable and an acre of pasture were included in the grant of the rectory to Thomas Stephens in 1538.[53] The land presumably passed with the rectory to Nicholas Vilett in 1602 and was probably sold by his successor, Thomas Vilett, to Thomas Goddard in 1633.[54] The chief value of the rectory, therefore, lay in the great tithes and throughout the 17th and 18th centuries these were the subject of numerous leases and conveyances between the Viletts, Goddards, Martins, Webbs, and other Swindon landowners.[55] The rectors claimed all the great tithes except those from one yardland which had been assigned to the vicar.[56] In 1608 Henry Martin was withholding all tithes from his farm at Eastcott, claiming a right to do so granted by the Crown.[57] How far he was successful in his claim is unknown, but when Eastcott was inclosed in 1657 Thomas and John Vilett were allotted 46 a. at the south end of Eastcott Marsh in lieu of tithes due to them in Eastcott, Nethercott, and Westcott.[58] In 1842 annual rent-charges in lieu of tithes were awarded to some 16 landowners.[59] The rest of the great tithes had already been compounded for at this date.[60]

[23] B.M. Add. MS. 33280, f. 261. On f. 121 it seems that Robt. was merely confirming a gift already made by his father, Wm. Pont de l'Arche.
[24] See below.
[25] Cal. Pat. 1324–7, 122.
[26] B.M. Add. MS. 33280, f. 261.
[27] Ibid. f. 264.
[28] Curia Regis R. iii. 65, 192, iv. 33.
[29] Cal. Pat. 1225–32, 213.
[30] Phillipps, Wilts. Inst. i. 4.   [31] Ibid. 65.
[32] Cal. Pat. 1547–8, 29.
[33] Goddard MS. 2.
[34] Phillipps, Wilts. Inst. sub anno.
[35] For conveyances of the rectory see below.
[36] Phillipps, Wilts. Inst. ii. 12, 17.
[37] Crockford, Clerical Dirs.
[38] C 3/141/14.
[39] Goddard MS. 2.
[40] C 142/247/101.

[41] C.P. 25(2)/242/44 Eliz. I East.
[42] C.P. 43/79 rot. 9.
[43] Hist. MSS. Com. Var. Coll. i. 73.
[44] Christ Church Swindon 1851–1951, Centenary Souvenir (pamphlet in Swindon Pub. Libr.).
[45] Ibid.   [46] Tax. Eccl. (Rec. Com.), 190.
[47] Inq. Non. (Rec. Com.), 162.
[48] S.C. 6/Hen. VIII/3340 m. 30.
[49] See above.   [50] C 3/141/14.
[51] Inq. Non. (Rec. Com.), 162.
[52] See below.
[53] Goddard MS. 2.   [54] Ibid. 20.
[55] Many of the conveyances are to be found among the Goddard MSS., and see Swindon Studies, 40, 134.
[56] See below.
[57] Sar. Dioc. R.O. Glebe Terrier, 1608.
[58] Morris, Swindon, 508–9.
[59] W.R.O. Tithe Award.
[60] Ibid.

The rectory house stood on the east side of the Square. It was occupied by the Viletts as lay rectors and by William Vilett Rolleston who succeeded his uncle William Vilett. But W. V. Rolleston left Swindon at the beginning of the 20th century[61] and in 1964 the house was derelict.

The ordination of the vicarage in 1378 allotted a generous share of the profits of the church to the vicar.[62] In 1535 the vicarage was worth £15 7s. 2d., about £5 more than the rectory.[63] In 1835 the average net income of the benefice over the past three years was £302.[64]

By the terms of the ordination, the vicar was entitled to the great tithes from one yardland belonging to the rectory as well as to all the lesser tithes of the parish.[65] An annual composition of £5 for the lesser tithes due from Broome Farm was made about the beginning of the 17th century,[66] and in 1650 Thomas Goddard compounded with an annual payment of £20 for the tithes from his manor of Lower Swindon.[67] Besides these two payments the vicar in 1671 was entitled to tithes in kind from the tithing of Walcot, West Swindon Closes, Okus Farm, and most of Eastcott. He also had the tithe of sheep, wool, and lambs from West Swindon Fields, 25s. for 18 beast leazes on Mandown, and about £3 for 88 beast leazes on Siddown.[68] In 1704 the tithes due to the vicar were valued at £56 12s. 7d.[69] In 1842 366 a. were found by the tithe commissioners to be free by prescription from the payment of vicarial tithe. All other vicarial tithes were commuted for £269.[70]

In 1378 the vicar was granted, besides a curtilage and garden, some meadow, pasture, and arable land.[71] In the 17th and 18th centuries the vicar's glebe amounted to some 20 a.[72] and was about the same size in 1887.[73] The vicar was also granted in 1378 as his dwelling certain houses 'in the rectory'.[74] This apparently meant within the grounds of the rectory house. In 1671 the vicarage was described as a substantial house in the Planks, built chiefly of stone.[75] It was enlarged by the Revd. Edmund Goodenough in c. 1790 who also enclosed part of the garden with a wall.[76] In 1848, at the time when the new church was being designed, the house was considered unsuitable as a residence for the vicar and was offered for sale.[77] In 1965 the former vicarage house still stood immediately south of the rectory garden near the junction of the Square and the Planks. The oldest part is an **L**-shaped stone house probably dating from the 17th century. Late-18th-century work includes internal alterations, a garden door with an open pediment and fanlight, and a tall brick wing to the south. The building was further extended for industrial purposes in the 20th century and in 1965 was used as storerooms and offices.

The church was charged with certain pensions and payments. An annual rent of £5 to Southwick Priory was ordained in 1198–9 soon after the church was granted to the canons.[78] This was still paid in 1291 and 1341[79] but is not heard of thereafter. By 1291 a pension of 13s. 4d. was being paid to Wallingford Priory (Berks.).[80] It is mentioned again in 1341[81] and may be represented by the payment of 8s. in lieu of tithes which was due to the priory from the Vicar of Swindon in 1538.[82] Annual pensions of 13s. 4d. to the Bishop of Salisbury and 6s. 8d. each to the Archdeacon of Wiltshire and Salisbury Cathedral Chapter were ordained when the church was appropriated in 1357.[83] The 6s. 8d. was still being paid to the chapter in 1535.[84] At this date there is mention of yet another payment from the church, namely £2 annually to Malmesbury Abbey.[85] This presumably originated in the payment of 2 lb. of wax which it was agreed in the 13th century should be paid annually to Malmesbury for tithes from land in Swindon.[86] In 1532 a portion of 16s. from the church was granted by the king to St. George's Chapel, Windsor, but no more is known of this payment.[87]

In 1547 a small rent from land on Eastcott Down was assigned for the maintenance of the rood light in the church.[88] The land was probably the half acre called 'le Rode' which was conveyed in 1565–6 to William Gryce. Included in the grant were two houses in Swindon called Trinity Houses which had likewise at some time been given for the maintenance of a light in the church.[89] At unknown dates several pieces of land were given for the repair of the church. These lay scattered throughout the parish and in Stratton St. Margaret. There were also a number of houses in the town which had been given for the same purpose. In 1748 some of the land was sold to pay, it was thought, for the rebuilding of part of the church.[90] Rent from church property amounted to £17 12s. in 1783 and an investment of £100 produced £4 10s. in interest.[91] All the land was sold and the proceeds invested between 1841 and 1884, but in 1888 four houses, nos. 31–34, Cricklade Street, were bought. The rents of the houses, and the profits of £3,297 stock were used for the repair of the church and to supplement the salaries of the parish clerk and caretaker.[92] In 1953 nos. 33 and 34 Cricklade Street were sold and £332 invested. The other two houses were still held by the repair fund, then known as the Church and Poor Lands Charity.[93]

Few of the vicars of Swindon achieved renown beyond the parish. Narcissus Marsh (d. 1713), mathematician and divine, who became Provost of Trinity College, Dublin, and eventually Archbishop of Armagh, was a Wiltshireman by birth and held

[61] W.A.M. xlii. 84. [62] B.M. Add. MS. 33280, f. 262.
[63] Valor Eccl. (Rec. Com.), ii. 126.
[64] Rep. Com. Eccl. Revenues, H.C. 54, p. 850 (1835), xxii.
[65] Sar. Dioc. R.O. Glebe Terriers, 1588, 1608.
[66] W.N. & Q. vii. 572–3; Sar. Dioc. R.O. Glebe Terriers, 1608, 1671.
[67] Goddard MS. 1325.
[68] Sar. Dioc. R.O. Glebe Terrier, 1671.
[69] Ibid. 1740. [70] W.R.O. Tithe Award
[71] B.M. Add. MS. 33280, f. 264.
[72] Sar. Dioc. R.O. Glebe Terriers.
[73] Retn. of Glebe, H.C. 307, p. 56 (1887), lxiv.
[74] B.M. Add. MS. 33280, f. 264.
[75] Sar. Dioc. R.O. Glebe Terrier, 1671.
[76] W.A.S. Libr., Devizes, Wilts. Misc. MSS. ii. 7.

[77] Ibid.; Morris, Swindon, 183.
[78] B.M. Add.MS. 33280, f. 262.
[79] Tax. Eccl. (Rec. Com.), 190; Inq. Non. (Rec. Com.), 162.
[80] Tax. Eccl. (Rec. Com.), 190.
[81] Inq. Non. (Rec. Com.), 162.
[82] L. & P. Hen. VIII, iv, p. 1957.
[83] B.M. Add. MS. 33280, ff. 262–3.
[84] Valor Eccl. (Rec. Com.), ii. 80. [85] Ibid. 121.
[86] Reg. Malm. (Rolls Ser.), ii. 16–17.
[87] L. & P. Hen. VIII, v, p. 579.
[88] W.A.M. xii. 382. [89] C 66/1025 m. 15.
[90] Endowed Char. Wilts. H.C. 273, p. 922 (1908), lxxx.
[91] Sar. Dioc. R.O. Glebe Terrier, 1783.
[92] Endowed Char. Wilts. (1908), pp. 929–31.
[93] Char.Com. File 50259.

the living for a year (1662–3).[94] Some incumbents are known to have been non-resident and may have played but a small part in church life. Richard Hagheman, presented in 1302, was immediately given leave to study at Oxford for 7 years.[95] Thomas Smith (1758–90) had dispensation to hold the rectory of Codford St. Mary with the vicarage of Swindon,[96] and, for a time at least, while Vicar of Swindon he served the chapelry of South Marston, about 3 miles distant. He resided in Swindon, however, and employed a curate to assist him, who also lived in Swindon.[97] Matthew Surtees (1809–23) did not reside, and throughout his incumbency a curate lived in the vicarage house.[98]

One of the vicars to make the most impact upon the parish was H. G. Baily (1847–85). He came to Swindon just as the new town was being established, and worked vigorously for the parish of the old town in its greatly altered circumstances. He was a member of the first Swindon School Board and opposed its undenominational policy: during his incumbency new church schools were built in King William Street and the old parish church replaced. Baily farmed the glebe himself. He resigned from Swindon in 1885 to become Rector of Lydiard Tregoze. An obituary notice described him as a vigorous and popular preacher of uncompromisingly evangelical views.[99]

In 1672 there were 572 communicants in the parish.[1] In 1783 there was a service with prayers and a sermon on Sunday mornings and prayers in the afternoons. Communion was celebrated 7 times a year and it was reckoned that there were generally 40 to 50 communicants at the Easter celebration.[2] Church attendance was not considered by the vicar to be very good in spite of the fact that there was little dissent in the town at the time.[3]

The need for a church for the new town was met in 1845 when St. Mark's was dedicated.[4] But a bigger and more substantial church was clearly needed in the old town too. Thus in 1850 work was begun on the large and imposing church of Christ Church at the top of Cricklade Street, on land given by Ambrose Goddard.[5]

On 30 March 1851 380 people attended morning service and 440 were present in the afternoon.[6] From the outset the strongly evangelical traditions of the old church were observed in the new one. There was no surpliced choir, altar lights were never used, and the preacher preached in a black gown.[7] An attempt to introduce altar lights and surplices by the vicar, H. Armstrong Hall, in 1885 met with such determined opposition that the experiment had to be abandoned and Hall retired soon afterwards.[8]

In 1913 congregations were sometimes so large on Sundays that the church hall in Devizes Road, built in 1912, had to be used as extra accommodation.[9] In 1926 it was believed that another church was needed within the parish, and St. Mary's, Commonweal Road, was built as a mission church.[10] Only a temporary structure was erected and this has not been replaced by any more permanent building, possibly because the need for it has been entirely justified. After the Second World War the Walcot area of the parish began to be built over with new housing estates. In 1956 two representatives were co-opted to represent Walcot on the Christ Church church council and two years later the new church of St. Andrew, in Raleigh Avenue, Walcot, was opened as a daughter church of Christ Church.[11]

The church of HOLY ROOD stood immediately to the south of the Lawn. It was apparently a humble structure by any standards. Morris, who knew it well, described it as the most insignificant ecclesiastical building in the whole neighbourhood and it was, moreover, 'hopelessly out of condition.'[12] At the time of its abandonment it consisted of a nave with clerestory and steep pitched roof, side aisles, chancel with a north aisle and vestry, north and south porches, and a somewhat stunted west tower rising in two stages and surmounted by a small bell-cote.[13] The nave was separated from its north aisle by an arcade of two bays with double-chamfered arches of the later 13th century. The arches sprang from a short round pier adorned with either dogtooth or 'nailhead' decoration. The pointed chancel arch sprang from corbels carved with a male and a female head. The 14th-century nave arcades of four pointed arches were supported on octagonal piers without capitals.[14] The exterior, apart from the chancel, appears to have been of 15th-century date.

The church was partly rebuilt in 1748 when a brick tower was added.[15] According to Morris this tower was supported within at the four corners by the trunks of four yew trees growing in square formation. It was presumably at this time that the chancel with its round-headed windows was rebuilt and the roofs of nave and chancel ceiled. A vestry was added in 1820 and a gallery in 1823. By 1845 there were galleries over the north and south aisles and at the west end. The west gallery contained an organ. About 1800 box pews flanked a central aisle, which was paved with large flags, a two-decker pulpit stood at the junction of nave and chancel, and hatchments of arms hung on either side of the east window.[16]

The faculty of 1852 providing for the closing of the church stipulated that it should be taken down with the exception of the chancel which was to be maintained by the parish. In fact it appears that the nave was allowed to fall into ruin and little was done to preserve the chancel before 1949 when the corporation assumed responsibility for it.[17] In 1964 the chancel was roofed and had been made weather-

[94] D.N.B.   [95] Reg. Ghent (Cant. and York Soc.), ii. 857.
[96] W.N. & Q. ii. 55.
[97] Sar. Dioc. R.O. Vis. Queries, 1783.
[98] W.A.S. Libr., Devizes, Wilts. Misc. MSS. ii. 7.
[99] W.A.M. xxxi. 92; Wilts. Cuttings, xvi. 357.
[1] W.N. & Q. iii. 535.
[2] Sar. Dioc. R.O. Vis. Queries, 1783.   [3] Ibid.
[4] See below.
[5] Christ Church, Vestry Min. Bk. 10 July 1847.
[6] H.O. 129/250/2/8/18.   [7] Ibid.
[8] Christ Church 1851–1951, Centenary Souvenir (see n. 44 above).
[9] Ibid.   [10] Ibid.

[11] Christ Church Parish Mag. Aug. 1956, Feb. 1958.
[12] Morris, Swindon, 160, 173.
[13] This account of the exterior of the church is based upon a north-west view painted by John Buckler, c. 1810 (in W.A.S. Libr., Devizes) and a print of 1850 giving south-west view, see pl. facing p. 108.
[14] Description of interior from ground-plan of 1798 reproduced in Swindon Studies facing p. 49 and notes in W.A.M. xlii. 295–6.
[15] Morris, Swindon, 164–5, 173.
[16] A painting of c. 1800 by Ric. Kemm, reproduced in Swindon Studies facing p. 33.
[17] Christ Church 1851–1951 Centenary Souvenir.

proof by blocking in the chancel arch. The bays separating the chancel from its aisle were also then blocked. Of the nave only a fragment of the 14th-century arcades of octagonal piers survived.

It is thought that the gazebo in the grounds of the Lawn was built with stones from the church tower as nearly as possible to the same dimensions.[18]

The large stone church of *CHRIST CHURCH* was designed by George Gilbert (later Sir Gilbert) Scott in the style of the late 13th century.[19] It was dedicated in 1851. It comprises chancel, clerestoried nave of three bays with aisles, transepts, and a western tower with broach spire. Tower and spire, which are a land mark for many miles around, are said to be copied from the church of Buckworth (Hunts.).[20] The chancel was refurbished in 1883 and an oak screen added to the west porch in 1888.[21] The south porch was added in 1916 in memory of Henry and Harriet Kinneir. In 1935 a side chapel, designed by Sir Harold Brakspear, was added on the south-east and by 1964 was known as the Lady Chapel.

The elaborate reredos, font, and pulpit, all of alabaster and marble, were presented at different dates by members of the Goddard family: the reredos in 1891 by Pleydell and Jessie Goddard in memory of their brother, Ambrose Ayshford Goddard; the font in 1905 by Edward Hesketh Goddard in memory of his wife, and the pulpit in 1906 by Pleydell Goddard and his sister, Jessie, in memory of their parents. A window in the north transept, designed by Martin Travers, commemorates F. P. Goddard (d. 1927), the last lord of the manor to live in Swindon. In it is a view of Liddington seen through the flowers in the garden of the Lawn.

Five bells of 1741 by Abraham Rudhall were brought from the old parish church in 1851 and a 6th was added that year.[22] Two trebles were added in 1883. In 1924 all the bells were re-cast and a 9th and 10th were added, making the second ring of 10 bells in Wiltshire.

In 1553 a chalice of 12½ oz. and plate of 57 oz. were taken from the old church for the king's use.[23] With the exception of a massive tankard-shaped flagon, hall-marked 1738 and presented to the old parish church in memory of John Neate (vicar 1703–19), all the plate in Christ Church is of 19th-century date. It includes a pair of bell-shaped chalices with patens, hall-marked 1851, a credence and paten given by James Edward Goddard Bradford and his wife, Charlotte, in 1886, and three brass almsdishes inscribed 1885. The registers date from 1640 and are complete.

In 1842 G. H. Gibbs, a director of the G.W.R. Company, died, leaving £500 towards building a church and a school for the company's new housing estate in Swindon.[24] The company whole-heartedly supported the project, although unable to finance it, and issued an appeal for subscriptions. By 1843 a substantial part of the money needed had been raised and a site for the church presented by the Vilett family.[25] *ST. MARK'S* was consecrated in 1845 and early in 1846 the district chapelry of Swindon New Town was formed.[26] The patronage of the living, which has always been a vicarage, was given to the Bishop of Bristol.[27] For the first few years the G.W.R. Company paid the vicar's stipend, but the need for this ceased when a succession of grants from the Ecclesiastical Commissioners endowed the benefice.[28]

Attempts to introduce ritualistic forms of worship seem to have made the church unpopular in its early days (see below). But by the beginning of the 1880s this unpopularity had largely disappeared, and with a rise in the population of the parish it was said to be impossible to provide enough accommodation in the church for all those wishing to attend the Sunday evening services.[29] Additional seating had to be provided in the parochial hall, where full evensong with a sermon was held.[30] The pressure upon St. Mark's was relieved in 1881 when part of the parish was transferred to the newly created parish of St. Paul, New Swindon.[31] In 1883 a daughter church, St. John's, was opened to serve the by then populous Queenstown district.[32] But at about this time St. Mark's temporarily assumed responsibility for the spiritual needs of residents in the Rodbourne district, which in point of fact lay outside the parish boundary (see below).[33] In 1890 a second daughter church, St. Saviour's, was opened in the south-west of the parish.[34]

To deal with the continually increasing parochial work the first assistant priests were appointed in 1880.[35] A few years later there were five assistants and from then until about the middle of the 20th century five or six was the usual number. Since the Second World War there have generally been only two.[36] To help with parochial work two sisters from the Community of St. Mary the Virgin, Wantage (Berks.) were sent to Swindon in 1891.[37] In 1896 a house was built for them in Milton Road, and after that date a few sisters from Wantage worked in St. Mark's parish. They were most active about the beginning of the 20th century when they ran a day school in Maxwell Street and organized various clubs in the parish. In 1965 there was a greatly reduced demand for their services.

The last of St. Mark's daughter churches, St. Luke's, was opened in 1903 in the east of the parish.[38] With this the final need for mission churches within the parish boundary had been met. The parish was by then almost completely built over

[18] *W.A.M.* xlix. 486.
[19] Pevsner, *Wilts.* (Bldgs. of Eng.), 456.
[20] *Swindon Studies*, 179.
[21] Unless otherwise stated, all information from *Christ Church 1851–1951. Centenary Souvenir*.
[22] Inf. about bells from *Christ Church 1851–1951, Centenary Souvenir*, and Morris, *Swindon*, 175–6.
[23] Inf. about plate from Nightingale, *Wilts. Plate*, 189–90 and local inf.
[24] *St. Mark's 1845–1945, Record written by Priests and People* (Swindon priv. print. 1945), 5.
[25] Ibid.
[26] Ibid. 22–23; *Lond. Gaz.* 30 Jan. 1846 (p. 324).
[27] *Kelly's Dir. Wilts.* (1903).

[28] *St. Mark's 1845–1945*, 23; *Lond. Gaz.* 4 May 1849 (p. 1464), 9 June 1854 (p. 1770), 7 Aug. 1868 (p. 4391), 27 Nov. 1874 (p. 5726).
[29] *St. Mark's 1845–1945*, 36.
[30] Ibid.
[31] See p. 149.
[32] See p. 149.
[33] See p. 150.
[34] See p. 150.
[35] *St. Mark's 1845–1945*, 117–18.
[36] Ibid.
[37] All inf. about the sisters from *St. Mark's 1845–1945*, 83–91 and ex inf. the vicar.
[38] See p. 150.

Railway works and estate from the south-west, 1959. St. Mark's church is among the trees to the left. The Mechanics' Institute is in the centre with the 'Barracks' to its right

Sussex Square, Walcot, in 1958. The sarsen stone found on the site is seen in the foreground

SWINDON

Junction Station, first-class refreshment room in 1852

Queenstown Bridge over Wilts. and Berks. Canal in 1885

SWINDON

and had a population of *c.* 20,000.[39] It was still chiefly residential, but as the 20th century progressed residents began leaving for the new housing estates on the outskirts of the town and much of the centre of the parish around St. Mark's was taken over by commercial and industrial concerns.[40] These developments and the consequent decline in resident population were even more marked in the neighbouring parish of St. Paul and in 1965 St. Mark's and St. Paul's were united to form the single parish of Swindon New Town.[41]

St. Mark's was consecrated when the Oxford Movement was at its height,[42] but attempts to introduce Tractarian teaching and practices were at first much resented by the congregation. Of the first vicar, Daniel Gooch wrote 'he seems to do one thing after another to bring himself and the church into discord with the men'.[43] The next incumbent was equally unsuccessful and himself reported in 1851 that the congregation had fallen off very much since his appointment, owing to a cry of Tractarianism raised against him.[44] Attendance on 30 March that year was in fact about 104 at morning service and 122 in the evening.[45] Attempts to introduce High Church ritual at this date led to the strongest opposition and even disturbances, and it has been said that when the vicar ventured to preach in a surplice, half the congregation walked out.[46]

High Church ritual was introduced into St. Mark's during the incumbency of J. M. G. Ponsonby (vicar 1897–1903).[47] In the 1880s daily services began to be held,[48] and in 1889 the Communion service was sung for the first time.[49] In 1897 mass vestments were used.[50] Parochial organization was carried out along Anglo-Catholic lines: special communicants' classes and guilds were introduced: retreats and quiet days were held, and a branch of the English Church Union was formed.[51] Canon Ponsonby's religious beliefs and observances were maintained and strengthened by his successor, A. G. G. Ross (vicar 1903–37).[52] In 1916 incense was first used and since 1924 the Sacrament has been perpetually reserved.[53] High Church traditions have persisted into the 1960s.

St. Mark's church was designed by Messrs. Scott and Moffatt in the Decorated style and belongs to the earliest period of George Gilbert (later Sir Gilbert) Scott's work.[54] It is built of stone with a tower with broach spire, 140 ft. high, at the north-west corner. It has a clerestoried nave of six bays, aisles, and north and south porches. The north porch is formed by the base of the tower. The chancel was extended and embellished by Temple Moore in 1897 and a north vestry and south Lady Chapel were added at the same time.[55] Attempts have been made from time to time to lighten the lofty, but rather gloomy interior. The large rood, designed

by T. H. Lyon and carved by Herbert Read of Exeter, was erected in 1928.[56] A new east window was inserted after the Second World War. In 1904 six bells were hung in the tower in memory of J. M. G. Ponsonby (vicar 1879–1903). Two more were added in 1927.[57]

The church of *ST. PAUL* was built in 1881 to serve the district chapelry of St. Paul, New Swindon, formed that year out of parts of the parishes of Christ Church and Swindon New Town.[58] The living was a vicarage in the gift of the Bishop of Bristol.[59] Although a separate parish, St. Paul's was closely connected with St. Mark's, and High Church rituals were similarly observed.[60] These were apparently unpopular at first, but they were not so violently resented as those at St. Mark's.[61] Morris, writing in *c.* 1885, remarked that on special occasions the altar was 'ablaze with candles' and drew the contrast between the High Church services in the two new town churches and those in Christ Church where a strongly Evangelical tradition prevailed.[62]

The effects of the re-development of the town centre and the departure of the resident population for the new estates were felt most acutely in St. Paul's parish. In 1962 when £90,000 was offered for the sites of the church, vicarage, and church hall, it was estimated that some 4,500 people were to be moved out in the course of the re-developments planned.[63] In 1964 the demolition of the church was approved, and soon after its clergy left to work in the new housing estate at Covingham, which was created the conventional district of St. Paul, Covingham.[64] The church was demolished early in 1965 and the parish was absorbed into that of St. Mark's.[65] The site was acquired by Messrs. F. W. Woolworth & Co., who surrendered one corner of it, on which it was intended to build a small chapel of ease for meetings and occasional week-day services.[66]

St. Paul's was designed by Edmund Ferrey, and the chancel, added in 1883, by John Bevan. It was built of brick in the Early English style, without a tower.[67]

The church of *ST. JOHN THE EVANGELIST*, Aylesbury Street, was built in 1883 as a daughter church of St. Mark's to meet the needs of the then developing Queenstown district of the parish.[68] Before the church was built a room in a house in Oriel Street was used as a temporary church.[69] The foundation stone of the permanent building was laid by the deputy chairman of the G.W.R., thus preserving the link between the company and St. Mark's parish.[70] In 1884 full congregations were reported and there were 150 pupils in the Sunday school.[71] Here as at St. Mark's High Church ritual was observed.[72] After the First World War numbers attending St. John's declined, presumably because

[39] *Clergy List* (1921).
[40] See p. 144.
[41] *St. Mark's Parish Mag.* Sept. 1963, and Mar. 1964.
[42] *St. Mark's 1845–1945*, pp. 11 sqq.
[43] Brit. Trans. Hist. R.O. HL 1/29 f. 23.
[44] H.O. 129/250/2/8/19.
[45] Ibid.
[46] *St. Mark's 1845–1945*, 25.
[47] Ibid. 14, 35.
[48] Ibid. 18.
[49] Ibid. 17.
[50] Ibid. 20.
[51] Ibid. 19, 102–3.
[52] Ibid. 43.
[53] Ibid. 21.
[54] Ibid. 22.
[55] Ibid. 26–27.
[56] Ibid. 29.
[57] Ibid. 28.

[58] *Lond. Gaz.* 2 Sept. 1881 (p. 4538); *Home Mission Field*, Nov. 1913, 100.
[59] *Kelly's Dir. Wilts.* (1903).
[60] *St. Mark's 1845–1945*, 16
[61] Ibid. 16–17.
[62] Morris, *Swindon*, 191.
[63] *Daily Telegraph*, 23 Nov. 1962.
[64] *St. Mark's Parish Mag.* Mar. 1964.
[65] *Evening Advertiser*, 5 Jan. 1965, and see p. 148.
[66] *St. Mark's Par. Mag.* Mar. 1964.
[67] Pevsner, *Wilts.* (Bldgs. of Eng.), 458.
[68] *St. Mark's 1845–1945*, 49.
[69] Ibid.
[70] Ibid. 50.
[71] Ibid.
[72] Ibid. 57.

St. Luke's[73] was by then serving an area formerly served by St. John's.[74] In 1921 St. John's was closed for some years.[75] It was reopened in 1926, but the neighbourhood from this date was ceasing to be a residential one, and in 1956 the church was finally closed and was pulled down soon after.[76] St. John's was designed by F. B. Wade. It was an aisle-less building with a raised chancel, built of variegated brick. It seated 300.[77]

ST. SAVIOUR'S church was built in 1889 as a daughter church of St. Mark's to serve the south-western corner of the parish.[78] It was built in wood in just over six months by the voluntary labour and in the spare time of men already working full-time in the G.W.R. factory.[79] The accommodation, which was for 180, soon became inadequate, as this part of the parish continued to be developed. In 1904 a new aisle and vestry were added, again by voluntary labour.[80] During the early 20th century a number of interior improvements were made.[81] But the structure was only a temporary one. Eventually in *c.* 1960 it was decided to build a stone church around the original one, encasing it completely.[82] The work, designed by R. E. E. Beswick, was completed and the church re-opened in 1961.[83]

ST. LUKE'S church originated in a temporary building in Broad Street begun in 1901 and opened in 1903.[84] In 1908 the need for a larger church was considered urgent, but for lack of money building did not begin until 1910, and the architect's original plans had to be modified for the sake of economy.[85] The new church was dedicated towards the end of 1911.[86] The district it served continued to be a mainly residential one and in 1965 St. Luke's and St. Saviour's, the two daughter churches of St. Mark's, were in many ways more active than their parent church. The church, designed by W. A. H. Masters,[87] is built of rustic-faced stone in the style of the 15th century. It comprises chancel, nave of five bays, south aisle, and south porch. The north aisle has not been built although allowed for in the plan.

ST. BARNABAS'S church began in a temporary building in Gorse Hill in 1874.[88] It has been said that the High Church forms of worship, later observed in the parishes of St. Mark and St. Paul, were first introduced here.[89] In 1875 Holy Communion was celebrated daily and all services were said to be highly ritualistic.[90] In 1885 work began on a permanent church and in 1890 a separate parish was formed for it.[91] The living is a vicarage in the gift of the Bishop of Bristol.[92]

The church was designed by J. P. Seddon[93] and is built of stone with lancet windows in the style of the 13th century. It has a lofty clerestoried nave, low

lean-to aisles, and a spirelet at the east end of the nave roof; the design allows for a tower beyond the south porch, of which two stages have been built.

In *c.* 1883 a mission room in Rodbourne was licensed for religious services.[94] Rodbourne at this date lay within the parish of St. Mary, Rodbourne Cheney, although most of its residents worked in Swindon, and the mission room was nearer to St. Mark's, Swindon, than to St. Mary's, Rodbourne Cheney.[95] For some time during the 1880s the temporary church was served by clergy from St. Mark's.[96] In 1908, by which date Swindon's boundary had been extended to include Rodbourne, a permanent church, dedicated to *ST. AUGUS-TINE*, was built, and a separate parish for it formed out of parts of the parishes of Rodbourne Cheney and St. Mark's.[97] The living is a vicarage in the gift of the Bishop of Bristol. In 1910 there were said to have been 266 communicants on Easter Day, and nearly 3,000 throughout 1909.[98] In 1929 it was reckoned that there were over 5,000 communicants in the parish.[99] During the 1930s the former mission room, used for meetings and social functions, was enlarged.[1] The church was designed by W. A. H. Masters.[2] It is built in red brick with Romanesque windows and has a small polygonal apse and north-east bell-turret. Aisles and chancel have not been completed.

ALL SAINTS, Southbrook, was consecrated in 1908.[3] Its first building was a temporary one designed so that it could later be used as schoolrooms.[4] The area to be served was expanding rapidly in the 20th century, although in 1908 the church could still be reached by 'country paths' from the centre of Swindon.[5] All Saints was at first a mission district closely connected with St. Mark's and services were conducted on the same lines in the two churches.[6] In 1929 a separate parish was formed. The living is a vicarage in the gift of the Bishop of Bristol.[7] The foundation stone of a permanent church was laid in 1937. The architect was Hartland Thomas of Bristol.[8] The church is a severely plain building of white brick with tall narrow windows. Above the porch is a bell spirelet.

ST. MARY'S mission church was built in Commonweal Road in 1926 as the first daughter church of Christ Church, Old Swindon.[9] It was believed that a church nearer than Christ Church was needed for parishioners living in the west of the parish.[10] A temporary structure of wood was provided and has not been replaced.

ST. ANDREW'S, Walcot East, was consecrated in 1958 as the second daughter church of Christ Church, Old Swindon.[11] Representatives of the new housing estate of Walcot had sat on the Christ

[73] See below.
[74] *St. Mark's 1845–1945*, 56.   [75] Ibid.
[76] *St. Mark's Par. Mag.* Dec. 1956.
[77] *St. Mark's 1845–1945*, 49–50.
[78] *St. Mark's 1845–1945*, 59.
[79] Ibid. 59–61.   [80] Ibid. 63.
[81] Ibid. 65–66.
[82] *St. Mark's Parish Mag.* July 1961.
[83] Ibid. Aug. 1961.
[84] *St. Mark's 1845–1945*, 27.
[85] Ibid. 71–75.   [86] Ibid. 75.
[87] Pevsner, *Wilts.* (Bldgs. of Eng.), 458.
[88] *St. Mark's 1845–1945*, 13.
[89] Ibid.   [90] Ibid. 13–14.
[91] *Clergy List* (1891); *Kelly's Dir. Wilts.* (1939).
[92] *Kelly's Dir. Wilts.* (1903).

[93] Pevsner, *Wilts.* (Bldgs. of Eng.), 457–8.
[94] *Story of St. Augustine's Swindon*, 6 (pamphlet in Swindon Pub. Libr.).
[95] *St. Mark's 1845–1945*, 36.
[96] *Story of St. Augustine's*, 7.
[97] Ibid. 9–11; *Home Mission Field*, 3 Feb. 1910, 7.
[98] *Home Mission Field*, 3 Feb. 1910, 7.
[99] *St. Augustine's Ch. Annual Rep.* 1929.
[1] *Story of St. Augustine's*, 15.
[2] Pevsner, *Wilts.* (Bldgs. of Eng.), 457.
[3] *St. Mark's 1845–1945*, 29.   [4] Ibid. 28.
[5] Ibid. 29.   [6] Ibid.
[7] *Crockford* (1931).   [8] Inscription on ch.
[9] *Christ Church, Swindon, 1851–1951, Centenary Souvenir.*
[10] Ibid.   [11] *Christ Church Parish Mag.*, Feb. 1958.

Church parish council since 1956 and services were sometimes held in a hut in Raleigh Avenue on the estate before the church was built.[12] St. Andrew's was designed by R. J. Beswick and Son[13] and has a steep glazed gable front.

The church of *ST. PETER*, Penhill, was consecrated in 1956.[14] The living is a vicarage in the gift of the Bishop of Bristol.[15] The church, which is of brick with a tower with a slender spire, was designed by Harold Brakspear.[16]

The church of *ST. JOHN THE BAPTIST*, Park North, was consecrated in 1961. The living is a vicarage in the gift of the Bishop of Bristol.[17] The church, built in a 20th-century style, was designed by Harold Brakspear. It has a slim high tower surmounted by a cross.[18]

ROMAN CATHOLICISM. There were 6 Roman Catholic families in Swindon in 1848, who attended mass at Horcott, near Fairford (Glos.), some 13 miles away. Later in the same year the priest from Horcott came to Swindon once a month to say mass at the Greyhound Inn in Westcott Place.[19] In 1850 the Swindon mission was served from Woodchester (Glos.) and then for six years was dependent upon Fairford.[20] In 1851 a chapel was opened on a site between Regent and Sanford Streets.[21] Seven years later Swindon had its first resident priest.[22] The first Roman Catholic school in the town was opened in Regent Street in 1878.[23] In 1882 the church between Regent and Sanford Streets was closed and a move made to a former nonconformist chapel in Regent Circus. This was used until 1905 when the church of Holy Rood in Groundwell Road was built.[24] The architect was E. Doran Webb[25] and the building he designed is of flint with a low, broad tower at the crossing.

With the growth of suburban Swindon after the Second World War another church was needed and in 1953 St. Mary's, Tovey Road, was built to serve the Rodbourne Cheney, Pinehurst, Penhill, and Stratton St. Margaret areas.[26] Three years later a mass centre was opened at Penhill, served by a priest from St. Mary's. At first mass was celebrated in the Penhill Community Centre, but this soon proved to be too small, and in 1966 an invitation from the Vicar of Penhill to use the Anglican church hall as a temporary mass centre was accepted. A parish of the Holy Family was formed in 1962 for the new housing estates to the east of the town, but in 1966 the parish had no church and parishioners attended mass in the Roman Catholic school in Marlowe Avenue.

In 1938 a mass centre at Wootton Bassett began to be served from Holy Rood, Swindon.[27] The mass centre at Stratton St. Margaret, opened and at first served from Holy Rood, was taken over by St.

Mary's, Tovey Road, in 1956, and after the closing of the mass centre at Highworth in 1965, an extra mass was said at St. Mary's on Sundays.

Three sisters of the Community of the Poor Servants of the Mother of God came to Swindon in 1922. One taught in the Groundwell Road school and the others visited in the parish. They moved into their convent in Groundwell Road in 1924. Some sisters from the Community of Presentation Sisters, living in Wroughton, taught in the Groundwell Road school after 1960. In 1964 the sisters moved from Wroughton to a convent in Marlowe Avenue. Missionary work in Swindon has been undertaken since 1964 by sisters of the Holy Spirit Missionary Congregation living in Wroughton.

A resident Polish priest came to serve the Polish community in Swindon in 1949 and until 1965 said mass for the community in Holy Rood. In 1965 the Polish Centre in Whitbourne Avenue was built and this provided the Poles in Swindon with a church as well as accommodation for social and educational activities. After 1965 the Italian community in Swindon had a priest living in the Italian Centre in Park Lane, and since 1951 a visiting priest has said mass at Holy Rood once a month for the Ukranian community living in the town and its neighbourhood.

In 1966 there were said to be 12,000 Roman Catholics in Swindon. Besides the parish priest there were 3 assistant priests at Holy Rood. St. Mary's parish and the Holy Family parish each had a priest and an assistant.

PROTESTANT NONCONFORMITY.[28] The north-eastern part of Wiltshire, in which Swindon lies, was not a region where religious dissent was particularly active before the later 18th century. In Swindon in 1676 there were 8 sectaries.[29] These are likely to have been Baptists and Quakers, sects known to have been influential in the district.[30] In 1741 John Cennick, sometimes called the Evangelist of North Wiltshire, visited Swindon in the course of his evangelistic campaign of the region. He was accompanied, amongst others, by the Welsh evangelist, Howell Harris, and attempted to hold a preaching and prayer meeting at the Grove (a site somewhere off the later Drove Road). But Cennick and his followers were given a particularly antagonistic and violent reception, inspired, apparently, by the lord of the manor, Pleydell Goddard.[31] Cennick was beleaguered by a Swindon mob again a few months later on his way to preach at Stratton St. Margaret.[32]

This early, apparently exceptionally fierce opposition seems effectually to have discouraged the introduction of nonconformity into Swindon during the 18th century. A house there was licensed as a meet-

[12] Ibid. Aug. 1956.
[13] Pevsner, *Wilts.* (Bldgs. of Eng.), 457.
[14] St. Peter's Parish Mag. July 1956.
[15] Crockford.
[16] Ex inf. Swindon Pub. Libr.
[17] Crockford.
[18] Evening Advertiser, 21 July, 1961.
[19] V.C.H. Wilts. iii. 98.
[20] Reginald Bearne, 'Catholic Church in Swindon' (TS in Swindon Pub. Libr.).
[21] Swindon Advertiser, Supp. 5 Feb. 1904.
[22] Bearne, op. cit.
[23] See p. 163.
[24] Bearne, op. cit.; V.C.H. Wilts. iii. 98.
[25] Swindon Guide (1905).
[26] Except where otherwise stated, this and all subsequent information supplied by the Very Revd. Canon J. P. Leahy, Holy Rood Presbytery, Swindon, to whom grateful thanks are due.
[27] See p. 203.
[28] Thanks are due to Mrs. Ada F. Tanner, Swindon, for much help with this section.
[29] W.N. & Q. iii. 535.
[30] V.C.H. Wilts. iii. 115.
[31] Morris, Swindon, 369–79.
[32] Ibid. 374.

ing-place for protestant dissenters in 1745, but for how long it was used, and by whom, is unknown.[33] Throughout the century the only permanent meeting-place for Swindon nonconformists was the Baptist church in the neighbouring village of Stratton Green.[34]

After Cennick and his followers, George Pocock, a friend of John Wesley, visited Swindon in the course of his preaching tours of north-east Wiltshire.[35] The first serious following Pocock mustered in the Swindon neighbourhood was at Hodson, in Chiseldon[36] but he also seems to have inspired a number of people to begin meeting in a house in Lower Town, Swindon (see below).

At the beginning of the 19th century, therefore, Swindon, a small market town of just over 1,000 people, had no nonconformist chapel. The first to be built was in Newport Street in 1804 by a group of Independents.[37] Foremost among them were several members of the family of Strange, who had a drapery business in the high street, and who were also responsible for the establishment of the first bank in Swindon.[38] In spite of some opposition Newport Street soon began to draw large congregations from Swindon, and became the headquarters for missionary work in some of the surrounding villages.[39] A group of Wesleyan Methodists, who, inspired by the visits of George Pocock, had been meeting in the house of a Mr. Noad in Lower Town,[40] began to build a second chapel on a site off the Planks in 1813.[41] It was many years before the building could be completed although a preacher was appointed in 1814, and the Swindon Circuit formed out of the Hungerford Circuit in 1817.[42]

Towards the end of the 1820s Primitive Methodism was introduced into Swindon by preachers from Brinkworth, where a circuit had been formed in 1826.[43] The early meetings in Swindon were held in a number of humble cottages on Eastcott Hill, particularly those occupied by Robert Sharps, Henry Gilmore, and John and Mary Pike.[44] By 1828 it had become customary to hold two services somewhere in Swindon on Sundays, and the Eastcott society had 15 members.[45] That year Charles Morse, of Stratton St. Margaret, joined the plan as exhorter, the first of a family which was to play a leading part for many years in Primitive Methodism in Swindon. Morse had his business premises at the foot of Eastcott Hill and from there conducted praying and singing meetings.[46] In 1840 Hugh Bourne visited Swindon and addressed a crowded meeting in the cottage of Thomas Edwards on Eastcott Hill.[47] The Edwards family produced several leaders in the early days of Primitive Methodism in Swindon, and Thomas and James Edwards provided the site for the Primitive Methodist chapel opened in 1849.[48]

With the opening of the G.W.R. works in 1843, and the building of the first housing estate for the workers, members of the Stratton Baptist church began to visit the new settlement on Sundays to hold missionary services there[49] and in 1849 a chapel was built on the east side of the estate.[50] For a time the Swindon church remained a mission church of Stratton Green, the two congregations sharing a minister.[51]

Nonconformity quickly took a hold in the new town, colonized, as it was, by workers, many of them nonconformists, from all over the country. Chapel building, however, could not keep pace with the rate at which the new town's population grew. The Particular Baptists built a chapel in the old town in 1845[52] but accommodation in this and the old town's other two chapels was soon inadequate. In the new town the Wesleyan Methodists built a chapel in Bridge Street in 1849 and the Unitarians one in Regent Street in 1861.[53] But the shortage of accommodation remained acute and halls and rooms all over the town, designed for other purposes, were used for religious services.

Between 1861 and 1871 several chapels were built, or rebuilt on a larger scale. The Wesleyan chapel off the Planks and the Congregational chapel in Newport Street were completely rebuilt in 1862 and 1866 respectively.[54] In spite of the demands of the new town both were rebuilt in Old Swindon, then thriving as a shopping and commercial centre. The congregation of the Wesleyan chapel, originally in Bridge Street, was moved to a larger building for the second time in 1869 when it acquired the large block known as the 'Barracks' with accommodation for well over 1,000 people.[55] The Primitive Methodist chapel in Regent Street was completely rebuilt in 1863 and in 1870 a new Primitive Methodist church was built in Prospect Place.[56] In 1866 a Welsh Baptist church was provided for the many Welsh families who came to Swindon during the 1860s.[57]

From 1870 until the end of the century the story is one of chapel building and enlargement as the town grew. In 1876 the Regent Street Primitive Methodist chapel was enlarged for the third time since its opening in 1849.[58] The Wesleyans in Old Swindon moved in 1880 to their large, and architecturally impressive church in the Bath road—still in the old town.[59] The Congregationalists built their first church in the new town in Sanford Street in 1877.[60] In response to the growth of Swindon north of the railway line both the Wesleyan and the Primitive Methodists established places of worship in 1871 at Gorse Hill. These congregations quickly grew and prospered, and by 1890, when Gorse Hill became part of Swindon, both had quite large chapels there.[61] The Baptists began mission work in Gorse Hill only in 1883, but they, too, had to

[33] W.R.O. Certs. Dissenters' Meeting-Places, 1706–45.
[34] V.C.H. Wilts. iii. 115.
[35] Morris, Swindon, 393–6.
[36] See p. 22.   [37] See p. 153.
[38] Norman Charlton, Immanuel Congregational Church, Swindon, 7.
[39] Ibid. 8.
[40] Morris, Swindon, 396.
[41] Ibid. 401–2.
[42] Ibid. 402, 395.
[43] S. J. Averies, Regent St. Methodist Church, 1849–1949, 3.
[44] Morris, Swindon, 416; Averies, op. cit. 5.
[45] Averies, op. cit. 3, 6.
[46] Ibid. 6.
[47] Ibid.; Morris, Swindon, 417.
[48] Averies, Regent St. Methodist Church, 7.
[49] F. W. T. Fuller, Baptists of Stratton Green, 23.
[50] See p. 156.
[51] Fuller, op. cit. 23–24.
[52] See p. 157.
[53] See p. 157.
[54] See p. 154.
[55] See p. 155.
[56] See p. 156.
[57] See p. 157.
[58] See p. 155.
[59] See p. 155.
[60] See p. 154.
[61] See pp. 155, 156.

build a bigger chapel there early in the 20th century.[62] At Even Swindon the Wesleyan and Primitive Methodists had chapels by c. 1882,[63] and the Baptists began missionary work in the neighbourhood not long after that.[64]

The 1880s saw a continuation of building activity, partly to keep pace with the town's growth, but also to establish more securely congregations formed in a modest way earlier. Two new churches became more firmly established in the town, both introduced there originally by workers settling in Swindon from other parts of the country. In 1898 the large and imposing Presbyterian Church of England was built, and a group of Moravians moved into the hall in Dixon Street vacated by the Presbyterians.[65]

The Primitive Methodists were particularly active during the last 20 years of the 19th century. A movement, described as a 'great revival', swept through the town in 1880–1. Many camp meetings took place, all-night meetings of prayer and praise were held, and processions marched through the streets, usually ending at the Regent Street chapel, the membership of which was increased by over 200 that year.[66] Between 1880 and the end of the century five new Primitive Methodist chapels were built.[67] In 1890 the Swindon Primitive Methodist circuit, which had been formed in 1877, was split into two and Prospect Hill became the parent-church of number one circuit, and Regent Street of number two circuit.[68]

In the last 20 years of the 19th century the Wesleyan Methodists opened four new chapels[69] and the Baptists built their large Tabernacle church in the classical style with seating for 1,000.[70] In the same period the Christian Brethren, the Salvation Army, and the Railwaymen's Christian Association established themselves in the town. A small group of Brethren came to Swindon in 1880. At first their headquarters was a tent pitched in Regent Place. Meetings held in the street near the G.W.R. works in the dinner hour sometimes caused obstructions. In 1889 there was a split among the members and about 40 broke away to join the 'Open Brethren'.[71] It was this group which flourished in Swindon and built the chapel in Regent Place in 1899.[72] Disturbances in the streets caused by the Salvation Army were reported in the local press in 1883 and 1884.[73]

A few new chapels were built during the early years of the 20th century and some existing chapels were enlarged.[74] These catered mainly for congregations in the suburbs, which were spreading steadily northwards. But the Primitive Methodists built a chapel in Manchester Road, near the station, and the Wesleyans built the Central Mission Hall in the very centre of the town.[75] A single Swindon Wesleyan Methodist Circuit, with the Bath Road church at its head, was formed in 1911 for all the Swindon Wesleyan chapels. Before that they had belonged

either to the Swindon and Marlborough Circuit or to the Wantage Circuit. After the Methodist Union of 1933 there were three Swindon Circuits, namely Bath Road, Prospect, and Regent Street. By 1959 there was again a single Swindon Methodist Circuit.[76]

From about 1900 many houses and rooms were registered as meeting-places for denominations quite new to the town, some of which flourished for only a few years, while others eventually established themselves in their own churches or chapels. Since the First World War five chapels have been built for denominations established in the town during the 19th century: in 1928 a small Methodist church was built on the Pinehurst estate; in 1939 the Congregationalists closed their church in Victoria Street and moved to a new one built for them in Upham Road, Walcot; in 1959 a Free Church was opened at Penhill; in 1961 a Methodist church was built in Queen's Drive, Walcot, and in 1961 the Methodists in Cheney Manor Road left their church for a new one in Moredon Road.[77] All these were situated in the new residential suburbs of the town. The earlier chapels, built to serve the residents of New Swindon, were by the mid 20th century becoming more and more isolated from their congregations. In 1957 one of the largest chapels in the town, the Methodist chapel in Regent Street, was demolished, and the money used to build the Methodist chapel in Queen's Drive, and improve one or two of the smaller 19th-century chapels.[78] A few years later the large Methodist church in the 'Barracks' in Faringdon Street was closed.[79] Two smaller Methodist chapels have also been closed, and at Gorse Hill the former Primitive and Wesleyan Methodist churches have been amalgamated, making it possible to dispense with one building.[80]

Congregational Churches

NEWPORT STREET. This, the first chapel to be built in Swindon, was opened in 1804.[81] George Mantell of the Upper Meeting House, Westbury, was its first minister. The congregation grew rapidly and quite soon more accommodation had to be provided by the addition of side-wings to the gallery. Mantell died in 1832 and was succeeded by S. B. Meons. Meons had been a Dutch merchant, who had lost his livelihood in Holland after the Napoleonic Wars. Shortly after his appointment to Swindon, some trouble developed between him and his congregation, and he was obliged to resign.[82] A new minister was appointed at once but the congregation was disunited and 15 members left it. These, thought by some to be the 'most lively and energetic members of the church', continued to worship together in a private house, and later formed the nucleus of the Particular Baptist congregation, for whom a chapel was built in South Street in 1845.[83]

By 1840 accommodation in the Newport Street

---

[62] See p. 157.
[63] See pp. 155, 156.
[64] See p. 157.
[65] See p. 158.
[66] S. J. Averies, *Regent St. Methodist Church*, 15–16.
[67] See p. 156.
[68] Averies, op. cit. 15, 17.
[69] See p. 154.
[70] See p. 157.
[71] D. J. Beattie, *Brethren, the Story of a Great Recovery*, (1940), 159–61.

[72] Date on bldg. and G.R.O. 37721.
[73] *Swindon Advertiser*, 23 Apr. 1883, 2 Feb. 1884.
[74] See pp. 155–8.   [75] See pp. 155, 156.
[76] All information from *Swindon Dirs.*
[77] See pp. 154, 156.   [78] See p. 156.
[79] See p. 159.   [80] See p. 156.
[81] Norman Charlton, *Immanuel Congregational Church.* Unless otherwise stated, information about this chapel from this source.
[82] Swindon Pub. Libr., Min. Bk. Cong. Ch. 1833–54.
[83] See p. 157.

chapel had become inadequate and the building needed attention. But although this was obviously a cause for discontent among the congregation, no move was made until 1866, when a new chapel was built at the corner of Bath Road and Victoria Street. Disagreement about the site may account for the long delay. There was clearly disagreement about something, for when at last the move was made, only five members transferred to the new chapel, and their minister did not go with them.

The old chapel stood on the north side of Newport Street. When it was built a neighbouring house was converted into a manse. The chapel seems to have been a small, octagonal building, with arched windows at ground and first-floor levels. Above the entrance door there was a round window and above this an inscribed medallion bore a date.[84] In the 1830s the schoolroom of a British School was built on to the chapel's east side and the chapel burial ground was used as a playground. When opened in 1804, the chapel was described as 'neat and commodious', but shortly before its closure it was called a 'dismal cell'. The ceiling was so low that the minister in the pulpit, and the occupants of the semi-circular gallery, could touch it. A harmonium stood in the centre of the gallery which was approached by a winding staircase.

VICTORIA STREET. Although it had become apparent by 1840 that the Newport Street chapel was too small, a new chapel was not built until 1866. That year a chapel built on a site at the corner of Victoria Street and Bath Road, in Old Swindon, was opened with accommodation for 550.[85] Only five members moved to the new chapel from Newport Street.[86] After the move, however, membership increased fairly rapidly and was 154 by 1867.[87] But the siting of the new chapel in Old Swindon had been ill-judged, for it was in New Swindon that there was the greatest need for a chapel, and in 1877 56 members left the Victoria Street chapel to form a new congregation in Sanford Street. In 1916 the Victoria Street congregation was split by disagreement over the appointment of a minister, and a number of members left to form the Evangelical Free Church.[88] Soon after this, serious defects in the fabric of the chapel appeared, and in 1925 its existence was threatened by a street-widening scheme.[89] Plans to move were followed by delays and protracted deliberations and it was not until 1938 that a site in Upham Road, Walcot, was chosen and work begun on building a chapel there.[90] The Victoria Street chapel was eventually demolished shortly after the Second World War.[91]

The chapel was built in undressed stone with heavy stone dressings.[92] At its south end was a large 'rose' window and at the south-east corner there was a square tower, rising above the top of the chapel roof.

SANFORD STREET. To meet the need for a chapel in New Swindon, the members of the Congregational chapel, Victoria Street, Old Swindon, in 1877 erected an iron chapel in Sanford Street.[93] This had 800 sittings and the new congregation was formed around 56 members from Victoria Street, who transferred to the new chapel.[94] In 1894 a permanent chapel was built on the same site with accommodation for 550. The architect was T. B. Silcock of Bath,[95] and the building was described locally as in 'a late Gothic style, slightly modified by Jacobean peculiarities'.[96] A Sunday schoolroom was added in 1898.[97] In 1964 there were 105 church members.[98]

UPHAM ROAD, IMMANUEL CHURCH. This chapel was built in 1938–9 to replace the Victoria Street Congregational chapel.[99] Membership had declined during the last years at Victoria Street and when the new chapel opened was only 21.[1] The site in Upham Road had been chosen in order to serve the rapidly expanding Walcot area of Swindon. Membership increased to about 100 members in 1943,[2] but, despite this, it was felt that the chapel had not made the impression upon the new neighbourhood that had been hoped.[3] Between 1949 and 1954 the chapel grounds were laid out as a family sports club, and church services and activities organized to make the chapel a Christian community centre.[4]

The chapel was designed by a Mr. Houchin[5] and is built in red brick in a style typical of the 1930s. Several Sunday schoolrooms and an assembly hall adjoin it at the back.

PENHILL FREE CHURCH. This was established largely through the efforts of the congregations of Immanuel and Sanford Street Congregational chapels.[6] In 1954 services were held in Penhill farmhouse and in 1959 the church in Penhill Drive with seating for 150 was opened.[7] The architects were Eric Cole and Partners of Swindon.[8]

Wesleyan Methodist Churches

THE PLANKS. In 1813 a group of Wesleyan Methodists, who had been meeting in a house in Lower Town, began to build a chapel on a site leading off the Planks.[9] Shortage of money brought many difficulties and prevented the completion of the building until 1824.[10] That year Thomas Bush, of Lambourn (Berks.), a well-to-do and ardent supporter of Methodism in the neighbourhood,[11] paid off the debt on the chapel and built two cottages adjoining it, one as a manse.[12] In 1842 an extra gallery was added to the chapel, making accommodation for 170, 30 more than before, and a schoolroom was added at the side.[13] In 1862 the first chapel was pulled down and a new octagonal-

[84] The history of the chapel by Norman Charlton (see n.81 above) has a picture.
[85] *Kelly's Dir. Wilts.* (1927).
[86] Charlton, *Immanuel Congregational Church*, 16–18.
[87] Ibid. 23.
[88] Ibid. 28, and see p. 158.
[89] Charlton, op. cit. 28.
[90] Ibid. 28–29.
[91] Ex inf. Mrs. Ada F. Tanner, Swindon.
[92] Photograph in Charlton, *Immanuel Congregational Church*, and see pl. facing p. 138.
[93] Charlton, op. cit. 24.
[94] Ibid.
[95] Wilts. Cuttings, v. 104.
[96] *Swindon Advertiser*, Supp. 5 Feb. 1904.
[97] *Sanford St. Congregational Church Yr. Bk.* (1957–8).
[98] *Congregational Yr. Bk.* (1964–5).
[99] Charlton, *Immanuel Congregational Church*, 28–29, 31.
[1] Ibid. 30.　[2] Ibid. 33.
[3] Ibid.　[4] Ibid. 34, 35.
[5] Ibid. 30.
[6] Ibid. 37.
[7] Ex inf. Mrs. Ada F. Tanner, Swindon; G.R.O. 66539.
[8] *Evening Advertiser*, 26 June 1957.
[9] Morris, *Swindon*, 401; *Swindon Advertiser*, Supp. 5 Feb. 1904.
[10] Morris, op. cit.
[11] Ibid. 398.
[12] Ibid. 402.
[13] *Swindon Advertiser*, Supp. 5 Feb. 1904.

shaped one was erected on the same site with seating for 300.[14] This chapel served the Wesleyan Methodists in Swindon until 1880 when another new chapel, with accommodation for 600, was built in Bath Road.[15]

After 1880 the chapel of 1862, sometimes called the 'Octagon', was converted and used for a time as stables, but by 1885 it had been acquired by the Salvation Army.[16] In 1965 the site had been com-completely cleared but a small piece of arcading, once part of an inside wall of the chapel, could still be seen against the wall of an adjoining building.

BRIDGE STREET. This was the second Wesleyan chapel to be built in Swindon, and the first in the new town. It was built in 1849 on the site later occupied by 'Mr. Clapper's shop' in Bridge Street and could accommodate 160.[17] In 1858 this chapel was pulled down and a larger one, with 550 seats, built nearby in Faringdon Road. In 1869 this chapel also was pulled down and a large building in Faringdon Road, known as the 'Barracks', was converted for use as a chapel. The 'Barracks', originally built by the G.W.R. as a lodging house, was converted as a chapel by T. S. Lansdown, of Swindon, and could accommodate 1,000.[18] The chapel was closed in c. 1959 and in 1962 the building became a railway museum.[19]

GORSE HILL. A mission hall was built by the Wesleyan Methodists in Gorse Hill in 1871.[20] In 1883 a chapel was built in front of this which could seat about 180. By 1900 the chapel was too small for the neighbourhood it served and was enlarged that year to accommodate 600. It later became called the Trinity Methodist Church.[21] In 1964 the congregation was joined by that from the Russell Memorial church (formerly Primitive Methodist) in the Cricklade road, which was then closed and demolished.[22]

PERCY STREET. An iron chapel with 200 sittings was erected in Percy Street in 1877.[23] In 1898 a new building was added to give accommodation for 450.[24] The chapel was closed c. 1956.[25]

BATH ROAD. The congregation from the chapel known as the 'Octagon' in the Planks moved in 1880 to a new chapel built for it in Bath Road at the corner of Wesley Street.[26] This was designed by Messrs. Bromilow and Cheers of Liverpool and had accommodation for 800. Beneath the chapel a basement was equipped as a Sunday school and there was space for public meetings. At the time of opening the chapel was described as a 'particularly handsome structure'. The chapel was still in use in 1964.

WILLIAM STREET. A mission hall was opened in this street in 1887.[27] In 1904 its 400 sittings were said to be 'hardly enough'. About 1951 the hall was acquired by the Christian Brethren.[28]

WESLEYAN CENTRAL MISSION HALL, CLARENCE STREET. A mission hall was built in 1884 in Princes Street with seating for 240.[29] In 1907 this was replaced by the Central Mission Hall built in Clarence Street.[30] This was extensively enlarged in the 1960s to provide accommodation for lectures and meetings.[31]

Primitive Methodist Churches

REGENT STREET. In 1848 Thomas and James Edwards, who had long been connected with Primitive Methodism,[32] sold a field, through which Regent Street later ran, as a site for a chapel.[33] The following year a small brick chapel accommodating about 150, with a burial ground to its east, was built.[34] Membership was 27.[35] In 1850 the congregation's first resident minister came to live in a thatched cottage in what later became Regent Circus.[36] By 1863 the chapel had become too small, and that year a larger one, with an adjoining schoolroom, was built on the same site.[37] By 1875 membership was 112 and again the chapel was found to be too small.[38] The following year a third chapel was built on the site, with accommodation for 600.[39] It was an ornate brick building with quoins of Bath stone and at its opening was described as 'one of the prettiest and best arranged public buildings in Swindon'.[40] In 1877 Regent Street was the largest of the three Primitive Methodist churches that were formed that year into the Swindon Circuit, and was the focal point for the missionary activities of the Primitive Methodists in Swindon in the 1880s.[41] In 1882 membership was well over 200.[42] In 1887 road improvements in Regent Street made it necessary to make certain structural alterations.[43]

When the Swindon Circuit was divided into two in 1890 Regent Street became the parent church of the second circuit.[44] Five years later a large Sunday school was built behind the chapel for 356 pupils and 32 teachers.[45] In the earlier 20th century a number of men prominent in civic affairs were active members of the congregation. Among them were Levi Lapper Morse and his son, William Ewart Morse, son and grandson of Charles Morse, both of whom were mayors of Swindon, county councillors, and M.P.s.[46] In 1904 membership was 200.[47] But as this part of the town developed as a shopping and commercial centre, the position of the chapel in Swindon's busiest shopping street became more

[14] Ibid; Morris, *Swindon*, 404.
[15] *Swindon Advertiser*, Supp. 5 Feb. 1904.
[16] Morris, op. cit. 411.
[17] Except where otherwise stated, information about this chapel from *Swindon Advertiser*, Supp. 5 Feb. 1904.
[18] Morris, *Swindon*, 411.
[19] Ex inf. Mrs. Ada F. Tanner, Swindon, and see p. 141.
[20] Except where otherwise stated, information about this chapel from *Swindon Advertiser*, Supp. 5 Feb. 1904.
[21] Ex inf. Mrs. Ada F. Tanner, Swindon.
[22] See p. 156.
[23] *Swindon Advertiser*, Supp. 5 Feb. 1904.
[24] Ibid.
[25] G.R.O. 35014.
[26] All information from Morris, *Swindon*, 411.
[27] Except where otherwise stated, information from *Swindon Advertiser*, Supp. 5 Feb. 1904.
[28] G.R.O. 63124.
[29] *Swindon Advertiser*, Supp. 5 Feb. 1904.

[30] Ex inf. Mrs. Ada F. Tanner, Swindon.
[31] Ibid.
[32] See p. 152.
[33] S. J. Averies, *Regent St. Methodist Church, 1849–1949*, 7; Morris, *Swindon*, 417.
[34] Averies, op. cit. 10.
[35] Ibid. 11.
[36] Ibid. 12.
[37] Ibid.
[38] Ibid.
[39] Ibid. 13.
[40] Ibid. 13–14.
[41] Ibid. 15. The other two were Prospect and Gorse Hill (later known as the Russell Memorial ch.).
[42] Ibid. 16.
[43] Ibid. 17.
[44] Ibid.
[45] Ibid. 19.
[46] Ibid. 6.
[47] *Swindon Advertiser*, Supp. 5 Feb. 1904.

and more unsuitable. In 1957 the chapel was demolished and its funds used to improve other Methodist churches in Swindon and to build a new chapel in Queen's Drive on the Walcot estate.[48]

PROSPECT PLACE. After the building of the Regent Street chapel in 1849 the Primitive Methodists in Old Swindon continued to meet in cottages and in the open air. A cottage in Albert Street was particularly popular as a meeting-place.[49] In 1870 a site in Prospect Place was acquired and a chapel built.[50] Between that date and 1904 the church was twice enlarged to make accommodation for 420.[51] In 1910 it had 108 members.[52] When the Swindon Circuit was divided into two in 1890, Prospect became the parent church of the first circuit.[53] In 1964 the chapel was still in use, although no longer the head of a circuit.

CRICKLADE ROAD (RUSSELL MEMORIAL CHURCH). The first Primitive Methodist chapel in Gorse Hill was built in 1871.[54] But as the district was developed, it soon became too small. In 1890 a new site at the corner of Edinburgh Street and Cricklade Road was acquired and a chapel built to seat 390. It had a schoolroom attached with accommodation for 300. In 1910 membership was 109. In 1964 the chapel was closed and the congregation joined that of the Trinity Methodist Church, formerly Wesleyan, on the opposite side of Cricklade Road.[55] In 1965 the chapel was sold for use as a warehouse.[56]

RODBOURNE ROAD. This church was formed with 7 members in 1882 and in 1883 a small chapel was built in Rodbourne Road.[57] A larger chapel was built in 1900 and the old building was converted into a schoolroom. In 1910 there were 59 members. In 1964 the church was still in use.

CLIFTON STREET. A small building was erected in Clifton Street in 1882, leaving space on the site for future expansion.[58] The building was enlarged in 1900 to make accommodation for 360.[59] In 1910 membership was 86.[60] After the demolition of the Regent Street chapel in 1957, Clifton Street received a grant from the funds of that chapel and with it built a Sunday schoolroom to accommodate 100.[61]

BUTTERWORTH STREET. This was the first church formed after the Swindon Circuit was divided into two in 1890.[62] At first services were held in a shop at the corner of Marlborough Street and Westcott Place, but in 1893 the chapel in Butterworth Street was opened. In 1910 it had 39 members. It was still in use in 1964.

RODBOURNE CHENEY. Services were held in the house of a Mrs. Matthews in Rodbourne Cheney in 1891.[63] In 1894 Levi Lapper Morse, a member of

the Regent Street chapel, gave some land in the same place on which a chapel was built. In 1906 this was converted into a schoolroom and a new chapel with seating for 230 was built at the northern end of Cheney Manor Road. In 1910 membership was 46. In 1961 a new church, dedicated to St. Andrew, was built for the Methodists a short distance away in Moredon Road, and their chapel in Cheney Manor Road was taken over by the Baptists.[64] The inscribed stone on the front of the chapel in Cheney Manor Road was then amended to read 'Rodbourne Baptist Church 1906'.[65]

DEACON STREET. An iron church was e ected in 1899, although the site seems to have been secured about five years earlier.[66] In 1910 there were 28 members.[67] A successful Sunday school was conducted for some years after this, but the congregation gradually dwindled and in 1920 the chapel was closed.[68]

MANCHESTER ROAD. The chapel was built in 1902 as the result of the activities of a group of Methodists who, during the 1890s, had met together at numerous camp and open-air meetings.[69] At the time of its opening it had 27 members and in 1910 41. In 1960 money from the sale of the Regent Street church was used to enlarge the chapel.[70]

FERNDALE ROAD. Services were held in temporary accommodation in this neighbourhood in 1903.[71] In 1904 a site for a chapel was bought and in 1907 a chapel was opened with 21 members. As this was the Connexional Centenary year, the chapel was sometimes called the Centenary Hall. In 1910 membership was 30. The chapel was still in use in 1964.

Methodist Churches

PINEHURST. Open-air services were held in a house in Linden Road in this neighbourhood in the 1920s.[72] In 1928 a small chapel was built, but for many years the church did not thrive. With the development of this part of the town after the Second World War, however, a larger congregation was gathered together, and in *c.* 1950 a deaconess for the district was appointed for the first time.

QUEEN'S DRIVE. This church was built in 1959–60 to serve the Walcot estates.[73] Money from the sale of the site of the former Primitive Methodist chapel in Regent Street was transferred for the use of the new church.[74] The building was designed by W. H. Cripps.[75]

General Baptist Churches

FLEET STREET. This was the first General Baptist chapel in Swindon and was opened in 1849.[76] Its

[48] Ex inf. Mrs. Ada F. Tanner, Swindon.
[49] Morris, *Swindon*, 417; Averies, *Regent Street Methodist Church, 1849–1949*, 11.
[50] *Swindon Advertiser*, Supp. 5 Feb. 1904.
[51] Ibid.
[52] *Prim. Meth. Ch. Souvenir Handbk.* (1910) (Swindon Pub. Libr.).
[53] Ibid.
[54] Except where otherwise stated, information from *Prim. Meth. Ch. Souvenir Handbk.* (1910).
[55] Ex inf. Mrs. Ada F. Tanner, Swindon.
[56] Personal observation.
[57] All information from *Prim. Meth. Ch. Souvenir Handbk.* (1910).
[58] *Prim. Meth. Ch. Souvenir Handbk.* (1910).
[59] Ibid. [60] Ibid.
[61] Ex inf. Mrs. Ada F. Tanner, Swindon.
[62] All information from *Prim. Meth. Ch. Souvenir Handbk.* (1910).

[63] Unless otherwise stated, information from *Prim. Meth. Ch. Souvenir Handbk.* (1910).
[64] Ex inf. Miss Joan Tanner, Swindon.
[65] Ibid.
[66] *Prim. Meth. Ch. Souvenir Handbk.* (1910).
[67] Ibid.
[68] Averies, *Regent St. Methodist Church, 1849–1949*, 41.
[69] Unless otherwise stated, information from *Prim. Meth. Ch. Souvenir Handbk.* (1910).
[70] Ex inf. Mrs. Povey, Swindon.
[71] All information from *Prim. Meth. Ch. Souvenir Handbk.* (1910).
[72] All information from Averies, *Regent St. Methodist Church, 1849–1949*, 41.
[73] Ex inf. Mrs. Ada F. Tanner, Swindon.
[74] See p. 155.
[75] Pevsner, *Wilts.* (Bldgs. of Eng.), 458.
[76] Ex inf. the Revd. C. S. Hall, Swindon; *Swindon Advertiser*, Supp. 5 Feb. 1904.

Town Hall, Regent Circus, built 1891

Baptist Tabernacle, built 1886

SWINDON

View from south, 1963, showing the old town in the foreground, Christ Church to the right of
centre and the new town beyond

SWINDON

earliest congregation consisted mainly of Baptists who had formerly attended the Stratton Green chapel, and for the first few years the Revd. Richard Breeze superintended both chapels.[77] Fleet Street remained subordinate to Stratton Green until 1855 when an independent church was formed with 24 members and Breeze became its first pastor.[78] In 1868 the chapel was enlarged to seat 520 and a schoolroom was added.[79] Soon after this mission work was begun in the Gorse Hill district and in 1882 a mission church, dependent upon Fleet Street, was built there. In the same year the Baptist chapel in Cambria Place also became dependent upon the Fleet Street church.

By 1879 accommodation had become inadequate and in 1886 the congregation moved to the Tabernacle in Regent Circus, opened that year.[80] The Fleet Street chapel was demolished, although the schoolroom was left and was still standing, used as a store, in 1951.[81]

CAMBRIA PLACE. This chapel was built in 1866 for the Welshmen and their families who came to Swindon about the middle of the 19th century to work in the G.W.R. works.[82] For many years sermons were preached in Welsh.[83] The chapel could accommodate 250.[84] In 1882 the church placed itself under the superintendence of the Fleet Street Baptist church, which later moved to the Tabernacle, Regent Circus, and in 1964 was still a dependent church of the Tabernacle.[85] A schoolroom was provided in 1905.[86]

REGENT CIRCUS TABERNACLE. The Tabernacle was built in 1886 with seating for 1,000, at a cost of over £6,000.[87] The Baptist chapel in Fleet Street was then closed and the congregation moved to the new chapel. Membership at this date was 305, and over 1,000 people attended the tea-party held on the day the chapel was opened.[88] Missions were soon established at Mill Street and Wroughton,[89] and in 1901 mission work was begun at Rodbourne.[90] In 1906 the debt on the building was paid off and membership was 780.[91] At the same date the constitution and organization of the church was overhauled and a body of 12 elders and 12 deacons appointed for the first time.[92] In 1909 the chapel was thoroughly renovated and in 1911 an organ was installed.[93] In 1964 it had 275 members.[94]

The chapel, designed by W. H. Read,[95] is in a purely classical style and has a massive portico of 6 Tuscan columns carrying a pediment.[96]

GORSE HILL. A small chapel was built at Gorse Hill c. 1883 as a result of mission work by the Fleet Street Baptist congregation. It stood at what later

became the junction of Ferndale and Cricklade Roads.[97] In 1904 a larger chapel was built at the corner of Beatrice Street and Cricklade Road, and the original chapel was given up, but not demolished.[98] In 1913 Gorse Hill was constituted a separate church, having been until then dependent upon the Tabernacle.[99] It was still in use in 1964.

RODBOURNE. Mission work by the congregation at the Tabernacle Baptist church was begun in the Rodbourne area early in the 20th century.[1] In 1907 an iron church and schoolroom, formerly used by troops on Salisbury Plain, was erected in Rodbourne Road as a mission chapel. Many attempts were made to improve the building and in 1930 a fund was started to provide for a new church. But no move was made until 1964 when the iron church was closed and the congregation moved to the former Primitive Methodist chapel in Cheney Manor Road.[2]

Particular Baptist Churches

PROVIDENCE CHAPEL, SOUTH STREET. The members of the Newport Street Congregational chapel, who left that church in *c.* 1840, continued to meet together for worship. Out of these meetings a Particular Baptist congregation was formed for which a chapel was built in South Street in 1845.[3]

The chapel, which in 1964 was still in use, is a long low building of stone with a slate roof. At either end are two slightly projecting wings. Above the door the date 1845 is inscribed. In front is a small burial ground and a path bordered by 6 pleached trees leads to the entrance door.

PROSPECT HILL, REHOBOTH CHAPEL. This chapel, which was still in use in 1964, was registered as a meeting-place for Particular Baptists in 1882.[4]

Unitarians. An iron church was erected in Regent Street in 1861.[5] This eventually was found to be too big for the dwindling congregation and a new church was built in Regent Circus.[6] By 1878 the congregation was even smaller and the church was closed and taken over by the Roman Catholics.[7]

The Salvation Army. In 1881 the army was operating from the Peoples' Hall in Old Swindon, probably another name for the former Methodist chapel in the Planks which it acquired at about that time.[8] By 1898 this had been given up and the Salvation Army Temple opened in North Street.[9] In the 1880s various premises in New Swindon were occupied and in 1891 the Citadel in Fleet Street was built.[10] This was reconstructed and rededicated

[77] F. W. T. Fuller, *Baptists of Stratton Green*, 23. For Stratton Green chapel see p. 152.
[78] F. E. Lovesey, *Baptist Tabernacle Church*, 9, 10, 15.
[79] Ex inf. the Revd. C. S. Hall, Swindon; Lovesey, op. cit. 19.
[80] Lovesey, op. cit., 23, 28–33.
[81] Ex inf. the Revd. C. S. Hall, Swindon.
[82] Inscription on building.
[83] *V.C.H. Wilts.* iii. 139.
[84] *Kelly's Dir. Wilts.* (1939).
[85] Lovesey, *Baptist Tabernacle Church*, 23.   [86] Ibid.
[87] Ibid. 33; *Swindon Studies*, 143.
[88] Lovesey, *op. cit.* 31, 33.
[89] Ibid. 40.
[90] Ibid. 41.
[91] Ibid. 44.
[92] Ibid.
[93] Ibid. 46.
[94] *Baptist Handbk.* (1964).
[95] Pevsner, *Wilts.* (Bldgs. of Eng.), 458.
[96] See pl. facing p. 156.
[97] *Swindon Advertiser*, Supp. 5 Feb. 1904, and ex inf. Mr. A. W. Billet, Swindon.
[98] Ex inf. Mr. A. W. Billet, Swindon.
[99] F. E. Lovesey, *Baptist Tabernacle Church*, 47.
[1] Unless otherwise stated, information from *Jubilee of Rodbourne Road Baptist Church*, leaflet in possession of Mr. A. W. Billett, Swindon.
[2] G.R.O. 69408.
[3] Norman Charlton, *Immanuel Congregational Church*, 15; G.R.O. 21112.
[4] G.R.O. 26323.
[5] F. Large, *A Swindon Retrospect*, 12 and photograph facing p. 34.
[6] Ibid. 34.   [7] See p. 151.
[8] G.R.O. 25652, and see p. 155.
[9] G.R.O. 36578.
[10] G.R.O. 33305.

in 1955.[11] In 1898 a hall in Chapel Street, Gorse Hill, was registered for use by the Salvation Army.[12] In 1961 a move was made to another hall in the same street.[13] In 1964 besides the Citadel, the army had premises in Gorse Hill and in North Street, Old Swindon.[14]

Railway Mission. The Railwaymen's Christian Association established itself in the town in the 1880s.[15] In 1887 Sunday afternoon and evening services were said to be well attended. For some years in the 1890s the movement flagged but it revived after the appointment of Emily Cowie as superintendent in 1899. Services were held in the Swimming Baths Hall or in the Mechanics' Institute until 1903 when the Mission Room in Wellington Street was built. Between that year and 1937 the mission was organized and run almost entirely by women. In 1938 the Revd. D. J. Laurie was appointed as the first male superintendent.

In 1965 there was a morning and evening service on Sundays and a Sunday school in the afternoons. On at least three evenings during the week there were social or educational meetings.

Presbyterian Church of England. Workers from the north of England coming to work in Swindon were responsible for the establishment of this church.[16] At first meetings were held in the Mechanics' Institute,[17] but in 1885 a lecture hall, accommodating 250, was opened in Dixon Street.[18] By 1898 it was clear that, contrary to expectation, the town was not expanding in this direction and a more central site was sought. The lecture hall was sold to the Moravian Church and in 1899 Trinity Church was built in Victoria Road.[19]

In 1939 church membership was 110 but there was no minister and the church had fallen into disrepair.[20] The 1950s were a time of considerable activity for this church. The building was restored and membership rose to 160. The church of 1899, known as Trinity Presbyterian Church, was designed by William Wallace, of London, and is built of red brick with Bath stone dressings in a 13th-century style. It has accommodation for 400 with schoolrooms and vestry in the basement.[21]

Moravian Church. Although John Cennick was active in the neighbourhood in the mid 18th century, the Moravian Church was not established in Swindon until the 1890s.[22] Then a group of Moravians, who had come to work in the G.W.R. works, formed themselves into a church, meeting at first in a hall in Regent Street.[23] In 1899 the chapel in Dixon Street, built originally for the Presbyterian Church of England, became available (see above) and was

acquired by the Moravians. This was still their church in 1966 when membership was 51.[24] After 1961 the minister in charge in Swindon had oversight of the Moravian congregation at East Tytherton.[25]

Society of Friends. A meeting was established in Swindon by 1899.[26] Two years later a meeting-house on Eastcott Hill was built. At the end of the 19th century there were 10 members and 18 attenders. By 1956 there were 55 members and in 1964 there were 26.

Fellowship of Independent Evangelical Churches. This congregation grew out of the group which left the Victoria Street Congregational church in 1916.[27] By 1923 premises in Devizes Road had been acquired and that year were licensed as an Evangelical Church and Bible Institute.[28] In 1962 another congregation was formed which left the Fellowship of Independent Evangelical Churches to form the Bethesda Church with premises in Malvern Road.[29]

Christian Brethren. A group of Christian Brethren, who had been active in Swindon for some time, built a mission hall in Regent Place in 1899.[30] In 1918 another group took over a hall in Florence Street which had been built as an independent mission in 1905.[31] The same group built a hall in Liddington Street in 1951[32] and the same year a fourth group acquired the former Wesleyan Methodist chapel built in 1897 in William Street.[33] In 1965, besides the halls mentioned above, there were three other halls in Swindon belonging to the Christian Brethren, all of whom were 'open'.[34]

Christadelphians. A room in Temple Street was registered for worship in 1913.[35] In c. 1936 this was given up for a church on Eastcott Hill which was still in use in 1964.[36]

Christian Science Society. A hall for use by this society was registered in Rolleston Street in 1924.[37] In 1958 this was relinquished for premises in Victoria Road still used in 1964.[38]

Church of Christ. A church was built in Broad Street and registered for worship in 1901.[39] A house in the same street was registered as a Sunday school in 1956 but the registration was cancelled in 1964.[40] The church was still in use in 1964.

Assemblies of God in Great Britain and Ireland. This congregation registered its Full Gospel Church in King William Street in 1938 and still occupied it in 1965.[41]

[11] Ex inf. Mrs. Ada F. Tanner, Swindon.
[12] G.R.O. 36443.   [13] G.R.O. 68099.
[14] *Swindon Dir.* (1964).
[15] All information from *Swindon Railway Mission. Souvenir of Festival Year 1948* (pamphlet in Swindon Pub. Libr.).
[16] *These 50 Years. Story of the Rise of Presbyterianism in Swindon* (pamphlet in Swindon Pub. Libr.).
[17] *Swindon Advertiser*, Supp. 5 Feb. 1904.
[18] 'These 50 Years' (see n. 16 above).   [19] Ibid.
[20] All information in this paragraph supplied by the sessions clerk.
[21] Wilts. Cuttings, vii. 268.
[22] All information from *Swindon Advertiser*, Supp. 5 Feb. 1904.
[23] Ex inf. the minister in charge.
[24] Ibid.   [25] Ibid.
[26] All information supplied by the clerk of the meeting.
[27] See p. 154.
[28] G.R.O. 48729.   [29] G.R.O. 68562.
[30] Date on building and G.R.O. 37721. For their earlier activities, see above p. 153.
[31] Ex inf. Mr. R. B. Blaylock, Swindon, and G.R.O. 47474.
[32] Ex inf. Mr. R. B. Blaylock and G.R.O. 62924.
[33] See p. 155.   [34] *Swindon Dir.* (1965).
[35] G.R.O. 45703.
[36] Ibid. 57013.   [37] Ibid. 49147.
[38] Ibid. 66609.   [39] Ibid. 38422.
[40] Ibid. 65316.   [41] Ibid. 58482.

Elim Foursquare Gospel Alliance. The Coronation Temple in Osborne Street was registered for worship in 1942 and the congregation was still represented in the town in 1965.[42]

Seventh Day Adventists. Premises were licensed in Cheney Manor Road in 1954.[43]

Ancient Catholic Church (Syrian). Premises in Regent Street were registered for use by this church in 1955 and in 1965 had been relinquished for others in Victoria Road.[44]

EDUCATION.[45] The first attempt to provide some form of public education in Swindon came in c. 1764 when the free school was opened in Newport Street.[46] Sunday schools connected with the Independent and Wesleyan chapels in the early 19th century provided some additional schooling and in the early days of the Independent chapel there was an 'academy' conducted by the minister for about 16 pupils.[47] For a few years after 1835 there was also a British school for girls held in a room adjoining the Newport Street chapel.[48] The early-19th-century town also had a fair number of small private schools.[49]

This provision was probably not inadequate for a town of some 2,000 persons, which Swindon was in 1841. But the arrival of the G.W.R. works in 1843 created a demand for schooling which could not be supplied by the schools of the old town. This the G.W.R. Company recognized and in 1845 it opened its own school in Bristol Street.[50] The school was intended at first for employees' children only but it was soon admitting others and very quickly outgrew the accommodation available. There was also in the mid 19th century a mixed school run by the Unitarians behind their chapel in Regent Street.[51]

After the Education Act of 1870 a new National school was built in the old town to replace the former free school[52] and in 1874 the G.W.R. Company built a larger school in College Street.[53] But by 1877, with the enforcement of school attendance by the Act of 1876, there was a deficiency of 1,196 school places and a school board was set up covering the two districts of Old and New Swindon. Among its first members were the manager and chief accountant of the G.W.R. works.[54] At this time 1,200 children were attending the G.W.R. schools and 670 the

National school.[55] Within three years of its formation the school board built four new schools and was leasing at a nominal rent from the G.W.R. its school in College Street.[56] In 1878 the first Roman Catholic school in the town was opened.[57] By 1881 there were places for 2,415 children in the board schools and 794 in voluntary schools.[58]

Between 1881 and 1891 the school board opened two new schools and extended two others[59] but school building could not possibly keep pace with the growth of the town and much use had to be made of temporary accommodation. In 1891 the total number of school places in the old and new towns was 6,777.[60] With the boundary changes of 1890 schools at Gorse Hill and Even Swindon were transferred to the Swindon School Board[61] and between 1891 and 1901 the board built one new school and extended four others.[62] Immediately following the Education Act of 1891 fees ceased to be charged in elementary schools in Swindon.[63]

The standard of education provided by the Swindon schools was high. In 1894 all were graded excellent and in 1898 the level of exemption from school was raised to standard VII while the rest of the county had a standard V level of exemption.[64] Evening schools were begun by the school board in 1893.[65] A Higher Grade School for boys was opened in 1891 and in 1898 was followed by a similar school for girls.[66] A Central Higher Grade School was moved to the school built in Clarence Street in 1897.[67] At this time there were over 100 pupil teachers in the Swindon schools and a Pupil Teacher Centre was opened in 1897 where they were instructed on two or three half-days a week.[68]

Until 1891 all further technical education in the town was provided by the Mechanics' Institute.[69] In 1887–8 nearly 500 students were attending technical classes and extra room had to be found in the town's schools.[70] In 1891 the Swindon and North Wilts. Technical Instruction Committee was formed to administer the Further Education Acts of 1889 and 1891. This committee then took over the technical classes previously run by the Mechanics' Institute and in 1896 opened the Swindon and North Wilts. Technical Institute in Victoria Road.[71]

After the Education Act of 1902 Swindon became a Part III authority responsible for elementary education.[72] By arrangement with the county council, the authority for higher education, the borough council also took over the functions of the Swindon and North Wilts. Technical Instruction

[42] Ibid. 60156.
[43] Ibid. 64210.
[44] Ibid. 65410 and *Swindon Dir.* (1965).
[45] This introduction is based upon one supplied by Dr. N. B. Mortimer in a somewhat extended form and his work for the *Wiltshire History* is most gratefully acknowledged. Except where otherwise stated, the information comes from Dr. Mortimer's thesis 'Part III Authorities in Engl. Educational System' (Lond. Univ. Ph.D. 1946) and his personal knowledge as Deputy Education Officer for the borough of Swindon. The short notes on individual schools which follow are based upon research undertaken by Miss Joan Tanner, head mistress of the Lawn Primary School.
[46] See p. 160.
[47] N. Charlton, *Immanuel Congregational Church, Swindon,* 10; *Swindon Advertiser,* Supp. 5 Feb. 1904.
[48] Charlton, op. cit. 14.
[49] See p. 166.   [50] See p. 161.
[51] F. Large, *Swindon Retrospect, 1855–1930,* 32.
[52] See p. 161.

[53] See p. 162.
[54] *Rep. Schl. Bd.* 1877–80.   [55] Ibid.
[56] *Final Rep. Schl. Bd.* 1901–3. The four schools were Queenstown. Gilbert's Hill, Sanford St., and Westcott.
[57] See p. 163.
[58] *Final Rep. Schl. Bd.* 1901–3.
[59] Ibid. Clifton St. and Lethbridge Rd. opened; Queenstown and Gilbert's Hill extended.
[60] *Final Rep. Schl. Bd.* 1901–3.
[61] Mins. Schl. Bd.
[62] *Final Rep. Schl. Bd.* 1901–3. Clarence St. built; College St., Even Swindon, Gorse Hill, and Westcott extended.
[63] *Rep. Schl. Bd.* 1889–92.
[64] *V.C.H. Wilts.* v. 355.
[65] *Rep. Schl. Bd.* 1889–92.
[66] Ibid. 1889–92, 1895–8.
[67] Ibid. 1895–8.   [68] Ibid.
[69] See p. 142.
[70] *Mech's Inst. Centenary Souvenir,* p. iii.
[71] See p. 165.   [72] *V.C.H. Wilts.* v. 355.

Committee and a higher education sub-committee of the borough education committee was eventually formed on which sat representatives of the county council.[73] The borough council then levied a penny rate, the maximum permitted, and asked the county council to impose a special rate upon the town of a further $\frac{1}{2}d.$ in the £ towards the cost of secondary and technical education.[74] This special rate rose gradually to $6\frac{1}{4}d.$ in the £ and, amongst other things, made possible a wide distribution of scholarships and free places in the secondary schools.

Encouragement to broaden the school curriculum was given by the extra grants offered by the Department of Education for the introduction of various new subjects, including practical instruction. Provision for the teaching of practical subjects had been made in the Central Higher Elementary School, opened in Euclid Street in 1904,[75] and a manual workshop had been added to the Technical Institute in 1899, but the elementary schools had no such facilities. The schools in Ferndale Road, built in 1907,[76] included a domestic centre and similar centres were provided at three other schools within the next few years. Woodwork classes were begun for boys in 1913.[77] After the Education Act of 1918, which required authorities to provide practical instruction for older pupils, centres for this were added to schools at Lethbridge Road in 1924 and Broad Street in 1925.[78]

Swindon was one of the five or six areas in the country to set up a Day Continuation School under the Education Act of 1918. It was opened in 1920 and ran for two or three years before closing.[79]

The Education (Provision of Meals) Act of 1906 was put into operation in Swindon in 1907–8 and to a greater extent in 1908–9. In 1910–11 the service was considered unnecessary, although it continued over the years on a small scale and could be extended in times of need, as it was during the General Strike of 1926. It was further developed during the Second World War before becoming the school meals service after the Education Act of 1944.[80]

The medical inspection of school children in Swindon had been carried out to a limited extent for some time before the Education (Administrative Provisions) Act of 1907 made it obligatory.[81] After the Act the town's medical officer of health conducted inspections until 1914 when a full-time school medical officer was appointed. A school nurse was employed in 1910. In 1913, under optional powers granted by the 1907 Act, a school clinic was begun in a classroom converted for the purpose and a part-time school dentist was appointed. Some arrangements for the education of physically or mentally handicapped children had been made by the school board and in 1916 the education committee started a special class in Westcott infants' school for the mentally handicapped. The physical welfare of children in Swindon schools benefited greatly from the voluntary work of the Swindon

Schools Athletic Association formed in 1912 to promote organized school games and sports.[82]

When in 1927 the Commonweal Secondary School was opened, this with the Euclid Street, and College secondary schools gave Swindon three secondary schools.[83] In 1933 all places in these schools were opened to competitive examination and fees were remitted on a scale fixed in proportion to income.[84]

The growth of the town north of the railway in the 1920s and the boundary extensions of 1928 created an urgent demand for more school places. Schools were particularly needed for the council's first large housing estate at Pinehurst.[85] In c. 1926, in accordance with the requirements of the Board of Education, the education committee drew up a three-year programme of educational development based on the recommendations of the Hadow Report. But much new building was required before the programme could be carried out and this was prevented by the economic slump of the 1930s. Between 1935 and 1939, however, two new schools were built and some existing schools were either enlarged or modernized.[86]

By the Education Act of 1944 Swindon ceased to be a local education authority for elementary education but became the only excepted district within the county.[87] Many functions were then delegated to the borough. The 1944 Act gave the force of law to the recommendation of the Hadow Report and with the completion of the Drove Secondary School in 1946, schools in Swindon were reorganized on the lines which had been planned in c. 1926. After the raising of the school leaving age in 1947 additional buildings were provided at many schools.

After 1953 the number of children attending Swindon schools increased from just over 10,000 at the rate of 1,000 a year. As the housing estates to the north and east of the town were built schools had to be provided for them. In 1965[88] the grammar and secondary modern schools were reorganized on a 'two-tier' comprehensive basis. Selection at eleven-plus was abolished. The secondary modern schools became high schools for the 11 to 14 age group and the grammar schools became senior high schools for pupils prepared to remain at school for at least two years after the age of 14. In 1966 there were over 20,000 children in the Swindon schools.

Church of England Junior and Infants' Voluntary Controlled School. Some time before 1764 a fund was raised by voluntary subscription to found a free school.[89] Here it was intended to instruct 20 poor children in religion, according to Church principles, and in arithmetic, but in no other subject.[90]

In 1764 a small house with a garden in Newport Street was bought as school premises.[91] The Horne and Cooper endowments (see below) enabled a few girls to be taught in addition to the 20 boys originally

[73] *Rep. Educ. Cttee.* 1903–4.
[74] Ibid.
[75] See p. 165.
[76] See p. 165.
[77] *Reps. Educ. Cttee.* 1903–13.
[78] See p. 165.
[79] *Swindon Studies,* 114.
[80] For source of information see n. 45 above.
[81] *Rep. Schl. Bd.* 1898–1901.
[82] Inf. in this para. from *Reps. Educ. Cttee.*
[83] See pp. 164, 165.
[84] For source of information see n. 45 above.
[85] See p. 165.
[86] New schls. Drove and Ferndale Rds. Modernized Sanford St. and Queenstown. Extended Pinehurst.
[87] For this and subsequent information see n. 45 above.
[88] This article on Education was prepared and written in 1964 and this brief statement about the reorganization of 1965 is an addition.
[89] *Endowed Char. Wilts.* H.C. 273, p. 919 (1908), lxxx.
[90] Ibib.
[91] Ibid. p. 920.

provided for.[92] In 1819 the school had 37 boys and 11 girls.[93] The master's salary for teaching the boys was £34 a year with £3 3s. for coal. For the girls he received another £10.[94] In 1834 boys were admitted as soon as they could read and were allowed to stay in the school for 5 or 6 years. A small charge was made for books and stationery.[95]

In 1836 the first school house was pulled down and a new one built on the same site. The Government and the National Society made grants.[96] By 1853 the building was considered hardly big enough for the then 78 pupils.[97] Five years later there were 100 pupils, one certificated master, and some pupil teachers. The one classroom measured 60 ft. × 30 ft. and was equipped with parallel desks. The school was said to be fairly well supplied with books and apparatus; discipline and instruction were good.[98]

In 1863 the school was divided into three departments, girls, boys, and infants.[99] A few years later the accommodation was quite inadequate and in 1870 the school was closed. New buildings in King William Street were opened in 1871[1] and were described as 'very impressive'.[2] In 1872 fees were 3d. for boys and girls, 2d. for infants, and 4d. for tradesmen's children. Would-be pupils were being turned away in 1881 for lack of space. In 1886 the vicar introduced a morning religious service. Classroom accommodation was enlarged in 1890.

In 1903, when average attendance was 607,[3] the school came under the control of the Swindon Education Committee.[4] In 1938 average attendance was 276. The school became a mixed junior and infant school (Church of England, voluntarily controlled) in 1946.[5] In 1964 there were 176 children on the roll.[6]

The school received a number of endowments. Thomas Goddard, lord of the manor, by a deed dated 1764, granted a rent-charge from a meadow in Eastcott.[7] William Nash granted another rent-charge, but after his death in c. 1787 £200 was invested instead for the benefit of the school. The interest on both these endowments was used in 1903 for the maintenance of the school buildings.[9]

Soon after the school was founded Mary Horne left £100 to provide for the teaching of a number of poor girls. After Mary's death her sister Elizabeth (d. 1793) distributed £5 annually to educate 5 girls selected by her.[10] To augment Mary Horne's endowment, Joseph and Elizabeth Cooper conveyed in 1796 about 9 a. in Stratton St. Margaret so that half the annual income arising from the land might provide for the education of some more poor girls in the school. The other half was to be spent upon the poor. In 1834 the income from the educational

part of the charity was £23 16s. and for the past 18 years the schoolmaster had received £9 a year for teaching 10 girls. In 1896 all the property was sold and £1,034 was invested.[11]

In 1849 Elizabeth Kemble bequeathed £100 to the school. This was added to William Nash's gift and both were drawn upon in 1870, and later, for the buildings of the school in King William Street.[12] A gift of £200 made in the will of Alexander Anderson, dated 1874, was also used to improve accommodation in the school.[13]

A Scheme of 1905 provided that a body of trustees, who were to include the lord of the manor and the Vicar of Swindon, were to administer all the school's endowments which were to be known jointly as the Old School Foundation.[14] The site in Newport Street was sold in 1909 and the proceeds invested. Income was used to maintain the King William Street school and to provide scholarships to secondary schools. The scholarships were supplemented by maintenance grants which in 1930 were usually of about £2 and were used to buy school books. In 1962 the income of the foundation was £38.[15]

G.W.R. School, Bristol Street, later Sanford Street. By his will, proved 1842, G. H. Gibbs, a director of the G.W.R., left £500 towards building a church and a school for the housing estate then growing up around the railway works.[16] The company appealed for more funds and the response was so good that both church (St. Mark's) and school were opened in 1845.[17] The school was to be non-sectarian and was intended for children of the G.W.R.'s employees. It was supervised by the company's board but was open to government inspection. Reading, writing, arithmetic, some geography, history, and scripture were taught. Fees were 4d. a week for juniors and 2d. for infants. Children of parents not connected with the G.W.R. were admitted at 1s. a week.[18]

In 1847–8, when there were two masters and 168 pupils, the school was rather unfavourably reported upon by a government inspector, although he found 'abundant means and appliances for instruction'.[19] Next Year, however, an improvement was noted. There was then an infant school of 127 and a mixed school of 90, taught by a master and 2 pupil teachers.[20] In 1850 the standard of education was said to be praiseworthy.[21] There were 180 children in the mixed department in 1859, taught by a certificated master and pupil teachers. The building was described as excellent, discipline good, and instruction sound and comprehensive. All arrangements were said to be on a most 'liberal scale'. The

[92] See below.
[93] *Digest of Retns. to Cttee. of Educ. of Poor*, H.C. 224, p. 1038 (1819), ix (2).
[94] *Endowed Char. Wilts.* (1908), pp. 920, 921.
[95] Ibid. p. 920.
[96] Ibid. p. 935.
[97] Rept. of H.M.I. quoted in Centenary Pageant Programme.
[98] *Acct. of Wilts. Schools*, H.C. 27, p. 107 (1859 Sess. 1), xxi (2).
[99] Schl. Log Bk.
[1] *Endowed Char. Wilts.* (1908), p. 935 and Log Bk.
[2] This and rest of information in this paragraph from Log Bk.
[3] *List of Schools under Administration of the Bd. 1903–4* [Cd. 2011,] p. 395, H.C. (1904), lxxv.
[4] Log Bk.
[5] Ibid.

[6] Ex inf. the head mistress.
[7] *Endowed Char. Wilts.* (1908), pp. 919, 937.
[8] Ibid. p. 920.   [9] Ibid. p. 938.
[10] Ibid. p. 920.
[11] Ibid. pp. 920–1, 925, 926.
[12] Ibid. p. 936.
[13] Ibid. p. 938.
[14] Ed. 47/8265 file 5401 (pt. 2).
[15] Reg. Educ. Char. Lansdowne House, Berkeley Sq. W.1.
[16] *Swindon Studies*, 111.   [17] Ibid.
[18] J. B. Lloyd 'Development of Education in Swindon', (Bristol Univ. M.A. Thesis(Educ.), 1955), 96, 98.
[19] *Mins. of Educ. Cttee. of Council, 1847–8* [998], pp. 190–1, H.C. (1847–8), l.
[20] Ibid. 1850, vol. i [1215], p. 665, H.C. (1850), xliii.
[21] Ibid. 1850–1, vol. i [1357], pp. 432–3, H.C. (1851), xliv.

infant department was housed in an excellent class-room, recently built, with boarded floors and galleries.[22]

In 1858 a local committee was set up to supervise the school.[23] Early in the 1870s it was clear that the building was too small to meet the demand for places in it.[24] Towards the end of the decade the girls were moved, first to temporary accommodation, and later to new premises on a site acquired by the G.W.R. in College Street.[25] In 1881 the boys were transferred from Bristol Street to a new school in Sanford Street, one of the first to be built by the Swindon School Board.[26] About this time a per-sistent feud between the boys of the G.W.R. school and those of the National school in Old Swindon[27] broke into active rioting, which lasted several days.[28]

Although after 1881 the boys of Sanford Street ceased to come under the direct control of the G.W.R., the school's curriculum was influenced to some extent by the needs of the company.[29] In 1888 science began to be taught and special attention was paid to drawing.[30] In the 1880s a few pupils, who stayed at school after the age of 13, were formed into a special 'science' class, taken for the most part out of school hours by a pupil teacher. At this time too the older boys with some of the girls from the College Street School gave Christmas concerts in the Mechanics' Institute and the money thus raised was used to provide cash prizes, known as 'scholar-ships'.[31] In 1909 average attendance was 780.[32] In 1946 the school became a boys' secondary modern school.[33]

The G.W.R. continued to use the Bristol Street buildings for other purposes after the school closed. In 1965 they housed a research laboratory of British Rail.[34]

College Street School. The girls of the G.W.R. school in Bristol Street were organized as a separate department with their own classrooms by 1863.[35] In 1871 overcrowding in the school was so bad that girls and infants were moved to temporary accom-modation in the 'Wesleyan room'. This was pre-sumably the nearby 'Barracks' in Faringdon Road.[36] Next year they moved again to the Drill Hall in Church Place, which the inspectors considered to be most unsatisfactory as accommodation.

In 1874 girls and infants moved to premises built for them by the G.W.R. in College Street. The Wilts. and Berks. Canal, which ran immediately behind the school, proved to be a great hazard for the children. The G.W.R. handed over management of the school to the school board in 1881.[37] In the 1890s alterations were made to the buildings, in-cluding the addition of a new classroom and a

teachers' room. In 1897, when average attendance was 785,[38] the headmistress complained that because her pupil teachers were attending the special central classes held for them elsewhere, there were 99 girls with only one teacher in standards VI and VII, and 98 in standard II. Next year part of the school was used as a Higher Grade School for girls, but this, which at one time had 70 pupils, was transferred to Clarence Street in 1903.[39]

In 1946 the school became a mixed junior school with 11 classes. In 1961 the site of the school was required for the development of Swindon's new shopping centre, and the building was demolished. The 295 children and their teachers were then transferred to the Clarence Street school.[40]

Queenstown Infants' and Girls' Schools. This was one of the first schools to be built by the Swindon School Board.[41] It was opened in 1880 as an infants' school for 204 children.[42] Attendance three years later was said to be 293.[43] In 1885 a girls' school was opened on the same site with accommodation for 250.[44] Numbers in the school remained fairly constant until the 1920s, although the infants' acc-ommodation consisted only of one long room with a recess and two classrooms.[45] In 1938, because of rebuilding, the infants were moved to the College Street Infants' School, and in 1939 the two infants' schools were amalgamated in the College Street premises.[46] After 1939 and until 1946 Queenstown was a girls' school. In 1946 it became an infants' school.[47]

Westcott Infants' and Primary Mixed Schools, Birch Street. This was one of the three infants' schools built by the school board immediately after its formation in 1877.[48] Until permanent buildings were ready, the school was housed in the Drill Hall.[49] The school was eventually opened in 1881 with accommodation for 286.[50] In 1892 a mixed school for 491 children was added and in 1893 there was a total of 894 children.[51] In 1897 the infants' school was enlarged.[52] In 1964 it had 130 children on its roll.[53] In 1946 the mixed school became a secondary modern school for which more rooms were added in 1956.[54] In 1964 the Westcott and Jennings Street Secondary Modern Schools were united to form the Westbourne Secondary School. The buildings of both schools were then used and there were 375 children on the roll.

Gilbert's Hill Girls' and Infants' Schools. These schools, in Dixon Street, opened in 1880 with a head teacher, an assistant mistress, and 42 children

[22] *Acct. of Wilts. Schools*, H.C. 27, p. 107 (1859 Sess. 1), xxi (2).
[23] Lloyd, 'Development of Education in Swindon , 97.
[24] Ibid. [25] See below.
[26] Lloyd, 'Development of Education in Swindon', 106, 108.
[27] Ibid. 108.
[28] F. H. Spencer, *An Inspector's Testament*, 54. This book contains a graphic account of the school in the later 19th century.
[29] Lloyd, 'Development of Education in Swindon', 112.
[30] Ibid. 112, 113.
[31] Spencer, *An Inspector's Testament*, 59, 60.
[32] *Bd. of Educ. List 21, 1909.*
[33] Ex inf. Miss J. Tanner.
[34] Personal observation.
[35] Except where otherwise stated, information from Schl. Log Bk.

[36] See p. 155.
[37] Lloyd, 'Development of Education in Swindon , 106.
[38] *Schools in receipt of Parl. Grants 1896*, [C. 8178], p. 248, H.C. (1896), lxv.
[39] *V.C.H. Wilts.* v. 356. [40] See p. 164.
[41] Lloyd, 'Development of Education in Swindon', 105.
[42] Ibid. 107. [43] Ibid. 109.
[44] Ibid. 132. [45] Schl. Log Bks.
[46] Ibid.
[47] Ex inf. Miss J. Tanner.
[48] Lloyd, 'Development of Education in Swindon', 105.
[49] Ibid. 107.
[50] Ibid. 108.
[51] Ibid. 132; ex inf. the Head Teacher.
[52] Lloyd, op. cit. 118–19.
[53] Ex inf. the Head Teacher.
[54] This and subsequent information supplied by head teacher.

under nine.[55] Fees were 2d. a week for infants, and 3d. for children in the first standard. In 1881 the school become a mixed infants' and girls' school. Accommodation seems to have been inadequate from the early days, and in the early 1880s cloak-rooms had to be used as classrooms. From 1886 the school was conducted as two separate departments, but under one head teacher. In 1890 some extensions were made to the buildings and separate head teachers were appointed for the two departments. In 1895 average attendance was 458.[56] For a time in 1914 the school was transferred to Dowling Street Mission Hall, because its premises were required by the military authorities. Throughout the 1920s the inspectors were criticizing the fact that three classes were taught in the main room, but no change was made. In 1938 average attendance was 227.[57] In 1946 the older girls were transferred either to Clarence Street Junior School, or to the Drove Secondary School, and the Gilbert's Hill School has since been used for infants only. In 1964 there were 65 children on the roll.[58]

Holy Rood School. This school was opened as a fee-paying school attached to the Roman Catholic church in Regent Street in 1878.[59] In 1899 it moved to new buildings in Groundwell Road and in 1905 changed its name to the Swindon Holy Rood Roman Catholic School. Average attendance in 1906 was 124 pupils[60] and in 1932 227.[61]. After 1946 the school was reorganized to become an infants' and junior school. A few years later the school began to be seriously overcrowded and temporary accommodation had to be used in various parts of the town. For a time some classes were held in huts at the Lawn, Old Swindon. A new infants' wing was added to the Groundwell Road school in 1953 but the school remained overcrowded. In 1957 there were 980 children on the school register and there were 24 classes spread over 5 centres in the town. The opening of new Roman Catholic schools in Swindon in 1958, 1961 and 1963 gradually reduced the pressure on the accommodation at Groundwell Road and in 1964 there were 445 children there in 12 classes.

Clifton Street Junior and Infants' School. This school began in the Drill Hall, Church Place, in 1883 with 37 boys and 8 girls.[62] The staff comprised a head master, a certificated assistant mistress, and 2 pupil teachers. Infants were admitted a few months later. The site on the corner of Clifton and Radnor Streets was bought by the Swindon School Board in 1884 and a school built to accommodate 625 children.[63] The boys' department (downstairs) was completed in 1884, the girls' (upstairs) in 1885, and the infants' building in 1886.[64] The infants' school was slightly enlarged in 1890.[65] Average attendance for

the whole school in 1909 was 839.[66] The older children continued to be taught in separate departments until 1939, when boys and girls were combined to form the Clifton Street Mixed School with 270 children between the ages of 7 and 14 on the register. In 1946 the school became a mixed junior and an infants' school. In 1950 it was much enlarged and altered.[67] In 1964 there were 264 juniors and 110 infants on the roll.[68]

Lethbridge Road Junior and Infants' School. This school in Lethbridge Road, Old Swindon, was opened in 1891 on a site offered at a low rent by A. L. Goddard, lord of the manor, after a long controversy between Goddard and the school board.[69] It had 8 classrooms and a hall and opened with 64 girls and 80 boys between the ages of 7 and 14. The staff comprised a head master, one assistant, and one first-year pupil teacher.[70] Numbers increased rapidly and only a year after opening there were 282 children on the register. Between 1890 and 1892 an infants' school to serve this district was held in the Sunday schoolroom of the Wesleyan Methodist chapel in Bath Road. In 1892 the infants moved into the Lethbridge Road school, using one classroom and a hall, partitioned by curtains into 3 classrooms. In 1893 there were 198 infants in the school. The early log books reveal much concern over truancy and bad attendance. A 'parents' day' was instituted in 1896, but to the first of these, held on a very wet afternoon, not a single parent came. In 1896 pupils in standard III were being taught science. In 1935 the infants were moved into wooden huts, which were still being used in 1964 when there were 180 children on the roll. The mixed school became a mixed junior school in 1946 and in 1964 had 250 pupils on the register.[71]

Gorse Hill. This school in Avening Street, Gorse Hill, then a tithing of Stratton St. Margaret, was opened in 1878 by the Stratton St. Margaret School Board to accommodate 450 boys, girls, and infants.[72] The infants' department had a hall and 8 classrooms built for it in 1882. In 1890, when Gorse Hill came within the Swindon boundary, the school was taken over by the Swindon School Board. The following year a new boys' and girls' department was opened.[73] The accommodation in the infants' school was considered suitable for 573 children, but in 1906 there were 735 on the register, and the average attendance for the whole school was 1,258.[74] In 1910 the school was still overcrowded in spite of the building of the Ferndale Road school nearby, and it was not until this school was enlarged after the First World War that attendance figures at Gorse Hill began to adjust themselves to the accommodation available.[75]

In 1946 the older children were removed from the school, leaving separate infants' and junior schools

[55] Except where otherwise stated all information from Schl. Log Bks.
[56] *Schools in receipt of Parliamentary Grants, 1896* [C. 8179], p. 248, H.C. (1896), lxv.
[57] *Bd. of Educ. List 21, 1938.* [58] Ex inf. the head mistress.
[59] Except where otherwise stated, information about this school was supplied by the Very Revd. Canon J. P. Leahy, Holy Rood Presbytery, Swindon.
[60] *List of Public Elem. Schools, 1906* [Cd. 3182], p. 677, H.C. (1906), lxxxvi.
[61] *Bd. of Educ. List 21, 1932.*
[62] Unless otherwise stated, information from Schl. Log Bks.

[63] Lloyd, 'Development of Education in Swindon', 11.
[64] Ibid.   [65] Ibid. 111, 1320.
[66] *Bd. of Educ. List 21, 1909.*
[67] Ex inf. the head teacher.   [68] Ibid.
[69] Lloyd, 'Development of Education in Swindon', 113.
[70] This and all subsequent information from Schl. Log Bks.
[71] Ex inf. the head teacher.
[72] Lloyd, 'Development of Education in Swindon', 105.
[73] Ibid. 132.
[74] Information supplied by the head teacher.
[75] *Bd. of Educ. List 21, 1909* and subsequent *Lists*; Lloyd, op. cit. 134.

at Gorse Hill.[76] For some years before schools were opened at Penhill (in the 1950s), children from that estate were taken by bus to Gorse Hill. Even after the Penhill schools were opened, classrooms in the Gorse Hill Junior School had to be used to relieve overcrowding in the new schools. In 1964 there were 202 children on the roll.

Even Swindon Junior and Infants' Schools. These schools lay outside the Swindon boundary until 1890. In 1880 a school for boys and girls of all ages was built by the Rodbourne School Board at the junction of Hughes Street and Rodbourne Road.[77] This originally had 6 classrooms, but 2 more and a central hall were added in 1895. An infants' school was built on the same site in 1884. The head master found that of the 138 children admitted in 1880, nearly 30 could not say the alphabet. He had difficulty in persuading parents to buy copy-books and slates, and in 1881 the board decided to provide these free of charge. Absences were caused from time to time by the inability of parents to pay 'school pence', but when these were abolished in 1891, attendance was 'the best . . . for many months'. The first head master served the school for 39 years. He showed great initiative in approaching firms for books and equipment. In 1890 the school was transferred to the Swindon School Board when Even Swindon was taken within Swindon's boundary. In the winter of 1908 free breakfasts of bread and milk were supplied at the school and during the Christmas holidays. The school comprised about 300 pupils aged between 7 and 14 years until 1946 when it became a junior mixed school and the older children were sent to the Jennings Street (later Westbourne) Secondary School.[78] In 1964 there were 213 children on the roll.[79]

Clarence Street School. This school with accommodation for 885 children was built in 1897 at the corner of Clarence and Euclid Streets. To it was moved a Central Higher Grade School which had been using temporary accommodation in Regent Street.[80] The school opened with 235 boys and 115 girls and a staff consisting of a head master, 3 certificated assistants, 2 other assistants, and 3 pupil teachers.[81] A separate infants' school was built in 1903.[82] The extra places that this gave in the mixed school were used to enlarge its standard VII, and for a time the school was overcrowded.[83] With the opening of the Euclid Street Higher Elementary School in 1904, however, some of the senior children were sent there.[84] Clarence Street was then divided into two separate boys' and girls' departments.[85] In 1909 average attendance was 891.[86] In 1946 Clarence Street became a junior mixed school. Children from the Walcot and Park estates attended the Clarence

Street School until schools were built nearer their homes and in 1958 there were over 1,000 children in the Clarence Street School which used the by then disused school building in Euclid Street as an annexe. In 1961, when the College Street School was closed, the pupils and staff from there were transferred to Clarence Street.[87] In 1964 there were 430 children on the roll.[88]

The College Secondary School. A Higher Grade School for boys in Swindon was begun in temporary accommodation in 1891.[89] In 1896 a Day Secondary School for boys was opened in the newly built Technical Institute in Victoria Road which thenceforth and until 1952 housed both technical college and secondary school.[90] At first the school was known as the Technical Secondary School, but in 1926 it came to be called the College Secondary School.[91] After 1897 the school began to admit girls as well as boys and scholarships awarded by the county council enabled children living outside the town to attend.[92] A workshop and engineering laboratory were added in 1899 and further additions were made in 1902.[93] In 1905 there were 196 pupils: in 1924 there were 480.[94] In 1927 when the Commonweal Secondary School in the Mall, Old Swindon, was opened,[95] a number of pupils from the College School were transferred to form the nucleus of the new school.[96] In 1943 the College and Euclid Street secondary schools were amalgamated to form the Headlands Secondary School.[97] The buildings of the two schools, which were only a short distance apart, continued to house the newly amalgamated school until 1952 when it moved to new premises built for it in Headlands Grove.[98]

Euclid Street School. In 1897 a day training centre was opened in Euclid Street for the many pupil teachers employed in Swindon's board schools.[99] In 1904 the Euclid Street School became a Central Higher Elementary School and to it were sent many of the pupils from the former Central Higher Grade School in Clarence Street.[1] The school opened with a staff of 14 teachers and 305 pupils.[2] At first children could enter the school between the ages of 10 and 12 and stay from 1 to 3 years. But in 1907 the age of entry became 12, and the duration of the course 3 years. Among other subjects physics, chemistry, French, woodwork, cookery, and technical drawing were taught. The head master took pains to find work for his pupils when they left the school, but there was little for girls to do in the town before 1911 when the G.W.R. began to employ girl clerks. In 1919 the school became a secondary school, providing the same standard of education as the College Secondary School.[3] In 1943 these two secondary schools were amalgamated to form the

---

[76] All information in this paragraph supplied by Miss J. Tanner, Swindon.
[77] All information, unless otherwise stated, from the Schl. Log Bks.
[78] Ex inf. the head master.   [79] Ibid.
[80] Lloyd, 'Development of Education in Swindon', 119, 132.
[81] Schl. Log Bk.   [82] Ibid; Lloyd, op. cit. 127.
[83] Ibid.   [84] Ibid.
[85] Except where otherwise stated, this and subsequent information from Schl. Log Bks.
[86] *Bd. of Educ. List 21, 1909.*
[87] See p. 162.
[88] Ex inf. the head master.

[89] Lloyd, 'Development of Education in Swindon', 115.
[90] Ibid. 118, 203; for Technical Institute, see p. 165.
[91] Lloyd, op. cit. 138.   [92] Ibid. 125, 120–1.
[93] Ibid. 122, 124–5.   [94] Ibid. 131.
[95] See p. 165.
[96] Lloyd, op. cit. 139.
[97] Ex inf. Miss J. Tanner.
[98] Ibid.
[99] Lloyd, 'Development of Education in Swindon', 204.
[1] Ibid. 121, and Schl. Log Bk.
[2] Except where otherwise stated, this and subsequent information from Schl. Log Bks.
[3] Lloyd, 'Development of Education in Swindon', 135.

Headlands Secondary School, and the buildings of both were used for the combined school. In 1952 the school moved to new buildings specially built for it in Headlands Grove.[4] The Euclid Street buildings were then used as temporary accommodation to relieve overcrowding in other schools. In 1964 they housed a day training centre run by the Newton Park Training College, Bath, for mature students intending to become teachers.

Jennings Street School. This school to serve the Rodbourne district was opened in 1904 with accommodation for 580 boys and girls and 198 infants.[5] In 1909 average attendance was 575.[6] In 1946 it became a mixed secondary modern school and in 1964 was amalgamated with the Westcott Secondary Modern School to form the Westbourne Secondary Modern School.[7]

Ferndale Schools. The expansion of Swindon north of the railway line in the early 1900s created the need for another school to serve that area, and in 1905 a site was acquired in Ferndale Road.[8] The school was opened in 1907 as a mixed and infants' school.[9] Numbers rose quickly and by 1910 there were 725 children in the school.[10] In 1926 a new building was provided for the infants, and all the earlier buildings were used for the older children.[11] In 1932 average attendance was 1,048.[12] A domestic science centre was opened in 1942 and enlarged in 1963.[13] Just before the Second World War new buildings were added, and in 1946 the school was reorganized as separate junior and secondary schools. In 1964 there were on the roll 246 children in the infants' school, 282 in the junior school, and 399 in the secondary school.

Commonweal Grammar School, the Mall. This school was opened in 1927 as a secondary school with accommodation for 276 children.[14] To form a nucleus, 156 children from the College Secondary School and 41 from the Euclid Street Secondary School were transferred to the new school, which also took 76 new entrants.[15] The buildings included 13 classrooms, numerous specialist rooms, a gymnasium, dining hall, and kitchen arranged around two courtyards. Numbers increased with the expansion of Swindon, but were reduced by the opening of Park Grammar School in 1960. In 1964 there were 718 pupils. The buildings were extended, mostly after 1950, and in 1964 had an additional 6 laboratories, a needlework room, music room, and 8 more classrooms.

Rodbourne Cheney School. A school at Rodbourne Cheney was opened in 1892 with 34 children, of whom 22 were infants.[16] The site and the extent of the premises are unknown but references in the log book to 'the room' suggest but a single classroom. In 1894, when there were 80 children on the register,

a new school was opened at the junction of what in 1964 was Broadway and Moredon Road. Numbers rose quickly and reached 160 in 1895. In 1904 the infants' class became a separate infants' school and the next year there were 201 children between 7 and 14 years of age in the school. In 1906 2 new classrooms were added and new subjects such as swimming, gardening, and domestic subjects began to be taught. In 1912 the present (1965) infants' school was built. The school was transferred to the Swindon Education Committee in 1928 when the Swindon boundary was extended to take in Rodbourne Cheney. After the re-organization of the Swindon schools in 1946 Rodbourne Cheney School took infants and juniors only. With the growth of Swindon's northern suburbs after 1930 numbers in the school rose considerably and the building was overcrowded. This was remedied when new schools were opened at Pinehurst (1935) and Moredon (1953). Between 1953 and 1955 Rodbourne Cheney was used as an annexe to the Pinehurst schools. But in 1955 the buildings were modernized and Rodbourne Cheney again became a separate school. In 1964 it had 148 infants and 144 juniors on the roll. Entries in the log books show that in its early days this was a village school, unaffected, unlike most of the Swindon schools, by the requirements of the G.W.R.

Pinehurst Schools. After the boundary extensions of 1928 there was urgent need of new schools to serve the northern parts of the borough. The need was greatest on the Pinehurst housing estate which had been built by the corporation after the First World War. In 1930 Pinehurst Infants' School was opened for 210 children in temporary accommodation.[17] Permanent buildings were ready in 1934. In 1935 Pinehurst Junior School for 449 children and Pinehurst Secondary School with 425 pupils were opened. As this part of Swindon was developed during the 1950s children from other housing estates came to the Pinehurst schools until new schools were built for them. In 1955 there were over 650 children in the infants' school, 817 in the junior school, and over 800 in the secondary school. In 1964 the numbers were 336, 527, and 576.

The Drove Infants' School. This school was opened in 1941 with 246 children transferred from Clarence Street Infants school. In 1964 there were 101 children on the roll.[18]

Swindon and North Wilts. Technical Institute, later the College. This was opened by the Swindon and North Wilts. Technical Instruction Committee in 1896 in Victoria Road on a site presented by W. V. Rolleston.[19] Grants were made by the Department of Science and Art and the county council and the institute was open to a certain number of pupils outside Swindon.[20] Day and evening classes were

[4] Ibid. 156.
[5] Lloyd, 'Development of Education in Swindon', 127.
[6] Bd. of Educ. List 21, 1909.
[7] Ex inf. Miss J. Tanner.
[8] Lloyd, 'Development of Education in Swindon', 130.
[9] Ibid.
[10] Bd. of Educ. List 21, 1910.
[11] Ex inf. the head master.
[12] Bd. of Educ. List 21, 1932.
[13] This and subsequent information from the head master.
[14] Lloyd, 'Development of Education in Swindon', 139.
[15] This and subsequent information supplied by the head master.
[16] All information from the head teacher and the Schl. Log Bks.
[17] All information about these schools from Schl. Log Bks. and head masters.
[18] All information supplied by the head teacher.
[19] Swindon Advertiser, Supp. 5 Feb. 1904.
[20] Lloyd, 'Development of Education in Swindon' 202–5.

provided and the first day classes were attended by between 50 and 60 pupils.[21] From soon after its opening until 1952 the institute also housed a secondary school for boys and girls.[22] In 1926 the institute was reorganized as a college of further education and the following year was renamed the College. In 1928–9 it had 1,995 students in day and evening classes.[23] In 1961 extensive new buildings were opened by the Duke of Edinburgh.[24] In 1966 there were 4,639 full-time and 511 part-time students.[25]

The first building in Victoria Road was designed by Messrs. Silcock and Reay[26] and is of red brick with symmetrically placed gables. Additions were made to the building from time to time but in 1958 work was begun on a site overlooking Regent Circus on a large new block which was to overshadow the original building completely.[27] It is a six-storied building of reinforced concrete with flank walls of charcoal-coloured brick designed by Charles Pike and Partners.[28]

Schools opened between 1946 and 1964.[29] Twenty seven schools were opened between these years and are listed below. The date of opening is given in brackets and is followed by the number of children on the roll at April 1964: Central Special School E.S.N. (1946), 120; Drove Girls Secondary (1946), 598; Headlands Grammar (1952), 536; Moredon Infants (1952), 167, Junior (1953), 288, Secondary (1955), 550; Penhill North Infants (1955), 412, Junior (1957), 529, Secondary (1958), 440; Walcot East Infants (1957), 342, Junior (1959), 450; Walcot West Infants (1957), 312, Junior (1959), 382; Walcot Secondary (1958), 532; Lawn Infants (1958), 353, Junior (1958), 437, Secondary (1964), 244; Park North Infants (1959), 609, Junior (1961), 536; Park South Infants (1963), 434, Junior (1964), 347; Park Grammar (1960), 570; Merton Fields (Penhill South) Secondary (1963), 134, Penhill South Infants (1963), 217, Junior (1964), 289. Three Roman Catholic schools were opened: St. Joseph's Secondary (1958), 702; St. Mary's Infants and Juniors (1961), 436; Holy Family Infants and Juniors (1964), 512.

PRIVATE SCHOOLS. In 1835 there were five private schools catering between them for 105 children.[30] George Nourse's Classical and Commercial School for boys, established in Prospect Place by 1830, survived until *c.* 1867.[31] After the 1840s, when there was a great shortage of school places in the new town, numerous private schools opened in the old town for the children of more prosperous parents. Most lasted for a few years only but the Classical Commercial and Mathematical School begun by S. Snell in 1869 survived in 1964.[32] In 1881 it became known as Swindon High School. It was

recognized by the Board of Education in 1907. Sandhill House School, founded by the Revd. Richard Breeze in 1855, continued until at least 1882.[33] Mr. Fentiman's Academy which flourished in the mid 19th century was attended by Richard Jefferies.[34] Among private schools for girls Colville House School, begun by Ellen and Clara Cowell, lasted from 1881 until 1945.[35]

CHARITIES. By a Scheme of 1906 the Charity Commissioners united the following thirteen charities for the poor of the ancient parish.

John Burgess, Vicar of Manningford Bruce, directed in his will, made before 1559, that 7s. 5d. should be distributed annually on the feast of St. Gregory among the poor.[36] Out of this 1s. 2d. was to be paid to the five most deserving cases and the rest distributed among other poor persons. The charity was dispensed regularly until 1782, when, by mistake, it was included in the church account. In 1795, and for some years after, it was not paid at all but in 1826 Ambrose Goddard paid the arrears.

Eleanor Hutchins, James Lord, and Henry Cuss, according to an inscription on Eleanor's monument in the parish church (Holy Rood), each gave £20 to be invested for the benefit of the poor at Easter.[37] In 1737 £3 was distributed. The income was said to derive from land in 1786. The charity payments had evidently lapsed by 1834 when it was decided to distribute £3 yearly again. In 1903 the charity was represented by a rent-charge of £2 10s. from West Swindon Mead.

Before 1701 Edmund Goddard devised an annual rent-charge of 20s. from North Laines Farm to be paid on Shrove Tuesday to the poor.[38]

Richard Goddard, by his will dated 1650, devised a tenement in Wroughton, known as Arnold's Estate, for the benefit of the poor.[39] The gift was overlooked until 1730 when the testator's grandson, Richard Goddard, paid the arrears of rent. In 1834 the total rent was £11. The property was later sold and the proceeds invested with those arising from the sale of the Brind and Broadway charity lands (see below).

Margaret Brind, by will dated 1740, bequeathed £100 for the poor. The interest was to be distributed yearly on 20 July.[40] Mary Broadway, also by will dated 1740, bequeathed £20 to be invested for the benefit of poor widows and the interest to be distributed yearly on 13 April.[41] In 1757 the bequest, together with the capital of Brind's Charity (see above), was used to buy a small amount of land in Stratton St. Margaret. In 1831 the rent from this brought in £9. When the open fields of Stratton St. Margaret were inclosed an allotment in Upper Stratton was made to Swindon church. The share of the poor, known as the Poor's Allotment, was

[21] Ibid. 205.
[22] See p. 164.
[23] Lloyd, 'Development of Education in Swindon', 213, 214.
[24] Swindon Pub. Libr., Official Programme of Visit.
[25] Figures supplied by Swindon Pub. Libr.
[26] Pevsner, *Wilts.* (Bldgs. of Eng.), 458.
[27] *Architect and Building News,* 6 Sept. 1961.   [28] Ibid.
[29] All information supplied by head teachers.
[30] *Educ. Enq. Abstract,* H.C. 62, p. 119 (1835), xliii.
[31] Morris, *Swindon,* 285.
[32] *Astill's Swindon Almanack* and other local dirs. all for 1869–1964. Thanks are due to Mr. R. G. H. Scrope-Howe for searching these and other directories.
[33] *Loyal Almanack* (1855); *Astill's Swindon Almanack* (1870–82).
[34] *Loyal Almanack* (1860–1); Lloyd, 'Development of Education in Swindon', 100.
[35] *Astill's Swindon Almanack,* (1881–9) and other local dirs.
[36] All inf. in this paragraph from *Endowed Char. Wilts.* (1908), pp. 917, 927.
[37] Ibid.
[38] Ibid.
[39] Ibid. pp. 918, 925.
[40] Ibid. p. 918.
[41] Ibid. pp. 918, 925, 927–8.

reckoned at two-fifths of the land allotted. In 1800 4 a. at the southern end were set apart for the benefit of the second poor.

In about 1884 all land belonging to the Richard Goddard, Brind, Broadway, and Poor's Allotment charities was sold.[42] Of the proceeds, £1,171 was invested as a fund for the poor and £203 as a fund for widows. In 1903 the gross annual income of the poor fund was £30 and of the widows' fund £5. That year the money available for widows was distributed among 37 women, of whom 12 received 3s. 1d. and 25 3s. each.

Richard Gray, by his will proved in 1807, gave £400 for the benefit of the second poor, the money to be distributed about March every year to widows, widowers, and single men and women over 60 years of age.[43] In 1903 the gross annual income of this charity was £10 and about 40 persons received 5s. 6d. each.

Elizabeth Evans bequeathed £70 to provide 6 poor women of over 60 years of age with new gowns on the feast of St. Thomas every year.[44] The capital was invested in 1787. In 1834 the interest had been received and applied regularly and, because cloth was cheap, eight rather than six gowns were distributed. In 1903 the income of this charity was £2 10s. and six linsey gowns were given away.

Mary Horne by a testamentary paper gave £100 for poor householders not receiving relief from the parish, as well as £100 for the free school. In 1784 Mary's sister, Elizabeth, distributed the interest on this legacy and when she died in 1793 desired in her will that all her sister's bequests should be regularly paid. Joseph and Elizabeth Cooper augmented the Horne charities by settling certain land upon the trusts of Mary Horne's will. In 1796 they conveyed 9 a. in Stratton St. Margaret to James Crowdy, who was to pay half the income to the schoolmaster of the free school for teaching a number of girls, and to distribute the other half among the poor. In 1834 the income was £23 16s., of which £9 was paid to the schoolmaster and the remainder was distributed among poor householders in sums of 2s. 6d. or less. In 1896 all the property was sold and £1,034 invested. The annual income was then divided equally between the poor and the free school. In 1903 £12 18s. 6d. was distributed among the poor.[45]

Harriet Rolleston, by her will proved in 1870, settled £300 in trust to provide, under the name of the Vilett Charity, coal and blankets for the poor at Christmas.[46] The gross annual income in 1903 was £8 2s. 4d.

John Harding Sheppard, by his will proved in 1877, gave £200 to be invested for the benefit of 12 aged poor persons at Christmas.[47] In 1904 the gross annual income, known as Sheppard's Dole, was £5 2s. 6d. and was distributed among 12 beneficiaries.

Richard Bowly, by his will proved in 1885, gave £200 to provide for a distribution of blankets at Christmas.[48] In 1903 22 recipients received a blanket each.

All the above charities for the poor were in 1903 advertised in Old Swindon only, although residents in the new town could apply.[49] More beneficiaries, it was explained, came from the old town because at that time there was more regular employment and consequently less poverty in the new town. Between three and four hundred people usually applied for coal and blankets, and that year (1903) 250 people received 2 cwt. of coal each and 50 people a blanket. No account was taken of religious denominations.

Alexander Anderson, by his will dated 1865, bequeathed about £1,636 for the benefit of the poor.[50] This money, with £32 given by the local board, was used to build 4 almshouses in Cricklade Street. The almspeople could be men or women over 60, widowed or single, residents in Swindon for more than 3 years, and not in receipt of poor relief. Preference was given to people reduced by misfortune from better circumstances. The inmates of houses no. 1 and no. 2 received small weekly pensions. In 1897 John Chandler by declaration of a trust gave £100 to provide a pension for the inmate of house no. 3. In 1903 all four inmates were women. Because each newly-elected almsperson was placed in house no. 4, which had no pension attached, there was no great demand for admission.

In 1906 a Scheme of the Charity Commissioners united all the above-mentioned charities under the title of the United Charities.[51] It was directed that certain of these, namely, the Bowly, Evans, and Gray charities, together with Sheppard's Dole (now raised to a minimum payment of 10s.), should be applied for their original purposes. The main purpose of the Scheme, however, was to amalgamate the remaining charities, thenceforth to be called the Almshouse and Nursing Charities, so that the joint income could be used to meet the increasing cost of maintaining Anderson's Institution (by this time called Hostel). Any residue might be distributed to the poor in other ways. A small benefaction to Anderson's Hostel was included in the will of J. E. G. Bradford, proved in 1912. In 1952 this produced an income of £9. Stipends to the inhabitants of Anderson's Hostel ceased to be paid in 1954 and were replaced by additional grants from the National Assistance Board. An additional Scheme of 1960 provided that almspeople should make a maximum weekly contribution of 7s. 6d. towards the maintenance of the almshouses. An extraordinary repair fund was also established at this date. The houses are of stone with north-facing windows overlooking the churchyard. The date 1877 is inscribed on the building. Each house has a living room and pantry on the ground floor with a large bedroom above.

Assets of the United Charities in 1960 comprised the four almshouses, a £1 rent-charge issuing from North Laines Farm (Edmund Goddard's Charity), another of £2 10s. from West Swindon Mead (Hutchins, Lord, and Cuss Charities), and unspecified stock. In 1962 the charities had an annual income of £110 and only residents in the ancient parish of Swindon were eligible to benefit.

Three charities were founded for the poor of the municipal borough. Henry James Deacon, by his will proved in 1916, bequeathed money to be dis-

[42] Ibid.
[44] Ibid. pp. 919, 928.
[45] Ibid. pp. 920-1, 925-6, 928.
[46] Ibid. pp. 926-7.
[47] Ibid. pp. 926, 928.

[43] Ibid. pp. 919, 927.

[48] Ibid.
[49] Ibid. p. 928.
[50] Ibid. pp. 931-5.
[51] All inf. in this paragraph from Char. Com. Files 210989/A2, 210989.

tributed amongst the poor of Swindon not in receipt of poor relief. The income amounted to £24 in 1966 and was distributed amongst 34 aged poor persons.[52] Arthur Joseph Colbourne's charity for the sick poor, founded at an unknown date, was governed by a Scheme of 1953. In 1965 the income

was £256.[53] Charles Langley Brooke, by his will proved in 1916, bequeathed money to be invested and the income used to apprentice two poor boys born and living in the borough. The income amounted to £70 in 1965.[54]

TOCKENHAM

THE PARISH of Tockenham lies 3 miles south-west of Wootton Bassett and covers 779 a.[1] It is a narrow oblong and measures some 2 miles in length and ¾ mile in breadth. The small village lies along the western boundary of the parish, and all the buildings on the west side of the village street are situated geographically in the adjoining parish of Lyneham. South of the village the street is known as Greenway after the farm of that name.[2] In 1968 there were plans to extend the south-western boundary of Tockenham in order to bring more land in this area, as well as West Tockenham (in Lyneham), within the civil parish.[3] It seems probable that until the 16th century, when certain common lands within Tockenham manor were taken into the Little Park of Vastern (Wootton Bassett), the north-eastern boundary of the parish extended further to the east.[4] Although no substantial estate existed at Tockenham in 1086, it is likely that the 13th-century manor of Tockenham extended over most of the ancient parish, which was also known by this date as East Tockenham to distinguish it from West Tockenham, which lay in Lyneham.[5] Tockenham Wick, in the extreme north of the parish, was probably never more than a cluster of cottages. By the 16th century the parish was, as far as is known, no longer referred to as East Tockenham, but by this date both parish and manor were known interchangeably as Tockenham or Tockenham Wick.[6]

Except for a narrow bed of Oxford Clay which stretches the length of the northern boundary of the parish, Tockenham lies entirely on the Corallian ridge and its soils range from an extensive bed of Coral Rag around Tockenham Wick to alternating beds of Red Down Clay and Red Down Iron Sand, which extend southward to Greenway and Tockenham Farms. There are outliers of Coral Rag north-west of Queen Court Farm, and immediately north of Greenway Farm, while east of Shaw Farm (Lyneham), there is an outlier of Red Down Iron Sand. The soils of Red Down Iron Sand are generally made up of a red or brown loam and are comparatively dry when well-drained, but rather wetter where the clay lies close beneath. Around Tockenham the fields show small pieces of dark brown ironstone.[7]

In the extreme north of the parish the Oxford Clay gives rise to a narrow valley, which is flanked

to the north by Grittenham Hill (in Brinkworth). The main railway line from Paddington to Bristol and the Wilts. and Berks. Canal both pass through this gap. South of the low-lying clay vale the scarp slope of the Corallian ridge causes the ground to rise steeply until it reaches a height of over 400 ft. at Tockenham Wick. The extensive parkland which surrounds the house now known as Tockenham Manor stretches from the scarp slope across the Corallian plateau and is bounded to the south by the Swindon-Chippenham road. The dip slope of the ridge drops away to the clays and sands of the southern part of the parish, but nowhere does the level of the land fall below 350 ft. The land around Tockenham Wick carries a fairly large cover of trees, especially north-east of the Swindon-Chippenham road, where the woodland which skirts Tockenham park is known as Teagle's Copse. The land under cultivation in 1968 was largely devoted to pasture, especially on the wetter, heavier clays around the area in the north-west of the parish known as Shaw.

There may have been a small settlement at Tockenham in Roman times, since a stone relief of this period is set into the exterior wall of Tockenham church.[8] But it is unlikely that there was more than random settlement there before the Middle Ages. When assessed for the 15th of 1334 East Tockenham made a contribution which was the third highest in Kingsbridge hundred, as then constituted, after those of Hilmarton and Lyneham.[9] In 1377 East Tockenham had 64 poll-tax payers.[10] Fifteen persons contributed to the royal loan in 1523[11] and there were 3 contributors to the subsidy of 1576.[12] No more is known of the population of Tockenham until 1801 when there were 124 inhabitants in the parish. This number rose steadily thereafter. In 1841 it was 263 but this included an influx of labourers laying the G.W.R. line in Tockenham and in the neighbouring parishes. By 1851 the population had fallen to 190 and by 1871 to 136 persons. It increased to 173 in 1911 but by 1931 this number had fallen to 131. By 1951 there were 212 inhabitants,[13] but in 1961 the population had declined to 119 persons.[14]

In the 18th century the main road from Wootton Bassett to Chippenham took a more southerly course

[52] Char. Com. File 243942.
[53] Ibid. 244805.
[54] Reg. Educ. Char. Lansdowne House, Berkeley Sq., London, W.1.
[1] Much of the preliminary work for this article was done by M. R. Pickering, whose work is gratefully acknowledged.
[2] Maps used include: O.S. Maps 1″, sheet 157 (1958 edn.); 1/25,000, SU 07 (1959 edn.); 6″, Wilts. XIV, XXI (1st edn.).
[3] Ex inf. Clerk of County Council, Trowbridge, and see p. 93.
[4] See p. 171.

[5] V.C.H. Wilts. ii, p. 161; C.P. 40/106 rot. 162d.
[6] C 3/13/106.
[7] For an acct. of the geology of the parish see W. J. Arkell, 'Geology of Corallian Ridge near Wootton Bassett and Lyneham', W.A.M. liv. 1–18.
[8] See p. 173.
[9] V.C.H. Wilts. iv. 300; see p. 3
[10] V.C.H. Wilts. iv. 309.
[11] L. & P. Hen. VIII, iii (2), p. 1490.
[12] Taxation Lists (W.A.S. Rec. Brch.), 106.
[13] All above figures from table in V.C.H. Wilts. iv. 359.
[14] Census, 1961.

through Tockenham than it did in 1968. The road entered the parish north-east of the village in 1773, whence it turned sharply northwards and left the parish south of the 'Red Lion', which lies on the Lyneham side of the parish boundary.[15] In 1790–1, when a turnpike trust was created, a new stretch of road from Hunt's Mill Bridge (in Wootton Bassett), to the 'Red Lion' was built.[16] The new road ran south of Teagle's Copse on a direct westerly route from Wootton Bassett along a shelf formed by a narrow monoclinal fold at the junction of the Coral Rag and Red Down Clay. This road carried most west-bound traffic from Swindon in 1968. In 1968 the south-western boundary of Tockenham lay immediately west of the minor road from Clyffe Pypard to Dauntsey. It is probable that this boundary was not established as a division between East and West Tockenham until the later 14th century, by which date the Prior of Bradenstoke had consolidated his estate at West Tockenham.[17] It was the duty of the parishioners of Tockenham to repair this road in 1562.[18] The Wilts. and Berks. Canal had been constructed across the parish by 1801. The canal was closed in 1914.[19] The G.W.R. Paddington-Bristol line was laid to the north of the canal and was completed by 1841.[20]

The village of Tockenham is grouped around the winding lane which branches eastwards from Greenway. It is likely that this was the area which formed the medieval, as well as the modern, nucleus of the parish. To the south-east stands Queen Court Farm on a partly moated site, while the church stands south-west of the farm. The western side of the village street of Tockenham, which, as explained above, lay in Lyneham, contained several brick houses, a shop, and a derelict Primitive Methodist chapel in 1968. To the east of the village street stood several bungalows at this date. South of the village and east of Greenway stood Greenway Farm, an early-18th-century, two-storied building of brick, with a symmetrical stuccoed front and a hipped roof of stone slates. Nearby were a few council houses in 1968. There was a small settlement at Tockenham Wick in the 18th century,[21] which presumably grew up around the house built there by Richard Danvers shortly before 1604.[22]

John Ayliffe, a member of the Ayliffe family of Grittenham, was born at Tockenham in c. 1718–19. He was educated at Harrow and on his return to Tockenham, taught for a while at the recently-founded free school at Lyneham. Soon afterwards, hoping to acquire an interest in the Grittenham estate, he became estate manager there. Subsequently, in his attempts to secure the Grittenham estate, Ayliffe was guilty of many frauds, and was executed for forgery in 1759.[23]

MANOR AND OTHER ESTATES. There were 3 small estates at Tockenham in 1086. Alfric the little, the king's thegn, held 1 hide there, another one-hide estate was held by Algar, while Alric, also the king's thegn, held ½ hide in Tockenham.[24] No more is known of these Domesday estates, but it is probable that they merged to form the estate held some time in the 12th century by William Pinkney. By 1194 the lands had escheated to the Crown.[25] Presumably either William Pinkney, or Walter Pinkney, possibly his son, regained the estate at a later date, since in 1242–3 Herbert, son of Peter, held an estate at Tockenham which had come to him from Walter Pinkney through the wish of the king.[26] On the death of Herbert without issue at an unknown date the manor of *TOCKENHAM* passed to his brother Reynold, who, again at an unknown date, conveyed it to Amy de Stanford.[27] She apparently died without issue and her estate passed to her sister Isabel, who by c. 1295 had been succeeded by her son John de Stanford.[28] By 1300 the manor formed part of the demesne lands of Hugh le Despenser,[29] and thereafter Tockenham descended as the manor of Wootton Bassett until 1553.[30]

In 1553 the Crown granted the manor of Tockenham to John Wright and Thomas Holmes, and in the same year they were given licence to alienate the estate to William Allen.[31] In 1560 William Allen was licensed to convey the manor of Tockenham to John Sturgis the elder,[32] who died seised in 1571. His heir was his son John the younger,[33] who in 1575 sold the manor to Roger Newborough the elder, probably a member of a cadet branch of the family of Newborough of Berkley (Som.).[34] Roger Newborough had apparently died by 1604, when his widow Anne held the manor for life as her jointure.[35] Roger Newborough was succeeded by his son Roger Newborough the younger, who was seised of the manor of Tockenham in 1617.[36] It was presumably Roger Newborough the younger who at some date conveyed the manor to William Wallis, who was lord in 1641.[37] Henry Wallis, presumably his son, was seised of the manor by 1655.[38] By 1702 Henry Wallis had been succeeded at Tockenham by his son, William (II) Wallis.[39] In 1719 William (II) Wallis and Lucy his wife conveyed the manor of Tockenham to John Jacob (d. 1728).[40] The manorial estate was augmented in 1746 by an estate at Shaw previously carved out of the ancient manor of Tockenham, and brought to John Jacob by his second wife Mary Smith (see below). John Jacob was succeeded by his son John the younger (d. 1776). He in turn was succeeded by his nephew and heir, Sir Robert John Buxton of Shadwell Court, Rushford (Norf.), the son of his sister Elizabeth (d. 1765) the wife of John Buxton.[41] On

15 *Andrews and Dury, Map* (W.A.S. Rec. Brch.), pl. 14.
16 *W.A.M.* xxix. 195; *V.C.H. Wilts.* iv. 270–1.
17 See pp. 95–96.
18 S.R.O. Button-Walker-Heneage Mun. 1446, Ct. R. for West Tockenham manor, 1562.
19 *V.C.H. Wilts.* iv. 273–7.   20 Ibid. 281–2.
21 W.R.O. 248/184, Estate Map of Tockenham manor, 1764.
22 W.A.S. Libr., Devizes, Story-Maskelyne Papers, J/52, Will of Ric. Danvers, 1604, and see p. 170.
23 *W.A.M.* xxi. 199–204.
24 *V.C.H. Wilts.* ii, p. 161.
25 *Pipe R.* 1194 (P.R.S. N.S. v), 18, 200.
26 *Bk. of Fees*, ii. 729.
27 C.P. 40/21 rots. 87, 89.

28 C.P. 40/106 rot. 162d.
29 *W.N. & Q.* vii. 520.
30 See pp. 190–1.
31 *Cal. Pat.* 1553, 262–4, 109.
32 Ibid. 1558–60, 264.
33 C 142/159/86.
34 *W.N. & Q.* viii. 282; Hutchins, *Hist. Dors.* i. 429.
35 C 142/289/81.
36 C 2/Jas.1/W 25/33.
37 *Wilts. Inq. p.m.* 1625–49 (Index Libr.), 322–3.
38 W.R.O. 212B/Tock. 7/31, Survey of leases in manor of Tockenham, 1719.
39 Ibid.
40 C.P. 25(2)/1078/5 Geo. 1 Trin.
41 *W.N. & Q.* iv. 469, 471.

his death in 1839 Sir Robert John Buxton was succeeded by his son Sir John Jacob Buxton (d. 1842). He in turn was succeeded by his son Sir Robert Jacob Buxton (d. 1888), whose heir was his daughter, Maud Isabel Buxton.[42] She married Gerard James Barnes, who assumed the name of Buxton in 1902.[43] Maud Isabel Buxton died in 1951.[44] She conveyed her estate to her husband at their marriage, and on his death in 1963 Tockenham passed to his great-nephew, Mr. David Barnes, who owned the estate in 1968.[45]

The capital messuage of the ancient manor of Tockenham may be identified with the site of Queen Court Farm, which lies south of the old turnpike road from Wootton Bassett to Chippenham, near the church and the western boundary of the parish. It was presumably always used as a farm-house. The present house, which is partly of rough-cast stone, has external features of the early 18th century, including a hipped roof of stone slates with dormer windows, a weather-mould at first-floor level, a door-hood on brackets, and more or less regular fenestration. The asymmetrical plan, however, suggests that a house of the 17th century or earlier may have been remodelled in the 18th century. Two arms of a moat survive to the north and west of the house.

During the 17th century Thomas Smith (d. 1668) accumulated an estate, situated in the north of the parish around Tockenham Wick and Shaw, which after 1746 became part of the Tockenham manor estate. In 1616 Roger Newborough and Joan his wife conveyed a messuage, 40 a. of land, 30 a. of pasture, and 6 a. of meadow to Thomas Walter (d. 1641).[46] This estate lay at Shaw south-west of Tockenham Wick.[47] Thomas Walter was succeeded by his son John, a minor,[48] and on John's death in 1649 the estate passed to John's niece Mary Pinnell, who was seised of the estate at Shaw at the time of her marriage to Thomas Smith (d. 1668) in c. 1656.[49]

By the time of his death in 1604 Richard Danvers had acquired a small estate at Tockenham Wick, which he devised to his wife Mary for life, and which, after her death, was to pass to his son William.[50] Mary died c. 1623[51] and was presumably succeeded at Tockenham Wick by William, who died childless at an unknown date. By 1656 the capital messuage at Tockenham Wick, together with its appurtenant estate, had passed to John Danvers of Corsham (d. 1699), the great-nephew of Richard and Mary Danvers.[52] In this year John Danvers conveyed the estate to Thomas Smith (d. 1668).[53] Thomas Smith was succeeded in his newly-acquired estate by his son Matthew (d. 1733), who was in turn succeeded by his son Goddard Smith (d.s.p. 1746). His heir was his sister Mary (d. 1762), who married first, in

1711, John Jacob (d. 1728), lord of the manor of Tockenham. Through her the estate passed to her son John Jacob the younger (d. 1776), and thereafter descended with the manor of Tockenham.[54]

Before his death in 1604 Richard Danvers built a house at Tockenham Wick on land known as 'Walters'.[55] This house can probably be identified with the oldest part of Tockenham Manor, a large rambling building which has been altered and extended at various periods. The core of the house is an early-17th-century stone structure with a **T**-shaped plan. The entrance range faces north-west and has a two-gabled front with a central porch; internally there is a massive central chimney and the original staircase was probably immediately behind it. The leg of the **T** is a rear wing, extending south-eastwards and having at its further end a room with a Jacobean overmantel and panelling, perhaps re-set. During the ownership of Thomas Smith (d. 1668) the house comprised a hall, parlour, kitchen, and pantry, while above were a hall chamber, parlour chamber, kitchen chamber, and a 'green chamber'.[56] Matthew Smith (d. 1733) appears to have made some internal alterations and to have added a finial to the porch bearing the date 1698 with his initials and those of his wife.[57] An alternative possibility is that the whole front range was built or rebuilt at this period in a somewhat old-fashioned style. In the 18th century two brick additions, a drawing room and library, probably the work of John Jacob the younger (d. 1776), more than doubled the size of the house. The tall single-storied library, which has late-18th-century fittings, continued the line of the entrance range towards the south-west. The Buxtons, successors to the Jacob family, did not live at Tockenham, and it is likely that the house was used as a farm-house after an earlier farm-house attached to the estate had been burnt down in 1787.[58] It was known as Manor Farm in 1887.[59] In the early 20th century, however, Maud Isabel Buxton and her husband came to live there, making extensive alterations and additions to the building.[60] The principal additions were a wing on the north-east side of the forecourt, and a gabled service wing north-east of the house, added in 1904 and 1912 respectively. In 1967 Mr. David Barnes started to reduce the size of the building and to modernize it internally. Work was in progress in 1968, the drawing room extension having already been demolished. In the stable court to the north of the house is a gabled stone building of the later 17th century surmounted by a cupola. The upper story was probably built as a dovecot and the lower part has been converted into a stable by the insertion of 18th-century wooden stalls in the classical style. The stalls may originally have belonged to a

[42] G.E.C. *Baronetage*, v. 332.
[43] Burke, *Peerage and Baronage* (1907), s.v. Buxton.
[44] Ex inf. Mr. E. C. Barnes, Hungerdown House, Seagry.
[45] Ex inf. Mr. D. Barnes, Tockenham Manor.
[46] W.R.O. 212B/Tock. 21A, Deed, Newborough to Walter.
[47] *Wilts. Inq. p.m.* 1625–49 (Index Libr.), 322–3.
[48] Ibid.
[49] W.R.O. 212B/Tock. 23A, Will of Thos. Walter; ibid. 212B/Tock. 62A, Settlement, Thos. Smith and Mary Pinnell.
[50] W.A.S. Libr., Devizes, Story-Maskelyne Papers, J/52, Will of Ric. Danvers.

[51] P.C.C. 19 Swann.
[52] F. N. Macnamara, *Memorials of the Danvers Family*, p. 539.
[53] W.R.O. 212B/Tock. 57A, Deed, Danvers to Smith.
[54] *W.N. & Q.* i. 425.
[55] W.A.S. Libr., Devizes, Story-Maskelyne Papers, J/52.
[56] J. Badeni, *Wilts. Forefathers*, 148–9.
[57] Ibid. 149. The date has sometimes been misread as 1608.
[58] Wilts. Cuttings, x. 290.
[59] O.S. Map 6″, Wilts. XIV, XXI (1st edn.).
[60] The 20th-century history of the house is from information supplied by Mr. David Barnes and from plans and photographs in his possession.

brick stable block of the 18th century which stands nearby. To the west of the house is a timber-framed barn with a thatched roof.

ECONOMIC HISTORY. Of the three Domesday estates in Tockenham, the one-hide estate held by Alfric had land for 1 plough, an appurtenant 6 a. of meadow, and 6 a. of pasture. It was worth 13s. in 1086. Another one-hide estate held by Algar had land for 1 plough as well as ½ plough with 1 bordar. This estate also had 6 a. of meadow and 6 a. of pasture, and was worth 13s. in 1086. Alric's half-hide estate had land for ½ plough, 3 a. each of meadow and pasture, and was worth 7s. in 1086.[61]

In 1330–1 the receipts of Tockenham manor amounted to £10 2s. 9d. No tenants within the manor are mentioned. At this date common pasture lay at 'Doddefeld', 'Thornyelese', 'Westlye', 'Mere-hegg', 'Combe', 'Inwode', 'Waterdich', and 'Estlye'.[62] In 1341 a water-mill at Tockenham rendered tithes worth 3s. yearly.[63] This is probably the same mill in which Henry de Badmynton and Eleanor his wife had an interest in 1340. In this year they conveyed two thirds of the mill to Robert Philipps.[64] No more is known of a mill at Tockenham. By 1369–70 manorial receipts had risen to £17 19s. 8d., and by this time certain lands within the manor were leased to William Bailly at £5 yearly. There were 16 customary tenants and 7 cottars on the manor during this period. All tenants owed bean-picking, sheep-washing, sheep-shearing, hoeing, weeding, hay-making, stacking, and harvest duties. Only the 16 customary tenants were liable to render ploughing and hay-carting duties.[65] It is likely that composition payments were made in place of services, as was the case in 1371–2.[66] In 1449–50 manorial receipts totalled £26 19s. 10½d., a sum which included the farm of certain demesne arable, pasture, and meadow leased to William Somerset for £4 yearly.[67]

Before 1602 the tenants of Tockenham manor had common pasture for cattle in 54 a. of pasture and wood known as Dodford Lawn and Dodford Wood. In the earlier 16th century these commons were taken into the Little Park of Vastern, and in exchange tenants were given common pasture in the Great Park of Vastern, from 25 March to 21 December.[68] Each tenant paid 1s. 6d. yearly and the Rector of Tockenham had free summer pasture there.[69] In 1671 certain common fields within the manor were known as Padmead, Little Field, Far Field, and West Lye.[70] In c. 1699 private inclosure of common land within Tockenham manor was agreed upon[71] and it was probably after this date that the manor, which covered some two thirds of the

parish, was consolidated into a number of farms. A wide ravine in Teagle's Copse was formerly known as the 'Vineyards'. The south-facing slope may have been terraced for vines in early times and Goddard Smith (d. 1746) probably replanted vines there in the early 18th century.[72] In 1764 the manorial estate at Tockenham, which by this date included the former estate of the Smith family at Tockenham Wick and Shaw, comprised 4 farms, Wick, Shaw, Queen Court, and Greenway Farms, besides a small amount of land which may be identified with the park attached to Tockenham Manor.[73] Tockenham Fields Farm was at this date known as 'Mr. Sheppard's farm'.[74] By the time of the tithe award it has passed to Jacob and Richard Smith.

In 1839 all the farms in the parish were occupied by tenant farmers. Greenway Farm (89 a.), Wick Farm (290 a.), Shaw Farm (39 a.), and Tockenham Fields Farm (87 a.), were under pasture at this date, although some mixed, as well as pasture farming was done at Queen Court Farm (179 a.).[75] By 1877 Tockenham Fields Farm had become part of the manorial estate at Tockenham and it was at about the same date that both Tockenham Fields and Greenway Farms were sold.[76] In 1968 the parish was mainly under pasture.

LOCAL GOVERNMENT. Records of views of frankpledge for the manor of Tockenham exist for 1546, 1547, and 1548,[77] but otherwise no records concerning the government of the parish are known.

CHURCH. A church in Tockenham is first mentioned in 1276.[78] In 1924 the benefice, which has always been a rectory, was united with those of Lyneham and Bradenstoke-cum-Clack.[79] In 1954 the rectory of Tockenham was separated from the united benefice and from that date has been held in plurality with the vicarage of Clyffe Pypard.[80]

Before 1276 the advowson of the rectory of Tockenham belonged to Herbert, son of Peter, who was lord of the manor.[81] After the death of Herbert some time in the 13th century the advowson descended with the manor of Tockenham until the 16th century. On the death in 1548 of Queen Katharine Parr, the last of the queens of England to hold the manor, the advowson reverted to the Crown, and remained with the Lord Chancellor in 1968.[82]

The rectory was taxed at £5 in 1291[83] and in 1341 the overall value of the benefice was £5 18s. 4d.[84] The church was again taxed at £5 in 1428.[85] In 1535 the value of the rectory was £6 6s.[86] Before certain common lands in the parish were inclosed in c. 1699 the rectory was reported to be worth £160,

[61] *V.C.H. Wilts.* ii, p. 161.
[62] S.C. 6/1057/3.
[63] *Inq. Non.* (Rec. Com.), 161.
[64] C.P. 25(1)/254/44/33.
[65] S.C. 6/1061/2.
[66] S.C. 6/1061/3.
[67] S.C. 6/1115/1.
[68] For the Great and Little Parks of Vastern, see p. 190.
[69] C 78/114 Entry 19; see p. 172.
[70] Sar. Dioc. R.O. Glebe Terrier, 1671.
[71] Ibid. Vis. Queries, 1783.
[72] *W.A.M.* xl. 364.
[73] W.R.O. 248/184, Estate Map of Tockenham manor, 1764.
[74] Ibid.

[75] Ibid. Tithe Award, 1839.
[76] W.A.S. Libr., Devizes, Sale Cat. 1877; ex inf. Mr. D. Barnes, Tockenham Manor.
[77] S.C. 2/209/69.
[78] C.P. 40/21 rot. 87.
[79] See p. 100.
[80] Ex inf. the Revd. F. E. Coward, Rector of Tockenham.
[81] C.P. 40/21 rot. 87.
[82] See pp. 169, 190–1; *Reg. Ghent* (Cant. & York Soc.), 822; Phillipps, *Wilts. Inst.* (see index in *W.A.M.* xxviii. 232).
[83] *Tax. Eccl.* (Rec. Com.), 190.
[84] *Inq. Non.* (Rec. Com.), 161.
[85] *Feud. Aids*, v. 285.
[86] *Valor Eccl.* (Rec. Com.), ii. 130.

but by *c.* 1744 the rector reported that as a result of inclosure the value of the benefice had declined to £85.[87] The rectory had an average yearly net income of £283 in 1835.[88]

In 1341 the great tithes arising from the demesne land of Queen Isabel in Tockenham were valued for purposes of taxation at £1, while certain other great tithes within the parish were worth £2 10s. The small tithes of Tockenham at this date were valued at £1 6s. 4d.[89] No more is known of either the great or small tithes until 1602 when the rector was allowed certain pasture rights in the Great Park of Vastern in place of great and small tithes in Dodford Wood and Dodford Lawn, which were formerly common pasture of Tockenham manor, but which had subsequently been inclosed in the Little Park of Vastern.[90] By 1650 the rector claimed that his parishioners rendered neither tithes in kind nor paid any modus in place of them.[91] By 1678 the pasture rights in the Great Park of Vastern, given in lieu of tithes from Dodford Wood and Dodford Lawn, were replaced by a yearly payment of £1 6s. 8d. made out of the Little Park of Vastern.[92] This payment was still made in 1704.[93] In *c.* 1699 when a private inclosure agreement was made at Tockenham, the landholders agreed to pay the rector a modus instead of rendering tithes in kind. Early in the 18th century the tithes, both great and small, were valued at £45. About 1770 the rector attempted to take tithes in kind. A dispute arose and eventually landholders at Tockenham agreed to allow him an additional £20 in order to make the modus more representative of the value of the tithes.[94] In 1839 the tithes arising from 762 a. in Tockenham were commuted for a rent-charge of £255 3s. payable to the rector.[95]

In 1341 the rector had a virgate of land and a meadow.[96] In the mid 16th century there was an unspecified amount of glebe-land attached to the church,[97] but no details about the rectorial estate are known until 1662 when there were 35 a. of glebe, which included 8 a. of pasture, known as Parsonage Close and which adjoined the parsonage house, as well as a parcel of 10 a. called 'Smallinges'.[98] This estate apparently remained intact and virtually the same amount of glebe-land was recorded in 1671 and 1678.[99] The rector in 1783 claimed that by reason of a private inclosure agreement made about 1699, his glebe-land had been considerably reduced.[1] A terrier of 1704, however, recorded 35 a. of glebe, which still included 9 a. called 'Smallingras'.[2] In 1764 the rectorial glebe was divided into two compact parcels, one of which lay south of the church and included Cowleaze Glebe and Glebe Mead, while the other, which included Great Smallingers, lay immediately north-west of the turnpike road from Wootton Bassett to Chippenham above Queen Court Farm.[3] The same estate was recorded in

1839.[4] A parsonage house is mentioned in 1662,[5] 1671,[6] and in 1704.[7] In 1887 the house, a large red-brick building, stood to the south-west of the church.[8] In 1968 it was used as a private house, since the incumbent lived in Clyffe Pypard.[9]

The rectors of Tockenham were probably resident in the Middle Ages. In the 17th and 18th centuries temporary arrangements were sometimes made for neighbouring incumbents to serve the cure. In 1686 the rector, William Durston, was described as a 'scandalous and disorderly man', who, besides neglecting his cure, had not provided a licensed substitute.[10] In 1692 the parishioners reported that Durston had visited Tockenham only once in the past six months, and that Christopher Symons, Vicar of Seagry, served the church at Tockenham, although he had no licence to do so.[11] After *c.* 1781 a prolonged illness prevented the rector, Algernon Frampton, from fulfilling his duties, and arrangements were made for neighbouring clergymen to serve Tockenham.[12] In 1864 there was no rector and the church was served by the Vicar of Wootton Bassett, assisted by a curate.[13]

In 1553 the parishioners complained that there was no preaching at Tockenham.[14] In 1783 the rector reported that before his illness prevented him, he had always taken a service on Sunday mornings, but that weekday services were never held since none would attend. Holy Communion, attended by an average of 7 people, was administered at Christmas, Easter, and Whitsun.[15] On Census Sunday 1851 it was reckoned that over the past year there had been an average congregation of 104 at the morning services and about the same number in the afternoons.[16] In 1864 services, at which sermons were preached, were held twice on Sundays, while weekday services were held on Ash Wednesday, Good Friday, and Christmas Day. There was an average congregation of 50 people at these services. Holy Communion was celebrated 4 times yearly and the communicants averaged 20 persons.[17] In 1968 Holy Communion was celebrated and Evening Prayer said each Sunday.

The church of *ST. GILES* (before 1928 dedicated to St. John the Evangelist)[18] is a 13th-century building consisting of a chancel and an unaisled nave with a wooden bell-turret at its west end. The west wall of the nave contains two lancet windows with a central buttress between them. Near the west end of the south wall is a two-light window with 13th-century tracery and opposite to it on the north side is a 14th-century window. Most of the other windows are of the 15th century. A curious arrangement which may have dated from the 13th century is shown at the east end of the chancel in a drawing of 1806 by John Buckler: two pointed windows, each of two lights, are combined under a single arch, the tympanum being pierced by a plain circular

[87] Sar. Dioc. R.O. Vis. Queries, 1783.
[88] *Rep. Com. Eccl. Revenues*, H.C. 54, pp. 850–1 (1835), xxii.
[89] *Inq. Non.* (Rec. Com.), 161.
[90] C 78/114 Entry 19.
[91] Hist. MSS. Com. *Var. Coll.* i. 121.
[92] Sar. Dioc. R.O. Glebe Terrier, 1678.   [93] Ibid. 1704.
[94] Ibid. Vis. Queries, 1783.
[95] W.R.O. Tithe Award, 1839.
[96] *Inq. Non.* (Rec. Com.), 161.   [97] C 1/1333/5.
[98] Sar. Dioc. R.O. Glebe Terrier, 1662.
[99] Ibid. 1671, 1678.   [1] Ibid. Vis. Queries, 1783.
[2] Ibid. Glebe Terrier, 1704.

[3] W.R.O. 248/184, Estate Map of Tockenham manor, 1764.
[4] Ibid. Tithe Award, 1839.
[5] Sar. Dioc. R. O. Ep. Vis. 1662.
[6] Ibid. Glebe Terrier, 1671.   [7] Ibid. 1704.
[8] O.S. Map 6", Wilts. XIV, XXI (1st edn.).
[9] See p. 38.   [10] Sar. Dioc. R.O. Chwdns.' Pres. 1686.
[11] Ibid. 1692.   [12] Ibid. Vis. Queries, 1783.
[13] Ibid. 1864, and see p. 202.
[14] Sar. Dioc. R. O. Bp's Detecta Bk. 1553, f. 147.
[15] Ibid. Vis. Queries, 1783.   [16] H.O. 129/251/1/3/6.
[17] Sar. Dioc. R.O. Vis. Queries, 1864.
[18] *Crockford* (1929).

opening.[19] The present east window, in the Decorated style, is work of 1876. At the west end of the nave two ancient posts supporting the bell-turret are incorporated in a timber-framed partition. The nave roof is of the trussed-rafter type. At rood-loft level a wooden door-frame has survived. The church contains a tub-shaped Norman font ornamented with flat arches and scallops.

In 1553[20] and 1686[21] the chancel was reported out of repair. The church, together with a 'tower', was said to be greatly out of repair in 1674,[22] but it is unlikely that anything larger than a turret ever existed at the west end. It may have been as a result of this report that the turret was rebuilt as shown by Buckler[23] and also part of the south wall of the nave below it; this bears the date 1699, together with the initials of two churchwardens. The south porch appears to be of the same period. A relief carving of Roman date, identified as a figure of Aesculapius or Hygea, has been built into the south wall west of the porch.[24] The church was restored in 1876, when the south wall of the chancel was rebuilt and the east window inserted, and again in 1908.[25] At one of these restorations the bell-turret was once more renewed. The most notable memorial in the church is a mural tablet with a portrait bust commemorating Mrs. Goddard Smith (d. 1726).

In 1553 the church retained a 6 oz. chalice for the use of the parish.[26] In 1692 the parishioners accused the absentee rector, William Durston, of taking away the communion vessels.[27] These were apparently returned to Tockenham eventually, and are probably to be identified with the chalice and paten, hallmarked 1681, which comprised the church plate in the 20th century.[28] In 1553 there were two bells. In the mid 20th century there was only one bell, that of c. 1480 from the Bristol foundry, inscribed 'Micael Celi Satrapa'.[29] A register of baptisms, marriages, and burials runs from 1653–1766. Another containing baptisms and burials covers the years 1767–1812, while banns of marriage (1765–1812), and marriages (1755–1816), are contained in another register. Yet another register contains marriages from 1814–36.[30]

NONCONFORMITY. In 1669 there was a group of Baptists at Tockenham Wick.[31] This may possibly be identified with the 7 nonconformists at Tockenham returned in Bishop Compton's census of 1676.[32] Thereafter nothing is known of nonconformity in the parish until the later 19th century, when a Primitive Methodist chapel, built in 1863, served the village.[33] The chapel, which stands on the west side of the village street, is thus geographically in Lyneham. By 1961 it was no longer in use and was derelict in 1968.[34]

EDUCATION. A Sunday school was established in Tockenham in 1828 and in 1835 17 boys and 15 girls were taught there. The school was supported by voluntary contributions, from which the master and mistress were paid a yearly salary of £6.[35] By 1859 a school at Tockenham was supported principally by Lady Buxton of Shadwell Court (Norf.). Here, in a good, recently-erected schoolroom 30 or 40 pupils were taught by an uncertificated mistress. A house in which the teacher lived adjoined the school.[36] A private school, presumably that formerly supported by Lady Buxton, had accommodation for 41 pupils in 1871. By this date a National school had been established at Tockenham.[37] This school had an average attendance of 56 pupils in 1906.[38] In 1926 it was closed and the children henceforth attended school at Lyneham.[39] From 1940 to 1946 the school was re-opened owing to danger of enemy attacks at Lyneham.[40] The former National school stood immediately south-west of the church and in 1968 was a private house.

CHARITIES. In 1780 Ann Jacob bequeathed £500 in trust for the endowment of charities in Hilmarton and Tockenham.[41] In Tockenham part of the profits was to be used for the upkeep of the family tombs in Tockenham church, while the remainder was to be distributed amongst certain poor people of the parish who did not receive alms. The recipients were to be chosen by the incumbent of Tockenham and the lord of Tockenham manor. In 1834 there were 22 parishioners who benefited from the charity. In 1896 £2, thenceforth to be known as Ann Jacob's Ecclesiastical Charity, was allotted for the upkeep of the Jacob tombs. The remainder of the income, to be called Ann Jacob's Parochial Charity, was to be given to the poor. The income from the Parochial Charity amounted to a little over £4 in 1904 and was distributed with Mary Clutterbuck's Charity.

In 1784 Mary Clutterbuck bequeathed £200 the interest on which was to be distributed yearly at Christmas amongst the poor of Tockenham.[42] In 1905 Ann Jacob's Parochial Charity and the Clutterbuck Charity were administered together and used to cover the expenses of coal and provident clubs in the village, and to supplement their dividends with cash bonuses. A few money doles were also paid to poor parishioners.

In 1962 Ann Jacob's Parochial Charity amounted to about £4 and was distributed in cash payments to the poor of Tockenham, presumably as need arose. The income of about £5 from Clutterbuck's Charity was distributed in either cash or goods in kind at this date.

In 1834 it was reported that a sum of £3 yearly was paid out of part of the Tockenham estate known

[19] W.A.S. Libr., Devizes, vol. iv. 44.
[20] Sar. Dioc. R.O. Bp's Detecta Bk. 1553, f. 147.
[21] Ibid. Chwdns.' Pres. 1686.
[22] Ibid. 1674.
[23] W.A.S. Libr., Devizes, vol. iv. 44.
[24] V.C.H. Wilts. i (1), 114.
[25] Kelly's Dir. Wilts. (1939); leaflet in church.
[26] Nightingale, Wilts. Plate, 143.
[27] Sar. Dioc. R.O. Chwdns.' Pres. 1692.
[28] Pevsner, Wilts. (Bldgs. of Eng.), 466.
[29] Walters, Wilts. Bells, 219.
[30] W.R.O. 907.
[31] V.C.H. Wilts. iii. 113.
[32] W.N. & Q. iii. 536.
[33] See p. 93.
[34] G.R.O. 15926.
[35] Educ. Enq. Abstract, H.C. 62, p. 119 (1835), xliii.
[36] Acct. of Wilts. Schools, H.C. 27, p. 109 (1859 Sess. 1), xxi (2).
[37] Retn. rel. to Elem. Educ. H.C. 201, p. 418 (1871), lv.
[38] Retn. of Non-Provided Schools, H.C. 178–xxxi, p. 834 (1906), lxxxviii.
[39] See p. 103.
[40] Ex inf. Chief Education Officer, Trowbridge.
[41] All inf. from Endowed Char. Wilts. (1908), pp. 945–9.
[42] All inf. from Endowed Char. Wilts. (1908), pp. 946, 948 and Char. Com. Files 204382, 204384.

as the 'Marsh'.[43] This sum was distributed by the churchwardens to certain poor parishioners who did not receive alms. In 1905 the Poor's Money, as this charity was called, was distributed shortly after

Christmas. A sum of £3 arising from Tockenham Marsh was still distributed, in an unspecified manner, to the poor of the parish in 1962.

WANBOROUGH

THE PARISH of Wanborough, 3 miles east of Swindon, is roughly rectangular in shape, some 5 miles long and varying from a mile to 2 miles in width.[1] Before 1884 a long narrow strip of land to the east, including Earlscourt Farm, was a detached portion of Wanborough situated geographically in the parish of Little Hinton. In the 11th century Wanborough and Little Hinton together formed a single estate, though the charter describing the boundaries is open to suspicion.[2] A charter of 854 apparently describes the boundaries of Little Hinton, and the Domesday entry suggests that Earlscourt, while formerly attached to Wanborough, had by 1086 been separated from it.[3] Its subsequent tenurial history renewed the connexion. In 1884 the detached part was absorbed into the civil parish of Little Hinton,[4] leaving Wanborough with an area of 4,514 a.[5] In 1964 an area in the extreme north-west of the parish, including Little Nythe and Covingham Farms, was beginning to be developed by the corporation of Swindon as part of its expansion programme.[6]

Geographically the parish is divided roughly in half, the southern section lying on the chalk downs. The shape of the parish conforms to a pattern found along the scarp slope of the Chalk both westwards into Wiltshire and eastwards into Berkshire, each parish having chalk uplands as well as greensands and clays for meadow and pasture.[7] Upper Wanborough, around the church, is on an Upper Greensand spur commanding a view north over Lower Wanborough and south over Liddington. The northern half of the parish towards the shallow valley of the River Cole is successively Gault, Lower Greensand, and Kimmeridge Clay.[8] The chalk scarp rises behind the village, reaching 800 ft. at Foxhill on the parish boundary. Most of the Chalk lies between 600 ft. and 700 ft. Two coombs pierce the eastern boundary between the Ridge Way and the Icknield Way, the larger containing two chalk pits. Below the scarp the land falls gently away to the river, to below 300 ft., and is drained by the Cole, its tributary stream the Lidd, and several smaller streams, providing abundant meadow land and marsh. There is little wood in the parish, although there is evidence of illegal felling during the 16th century.[9] Stone was quarried at Berrycombe in the

16th century[10] and marl was taken from Inlands at least from the end of the 13th century.[11]

Wanborough's reputation as the 'key of Wessex',[12] the site of two battles between rival Saxon kings,[13] is not accepted by modern scholars,[14] but the southern boundary follows the 'Folces Dic', or 'Thieves Way', the ancient hundred boundary,[15] which may represent the march between tribal spheres of influence. Archaeological and place-name evidence[16] confirms Neolithic and Bronze Age activity in the south of the parish and Early Iron Age coins have been found.[17] The parish lies athwart three ancient trackways which run along the line of the chalk downs. The 'Rogues Road', north of the 'Thieves Way', winds along the valley at the foot of the scarp, running south of Earlscourt, through the Breach and Horpit, skirting the Marsh and thence entering Liddington.[18] The road running west from Little Hinton towards Swindon, passing through Upper Wanborough, follows for part of its course the line of the Icknield, or Ickleton Way, and a mile to the south runs the Ridge Way.

The Roman occupation left considerable traces in the parish. Ermine Street runs diagonally through the whole length of Wanborough, the lower part of the village lying along its route. The Cunetio (Mildenhall) road, branching from Ermine Street, near Covingham Farm, forms part of the western boundary of the parish. At the junction of these roads lies a large settlement which has been tentatively identified as Durocornovium.[19] Considerable structural remains, for at least two centuries used as a stone quarry, as well as individual finds, including a large coin hoard, attest an occupation from the first century to the end of the Roman period.[20] Another theory places Durocornovium at Popplechurch in the extreme south of the parish, identifying the Covingham site as a trading site, the other being a staging post.[21] Pagan-Saxon material has been found in the parish, including a cemetery at Foxhill.[22]

The later settlement pattern of Wanborough is complex and its scattered nature seems to be of early origin. The position of Upper Wanborough, including the church, on the Icknield Way but west of Ermine Street, suggests that it might be the original nucleus of the village. In this respect

[43] All inf. from *Endowed Char. Wilts.* (1908), pp. 946, 949 and Char. Com. File 204483.
[1] The following maps have been used: O.S. Maps 6", XI, XVI, XXIII (1st edn.); 1/25,000, SU 18, 41/27–28; 1", sheet 34 (1st and later edns.).
[2] T.R. Thomson, 'Early Bounds of Wanborough and Little Hinton', *W.A.M.* lvii. 201–11.
[3] See p. 176.
[4] *V.C.H. Wilts.* iv. 359; M.H. 12/13764.
[5] *Census*, 1891.
[6] See p. 119.
[7] C.S. & C.S. Orwin, *Open Fields*, 25, 27.
[8] O.S. Geological Map, ¼" (1900), 19.
[9] S.C. 2/209/66.
[10] Ibid.

[11] Magdalen Coll., Oxford, Wanborough deeds, 34.
[12] *W.A.M.* xxiii. 113.   [13] Ibid.
[14] F. M. Stenton, *Anglo-Saxon Engl.*, 30, 70; *Anglo-Saxon Chron.*, ed. D. Whitelock, D. C. Douglas, and S. I. Tucker, 14, 26.
[15] *W.A.M.* lvii. 208, 210 and map.
[16] *P.N. Wilts.* (E.P.N.S.), 283–4; *W.A.M.* lvii. 204.
[17] *V.C.H. Wilts.* i (1), 117, 141, 194.
[18] *W.A.M.* lvii. 205, 207, and map.
[19] A. D. Passmore, *Roman Road from Caerleon to Silchester*; J. B. Jones, *New View on Ermine Street*; *W.A.M.* lii. 386.
[20] *V.C.H. Wilts.* i (1), 117.
[21] *W.A.M.* lvii. 207.
[22] *V.C.H. Wilts.* i (1), 118.

Wanborough follows its neighbours to the east, many of which are placed just above the spring line. The pattern of Lower Wanborough was governed to some extent by Ermine Street and the 'Rogues Road', but also by the position of the common land.[23] The distinction between East and West Wanborough occurs by the end of the 13th century, and suggests that Lower (presumably East) Wanborough was then of reasonable size.[24] This division persisted for administrative purposes during the 16th[25] and 17th centuries, although by the 18th century smaller areas, such as Hydes, Foxbridge, and Redlands were being used for the purposes of poor relief.[26] Some other areas of settlement in the parish probably precede this division: apart from Earls-court,[27] Horpit dates from the middle of the 13th century at the latest, and Nythe and 'La Hyde' occur as settlements by the end of that century. Moor Leaze also probably originated at this time, and the Breach occurs as a settlement a century later.[28]

The sites of several medieval houses lying away from the main areas of settlement are similarly identifiable. Cold Court, with the chapel of St. Katherine, surrounded by a moat and close to the great fishpond, was situated south of the stream known as the Lidd in Wanborough Marsh.[29] Hall Place, the home of the Polton family at the beginning of the 15th century and of Thomas Brind as late as 1633, seems to have been a little to the east of Lower Wanborough.[30] The chapel of St. Ambrose, probably attached to the house, has left traces in a field called 'Ambrose', which has visible evidence of disturbance.[31]

By the later 18th century, before the inclosure of the common, houses in Lower Wanborough were grouped around the edge of the common lands.[32] These were of irregular shape, straddling Ermine Street and providing, in effect, a large village green. The western boundary of the lands is marked by a line of houses stretching from the Marsh, through Warnage, to the foot of Kite Hill, the southern boundary by Rotten Row, and the eastern by the houses at Horpit. Many of these houses on the fringes of the former common still stand. Along Rotten Row there are three or four of the 17th or 18th centuries, which before inclosure would have faced north across the common. At Horpit, Elm Farm, a thatched stone-built farm-house, dates from the 18th century and close by there are one or two other houses with thatched roofs probably of 17th- or 18th-century date. There are also a few houses of about the same period in that part of Lower Wanborough which lies along Ermine Street at the bottom of Callas Hill. Among these are two thatched inns, the 'Plough' and the 'Harrow', both of which stand at right-angles to the road and were no doubt once of some importance as coaching inns. During the 19th century there was some expansion of Lower Wanborough along Berrycroft Row and northwards along Ermine Street.

The village of Upper Wanborough, which lies to the east of the church, contains buildings mostly of the 18th and 19th centuries but there are a few thatched cottages of earlier date. Kite Hill, which runs parallel to Ermine Street and is one of the roads linking Upper and Lower Wanborough, was built up with council houses between the two World Wars. In the mid 20th century there has been some private building development in Upper Wanborough on lands belonging to the former Warnage Farm. In 1968 there was a village shop in Upper Wanborough but the post-office was at Lower Wanborough.

The scattered settlement pattern necessitated a network of roads and tracks particularly across the meadows and common lands in the north of the parish. Thus a track from Berrycroft Row led north through Foxbridge to Swanhill and then west to the parish boundary at Wick Lane. This was also the line followed by the fencing around pasture land during the 16th century.[33] A green lane leading north from the bottom of Kite Hill, still clearly to be seen in the 1960s, joined the track at Berrycroft Row. Another track, since disappeared, linked Horpit with West Town, Little Hinton, in the 18th century.[34]

Wanborough, which was assessed as a whole, was the fifth most highly-rated fiscal unit in the county in 1334.[35] There were 201 poll-tax payers in 1377, making the parish the largest unit in the hundred of Thornhill.[36] In 1545 there were 5 tax-payers to the Benevolence of that year and to the subsidy of 1576 Wanborough contributed £4 15s.[37] In 1801 the population was 793, rising to over a thousand in 1831; partly as a result of emigration to Canada, the figure fell, amounting to 764 in 1911. By 1961 with many people who worked in Swindon making their homes in Wanborough, the figure had risen again to 972.[38]

Thomas Langley, Vicar of Wanborough (1563–1581), was chaplain to Archbishop Cranmer in 1548 and a member of the Geneva congregation in 1556. He wrote an abridged version of Polydore Vergil, a treatise on the Sabbath translated from the Italian, and various Latin verses.[39] Sir Charles Hedges (d. 1714), lord of the manor of Wanborough by 1704, was a judge of the Admiralty Court, Secretary of State (1700–6), and a judge of the Prerogative Court of Canterbury.[40] William Sandys Wright Vaux (1818–85), son of William Vaux, Vicar of Wanborough, was Keeper of the Department of Coins and Medals at the British Museum (1861–1870).[41] A. D. Passmore (d. 1958), the Wiltshire antiquary, lived in the parish. He contributed many articles to the *Wiltshire Archaeological and Natural History Magazine* and made a large collection of antiquities.[42]

MANORS AND OTHER ESTATES. According to a charter purporting to be of the time of Stigand,

[23] See below.
[24] Magdalen Coll., Oxford, Wanborough deeds, 13a, 33a.
[25] S.C. 2/209/66.
[26] See p. 181.
[27] See p. 176.
[28] *P.N. Wilts.* (E.P.N.S.), 284.
[29] See p. 184.
[30] Polton brass in par. ch.; Burial Reg. 15 Mar. 1633.
[31] Aubrey, *Topog. Coll.* ed. Jackson, 196.

[32] *Andrews and Dury, Map* (W.A.S. Rec. Brch.), pl. 15.
[33] S.C. 2/209/66.
[34] *Andrews and Dury, Map* (W.A.S. Rec. Brch.), pl. 15.
[35] *V.C.H. Wilts.* iv. 302–3.   [36] Ibid.
[37] *Taxation Lists* (W.A.S. Rec. Brch.), 22, 104.
[38] *V.C.H. Wilts.* iv. 359; *Census*, 1961.
[39] *D.N.B.*
[40] Ibid.   [41] Ibid.
[42] *W.A.M.* lvii. 255.

Bishop of Winchester (c. 1043–53), the area of the present parishes of Wanborough and Little Hinton formed part of that bishop's estates.[43] The manor of *WANBOROUGH* was still held by the Bishop of Winchester in 1086, and was then assessed at 19 hides.[44] In 1166–7 the Count of Perche was holding the manor.[45] This was Rotrou (III), son of Rotrou (II) by Hawise, sister of Patrick, 1st Earl of Salisbury. He may have inherited the property through his mother, or possibly through his grandfather, Geoffrey (II), Lord of Mortagne.[46] Rotrou (III) died in 1191 and was succeeded by his son Geoffrey (III); the sheriff rendered £4 three years later for the new count's lands in Aldbourne and Wanborough.[47] Geoffrey (III) died in 1202 and his son Thomas was killed at the battle of Lincoln in 1217, fighting for Prince Louis. His lands were taken into royal hands, but almost immediately Wanborough and other properties were granted to William Longespée, Earl of Salisbury, the king's uncle.[48] The overlordship then descended like that of the manor of Trowbridge.[49] In the same way it passed in 1366 to John of Gaunt, Duke of Lancaster, and became parcel of the Duchy of Lancaster when John's son became king in 1399.[50]

In 1086 Richer held a hide of land at Wanborough of the Bishop of Winchester.[51] By 1242–3 Stephen Longespée, nephew of William, Earl of Salisbury (d. 1250), held the manor of his uncle.[52] Stephen died in 1260 and his heirs were his two daughters by Emily, formerly Countess of Ulster (d. c. 1276), namely Ela, wife of Roger la Zouche, and Emily, wife of Maurice FitzMaurice.[53] The manor passed to Emily and in 1314 was settled upon her for life with successive remainders to Thomas, Earl of Lancaster, and Robert de Holand and Maud his wife, granddaughter of Ela la Zouche.[54] Emily died in 1331 and the manor passed to Maud, then a widow.[55] At Maud's death in 1349 the manor descended to her son, Sir Robert de Holand.[56] His heir at his death in 1373 was his granddaughter Maud, wife of John, Lord Lovel of Titchmarsh (d. 1408). From 1399 Lord Lovel held of the Duchy of Lancaster in right of his wife, who survived him until 1423.[57] Maud's grandson, William, succeeded to the estate and died in 1455 seised of Wanborough jointly with his wife Alice, later wife of Ralph Boteler, Lord Sudeley.[58] Alice survived until 1474, to be followed by her grandson Francis, later Viscount Lovel, who was attainted for high treason

in 1485. Between 1485 and 1511 the forfeited lands were farmed first by Sir John Cheney and then by Sir Richard Eliot, but in 1511 the manor was granted to Sir Edward Darell.[59]

This grant was renewed in favour of Darell and his wife in 1512 to form her jointure, and was again confirmed in 1515.[60] Darell died in 1530; his widow retained the property for her life and was succeeded by Darell's cousin, Edward Darell of Littlecote (in Ramsbury). He died in 1549 leaving the manor in the hands of his widow Elizabeth, since William Darell, his son and heir, was a minor.[61] By 1561 Elizabeth had re-married and William had succeeded to the property.[62] At his death his brother, Thomas Darell of Hungerford (Berks.), acquired the manor, and died in 1591 leaving a son, John, as his heir.[63] John Darell (cr. baronet in 1622), of West Woodhay (Berks.), sold the manor to Sir Humphrey Forster of Aldermaston (Berks.) in 1628.[64] In 1648 Forster sold it to Henry Gooding of Henley (Berks.).[65] Henry was succeeded by his son George, who still held the property in 1700.[66] Four years later it had been acquired by Sir Charles Hedges who retained it until his death in 1714 when he was succeeded by his son William.[67] Thomas, William's eldest son, sold the manor in 1768 to Samuel Sharpe of Bath. In the following year Sharpe settled it upon his son Samuel (d. 1781), who took the additional name of Pocklington. In 1800 Samuel's eldest son Henry Sharpe Pocklington sold the manor to John Strange, of London, and in 1809 Strange sold it to James Bradford of Swindon. Two years later Ambrose Goddard, lord of the manor of Swindon (d. 1815), purchased the manor from Bradford. Thenceforth Wanborough followed the same descent as Swindon until 1931 when the Goddard lands were broken up and sold in lots.[68]

By a spurious charter dated 854 Ethelwulf, King of the West Saxons, made a grant of land to the church of St. Peter and St. Paul at Winchester, which comprised an area covered by the modern parish of Little Hinton. This included that estate later known as the manor of *EARLSCOURT* which until the 19th century was a detached part of Wanborough.[69] The property was apparently in the hands of Stigand, Bishop of Winchester (c. 1043–1053),[70] but before the Conquest came into the hands of Earl Odo.[71] In 1086 it was held by Stephen the Carpenter, one of the king's serjeants.[72] The overlordship probably descended with that of the manor

43 *Cart. Sax.* ed. Birch, ii, pp. 80–81; H. P. R. Finberg, *Early Charts. of Wessex*, p. 105. The charter is available only in a later copy but its authenticity is not in doubt.
44 *V.C.H. Wilts.* ii, p. 120.
45 *Pipe R.* 1167 (P.R.S. xi), 132.
46 *L'art de vérifier les dates* (Paris 1818, 2nd ser. xiii), 172–82; *Complete Peerage*, xi. 374–5 and App. D; *Pipe R.* 1181 (P.R.S. xxx), 97; ibid. 1183 (P.R.S. xxxii), 128; *Lewes Cartulary Supp.* (*Wilts. Portion*), (Suss. Rec. Soc.), p. 5.
47 *Pipe R.* 1195 (P.R.S. N.S. vi), 199; *Red Bk. Exch.* (Rolls Ser.), ii. 748.
48 *Red Bk. Exch.* (Rolls Ser.), ii. 482; *Rot. Lit. Claus.* (Rec. Com.), 333.
49 *V.C.H. Wilts.* vii. 128–9.
50 Ibid.
51 Ibid. ii, p. 120.
52 *Bk. of Fees*, ii. 738; B.M. Harl. Ch. 53. B. 14.
53 *Rot. Hund.* (Rec. Com.), ii. 275–6.
54 Hist. MSS. Com. *4th Rep. Magdalen Coll.* 463; *Feet of F. Wilts.* 1272–1327 (W.A.S. Rec. Brch.), 126.
55 *Cal. Inq. p.m.* vii, pp. 312–13.
56 Ibid. ix, p. 179.
57 *Feud. Aids*, vi. 531, 629; *Cal. Close*, 1405–9, 413.
58 *Feud. Aids*, v. 278; C 139/158/28.
59 E 150/967/2; *L. & P. Hen. VIII*, i (1), pp. 442, 632; *Cal. Chart. R.* 1427–1516, 278; *Cat. Anct. D.* iii, C 3638.
60 *L. & P. Hen. VIII*, ii (1), p. 281.
61 C 142/51/2; C 142/92/111; E 150/982/7; *Cal. Pat.* 1550–3, 54–55.
62 C 3/10/73; C 3/49/57.
63 C 142/230/63.
64 C.P. 25(2)/508/4 Chas. I Mich.
65 W.R.O. 130/64 Simpson deeds.
66 T. Phillipps, *Collectanea de familiis diversis . . . apud Wanborough et apud Broadway . . .*, 611.
67 See W.R.O. 529, for the whole subsequent descent.
68 See p. 120.
69 *Cart. Sax.* ed. Birch, ii, pp. 78–79; H.P.R. Finberg, *Early Charts. of Wessex*, p. 74. Although thought to be fundamentally a fabrication, the charter may embody some authentic material. See also p. 174.
70 Ibid. pp. 80–81.
71 *V.C.H. Wilts.* ii, p. 159.
72 Ibid.

of Wanborough, for it was in the hands of Geoffrey (III), Count of Perche, at the beginning of the 13th century.[73] Ela, daughter of William Longespée, lord of the main manor, acquired it by 1228–9 as part of a settlement made between herself and Humphrey de Bohun, Earl of Hereford.[74] It was held by the earl in 1275.[75] At the death of the earl's direct descendant, Humphrey, in 1372, Earlscourt formed part of the inheritance of Mary de Bohun, one of his two daughters.[76] Her marriage to Henry Bolingbroke brought the overlordship to the Duchy of Lancaster and thence to the Crown.

In 1195 Stephen of Earlscourt was holding Earlscourt when his house was burned down.[77] He was later said to hold a third part of half a hide there of the gift of Geoffrey (III), Count of Perche.[78] By 1275 the land was held by Richard of Earlscourt.[79] In 1316 it was found by inquisition that Peter Doygnel and Agnes his wife held the property, with reversion to Peter, son of Thomas le Blount. But by the time of the inquisition the Doygnels and Peter le Blount were dead, and the land had passed to John, son of Nicholas de Cotteleye.[80] For the rest of the 14th century the descent of Earlscourt is obscure. In 1372 Gilbert Spencer was tenant; by 1381 John Garton and his wife, Maud, held the land.[81] It was in the hands of John, Lord Lovel, lord of the main manor, by 1402.[82] Lovel died in 1408 and his heir John was given livery. Three years later he successfully defended his right to the property against the heirs of Sir John Roches.[83] Lovel died in 1414, leaving the manor in the hands of his mother, Maud, who died in 1423 seised of Earlscourt held as of her manor of Wanborough.[84] In 1428 Maud's grandson, William, who had succeeded to both properties, had also taken actual possession, the lands having earlier been leased to William atte Welde.[85] Earlscourt was then settled on Lovel's second son, William, who married Eleanor Morley, daughter and heir of Robert, Lord Morley.[86] Lovel was summoned to Parliament in her right as William Lovel of Morley and died in 1476.[87] His son Henry (d. 1489) left as his heir Alice, whose second husband was Edward, second son of Thomas Howard, Duke of Norfolk (d. 1554). The property seems to have come into the duke's hands, for in 1540 Thomas Hinton of Wanborough had a lease for 21 years of 'a messuage called Erlescote' from the Crown which had lately been obtained from Thomas, Duke of Norfolk.[88] Hinton died in 1567 leaving Earlscourt to his heir Anthony.[89] Anthony was succeeded in 1599 by his son Thomas. Earlscourt was settled on his son Anthony (II) on his marriage to Mary, daughter of Sir Thomas Gresham, in 1619.[90]

The Hintons seem to have left Wanborough before the middle of the 17th century, and thereafter the descent of the property is difficult to trace. William Glanville held it in 1672 when it was leased to William Lancton.[91] In 1676 the estate, comprising 280 a., passed to John Lowe.[92] Elizabeth Astley, widow, proved her right to the manor in 1716.[93] The property seems to have been divided by this time, for the manor was then said to consist of 85 a. By 1780 John (later Sir John) Croft held Earlscourt, while Thomas Liddiard held Lower Earlscourt.[94] Sir John died in 1797[95] and his estate passed to John Croft of Worle (Som.), who died in 1822.[96] His heirs were his six daughters, four of whom still retained shares in 1843.[97] James Halls Croft died possessed of the estate in 1876, and was succeeded by Margaret Elizabeth, Baroness d'Etigny. In the same year she sold it to John William Bell of Gillingham (Dors.), who in 1877 sold it to Henry Kinneir of Swindon. Kinneir also acquired Lower Earlscourt, but at his death in 1917 the property was again divided, Earlscourt passing to the tenant, D. L. Manners, and Lower Earlscourt to M. R. Haskins of Wootton Bassett.[98]

The medieval manor-house was represented in 1965 by Earlscourt Farm. In 1423 the buildings consisted of a hall, two chambers, a barn, a stable, and a sheepfold.[99] Ponds to the west of the house suggest that it once had a moat. The house of 1965 was L-shaped, mostly of stone, with a stone-tiled roof. The north end of the west wing was originally timber-framed, part of the north wall having exposed framing with ogee braces, close studding, and herring-bone brick panels. The east wing was mid 19th century except for the west end which had a staircase of c. 1700, and a mullioned and transomed window of similar date on the first floor landing. It is possible that the original timber-framed house had an east-west axis; the quality of the framing suggests a substantial house, probably of the mid 16th century. The house was stripped of oak panelling reputed to have been Jacobean[1] and an oak beam with the initials of Anthony Hinton and his wife is said to have been taken to America.[2]

The manor of *WARDENAGE* or *WARNAGE* originated in the grant of some 60 a. of land made in 1270 by Emily Longespée, widow of Stephen Longespée, lord of the manor (d. 1260), to endow the chapel of St. Katherine.[3] Further small grants were made about the same time including land at Inland within the parish.[4] The foundress's executors added lands at Ashbury (Berks.) and at 'Ordestone' (?Bishopstone) in 1280.[5] Nearly 100 a. were added by Emily's daughter, Emily Longespée, widow of Maurice

[73] *Cur. Reg. R.* iii. 183, 241, 245.
[74] *Complete Peerage*, vi. 460.
[75] *Rot. Hund.* (Rec. Com.), ii. 275.
[76] *Cal. Inq. p.m.* xiii, p. 139.
[77] *Cur. Reg. R.* 1194–5 (Pipe R. Soc. xiv), 92.
[78] *Cur. Reg. R.* iii. 183, 241, 245; iv. 27, 86; v. 288.
[79] *Rot. Hund.* (Rec. Com.), ii. 275.
[80] *Cal. Fine R.* 1356–69, 171; *Cal. Close*, 1360–4, 286; *Cal. Inq. p.m.* xi, pp. 8–9.
[81] *Cal. Inq. p.m.* xiii, p. 139; *W.A.M.* xxxix. 89.
[82] *Feud. Aids.* vi. 632.
[83] *Cal. Close*, 1409–13, 259.   [84] C 138/8/30; C 139/6/51.
[85] *Feud. Aids*, v. 278.   [86] *Cal. Close*, 1429–35, 259.
[87] *W.A.M.* xxxix. 93; *Complete Peerage*, ix. 219–22; C 139/158/28; C 140/59/73.
[88] *L. & P. Hen. VIII*, xvi, p. 723.
[89] C 142/148/3; Wards 7/11/8; C 142/257/85; Wards 2/24/217.

[90] C 142/488/95. [91] Sar. Dioc. R. O. Glebe Terrier, 1672.
[92] C.P. 43/375 rot. 53.
[93] C.P. 25(2)/1077/3 Geo. I Mich.
[94] W.R.O. Land Tax Assessments.
[95] G.E.C. *Baronetage*, iv. 50.
[96] *Gent. Mag.* 1822 (ii), 190. The descent of the property during the 19th century is based on abstracts of deeds made by the Revd. A. E. Davies, *penes* the Vicar of Wanborough, the Revd. G. P. Powell. Thanks are due to Mr. Powell for much help with this article.
[97] Tithe award *penes* the vicar.
[98] W.A.S. Libr., Devizes, Sale Cat. 1917.
[99] C 139/6/51.
[1] W.A.S. Libr., Devizes, Sale Cat. 1917.
[2] Ibid. Notebook of A. D. Passmore.
[3] Magdalen Coll. Oxford, Wanborough deeds, 66a. and see p. 184.
[4] Ibid. 31a, 48.   [5] Ibid. 65a, 70.

FitzMaurice, in 1291[6] and the next year she made a
further grant which included common in the marlpit
at Inland, the great fishpond, and all profits of her
manor courts.[7] Additions were made to the estate
in 1308[8] and in 1329 Robert of Wanborough, clerk,
had licence to grant a mill and meadow to the chapel.[9]
In 1332 the land so accumulated seems to have been
in the hands of Robert of Wanborough and after his
death by 1334 in those of his brother John.[10] This
is probably because both Robert and John were at
this time concerned with the proposal to establish a
new foundation to pray for members of the Wanborough family.[11] But by 1336 the estate together
with a messuage called 'Colne', which John of
Wanborough had inherited from his brother Robert,
was again annexed to the chapel and was in the hands
of the warden.[12]

In 1483 Francis, Viscount Lovel, conveyed the
estate with the chapel to William Waynflete, Bishop
of Winchester, and in the same year the bishop conveyed both to Magdalen College, Oxford.[13] In 1535
it was described as a manor.[14] For the next 400 years
Warnage or Wardenage was held by the college. In
1922 part of the estate, comprising Moat Farm, Kite
Hill Farm, Pond Farm, and the Lynch Farm, was
sold to the tenants farming them.[15] The rest of the
estate was sold by the college in 1946 and 1957.[16]
The chief farm-house of the estate, Warnage Farm,
probably stood on or near the site of the farm called
Underdown Farm, a 19th-century building.

The manor of *HYDES* seems to have originated
in an estate held in 1177–8 by Sewall d'Oseville.[17]
Sewall was still alive in 1210–12, when his holding
was described as ¼ knight's fee.[18] By 1242–3 he had
been succeeded by Osbert d'Oseville who held the
fee of the Earl of Salisbury.[19] This is the first mention
found of the overlordship which thenceforth
descended like that of the main manor of
Wanborough.[20]

The d'Osevilles were succeeded by the St.
Amands. Amauri de St. Amand held two carucates
in Wanborough in 1275.[21] He had died by 1286
when his lands were taken into custody for the re-
payment of debts during the minority of Amauri (II),
his heir.[22] Amauri (II) entered into the estate in
1289[23] and was succeeded in 1310 by his brother
John.[24] John died by 1330, leaving his son, Amauri
(III), a minor; during the minority the lands were
farmed by the Crown.[25] In 1362 Amauri (III)
leased his estate to John atte Hyde and Alice his wife
for their lives; and his son, Amauri (IV), confirmed
the leases in 1380.[26] Hyde must have acquired the

estate soon after this, for he was holding it directly
of the Duchy of Lancaster, the overlords, in 1401–2
and still did so in 1428.[27] By 1485 it had passed to
Francis, Lord Lovel, lord of the main manor, and
was forfeited on his attainder.[28] It then descended
with the main manor to the Darells. It formed part
of the jointure of Elizabeth Darell whose husband,
Edward, died in 1549.[29] She leased the site of the
manor for her life to Anthony Disney, who in turn
leased most of the property to Thomas Essex of
Chelvey (Berks.).[30] When Elizabeth's son William
came of age in 1561 the manor passed to him and
became merged in the main manor.[31]

The land attached to the church of Wanborough
was acquired by Amesbury Priory when it appropriated the church in the later 13th century.[32] In 1315
the convent took £29 for corn and beans from this
estate and a further sum for wool.[33] In 1341 there
were 2 virgates of land in demesne and land and
other profits were valued for taxation at £8 12s. 2d.[34]
After the Dissolution the rectorial estate, valued
at £19, passed in 1541 to the newly constituted Dean and Chapter of Winchester.[35] Since
1523 it had been in the hands of Anthony Fetiplace
on a lease for 61 years and probably continued to be
leased out by the chapter.[36] In 1639 Henry Hedges
became tenant for 21 years.[37] In 1651 the Trustees
for the Sale of Church Property sold the rectory
house and 4½ oxgangs of land to John Stanton of
London.[38] The chapter recovered the property at
the Restoration and continued to lease it out during
the rest of the century.[39] Sir Charles Hedges, lord
of the main manor at the beginning of the 18th
century, was among the lessees.[40] By 1780 Samuel
Pocklington, also lord of the manor, was leasing
parts of the property known as Parsonage Farm,
Lotmead Farm, and part of Nythe Farm. Ambrose
Goddard was occupying these farms by 1783 and
the rest of the property known as Plain Farm came
into Goddard's hands by 1817.[41] Goddard's grandson, who was also lord of the main manor, became
tenant of most of this in 1857 and bought the
reversion of the tenancy in 1859.[42] Lotmead Farm
was retained by the chapter and was subsequently
transferred to the Church Commissioners.[43]

The rectory house in 1649 consisted of a hall, a
parlour, 2 kitchens, 2 butteries, a dairy house, and
8 chambers. Outbuildings included a barn, stable,
and carthouse.[44] This may already have become the
residence of the vicar, and is likely to be the
'mansion house' described in 1672 in similar
terms.[45] The property also included a small tene-

[6] *Wilts. Inq. p.m.* 1242–1326 (Index Libr.), 186–7.
[7] Magdalen Coll. Oxford, Wanborough deeds, 34.
[8] Ibid. 7a.
[9] Ibid. 1, 3, 29.
[10] Ibid. 26, 30, 63a.
[11] See p. 184.
[12] Magdalen Coll. Oxford, Wanborough deeds, 26.
[13] Ibid. 15, 74a.
[14] *Valor. Eccl.* (Rec. Com.), ii. 278.
[15] Ex inf. the Estates Bursar, Magdalen Coll.
[16] Ibid.
[17] *Pipe R.* 1178 (P.R.S. xxvii), 31.
[18] *Red Bk. Exch.* (Rolls Ser.), ii. 482.
[19] Ibid. 720.
[20] See p. 176.
[21] *Rot. Hund.* (Rec. Com.), ii. 275.
[22] *Cal. Pat.* 1281–92, 221.
[23] *Cal. Inq. p.m.* ii, pp. 351, 454.
[24] Ibid. v. pp. 148–9.
[25] *Cal. Fine R.* 1327–37, 251.

[26] *Cal. Close,* 1377–81, 351.
[27] *Feud. Aids,* v. 278; vi. 539, 629.
[28] *Complete Peerage,* viii. 225. [29] See p. 176.
[30] C 3/60/30; *Cat. Anct. D.* vi, C 6975.
[31] See p. 176. [32] See p. 182.
[33] Archives M. et L. Angers, Amesbury receivers' accts.
1315.
[34] *Inq. Non.* (Rec. Com.), 163.
[35] *L. & P. Hen. VIII,* xvi, p. 723. [36] See p. 182.
[37] *W.A.M.* xli. 29–31.
[38] C 54/3618 m. 6.
[39] *Docs. rel. to Winchester Chapter, 1636–83* (Hants
Rec. Soc. ii), 185.
[40] Hants R.O. 11M59/286627–8, Ch. Commrs. deeds.
[41] W.R.O. Land Tax Assessments; Hants R.O. 11M59/
59594, Ch. Commrs. deeds.
[42] Hants R.O. 11M59/286627–8, Ch. Commrs. deeds.
[43] Ibid. 11M59/286971.
[44] *W.A.M.* xli. 29–31.
[45] Sar. Dioc. R.O. Glebe Terrier, 1672.

ment known as Lynges House near the churchyard. Both existed in 1705.[46] The house to the east of the church, called Parsonage Farm in 1966, appears to be a square stone house of the early 18th century. It was probably refronted in brick about 100 years later. Traces of timber-framing in the walls suggest that it may be the house referred to in the 17th century subsequently thoroughly remodelled.

Rotrou, Count of Perche, gave a hide of land to Lewes Priory in 1135.[47] The grant was confirmed several times during the next 25 years.[48] In 1210 the monks drew rents from the land worth £1,[49] but there is no trace of the property in the 1535 valuation of their lands. The land was demised by the tenant, Robert son of Roger, in 1169 as security for a loan.[50]

A small estate granted by Geoffrey (III), Count of Perche, was confirmed to the canons of Bradenstoke in 1207, and consisted of 7s. rent.[51] Sewall d'Oseville gave the canons a load of grain every Michaelmas.[52] The rents were assessed at 19s. in 1535.[53] Stephen Longespée gave to Lacock Abbey 2 a. of his meadow in 'Niweham' c. 1232.[54] This was granted to John Goddard of Aldbourne in 1540.[55] In 1545 New College, Oxford, held the farm of certain lands in the parish.[56] Clement Harding gave some land there to the college, of which he was a Fellow, in 1507.[57] In 1738 the college leased Knight Moor or Knight's Meadow to Pleydell Goddard.[58]

ECONOMIC HISTORY. Even though the charter of King Ethelwulf to Winchester Cathedral in 854 may not be genuine, it seems likely that Winchester had an estate in Wanborough in the 9th century and that it comprised 20 hides.[59] By 1086 this had been divided, Wanborough then having 19 hides and Earlscourt a hide and a virgate. Nearly half of Wanborough was then demesne and there was land for 10 ploughs, three of which were on the demesne with 6 serfs. Nineteen villeins and 13 bordars had 5 ploughs. There were 40 a. of meadow, pasture measuring half a league long and 15 furlongs broad, and a mill. Earlscourt had land for 2 ploughs and there were 30 a. of meadow and 8 a. of pasture.[60]

The terrain of the northern half of the parish was not particularly well suited to open-field farming, and the comparatively small areas between the marsh lands were inclosed into 'crofts' for pasturage by the beginning of the 14th century.[61] 'Papwellescroft'

and 'Balicroft' occur by 1374.[62] Of the common fields East and West Fields are mentioned in 1270,[63] both of which lay in the south of the parish, and at the same date there was a meadow, probably common, known as 'Cotsettlemede'.[64] Beyond their existence little else is known of the fields during the Middle Ages.

The nuns of Amesbury, who held the rectory, were letting their demesne to farm by 1316[65] and probably continued to lease it until the dissolution of the house. Their successors, the Dean and Chapter of Winchester, certainly did so.[66] The demesne of Warnage was leased by 1545, and had probably been so since Magdalen College acquired the property in 1483.[67] There was very little demesne on St. Amand's manor, most of the property being in the hands of a number of free tenants by 1310.[68]

A feature of the economy in the late 14th century is the emergence of substantial tenants. The family of FitzWilliam, traceable in the parish from as early as 1318,[69] was clearly of some standing[70] and their status required a stone effigy in the church.[71] The family of Coventry, in existence by 1292,[72] seems to have acquired part of the manor of Hydes by marriage[73] and by 1439 Thomas Coventry was described as a gentleman when he stood surety for the keepers of Clatford Priory.[74] The family remained in the village until the 19th century.[75] The Poltons of Hall Place were also, evidently, a family of importance.[76] By the 16th century the family of Brind provided substantial tenants in the parish, Thomas Brind (d. 1559) standing second only to Thomas Hinton of Earlscourt in contributions to the Benevolence of 1545.[77] Brind was the largest tenant of the main manor by 1547, paying a total rent of nearly £9 for freehold and copyhold properties, amounting to more than a quarter of the total revenue.[78] By 1559 he was farming the Warnage manor and his son succeeded him.[79] Thomas Brind the younger headed the subsidy list of 1576 with an assessment of over £11, followed by Anthony Brind with over £8.[80] The name of Brind continued in Wanborough until 1932.[81]

By the second decade of the 17th century a clearer picture of the agricultural activities in the parish can be obtained from a detailed survey of the main manor.[82] There were 15 fields of varying size: the field next Liddington, West Middle Field,

[46] Ibid. Glebe Terrier, 1705.
[47] *Lewes Cartulary Supp.* (Wilts. Portion), (Suss. Rec. Soc.), p. 25.
[48] Ibid. pp. 30, 31; *Cal. Doc. France*, ed. Round, p. 509.
[49] *Interdict Doc.* (P.R.S. n.s. xxxiv), 18, 29.
[50] *Lewes Cartulary Supp.* (Wilts. Portion), (Suss. Rec. Soc.), p. 5.
[51] *Rot. Chart.* (Rec. Com.), 169.
[52] *V.C.H. Wilts.* iii. 280.
[53] *Valor Eccl.* (Rec. Com.), ii. 123.
[54] Lacock Abbey MSS. Older Cartulary, f. 25; Newer Cartulary, f. 86v; ex inf. Mr. K. H. Rogers.
[55] *L. & P. Hen. VIII*, xv, pp. 293, 296.
[56] *Valor Eccl.* (Rec. Com.), ii. 258.
[57] Aubrey, *Topog. Coll.* ed. Jackson, 196.
[58] Swindon Pub. Libr., Goddard MS. 615.
[59] *V.C.H. Wilts.* ii, p. 85.   [60] Ibid. pp. 120, 159, 206–7.
[61] *Wilts. Inq. p.m.* 1242–1326 (Index Libr.), 380.
[62] *Cal. Close*, 1374–7, 100.
[63] Magdalen Coll. Oxford, Wanborough deeds, 18–19.
[64] Ibid. The name was retained as Cossical or Cotsettle Marsh.
[65] Archives M. et L. Angers, Amesbury receivers' accts. 1316.

[66] See p. 182.
[67] *Valor Eccl.* (Rec. Com.), ii. 278; see p. 178.
[68] *Wilts. Inq. p.m.* 1242–1326 (Index Libr.), 380.
[69] Magdalen Coll. Oxford, Wanborough deeds, 8a.
[70] *Cal. Close*, 1374–7, 100; Aubrey, *Topog. Coll.* ed Jackson, 195, 199.
[71] Aubrey, *Topog. Coll.* ed. Jackson, 198.
[72] Magdalen Coll. Oxford, Wanborough deeds, 34.
[73] *Cal. Close*, 1413–19, 354.
[74] *Cal. Fine R.* 1437–45, 115–16.
[75] MSS. Notes by the Revd. A. E. Davies *penes* the Vicar of Wanborough, the Revd. G. P. Powell.
[76] Aubrey, *Topog. Coll.* ed. Jackson, 200–1.
[77] *Taxation Lists* (W.A.S. Rec. Brch.), 22. The Brinds also had property outside the parish: Aubrey, *Topog. Coll.* ed. Jackson, 195.
[78] S.C. 12/1/35.
[79] Magdalen Coll. Oxford, Estates Bursary, General Court Bk. (unpaginated).
[80] *Taxation Lists* (W.A.S. Rec. Brch.), 104.
[81] MSS. of the Revd. A. E. Davies (see n. 75 above).
[82] W.A.S. Libr., Devizes, Smith Papers. The survey is wrongly dated 1720; it must have been made between 1622 and 1628.

Middle Field, and the field next Hinton were the largest, the first three being over 200 a. in extent. Ham Field, Cornmarsh Field, and West Berrycroft were smaller, with some 50 a. each, and smaller still were, for example, Binnland and Hitchen with about 40 a. Even the smallest were divided into strips. West Middle Field, with over 250 a., had at least 370 separate holdings, held by 23 leaseholders and 19 copyholders. Thomas Brind held 18 parcels in this field all on lease, comprising 13½ a. In Binnland and Hitchen together there were at least 29 holdings divided into 77 parcels, and in West Berrycroft 32 holdings in 131 parcels, together with a plot for the hayward. Leaseholds predominated over copyholds save in Swanhill Mead.

Land in the Nythe at the northern end of the parish, and elsewhere, was by this time held by a syndicate of tenants and known as the Great Bargain. The property included meadow land at the Nythe and other lands in the Breach, Cornmarsh, the Hide Field, stretching above the village, and also in the East and West Fields.[83] There were at least 18 joint tenants by 1628 although it is not clear how many divisions originally existed. The holder of each part was entitled to one lot in the meadow (hence Lotmead), five common leases on the east side of the parish, sheep commons, and common on the lord's down.[84] These lots were gradually consolidated[85] and in 1712 half were united in one hand.[86]

The progress of inclosure is difficult to trace, though at least three open fields were certainly still in existence in 1712.[87] The inclosure award of 1779[88] concerned only the commons and wastes and therefore indicates only the final stage of the process. Consolidation of holdings is reflected in the emergence of individual farms: Cally Farm occurs in 1692,[89] Hill and Parsonage Farms by 1780, Nythe Farm by 1783, and Plain Farm by 1817.[90] Between 1780 and 1815 Ambrose Goddard[91] carried through a piecemeal acquisition of property in the parish. Beginning with parts of Hill Farm and the Nythe in 1780 he acquired, by purchase or tenancy, Cossicle Marsh and Parsonage Farms by 1786, Hill Farm completely by 1790, the farm by the warren by 1798, and Plain Farm by 1817.[92] Much of this had formerly been in the hands of the Pocklingtons, lords of the manor until 1800; Goddard acquired the lordship in 1815.[93] Most of these farms lay on the arable land to the south of the village; holdings in the north, mostly grass farms, continued to be small. The Magdalen College estate, which was offered for sale in 1922 but not finally sold until 1957, consisted of seven farms, the largest of 75 a., besides a number of much smaller units.[94] In 1873

369 a. of this estate were held on a beneficial lease and 272 a. by copyhold.[95]

Little can be said of the details of agriculture beyond the rearing of sheep, memory of large flocks on the downland persisting to the present century.[96] Sheep were evidently kept in some numbers by the earlier 13th century.[97] Pasture for 100 sheep was given to the warden of St. Katherine's chapel in 1291 and it is likely that the donor retained twice as much.[98] They were still an important part of the economy in the 16th century and at shearing time four tellers were required to number them.[99] One individual, Thomas Brind, claimed to have feeding in common and pasture for 252 sheep on the lord's down, a claim challenged by the lord of the manor.[1] On his death in 1559 Brind had over 200 sheep 'on the East Field on the Hill'.[2] Each shareholder in the Great Bargain had 54 sheep commons as well as a share in the lord's down.[3] References to shepherds are frequently found in the parish registers, including one to Thomas Horne who was described at his death in 1643 as 'a rich old man'.[4] In 1692 Alexander Popham was said to have 500 beasts in the parish and Mrs. Mary Hipsley 300, almost certainly sheep,[5] but a plaintive memorandum in the register of baptisms under the year 1729 suggests that sheep were then a declining interest. The vicar noted that there were about 364 'east side common leases' and that one hundred or more were every year stocked with cattle from other parishes which therefore yielded nothing to the parson 'either by plough or pail'. By this time the village seems to have had more pasturage than was required.

Wanborough's position on the Ridgeway may perhaps in part explain the cattle from outside the parish. In the early 20th century cattle and sheep droves were still remembered, about 800 cattle passing through every week.[6] An annual cattle fair was then held in the village.[7] Cottage industries, however, were still concerned with wool, though it was sent to Oxfordshire to be dyed, brought back to be woven, and sent away again for milling. Straw plaiting, blanket and carpet weaving, and soap and candle making were also practised on a small scale.[8] John Smith (1722–94) and his sons John (1751–1815), and Thomas, were soap boilers and tallow chandlers, and in their premises at Kite Hill the first meeting of Methodists took place in the village.[9] Thomas Honeybone (d. 1796), clockmaker, lived and worked in the parish, having a house in the Marsh.[10]

In 1252 Stephen Longespée was granted a fair on Whit Monday and for the two days following.[11] By 1798 a fair was held on 4 September.[12] This was usually followed by revels, back-sword play, and

[83] W.R.O. 130/31B, Wanborough deeds, 1712–61.
[84] W.A.S. Libr., Devizes, Smith Papers, Survey of Wanborough.
[85] W.R.O. 201/21, Release, Boult to Goodinge.
[86] Ibid. 130/31B, Wanborough deeds, 1712–61.
[87] Ibid.
[88] Ibid. Inclosure Award.
[89] Ibid. 212B/Wan. 9, Land Tax.
[90] Ibid. Land Tax Assessments.
[91] See pp. 120, 176.
[92] W.R.O. Land Tax Assessments
[93] See p. 176.
[94] W.A.S. Libr., Devizes, Sale Cat. 1922.
[95] Ibid. 1873.
[96] Alfred Williams, *Villages of the White Horse*, 154.
[97] Magdalen Coll. Oxford, Wanborough deeds, 42a.
[98] *Wilts. Inq. p.m.* 1242–1326 (Index Libr.), 186–7.
[99] S.C. 2/209/66.
[1] C 1/1212/19.
[2] Magdalen Coll. Oxford, Estates Bursary, General Court Bk.
[3] W.A.S. Libr., Devizes, Smith Papers, Survey of Wanborough.
[4] Parish Reg. Bur. 1643, *penes* the Vicar of Wanborough.
[5] W.R.O. 212B/Wan. 9, Land Tax.
[6] Williams, *Villages of the White Horse*, 153.
[7] Ibid.   [8] Ibid. 148.
[9] See p. 185.
[10] *W.A.M.* l. 92; W.A.S. Libr., Devizes, A. D. Passmore's Notebook.
[11] *Cal. Chart. R.* 1226–57, 386.
[12] *Univ. Brit. Dir.* v. 206.

performances by the village band.[13] At mowing time a celebration was held at Lotmead when the lord of the manor wore garlands of flowers and the mowers were given beef and garlic. By the 17th century horse-racing was also included in the festivities.[14] Dobbin Sunday, when the village charities were paid out, was also an occasion for celebrations.[15]

In 1086 the mill at Wanborough was worth 5s.[16] A mill-pool was mentioned in 1292.[17] William atte More proved his right to a mill and other property in 1305 against Richard Costard, but the latter subsequently regained possession.[18] The estate of Amauri de St. Amand in 1310 included a water-mill held by Ellis Bede and a windmill.[19] In 1318 Bede's son, John, gave the mill to his sister, who released it to John FitzWilliam of 'Bydemylle' as security.[20] In 1321 it came into the hands of Robert of Wanborough, who gave it in 1329 to the warden of St. Katherine's chapel.[21] This mill was near the chapel, between the mill-pool mentioned in 1292 and the great fishpond which it fed, the water then flowing into the moat around the Longespée manor house.[22] In 1363 Henry Podyfat granted two mills on lease to John Coventry, and the property remained in the Coventry family until 1502.[23] John Yate, who then acquired part of the mill, was still in possession in 1509; Thomas Yate sold a mill and a fishery to Thomas Brind in 1549 for £340.[24] The Brind family retained their interest until 1577, when it passed to Alexander Staples, and then to Thomas Fisher.[25] The mill, together with lands in Liddington, passed through several hands during the later years of the 17th century, and in 1731 was sold to William Stanley for £400.[26] The property consisted of a mill-house, a water grist-mill and mill-bank, and a little orchard by the close called Court Close, and two closes called Mill Closes. By his will dated 1743 Stanley declared that Edward Stanley could have the mill if he wished at the price of £400.[27] Thomas Robins (d. 1760), miller at Wanborough, received the commendation on his tombstone:

> God works his wonders now and then,
> Here lies a miller, an honest man . . .

The succession of millers ended with the death of Herbert Reynolds in 1876.[28]

LOCAL GOVERNMENT. Court rolls of the manor of Wanborough survive for 1564–6, 1571, and 1585,[29] and there is a printed edition of rolls for 1649–76,

1690–6, 1700–6.[30] During the 16th century courts seem to have been held four times a year, alternately courts baron and views of frankpledge, and these were presided over by a steward. The officers of the court consisted of a bailiff, a constable, a tithingman, and a hayward, together with two assessors of fines. By the later 17th century courts baron and views of frankpledge were usually combined and were held, for the most part, annually. By 1650[31] a carner ('carnerius') and ale-taster was regularly appointed in the court and continued, like the other officers, at least until the beginning of the 18th century. Encroachments, strays, the maintenance of ditches and hedges, the admission of tenants, probate, and petty infractions of the peace provided the main business of the courts in the 16th century. Later, tenancy business became less important, while more detailed control was maintained over the exercise of common rights.

Magdalen College, Oxford, held a court baron for their manor of Warnage at their pleasure.[32] Records of the court have survived in general court books for 1536, 1549–63, 1611, 1659–69, 1682–91, 1703–15, 1727–43, and 1764–77.[33] The court, under a steward, was held annually during the 16th century, irregularly during the 17th, and biennially during the eighteenth. Special courts might be summoned at other times to take surrenders. Business consisted principally of tenancy changes and the levy of entry fines and heriots. Wills and administrations were occasionally dealt with and inventories taken. Only occasional orders were recorded for making improvements or dealing with encroachments. No manorial officers were appointed.

Two surveyors of ways were employed by the vestry by 1611, and ten years later these were responsible for the east and west sides of the parish respectively.[34] By 1736 their number had increased to four.[35] In 1721 a man agreed in the vestry to maintain and repair a number of gates, a stile, and a bridge in the parish.[36] By 1735 the vestry had appointed two overseers of the poor.[37] Others were sometimes added for particular areas: in 1745 the two overseers were aided by three others for Hydes, Foxbridge, and college lands.[38] By 1788 there was a poorhouse in the village at a place unknown, under the charge of the parish officers.[39] Between 1816 and 1824 expenditure on the poor varied between £723 in the former year and £1,965 in 1819.[40] The average expenditure for 1833–5 was £1,097.[41]

CHURCH. The church of Wanborough with its

13 Williams, *Villages of the White Horse*, 154.
14 Ibid.; Aubrey, *Topog. Coll.* ed. Jackson, 198.
15 Williams, *Villages of the White Horse*, 155. Dobbin is an old Wiltshire word for a small loaf, see p. 186.
16 *V.C.H. Wilts.* ii, p. 120.
17 Magdalen Coll. Oxford, Wanborough deeds, 34.
18 *Feet of F. Wilts.* 1272–1327 (W.A.S. Rec. Brch.), 53, 58.
19 *Cal. Inq. p.m.* v, p. 149. William le Wyndmuleward of Wanborough was hanged in 1334 for stealing wax from the church (J.I. 3/120 m. 5). Windmill Post occurs in 1592 (Par. Reg. Bur.).
20 Magdalen Coll. Oxford, Wanborough deeds, 8a, 27a.
21 Ibid. 10a, 23a, 24a.   22 See p. 184.
23 C.P. 25(1)/255/50/27; C.P. 25(1)/256/57/21; C.P.25(1)/256/66/32.
24 C.P. 25(2)/65/532/3 Edw. VI Mich.
25 C.P. 25(2)/81/695/4 & 5 Phil. & Mary; C.P. 25(2)/239/1 Eliz. 1 East.; C.P. 25(2)/240/19 Eliz. 1 Hil.; Req. 2/206/70; C 142/258/139.

26 C.P. 25(2)/803/1 Jas. II Mich.; C.P. 25(2)/889/8 Wm. III Trin; C.P. 25(2)/980/10 Anne Hil.; W.R.O. 130/31B, Wanborough deeds, 1712–61.
27 W.R.O. 130/31B, Wanborough deeds, 1712–61.
28 Par. Regs.
29 S.C. 2/209/66–67; S.C. 2/214/74.
30 Phillipps, *Collectanea (Wanborough)*, 501–90, 601–60.
31 Ibid. 505.
32 Magdalen Coll. Oxford, Estates Bursary, Customs of Wanborough.
33 Ibid. Liber Curiarum (1536) and General Court Bks.
34 Phillipps, *Collectanea (Wanborough)*, 825, 827.
35 Ibid. 832.   36 Ibid. 659.
37 Ibid. 832.   38 Ibid.
39 W.R.O. Land Tax Assessments.
40 *App. Rep. Sel. Cttee. Poor Rate Retns.* H.C. 556, p. 188 (1822), v.
41 *App. 1st Rep. Commrs. Poor Law Amendment Act*, H.C. 500, p. 559 (1835), xxxv.

tithes and some land attached to it was among those granted by St. Osmund to Salisbury Chapter in 1091.[42] It was still held by the chapter in 1146, but apparently not in 1158.[43] The advowson was presumably included in the grant of the church to the chapter but its descent over the next 200 years is obscure. It may have passed to the overlords of the main manor of Wanborough, the counts of Perche, and from them to the Cluniacs of Nogent-le-Rotrou (Eure-et-Loir), for whom the counts had a special devotion.[44] It was not among the possessions of that house confirmed in a bull of 1182,[45] but in 1290 the Prioress of Amesbury asserted that Nogent-le-Rotrou had held the advowson of Wanborough for 100 years and had then granted it to her.[46] She was at the time claiming it against the lord of the manor, Stephen Longespée, who had, she alleged, wrongfully presented to the church some years earlier.[47] Six years later, however, in 1296 it seems to have been established that the advowson belonged to the overlords of Wanborough, for that year the Earl and Countess of Lincoln conveyed it to Amesbury Priory.[48] The rectory was probably appropriated by the priory shortly after this.[49] In 1305 the abbey of Fontevrault, the mother house of Amesbury, unsuccessfully claimed to present a vicar to the church.[50] Amesbury continued to present until the Dissolution, although in 1523 the convent leased the advowson with the rectory to Anthony Fetiplace for 61 years.[51] After the Dissolution rectory and advowson were granted in 1541 to the Dean and Chapter of Winchester.[52] John Snowe of Wilcot and Ellis Wyn of Winchester presented in 1543 and 1551 respectively, probably as farmers of the rectory.[53] In 1639, however, the lease of the rectory estate to Henry Hedges expressly excluded the right of presentation.[54] The queen was patron by lapse in 1583.[55] The chapter continued as patrons until 1908 when they transferred their rights to the Lord Chancellor.[56]

In 1291 the appropriated rectory was valued for taxation at £20[57] and it was reckoned to be worth the same in 1535.[58] At the later date payments of 5s. 5d. to the lord of the manor and 20s. to the Vicar of Wanborough were charged upon it. In 1341 a ninth of the value of corn, wool, and lambs was reckoned to be £15.[59] The tithe of certain meadows valued at £6 6s. 8d. also belonged to the rectors at this date. During the 16th and 17th centuries the great tithes were leased by the lessees of the rectory estate. In 1649 the tithes due to the

farmer of the estate were valued at £135 12s. 6d. and comprised all the great tithes in the parish except those from Earlscourt and Hide Field, which belonged to the vicar.[60] All the rectorial tithes were extinguished by the Inclosure Act of 1779 when land was allotted to the appropriators in their stead.[61]

Some land was already attached to the church when it was granted to Salisbury Chapter in 1091.[62] In 1341, by which date the church had been appropriated by Amesbury Priory, it was reckoned that the rectorial estate with all its profits was worth £8 12s. 2d.[63] In 1649 it comprised 69 a. of arable, 11 a. of pasture, a rectory house and farm buildings, 2 cottages, and grazing for 23 cows or horses. It was valued at £180 but was charged with certain payments totalling £23.[64] An account of the descent of this property is given above.[65]

In 1291 the vicarage was valued at £5.[66] In 1535 its value, which lay in land, tithes, a payment of 20s. from the rector, and other emoluments, was reckoned to be £21 10s. 6d. net.[67] It was valued at £100 in 1649[68] and in 1835 the average net income of the benefice was £375.[69] By 1649 besides the lesser tithes, the vicar had the great tithes of Earlscourt and Hide Field[70] and by 1672 he also had the great tithes from a few other scattered fields.[71] All the vicarial tithes, except the great tithes from Earlscourt and Hide Field, were extinguished by the Inclosure Act of 1779 when land was given as compensation.[72] The tithes from Earlscourt and Hide Field were commuted for a rent-charge of £25 2s. 9d. in 1843.[73]

Most of the vicar's glebe in 1672 lay in East Field and amounted to over 30 a.[74] By 1887 the acreage had increased to 84 a.[75] Further additions were made before 1912, principally by the purchase of Mount Pleasant Farm in Little Hinton.[76] In 1925 the Ecclesiastical Commissioners purchased 165 a. of glebe for £4,050.[77]

In 1668 it was said that a former vicar had allowed the vicarage house to fall into disrepair and had added to it without licence from the bishop.[78] The house was said to be in good repair in 1686.[79] In 1812 the curate was living in the vicarage house which was described as 'new and small'.[80] The vicarage house of 1966, built in part of the grounds of the early-19th-century house, was designed by Oswald Brakspear and erected in 1959.[81]

At a visitation in 1584 the minister was reported for not wearing a surplice.[82] Two years later the

[42] Reg. St. Osmund (Rolls Ser.), i. 199; V.C.H. Wilts. iii. 157.
[43] V.C.H. Wilts. iii. 159 and n. 43.
[44] W.A.M. xxxv. 95.
[45] Chart. of Nogent-le-Rotrou, ed. C. Metais, 226–31.
[46] W. Prynne, Supreme Eccl. Jurisdiction, iii. 438.
[47] Ibid.
[48] Feet of F. Wilts. 1272–1327 (W.A.S. Rec. Brch.), 42.
[49] V.C.H. Wilts. iii. 250.
[50] Phillipps, Wilts. Inst. i. 6.
[51] Doc. rel. to Winchester Chapter, 1541–7 (Hants Rec. Soc.), 101.
[52] Ibid. 73; L. & P. Hen. VIII, xvi, p. 147.
[53] Phillipps, Wilts. Inst. i. 210, 215.
[54] W.A.M. xli. 29–31.
[55] Phillipps, op. cit. 231.
[56] Lond. Gaz. 6 Oct. 1908 (p. 7203).
[57] Tax. Eccl. (Rec. Com.), 190.
[58] Valor Eccl. (Rec. Com.), ii. 94.
[59] Inq. Non. (Rec. Com.), 163.
[60] W.A.M. xli. 29–31.

[61] Wanborough Incl. Act, 19 Geo. III, c. 75 (priv. act).
[62] Reg. St. Osmund (Rolls Ser.), i. 199.
[63] Inq. Non. (Rec. Com.), 163.
[64] W.A.M. xli, 29–31.
[65] See p. 178.
[66] Tax. Eccl. (Rec. Com.), 190.
[67] Valor Eccl. (Rec. Com.), ii. 126.
[68] W.A.M. xli. 29–31.
[69] Rep. Com. Eccl. Revenues, H.C. 54, p. 852 (1835), xxii.
[70] W.A.M. xli. 29–31.
[71] Sar. Dioc. R.O. Glebe Terrier, 1672.
[72] Wanborough Incl. Act, 19 Geo. III, c. 75 (priv. act).
[73] Tithe Award, penes the vicar.
[74] Sar. Dioc. R.O. Glebe Terrier, 1672.
[75] Retn. of Glebe, H.C. 307, p. 66 (1887), lxiv.
[76] Abstract of Title, penes the vicar.
[77] Ex inf. Principal Officer, Ch. Com.
[78] Sar. Dioc. R.O. Chwdns.' Pres. 1668.
[79] Ibid. 1686.
[80] W.A.M. xli. 136.
[81] Ex inf. the vicar.
[82] Sar. Dioc. R.O. Ep. Vis. 1584, f. 21.

SWINDON OLD TOWN: HIGH STREET LOOKING SOUTH IN 1942
The Goddard Arms Hotel is on the left

WANBOROUGH: CHURCH OF ST. ANDREW IN 1810

offence was again noted.[83] Not until 1595 apparently was the fault remedied when the churchwardens paid 10s. to the incumbent of Little Hinton for a surplice.[84] In 1668 the churchwardens presented themselves for failing to provide a Book of Homilies and a Book of Canons.[85] The homilies were still wanting in 1674.[86] Preachers at the church in 1686 were said to be so well known that it was unnecessary to keep a register of their names and licences. The vicar at the time was resident and had a curate. The parishioners attended well on Sundays and other days, as commanded by law, but not on saints' days. Most behaved with decency during service except two or three old men who, in cold weather, wore their hats during the sermon.[87] A century later services were held on Sunday mornings and afternoons and prayers were said on Wednesdays and Fridays before Sacrament Sundays. Communion was celebrated five times a year when 20 or 30 people attended. The church was then served by a curate who lived in Swindon; the vicar lived at Chiddeston (Hants).[88] In 1812 the church was served by a resident curate who also served the church of Little Hinton. Services were then held only once on Sundays in winter, but twice in summer.[89] Some 30 persons attended Communion four times a year. By 1851 services were held on Sunday mornings and afternoons, and on Census Sunday that year 180 people were present in the morning and 200 in the afternoon.[90]

In the 15th century there was a chantry with a priest at the altar of St. Mary in the church. In 1434 Nicholas Palmer and Agnes his wife released the advowson of this to Sir Walter Hungerford and others.[91] Churchwardens' accounts for 1530–1640 and 1735–68 survived until the 19th century and were transcribed.[92] They include information about various lights in the church which were supported either by alms or property. In c. 1541–2 All Souls light was endowed with 4s., 2 sheep, and a lamb.[93] Somewhat later Our Lady's light had, besides a small sum of money, the income from a few sheep and a cow.[94] By 1566 the churchwardens were responsible for a church house which was let for 6s. 8d.[95] and from 1591 they accounted regularly for the Whitsun church ale.[96]

The church of ST. ANDREW occupies a commanding position at Upper Wanborough, the ground falling away steeply to the south and west. It is built largely of local chalk-stone and consists of a chancel with a vestry to the north of it, an aisled nave, north and south porches, and a west tower. It possesses some of the features of a cruciform plan, having an extra bay between nave and chancel, divided from both by transverse arches. Above this bay or 'crossing' rises a slender hexagonal tower with a stone spire. Flanking the crossing are small 'transepts', which are divided from the aisles by arches but do not project beyond their outer walls. The south

transept contains an original piscina and is now used as a chapel with a modern dedication to St. Katherine. Above the crossing small additional arches to north and south help to provide a square support for the tower. Both tower and spire have windows on each face, giving light to the area below. All this work dates from the 14th century when the rest of the nave, which is of four bays, was also rebuilt. It is possible that the curious arrangement between nave and chancel perpetuates the plan of an earlier cruciform church. The only survivals from the earlier building are the Norman font and some re-used stones in the walls of the nave. It has been suggested that the north doorway of the nave, with its elaborate 14th-century carving to arch and jambs, was brought from the former chapel of St. Katherine at Wanborough.[97]

The chancel, the north porch, and the embattled west tower of three stages were built in the 15th century. A brass plate on the tower records that it was begun in 1435, mentioning Thomas Polton, his wife Edith, and others as benefactors. Various legendary explanations have been given for the existence of two towers to the church, one at each end of the nave. It was not uncommon, however, for imposing west towers to be added to parish churches in the 15th century, largely in order to accommodate the number of bells then thought necessary.[98] In the case of Wanborough the earlier and smaller tower may have continued to house the sanctus bell. The present chancel is of later-15th-century date and it is possible that a rebuilding of the nave in the same style, involving the demolition of the central tower, was contemplated but never carried out. At some period after the west tower was in existence the nave roof was given a lower pitch;[99] it may have been at this time that a shallow clerestory was added. The clerestory no longer contains windows although one window on the north side survived into the 19th century.[1]

A restoration of the church was carried out in 1887 during which internal whitewash and plaster were removed, revealing 15th-century wall paintings;[2] one of these, depicting the Entry into Jerusalem, has been preserved on the north wall of the nave. Monuments in the church include a brass with figures of Thomas Polton and his wife Edith (both d. 1418) and a mural tablet with a long inscription which probably commemorates Anthony Hinton (d. 1598).[3] A tablet in the vestry is in memory of Thomas Gray (d. 1725). Housed in the south porch are two incomplete stone effigies of the 14th century. A painted notice in the north porch requests all 'females' to take off their pattens on entering the church.

In 1370 the church possessed a portas, a psalter, and a corporal which had recently been stolen by a former servant of the vicar.[4] The king's commissioners took 17 oz. of plate in 1553 and left a chalice

[83] Ibid. 1586, f. 42v.
[84] Phillipps, Collectanea, 823.
[85] Sar. Dioc. R.O. Chwdns'. Pres. 1668.
[86] Ibid. 1674.   [87] Ibid.
[88] Ibid. Vis. Queries, 1783.
[89] W.A.M. xli. 136.
[90] H.O. 129/250/2/3/5.   [91] C.P. 25(1)/257/62/29.
[92] Phillipps, Collectanea, 819–33.
[93] Ibid. 820.   [94] Ibid.
[95] Ibid. 822.
[96] Ibid. 821.

[97] Guide to church. For St. Katherine's chapel see below.
[98] A similar arrangement is found at Purton where a 14th-century central tower survived the building of a west tower in the 15th century.
[99] The line of the steeper roof is visible on the east face of the tower.
[1] Watercolour of 1810 by John Buckler in W.A.S. Libr., Devizes, see pl. facing p. 182.
[2] Guide to church.
[3] Ibid.; Pevsner, Wilts. (Bldgs. of Eng.), 487.
[4] J.I. 3/161 mm. 16, 20d.

weighing 9 oz.[5] In 1966 the plate comprised a chalice and cover of 1577, a paten of 1690, and a flagon of 1615, the gift of Martha Hinton of Earlscourt.[6]

Four bells and a sanctus bell were delivered to the king's commissioners in 1553. In 1966 there were 6 bells and a sanctus bell. Three dated from the later 17th century, two from the 18th century, and one from 1950 when all the bells were recast or retuned. The sanctus bell dates from 1783.[7] The registers begin in 1582 and are complete except for the years 1653–65 in the register of baptisms, 1651–1665 in the marriage register, and 1653–65 in the burial register.[8]

A chapel dedicated to St. Katherine was founded in 1270 by Emily Longespée (d. c. 1276), widow of Stephen Longespée, lord of the manor.[9] She endowed it with a small estate to support two chaplains and a clerk who were to say matins and vespers and celebrate mass daily.[10] The senior chaplain was apparently appointed for life and was called warden, the other was said to be 'elected'.[11] Further small grants followed, including some land for extensions to the chapel.[12] In 1280, when more land was granted, another priest was added who was to spend 1 mark each year upon clothing the poor and was to distribute 20s. in alms.[13] In 1329 more property was granted by Robert of Wanborough for the maintenance of another chaplain.[14] At the time of Robert's death in c. 1334 there seem to have been proposals to use some of the land for a new foundation to support two chaplains either in the parish church or in St. Katherine's chapel, to pray for the overlord of the manor, for John of Wanborough, Robert's brother, and the souls of Emily Longespée, Robert of Wanborough, and Robert of Hungerford.[15] Nothing more is heard of these proposals and in 1336 the chapel's endowments were maintaining two chaplains and a warden following the rules of the original foundation and celebrating mass for the Bishop of Salisbury and members of the Wanborough family.[16] Obits were also kept in the chancel of the chapel for Emily Longespée and Robert of Wanborough.[17]

By agreement with the rectors of the parish church offerings made at the chapel could be retained on condition that none of the parishioners was admitted to the sacraments.[18] In 1273 the chaplains were exempted from archidiaconal jurisdiction[19] and at about the same time from all exactions of the overlord.[20]

The advowson of the chapel descended from the founder to successive lords of the manor of Wanborough,[21] although in 1361 the Bishop of Salisbury presented.[22] In 1483 Francis, Viscount Lovel, sold the chapel and its estate to William Waynflete, Bishop of Winchester.[23] In the same year Waynflete conveyed the property to Magdalen College, Oxford. The last recorded presentation of a warden was made that year,[24] although college fellows continued to preach there on St. Katherine's Day and at other times.[25] Offerings were still made there in 1535[26] but the chapel was otherwise little used and was probably demolished in 1549.[27]

The chapel stood within Emily Longespée's court, and a chamber and wardrobe for the priests and for the chapel ornaments were built nearby 'in her courtyard near the marsh on the south side of the granary'.[28] The wardrobe was built on the south side of the court, with ditches on both sides connected to the marsh.[29] Access to the chapel in 1292 was by a gate between the 'great fishpond' and the boundary of the warden's property.[30] It seems likely, therefore, that the chapel was situated on the moated site at Cold Court at the Marsh, more than a mile north-west of the parish church.[31] It was evidently of considerable size, having a chancel and more than one altar. An inventory of goods taken from the chapel to the vicarage house in 1484 included at least eight service books, a silver-gilt chalice engraved with the Lovel arms, various vestments and ornaments, and a casket of relics including the girdle of St. Katherine with her vial of holy oil.[32]

In 1334 Maud de Holand, great-grand-daughter of the founder, gave a rent of 14 marks from her manor of Market Lavington to the Warden of St. Katherine's to celebrate masses for herself and her husband in the chapel of St. Mary, presumably in St. Katherine's chapel.[33] After 1368 this rent was payable by Edington Priory.[34] Magdalen College successfully defended its right to it in 1496[35] and the property was valued at £9 6s. 8d. in 1535.[36]

It has been said that there was a chapel dedicated to St. Ambrose at Hall Place and its existence is supported by the survival of the name as a field-name.[37]

NONCONFORMITY. In 1660 two couples in Wanborough were presented at the Quarter Sessions as Anabaptists.[38] In 1668 they were said to have refused to have their children baptized publicly,

[5] Nightingale, *Wilts. Plate*, 191–2.
[6] Ibid.; *W.A.M.* xli. 136.
[7] *W.A.M.* i. 93–94; Walters, *Wilts. Bells*, 225–6; *Guide to church*.
[8] Ex inf. the vicar.   [9] See pp. 176, 177.
[10] Magdalen Coll. Oxford, Wanborough deeds, 66a. and see p. 177.
[11] Ibid. 22, 23.   [12] See pp. 177–8.
[13] Magdalen Coll. Oxford, Wanborough deeds, 65a.
[14] Ibid. 3.
[15] Ibid. 62a.
[16] Ibid. 4, 26.
[17] Ibid.
[18] Ibid. 6, 37a, 40a.
[19] Ibid. 35a.
[20] Ibid. 27.
[21] Phillipps, *Wilts. Inst.* i. (see index in *W.A.M.* xxviii).
[22] Ibid. 55.
[23] Magdalen Coll. Oxford, Wanborough, deeds, 8, 9, 11, 12, 16, 29a.

[24] Ibid. 28.
[25] W. D. Macray, *Reg. Magd. Coll.* i. 15, 20, 68, 100, 127. A missal was bought for the chapel in 1512–13.
[26] *Valor Eccl.* (Rec. Com.), ii. 278.
[27] Macray, op. cit. ii. 30.
[28] Magdalen Coll. Oxford, Wanborough deeds, 66a.
[29] Ibid. 24.
[30] Ibid. 34.
[31] Ibid. 26: 'Colne' was the name of a messuage which formed part of the grant of John of Wanborough (see p. 178). In July 1866 paving tiles of 14th-century date were found at the site, covering a lead coffin: Wilts. Cuttings, xvi. 371.
[32] Magdalen Coll. Oxford, Wanborough deeds, 31.
[33] *Wilts. Inq. p.m.* 1327–77 (Index Libr.), 106.
[34] Ibid. 349.
[35] Magdalen Coll. Oxford, Wanborough deeds, 79a.
[36] *Valor Eccl.* (Rec. Com.), ii. 278.
[37] Aubrey, *Topog. Coll.* ed. Jackson, 196, and see p. 175.
[38] *V.C.H. Wilts.* iii. 115.

and to have remained excommunicate for three years.[39] They were presented again in 1671, 1674, 1683, and 1684,[40] and were included in Bishop Compton's census of 1676.[41] In 1686 only one family was presented.[42] One Roman Catholic was reported in the parish in 1780,[43] but three years later neither papist nor dissenter could be found.[44]

Before the end of the century Methodism had taken a hold in the parish and a dwelling-house was licensed for worship in 1798.[45] It was probably introduced by George Pocock, one of Wesley's friends, and was later supported by Thomas Bush of Lambourn (Berks.).[46] Preaching was said to have begun in a soap-boiling room owned by Thomas Smith.[47] Further licences for Methodist meetings were issued in 1799, 1811, and 1814, and in 1818 a Wesleyan chapel was built, licensed in the name of James Spicer.[48] This chapel had 120 members in 1829.[49] In 1851 it was reckoned that over the past year there had been an average general congregation of 278 at morning and evening services on Sundays, while those occupying separate sittings numbered 46 at morning and 47 at evening service.[50] The chapel remains in use. It is a plain building of brick with a cemented front. A schoolroom was added in 1892 and a porch in 1901.

Early in the 19th century an Independent cause began in the parish and a chapel was built in 1806.[51] This was fostered by John Strange, lord of the manor, who provided a site, and was a member of that family of nonconformists who were so active in Swindon at this date.[52] At the opening of the chapel preachers came from 'Lavington', Wantage (Berks.), and Devizes. It was under the care of an itinerant minister and a Sunday school was held there. A Mr. Cannon was described as the 'missionary' at this chapel in 1826 and a building for the use of Independents was licensed two years later in the name of Charles Cannon.[53] In 1829 there were 60 members.[54] No further reference to this church has been found, however, and it may not have survived for very long after this date.[55]

In 1829 Thomas Smith was permitted to use his house as a place of worship for Methodists, apparently of the Primitive connexion.[56] In the same year there were 150 members.[57] Three licences were issued in 1835 including at least one for Particular Baptists,[58] who in 1856 opened Adullam Chapel in Rotten Row (Lower Wanborough).[59] In 1883 this was taken over by the Primitive Methodists[60] and was eventually closed several

years before its demolition in 1965.[61] It was a plain brick building with stone dressings.

EDUCATION. In 1622 Anthony Smith, described as a schoolmaster, was living in the parish, although there is no evidence that he taught there.[62] By 1686 there was a licensed schoolmaster who was described as a very poor man.[63] In 1783 the churchwardens reported that there was neither a free nor a public school.[64] In 1819 there were said to be no endowments for education, but there was a Sunday school of 150 children supported by voluntary contributions, which were then declining 'with the prospect of getting worse every year'.[65] In 1833 there were two day schools attended by 65 children at their parents' expense, and a Sunday school for 85 children supported by subscription.[66] In 1852 the site for a school was acquired by the vicar and churchwardens, acting as trustees, aided by a grant of £50 from Magdalen College.[67] It was to be 'a school for adults and children, or children only, of the labouring, manufacturing or other poor classes' and was to include a residence for the teacher. It was to be run in union with the National Society.[68] In 1858 it was reported that 'the school is now taught with method and success'.[69] Fifty pupils were being taught by a certificated master and a pupil teacher in 1859; the schoolroom was reported as good, having a boarded floor and parallel desks.[70] In 1903–4 there were 201 places available and the annual average attendance was 90.[71] After the school in Liddington was closed in 1962 the children from that parish came to school in Wanborough.[72] In 1966 there were 125 children in the school.[73]

CHARITIES. Benefactions recorded on a tablet in Wanborough church show that three separate gifts were made to the parish during the 18th century. William Stanley bequeathed £50 in 1745 for a sermon, and bread and money for the poor. Out of this 20s. was to be paid to 20 poor families not receiving alms who attended church, 10s. was to be given to the minister for a sermon, and the remainder spent on bread. This was to be distributed on the Sunday following the day of Stanley's burial (19 Feb.). In 1747 Margaret Brind gave £100 and in 1748 Mary Broadway bequeathed £20 to the poor, the interest to be given annually to poor widows.[74] These three sums, together with £9

39 Sar. Dioc. R.O. Chwdns.' Pres. 1668.
40 V.C.H. Wilts. iii. 115.   41 Ibid.
42 Sar. Dioc. R.O. Chwdns.' Pres. 1686.
43 V.C.H. Wilts. iii. 96.
44 Sar. Dioc. R.O. Vis. Queries, 1783.
45 G.R.O. Retns. of Regns.
46 V.C.H. Wilts. iii. 141–2.
47 William Morris, Swindon Fifty Years Ago, 397.
48 Ibid. 215–6.
49 W.R.O. Retns. Dissenters' Meetings, 1829.
50 H.O. 129/250/2/3/6.
51 G.R.O. Retns. of Regns.   52 See p. 152.
53 W.R.O. Retns. Dissenters' Meetings, 1829.
54 Ibid.
55 It is not listed in the Congregational Yr. Bk. for 1846 or any subsequent years.
56 G.R.O. Retns. of Regns.
57 W.R.O. Retns. Dissenters' Meetings, 1829.
58 G.R.O. Retns. of Regns.   59 Ibid.
60 Ibid.   61 Ex inf. the vicar.
62 Par. Reg. Bur.

63 Sar. Dioc. R.O. Chwdns.' Pres. 1686.
64 Ibid. Vis. Queries, 1783.
65 Digest of Returns to Cttee. of Educ. of Poor, H.C. 224, p. 1039 (1819), ix (2).
66 Educ. Enq. Abstract, H.C. 62, p. 1050 (1835), lxiii. Magdalen Coll. paid a subscription in 1844, see Macray, Reg. Magd. Coll. iv. 24.
67 Macray, op. cit. vi. 36. The college continued to support the school until it was transferred to the School Board in 1881 (Macray, op. cit. vii. 3). The D. and C. of Winchester also gave money towards expenses (D. & C. Winchester, Chapter Mins., Jan. 1876).
68 Endowed Char. Wilts. H.C. 319–xvi (1904), lxxiv.
69 Acct. of Wilts. Schools, H.C. 27, p. 46 (1859 Sess. 1), xxi (2).
70 Ibid.
71 Endowed Char. Wilts. (1904); School deeds penes the vicar.
72 See p. 75.   73 Ex inf. the vicar.
74 All inf. about these gifts, unless otherwise stated, from Endowed Char. Wilts. (1908), pp. 1013–5, and the vicar.

arrears of interest and about £21 advanced by parishioners, were used to purchase 3½ a. of pasture in the Marsh called the Poor's Closes (also known as the Poor's Mead), producing £10 10s. in 1786. In 1834 this property was let at £12, two fifths of which were distributed to all poor widows in the parish, of whom there were then about 20. The rest was spent on bread, given in church to all the poor, together with 10s. to the minister for a sermon and 1s. to the sexton. The remainder of the rent was distributed to all poor who attended church on Good Friday. In 1881 the trustees appealed successfully to the Charity Commissioners to have the date and place for distribution of bread changed to avoid unseemly disturbances in church. In 1903 these charities were distributed as follows: 10s. to the vicar, 1s. to the sexton, £1 in gifts of 1s. to 20 poor people, and a varying sum in gifts of 4s. to poor widows. The balance was used to buy bread. In 1903 448 loaves were distributed. Bread to the

value of £6, marked 'Dobbin' (meaning a small loaf),[75] was given in 1965; in the previous year the whole charity was worth £45.[76]

By his will, proved in 1882, John Jenner bequeathed £300 in trust for paupers or labourers to be invested for the distribution of coal.[77] In 1892 £270 was invested, which produced about £8 in 1903 when there were 54 recipients. In the 1960s the income was distributed every three years.[78]

Henry James Deacon, a native of Wanborough, bequeathed £500 in 1916 for the benefit of the poor, together with £100 for the repair of the parish church.[79] This was invested and produced over £15 in 1966, and was given to the poor in need during the year and particularly at Christmas.[80]

In 1967 an anonymous donation of £500, known as St. Andrew's Wanborough Trust Fund, was made for the relief of needy parishioners.[81] In the same year the charity yielded an income of £25.

WOOTTON BASSETT

WOOTTON BASSETT lies about 5¾ miles south-west of the centre of Swindon. The parish is roughly triangular in shape and covers some 5,106 a. of land.[1] From the base of the triangle to its tip in the north is about 3½ miles and the distance along the base is approximately three miles. The northern part of the parish lies on the Oxford Clay and the southern on the Kimmeridge Clay. Through the middle, dividing the clays, runs the Corallian ridge, which extends from Wheatley, near Oxford, in the east, almost to Calne, in the west.[2] In the north and south of the parish, therefore, the ground is fairly flat and low-lying with good pasture suitable for dairy farming. But from the Oxford Clay in the north the land rises steeply up the side of the ridge, which on its crest is some 400 ft. above sea level. Towards the south the drop from the ridge to the Kimmeridge Clay is more gradual. Along the top of the ridge Wootton Bassett high street runs for nearly a mile. Immediately south-west of the town the ridge narrows and dips where the Brinkworth Brook cuts through and on the high ground beyond this dip Gilbert Basset built his great house of Vastern in the 13th century. Numerous wells and springs occur along the length of the ridge and the frequent exposures of Coral Rag have led in the past to the quarrying of stone for use locally for roads and building.

Two mineral springs in the parish have attracted some attention.[3] One on the land of Whitehill Farm, just south of the railway line, is probably the one claimed by John Aubrey c. 1670 to produce 'petrifying water'. It drew a certain number of visitors in the later 19th century. There is also a

chalybeate well near Hunt's Mill, which is reputed to turn leaves red.

The southern part of the parish is roughly divided into two by the Brinkworth Brook, which is one of the headwaters of the Bristol Avon, and rises further south at the foot of the chalk escarpment. Having penetrated the Corallian ridge at its narrowest point, just south-west of Wootton Bassett town, the stream flows out of the parish in a north-westerly direction. Another stream, flowing in the same direction, and eventually joining the Brinkworth Brook, forms the western boundary of the parish for about 3 miles. Two other streams, one of which is the Thunder Brook, flow westward through the northern part of the parish and likewise join the Brinkworth Brook.

From the 12th to the beginning of the 17th century all the northern part of the parish was occupied by Vastern Park,[4] which probably accounts for the fact that only one road runs through it. This was called Whitehill Lane in the 17th century and left the parish on the west by a gate called Faafe, later Hookers, Gate.[5] Here in 1602 it was said 'the Duke had his way forth'.[6] The southern part of the parish was divided by the Brinkworth Brook into the tithing of Woodshaw on the east and the tithing of Greenhill on the west.[7] Until the early 19th century a feature of the southern part of the parish were the commons which survived long after the rest of the parish was inclosed.[8] The largest was Greenhill Common in the west. Further east were Dunnington, Nore Marsh, second in size to Greenhill, and Woodshaw.[9] Numerous lanes converged upon these commons, some of which became disused

---

[75] For Dobbin Sunday see p. 181.
[76] Ex inf. the vicar.
[77] Inf. about this charity until 1903 from *Endowed Char. Wilts.* (1908), p. 1016.
[78] Ex inf. the vicar.   [79] *W.A.M.* xxxix. 416.
[80] Ex inf. the vicar.
[81] All inf. from Char. Com. File 254529.
[1] Maps used include O.S. Map 1/2,500 Wilts. XIV. 7, 8, 11, 12, XV. 5, 9 (1st and later edns.); 6", Wilts. XIV, XV, XXI, XXII (1st and later edns.).
[2] For fuller account of the geology of the region, see W. J. Arkell, 'Geology of Corallian Ridge, near Wootton

Bassett', *W.A.M.* liv. 1–18, also Fry, *Land Utilization Wilts.* 151.
[3] J. H. P. Pafford, 'Spas and Mineral Springs of Wilts'. *W.A.M.* lv. 1–10.
[4] See p. 189.
[5] *W.A.M.* xxviii. 173; W.R.O. 130/79/89, Map of Lord Hyde's Estate, 1773.
[6] *W.A.M.* xxviii. 173. It is not clear which duke is meant, but perhaps the Duke of York (d. 1415): see below, p. 191.
[7] *W.A.M.* xxix. 194.   [8] See p. 195.
[9] W.R.O. 130/79/89, Map 1773 and see also *Andrews and Dury, Map* (W.A.S. Rec. Brch.), pl. 14.

and disappeared after the commons were inclosed in 1821. A lane called in 1773 Bushey Fowley Lane, which in 1967 was in places a mere footpath, forms for about 1½ mile the eastern boundary of the parish.[10]

The main road from Cricklade to Chippenham runs through the middle of the parish and for about half a mile forms the high street of the town. In 1773, after crossing the Brinkworth Brook at Hunt's Mill, the road crossed Greenhill Common and left the parish along Roger Lane for Tockenham on a rather more southerly route than that of 1967.[11] The more northerly course was made when the common was inclosed in 1821.[12] During the 19th and very early 20th centuries three bridges had to be built on less than a mile stretch of this main road to Chippenham after it left the town to carry it over two railway lines and a canal. The road leading off the high street for Marlborough was turnpiked early in the 19th century.[13] In 1773 it skirted Dunnington Common and left the parish as Marlborough Lane.[14] A road called New Road was built early in the 20th century to make a way from this road to the main road to Chippenham, avoiding the town.[15]

The Wilts. and Berks. Canal reached the parish boundary from the west in 1801 and before 1804 had been constructed right across the parish.[16] A wharf was built at Vastern, where coal could be unloaded and local produce taken away.[17] There was no traffic on the canal after 1906.[18] Its course was clearly to be seen in 1967, although it had been filled in. The railway line from London to Bristol was constructed through the parish in 1841.[19] A station, known as Wootton Bassett Road, was opened in the adjoining parish of Lydiard Tregoze at the end of 1840 and served Wootton Bassett until its own station about ¾ mile south of the town was opened in 1841.[20] Some of the heaviest engineering works on the whole line were required on the stretch west of the station known as the Wootton Bassett incline. Here the line had to cross the Corallian ridge and make a steep descent, which required the construction of deep cuttings and long embankments.[21] In 1903 a new main line to South Wales, via Patchway, was opened from a junction on the old line just west of Wootton Bassett station.[22] In 1967 both lines were operating but Wootton Bassett station was closed in 1965.[23]

Apart from the town the only other centres of settlement within the parish were those at Vastern, at Hunt's Mill and the farmsteads around Greenhill Common, and around the other commons of Dunnington, Nore Marsh, and Woodshaw, all in the southern half of the parish. Vastern, as is shown below, was once the administrative centre of the whole parish.[24] At Hunt's Mill a kiln of Norman date was discovered c. 1893, which may have supplied

pottery over quite a wide area locally.[25] At all the commons there were farm-houses and a map of 1773 shows a few other small houses around the edges.[26] In 1967 the farm-houses remained, although those at Dunnington and Nore Marsh were almost engulfed by the housing development on that side of the town. Greenhill Common Farm, probably dating from the 17th century, once had an imposing entrance through stone gateposts with ball finials, but was deserted and ruinous in 1967. Nore Marsh House, outwardly of the earlier 18th century, has a projecting porch and gateposts with ball finials. According to tradition wool for spinning was once stored in its attics.[27] Upper Woodshaw was burnt down in the 20th century. Lower Woodshaw and Harriscroft have timber framing and date from the 17th century. In the northern half of the parish, which for so long was covered by Vastern Park, there were no similar settlements, although after the break-up of the park in the 17th century several quite large farms, such as Whitehill Farm, Park Ground Farm, and Callow Hill Farm were developed.

When assessed for taxation in 1334 the parish was returned under the name of Vastern and contributed 86s. 8d., the next highest contribution to that of Swindon in the hundred of Kingsbridge.[28] In 1377 there were 207 poll-tax payers in the parish and only Swindon in the same hundred had more.[29] To the Benevolence of 1545 Greenhill and Wootton Bassett returned two contributors each. Woodshaw had five contributors.[30] For the subsidy of 1576 borough and manor were assessed separately. There were then 10 tax payers in the borough and 17 on the manor.[31] In 1801 the population of the parish was 1,244.[32] It then rose steadily and in 1841 was 2,990, but this included 800 labourers constructing the railway line through the parish.[33] Consequently in 1851 it had dropped to 2,123. In 1871 it was 2,392, and although this increase was in part attributed to a general prosperity in trade, some of it was accounted for by the presence of 13 workmen repairing the parish church and 50 people attending the fair.[34] In 1881 it was 2,237 and then began to drop slightly until 1911 when it was 1,991. Thereafter it began to rise and in 1951 was 3,419. By 1961 it was 4,390.[35]

The plan of Wootton Bassett with its long, straight street, flanked by plots of burgage character, suggests a town that was at some time deliberately planted, presumably as an extension to a small settlement around the church, which lies towards the south-western end of the street. It seems reasonable to suggest that this may have been done in the 13th century, perhaps to meet the needs of the rural community on the estate the Bassets were developing at Vastern.[36] According to tradition the priory, founded by Sir Philip Basset in 1266, stood just to

[10] W.R.O. 130/79/89, Map 1773.
[11] Ibid.
[12] W.R.O. Inclosure Award.
[13] V.C.H. Wilts. iv. 263.
[14] W.R.O. 130/79/89, Map 1773.
[15] Ex inf. Mr. W. G. W. Hunt, Wootton Bassett. Thanks are due to Mr. Hunt for much help given.
[16] V.C.H. Wilts. iv. 273.
[17] Charles Hadfield, Canals of S. England, 156–7.
[18] V.C.H. Wilts. iv. 273.
[19] Ibid. 282.
[20] Ibid.
[21] Ibid.
[22] Ibid. 289.

[23] Local information.
[24] See p. 198.
[25] W.A.M. xxviii. 263–4.
[26] Andrews and Dury, Map (W.A.S. Rec. Brch.), pl. 14; W.R.O. 130/79/89, Map 1773.
[27] W. F. Parsons in Wootton Bassett Almanack, 1896.
[28] V.C.H. Wilts. iv. 297.
[29] Ibid. 306.
[30] Tax. Lists (W.A.S. Rec. Brch.), 21.
[31] Ibid. 105–6.
[32] V.C.H. Wilts. iv. 361.
[33] Ibid. 320.
[34] Ibid. 325.   [35] Ibid. 361.
[36] See p. 194 and pl. facing p. 193.

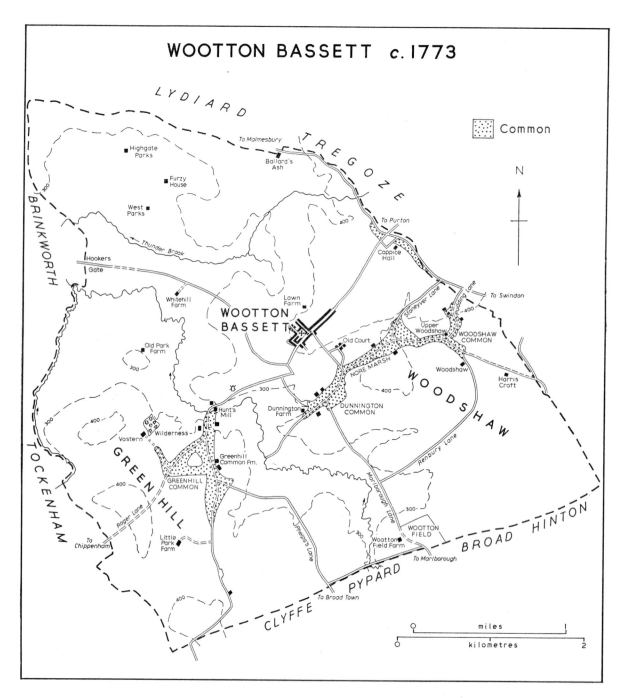

WOOTTON BASSETT c. 1773

Common

the north of the church, and so would have been situated in what was the nucleus of the town. No trace of the priory, which only survived until *c.* 1406,[37] remains above ground, but a house in Wood Street, probably of the 17th century, is called Priory Cottage and is thought to adjoin the site.

Shops in the town are mentioned in account rolls of the late 15th and early 16th centuries.[38] One was in a house called the House of St. Mary (*domus beate Marie*).[39] By the same time there were several plots in the middle of the street for which rents were paid.[40] These may have been connected with the market, which, so far as is known, was always held in the street, and for which at some time shambles were built. In 1773 these stood in the street im-

mediately west of the Town Hall. They were removed in 1813.[41] On the other side of the Town Hall there was a pond, which is shown in a print of 1808, but was filled in in 1836.[42] The Town Hall, which stands in the middle of the street, is traditionally said to have been provided by Lawrence Hyde in 1700.[43] It was extensively restored by Sir Henry Meux in 1889, and presented by Lady Meux to the town in 1906.[44] The mayor and aldermen held their petty sessional courts in it until 1886 and it subsequently has been used to house the property of the Town Trust and a branch of the County Library.[45] It is a small half-timbered building supported on 15 stone columns and reached by an open staircase. Under the staircase there was, until

[37] *V.C.H. Wilts.* iii. 368–9.
[38] S.C. 6/1115/1; S.C. 6/Hen. VII/878.
[39] Ibid.
[40] Ibid.
[41] W.R.O. 130/179/89, Map 1773 and see p. 197.

[42] W.A.S. Libr., Devizes, Parsons Papers. The print is reproduced in *V.C.H. Wilts.* v. facing p. 226.
[43] E. H. Goddard and W. Gough, *Notes on the Town Hall,* ii. 8, and see pl. facing p. 193.
[44] Ibid.
[45] Ibid.

the restoration of the hall, a lock-up or blind house. Beneath the hall in 1967 stood a pair of stocks and an ancient fire engine.

Until the mid 19th century the town was virtually limited to the high street, the narrow streets running off its north-west side, and the small street behind the church called Butt Hay. The three side streets, which are connected by a footpath, known locally as Row Dow,[46] end abruptly where the escarpment, on which the town stands, begins its descent. On the southern side of the town, but, until the 19th century, quite separate from it, there was the small group of buildings known as Old Court, which, as has been suggested below, may have marked the site of the earliest manor of Wootton.[47]

The wide high street extends for about ½ mile and is closely lined on both sides by houses fronting directly upon the pavement. Most of the houses are of red brick from the local brickyards with stone roofs and appear to date from the 18th and early 19th centuries. One or two timber-framed houses, however, survive at the western end of the street. For the most part the 18th- and early-19th-century houses are modest buildings of two stories with attics and many have had shop fronts inserted on the ground floor. On the south-east side, however, there are two more substantial houses. No. 141 dates from the early 18th century. It is thought to have belonged to the Maskelyne family in the late 18th and early 19th centuries, and housed a bank and the offices of Messrs. Bevir and Sons, solicitors, from 1867 onwards. The bank closed in 1930.[48] It is a stone house of seven bays with several distinguished features, notably the shell hood on carved brackets above the central doorway. Within is the original staircase. No. 137 is of brick and has five bays. It also dates from the 18th century and has some architectural distinction, including a broken pediment with urn above its front door. Lime Kiln House at the east end of the town is another fairly substantial house of the early 18th century. It was for a time the home of the Bevir family.

Lying along an important highway and having been the site of a weekly market, the high street is well supplied with inns. One or two were clearly quite substantial coaching inns in the 18th century and these are among the street's more prosperous-looking buildings. The Angel Hotel, on the north-west wide, is of chequered brick and has six bays and two stories. On the other side of the road the Crown Hotel has a parapet with ball finials and central doorway with fanlight, pilasters, and pediment. The 'Crosskeys', nearby, is dated 1742 but incorporates earlier building. It has a central arched entrance for carriages. Among the more modest inns were two older buildings at the west end of the street, namely the 'Waggon and Horses' and the 'Curriers Arms', both of which had parts dating from the 16th and 17th centuries. The 'Currier's Arms' was rebuilt in 1953.[49] The coming of the canal and the railway added at least two more inns, namely the Bridge

Inn, standing where the Marlborough road crosses the canal, and the Railway Hotel at the bottom of Station Road. The Bridge Inn was closed in 1956.[50] A new hotel was built in the high street on the site of an earlier one in c. 1864.[51] This was the 'Royal Oak' built for Sir Henry Meux by Thomas Barratt of Swindon.[52] It served the neighbourhood as a hunting inn for some years but was closed in c. 1910.[53] In 1967 it housed a branch of the Midland Bank.

The expansion of the town began in a very small way with the coming of the railway in the 1840s. The canal, which came earlier, passed so far south, that it made no changes in the appearance of the town. But some cottages were built for the wharf at Vastern about a mile away. There was some early 19th-century building in the high street, mostly of smaller houses. A row of 15 cottages, called Victory Row, at the end of Wood Street is said locally to have been built in c. 1817 by William Cripps to celebrate a Whig victory. But it seems more likely that it was to celebrate the victory over France. The building of the station nearly ¾ mile from the high street in 1841 prepared the way for the building up of Station Road, formerly the northern end of the Marlborough road. The National Schools and the vicarage were built here in the 1860s. The Beaufort Brewery, near the station, was built in c. 1886.[54] There was also some late-19th-century building or rebuilding in the high street, notably the large house at the north-east end, once known as Troy House, later the Manor House, and in 1967 the offices of the Cricklade and Wootton Bassett R.D.C.

The opening of the Dairy Supply Company's factory near the station in 1908, resulted in a little more building in this direction. The R.D.C.'s first council houses were built in Station Road in 1921 and others were added in the same neighbourhood before the Second World War.[55] But Wootton Bassett's greatest expansion has taken place since the early 1950s when it has to some extent become a dormitory town for Swindon and a place of residence for personnel from the R.A.F. station at Lyneham. Almost all this new building, both private and council, has been to the south of the town, although in 1967 new estates were being laid out on either side of the Swindon road.

VASTERN PARK. The park of Vastern, which at its greatest extent covered virtually the whole of the north-western half of the parish, has been treated elsewhere in the *History*.[56] It will, therefore, only be touched upon briefly here.

So far as is known, the park first came into being c. 1229 when Alan Basset (d. 1232–3) was allowed to inclose 3½ a. of his wood of Wootton, which lay within Braydon Forest, together with his wood of Vastern, which lay outside the forest.[57] The park so formed was ordered to be destroyed by Henry III,[58] but on the reconciliation of the king and Gilbert Basset in 1234, permission was given for it

[46] *W.A.M.* xxviii. 174.   [47] See p. 192.
[48] Ex inf. H. Bevir & Son, Wootton Bassett.
[49] Swindon Public Libr., Scrapbk. [50] Local information.
[51] The earlier one was the 'Old Royal Oak', Pigot, *Nat. Com. Dir.* (1844).
[52] W.A.S. Libr., Devizes, Parsons Papers, newspaper cutting.

[53] Ex inf. Mr. F. Blackwall, Wootton Bassett.
[54] W.A.S. Libr., Devizes, Parsons Papers, newspaper cutting.
[55] Ex inf. Clerk to the R.D.C.
[56] *V.C.H. Wilts.* iv. 402–4.
[57] *Cal. Chart. R.* 1226–57, 115.
[58] *Cal. Pat.* 1226–40, 228.

to be re-inclosed.[59] Over the next ten years there were several royal gifts of venison to stock it as well as permission to enlarge it somewhat.[60]

The two woods inclosed in 1229 may have retained their separate identity and have been regarded as forming two parks. More than one park is mentioned in 1267 when Philip Basset was permitted to inclose a further 50 a.[61] This was then called the New Park of Wootton and was described as lying beneath the town of Wootton, while the Old Park of Vastern apparently lay under the manor of Vastern.[62] Old Park Farm, still so called in the 20th century, presumably indicates roughly where the Old Park lay. It is thought to have included also land later belonging to Whitehill Farm, Hart's Farm, and Hunt's Mill Farm.[63] The exact location of the New Park is not known. In 1271 and 1281 there were said to be three parks, and at the earlier date there was said to be a 'foreign' wood as well, which presumably lay outside the confines of the parks.[64] But finally two parks emerge, namely the Great and the Little Park of Vastern. Assuming that the present (1967) Little Park estate represents approximately the region of the Little Park of Vastern, the Great Park occupied the most northerly parts of the parish.

Under Hugh le Despenser the parks were further enlarged. A large extension was made in 1320 when some 600 a. were taken from the manor of Midgehall (in Lydiard Tregoze) in the north and the manor of Brinkworth in the west.[65] Another enlargement took place in 1363 when 120 a. were taken in and as late as the earlier 15th century 54 a. were added.[66] By this date the park must have reached its greatest extent. A survey made in 1602, by which time the disparkment of the park had begun, but based on an earlier perambulation, shows the park to have covered almost all the land of the parish north-west of the present main road to Chippenham, coming right up to the western outskirts of the town.[67] It must also at one time have extended south of the road where Little Park lay. The disparkment of Vastern began, as is shown below, soon after the middle of the 16th century when the manor belonged to the Englefields.

MANORS AND OTHER ESTATES. Before tracing the descent of the manor some explanation of the manorial structure and changes of name seems necessary. Until the earlier 13th century there is firm evidence for only a single estate.[68] By 1210, as the manor of *WOOTTON*, this was held by Alan Basset. During the earlier 13th century, however, the Bassets, with royal consent, created the park of Vastern and by 1269 another manor, called

VASTERN emerges.[69] By 1281 this was the main manor in the parish with the manor of Wootton described as one of its members. The two were for a time administered as separate manors but were always held of the same lord. Then towards the end of the 15th century the two manors were merged to form the manor of Wootton, and the name Vastern is applied only to the manor-house and its associated buildings and to the adjoining park. At roughly the same time the town or borough of Wootton begins to be distinguished in conveyances as a separate place and, to differentiate the manor from the town, the manor is usually called *OLD WOOTTON*, although occasionally the borough is also so called. At the beginning of the 16th century the name of Old Wootton is gradually replaced by the name *WOOTTON BASSETT*.

Charters of 680, 745, and 937 all purport to grant a 10-hide estate in Wootton to Malmesbury Abbey.[70] A 10-hide estate there is also included in Edward the Confessor's charter of 1065, confirming all its possessions to the abbey.[71] But Malmesbury did not hold Wootton at the time of the Conquest. In 1066 it was held by Leofnoth and in 1086 it was one of the estates of Miles Crispin.[72] Miles, in a way described elsewhere, subsequently acquired those lands which later formed the honor of Wallingford.[73] Wootton, like most of Miles's other Wiltshire estates, then became part of that honor and was held of its lord as overlord.[74]

By 1210 Wootton was held as 2 knights' fees of the honor of Wallingford by Alan Basset.[75] Alan died in 1232–3 and was succeeded by his son Gilbert, who was deprived of his estates for a short time after taking part in the rebellion against Henry III.[76] They were, however, restored to him in 1234. Gilbert was succeeded c. 1241 by his brother Fulk, then Dean of York and later Bishop of London, and Fulk was succeeded by another brother Philip.[77] Philip died in 1271, at about which date the Bassets' family name was occasionally, although not often, attached to that of Wootton.[78] Philip's heir was his daughter Aline, then the wife of Roger Bigod, Earl of Norfolk (d. 1306), but formerly the wife of Hugh le Despenser, the justiciar who was killed at the battle of Evesham in 1265.[79] Aline died in 1281 and her son by her first marriage succeeded to her lands.[80] This son was Hugh le Despenser, later known as the Elder, the favourite of Edward II. In 1300 Despenser was granted free warren in all his demesne lands which included Wootton and Vastern.[81] As an important Wiltshire residence of the Despensers, Vastern may have been singled out for plunder by their opponents. It was certainly plundered along with the Despensers' other Wiltshire property during their banishment in 1321.[82]

[59] *Cal. Close*, 1231–4, 441.
[60] For e.g. ibid. 1234–7, 24; 1237–42, 420.
[61] *Cal. Pat.* 1266–72, 116–17.
[62] Ibid. 177.
[63] *W.A.M.* xxviii. 174.
[64] *Wilts. Inq. p.m.* 1242–1326 (Index Libr.), 64, 134.
[65] *Cal. Pat.* 1317–21, 431.
[66] *Wilts. Inq. p.m.* 1327–77 (Index Libr.), 361.
[67] *W.A.M.* xxviii. 173 used with W.R.O. 130/79/89, Map 1773.
[68] It has been suggested that one of the many places called Clive in the Wiltshire Domesday may refer to the estate in Wootton which became called Vastern. But this is only conjecture: *Dom. Bk. Wilts.* ed. Jones, 208.
[69] *Cal. Pat.* 1266–72, 116–17.

[70] *V.C.H. Wilts.* ii, pp. 3, 4, 90.
[71] Ibid. p. 90; ibid. iii. 214.
[72] Ibid. ii, p. 145.
[73] Ibid. pp. 102, 111.
[74] For the honor of Wallingford, see *V.C.H. Berks.* iii. 523–8.
[75] *Red Bk. Excheq.* ii. 485.
[76] *V.C.H. Bucks.* iii. 123; *Cal. Lib.* 1226–40, 228.
[77] *V.C.H. Bucks.* iii. 123; *Cal. Close*, 1237–42, 420. For Fulk Basset, see *D.N.B.*
[78] *Wilts. Inq. p.m.* 1242–1326 (Index Libr.), 64.
[79] Ibid.; *Complete Peerage*, Despenser.
[80] Ibid; *Wilts. Inq. p.m.* 1242–1326 (Index Libr.), 134.
[81] *Cal. Chart. R.* 1257–1300, 489.
[82] *Cal. Close*, 1318–23, 543; *Cal. Pat.* 1321–4, 166, 168.

With the final overthrow of the Despensers in 1326, the manors of Vastern and Wootton passed with the rest of the Despenser lands in Wiltshire to Isabel, the queen mother.[83] On Isabel's downfall at Nottingham in 1330, the two manors were bestowed upon Edward de Bohun in recognition of the part he played at Nottingham,[84] but they were restored to Isabel after Bohun's death in 1334.[85] On Isabel's death in 1358 Edward III granted the two manors to his queen, Philippa, for life and workmen were sent to restore the houses and other buildings on the manor of Vastern.[86] Philippa died in 1369 and in 1376 the king granted the manors of Vastern and Wootton to his son Edmund, Earl of Cambridge.[87] Edmund, created Duke of York in 1385, died in 1402 seised of the manor of Vastern, with the manor of Wootton as a member, and was succeeded by his son Edward.[88] In 1404 the younger Edward was arrested and his lands seized, although licence was granted to his wife Philippa to occupy the manor of Vastern.[89] One year later Edward's lands were restored to him and in 1415 he obtained permission to mortgage the manors of Vastern and Old Wootton and the town of Wootton to raise money for the building of his college at Fotheringhay (Northants.).[90]

Edward, Duke of York was killed in 1415 at Agincourt and the trustees, to whom the manors had been conveyed, granted a third of them to his widow Philippa.[91] After Philippa's death in 1431 both manors were restored to her husband's heir, who was his nephew Richard, Duke of York (d. 1460), father of Edward IV.[92] At the time of Richard's defeat by the Lancastrians, and before Edward's succession, several of Henry VI's supporters were rewarded from the issues of the two manors.[93] But on his succession Edward IV granted both to his mother Cecily, Duchess of York, for life.[94] On Cecily's death in 1495 all manors granted by Edward III and Richard II to Edmund, Duke of York (d. 1402) were resumed by the Crown, and Wootton was granted by Henry VII to his queen.[95] Henceforth for about the next half century the manor of Wootton, including the borough of Wootton and the park or pasture of Vastern, formed part of the jointure of the queens of England. In 1509 it was granted to Katharine of Aragon;[96] in 1540 to Anne of Cleeves;[97] in 1541 to Katharine Howard;[98] in 1544 to Katharine Parr.[99] Just before the death of Katharine Parr the reversion of the manor was granted by Edward VI to his uncle, the Duke of

Somerset,[1] and in 1550 the duke succeeded to it.[2] After the execution of Somerset in 1552 the manor was granted to John, Earl of Warwick, who was attainted the following year and died in 1554.[3]

In 1555 Queen Mary granted the manor to Sir Francis Englefield of Englefield House (Berks.), with remainder to his brother John.[4] Englefield was an officer of the queen's household and a zealous papist. On the accession of Elizabeth I he was obliged to withdraw to the continent and spent the rest of his life working in league with the English Roman Catholics there.[5] By 1571 Wootton Bassett had been taken into the queen's hands and part of its revenues confiscated.[6] For intriguing on behalf of Mary, Queen of Scots, Englefield was attainted in 1585 and all his lands were formally forfeited to the Crown. Two years later he died.[7] Wootton Bassett then passed to his nephew Francis, son of his brother John.[8] Francis (II) Englefield was made a baronet in 1611, died in 1631, and was succeeded by his eldest surviving son, also called Francis.[9] Francis (III) Englefield died in 1656 and was succeeded by his son Francis (IV). Francis (IV) died without surviving issue in 1665 and his heir was his uncle Thomas Englefield.[10] Francis (IV's) widow, Honoria, upon whom Wootton Bassett was settled for life, married secondly Sir Robert Howard, politician and dramatist (d. 1698).[11] After Honoria's death in 1676[12] Wootton Bassett should have reverted to Sir Thomas Englefield, but, upon the marriage of Honoria and Howard, the reversion was acquired from Sir Thomas by Howard, a transaction which led to a long legal dispute.[13] In 1676 Howard sold Wootton Bassett to Lawrence Hyde, cr. Earl of Rochester 1682 (d. 1711).[14] It passed to Lawrence's son Henry, who succeeded to his grandfather's earldom of Clarendon in 1723, and died in 1753 without a surviving male heir. Henry's estates then passed to his granddaughter Charlotte Capel, wife of Thomas Villiers, who was created Earl of Clarendon in 1776.[15] Thenceforth Wootton Bassett passed with the earldom of Clarendon until 1866 when it was sold to Sir Henry Meux.[16] Sir Henry died in 1883 and was succeeded by his son Henry Bruce Meux, who on his death in 1900 demised all his estates to his wife Valerie Susie Bruce Meux. Lady Meux died in 1910 having demised the manor to Ferdinand Marsham-Townshend, a grandson of the Earl of Romney (d. 1845).[17] F. Marsham-Townshend sold the estate in lots in 1913.[18]

In 1338 Gilbert of Berwick, who in 1331-2

[83] Cal. Pat. 1327-30, 67.
[84] Cal. Chart. R. 1327-41, 200.
[85] Wilts. Inq. p.m. 1327-77 (Index Libr.), 102; Cal. Pat. 1334-8, 60, 76, 105.
[86] Cal. Pat. 1358-61, 238, 472; ibid. 1361-4, 146, 156, 333.
[87] Ibid. 1374-7, 474.
[88] C 137/32/23.
[89] Cal. Close, 1402-5, 435.
[90] Cal. Pat. 1413-16, 349-50; V.C.H. Northants. ii. 170.
[91] C 138/14/27; Cal. Close, 1429-35, 264.
[92] Cal. Pat. 1452-61, 574, 575.
[93] Ibid.
[94] Ibid. 1461-7, 131.
[95] Rot. Parl. vi. 460, 462.
[96] L. & P. Hen. VIII, i (1), p. 49.
[97] Ibid. xv, p. 52.
[98] Ibid. xvi, p. 240.
[99] Ibid. xix (1), p. 83.
[1] Cal. Pat. 1547-8, 124.
[2] Ibid. 1549-51, 430.

[3] Ibid. 1553, 242.
[4] Ibid. 1554-5, 52; W.R.O. 212A/37/5, Abstract of title.
[5] For an account of his life, see V.C.H. Berks. iii. 407.
[6] Cal. Pat. 1569-72, 194.
[7] V.C.H. Berks. iii. 407.
[8] W.R.O. 212A/37/5, Abstract of title.   [9] Ibid.
[10] Ibid. For pedigree of Englefields, see Burke, Commoners, ii. 646; Ext. and Dorm. Baronetcies (1844), 185, and G. E. C. Baronetage, i. 91. These works differ in the date ascribed to death of Francis (III).
[11] W.R.O. 212A/37/5, Abstract of title; N. & Q. clxxvii. 7; D.N.B.
[12] N. & Q. clxxvii. 7; Hist. MSS. Com., Rutland MSS. ii. 29.
[13] Hist. MSS. Com. 14th Rep. pt. 6, p. 256; W.R.O. 212A/27/12/1, Deed Englefield to Howard.
[14] W.R.O. 212A/27/12/2, Deed Howard to Hyde; Complete Peerage, Rochester, see pl. facing p. 28.
[15] Complete Peerage, Clarendon.
[16] Notes from Sale Cat. of Dauntsey Estate (1913).
[17] Ibid.   [18] Ibid.

accounted as bailiff for both Wootton and Vastern,[19] held both manors at farm of Queen Isabel.[20] In 1369 the two manors were leased for 10 years to William Wroughton.[21] By the mid 15th century there was a considerable amount of leasing of the manorial lands, including parts of the demesne. Vasternclose, which represented the site of manor, including its buildings and a certain amount of land, was among the holdings leased out.[22] When the manor was in the hands of Katharine Parr, Vastern was leased to Sir Henry Long, who surrendered his lease when the estate passed to the Duke of Somerset in 1555.[23] By 1573 a house called the Gatehouse, apparently the manor-house, was leased to Richard Rowsewell.[24] In 1587 the Gatehouse, some associated buildings, and about 112 a. of land were leased to John Rowsewell for 21 years.[25] In c. 1641 Thomas Jacobs occupied the manor-house and was styled of Vastern.[26] In 1664–5 the capital messuage, site, and manor-house of Vastern were in the tenure of Thomas Brinsden, who probably still held them in 1670.[27] In 1674 the manor-house was in the hands of the lord of the manor, Sir Robert Howard, who may have occupied it for a time.[28] Under the earls of Clarendon Vastern was occupied as a farm-house by members of the Franklyn family.[29] After the restorations of Sir Henry Meux (see below) the house again became a more sophisticated residence. In 1967 it belonged to Mr. E. Le Q. Herbert.

MANORIAL BUILDINGS. A chapel in the court of Wootton is mentioned in Alan Basset's lifetime (d. 1232–3).[30] Its whereabouts are unknown and it seems reasonable to suggest that the early buildings at Wootton were supplanted by the great house at Vastern built by the Bassets during the 13th century (see below). The Old Court mentioned in 1281 as a member of the manor of Vastern[31] may be a reference to these early buildings, and, even after Vastern had become established as the main manor-house of the estate, there continued to be some manorial buildings at Wootton at least during the period when Wootton and Vastern formed separate manors. In 1331 a great storm damaged a roof at Vastern and a grange at Wootton and in 1334 there were said to be capital messuages on both manors.[32]

A great house at Vastern is first heard of in 1233 when, because of Gilbert Basset's part in the rebellion against him, Henry III ordered it to be demolished.[33] The house, as its name implies, was almost certainly fortified.[34] Consideration of the site indeed confirms this supposition, for the house stood aloft on the limestone ridge in an excellent defensive position, with the land falling away not only to the north and south, but also to the east where the ridge

dips suddenly before climbing again to the town of Wootton Bassett. How far the demolition ordered in 1233 was carried out is not known for in the following year Gilbert Basset was restored to favour.[35] But the Constable of St. Briavels (Glos.) was ordered to send 10 workmen to undertake the task and the Sheriff of Wiltshire was commanded to pay and provide them with the necessary tools.[36] If demolished, Vastern was quickly rebuilt and became and always remained the manor-house of the combined estate which came to be called the manor of Wootton (see above).

By 1355, when the manor had been restored to Queen Isabel, the manorial buildings at Vastern were in disrepair and carpenters, masons, sawyers, and other workmen were dispatched there.[37] More repairs were necessary in the 1360s when the manor formed part of the lands of Queen Philippa.[38] Between 1369 and 1376, when Vastern was leased to William Wroughton, the king retained responsibility for the upkeep of all buildings within the great gate of the manor, special mention being made of the great grange there.[39] A series of account rolls covering this period suggests a considerable conglomeration of buildings, requiring fairly constant maintenance.[40] Roofs in particular needed the attention of many tilers and women were employed to collect moss to line them. Two high towers were covered with lead. A fireplace (caminus) in the great hall was repaired. Drains and a water tank were made. There were rooms, with a garderobe, above and next to the gate of the manor. Various other garderobes were repaired. Rooms named within the manor-house were the 'Shyngledechamber' and 'Halones-chamber'. A great oven (furnus) is mentioned, as well as a kitchen, bakehouse, brewhouse, and malthouse. An account roll of 1449–50, when the manor had passed to Richard, Duke of York, mentions at Vastern a cellar, a little kitchen, and a porter's chamber.[41]

By 1501–2 there were on the site of the manor a great barn and an outer court, in which were a granary and another barn.[42] In 1573 the manor-house was evidently represented by a house known as the Gatehouse,[43] which may have evolved from the great gate of the manor mentioned in 1369 (see above). In 1587 besides the Gatehouse, there was a building called the 'Garnerhouse' with a small stable adjoining, and a granary (horreum) of 5 bays (spacii), to which was annexed a building, or perhaps a piece of ground, called the 'cutting'. There were also an orchard, a garden, called the courtgarden, of 3 a., as well as fields and pastures adjoining the site of the manor.[44] A rental of 1674, made for Sir Robert Howard, estimates that the manor-house,

[19] S.C. 6/1057/3. [20] Cal. Pat. 1338–40, 47.
[21] Cal. Fine R. viii, pp. 30–31; Wilts. Inq. p.m. 1327–77 (Index Libr.), 361.
[22] S.C. 6/Hen. VII/878; S.C. 6/Hen. VIII/3803.
[23] W.A.M. xxii. 177. [24] E 178/2395.
[25] C 66/1291 mm. 15, 16.
[26] Wilts. Inq. p.m. 1625–49 (Index Libr.), 321.
[27] W.R.O. 212A/37/4, Abstract of title; W.N. & Q. iv. 470.
[28] W.R.O. 212A/37/5, Rental of 1674; W.A.M. xxiii. 179.
[29] 'Diary of Goddard Smith', MS. copy in W.A.S. Libr., Devizes; W.A.M. xxiii. 179.
[30] Cat. Anct. D. iii, A 4821.
[31] Wilts. Inq. p.m. 1242–1326 (Index Libr.), 134.
[32] S.C. 6/1057/3; Wilts. Inq. p.m. 1327–77 (Index Libr.), 102–3.
[33] Cal. Lib. 1226–40, 228.
[34] Probably from OE fæstærn, meaning stronghold: P.N. Wilts. (E.P.N.S.), 273.
[35] See p. 190. [36] Cal. Lib. 1226–40, 228.
[37] Cal. Pat. 1354–8, 173.
[38] Ibid. 1358–61, 472; 1361–4, 146, 156, 333; 1367–70, 116.
[39] Cal. Fine R. 1369–77, 31.
[40] S.C. 6/1052/3–9; S.C. 6/1270/9. Sums spent on repairs appear on all the rolls but S.C. 6/1270/9 gives details of expenditure and unless otherwise stated, information in this paragraph comes from it.
[41] S.C. 6/1115/1.
[42] S.C. 6/Hen. VII/878.
[43] E 178/2395.
[44] C 66/1291, mm. 15, 16.

CLYFFE PYPARD
View from the escarpment looking north towards Tockenham

WOOTTON BASSETT: VASTERN MANOR
The 15th-century doorway and window brought from Berwick Bassett Manor are seen in the south-west wing

View looking north-east along the high street, 1932

Town Hall probably built in 1700; restored in 1889

WOOTTON BASSETT

with its outbuildings and gardens, including bowling greens and wildernesses, covered 10 a. of ground.[45] The bowling green at Vastern was evidently a meeting-place for the local gentry in the 18th century, who gathered there to play for money prizes.[46] The Wilderness, a wooded area to the east of the manor-house and comprising c. 5 a., is marked on a map of 1773[47] and is still marked on maps of the 20th century.

Little is known of the plan or appearance of the early manor-house at Vastern, beyond the fact that it was extensive. Since there was a great gate, the buildings were probably contained within a surrounding wall and it is known that there was a prison there in the earlier 14th century.[48] James Waylen, visiting in 1840, speaks of foundations of large proportions, still to be seen at the rear of the house, but by then nearly destroyed. The house of 1840 he surmised, was 'but a shadow of its former self'.[49] In 1967 there was no trace of these foundations, although the irregular levels of the ground round about, and especially to the north-east, made it possible to guess at their whereabouts. The central block of the present house, which is built of stone, is apparently of medieval origin and may perhaps once have formed part of the gatehouse mentioned in documents from the 14th to 16th centuries. Its position, a little below the crest of the ridge where the rest of the buildings probably stood, lends weight to this suggestion. The block has a rectangular plan and is of two stories. A projection at the south-west angle may represent the remains of a small turret or of a garderobe. Internally one of the two ground-floor rooms has heavily moulded ceiling beams with a foliage boss of late medieval date at their intersection. The house, or gatehouse, was evidently remodelled in the later 16th century when it was given a Tudor-arched doorway on its west side. The massive stone chimney in the centre of the rear wall may also have been added. A carved stone chimney-piece of this period carries the arms of the Englefields, who acquired Vastern in 1555. It is believed that the chimneypiece was originally on the upper floor, where there may have been a single lofty room.[50] The addition of small wings on the north, east, and west sides of the building probably took place in the late 17th and 18th centuries. Under Sir Henry Meux the house was much restored and certain additions were made to the back premises. At this period a 15th-century doorway and a single-light window were brought from Berwick Bassett Manor House and inserted in the south-west wing.[51] The drive leading up to the house was in 1967 flanked by a tall clipped hedge, mainly of box, but containing also a few ancient yew trees.

After the attainder of Sir Francis Englefield in 1585 Little Park, until then part of the manor of Wootton Bassett and known as the Little Park of Vastern, was granted by the queen to Thomas Knyvett, a groom of her privy chamber.[52] In 1596 Knyvett sold the estate to Francis (II) Englefield, who had succeeded to his uncle's lands in 1587, and thus Little Park again became part of the manor.[53]

In 1676, at the time of the sale of the manor to Lawrence Hyde, Little Park was sold separately and was acquired by Francis Moore.[54] Moore subsequently got heavily into debt and an Act of Parliament was obtained vesting Little Park in the hands of trustees for sale.[55] In 1714 it was sold to Ralph Broome of Lyneham.[56] On his death in c. 1715 Ralph devised to his nephew John Broome Little Park House and 277 a., and to John's younger brother Jacob Broome 95 a. called Upper Bargain.[57] Jacob died unmarried and the 95 a. then reverted to John.[58] In 1758 John Broome sold Little Park to Sir Mark Stuart Pleydell (d. 1768).[59] It subsequently passed, like all Sir Mark's estates, to his grandson Jacob, Earl of Radnor (d. 1828).[60] It then descended with the Radnor title until 1914 when it was sold.[61] In the later 18th century the Pinneger family were tenants first under the Broomes then under the earls of Radnor.[62]

Little Park Farm appears to date from the 17th century, remodelled in the 18th century and possibly again in the early 19th century. It has a symmetrical front with two short-gabled angle projections and a gabled central porch. In the front of the house a walled forecourt is entered through a gateway with ball finials. An elaborate painted and gilded chimney-piece in one of the upper rooms was removed to Longford Castle by one of the earls of Radnor during the 19th century. It was said to be decorated with the arms of the Moore and Dancastle families.[63]

Land in a close called Privetthay was granted in 1325 by Hugh le Despenser to Ralph Bolle, his cook.[64] The following year Walter Cannings of Stratton conveyed all his right in tenements and land at Privetthay to Walter Berton of Highworth.[65] By 1385 Walter Berton had been succeeded by his son Richard who conveyed Privetthay to John Cole and William Hertheneve.[66] John Cole then apparently conveyed the lands to Walter Chapman, for in 1386 Katharine Freebody, widow of Walter Berton, relinquished her right of dower in them to Chapman.[67] By 1402 the Privetthay lands had passed to John Chapman, Walter's son.[68]

Besides the Privetthay lands Walter Chapman and Alice his wife had acquired a messuage with curtilage in Wootton Bassett from Thomas Castletown, merchant of Salisbury, in 1378,[69] and more messuages and land from John Wyke and Margaret his wife in 1389.[70] By 1407 the lands conveyed by John Wyke had passed to Nicholas Wootton, who

[45] W.R.O. 212A/37/5, Rental 1674.
[46] 'Diary of Goddard Smith', MS. copy in W.A.S. Libr., Devizes.
[47] W.R.O. 130/79, Map 1773.
[48] Rot. Parl. ii. 416.
[49] James Waylen, 'Wilts. during the Civil War', Wilts. Independent, May, 1840 (copy in W.A.S. Libr., Devizes).
[50] W.A.M. xxxiii. 179.
[51] Pevsner, Wilts. (Bldgs. of Eng.), 532 and see pl. facing p. 192.
[52] W.R.O. 212B/64/1A.
[53] Ibid. 212B/64/3, and see above p. 191.
[54] W.A.M. xliv. 31.
[55] Ibid. 33.
[56] Ibid.
[57] Ibid. 34.
[58] W.R.O. 212B/64/11/47.
[59] W.A.M. xliv. 37.
[60] Burke, Peerage (1959), Radnor.
[61] W.A.S. Libr., Devizes, Cuttings, xvi. 380.
[62] W.A.M. xliv. 42; W.A.S. Libr. Devizes, Cuttings, xvi.
[63] W.A.M. xliv. 41. Francis Moore of Little Park married a daughter of John Dancastle.
[64] Cat. Anct. D. iii, A 4812.
[65] Ibid. C 3310.
[66] Ibid. C 3300, C 3703.
[67] Ibid. vi, C 4581.
[68] Ibid. C 5788.
[69] Ibid. i, C 858.
[70] C.P. 25(1)/256/56/8.

was the son and heir of Walter Chapman, and presumably the brother of the John Chapman mentioned above.[71] In 1418–19 Nicholas Wootton acquired more land in Wootton Bassett from Richard By-the-water and Joan his wife.[72] After Nicholas's death his estate in Wootton Bassett, said to comprise 20 messuages, 3 virgates of land, 6 a. of wood, and 3 a. of meadow was divided equally some time before 1454 between his daughter Agnes, wife of William Yorke, and his granddaughter, Emmot, who was the wife of Henry Ogdun.[73] The two moieties may have been later united, for only a holding belonging to the Yorkes has been traced further. In 1476 John Yorke, son of William, conveyed some land in Wootton Bassett to the chaplain of the chantry, which he founded in Ramsbury church, called the Wootton and Yorke chantry.[74] John Yorke was succeeded before 1512 by his son Thomas, who leased out land in the parish that year and in 1524.[75] In 1539 a Thomas Yorke, presumably the same, again acquired the land which had been granted to the chaplain of the chantry in Ramsbury church.[76]

ECONOMIC HISTORY. Although for much of its history Wootton Bassett has been the site of a weekly market it has never been other than a town on the smallest scale. The cloth industry of the 16th and 17th centuries made almost no impression upon it and until the 20th century the main occupation of its inhabitants was agriculture. The failure to develop any truly urban characteristics may always have been due to the proximity of Swindon with its more important market. Since the later 19th century the expansion of Swindon has certainly determined the course of Wootton Bassett's development.

AGRICULTURE. Of the 12 hides which made up the estate of Wootton in 1086 6 were in demesne. Here there were 3 ploughs and 5 serfs, while elsewhere on the estate there were 11 villeins and 14 bordars with 6 ploughs, making a total of 9 ploughs, although there were teamlands for 12. There were 24 a. of meadow, 33 a. of pasture, and a wood 2 leagues long by 1 league broad. Before the Conquest the value of the estate had been £10 but in 1086 it was only £9.[77]

As has been shown above, early in the 13th century the Bassets began to create the park of Vastern by inclosing land which lay partly in Braydon Forest and partly in Vastern.[78] These inclosures could be made either for the enlargement of the park or to bring land into cultivation and by the later 13th century an agricultural estate at Vastern appears to have been developed.[79] When Philip Basset died in 1271, however, only a single manor, called the free manor of Wootton Bassett, was extended. Here there were 560 a. of arable, 65 a. of meadow, and pasture for 3 oxen, 20 cows, and 100 sheep. There was also pasture in 3 parks and a 'foreign' wood. Members of the manor are mentioned, but not named, and manor and members

together were worth £44 6s. 7d.[80] By 1281 a manor called Vastern was the Bassets' main manor in the parish with the manor of Wootton expressly said to be one of its members. The other members were Old Court and an estate in Swindon.[81] Vastern by this date was reckoned to have 616 a. of arable and 173 a. of meadow, and pasture for 85 beasts and for 80 more in 3 parks. Manor and members were worth £53 11s. 8¼d.[82]

In the 14th century the manors of Vastern and Wootton seem to have been organized separately. In 1326 Wootton was valued at £30 and £28 for the goods and stock upon it; Vastern was valued at £20 with £40 10s. for goods and stock.[83] In 1334 the manors were extended separately. At Vastern there were 324 a. of arable, 134 a. of meadow, a several pasture, and the 2 inclosed parks. At Wootton there were 241 a. of arable, a several pasture of 29 a., 25½ a. of common meadow, and 2 common pastures called 'Windmillhill' and 'Pushill'.[84]

Although the two manors were apparently for a time organized separately, each with its own court and reeve, and growing its own grain, Vastern seems to have relied upon Wootton for its labour.[85] During a five-week period in 1331–2, Vastern received from the reeve of Wootton 379 labour services, which were used mainly for ploughing, for repairing the palings around the park and inclosing it in places with hedges, and for tending the royal horses. A surplus of services not required was sold. At Wootton, besides the services supplied to Vastern, 214 services were performed upon the manor and 219 sold. All these services came from 16 virgaters, 19 half-virgaters, and 19 cottars at Wootton. In 1334 the labour force available for both manors was reckoned at 16 virgaters, 16 half-virgaters, 8 quarter-virgaters, and 6 cottars, holding a cottage a-piece, all of whom paid no rent but owed services according to the size of their holdings. There were also 11 cottagers, 7 cottars, and an unspecified number of other tenants, who held newly arrented tenements, all of whom paid rent but owed no service.[86] In 1449, by which date the two manors had been amalgamated, there was besides the same classes of virgater, a class of tenant called Monday-men. But by this time the service due from them and all other customary tenants had been commuted for money payments.[87]

For a time in the 14th and 15th centuries there was a royal stud at Vastern. In 1331–2 both the king and queen had horses there.[88] In 1360 3 stallions were sent to sire the king's mares and the following year all but 10 of the royal horses at Vastern were sold.[89] In 1449–50 the king had a stallion there called Balle Roos.[90]

The management and maintenance of the parks at Vastern formed a special department of the manorial economy, which in the 14th century was administered by the reeve of the manor and the keeper of the parks. At this date the keeper received 4d. a day out of the issues of the manor.[91] Later this

71 Cat. Anct. D. i, C 1329.
72 C.P. 25(1)/256/60/26.
73 Cal. Close, 1454–61, 10, 11, 315.
74 Cal. Pat. 1476–85, 11; Cat. Anct. D. vi, C 6194.
75 Cat. Anct. D. vi, C 7428, C 7330.
76 Ibid. iii, C 3630.
77 V.C.H. Wilts. ii, p. 145.   78 See p. 189.
79 Cal. Pat. 1266–72, 116–17.
80 Wilts. Inq. p.m. 1242–1326 (Index Libr.), 134–5.

81 See p. 199.
82 Wilts. Inq. p.m. 1242–1326 (Index Libr.), 134–5.
83 E 142/33 m. 5.
84 Wilts. Inq. p.m. 1327–77 (Index Libr.), 102–4.
85 S.C. 6/1057/3.
86 Wilts. Inq. p.m. 1327–77 (Index Libr.), 103–4.
87 S.C. 6/1115/1.   88 S.C. 6/1057/3.
89 Cal. Close, 1360–4, 3; Cal. Fine R. vii. 134.
90 S.C. 6/1115/1.   91 Cal. Pat. 1364–7, 235.

became 2d. a day and continued to be a charge upon the manor, although the office became a mere sinecure bestowed as a piece of patronage. During the later part of the century, when the manor was leased to William Wroughton, the parks remained in the hands of the king, who also retained responsibility for the upkeep of the manorial buildings at Vastern. For the years 1367–75 accounts of the reeve survive for income and expenditure on both buildings and parks,[92] and for the period 1370–6 these accounts are supplemented by more detailed ones kept by the reeve and the keeper of the parks.[93] Only the barest summary of their contents can be given here. Income came from the agistment of animals pastured in the parks at certain times of the year and from the sale of trees, crop and lop, and bark. The agistment was usually leased out. Outgoings, in addition to wages, and expenses on buildings, which have been mentioned elsewhere,[94] included the maintenance and renewal of the palings and hedges surrounding the park and the upkeep of its numerous bridges and gates. Little can be said about the park as a royal chase. According to Leland Henry VII hunted deer there in 1489.[95] In 1449–50, when the manor was in the hands of the Duke of York (d. 1460), the parks were being administered by the reeve as part of the manorial estate.[96] In 1526–7 the palings round the park were still being maintained.[97]

The arrangements for common field cultivation and for grazing on both manors were clearly considerably affected by the development of the park, which eventually covered most of the northern half of the parish. In 1363 Park Field, containing 120 a. of arable, meadow, and pasture, which belonged to the manor of Wootton, and was let to tenants there, was inclosed and taken into the park.[98] Vastern manor had meadows both inside and outside the park. One of these, called 'Titele', lay uninclosed within the park in 1369 and was grazed in common by tenants of that manor.[99] The inhabitants of the town had grazing rights for their beasts like the rest of the manorial community. In 1562–3 these lay within the park and comprised 100 a. at Wootton Lawn and a parcel of ground towards the park's east boundary.[1] But in the later 16th century, when the Englefields began to inclose the park, the townspeople were deprived of all but their rights in Wootton Lawn.[2] New arrangements for commoning were made, allotting to every householder a specified amount of grazing in the limited area available.[3] But this in turn was taken from them in the earlier 17th century when the Englefields were stocking the Lawn with their own beasts and acquiring releases of common rights.[4] A full account of the

townspeople's grievances is contained in a petition they addressed to Parliament in c. 1632.[5] By then, however, they were left with only the commons in the southern part of the parish.

Little is known of the common arable fields of the parish. The inhabitants of the town clearly had a share in them and in 1408 the conveyance of a burgage tenement and garden in the town included land in a North Field.[6] This may have been the field called Coxstalls on a map of 1773,[7] which lay outside Vastern Park, immediately north of the town, and where part of the glebe arable lay in the 17th century.[8] In the 16th century East and West Fields are mentioned.[9] The East Field lay in the southeast corner of the parish,[10] much of it represented in 1968 by the land of Wootton Field Farm. The West Field may have adjoined it, for it seems to have been in the neighbourhood of the Greenhill farms.[11]

There were inclosed meadows and a considerable amount of inclosed arable on both manors in 1334.[12] The break-up of the park for inclosure and leasing apparently began in the later 16th century, after Sir Francis Englefield acquired the manor, and some of the farms in the north of the parish, such as Whitehill, date from this time.[13] Early in the 17th century rights of common within the park were being extinguished and later in the century much of the land was evidently being ploughed.[14] The inclosure of the common fields outside the park probably took place over roughly the same period. In 1671 53 a. of glebe in the East Field had been inclosed to form three fields called the 'new inclosure'.[15] In 1699 there were two closes of 'new inclosed ground' in the West Field similarly named.[16] By this date inclosure, except for the commons at Greenhill, Dunnington, Nore Marsh, and Woodshaw was probably almost complete. The commons were inclosed by Act of Parliament in 1821, but by then rights in them were so inconsiderable that no allotments were made and the land was merely added to the adjoining farms.[17]

By the mid 15th century a considerable amount of the manorial land seems to have been leased out to various tenants.[18] A series of rentals for the period 1665–76 show that by then almost the entire demesne was rented out in lots.[19] Only just over 300 a. out of 2,823 a. were in hand in 1674.[20] The rest, broken up into some 40 lots, produced about £1,977 a year in rents.[21] Outside the demesne there were in 1671 1,068 a. held by copy- and leaseholders and 1,200 a. held by freeholders.[22]

In the mid 19th century almost the entire parish was given over to dairy farming. In 1842 there were 550 a. of arable against 4,225 a. of meadow and pasture.[23] All but about 1,000 a. of the parish belonged to the Clarendon estate. The only other

[92] S.C. 6/1052/3–9.
[93] S.C. 6/1270/9.   [94] See p. 192.
[95] Leland, Collect. iv. 248.
[96] S.C. 6/1115/1.
[97] S.C. 6/Hen. VIII/3808.
[98] Wilts. Inq. p.m. 1327–77 (Index Libr.), 361.
[99] Cal. Fine R. 1369–77, 30–31.
[1] E 178/2395.   [2] See below.
[3] These arrangements are set out in the petition addressed to Parliament by the townspeople in c. 1632, see n. 5.
[4] C 2/Jas. I/W30/53. For the releases of common rights see W.R.O. 212A/37/5, Releases of Common Pasture.
[5] This exists as a printed broadsheet in W.A.S. Libr., Devizes. There is no record of it ever having been presented. It is printed in Topog. and Geneal. iii. 22–25.
[6] Cat. Anct. D. i. C 1205.

[7] W.R.O. 130/79/89, Map 1773.
[8] Sar. Dioc. R.O., Glebe Terrier.
[9] S.C. 6/Hen. VIII/3808; E 178/2395.
[10] Sar. Dioc. R.O. Glebe Terriers, 1698, 1671, 1783 and W.R.O. 130/79/89, Map 1773.
[11] W.R.O. 529/7/53, Deed Jacob to Jacob.
[12] Wilts. Inq. p.m. 1327–77 (Index Libr.), 102–4.
[13] E 178/2395.
[14] W.R.O. 212A/37/5, Rental 1671.
[15] Sar. Dioc. R.O., Glebe Terrier.
[16] W.R.O. 529/7/53, Deed Jacob to Jacob.
[17] W.R.O. Inclosure Award.
[18] S.C. 6/1115/1; S.C. 6/Hen. VII/878; S.C. 6/Hen. VIII/3803.
[19] W.R.O. 212A/37/5, Estate Papers.
[20] Ibid. Rental 1674.   [21] Ibid.
[22] Ibid.   [23] Ibid. Tithe Award.

farms of any size were Lower Woodshaw and Lower Greenhill, belonging to Sir John Jacob Buxton, Bishops Fowley Farm and Harris Croft, belonging to Robert Hughes, and Little Park, belonging to Lord Radnor.[24] In 1846 a labouring man reported that about two-thirds of the population of the parish were only occasionally employed and the other third, although employed about the farms, could only work in good weather. The highest wage was 8s. a week, or very occasionally 9s., and the usual rate was 6s. to 7s.[25] After the sale of the manor to Sir Henry Meux in 1866, Wootton Bassett became part of the large estate belonging to the Meux family, centred on Dauntsey, and a period of improved estate management began. Most of the farm-houses were renovated and many new buildings, including 40 labourers' cottages, were erected.[26] When the estate was finally sold early in the 20th century, all farms were let at a total annual rental of £7,560. The estate was broken up at the sale and sold in lots.[27] In the 1960s an associate company of the agricultural engineers, Blanch-Lely, bought several of the farms in the parish partly to farm for profit, but also to use for testing new agricultural machinery.[28]

TRADE AND INDUSTRY. As has been suggested above, a small settlement of craftsmen and traders dwelling around the parish church may have been encouraged to expand during the 13th century to meet the needs of the large rural estate and great house which the Bassets were creating at Vastern nearby.[29] The market granted to Alan Basset in 1219 may well have been held here from its beginning.[30] Almost nothing is known of the small town which developed during the Middle Ages and its growth was probably very slow. In the mid 15th century there were several shops. There was also a common bakehouse, which when leased out was worth 3s. 4d. to the lord of the manor.[31]

Wootton Bassett lay towards the edge of Wiltshire's cloth manufacturing region but there was a fairly flourishing industry in the parish in the 16th and earlier 17th centuries. The name of the first mayor known, John Wollmonger, suggests that the trade of woolstapling existed in the parish in the early 15th century.[32] In the early 16th century two inhabitants of the parish were accused of the offence of buying woollen yarn without intending to make it into cloth.[33] In 1631 Wootton Bassett was one of 14 Wiltshire towns suggested as a centre for the inspection of broadcloth,[34] but by then the industry was probably already dwindling. An early-19th-century gazetteer speaks of a former 'considerable trade in broadcloth', which was, however, by then extinct.[35]

In spite of its weekly market the town never really became a flourishing centre for the surrounding countryside. In the earlier 19th century the market's trade was so bad that it ceased to be held for some years[36] and in 1814 the town was said to have 'much dwindled'.[37] This may possibly be accounted for by the proximity of Swindon with its then flourishing market. Nineteenth-century directories show that Wootton Bassett had virtually no trades or industries beyond those required to meet the modest needs of the immediately neighbouring farming community. In 1844 among the town's tradesmen were 4 blacksmiths, 3 wheelwrights, 2 coopers, and 2 saddlers and harness-makers.[38] It must be said, however, that a bank was probably opened in the town either at the end of the 18th or early in the 19th century,[39] and by 1838 both the North Wilts., and the Wilts. and Dorset Banking companies had branches there.[40] There was by that year also a post office.[41] The numerous inns along the whole length of the high street are evidence of a certain amount of business created by the weekly market. They were also called for by the travellers on the highway, along which the town lay. In 1755 15 persons were licensed to keep alehouses.[42] In 1822 there were 11 inns, many of which existed under the same name in 1968.[43]

The coming of the Wilts. and Berks. Canal in 1801 probably made little difference to the economic life of the parish, although coal for the surrounding countryside was unloaded at Vastern wharf.[44] Likewise the coming of the G.W.R. line with a station at Wootton Bassett seems to have made no very striking change, but by giving easy access to Swindon it opened up new possibilities for employment in that rapidly expanding town. After 1845 special early morning workmen's trains were run from the station.[45] Throughout the 19th century, however, agriculture remained the main occupation of the parish.

In the later 19th century there were two or three small breweries in the town.[46] The largest was that started by Howard Horsell in c. 1878, for which the Beaufort Brewery in Railway Road was built in the 1880s.[47] There was also a brickmaking business belonging to a family called Boulter in Church Street, which had three brickyards and continued into the early years of the 20th century.[48] Charles Rouse was making ropes in the town in 1890[49] and the family hardware business survived in 1967. The first substantial business, apart from the earlier cloth trade, to come to the town was the Dairy Supply Company, which opened a factory in c. 1908 and acquired as part of its premises the former Beaufort Brewery.[50] This company was taken over in 1915 by United Dairies Ltd., which merged in 1959 with the Cow & Gate Company to form Unigate

[24] Ibid.
[25] The Times, 3 Feb. 1846.
[26] E. H. Goddard and W. Gough, Notes on the Town Hall, ii. 16–17.
[27] W.A.S. Libr., Devizes, Sale Cat.
[28] Ex inf. Blanch-Lely Ltd.
[29] See p. 194.
[30] See p. 197.
[31] S.C. 6/1115/1.
[32] Cat. Anct. D. i, C 1205.
[33] Early Stuart Tradesmen (W.A.S. Rec. Brch.), 93.
[34] G. D. Ramsay, Wilts. Woollen Industry, 86–87.
[35] Beauties of Eng. and Wales (1814), xv. 641.
[36] See p. 197.
[37] Beauties of Eng. and Wales (1814), xv. 641.

[38] Pigot, Nat. Com. Dir. (1844).
[39] W. N. & Q. i. 568–9.
[40] Robson, Wilts. Dir. (1838).
[41] Ibid.
[42] W.R.O. Reg. of Alehousekeepers' Recogs.
[43] Ibid.
[44] Charles Hadfield, Canals of S. Eng. 156–7.
[45] A. L. Baker, 'Life and Work in Wootton Bassett in 19th century', Thesis 1966 for Redland Teachers' Training Coll., Bristol.
[46] Kelly's Dirs. Wilts. (1878–90).
[47] Owen's Wilts. Dir. (1878) and for date of Beaufort Brewery, see Parsons Papers in W.A.S. Libr., Devizes, Scrapbk. 3.
[48] Kelly's Dirs. Wilts. (1880–1911).
[49] Ibid. (1890).
[50] V.C.H. Wilts. iv. 227.

Creameries Ltd.[51] For a time the Wootton Bassett depot specialized in the production of dried milk.[52] In 1967 a fleet of milk-tankers was operated from the depot, which employed about 175 people.[53] A new industry came to the town in 1962 when Blanch-Lely Ltd. of Crudwell, makers of agricultural machinery, built a factory in Whitehill Lane.[54] In 1967 this covered some 12 a., on which stood the shops for assembling parts made in Crudwell. There was also accommodation for a development section and drawing office. About 100 persons were employed.[55] In 1967 a timber-yard at Vastern employed a small number of men making coffin-boards.

It was not, however, the arrival of new industry which accounted for the town's marked physical expansion in the 1960s. This was due in large measure to the huge development of Swindon only 6 miles away and the need for housing for personnel employed at the R.A.F. station at Lyneham about 4 miles away. The proximity of Swindon also meant that while extensive housing estates increased the size of Wootton Bassett, there was little corresponding development as a shopping or commercial centre.

MARKETS AND FAIRS. A weekly market on Fridays in his township (*villa*) of Wootton was granted to Alan Basset in 1219.[56] The tolls from this, valued at 50s., were reckoned among the profits of the manor of Wootton in 1271,[57] and in 1281 tolls of market and fairs together were estimated at 30s. and were again included among the profits of the manor.[58] This manorial market may have played an important part in the development of Wootton Bassett in the 13th century. But it possibly did not flourish for very long. Nothing more is known of it during the Middle Ages.

According to the reputed charter of 1561, a weekly market on Tuesdays was that year granted to the mayor and burgesses.[59] Such a market was certainly granted in 1571.[60] No market is mentioned in the charter of incorporation of 1679[61] but there is no reason to doubt that the Tuesday market continued. But the market-place, which was in the main street, belonged to the lord of the manor and this situation seems to have led to a certain amount of difficulty and uncertainty. In the earlier 17th century one of the complaints of the inhabitants against Sir Francis (II) Englefield (d. 1631) was that he had removed their shambles, which stood in the middle of the street in the market-place, and had given them to a 'stranger', not resident in the town.[62] There is nothing to suggest that the weekly market was ever a particularly

flourishing one and it may have been overshadowed by the more successful one at Swindon only six miles away. In 1673 it was described as 'indifferent'.[63] In the 18th century the day for holding it was changed to Thursday.[64] The tolls were probably frequently leased out and in 1752 it was laid down that the mayor had to provide the necessary boards and tressels, and the person to whom the tolls were let had to maintain them.[65] Early in the 19th century the market had so far declined that it was decided to sell the shambles. But no buyer could be found and the corporation was obliged to take them down at its own expense.[66]

In 1836 the market was revived after a lapse as a monthly event, held on Wednesdays.[67] At the first monthly market some 772 beasts were sold and trade was said to have 'fully realized expectations'.[68] The market-place continued to be regarded as belonging to the lord of the manor and after the corporation was dissolved in 1886 the market was said to belong to him.[69] This monthly market survived into the 20th century and was said shortly before the First World War to be very flourishing, although in 1903 auctioneers' fees and tolls only averaged £16 17s. 5d. a year.[70] Four firms of auctioneers regularly conducted sales of cattle, sheep, calves, and pigs.[71] But by c. 1938 business had declined so much that the market was closed.[72]

Fairs are first mentioned in 1281 in an extent of the manor of Vastern, when their tolls, with those of the market, were valued at 30s.[73] Three fairs with a court of piepowder were granted to the town by the reputed charter of 1561.[74] These were on the feast and morrow of St. George (23 Apr.), the feast of St. Bernard (21 Aug.), and the feast and morrow of the Conception of the Virgin (8 Dec.). The grant of privileges of 1571 confirmed the April and December fairs but made no mention of that on the feast of St. Bernard.[75] Two new fairs were granted in the charter of incorporation of 1679, namely on Whit Monday and on the Monday after the feast of St. Bartholomew (24 Aug.).[76] In 1792 there were three fairs: on 4 May, 13 November, and 19 December.[77] By 1888 there were only two, the spring fair, held at the beginning of April, and the Michaelmas fair, held early in October.[78] Both these for a time in the 19th century were partly hiring fairs and were said to have been of considerable importance.[79] But by the end of the century they were very small amusement fairs and only survived for a few years into the 20th century.[80]

MILLS. In 1086 there was a mill paying 30d. on Miles Crispin's estate at Wootton.[81] In 1271 there

[51] Ibid. and ex inf. the Manager, Unigate Creameries Ltd., Wootton Bassett.

[52] *V.C.H. Wilts.* iv. 227 which gives a somewhat fuller account of the Wootton Bassett depot up to 1959.

[53] Ex inf. the Manager, Unigate Creameries Ltd., Wootton Bassett.

[54] Ex inf. the Works Manager, Blanch-Lely Ltd., Wootton Bassett.

[55] Ibid.   [56] *Rot. Lit. Claus* (Rec. Com.), 385.

[57] *Wilts. Inq. p.m.* 1242–1326 (Index Libr.), 64.

[58] Ibid. 134.   [59] See p. 199.

[60] *Cal. Pat.* 1569–72, 235.

[61] See p. 199.

[62] J. Britton, *Beauties of Wilts.* iii. 41.

[63] Blowes, *Brittania* (1673).

[64] *Rep. Com. Mrkt. Rights* [C 5550], H.C. p. 215 (1888), liii (1).

[65] W.R.O. 253/1, Ct. Bk. 1751–2.

[66] W.R.O. 253/2, Ct. Bk. 1785–1856.

[67] Wilts. Cuttings, xviii. 33.   [68] Ibid.

[69] *Rep. Com. Mrkt. Rights* [C 6268–vi. A], vol. xiii. pt. ii, p. 544, H.C. (1890–1), xl.

[70] *Endowed Char. Wilts.* (1908), p. 10.

[71] *Wootton Bassett and its Amenities*, Guidebk. (n.d.).

[72] Letter from W. Gough *penes* Mr. E. le Q. Herbert, Vastern Manor.

[73] *Wilts. Inq. p.m.* 1242–1326 (Index Libr.), 135.

[74] See p. 199.

[75] *Cal. Pat.* 1569–72, 235.

[76] *Cal. S.P. Dom.* 1679–80, 279–80. For transcript of this, see Wilts. Cuttings, xvi. 381.

[77] *Rep. Com. Mrkt. Rights* (1888), 215.   [78] Ibid.

[79] *Wootton Bassett and its Amenities*, Guidebk. (n.d.).

[80] Swindon Pub. Libr., Wootton Bassett, Scrapbk. Fair Posters.

[81] *V.C.H. Wilts.* ii, p. 145.

were a water-mill and two windmills on the manor of Wootton.[82] Ten years later in addition to these three mills, there was also a horse-mill,[83] which is mentioned again in 1334.[84] In 1331 and 1334 when Vastern and Wootton formed separate manors, the water-mill belonged to Vastern and each manor had one windmill.[85] The water-mill was undoubtedly that known later as Hunt's Mill, lying on the Brinkworth Brook, less than ½ mile from Vastern Manor House. The first reference to it by that name found occurs in 1449–50.[86] The two windmills are marked on a map of 1773.[87] One stood at the end of Wood Street, the other stood just north of Hunt's Mill on the high ground above the main road to Chippenham and was blown down in 1781.[88] In 1674 Hunt's Mill with some 36 a. of land was let to Andrew Wharton for £20 a year but was reckoned to be worth £30.[89] When it was sold with the rest of the Meux estate in 1906 it had three floors and was fully equipped with two pairs of millstones.[90] The mill ceased working in c. 1906 and was pulled down in c. 1964.[91]

PARLIAMENTARY REPRESENTATION. This topic has been dealt with in another volume of the *Wiltshire History* and will, therefore, only be treated summarily here.[92] Wootton Bassett first sent representatives to Parliament in 1446–7 and so was among the last of the Wiltshire boroughs to do so.[93] From 1446–7 two representatives were summoned regularly until 1832 when the borough was disfranchised.[94] The franchise lay with resident householders paying scot and lot.[95]

Until about the middle of the 17th century no particular influence or influences dominated the borough, thus giving strangers a rather better chance of being returned than in most Wiltshire boroughs.[96] From the middle of the 17th century the borough was generally, although not completely, dominated by the influence first of the Pleydells and the St. Johns, both local families, and then by the St. Johns and the Hydes (later Hyde-Villiers), who after 1676 were lords of the manor.[97] Until 1780 the members were almost all local men while after 1780 few local men sat for the borough other than members or connexions of the St. John family.[98] Towards the end of the 18th century, by which time the St. John family were in financial difficulties, Lords Bolingbroke and Clarendon came to an agreement by which each returned one member.[99] But twice in the early 19th century their interests were defeated by those of James Kibblewhite, a London attorney, who mainly by bribery managed to get both members returned. Among the measures

taken by Kibblewhite was the building of a number of houses in the town, all bestowing the right to vote. These he later sold to Joseph Pitt, of Cricklade, who succeeded in returning two members in 1818.[1] On the eve of the Reform Bill Lord Clarendon had regained the patronage but held it precariously.[2]

The franchise, depending upon residence and contribution to municipal expenses, resulted in an electorate of about 250.[3] The corporation, and particularly the mayor, who was returning officer, wielded very considerable power at elections. It was because the St. John family usually had control over the corporation that their influence was on the whole greater than that of the Hydes, in spite of the fact that Lawrence Hyde acquired the lordship of the manor for the family in 1676 and bestowed several generous gifts upon the town.[4] Wootton Bassett was not the most corrupt of the Wiltshire parliamentary boroughs, although there were some particularly bad cases of bribery during the 18th century.[5] Probably the most dramatic attempt at corruption occurred in the early 1750s when Robert Neale was seeking election with the support of the Hyde interest.[6] Neale succeeded in appointing himself deputy town clerk and gaining possession of all the corporation records. His efforts to win over the mayor, William Hollister, and 'pack' the corporation with his supporters did not, however, succeed. Hollister, who was seven times mayor, remained loyal to the St. John candidates, who were said to have bought 135 votes at over 30 guineas a head and to have incurred bills at 11 public houses amounting to over £1,000. Neale claimed to have spent over £1,800 and his fellow candidate probably not much less. 'We hear from Wootton Bassett' reported a contemporary newspaper 'that there has been such rioting about the election as never was known in so small a town . . . there were guns, pistols and swords on both sides, but nobody was murdered. Eight men are already in Salisbury jail'.

LOCAL GOVERNMENT AND PUBLIC SERVICES. In 1274 the Earl Marshal, as lord of the honor of Wallingford, had a gallows and the assize of bread and ale in Wootton, which formed part of the honor.[7] Vastern may have been one of the more important of the Wiltshire estates of the Despensers, for in the earlier 14th century the elder Despenser had a prison there, in which he was alleged to have imprisoned a neighbour for a week without trial.[8]

In 1281 there were three members attached to the manor of Vastern, which was evidently at this date the main manor of the parish.[9] These members

[82] *Wilts. Inq. p.m.* 1242–1326 (Index Libr.), 64.
[83] Ibid. 135. [84] Ibid. 1327–77, 103.
[85] S.C. 6/1057/3. [86] S.C. 6/1115/1.
[87] *Andrews and Dury, Map* (W.A.S. Rec. Brch.), pl. 14.
[88] *Wootton Bassett Almanack*, 1896 (copy in W.A.S. Libr., Devizes).
[89] W.R.O. 212A/37/5, Survey 1674.
[90] W.A.S. Libr., Devizes, Sale Cat.
[91] Ex inf. Mr. W. Coleman, Wootton Bassett.
[92] *V.C.H. Wilts.* v. 73, 78, 112, 121, 226–7.
[93] Ibid. 73.
[94] *Wilts. Borough Rec.* (W.A.S. Rec. Brch.), 103.
[95] Oldfield, *Hist. of the Boroughs*, iii. 201.
[96] *V.C.H. Wilts.* v. 121.
[97] J. A. Cannon, 'Wilts. Boroughs 1754–90' (Ph.D. Thesis, Bristol Univ. 1958), 297.

[98] *V.C.H. Wilts.* v. 226.
[99] Ibid. 227; Oldfield, *Rep. Hist.* v. 231.
[1] Ibid.
[2] Anon. *Key to both Houses of Parl.* (1832), 426–7.
[3] J. A. Cannon, 'Wilts. Boroughs 1754–90' (Ph.D. Thesis, Bristol Univ. 1958), 310; Namier and Brooke, *Hist. Parl.* 1754–90, i. 421.
[4] Ibid. 309 and see below p. 199.
[5] *V.C.H. Wilts.* v. 226.
[6] For a full account of the affair, see J. A. Cannon, 'Wilts. Boroughs 1754–90' (Ph.D. Thesis, Bristol Univ. 1958), 309–21.
[7] *Rot. Hund.* (Rec. Com.), ii (1), 244, and see above p. 190.
[8] *Rot. Parl.* ii. 416.
[9] See p. 190.

were named as the manor of Wootton, Old Court, and an estate which lay partly in Swindon and partly in Westlecott (Wroughton).[10] Nothing more is known of Old Court as a member of the manor, although its possible identity is discussed above.[11] Nor is the estate in Swindon and Westlecott mentioned again as a member of the manor, although in the 15th century the steward of Wootton Bassett held an annual court at Nethercott (Swindon) for the tenants there and court silver was still paid to the lords of Wootton Bassett in the 17th century.[12] A single court may have been held for Vastern and its members in 1281, but by 1331 there were three separate courts for Vastern, Wootton, and the borough.[13] But although separate courts were held, all three were held on the same day by the steward of the lord of the manor and borough.[14] By 1449–50 the manors of Vastern and Wootton had become merged, as shown above, and a court for the combined manor was held twice a year, while a court leet was held on the same days for the borough.[15]

As has been suggested above, it is probable that the town of Wootton Bassett was deliberately created some time in the 13th century.[16] The first sign of the development of any urban characteristics occurs in 1236 when reference to burgesses of Wootton suggests the existence of burgage tenure there.[17] The freemen of the manor of Wootton, paying £6 4s. 1d. rent to the lord of the manor in 1281,[18] may also have been holders of burgages, although specific mention of burgages has not been found before 1334.[19] That year an unspecified number of burgesses holding burgages in Wootton paid the lord of the manor £7 3s. 3d. annually for all services.[20] By 1331–2 the settlement at Wootton had developed sufficient urban attributes for it to be called 'burgus' and for a special court to be held for it.[21] Called the court of the borough, it was in fact a view of frankpledge held by the steward of the lord of the manor on the same day as the manor court was held. It is, indeed, clear that in spite of burgage tenure, the eventual development of a conventional borough constitution, parliamentary representation, and a grant, or possibly grants, of privileges, Wootton Bassett never achieved truly effective borough status, and the real business of government was conducted either in the courts leet of the lord of the manor or else by the parish officers. Even the market-place, in which the markets granted to the mayor and corporation in 1571 were held, always belonged to the lords of the manor.[22]

Nevertheless, some form of borough organization was established by the early 15th century. Reference to a mayor has been found in 1408, and, from such records as survive, it seems that throughout the 15th century the office was filled annually.[23] In 1446, for the first time, representatives from Wootton Bassett were summoned to Parliament, and it has been said that the borough received a charter of privileges that year.[24] But no evidence has been found for this. There is a 17th-century copy of a reputed charter dated 1561, granting wide privileges.[25] But, again, no enrolment or other trace of its existence has been found,[26] although the complaint by the inhabitants of the town in c. 1631 that besides depriving them of their common rights, Sir Francis (II) Englefield had confiscated their charter, is conceivably evidence that a charter existed.[27] According to the 17th-century copy, the charter of 1561 confirmed a corporation consisting of a mayor, 2 aldermen, and 12 capital burgesses, all of whom were named.[28]

The first grant of privileges for which there is definite evidence is one of 1571 which merely granted a market and two annual fairs.[29] But in 1679 the borough received a charter of incorporation from Charles II.[30] This confirmed all earlier charters and the existing corporation, which was constituted as that laid down in the reputed charter of 1561. A common clerk was to be appointed, approval for the appointment first being obtained from the Crown. The corporation was to have a common seal and could hold property to the value of £40. A weekly court of record was authorized for the recovery of small debts and the trial of trespasses not involving more than £20. Exemption from toll was granted and trade within the borough restricted to freemen thereof. This charter was removed in 1752 by the town clerk with all the other borough records in the course of the intrigues between the rival political interests to gain control of the corporation.[31] It was recovered in 1859 but lost again in 1866, when another town clerk absconded.[32]

There can be little doubt that the charter of 1679 was obtained for the borough by Lawrence Hyde, lord of the manor, with his political interests in mind.[33] He probably presented the town hall too, and certainly gave a seal in 1682.[34] But the charter did not result in the development of any effective borough government and practically the only function of the corporation continued to be the returning, through the mayor, who was the returning officer, of the borough's two representatives to Parliament.[35] The court of record was never established and in 1804 the town's entitlement to it was said to have been only recently discovered.[36] Meetings of the corporation were known as a borough court, for which court books survive covering the periods 1751–2, 1785–1886.[37] But almost the only business of the court was the election and regulation of the corporation and its officers, although in the 19th century some action concerning the market and fairs was taken.[38] A constable and two serjeants-at-

[10] *Wilts. Inq. p.m.* 1242–1326 (Index Libr.), 134–5.
[11] See p. 192.
[12] W.R.O. 212A/37/5, Rental 1674.
[13] S.C. 6/1057/5.   [14] Ibid.
[15] S.C. 6/1115/1.   [16] See p. 187.
[17] *Cal. Close,* 1234–7, 223.
[18] *Wilts. Inq. p.m.* 1242–1326 (Index Libr.), 134.
[19] Ibid. 1327–77, 103.   [20] Ibid.
[21] S.C. 6/1057/3.
[22] See p. 197.
[23] *Cat. Anct. D.* i, C 1205.
[24] J. Britton, *Beauties of Wilts.* iii. 37; Aubrey, *Topog. Coll.* ed. Jackson, 202–3.
[25] W.R.O. 253/4. For further acct. of the borough's charters see *Wilts. Borough Rec.* (W.A.S. Rec. Brch.), 103.

[26] There was a similar situation in the borough of Calne: *Wilts. Borough Rec.* (W.A.S. Rec. Brch.), 1.
[27] See p. 195.   [28] W.R.O. 253/4.
[29] See p. 197.
[30] C 66/3209 no. 19.
[31] *W.A.M.* xxiii. 173; xl. 363; *Wilts. Borough Rec.* (W.A.S. Rec. Brch.), 103.
[32] Ibid.
[33] See p. 198.
[34] See below.
[35] J. A. Canon, 'Wilts. Boroughs 1754–90' (Ph.D. Thesis, Bristol Univ. 1958), 310.
[36] W.R.O. 253/2.
[37] W.R.O. 253/1, 2, 3.
[38] See p. 197.

mace were appointed, but their functions were mostly ceremonial.[39] A town crier paid £2 a year for the privilege of crying, but in the 19th century it was difficult to find anyone willing to pay the price.[40] Town clerks were appointed with royal approval in 1690, 1699, and 1700.[41] These early clerks were attornies-at-law. Subsequently the appointment became a purely political one, held on at least two occasions by the lords of the manor.[42] The appointment of the capital burgesses was likewise a matter of politics fought over by the rival political interests.[43] By the 19th century any administrative action required was undertaken by a deputy town clerk, whose only salary was the payment he received for acting as clerk to the magistrates.[44]

In the later 19th century the mayor and aldermen held a petty sessional court about once a fortnight, although the county magistrates had concurrent jurisdiction in the town.[45] With the disfranchisement of the borough in 1832 the corporation virtually ceased to have any function at all, but in spite of this it was not dissolved by the Municipal Corporations Act of 1835.[46] It survived until 1886 when Wootton Bassett finally lost its borough status as a result of the Act of 1883.[47] The corporation's only income at the time of its dissolution came from the tolls of the markets and fairs and the money paid by the town crier for his licence.[48] Besides the insignia and a few other objects in the town hall, it held no property. To administer such income as there was, the Wootton Bassett Town Trust, consisting of seven trustees, was established in 1889 by the Charity Commissioners.[49] A charity to administer the town hall was established in 1909.[50] In 1912 this charity was united with the Town Trust and known as the Town Hall and Trust Charity.[51] In 1962 the charity funds were augmented by a legacy of £15,000 from Richard Parsons of Hunt's Mill Farm.[52]

In the absence of any effective borough government, much of the business of the town and of the parish at least up to the 16th century was conducted in the manorial courts and the courts leet for the borough. The only records of these courts to survive are of 16th-century date and are but few.[53] The manor courts were then dealing with the usual agrarian matters, such as the regulation of common grazing and the payment of fines and heriots.[54] The court leet held for the borough dealt with offences by the town's bakers and brewers against

the assize of bread and ale and with irregularities in the trade of butchers.[55] This court continued to meet in the town until 1834 but by this date the meeting was probably little more than a formality.[56]

Almost no parish records survive for the administration of town and parish by the parish officers and there are no vestry minutes.[57] The parish was divided into the two tithings of Woodshaw and Greenhill, each with a tithingman, who acted as constable until replaced by the county police in 1839.[58] Each tithing also had its own surveyor of the highways.[59] In 1798 the overseers employed a doctor to attend to the poor, and that year he innoculated some children in Wootton Bassett against small-pox.[60] In 1835 the parish became part of the Cricklade and Wootton Bassett Poor Law Union and since 1895 has been part of the rural district of the same name.[61] A parish council met for the first time in January 1895 and in 1967 met once a month.[62]

The town was said to be well lit by gas in 1859.[63] The gasworks in Station Road were closed in 1934.[64] In 1878 £400 was spent on a drainage scheme for the town,[65] and the sewerage works in Marlborough Road were built in 1891.[66] These were modernized and enlarged in 1921 and still served the parish in 1967.[67] By 1880 the town was said to be paved from end to end.[68] The first piped water supply was provided in 1891 and was brought through 8 miles of mains from Clyffe Pypard.[69] Electric street lighting was first introduced in 1933.[70] In 1962, with the rest of the rural district, Wootton Bassett was transferred to the Swindon Corporation Water Co. for its water supply.[71] Under the Isolation Hospitals Act of 1893 Wootton Bassett became the head of a hospital district and a hospital was built there. This was closed in 1930.[72]

The town's insignia comprises two maces and a sword.[73] The maces are not an exact pair. They are of silver with iron cores and bear no hall-marks. One is 15 in. long, the other 14⅛ in. On the caps are engraved plain shields of the royal arms as borne by James I and above the shield is the date 1603. Both maces have the initials 'R.S.' on the under part of the bowl of the head.

The sword was presented by John Attersol, one of the members for the borough in 1812. It is 45½ in. in length. On the scabbard is a coat of arms, reputedly those of the borough, the arms of John Attersol, and those of James Kibblewhite, the other member for Wootton Bassett in 1812. At the same

[39] Rep. Com. Munic. Corps. [C 2490–1], H.C. pp. 125–7 (1880), xxxi (ii).
[40] Ibid.
[41] Cal. S.P. Dom. 1689–90, 565; 1699–1700, 287; 1700–2, 37.
[42] Rep. Com. Munic. Corps. (1880), 125; E. H. Goddard and W. Gough, Notes on the Town Hall, ii. 15.
[43] W.R.O. 253/1; Canon, 'Wilts. Boroughs 1754–90' (Ph.D. Thesis Bristol Univ. 1958), 315.
[44] Rep. Com. Munic. Corps. (1880), 125–6.   [45] Ibid.
[46] Wilts. Borough Rec. (W.A.S. Rec. Brch.), 103.   [47] Ibid.
[48] Endowed Char. Wilts. H.C. 273–i, pp. 1032–4 (1908), lxxxi.
[49] Ibid.   [50] Char. Com. File 203207/A1.
[51] Ibid. File 203207/A2.   [52] Ibid. File 203207.
[53] S.C. 2/209/69, 70.   [54] Ibid.
[55] Ibid.
[56] W. F. Parsons, 'Notes on Wootton Bassett', W.A.M. xxix, 196.
[57] Such records as survive, were, in 1967, kept in the parish chest in the vicarage. There were some early-

19th-cent. poor-rate assessment bks., a highway-rate bk. (1833–5), and chwdns.' accts. (1822–70).
[58] W.A.M. xxix. 194.
[59] The surviving highway-rate bk. (1833–5) is for Woodshaw tithing.
[60] Parish chest, Wootton Bassett vicarage, bill to overseers.
[61] V.C.H. Wilts. v. 294, 258.
[62] Ex inf. Clerk to the Parish Council.
[63] Kelly's Dir. Wilts. (1859).
[64] Ex inf. South Western Gas Board.
[65] Rep. Com. Munic. Corps. (1880), 125.
[66] Ex inf. Clerk to Cricklade and Wootton Bassett R.D.C.
[67] Ibid.   [68] Rep. Com. Munic. Corps. (1880), 125.
[69] Ex inf. Clerk to Cricklade and Wootton Bassett R.D.C.
[70] Ex inf. Clerk to the Parish Council.
[71] Ex inf. Clerk to Cricklade and Wootton Bassett R.D.C.
[72] V.C.H. Wilts. v. 277, 327, 345.
[73] The following paragraphs are based on E. H. Goddard, 'Corporation Plate and Insignia of Wilts.', W.A.M. xxviii. 60–62. Full descriptions are given.

time as Attersol presented the sword, Kibblewhite gave robes to the mayor, aldermen, and burgesses. Each gift is said to have cost 100 guineas. There is also a wooden constable's staff 4 ft. 10 in. long. The initials 'C.R.' and date '1678' appear on the head which is of gilt.

In 1894 the borough seals were said to have disappeared, although known to have been in existence within living memory. In 1893 one seal came up for sale locally and was bought by E. C. Trepplin. It was described as slightly oval in shape, 1 in. × $\frac{7}{8}$ in. in diameter, with an ivory moulded handle $2\frac{3}{4}$ in. high. It bore the 'spurious arms' and the legend:

MINOR SIGILLUM WOOTTON BASSETT
ALIAS WOOTTON VETUS

On the neck of the head was the inscription 'Ex dono Prenobil. L. Comitis Rochester 1682'. An endorsing stamp has the same arms with a buckled band inscribed 'Borough of Wootton Bassett'.

CHURCH. The church is first mentioned in 1200.[74] Licence for Stanley Abbey to appropriate it was granted in 1363 and the appropriation was confirmed by Boniface IX in 1399.[75] Before 1399 the abbey had appointed a vicar to serve the church and a vicarage had probably been ordained.[76] A hospital with a free chapel of the Virgin, St. John the Baptist, and All Saints was founded in the parish in 1266 by the lord of the manor, Sir Philip Basset. It was, however, in no way subject to the parish church and the rights of the parish were expressly protected in its foundation deed.[77] There was also a free chapel at Vastern in the 13th and 14th centuries. Since 1951 the benefice has been held in plurality with that of Broad Town, three miles distant.[78]

In 1200 the priory of Monkton Farleigh renounced a claim to the advowson of the church of Wootton in favour of Alan Basset, lord of the manor, and in return was granted an annual payment of one mark from the church.[79] From then until 1363, so far as is known, the advowson belonged to the lords of the manor. In 1363 it was conveyed to Stanley Abbey and leave to appropriate the church was granted a little later.[80] Stanley retained the advowson until the dissolution of the abbey in 1536. It then again became attached to the lordship of the manor and descended with it until c. 1926 when it was sold to the Martyrs' Memorial and Church of England Trust.[81] In 1935 it was purchased by the parishioners and transferred to the Diocesan Board of Patronage.[82]

In 1291 the church was valued for taxation at £16,[83] and in 1341–2 at £16 13s. 4d.[84] At the later date there were 4 a. of land belonging to the church; tithes of hay were worth £4 a year; tithes of mills 10s.; small tithes and alterage dues £2, and a ninth part of the tithes of corn, wool, and lambs £8. A ninth part of the tithe of corn from Queen Isabel's

demesne land, since it was not leased out, was valued at £3 a year. A similar tithe from the Abbot of Stanley's demesne at Bassetsclose was worth 5s.[85]

A re-allotment of the revenues of the church between Stanley Abbey, as rectors, and the vicar was probably made in 1467. But the evidence for this only survives in an extremely corrupt document, in a much later hand, purporting to be a copy of the record of an enquiry held in 1565 by the Dean and Chapter of Salisbury into the provisions of such a re-allotment.[86] So far as can be judged from this document, which is very detailed, the vicar's share in the profits of the church was increased in 1467 in return for certain regular annual payments to Stanley Abbey. Among these was a rent of £6 for the farm of the great tithes.[87]

In 1535 Stanley Abbey was receiving a rent of £7 for the rectory and £1 from the vicar.[88] After the Dissolution the rectory, the value of which lay entirely in the great tithes, continued to be leased out. In 1555 it was leased to Roger Blake for 21 years with certain reservations, including the payment of £1 from the vicar and the tithe of wild deer in the parks.[89] By 1572, at which date the manor was in the queen's hands, the rectory had passed to John Hooper, who died that year holding it of the queen.[90] In 1583 Hooper's son, also called John, Henry Hooper, and George Hooper conveyed the rectory to Robert Streynsham.[91] By 1615 it had passed to Richard Francklin, who died seised of it that year and was succeeded by a son Sir John Francklin.[92] In 1660 it was held by Sir Richard Francklin.[93] By 1671 it had probably passed to William Packer and in 1687 was held by John Packer.[94] In 1720–1 it was conveyed by Richard Frome, Anne his wife, and Grace Packer, widow, to William Pleydell, who was Vicar of Wootton Bassett.[95]

In 1721 William Pleydell sold the great tithes due from Little Park and Brinsden's Farm to William Bartlett and Francis Broome respectively and there were subsequent sales of these tithes.[96] Other of the great tithes must have been sold at unknown dates and in 1842 there were 5 impropriators.[97] The Earl of Clarendon (lord of the manor) had the great tithes from 3,400 a. which were commuted that year for an annual rent-charge of £439; Robert Hughes of Woodford from 675 a. (commuted for rent-charge of £130); Sir John Jacob Buxton from 240 a. (commuted for rent-charge of £12); Jasper Warman and Elizabeth his wife from 32 a. (commuted for rent-charge of £4), and the executor of Thomas Ripley, Vicar of Wootton Bassett (d. 1804) from 1 a. (commuted for rent-charge of 10s.). The Earl of Radnor (d. 1869) had a life estate in the great tithes from Little Park and these were extinguished by the Tithe Award.

In 1535 the vicarage was valued at £11 or

[74] *Cat. Anct. D.* iii. A 4861.
[75] *Cal. Pat.* 1361–4, 334; *Cal. Papal Lett.* v. 192.
[76] *Cal. Papal Lett.* v. 192.
[77] *V.C.H. Wilts.* iii. 368–9.
[78] A. R. J. Horn, *Guide to Church* (1960), 23.
[79] *Cat. Anct. D.* iii. A 4861.
[80] *Cal. Pat.* 1361–4, 328–9.
[81] Horn, *Guide to Church*, 8.   [82] Ibid.
[83] *Tax. Eccl.* (Rec. Com.), 189.
[84] *Inq. Non.* (Rec. Com.), 162.
[85] Ibid.
[86] W.R.O. 212B/64/1. The findings of the enquiry with a copy of the 1467 settlement were apparently recorded in

the Chapter Lease Bk. II, 5 Eliz. I–6 Jas. I, now (1967) missing, but for which there is an index in Sar. Mun. Rm. Press 2, showing what were its contents.
[87] W.R.O. 212B/64/1.
[88] *Valor Eccl.* (Rec. Com.), ii. 114.
[89] *Cal. Pat.* 1560–3, 591.   [90] C 142/162/165.
[91] C.P. 25(2)/260/25 Eliz. I Trin.
[92] C 142/349/166.
[93] C.P. 43/312 rot.52.
[94] W.R.O. 212A/37/5; C.P. 25(2)803/3 Jas. II Trin.
[95] C.P. 25(2)/1078/7 Geo. I Hil.
[96] *W.A.M.* xliv. 35, 36, 40.
[97] W.R.O. Tithe Award.

£9 8s. 10d. after payments of £1 to Stanley and 11s. 3d. to the Archdeacon.[98] In 1831 the average net income of the benefice over the last three years was £461.[99] At the end of the 18th century there was a protracted dispute over the small tithes due from Little Park.[1] By 1773 the small tithes due from Vastern, Old Park, and other demesne lands had been commuted for an annual modus of £35 12s. 4d.[2] In 1842 all the remaining small tithes in the parish were commuted for a rent-charge of £485 12s. 4d. payable to the vicar.[3]

According to the document purporting to record the settlement of 1467 (see above) the vicar had two pastures called High Mead and Sharps, a piece of arable called Parsonscroft lying in the common fields, and other strips of arable in Coxstalls.[4] He also had a house with a plot before it. He still had these lands in 1671 and had acquired additionally a small close called Pondclose, an arable close called Parklands, and some 53 a., formerly in the common fields, but by then inclosed.[5] The total glebe at this date comprised about 91 a. It was approximately the same in 1842 and consisted of 75 a. meadow and pasture and 16 a. arable.[6] In 1783 the vicarage house was of stone with a thatched roof.[7] This was pulled down in 1865 and replaced by a new vicarage in Station Road.[8] This was vacated by the vicar in 1959 when a smaller vicarage was built for him nearby.[9]

In 1563–4 there is mention in a conveyance of some land which had earlier been given by Nicholas Reeve to provide 5 lights in the church. Other land in Ashton Keynes, given for the same purpose, also at an unknown date, was included in the conveyance.[10]

In 1783 there were two services in the church on Sundays and one on Wednesdays and Fridays. Holy Communion was celebrated at the usual feasts.[11] There were then generally between 60 and 70 communicants. The corporation, it was reported, seldom went to church, and the mayor of that year was said to be an exception, for he, with three or four other officers, 'were not ashamed' to be seen there and 'behaved with decency suitable to their station'.[12] On a Sunday in 1851 the morning congregation numbered 300 and there was a slightly higher attendance in the afternoon.[13] In 1864 the vicar also served the church at Tockenham and was assisted at Wootton Bassett by a curate. Three services with sermons were held on Sundays and there were services on all the usual festivals. The average number of communicants at the great festivals was 60 and at other times 40.[14] When the benefices of Wootton Bassett and Broad Town were combined in 1951 a full-time assistant curate was appointed to help the vicar and regular services in the two parishes were maintained with the help of lay-readers.[15]

The church of *ST. BARTHOLOMEW AND ALL SAINTS* was extensively restored in 1870–1 by G. E. Street at the expense of Sir Henry Meux.[16] It is of stone and comprises chancel, nave of 5 bays, north and south aisles, south porch, and embattled west tower. The first impression on entering is of loftiness. Before restoration, it consisted of 2 naves only, of equal length and height, divided by an arcade of 8 pointed arches on circular piers, running the entire length of the church. Sir Stephen Glynne describing the church some time in the 19th century remarked that the east end presented a rather unusual aspect, having two east windows of the same size 'in one gable'.[17] There was a low west tower and a south porch with parvis above. The building was apparently entirely of the 15th century, except for an early-14th-century window in the easternmost end of the north wall.[18] There was evidently a screen with rood loft above, for the staircase leading to the loft survives in the south wall.

Some alterations were made early in the 18th century, probably by Lawrence Hyde. A new screen was erected between nave and chancel and certain alterations made to make a more satisfactory chancel, although this continued to be divided lengthwise by the eastern bays of the central arcade. At about the same time the ceilings of the naves were boarded over and painted with stars. In 1823 a medieval wall painting showing the murder of St. Thomas Becket was discovered on the south wall, but this was obliterated in 1856.[19]

At the restoration of 1870–1 the north wall of the church was pulled down and a north aisle built with vestry and organ chamber at its eastern end.[20] The one 14th-century window in the old north wall was then re-erected at the eastern end of the south wall of the south aisle, which was also partially restored, although its four 15th-century windows were preserved. Elsewhere Street inserted 13th-century style windows. The arcade east of the screen, which now divided the chancel from the south chancel aisle, was taken down and rebuilt and new arches were built from north to south across the chancel and chancel aisles. The tower was heightened and the bells rehung. The font and altar with its reredos by Thomas Earp date from this time. The pulpit is of the 15th century. Among the furnishings is a brass chandelier given in 1782 by Jane Hollister, who also gave 3 sconces, which have since disappeared.[21] A Lady Chapel was formed in the south chancel aisle in 1944.[22]

In 1553 the church had 4 bells and a sanctus bell. A peal of 5 bells was hung in 1633 and remained in position until the tower was rebuilt in 1870. In 1887, to mark the Golden Jubilee, three new bells were presented. The 2nd and 3rd bells of the old peal of 5 were recast and the 4th, 7th, and tenor of the existing peal of 8 are the old bells of 1633. A ringing chamber was formed in the tower in 1950 with choir vestry below.[23]

Edward VI's commissioners left the church a

[98] *Valor Eccl.* (Rec. Com.), ii. 130.
[99] *Rep. Com. Eccl. Revs.* H.C. 54, p. 855 (15), xxii.
[1] *W.A.M.* xliv. 42.   [2] W.R.O. 130/79/89, Map 1773.
[3] Ibid.   [4] W.R.O. 212B/64/1, and see n. 86 above.
[5] Sar. Dioc. R.O. Glebe Terrier, 1671.
[6] W.R.O. Tithe Award.
[7] Sar. Dioc. R.O. Glebe Terrier, 1783.
[8] *Wootton Bassett Almanack*, 1896.
[9] Horn, *Guide to Church*, 24.
[10] *Cal. Pat.* 1563–6, 89.
[11] Sar. Dioc. R.O. Vis. Queries, 1783.

[12] Ibid.   [13] H.O. 129/251/1/4/7.
[14] Sar. Dioc. R.O. Vis. Queries, 1864.
[15] Horn, *Guide to Church*, 23.
[16] Ibid. 12–13.   [17] *W.A.M.* xlii. 305.
[18] Sar. Dioc. R.O. Faculty. Plans and drawings by G. E. Street. Also S.E. view painted by John Buckler, 1806, in W.A.S. Libr., Devizes and pl. facing p. 62.
[19] Horn, *Guide to Church*, 11–12.
[20] Sar. Dioc. R.O. Faculty particulars.
[21] Described in *W.A.M.* lvii. 377.   [22] Horn. op. cit. 21.
[23] Walters, *Wilts. Bells*, 242; Horn, op. cit. 15–17.

chalice of 8 oz. and took 13½ oz. for the king.[24] Among the plate is a large chalice of silver gilt the stem and base of which are ornamented with rich mouldings. Engraved on the bowl is a shield of arms of the Bakers' Company of Exeter. An inscription records that it was given to the church by William Joburn in 1631. There are two patens, one of which was given by William Pleydell, vicar (d. 1724). An elaborately ornamented communion set was given in c. 1871 in memory of Thomas Hyde Ripley, vicar for 52 years, and of his daughter Caroline. The registers begin in 1584. They are complete except for a gap between 1700 and 1720 in the register of baptisms.

ROMAN CATHOLICISM. After the manor was granted by Mary Tudor to Sir Francis Englefield, Vastern may have become for a time something of a centre of Roman Catholicism, attracting other papists to the parish.[25] Three papists were returned to Bishop Compton's census in 1676.[26] Francis Moore, who acquired Little Park that year and held it until 1714, came from a Roman Catholic family.[27] The Cruse family, who occupied Greenhill Common Farm as tenants of the lord of the manor for most of the 18th century, were also Roman Catholics.[28] There were 6 Roman Catholics in the parish in 1767 and 4 in 1780.[29] The four Roman Catholics of 1780 were members of one family and were visited occasionally by a chaplain, who was attached to the household of a member of the Arundel family in Chippenham.[30]

A chapel of ease, served from the church of Holy Rood, Swindon, was founded in Wootton Bassett in 1938, and in 1954 the Sacred Heart Church, likewise served from Swindon, was opened.[31] In 1967 it had a priest residing in Wootton Bassett.

PROTESTANT NONCONFORMITY. There were reported to be 8 nonconformists in the parish in 1676.[32] In 1703 the dwelling house of William Norris, known as the 'Sign of the Bear', was registered as a meeting place for Quakers.[33] But the meeting did not become permanently established and no more is known of the Society of Friends in Wootton Bassett. A meeting-place for Independents was licensed in 1779[34] and probably served as a chapel until 1825 when a new chapel was built in Wood Street with aid from the Congregational Association.[35] In 1851 average attendance was reckoned to be 120 at both morning and evening services.[36] In 1967 services were still held regularly on Sundays.

Primitive Methodism was brought to Wootton Bassett during the 1820s by preachers from the Brinkworth Circuit.[37] Meetings were held in various cottages and sometimes at the 'Royal Oak'. In 1831 two cottages were converted to make a chapel and an intensive campaign of house to house visiting was pursued. In 1838 the old chapel was demolished and a new one built on the same site at the western end of the high street. This later became known as the Hillside Chapel. It is a simple building with two large arched windows below a pedimental gable. Hugh Bourne is said to have preached at Wootton Bassett. Schools connected with the chapel were opened next door in 1842.[38] A town mission was undertaken in 1870 when 4,500 calls were made. On a Sunday in 1851 there were 171 at morning service and 216 in the evening.[39] In 1967 services were held regularly on Sundays.

The Wesleyan Methodists held services in Wootton Bassett in 1851 but had no chapel at this date.[40] Average attendance at these services was 55 both in the morning and in the evening.[41] A chapel was built at the corner of Coxstalls and the high street in 1855.[42] In 1897 there was no resident minister but services were conducted by preachers from Swindon.[43] The chapel was pulled down in 1964, by which date the congregation had joined the Methodists at the Hillside Chapel.[44]

A Baptist church was formed in 1878[45] and in 1896 a chapel, known as the Hope Chapel, was built at the west end of the high street.[46] The following year there was no resident minister but visiting preachers conducted services.[47] The chapel, a plain red-brick building, was closed in 1939 and was subsequently used first as a timber-store and later as an additional schoolroom for the County Primary School.[48]

EDUCATION. A free grammar school for boys was founded c. 1696 as the result of a legacy of £300 in the will of Richard Jones, dated 1688.[49] With this money Jones's executors purchased a rent-charge of 30s. and land in Haydon Wick and Rodbourne Cheney to provide for a salary for a schoolmaster. Some 18 boys of the town were taught reading, writing, and arithmetic. By 1834 the rent-charge had been lost, but the master was receiving £25 a year rent from the land as a salary. By c. 1859 the school, which was held in the town hall, had fallen into disrepute and was closed. For about the next 40 years the income from the land was applied to the upkeep of the National Schools (see below), although attempts were made from time to time to include the British Schools within the scope of the charity. In 1898 a Richard Jones Foundation was established to provide exhibitions of between £5 and £20 a year tenable at any secondary school or technical college. In 1903 the income

24 Nightingale, *Wilts. Plate*, 145–6; Horn, op. cit. 15.
25 *V.C.H. Wilts.* iii. 89, and see p. 191.
26 *W.N. & Q.* iii. 536.
27 *W.A.M.* xliv. 41–42, and see p. 193.
28 W.A.S. Libr. Devizes, Story Maskelyne MSS.
29 *V.C.H. Wilts.* iii. 96.
30 Sar. Dioc. R.O. Vis. Queries, 1783.
31 Ex inf. the Very Revd. Canon J. P. Leahy, Swindon.
32 *W.N. & Q.* iii. 536.
33 W.R.O. Certs. Dissenters' Meeting-Places, 1695–1705.
34 *V.C.H. Wilts.* iii. 134.
35 Ibid. 140; W.R.O. Retns. of Regns.
36 H.O./129/251/1/4/8.
37 All information about this denomination, unless other-

wise stated, from W. C. Tonks, *Victory in the Villages*, 128–34.
38 See p. 204.
39 H.O./129/251/1/4/9.　　　40 H.O.129/251/1/4/10.
41 Ibid.　　　42 *Kelly's Dir. Wilts.* (1903).
43 *Wootton Bassett Almanack*, 1896 (copy in W.A.S. Libr., Devizes).
44 Local information.
45 *V.C.H. Wilts.* iii. 138 n.
46 Inscription on building.
47 *Wootton Bassett Almanack*, 1896.
48 Ex inf. Mr. J. Tugwell.
49 All inf. about this school from *Endowed Char. Wilts.* (1908), pp. 1–2, 4–6.

still came from land and amounted to £20 a year. Three exhibitions had been awarded that year. In 1920 the land at Rodbourne Cheney, which comprised 20 a. and was known as Tan Hill, was sold and the proceeds invested.[50] In 1967 the income (about £70 a year) was used to help apprentices to buy tools and those going to grammar schools and technical colleges to buy equipment.[51]

In 1819 there was also a school for 18 girls taught by a mistress, whose salary was paid by Lord Clarendon.[52] There were 4 other day schools attended by about 140 children paid for by their parents and a Sunday school with about 80 children.[53] The poor, it was said, were generally desirous of receiving instruction.[54] The school for 18 girls still existed in 1835 and there were then 6 other day schools, including the free boys' school, as well as 2 large Sunday schools.[55]

The Primitive Methodists opened a day school next to their chapel in the high street in 1842.[56] In 1858 this was transferred to the British and Foreign School Society and that year had 200 pupils.[57] The premises were extended and improved in 1867 and 1891[58] and in 1902 average attendance of infants was 66 and of older children 159.[59] After the Second World War the school was much enlarged by the erection of temporary buildings and in 1967, when the numbers were about 400, the school awaited removal to completely new buildings at Nore Marsh.[60]

By 1858 there were parochial schools for both boys and girls. Each had between 50 and 60 pupils and accommodation in both was said to be bad. In the boys' school premises, apparatus, and furniture were described as 'abominable'.[61] In 1859 Lord Clarendon gave a site in Station Road for new church schools and these were opened in 1861.[62] The architect was Isaac Lansdown and the plan allowed for infants on the ground floor with the older children above.[63] In 1902 average attendance was infants 91 and older children 77.[64] After the Second World War accommodation was much enlarged by the addition of temporary buildings.[65] In 1968 there were 280 children on the roll.[66] A County Secondary school was opened for 258 pupils in 1958. Numbers in 1968 were 608.[67]

The town has had a number of small private schools. In 1844 there were 2 boarding and day academies[68] and in 1858 2 dame schools.[69] In 1897 there was a preparatory school called the Lodge and 2 'seminaries for young ladies'.[70] In the 1920s there was also a preparatory school, known as Little Meads, in the house in the high street called the Manor House.[71]

CHARITIES. During the 17th and 18th centuries several charities for the poor of Wootton Bassett were founded. In 1700 Charles Compton left a third of the residue of his estate to the poor of Wootton Bassett and Lyneham. Land in Badbury (in Chiseldon) was bought with this some years later, and the income from it was distributed equally between the poor of the two parishes. Gifts of £40 from Charles Pynner (Vicar of Wootton Bassett 1584–1619) and of £100 made at an unknown date by Sir Francis Englefield were also used to purchase land in Brinkworth for the benefit of the poor.

Benefactions of £40 made at an unknown date by John Gallimore, of Wootton Bassett, and £200 bequeathed by Lord Clarendon (d. 1786) were invested together in stock. A bequest of £200 in the will of Alice Brothers, proved 1766, to provide bread was also invested in stock, as was one of £100 from Lord Clarendon (d. 1824). By 1903 these seven charities, known as the Second Poor's Money, were all administered together and the income used to provide bread and gifts of money. That year 965 people received help from these combined charities.

The charity estate at Brinkworth was sold in 1920 and the profits thereof reinvested, while in 1962 the land at Badbury was sold and the proceeds invested. The incomes of the charities comprising the Second Poor's Money were evaluated separately in 1961–2, but together provided a joint income of about £69 to be used for the benefit of the poor of Wootton Bassett. In 1958 it was stated that Compton's Wootton Bassett charity had been distributed in small money payments, and the remainder of the charity money was probably allotted in the same manner.[72]

John Jacob, by his will proved in 1706, bequeathed £20 for apprenticing 3 poor children born and living in the parish of Wootton Bassett. He also bequeathed £3 to be distributed every winter amongst 12 poor persons of the town and parish, not in receipt of alms.[73] No more is known of this charity.

William Savage, by his will proved 1882, bequeathed £100 in trust.[74] The income was to be used to apprentice orphan boys or girls of Wootton Bassett or Liddington, who were to be selected by the Vicar and churchwardens of Wootton Bassett together with two ratepayers elected annually for the purpose. Wootton Bassett was to have the first two appointments and for every child chosen from Liddington, two were to be chosen from Wootton Bassett. If no suitable orphans were forthcoming, the child of a widow, or other poor person, might be considered. If there were no suitable applicants at

[50] Char. Com. File 79298.
[51] Ex inf. Mr. W. G. W. Hunt, Wootton Bassett.
[52] *Digest of Returns to Cttee. of Educ. of Poor*, H.C. 224, p. 1042 (1819), ix (2).
[53] Ibid.   [54] Ibid.
[55] *Educ. Enq. Abstract*, H.C. 62, p. 123 (1835), xliii.
[56] W. C. Tonks, *Victory in the Villages*, 134.
[57] Ibid; *Acct. of Wilts. Schools*, H.C. 27, p. 115 (1859 Sess. 1), xxi (2).
[58] TS notes *penes* Mr. W. G. W. Hunt, Wootton Bassett.
[59] W.R.O. List of Schools, 1902.
[60] Ex inf. Mr. W. G. W. Hunt, Wootton Bassett.
[61] *Acct. of Wilts. Schools* (1859 Sess. 1), p. 115.
[62] Ibid.; TS notes *penes* Mr. W. G. W. Hunt, Wootton Bassett.
[63] TS notes *penes* Mr. W. G. W. Hunt, Wootton Bassett.

[64] W.R.O. List of Schools, 1902.
[65] Ex inf. the head master.
[66] Ibid.
[67] Ibid.
[68] Pigot, *Nat. Com. Dir.* (1844).
[69] *Acct. of Wilts. Schools* (1859 Sess. 1), p. 115.
[70] *Wootton Bassett Almanack*, 1897 in W.A.S. Libr., Devizes.
[71] Ex inf. Mr. W. G. W. Hunt, Wootton Bassett. For this house, see above p. 189.
[72] For an acct. of the charities known jointly as the Second Poor's Money, see *Endowed Char. Wilts.* (1908), pp. 1025–6, 1029–31; Char. Com. Files 201408/A1, 203909, 203906, 203908, 203907.
[73] *W.A.M.* xxxi. 164–5.
[74] *Endowed Char. Wilts.* (1908), pp. 1034–5; Reg. Educ. Char. Lansdowne House, Berkeley Sq., London, W.1.

all, the fund was to be allowed to accumulate. No child was apprenticed until 1903 when a boy of Wootton Bassett was apprenticed to an ironmonger. The charity still existed in 1963 and had an income of about £2 yearly.

By his will, proved 1894, John Wicke (Vicar of Wootton Bassett 1865–80) bequeathed £500 to be invested in stock.[75] The income was to be used to buy groceries and other provisions for the poor and provide a certain handicapped child with an annuity. In 1903 tickets worth 6s. or 8s. were distributed among the poor. By 1953 money grants were made to a fund for persons aged 65 years or more, to a patient suffering from tuberculosis, and to a coal club in Wootton Bassett. In 1963 the income of the charity was about £12.

[75] *Endowed Char. Wilts.* (1908), pp. 1035–6; Char. Com. File 214295.

INDEX

NOTE: A page number prefixed by a dagger (†) indicates a reference to a plate facing that page; a page number in italic denotes a line illustration. The pages containing the substantive history of a parish are set in bold-face type. A page number followed by *n* is a reference only to the footnotes on that page.

The following abbreviations are used: abp., archbishop; adv., advowson; agric., agriculture; Alex., Alexander; And., Andrew; Ant., Anthony; b., born; Bart., Bartholomew; Ben., Benjamin; bp., bishop; br., bridge; cast., castle; Cath., Catherine; cath., cathedral; cent., century; ch., church; chant., chantry; chap., chapel; char., charities; Chas., Charles; Chris., Christopher; Co., Company; coll., college; ctss., countess; d., died; D. and C., Dean and Chapter; Dan., Daniel; dchss., duchess; Edm., Edmund; Edw., Edward; Eliz., Elizabeth; fam., family; fl., floruit; Fred., Frederick; Geo., George; Geof., Geoffrey; geol., geology; Gilb., Gilbert; govt., government; Hen., Henry; ho., house; hosp., hospital; Humph., Humphrey; hund., hundred; inc., inclosure; ind., industry; Jas., James; Jos., Joseph; Kath., Katharine; Laur., Laurence; Lawr., Lawrence; Ld., Lord; m., married; man., manor; Marg., Margaret; Mat., Matthew; mchnss., marchioness; Mic., Michael; Nat., Nathaniel; Nic., Nicholas; par., parish; Parl. rep., Parliamentary representation; Pet., Peter; Phil., Philip; pop., population; prot. nonconf., protestant nonconformity; R. D., Rural District; Ric., Richard; riv., river; rly., railway; Rob., Robert; Rog., Roger; Rom. Cath., Roman Catholicism; Sam., Samuel; sch., school; Sim., Simon; soc., society; sta., station; Steph., Stephen; succ., succeeded; Thos., Thomas; Tim., Timothy; U.D.C., Urban District Council; univ., university; vct., viscount; vctss., viscountess; Wal., Walter; Wm., William.

INDEX

168; prot. nonconf., 173; Queen Court Farm, 168, 169, 170, 171; rly., 168, 169; rectorial estate, 172; rectors, 101, 171, 172; rectory, 100, 171; reservoir, 93; roads, 168-9; Roman remains, 168, 173; schs., 173; Shaw, 168, 169, 170, 171; tithes, 172; village, 168, 169; Wick, 168, 169, 170, 171, 173; woodland, 168, 171

Tockenham ('Toccansceaga'), West, in Lyneham, 68, 91, 168, 169; agric., 98; Court Farm, 96, 98; courts, 99; estates, 95-6; fields, 98; inc., 98; man., 95, 96; man.-ho., 96; Meadow Court, 96; mills, 99; pop., 91; roads, 93; tithes, 101

Toomer, John, 106, 115

Torperley, Nat., rector of Liddington, 72

Town and Country Planning Act (1947), 140

Town Development Act (1952), 106, 131, 140, 144

Townsend, — (18th cent. architect), 31

Towresley, Wm., 99

Travers, Martin, 148

Tregoze, Clarice, m. la Warre, 78; John, 4, 53, 78, 86; Rob., sheriff of Wilts. (d. by 1215), 78; Rob., (d. 1265), 53, 77, 78; Sybil (wife of Rob. I), see Ewias; Sybil, m. Wm. de Grandison, 78, 79, 83, 86; fam., 53

Trepplin, E. C., 201

Trevilines, — (fl. 1413), 121

Trowbridge, 39, 121; honor of, 55, 56, 95; man., 122, 176

Trowbridge Building Soc., 112

Tuchet, Geo., earl of Castlehaven (d. 1617), 55; Jas., earl of Castlehaven (d. 1684), 55; Lucy, see Mervyn; Mervyn, earl of Castlehaven (d. 1631), 55, 56

Tuck, Adam (fl. 1660), 97, 101; Adam (fl. 1744), 97; John, 57; Mary, see Selfe; Rob. (fl. 1660), 97, 101; Rob. (fl. 1719), 97; fam., 97

Tudor, Edm., earl of Richmond (d. 1456), 79; Marg., see Beaufort

Turchetil (fl. 1086), 56

Turner, Isaac, 103; Lucy, 54; Ric., 54; Revd. S., 90; Thos., 115; Wm., 54; fam., 130

Twittee, Thos., vicar of Chiseldon 48, 49

Tyeys, de, Alice, m. Warin de Lisle, 45, 83; Hawise, 45; Hen. (d. c. 1308), 45, 46, 83, 84; Hen. (d. 1321-2), 45, 83

Tymmes, Thos., 38

Tytherton, East, in Chippenham, 158

Uffcott, in Broad Hinton, 3, 4, 5

Ulfric (fl. 1060), 53

Ulvric (fl. 1086), 124

Ulward (fl. 1086), 122, 124

Unigate Creameries Ltd., 196-7

Unitarians, 152, 157, 159

United Dairies Ltd., 196

United Kingdom Land and Building Association, 112

Unwin, Sir Raymond, 116

Upham, in Aldbourne, 14, 120, 122

Valence, de, Aymer, 120, 131; Wm., earl of Pembroke (d. 1296), 4, 5, 105, 120; fam., 105

Vaux, Wm., vicar of Wanborough, 175; Wm. Sandys Wright, 175

Vergil, Polydone, 175

Vickers-Armstrong, aircraft manufacturers, 130

Victoria County History, 141

Vilett, Arthur, 131; John (fl. 1657), 122, 125, 145; John (fl. 1729), 122; Mary, see Goddard; Nic., 145; Thos. (fl. 1657), 122, 125, 145; Thos. (fl. 1773), 46, 108; Thos. Goddard, rector of Draycot Foliat, 48; Wm., 146; fam., 105, 112, 122, 145, 146, 148, 167

Villiers, Barbara, see St. John; Charlotte, see Capel; Sir Edw., 79 n; Geo. Wm. Fred., earl of Clarendon (d. 1870), 39; Thos., earl of Clarendon (d. 1786), 81, 87, 191, 204; Thos., earl of Clarendon (d. 1824), 85, 204; Sir Wm., 79 n

Wadard (fl. 1086), 121

Wade, F. B., 150

Wakeham fam., 64

Walcot, in Swindon, 108, 117; agric., 124, 125; ch., 144, 147, 150-1; estates, 123, 124; farms, 126; inc., 125; local govt., 134, 138; prot. nonconf., 153, 154, 156; schs., 166; tithes, 146; *and see* Swindon, housing estates

Walker, Clement, 94; Heneage, 94, 96, 101, 102; John (d. 1758), 29, 94; John (later Walker-Heneage, d. 1806), 94, 100, 101; Mary, see Button; Rob., 18; fam., 96, 102

Walker-Heneage, Clement, 94; Geo. (formerly Wyld), 94; Godfrey, 94; John (formerly Walker), 94; fam., 94, 96, 98, 100, 102

Wallace, Wm., 158

Wallingford (Berks.), 39; honor of, 12, 28, 44, 45, 47, 123, 190, 198; prior and priory of, 123, 146

Wallis, Hen., 169; Lucy, 169; Wm. I, 169; Wm. II, 169

Walrond, Edw., 121; Eliz., 12; Ingram, 12; Joan, 12; John, 12; Wm., 12; fam., 12

Walsham, Rob., canon of Salisbury, 72; Wm., prebendary of Liddington, 72

Walter, bp. of Bath and Wells, 11

Walter, abbot of Hyde, 12, 13

Walter, John, 170; Thos., 170

Wanborough, of, John, 178, 184; Rob., 178, 181, 184; fam., 178, 184

Wanborough, 1, 3, 4, 5, 46, 66, 119, **174-86**; adv., 182; agric., 179-80; area, 174; boundaries, 174; chant., 183; chap. of St. Ambrose, 184; chap. of St. Katherine, 177, 178, 180, 181, 183, **184**; char., 185-6; ch., 178, 181-4, †182; courts, 181; Earlscourt Farm, 174, 176-7, 179, 182; East and West, 175; estates, 175-9; fairs, 180-1; farms, 180; fields, 179-80; geol., 174; houses, 175; inc., 180; ind., 180; inns, 175; local govt., 181; Lower and Upper, 175; man.-ho., 177; mans., 175-9; mills, 179, 181; poor relief, 181; pop., 175; prehistoric remains, 174; prot. nonconf., 180, 184-5; quarries 174; rectorial estate, 178, 182; rectors, 182, 184; rectory, 179, 182; rectory ho., 178-9; roads, 174, 175; Rom. Cath., 185; Roman remains, 126, 174; Saxon cemetery, 174; schs., 75, 185; tithes, 182; trackways, 174, 175; vicarage, 182; vicarage ho., 182; vicars, 178, 182, 183; village, 175; wall paintings, 183; Warnage Farm, 178; worthies, 175

Wancy, de, Christine, 54; Geof., 4, 54; Ralph, 52, 54; Wm., 54; fam., 54

Wantage (Berks.), 153, 185; Community of St. Mary the Virgin at, 148

Ward, John, 46, 47; Mic. Foster, 46, 47

Warman, Eliz., 201; Jasper, 201; John, 74; Thos., 68

Warminster, 105

Warner, Hen., 54

Warre, le or la, Clarice, see Tregoze; John, 78; Rog., 53

Warry, Cath., see Stone; Wm., 12

Warry-Stone, Wm. Ellis, 12

Warwick, earl of, see Beauchamp, Dudley

Warwick, Eliz., 100

Waspail, Rog., 55

Watchfield (Berks.), 124

Watkins, Eliz., see Tame; Lewis, 120; Wm., 120

Watson, Geo., 86

Waylen, Jas., 193

Waynflete, Wm. of, bp. of Winchester 55, 178, 184

Wealsh, Jas., vicar of Hilmarton, 62

Weare, *alias* Browne, John, 83; Thos., 83

Weaver, Hen., 52, 63

Webb (Webbe), Dan., 57; E. Doran, 151; Eliz., m. Thos. Smith, 57; Marg., see Selfe; Mary, 47; Rob., 71; Thos., 49; — (fl. 19th cent.), 22; fam., 145; *and see* Evered, Richmond

Welde, Wm. atte, 177

Wells, Rob., 74

Wenman, Thos., 121

Wereman, Wm., 13

Wesley, John, 22, 152, 185

Wesleyan and General Insurance Co., 143

West, Thos., 123; Wm. (d. 1610), 123; Wm. (fl. 1617), 123

Westbury, 40, 105, 153; *and see* Heywood

Westcott, in Swindon, 109, 110, 111; agric., 124; man., 121-2, 124; mill, 131

Westlecott, in Wroughton, 3, 4, 5, 68 124, 127

Westminster Press and Provincial Newspapers Ltd., 144

Westrop, in Chiseldon, 5, 8, 14, 15

Weymouth (Dors.), 142

Wharton, And., 198

Whatley, Chas. W., 16; fam., 12, 17

Wheeler, Thos., 22

White, Thos., 145

Whitefield, Geo., 103

Whitley, in Calne, 51

Whitmore, Marg., m. Sir John St. John, 89

Wicke, John, vicar of Wootton Bassett 205

Wigmore (Herefs.), 96

Wilcot, 182

Wild Life in a Southern County (Richard Jefferies), 67

Willetts, Canon W. H., rector of Lydiard Tregoze, 89

Williams, Alfred Owen, 67, 130, 143; J. A., 95; Jos., 128

Wills (Chas.) and Sons, clothiers, 130

Wills, W. D. and H. O., tobacco manufacturers, 130

Wilson, Frances, see Goddard; Pet. Werden, 28; Wm., 28; Wm. Werden, 28

Wilson and Wilcox, architects, 132

Wilton, prior of, 4

Wiltshire, — (20th cent. quarrier), 128

Wiltshire, 42, 43, 127; archd. of, 39, 86, 146, 202; sheriff of, 192

Wiltshire Archaeological and Natural History Magazine, 175

Wiltshire Archaeological and Natural History Soc., 26, 141

Wilts. & Berks. canal, 8, 77, 78, 85, 93, 105, 108, 110, 112, 116, 119, 127,

219

PRINTED IN GREAT BRITAIN
BY ROBERT MACLEHOSE AND CO. LTD
THE UNIVERSITY PRESS, GLASGOW